Icons of sociology

Icons of sociology

Mart-Jan de Jong

Boom academic

Despite our best efforts we have not been able to find all rightful owners of the illustrations used in this book. Whoever feels infringed is requested to get in contact with the publisher.

Editor
Thea Daw

Cover design
BuroLamp, Amsterdam

Photo back cover
A.M.K. de Jong

Lay out
H&R Communicatieve vormgeving, Purmerend

ISBN 978 90 473 0007 6
NUR 756

www.boomonderwijs.nl
www.iconsofsociology.com

Contents

Preface

From my days as a student at the University of Utrecht, I cherished good memories of Lewis Coser's *Masters of Sociological Thought* in which he presented the work of 12 renowned sociologists or precursors of sociology. A similar book that I found inspiring was Raymond Aron's book about the stages of sociological thinking, in which he discussed the work of seven great founding fathers of sociology. Since the publication of the books of Raymond Aron and Lewis Coser new sociologists of great stature have presented their work and by doing so have overshadowed the work of some of the renowned sociologists of earlier decades. I am well aware that each sociologists has his own view on the people that belong to the canon of sociology, but I expect that the majority of the icons I have chosen figure on everybody's list. Students who want to major in sociology or to become a sociologist certainly will profit from studying the work of all the icons that are presented and discussed here. And practicing sociologists that are not familiar with all of them yet may also benefit from reading about them.

Almost two centuries ago, Auguste Comte, the man who coined the term sociology, argued that societies in transition urgently need a science that could explain and foresee fundamental social changes. He was not only concerned about the aftermath of the French revolution but also fretted about the disruptions caused by industrialization, urbanization and secularization. In his view, it must be possible to generate scientifically based knowledge that could channel processes of social change and prevent mayhem and revolutions. He strongly advocated that this new science of sociology should become a real science by copying the objective and rigorous methods of the physical sciences. He realized that to predict and explain the dynamics of social organizations, small communities and whole societies was very difficult. That was probably the main reason why sociology hadn't entered the field of science earlier. It might also be one of the reasons why progress is slow. Nevertheless, the history of sociology has produced some creative geniuses that have constructed a solid and multilayered basis for this new scientific discipline. There is widespread consensus that Karl Marx, Emile Durkheim and Max Weber form some kind of illustrious trinity that gave sociology a very good start. Also the work of Georg Simmel deserves mentioning here. Many of their insights are still valid today. They opened our eyes for the social effects of rapid industrialization, urbanization and rationalization. There are very few contemporary social theorists of international stature that have not tried to incorporate their major theories and insights in their own work in order to lift sociological theory to a higher plane. Good examples of the new generation of brilliant social theorists of the twentieth century are Talcott Parsons, Norbert Elias, Peter Berger, Jürgen Habermas, and Pierre Bourdieu. Furthermore I have studied the work of a very important contemporary female social scientist: Mary Douglas. I find her work very inspiring and have started to use it already many years ago for my course on cultural sociology. She has built quite a reputation with her work in social anthropology, but later on in her career she widened her scope to socio-logical topics and social issues of modern societies, showing that the borderline between anthropology and sociology is an artificial one.

After this short prelude, it will be no surprise that I start this book with a discus-sion of the life and scientific oeuvre of Auguste Comte (1797-1857). I will follow a more or less chronological order. Hence, the second chapter is about the life and works of Karl Marx, who lived from 1818 till 1883. In many respects he was the opposite of Comte. He was a theorist and propagandist of revolutions, whereas Comte put all his theoretical energy in the attempt to prevent revolutionary situ-ations. Marx wanted to destroy capitalist industrialism, whereas Comte wanted to direct it into a more humane direction with the help of a corporatist social system. But there are also strong similarities. Both did not make a professional career within the academic world and had to survive financially with the help of friends. Also, they both had great designs for a just and better organized world. The third chapter is devoted to the biography and studies of Émile Durkheim (1958-1917). He was the first professor of sociology in France. In many ways his work reminds us of the ideas and goals of Comte. He also wanted to study social facts as if they were material things and could be researched and analyzed ob-jectively. He shared the same concern as Comte with order, social cohesion and consensus. Both believed that if religion and the morals based on religion were losing their grip on society, they had to be replaced by moral education on a secu-lar basis. Durkheim also shocked his contemporaries by stating that deviant be-haviour, criminality and suicide are normal social facts that could and should be explained sociologically. The fourth chapter is about the life and work of Georg Simmel, a German sociologist who lived from 1858 to 1918. His approach to social or cultural science is rather different in that he did not aim for general law-like statements or theories, but wanted to detect the essential characteristics of social forms. He hoped to find basic features of social types that could be discovered in a wide range of social organizations or social relations. Simmel enriched sociol-ogy with brilliant essays about all kinds of people and their lifestyles and pro-duced very interesting theories about social conflicts, domination and money. He showed that conflicts also have positive social functions. The fifth chapter is about Max Weber, the most famous German sociologist, who lived from 1864 till 1920. Weber introduced the methodology of constructing ideal types, partly for the same kind of reasons that Simmel was searching for social forms. He want-ed to hold on to the positivistic approach of science in which hypotheses have to be presented and tested, but also recognized that the subject matter of sociol-ogy is very different from that of physical science. People have a mind of their own that makes their individual and group behaviour more difficult to predict than the speed of falling stones. No chapter on the work of Weber is complete without a presentation of his seminal study *The Protestant Ethic and the Spirit of Capitalism* in which he showed that there is an elective affinity between both systems. The sixth chapter is devoted to the work of Talcott Parsons, who trans-lated *The Protestant Ethic* and introduced the work of other famous European sociologists to an American audience. His widely known book *The Structure of Social Action* was presented as a synthesis of the work of Emile Durkheim, Max Weber, the Italian economist and sociologist Vilfredo Pareto and the English in-stitutional economist Alfred Marshall. For this reason we could say that Parsons (1902-1979) rounded off the classical sociology of the founders. His attempt to in-tegrate the work of these four scholars could also be viewed as a starting point for modern sociology. However, after a few decades of rising fame, his work was severely criticized by a new generation of sociologists from the sixties and seven-ties. The series of modern sociologists starts with a discussion of the work of Nor-bert Elias (1897-1990). Although he was born five years earlier than Parsons, his breakthrough in sociology occurred when Parsons' stardom already went down-hill. Like most sociologists Elias had interpreted the latter's work and his mod-els in a static mode, ignoring Parsons' focus on social processes, social change and evolution. To avoid any static and simplified interpretation of his own work, Elias emphasized the complex and dynamic character of social figurations. His major work, The Civilizing Process, sketched in great detail how the culture of European societies changed due to important structural, demographical, histori-cal, and political changes. He detected a steady and significant increase in self-constraint, rationalization, and individualization. The eighth chapter is devoted to the work of Mary Douglas, an English social scientist, born in 1920. Where-as Parsons has become famous for his fourfold model of basic social functions, Mary Douglas has drawn a lot of attention to her fourfold group-grid model of differently structured social systems. Group denotes the variable that indicates the level of social cohesion and social exclusion and grip denotes the variable that ascribes the level of regulation within groups. In her typology a low or high level of regulation is combined with either a high or low level of commitment to the group. The four combinations produce entirely different settings that are highly useful for the cultural analysis of societies or groups that resemble sects, markets, cohesive hierarchical organization like convents or non-cohesive sets of isolates. The following chapter is dedicated to the work of Peter Berger. His *Invitation to Sociology* has inspired me and numerous others to study sociology. Peter Berger was born in 1929. His approach to sociology is humanistic and features the mod-esty that our science still requires. His main topic is the social construction of social reality and the intertwining of individuals with society. His views tend to be very different from those of mainstream sociologists, so his explanations of secularization, the war on the family or the revolution of capitalism can come as a surprise. Another icon of sociology whose work certainly has to be repre-sented in a book like this is Pierre Bourdieu (1930-2002). He produced a stunning number of books and essays covering many fields inside and outside sociology. His most renowned sociological book is *Distinction*. Herein he sharply analyzed the relationship between cultural capital and social origin, and showed that this relationship helps to reproduce social inequality in each generation. Culture and lifestyles become markers that lead to exclusion and self-exclusion. He has fruit-fully refined and expanded the approach of Karl Marx by expanding the concept of capital to non-economic dimensions and by foregrounding culture as an important factor in processes of social reproduction. The last chapter renders the work of Jürgen Habermas, a German philosopher and sociologist, born in 1929. He has set himself the task of theoretically unraveling the deeper causes of the negative turns taken by modernity. His main objective is to contribute valuable insights that can help mankind emancipate itself from the wrong world in which it has maneuvered itself, because of the one-dimensional emphasis on instrumental reason. He believes that the project of modernity can still be salvaged. To achieve that we have to acknowledge that we not only must respect the validity claims of truth produced by positivistic science, but also the valid claims of social justice and psychological sincerity whenever major decisions have to be made. No longer should our private life-worlds be colonized by the imperatives of the economy or the tactics of power politics.

I hope the students and readers of this book will enjoy this tour through the history of sociology. A tour that brings them into contact with fascinating examples of social theory and empirical research of five German, three French, two American and one English sociologist. It has always been my aim to write didactically clear texts, especially when the subject matter is far from simple. In the last three years I have already used draft chapters for my courses in introductory sociology and modern sociology at the Roosevelt Academy, Middelburg, an international liberal arts and sciences college associated with Utrecht University. So far, the students have evaluated my drafts very positively, just like the earlier Dutch version was evaluated positively by my former students at Erasmus University Rotterdam.

Middelburg, March 5 2007

AUGUSTE COMTE

MAN WITH A MISSION

For some, Auguste Comte is the last of the great precursors of sociology, for others he is the *founding father* of sociology. Like all the forerunners and pioneers in sociology, Auguste Comte was very concerned about the consequences of modernization. In his case there was the extra worry about the aftermath of the French revolution. In his view, the revolution marked a turning point in the history of mankind. The Old Regime had failed to adjust to the social changes brought about by science and industrialization. Therefore, he assigned himself the monumental task of investigating the nature and causes of the demise of the antiquated structures and to search for ways that could lead to a peaceful reconstruction and revitalization of society.[1]

This chapter will start with a discussion of major conditions of a sociological approach. It will be followed with a sketch of the embryonic phase of sociology in France. There we will discuss some philosophers that had a strong influence on Comte's thinking. Section 1.3 offers a short biography of the man that fathered the new science of sociology and also gave it its name. This section will also tackle the reasons for his failure to build an academic career in spite of his considerable talents. Section 1.4 deals with the period in which he cooperated with Saint Simon. This relationship started as a master-student relation, but after a few years it ended rather abruptly when differences of opinion had soared to such a degree that the divorce of their intellectual marriage became unavoidable. Section 1.5 presents Comte's optimistic views on social engineering, planning and progress. The following section, section 1.6, delves deeper into his views on social dynamics. Here, his law of the three stages is explicated. This law states that all intellectual thinking passes through two stages, the theological and the metaphysical stage, arriving at the third stage of modern, positive science. In Comte's view, societies where in great need of a science that could come up with the right theories about social change, its causes and foreseeable consequences, so that politicians could apply them to channel social progress in such a way that order would be restored. Section 1.7 is devoted to his strong belief in positive science, its assumptions, methods, and functions. The section ends with a short discussion of critiques and counter-critiques. We remain focused on the topic of science, for section 1.8 discusses his classification of the sciences. In section 1.9 and 1.10 industrialization and the organic model of society are tackled. Section 1.11 renders a short overview of his plan to establish a secular religion that would fill the moral gap that emerged after a growing number of people had left the Catholic Church. The chapter ends with a short epilogue.

1.1   Forebodes of a new science

We can find prototypical forms of sociology in the classical texts of great historical cultures. The writings of Plato and Aristotle acknowledged that every form of society, however loosely organized, depends on a system of norms to bind its members and regulate their behaviour. Obedience or acquiescence to these norms must be achieved by a variety of means, by customs, religion or law. At the same time society must be organized to serve certain ends. So, already Plato and Aristotle implicitly used the equation:

$$\text{norms} + \text{organization} = \text{society}^2$$

These two great philosophers also argued that this equation is only valid if the culture and its organizational structure are adjusted to each other. Only then would a fully organized city-state be viable and could serve its allotted ends. In their view, the goal of any society was to be a good society, a society that offered the good life to its citizens. Social philosophy deals with questions about the chief characteristics of a good society, how it functions and to which degree it approximates the ideal of the good society, or if society deviates too much from the ideal state, what could be done to remedy this situation? This mix of empirical and normative questions still plays a prominent role in modern sociology and every sociologist has to come to terms with this mix.

Though Plato's theory of society also consisted in an empirical description and theoretical explanation of the structure of society and its division of labour, his heart was in demonstrating the imperfection of every existing form of human government and setting up an ideal and just society or utopia. Plato was the most critical analyst of his society. He was constantly showing that there was much need for improvement and always looking for a mythological lost Paradise. His devastating criticism sprang from a passionate zeal for the welfare of man, and the conviction that it was possible to bring about a far better state of affairs. In his view society was not static but a conscious process of continuous endeavor to achieve the good life, a process in which all members should participate for the common good and their mutual well-being. This ideal standard could be approximated with the help of human reason. Reason, the most highly rated human faculty, was continually at war with two other important faculties: spirit and appetite. In the good life, there is a harmonious coexistence of reason with feelings and desire.[3]

For Aristotle, society is a natural development of humans' social impulses. Humans are social beings. This is natural. Nature, according to his theory, produces nothing in vain: and man alone is furnished with the faculty of language. The mere making of sounds to indicate pleasure, fear and pain is a faculty that belongs to many species. But human language serves to declare what is advantageous or not and to decide what is just or unjust. Only human beings can make a distinction between good and evil, and it is participation in a common perception of these evaluations that make families and societies. For Aristotle, the social whole is prior to the part, that is, the individual. Isolated individuals cannot survive. Without society man is less than an animal: *'Man, when perfected, is the best of animals; but if he be isolated from law and justice he is the worst of all.'*[4] His whole progress in life is only possible within, and is determined by, his participation in a society of like-minded people. The modern idea of socialization – the process by which humans learn their roles in society, learn how to live with others and how to conform to the norms of society – are implicit in Aristotle's theory.

Besides norms societies also need a structure. For Aristotle it was quite in keeping with the natural order of things that society should be graded hierarchically, for the simple reason that not all human beings are gifted with the same intellect. Hence, societies have to be led by a few enlightened people at the top, who would be followed by others less favoured with a capacity for sound reasoning. In Aristotle and Plato's view, the slaves are by nature inferiour to all others. Therefore, they should be subordinate to all others. Though we can observe stratified societies everywhere, no modern sociologist will support these opinions on the 'natural' position of slaves or any other class or caste in society. However critical Plato and Aristotle might have been of their society, here they manifested a strong bias that only can be explained by their intensive socialization in a particular society and an era that fully accepted these naturalistic views about slavery.

Aristotle was impressed with the idea of natural growth and development. He thought of the growth of anything – plants, animals, and children – in terms of a latent potentiality that can be realized. Such realization can be viewed as the fulfillment of one's nature. Perhaps, it is natural that we should do what we can to achieve this state of fulfillment, if so the good society is a society that offers the required conditions for everyone to reach this state of self-realization. Aristotle gave one of the first sketches of a three-tiered society. He distinguished between the very rich, the middle class, and the very poor. To date, similar rough distinctions between high, middle and lower class are still very popular in sociological theory and research. In contrast to many modern sociologists, especially those with a Marxist inclination, Aristotle had a much higher esteem for the social role of the middle class. He took it as a general principle that moderation and the mean are always best and concluded that the middle class occupies the best position. He asserted that its members are the most ready to listen to reason and the less inclined to violence and serious crime. For him, it is a further merit of middleclass people that they suffer least from ambition. People nurtured in luxury never acquire a habit of discipline. On the other extreme, people who have been raised and live in poverty will grow mean and poor-spirited. At best they can be taught to obey the leaders. Aristotle did not think well of states that only consisted of slaves and masters, for it is impossible to build a sustainable society on envy, hate, and contempt. These states are missing out on the large benefits offered by a broad middle class. To build a good society you need friendship and co-operation. A viable society aims at being, as far as it can be, a society of equals and peers, who as such, can be friends and associates; and the middle class, more than any other, has this sort of composition. Thus, it contributes to the security of the state. The middle classes also enjoy a greater security themselves. As they do not plot against others, or against themselves, they live in freedom from danger. Where the middle class is large and outnumbers the rich and the poor there is the least likelihood of disagreement and conflict among the citizens.[5]

The fall of the Roman Empire led to an almost complete rupture with previous thought. Intellectual life in Europe became disorganized and fragmented. For this reason, and also for the sake of brevity, we have to take a large leap in our discussion of the forefathers of sociology and skip the scattered work of many thinkers produced in the following ages. In Europe, during one and a half millennium, Christian dogma prevailed over critical philosophy and independent scientific thinking. Dogma held it that the existing state of affairs which manifested huge differences in power and wealth was willed by God. It took much time, courage and effort to change this view, but once this critical process had gathered momentum it could not be reversed.

To be historically correct it is right to speak of forefathers, because only men have played a prominent role in the making of sociology. Besides this striking gender bias at the level of top-ranking sociologists, there is another bias and that is the near absence of a non-western influence. One exception should be made for Ibn Khaldun, who lived from 1332 till 1406. In the fourteenth century, Ibn Khaldun, who was ignorant of European philosophy, formulated an original and brilliant theory of change, in which he brought together a broad series of causal factors. Ibn Khaldun had witnessed the fall of North African society. The Maghreb had known great power and influence but had lost it all. He undertook to explain the reasons for this sudden decline. In his view, the Arabs defeated the settled populations of North Africa because of their great solidarity. Kinship and tribal ties reinforced by rigid and fanatical religious faith had formed a vigorous power that could defeat military forces that greatly outnumbered them. The victory was eased by the fact that the Maghreb dynasties had degenerated as a consequence of their sudden economic advance and their great appetite for refinement and luxury. Ibn Khaldun, who had studied the history of many great peoples, was convinced that history followed a cyclical process, in which nations would grow stronger and stronger until they reach a peak. After that they will fall back, further decline and finally be taken over by other nations.

Ibn Khaldun already stated that differences between groups are cultural and not innate. Many travelers who went from the Maghreb to the East, in search for learning, believed that the minds of the Easterners, the people from Egypt, Iraq, and Persia, were more developed than those of the Westerners. They believed that they were innately quicker and sharper. Moreover, they showed higher skills in science, art, and crafts. Ibn Khaldun rejected this idea of an essential difference in the nature of people, except for people living in extremely remote zones, and explained the higher levels of thought and skills by a difference in education, training and experience. Although formerly great centres of learning such as Baghdad, Basra and Kufa had been ruined, God almighty had compensated this loss with the emergence of new and even mightier cities such as Khorasan in Persia and Cairo in Egypt. Ibn Khaldun noticed similar prejudices among the townsmen. Since they had perfected certain skills, observed certain civilized codes and customs that were unknown to the nomads, they thought that they were born brighter than the nomads. But the difference only is a thin veneer brought about by a difference in culture.[6]

1.2   The embryonic stage of sociology in France

Johan Heilbron discerns three phases in the preparatory stage of sociology in France.[7] In the phase that runs from 1730 until 1775, philosophers like Montesquieu and Rousseau developed the first secular social theories. Until the late Middle Ages, societies were exclusively seen as homogeneous religious or political units, but Montesquieu and Rousseau helped to shift the focus from unitary concepts such as church and community, to terms and issues that underlined social differentiation and multiplicity such as cooperation and co-existence.
Charles de Montesquieu introduced the idea that each societal system has its own 'natural laws of development.' He contended that the knowledge of such laws could and should help statesmen. Only if they knew the nature and pace of institutional changes could they wisely issue new policies. In his famous treatise *On the spirit of the laws* he argued that new political laws should match the 'spirit of the nation,' otherwise they will fall on barren ground or encounter fierce resistance. In other words, if laws do no fit the prevailing culture, it will be very difficult to implement and control them as modern governors and policymakers learn everyday. Though Montesquieu still speaks the language of a spiritual or theological philosophy, we recognize that his approach already features the hallmarks of sociological insights. His main theory was a theory about the development of states and nations, which involved an entire psychological, institutional and historical analysis of the nature of these societies. In many respects Montesquieu was a remarkably modern precursor of sociology. For instance, he frankly discussed the nature of religion, and the social and psychological functions it fulfills.[8]
Presumably Jean-Jacques Rousseau, another great precursor of sociology, has introduced the word social. He spoke of a social contract and a civil society. No

longer was the term society restricted to elite groups which we associate with the idea of 'high society.' Rousseau recognized the great importance of the social environment for human beings. However, he had a very negative view of society. In his view, neither God nor human nature was to blame for the evil forces that seemed to prevail, in particular the evil of social inequality.[9] He believed that social forces that sprang from human needs had become so powerful that they now fully determined the lives of individuals. Societies left hardly any room for personal choices that deviated too much from socially prescribed laws and regulations. Rousseau, who originated from Geneva, Switzerland, always remained an outsider in French society. Somehow he sublimated his feelings of powerlessness into a convincing image of autonomous social forces that did put a lot of constraints on human behaviour. Also, in other respects Rousseau differed from his fellow philosophers in France. He had severe doubts about the tenets of The Enlightenment and did not share their idea that the expansion of education, cultural refinement, etiquette, and the love of art would lead to moral progress. In his view, there was no close link between good taste, literacy, or intelligence. He also rejected the idea of a natural or god-given hierarchical relationship between the leaders of the nation, such as the king and the bishops, and the commoners. He did not accept the idea that the people had handed over their power to the prince in exchange for security and protection. In his view, the social contract should be an agreement between all members of society for the common wealth of society. It should be a union of equals.[10]

The second stage started in 1775. In this period, social relations were no longer viewed as objects for purely rational ideas but as objects for empirical study. From then on, scientists attempted to support their social theories with the help of empirical research. This important intellectual shift emerged after Louis XVI seized power. Jean-Antoine de Condorcet, a mathematician, brought the new idea of progress into the center of all thought about man and society. This idea signified a far-reaching breakthrough in thinking. It definitely killed the assumption that the world and mankind were created for a stable and orderly worldly existence and a divine eternity. Condorcet had sketched his ideas about the progress of humankind from the first simple hordes to the more advanced stage that led to the French Revolution. In the years following the French Revolution, he became responsible for public education and used this position to put some of his ideas into practice. In his view, education was the most important vehicle for the advancement of civilizations. Modern education had to prepare new generations for the next stage in the history of mankind. He strongly believed that the reconstruction of society should focus upon the elimination of inequalities between nations and social classes, and upon the perfecting of human nature, physically, intellectually and morally.

The demise of Napoleon, in 1814, marked the start of the third embryonic phase. This period was characterized by a further expansion of social theories and a growing diversity in theoretical approaches and the emergence of the first specialists. Finally, the idea had emerged that human history could be regarded as an on-going process in which change was a normal phenomenon. It simply was a matter of society becoming different from what it had been before. Now it was thought correct to conceive of human history as a creative process in which civilization was a cumulative and advancing phenomenon.

In the third preparatory phase, the number of social theories expanded and sociology became established as an independent science, thanks to the hard and impressive work of Auguste Comte.[11] Of course it is a matter of opinion whether we see Comte as the last great scholar of the pre-sociological era, or as first great master and founder of sociology.[12] He constructed the word sociology by attaching a Latin word (*societas*) to a Greek one (*logos*), but certainly that is not the main reason for starting a book about the icons of sociology with Auguste Comte. There are far better reasons. For Ronald Fletcher the true reason is that:

> No one has more succinctly laid bare the many-sided nature of the dilemmas that are still alive in our experience, and still form the substance of our problems. No one has given a clearer historical account of the changing nature of European institutions …; no one has given a clearer intellectual appraisal of the many earlier strands and tendencies of European thought; all of which were culminating in the shaking of the foundation of the old order of society, and the coming into being of the new; and all of which remain highly relevant to our situation today. No one has given, within this context, a clearer picture of the nature and scope of the new science of sociology, and the significance of its place in the attempt to create a new polity appropriate to the conditions and tendencies of science and industrialization. And no one has formulated all this in so clear a plan of thought, feeling and action.[13]

Ronald Fletcher, that great admirer of the work of Comte, has set it as his task to restore the caricature that most sociologists tend to make of the latter and his positivism. Admittedly, Comte has proposed extremes, held positions, and possessed idiosyncrasies, which were and remain open to serious criticism. Undeniably, he has written thick treatises that have put off many potential readers. But large and complex themes tend to require large and intricate exercises of the mind. However, in Comte's case everything is plain. There is no obscurity in them. To look at his first major essay – the *Plan of the Scientific Operations Necessary for Reorganizing Society*, published in 1822 – is to see as clear a statement as can be found of his central vision that has been basic in the foundation and development of sociology. Here and in the majority of the books he published later, we really can watch and behold the birth of a new science, the actual start of sociology.[14]

Comte studied and elaborated the magisterial work of earlier thinkers, and did this in an ingenious and original way.[15] His awesome knowledge of history, philosophy and the natural sciences surprised everyone. And also the extent and clarity of his grasp and critical appraisal of the work of thinkers like Aristotle, Kant, Montesquieu, Condorcet, Hume, Adam Smith, and many others was astounding. This impressive familiarity with the essence of philosophy, history and the natural sciences enabled Comte to produce the first systematic approach to the study of society. In his *Course of Positive Philosophy* he meticulously rendered a dazzling perspective on society's shift from belief to proof, from intuition to reason, in other words, its gradual accommodation to science – as the dominant basis of our knowledge, – and to industrialization – as the new organization of techniques by which modern men attempt to increase human welfare; a perspective in which old social systems were falling apart and new systems were gradually emerging.

Another reason for discussing Comte's work is not only that his statement was the first, but also that it was basic and seminal. His sketches contained a great many of those seeds of insights, which later thinkers were to develop as the central ideas of their work. For example, the emphasis upon the change from the distinctive social bonds of traditional community to a modern 'contractual' society, later to be explored more deeply by Ferdinand Tönnies, was already there. Comte emphasized the 'dialectical' nature of social change, the significance of 'private property' and 'class relations' and the importance of the practical, productive activities of men 'working for the explication of historical change. Later, these insights became basic elements of Karl Marx' historical materialism. Similarly, the emphasis of Protestantism for the understanding of the growth of industrial capitalism – later developed by Max Weber – was present in his work. The same is true for the strong emphasis upon the distinctive level of 'social facts' and its implications for sociological theory and method. Emile Durkheim developed these insights further. All these, and many other seminal insights, were prominent in Comte's social theory. Much of his work remains highly relevant to our situation today.[16]

1.3   A biographical impression

Isodore Auguste Marie François Xavier Comte was born on the 20th of January 1798. He was raised in a pious Catholic family.[17] His father was a conscientious low-ranking civil servant with a modest income. A few decades earlier, such an income was not enough to pay the costs for secondary and higher education, but fortunately for Auguste, who showed a great aptitude for learning, the educational opportunities had increased by the revolutionary and Napoleonic régimes.

Auguste did not get on well with his siblings, kept a distance from his mother, was on bad terms with his father, turned most friends into foes, divorced his first wife, and lost his second and last love two years after he first met her. His life ended in a mess and was troubled by periods of grave mental illness. Twice he attempted suicide, though, in both cases he did it in such a halfhearted way that he could be saved. Despite his emotional difficulties he was able to work and accomplish great things, thanks to his strong ego-drive. At the Lyceum of Montpellier

Auguste proved to be an outstanding pupil. He already finished secondary education at the age of fifteen, but stayed one extra year to replace his math teacher.
He was admitted to the *École Polytechnique* in Paris, the Mecca of the Natural
Sciences. The school radiated a strong belief in the unlimited possibilities of science and technology. Unfortunately, Comte got in trouble with the academic authorities, because he could not stand the military style of the school. As bright
student he had great trouble in showing respect for authorities that had to rely
on power instead of respect for their knowledge and leadership. As a result he
was expelled and returned to Montpellier to do some serious study at the medical
faculty for a while.[18]

From 1817 till 1824, Comte was the assistant and secretary of Count Claude-Henri
de Saint-Simon. After a cooperation of more than six years Comte got the feeling
that he could learn no more from this master. Besides, he began to suspect that
the latter attempted to steal his ideas. Some specialists think it was the other way
around, but close reading of the publications of Saint Simon shows that Comte
only used some of the better ideas and sayings of Saint Simon as a basis for his
work, which was much more substantial than that of his former tutor and boss.[19]
In fact, one of the main reasons for their separation was a growing divide between
their social-philosophical and economic views.[20] There is no doubt that Comte
has been greatly influenced by Saint-Simon. In the beginning he was fascinated
by the extremely energetic aristocrat and eagerly absorbed all his shrewd ideas.
He admired Saint-Simon's huge ambitions, his staggering plans and projects,
and his indestructible belief in himself. On the other hand, he thought that Saint-
Simon showed too much haste in putting his ideas into practice, whereas Saint-
Simon thought that Comte was taking far too much time looking for secure
foundations.[21] Another reason for the break-up was that Comte could no longer
endure to be treated as a pupil. After he broke with Saint-Simon he started to give
private lessons in mathematics. For years this was his main source of income.
More than once he tried to become a professor at the *École Polytechnique*, but did
not succeed. He only functioned as a coach and admissions examiner for a while,
but failed to keep this position. He was often in deep financial trouble. Frequently
friends had to help him to make ends meet.

In 1825, he married Caroline Massin, a prostitute without any family or money.
He was convinced that other women were out of his league, because he lacked
a stable social position. Besides, he was very short, squinted and suffered from
an inferiority complex. Once he wrote: *'I was alone, and wasn't endowed with
anything that could please women.'* Near the end of his life he would evaluate his
marriage with Caroline Massin as the only *faux pas* of his entire life.[22] The couple did not solemnize their marriage in church, which displeased his pious parents. Later, when he was in a deep mental crisis, his mother forced him to have his
marriage confirmed for the Catholic Church. Only by giving in to this wish was
he allowed to leave the psychiatric institute.[23] Caroline Massin was an intelligent
woman who showed a great interest in his work and often turned up at his lectures. Comte always had the intention of helping her with her education, but his

inability to earn a decent income repeatedly forced her to return to her trade. The marriage went through some difficult periods and did not last. Caroline left him in 1842, just after he finished his *Cours de la Philosophie Positive*, a series of six books, to which he had devoted 12 years of his life. As a result Comte experienced a major nervous breakdown.

In April 1845, he met Clotilde de Vaux and quickly fell in love with her. This impoverished gentlewoman of thirty did not live with her husband, perhaps because he was imprisoned or because he had deserted her after he had fallen in love with a man. After one unsatisfactory sexual encounter, Clotilde demanded that their relationship should remain strictly platonic. Comte submitted and sublimated his desire into a quasi-religious worship of women, placing them on a pedestal while nonetheless denying them equality and freedom.[24] Clotilde was ill most of the time and died in April 1846. So, Comte only enjoyed her company and affection for one year, but he would always love her and visit her grave every Sunday for the rest of his life. For him, this one year with Clotilde de Vaux was the 'year without a parallel'. His adoration for this woman transformed into a kind of cult. Madame de Vaux had a great influence on his further development as a scholar. She managed to shift his focus from the rational to the emotional aspects of human existence. This became manifest in his *System of Positive Politics*.[25] Herein, he explicated how a positive religion of humanity could function as the binding force of society, as the moral cement of society. To distance himself from his former rationalistic period, he decided to call himself 'The Founder of the Universal Religion, High Priest of Humanity'. Thus he wanted to indicate that the era of Enlightenment had come to an end. No longer, was there a need for the prophets of rationality and individual liberty; the time had come for a secular 'religion of mankind'. Comte even believed that it would not take long before he would replace the pope and would preach his self-made religion from the pulpit of the Notre Dame.[26]

Comte's academic career was an outright drama. It never lifted off, despite the high quality of his books, essays, and lectures. In the beginning, his treatises were studied by the most prominent scholars, including members of the *Académie Française*. These renowned academics admired his *Cours de Philosophie Positive*. As a private lecturer he organized courses to present his ideas to a learned audience. Famous physical scientists such as Ampère, Gay-Lussac, Fourier, and Laplace attended his lectures. Unfortunately, a nervous breakdown forced him to abort these activities. It took a long time before he was cured and could start teaching again. However, by then his chances of an academic career had evaporated. Besides, a few influential professors disliked him and obstructed his plans. Partly, Comte himself was to blame for this course of events, for he often managed to spite his admirers, colleagues, and friends. For a long time, he enjoyed a close intellectual relationship with John Stuart Mill. They wrote letters to each other discussing each other's work, almost on a monthly basis from November 1841 to May 1847.[27] A close friendship grew between the two. Unfortunately, after a few years strong differences of opinion emerged that affected their relations and led to the termination of their correspondence.

In the end phase of his life he even lost the last remains of academic esteem. Some former colleagues started to doubt his mental health after he had declared that he had stopped reading the work of other scientists for reasons of 'cerebral hygiene'. His audience had dwindled and deteriorated. Most of his students were half-educated but admiring followers who did not dare to criticize him or to probe him with intelligent questions. Totally depraved from the stimulating encounters with intellectual peers, he lost his grip on reality. He now lashed against the intellectuals who failed to acknowledge his wisdom. Instead he praised the natural aptitude of simple workers who frequented his lectures.[28] This might sound rather negative, but we should credit Comte for his great ability to explain complex matters to a lay audience and for all the years he taught common people for free on Sunday afternoons. Thus he transformed his commitment with the plight of the poor in practical actions, for he strongly believed that education could be of great help to these people.

Comte loved debates about academic issues. He was relentless in his attacks when someone did not share his view on social reality and the task of sociology. But he had to pay a formidable price: losing most of his friends and forfeiting his chances of an academic career. However, his character and motivation left him no other option than to fight his opponents. In his view, industrial society was facing such a tremendous crisis that finding a valid explanation of its causes ought to have the highest priority with all social scientists. The constitution of a positive science of society really was a matter of life and death.[29]

During the last years of his life, Auguste Comte retreated to his study, devoting all his energy to his writings. His health was deteriorating. Besides he was weakened by the periods of fasting that he forced himself into to show solidarity with the hungry poor. His loyal maid looked after him until his death. He died on 5 September 1857. He was buried in the famous Paris churchyard Père Lachaise and honored with an impressive statue that can be admired at the Place de la Sorbonne. The statue shows Auguste Comte with Clotilde de Vaux on one side and a manual labourer on the other.

1.4   Under the wings of Saint-Simon

Also Bruce Mazlish situates the birth of sociology in the aftermath of the breakdown of the connections between Man and God, between Man and Nature, and between Man and Society. The first cracks had been dimly seen in the 17th and 18th century, and only became clearly evident in the 19th century. Then, everyone could witness the passage from tradition to modernity. This passage is deplored by conservatives and welcomed by liberals. Conservatives lamented about the loss of a romanticized rural community, while modern liberals and socialists only wished to mitigate the most vicious features of industrialization and capitalism. Revolutionaries wanted to go even further and planned to reconstruct society anew. In the eye of the lamenters all existing social links had been smashed, leaving the world in pieces. To the eye of the innovators things appeared quite differently. What others had seen as functional social connections, they had seen as chains, and in breaking these chains they had prepared the way for individual freedom and independence. Besides, they also believed that they had opened our eyes for new forms of connections and had revealed webs of new affinities and social attractions between people.[30]

Count Saint-Simon clearly was an innovator. He had revealed himself as an ardent admirer of the French Revolution and renounced his title. He was convinced that science would solve the great problems of a rapidly modernizing society; hence he liked to be surrounded by famous scientists and philosophers.[31] He wanted to reform society and the state of anarchy that had emerged after the French revolution.

Saint-Simon has published some of his revolutionary ideas in a famous parable about French society. Herein he boldly states that if France would lose three thousand of its best scholars and artisans overnight, then it would turn into a body without a soul. However, should thirty thousand members of the existing social elite, such as the marshals and generals, the cardinals and bishops, the noblemen and landowners suddenly disappear, then this would not cause the country any harm. On the contrary, then the elite could no longer steal from the burghers and enrich themselves through levies and taxes. No longer could these big scale thieves punish the petty thieves. No longer could this immoral and non-productive elite treat hardworking citizens as inferior people, and urge them to behave morally.[32]

The former count did see it all very clearly. As a consequence of the application of the inventions and discoveries of the natural sciences the whole system of production was changing fundamentally, making the structure of the old social system obsolete. It had turned everything upside down. It had revealed that the unskilled and good-for-nothing members of the traditional elite scandalously profited from the skillful and hardworking people. It was even worse: a useless class ruled over the useful. Clearly, a revolution was inevitable, a revolution that would erase all the privileges of the feudalistic elite. In the new social structure all people would be equal.

Saint-Simon believed that a social system merely is a system of ideas put into practice. Hence, new ideas will lead to a new type of society. New scientific theories will change religions and political systems. Saint-Simon and Comte both acknowledged that the development of science and technology were the prime movers of social transformation. They acknowledged that natural scientists had generated a systematic accumulation of knowledge and had solved many technical problems, but noticed that these eminent researchers did nothing to prevent that society ran into great trouble. Therefore, society needed a new type of science, 'social physics', to guard it against new crises and to lead it into a better organized and just society. The drive to transform society has always inspired and still inspires sociologists.

For Saint-Simon, progress is the most compelling fact of life. He was convinced that the mechanism of progressive development rules our lives. He had observed that industrialization had increased the interdependency of all people. This was a result of the division of labour into partial tasks. Therefore, he hoped that people, though occupying different social positions, would see that they had similar interests. He remained a hierarchical thinker, who transposed the aristocratic hierarchy into a meritocratic one. In his view, people who worked harder and achieved more deserved more prestige and income. Like Montesquieu, he also viewed compulsory education as an important condition for a meritocratic society.

1.5   A strong belief in planning, progress and the unity of mankind

Raymond Aron discerned three phases in the theoretical thinking of Comte. His three major works mark these phases. The first phase, from 1820 to 1826, is that of his early *Opuscules* or little works. Herein he gave a summary treatise on modern history and a plan for the reorganization of society. During the second phase, Comte mainly occupied himself with writing lectures for his *Course on Positive Philosophy* and the third stage concerns his work on the *System of Positive Policy*.[33] Comte's first analysis was inspired by the great problems of a rapidly modernizing society, a society already disorganized by the French revolution. Medieval society was united by the Christian faith as preached by the Catholic Church until the Protestants created a major schism. In medieval times, theological thinking and military actions dominated society. But in the emerging new society scientific theories replaced theological dogma, and industrialists, in the all-inclusive sense of businessmen, managers and bankers, gained prominence over idle noblemen and professional warriors. In no way the old and dying world could be reconciled with the new-born world. The world was in crisis as a result of the demise of the old social structures and the rise of entirely new ones. The only solution would be a victory of the positive scientists and the industrialists. For Comte, the function of sociology is to understand these inevitable historical evolutions, to support and to accelerate them. History has to follow its course, but it could do so in a less cumbersome way, if only historical processes would be better understood and its progress better planned. So, the most urgent thing was to sketch a clear plan. In view of the circumstances there was no time to waste.

Comte realized that this involved an awesome amount of intellectual work that had to be undertaken step by step. He thought that the best way to begin this huge project was to start with a systematic, critical reappraisal of earlier social theories and to rework this in a new synthesis. Secondly, he had to develop a theory of the nature and historical development of the human mind, which he later presented as his Law of Three Stages. Then, on this basis, he had to formulate an entire system of knowledge embracing all the sciences. Eventually, this third step culminated in the exposition of his model of the Hierarchy of Sciences. In the fourth place, he had to formulate and analyze the nature, scope, and essential elements of sociology. In the fifth step, on this basis, he had to venture on a detailed comparative and historical study of the development of major social institutions. All this formed the groundwork for a detailed outline of a new social system that would match the demands of the new era, an epoch in which science and industry would prevail over religion and military power. For Comte, this had to include a theory of a secular religion that could function as an important body of beliefs and rituals establishing the necessary social bonds to maintain this new society. Of course, this new body of beliefs had to come to terms with the new knowledge and practices produced by science and industry. Thus, the newly designed social system should offer a new institutional order for linking the feeling, thought and action of citizens within the new social conditions.[34] Even in his day and age hardly any ambitious and talented young man would think about such an audacious scheme, let alone seriously start it and produce the outcomes in a series of impressive books. Like Saint Simon, Comte asserted that the basic condition of social reform is intellectual reform. It is not by the accidents of a revolution or by violence that a society in crisis will be reorganized, but through a synthesis of the sciences and by the creation of positive politics. In the *Cours de Philosophie Positive* he presented a first overview of the social laws that could explain the diversity of social phenomena as well as the route of the evolution of societies. He embraced Condorcet's suggestion of progress governed by the advancement of the human mind and Bossuet's idea that mankind is a unity on the road to a single goal. Though Comte did not allow theological explanations within the realm of social science, he admired Bossuet's idea. It was eminently suited to indicate

> ... *a general goal which our intelligence must never cease to set itself, a final result of all our historical analysis, I mean the rational co-ordination of the fundamental sequence of the various events of human history according to a single design ...* [35]

This quotation shows that Comte was concerned with the fundamental sequence of historical events according to a single design. Theoretically, he sought to reduce the seemingly infinite variety of human societies and was eager to find proof for the unity of mankind. He was concerned with an ultimate state of mankind. So, according to Aron, the man who is regarded as the founder of positivism can also be described as the last disciple of theological providentialism, although he transformed the interpretation of human history in terms of divine providence into an explanation in terms of general (sociological) laws.[36] In the third and last phase of his intellectual odyssey, he worked on his *Système de Politique Positive*. In this period, he lost his academic audience, stopped writing in an academic style, and became less precise in his formulations.[37] Nonetheless, he stayed loyal to his way of thinking. He presented a philosophical foundation for his idea that mankind is a unity. Through the whole history of mankind all people share a vast number of invariable characteristics. This seems to imply that all societies are constructed on the same basis. Therefore, we should not delude ourselves by the superficial appearance of a huge variety of social forms between tradition-al and modern societies. It must be possible to deduct how historical evolution develops and to use this law of social evolution to support its course. In Comte's view, it is one of the main tasks of sociology to discover the route of historical de-velopment. However, sociology can only have a limited impact, because history will unfold itself along the lines that were predetermined from the beginning. Hence he speaks of a *fatalisme modifié*, a modified fatalism. Since each successive stage in the evolution of mankind necessarily grows out of the preceding one, the construction of the new system cannot take place before the destruction of the old, and not before the potentialities of the old order have been exhausted. The passage from one social system to another can never be continuous and direct.

> *There is always a transitional state of anarchy, which lasts for some generations at least, and lasts the longer the more complete is the renovation to be wrought. The best political progress that can be made during such a period is in gradually demolishing the former system, the foundation of which had been sapped before. While this inevitable process is going on, the elements of the new system are tak-ing form as political institutions, and the reorganization is stimulat-ed by the experience of the evils of anarchy. There is another reason why the constitution of the new system cannot take place before the destruction of the old: without that destruction no adequate concep-tion could be formed of what must be done. Short as is our life, and feeble as is our reason, we cannot emancipate ourselves from the in-fluence of our environment. Even the wildest dreamers reflect in their dreams the contemporary social state: and much more impossible is it to form a conception of a true political system, radically different from that amidst we live. The highest order of minds cannot discern the characteristics of the coming period till they are close upon it, and before that the incrustations of the old system will have been pretty much broken away, and the popular mind will have been used to the spectacle of its demolition.*[38]

This lengthy quotation reveals that Comte was the first of the great sociologists who acknowledged the strong influence prevailing ideas of an era have on indi-vidual minds. These collective ideas dominated the perception of problems as well as the discovery of possible solutions. This basic sociological view on the de-velopment of ideas and the role of a 'collective spirit', a collective conscience or a collective thought style, were later further developed by Emile Durkheim, Lud-wig Fleck, Thomas Kuhn and Mary Douglas. This quotation also reveals a dialec-tical mode of thinking, in which a social system has to degenerate first in order to trigger the necessary ideas, energy and motivation required for striving toward an antithetical new system.

1.6   Social dynamics

In contrast to the eternal repetition of events in the animal kingdom, the succession of human generations offers a fascinating spectacle of changes. An endless chain of causes and effects ties our contemporary situation with all the worlds that have preceded ours. All elements of human knowledge form a communal treasure that each generation hands over to the next. Moreover, in the course of time new knowledge has been added which replaced knowledge that had turned out to be false. Henceforth, the evolution of mankind could only go forward.

1.6.1   The progress of humanity

Until the 19th century, the process of social evolution went on in slow motion, but the growth of science and the expansion of education helped to speed it up. Thus, Comte believed that in the foreseeable future the last remains of superstition and clerical domination would be erased, and all men would become free citizens, thinking and acting more rationally than ever before. He ardently promoted his idea of the historical connection between all generations and the idea of social progress based on an accumulation of knowledge and new insights. His point of departure was the law of evolution that determined the actions of individuals as well as that of mankind as a whole. He discerned three important and invariant aspects or universals of human nature that determine our lives:

1 *Our feelings* – the impulses and emotions which prompt us to activity;
2 *Our thought* – which is undertaken in the service of our feelings, but also helps to govern them;
3 *Our actions* – which are also undertaken in the service of our feelings and in the light of our reflection.

Humans' first impulse is always based on a feeling, motive or emotion. In the next phase, a phase that is often skipped, humans start to think about these feelings, the events that gave rise to them and the directions in which they tend to push them. This moment of reflection can result in a redirection of the first reaction. In the third stage, people carry out their actions. According to Comte, thoughts and actions must harmonize with our feelings. For the existence and continuity of society (broadly defined as a system of shared and regulated behaviour amongst a group of individuals) there must be some order of institutions, knowledge, values, and beliefs which successfully relate the *feelings, thought, and activity* of its members. Comte did not share the view that progress could only manifest itself by an ever-growing subordination of emotions by reason.[39]

1.6.2   The Law of the three stages

In 1725, Giambattista Vico presented the view that intellectual evolution takes place in three stages. At first, only the power and creativity of God or gods are accepted as effective causes, feelings dominate the mind and the model of society is theocratic. In the next stage, explanations are based on heroic actions of people who hold on to highly respected values, such as courage, loyalty, and persever- ance. In the third phase, social phenomena are being explained by the actions of normal people and common sense. In this phase, theocracies are transformed into monarchies and republics. Political freedom is enlarged. For Vico, each subsequent step implies a higher level of thinking, a fuller consciousness of real- ity and one's role and place in that reality. Human intelligence matured, which manifested itself in a better understanding of nature and God. Supposedly, Vico was the first to present a model of historical progress in which later periods could profit from the achievements of earlier periods and elaborate them further. His idea that the maturation of the human mind was a collective process foreshadows the ideas that were later presented by Hegel.[40]

Comte's model of historical stages closely resembles that of Vico. He also dis- cerns three stages: the theological or fictive stage, the metaphysical or abstract stage, and the positive or scientific stage. He further divided the theological stage in three sub-stages: fetishism, polytheism and monotheism.

- Fetishism – In this state everything in nature is thought to be imbued with spiritual life and feelings analogous to our own
- Polytheism – In this stage unrestrained imagination fills the world with innu- merable gods and spirits
- Monotheism – In this phase many gods are unified into one almighty god, largely in the service of awakening reason, which qualifies and exercises con- straint upon imagination.[41]

Scheme 1.1   The three stages of explanatory thought

Vico	Comte
1 Acts of God	1 **Theological phase**
	– *fetishism/animism*
	– *polytheism*
	– *monotheism*
2 Heroic acts	2 **Metaphysical phase (Half-hypothetical phase)**
3 Normal human acts	3 **Phase of positive science (Hypothetical phase)**

For Comte, the necessity of the intellectual evolution lies in the primary tenden- cy of all human beings to transfer the sense of their own nature into an explana- tion of all phenomena whatsoever. In the childhood years of mankind, the only way that they could explain many phenomena is by comparing them to human or animalistic acts – the only ones whose production they could partly under- stand. They could only explain the intimate nature of phenomena in likening them, as much as possible, to the acts of human will, through a primary tendency to regard all beings as living a life analogous to their own. This is also true for the spirits or gods they invented: analogous to men, but far superior because of their greater power and energy. For many millennia, this anthropomorphic way of thinking or theorizing has been extremely influential. All the time, people believed that supernatural beings held extreme powers over them. History has shown that mankind had to fight hard to emancipate itself from this kind of reasoning.[42]

Fortunately, the roots for developing the alternatives lay within theological thinking itself. In the past, religious groups had instituted a special class of people that had to devote a significant part of their time, if not all, to interpreting tragic aspects of reality such as human suffering, death and natural disasters; by adducing the acts or feelings of supernatural beings as possible causes. Here we find the start of a caste that could free itself from practical chores to engage in theoretical issues. The establishment of this new caste of intellectual professionals was a major step in the development of human societies. It may have formed the principal model for the establishment of other new classes, castes or guilds. For Comte, who, like Saint-Simon, was convinced that all progress is directed by intellectual development, the constitution of this new class of sacred people was as important for mankind as the invention of the wheel. Also he thought that there could not be another way for establishing this division of labour except through the divide between theory and practice. There had to be very good reasons for discharging people from tiresome physical labour. The only acceptable reason was involvement in sacred activities, activities that were esteemed to be of far greater value than the mere gathering of food. Any spiritual expansion supposes the existence of a privileged class, enjoying the leisure indispensable to intellectual activity. This select group was urged to develop rituals and highly speculative activities that were supposed to keep people healthy and to bless hunting expeditions and harvests.[43] The emergence of a class of shamans and priests led to a steady refinement of thinking. Though many of these religious leaders used their great intellect to find ingenuous rationalizations for all kinds of dogmas that were hard to defend, a small group developed a highly rational and more convincing approach to problem solving, because from the beginning of mankind they had to convince all sensible people that used their common sense to question some of their doctrines and explanations. As a consequence, it was unavoidable that some of these shamans, priests and monks eventually became scientific thinkers.

In the beginning of the theological stage the forces or actions of an anthropomorphic God or other supernatural beings are used to explain all phenomena. This was the only kind of reasoning that made sense at this stage, in which people knew about themselves, their own feelings and drives; this was the only kind of reasoning that made sense. People believed in absolute knowledge, presented by 'animated' objects. Everyone thought that all objects in nature are endowed with a form of life that is very similar with their own existence. To the 'savage' the world in general is animate, and trees are no exception to the rule. For instance, the Wanika in Eastern Africa fancy that every cocoanut tree has a soul or houses a spirit. To them, the destruction of a cocoanut tree is the equivalent of matricide, because these trees give life and nourishment, such as a mother does her child. When the clove-trees are in blossom on the Moluccan isles they are treated like pregnant women. No noise must be made near them; no fire must be carried past them at night. These precautions are observed lest the tree should drop its fruit too soon, like a woman can lose her child prematurely. Sometimes, it is believed that the souls of their ancestors animate the trees.[44] I have dwelled a bit at this example of tree worship, to remind us that all these phases are still not entirely dead. Even in modern times, a number of people talk to trees and believe that they are communicating with them. Undoubtedly, we live in an age that is dominated by economy, science, and technology; yet many people still indulge in unscientific views. For some, it is a kind of revolt against the domination of the hard sciences; for others, it offers refuge from the hectic pace of modern society, a refuge in which they can indulge in pseudo explanations for the things that cannot be explained yet or never will.

Let us return to Comte's model. In the second sub-phase (polytheism) people start to believe in various kinds of supernatural forces. People imagine numerous gods and spirits that are specialized to act in specific domains: sea gods, forest gods, river gods, rain gods, fertility gods, et cetera. This led to an infinite proliferation of specialized gods and spirits that might come to represent conflicting interests. The accumulated experience of thousands of generations not only stimulates our imagination but also the further development of our common sense, which then starts to bridle our fantasies, including our wildest ideas about the power of specific gods or the possible conflicts between different gods. So, a few thousand years ago, in the Middle East, the huge number of specialized gods and spirits started to shrink until a point was reached in which only one almighty God was accepted and viewed as the one and only God that created the whole universe out of nothing. From then on, every remarkable event was attributed to the will of that one and only God.[45] Comte thought that once the reflective tendencies leading to monotheism have taken place, they cannot be held in check. They lead to the second stage of thought: the metaphysical stage. To him, this was only a transitional period.

In the metaphysical stage supernatural forces are still used to explain events, but they are criticized too. More and more, explanatory forces like gods and spirits are replaced by personified abstractions. Men now pursue meaning for and explanations of the world in terms of 'essences', 'the force of life', 'the nature of things', 'ideals', and 'forms': in short, in conceptions of some 'ultimate reality'. Neither the theological nor the abstract, metaphysical ways of explanation, their ways of relating feeling, thought, and action, are adequate. Intellectually, they are found to be wanting. They never resolve problems. They fail when brought to the test of practical experience. As human society becomes more complicated because of industrialization and urbanization, theological and metaphysical systems of thought become increasingly inadequate. Comte mentioned as an example of metaphysical thinking that opium supposedly causes sleep because of its 'sleepy virtue or essence.' Metaphysical concepts cannot provide reliable knowledge about physical, medical, technical, economic or political problems. Hence, they are overcome or will eventually be superseded by positive science.[46] Whereas imagination strongly prevailed during the theological and the metaphysical stage, the real strength of the positive stage lay in methodical observation. This powerful tool was going to kill all imaginative explanations that did not stand the test.

At the end of this section it is appropriate to say a little bit more about Comte's dynamic model of intellectual, historical or social change. Crucial is his tenet that major changes in our thinking and in the social and political structure of society cannot happen overnight. For most individuals the shock would be too great or even impossible to cope with. The same is true for societies as a whole, or for social groups who have been accustomed to traditional ways that have existed for decades or generations or even hundreds or thousands of years. To ensure a gradual and peaceful shift from one mode to a completely different one, we always need a transitory period or intermediate model to pave the way for the necessary new idea or practice. Common sense or more systematic critical analysis must have revealed some weak spots in the old system and produced new ideas that could constitute a valuable alternative. In the first stage of corrosion even the new ideas still resemble much of the old ideas, but they create a basis for further comments, critiques and the invention of alternatives. It takes time for the new ideas to gain support and to become a counterforce that would be strong enough to overcome the weakened forces of the past. Here, we see his model for analyzing historical change, be it great shifts in worldviews or great shifts in the structure of society. A convincing theory has to find evidence of processes that lead the process of corroding and weakening the old philosophy, regime, or practice and also provide evidence as to how new emerging ideas and joint efforts by groups of people have produced a significant change.

1.7   Comte: The staunch advocate of positivism

The creation of Social Science demands that Observation should preponderate over Imagination.

Within social science Comte was the first great champion of positivism. He invented this very term.[47] In positivism all scientific explanations are based upon facts. Only the facts that can be observed by our senses are acceptable. Phenomena that cannot be observed objectively fall outside the realm of science. This view on science was not original. It was introduced and put into practice by famous scholars like Bacon, Descartes, and Galileo, whom Comte regarded as the founders of the positive method of science.[48] Positivists shun all theological and metaphysical problems. Not because they are meaningless, but because they cannot be tested. As scientists, positivists are not at all interested in a search for initial or final causes, or in metaphysical questions about the meaning of life, or the essence of things. If one wishes to ponder on these types of questions, then by all means one should do so, but according to positive scientists these kinds of questions do not belong to science and will not be very helpful in solving practical problems and lead us to a new and better world.

The basic assumption of positivists is that all observable facts are submitted to fixed laws. It is the goal of science to discover those laws and to reduce them to a minimal number of basic laws. These laws are nothing more than statements about the way in which facts, that is data of observed phenomena, are related. There are laws concerning the static and dynamic aspects of social existence. The first type concerns the coexistence of phenomena, things that exist simultaneously. The second type concerns the phenomena that constantly appear after each other. Comte searched for the first type of laws when he started to study statical sociology and the second type for dynamical sociology.

Comte's fundamental doctrine of positive science consists of the following principles:

1   We have no knowledge of anything but observable phenomena.
2   Our knowledge of phenomena is relative, not absolute.
3   We do not know the essence, nor the real mode of production, of any fact but only its relations to other facts in the way of succession or similitude.
4   These relations are constant; that is, always the same in the same circumstances.
5   The constant resemblances which link phenomena, and the constant sequences which unite them as antecedent and consequent, are termed their laws.

These laws are all we know of them. Their essential nature, and their ultimate causes, either efficient or final, is unknown and inscrutable to us.[42]

Box 1.1

1.7.1   The methods of positive science

True positive science aims at the discovery of general laws that fit our observations. In particular, it intends to create a prevision with which we can make concrete predictions, as is already the case in the natural sciences. Comte expected that, in the long run, also sociology would reach this level of positive science.[50] He deemed the following four procedures necessary to arrive at valid and reliable social knowledge:

1   observation
2   experimentation
3   comparison
4   historical analysis.

Firstly, the scientific attitude is radically distinguished from the theological and metaphysical by the steady subordination of the imagination to observation. Positive science restricts itself to discovering observable facts and perfecting the theoretical connection between these observed facts. Despite this restriction it offers the vastest and richest field to human imagination.[51] Comte underlines that observations are only useful if they are done within the framework of a specific theory. Social facts become meaningful if they are related to other facts, at least within a provisional theory or hypothesis. Without the guidance of a preparatory theory, the observer would not know what facts to look for. No social fact can have any scientific meaning until it is connected with some other social fact by a preliminary theory.[52]

Secondly, theories should always be tested with the help of experiments, in the sense of controlled observations, that is, under controlled circumstances. Although a direct, unadulterated and carefully premeditated labouratorial experiment often is impossible or unethical in social sciences, we can still study pseudo-experiments. These kinds of experiments occur when the normal course of affairs is disturbed by unexpected events such as accidents, natural catastrophes such as floods, great outbursts of volcanoes, or periods of extreme cold that cut off people from the rest of society. Hence, pathological social situations offer great opportunities for scientists to test their theories, like diseases in plants and animals offer great opportunities for biologists.

Thirdly, the comparative method has the advantage of offering a powerful antidote against absolutism and unwarranted generalizations. Scrutinizing many social phenomena in different contexts can open our eyes to distinctions, but also to the general laws of human civilization. Comparisons of human groups or societies with collectivities of animals will give us precious clues for the first beginnings of social relations. Naturally, comparisons within the human species are more central to sociology. Though Comte was convinced that the human race as a whole has progressed in a single and uniform manner, various populations have attained extremely unequal degrees of development and we still don't know why. Hence, certain phases of development of which the history of Western civilization leaves no perceptible traces can be known only by comparative studies of 'primitive' societies.

The historical method is a special case of the comparative method. The only difference is that the historical method compares existing societies with societies of the past. The historical comparison is an essential device of sociology. Observation, experimentation and comparison are methods that are used in all positive sciences, but the historical comparison of societies or social phenomena is a new tool that is dearly needed in sociology. According to Comte, sociology is nothing if it is not informed by a sense of historical evolution.[53] Whether Comte himself was a meticulous applicant of historical comparisons is a matter of opinion. Fletcher admires him for his clear historical account of the shifting nature of European institutions – moving through a vast array of facts with such certain perspectives and analytical conceptions, whereas others have accused him of merely giving illustrative facts randomly picked from history. [54]

1.7.2   Why positive science is positive

According to Auguste Comte, there are many good reasons for using the epithet positive. In the first place the word indicates that positive science occupies itself with facts and not with fantasy. It occupies itself with everything that can be observed, with everything that can be understood with the help of sound reasoning or common sense. Positive science also refers to scientific work or problem solving that aims at being useful to mankind, and does not waste time with meaningless issues. In the third place Comte contends that positive sciences aim at a permanent improvement of our living conditions, an improvement that leads to positive developments for social groups or social wholes as well as for individuals. And fourth, the term positive points to the goal of science to produce precision in its statements and predictions in contrast to the vague statements of people in other fields such as in politics or in the theological or metaphysical stage of philosophy. Comte even adds a fifth reason by simply presenting positive science as the opposite of negative science. Positive science is directed towards organization, composition and construction and not towards creating chaos, destruction or decomposition. If the new positive science has been criticizing, falsifying and destructing old insights and convictions it only did so for the sake of clearing the way for more valid and more useful theories. Moreover, positive science aspires to approach and solve scientific problems without prejudice and to rid itself from the cultural biases as much as it can. And as far as positive science needs to be critical because it must criticize views and theories that no longer are tenable, it will do this with the help of sound arguments and respect and not by ridiculing, making caustic remarks and showing contempt.[55]

1.7.3   Critique and counter critique

Comte has been greatly criticized for his sweeping claims on behalf of positive science, but a careful examination of his work shows that his claims were rather modest. Besides, most of his views about methodology and epistemology are similar to those of modern philosophers of science. His positivistic approach does not exclude the role of intuition, feelings and imagination. All scientists have to use their creativity and imagination to produce new concepts, models, hypotheses and theories. They play an important role in the progress of science, but will be omitted as soon as they do not stand rigorous testing. They are subordinated to the positive methods of observation and testing. For Comte, science is a type of 'industry' that needs intuition, imagination and other forms of creativity to form or improve hypotheses about the way phenomena are connected. He was perfectly clear about the role played by hypotheses:

> *If it is true that every theory must be based upon observed facts, it is equally true that facts cannot be observed without the guidance of some theory. Without such guidance, our facts would be desultory and fruitless; we could not retain them; for the most part we could not even perceive them.*

So, all that Popper has said about 'conjectures and refutations' and the 'hypothet-ical-deductive method'; all that Parsons has said about 'theory before empirical investigation', was stated with perfect clarity by Comte, a hundred years earlier.[56]

Another point of critique regards his view on predictions. It is often thought that Comte conceived of 'prediction' as a matter of 'predicting future states of society' as though he wished sociology to possess a kind of historical clairvoyance. But he clearly acknowledged that such a thing is impossible. Societies are far too complex and sociological knowledge is light years away from completion. His notion of 'pre-vision' or 'prediction' was in every way the same as that of contemporary science.

> *Prevision is a necessary consequence of the discovery of constant re-lations between phenomena ... Thus the true positive spirit consists above all in seeing for the sake of foreseeing; in studying what is, in order to 'infer what will be, in accordance with the general dogma that natural laws are invariable.[57]*

He only meant to say that if you would have a valid theory about the relation be-tween two social phenomena, then you could predict what will happen to the second phenomenon if the first one changes, and other phenomena don't inter-fere. Such knowledge would offer you an instrument to interfere in the course of affairs of these particular phenomena. But Comte has never intended to predict inevitable historical trends for whole societies.[58] Such a tall order would require knowledge of the behaviour of hundreds of variables, most of them interfering with each other. Although he was a staunch advocate of positivism, Comte also was very keen in emphasizing its limits, restrictions, and pitfalls. It is simply im-possible to know the future of mankind. The future will be shaped by knowledge we have not yet discovered and by innovations that this new knowledge will en-gender, or by other spontaneous changes that might take place. Therefore, we can never be sure that certain insights we now believe to be true might be based on false observations or based on invalid conclusions. On the other hand, we can prepare ourselves somewhat better against all kinds of risks and dangers, thanks to the growth and accumulation of positive knowledge, including the improve-ment of methods of research.[59]

Frequently positivism is associated with a form of research that is completely focused on statistical analysis. Therefore, it is good to mention that Comte and Saint-Simon both had an aversion of statistics and statisticians. The latter often spoke of sad counters and calculators.[60] According to Comte, who always had excelled in mathematics, statistics could even endanger social science. The aura of science could prevent wrong conclusion from being exposed. Precisely his aversion for statistics urged him to invent an alternative name for this new social science. He renounced the name 'social physics' because the Belgian statistician Quetelet had published a book about social statistics entitled *Physique sociale*.

Therefore, in 1838, he proposed to call the new science sociology. Comte was the first to warn us against the danger of the degeneration of positive science into a frenzied collection of random facts with no other merit than being precise. Like all positive sciences sociology faces two great dangers. It balances between empiricism and mysticism, between an unstoppable, but unimaginative *bric à brac* of exact and concrete facts and an intangible mist of vague concepts and highly abstract theories. But true science does not solely rest on pure observations, how important they might be in themselves.

> *Facts in themselves, how exact and how numerous, merely form the basic material for the creation of science.*[61]

Among many strands of present-day sociology 'positivism' is a dirty word. By many it is regarded as a superficial and outmoded approach, and characterized as a naive and uncritical application of the methods of the so-called hard sciences as physics and chemistry, sciences that only have to deal with material objects. Since sociology has to deal with the subjective meanings of individuals, it needs a more profound, more penetrating and more 'interpretative' understanding of social action. With this type of critique whole generations have constructed a superfluous dichotomy between the positivistic approach and their own. But Comte never entertained for a moment any simple notion of 'natural science', which could be applied without qualification to the study of man and society. His positivistic sociology never rested upon any such conception. It was never deterministic and never postulated causal necessity. It was never confined to 'phenomena' in any narrow sense; never excluded 'action' or the 'interpretation of action' from the distinctive level of social facts. In Comte's own words: positive science

> *... is exclusively occupied in discovering laws, that is to say, the constant relations of similitude and succession which subsist between facts.* [62]

These scientific 'laws' are only statements of *constant concomitance* or *regularities of connection* among physical or social facts. No metaphysic of causality or determinism underlies them.

Positivistic prediction is no more than the clear statement of a law, and what could be expected to follow from it by way of deductions and inferred connections in particular cases under specified conditions. Prediction is the crucial test of knowing. Knowing the regular connections between particular facts means knowing what will happen in specified cases. But arrangements of social facts are modifiable by our actions as soon as we know the 'law like' connections between them. So, to see is to be able to foresee, and also to be able to prevent or to modify in the light of this foresight, but, even so, in all cases the extent to which we could modify people's actions depends upon the reliability of our knowledge of their inter-connections. [63]

The claims of positivism were and still are very modest, stemming from a clear recognition of the limitations of science. But, curiously, it was just this which gave them reliability and usefulness. It proved to be the most useful source of knowledge just because it discarded insupportable pretensions and deliberately limited its scope. It claimed no certainty; offered no final solutions of 'ultimate' questions. Yet, the revealed connections constituted the primary basis for effective actions and social improvement. The laws discovered and tested by positive science provided a clear and effective basis for foresight and deliberate action: a basis for practical and social use.[64]

1.8   Comte's classification of sciences

Comte did not reduce all the qualitative detail and distinctions of human experience to the kinds of phenomena studied by the natural sciences. There are distinctive differences of 'level' between the facts studied by biology and sociology. Biology can explain much about the nature of man as a species, and as an organism, and even about some basic, elementary characteristics of human grouping. But, from a certain point, it becomes clear that language, institutions, cultural traditions, etc. are facts of a different level: the outcome of the associational activities of men within shared collective conditions, and involving the different processes of historical continuity, accumulation, change, cultural transmission, social development and evolution. Therefore, Comte concludes that:

> ... considerations of primary importance demonstrate the absolute necessity of separating the study of collective phenomena of the human race from that of individual phenomena; while establishing, nonetheless, the natural relations that exist between these great sections of physiology.[65]

Still, social facts are of a qualitatively different level. Social facts are characterized by their cumulative, cultural and historical nature. Hence their investigation requires an autonomous science that uses distinctive methods to reveal the interconnections between these facts. Yet, sociology must remain in close touch with these biologically given starting points.

1.8.1   *Criteria for the classification of sciences*

Comte created a classification of sciences according to their advancement on the road to positivism. As criteria for this classification he chose historical age, decreasing generality and growing complexity of subject matter, the degree to which one science expanded on a preceding science and the degree to which it constituted the necessary precondition for the development of a succeeding science. Thus he arranged the sciences in a series of which each term represents an advance in specialty and complexity beyond the science preceding it. In his view they stand in the following order: mathematics, astronomy, physics, chemistry, biology, and finally sociology or social sciences.

After mathematics, which only studied abstractions like numbers and geometry with the help of logical reasoning, came the empirical sciences that studied dead matter such as astronomy, physics, and chemistry through observations. Mathematics provides the basic instruments for the study and the expression in formulas of the laws governing the movements of the stars, physical particles and forces. The study of physics helps to explain many chemical processes, and in turn the laws of physics and chemistry help scientists to get a better insight in the complex biological processes, though the explanation of all organic processes cannot be reduced to laws that explain the mechanics of inorganic matter. Each new class of science requires a more arduous inquiry than its predecessor. So, it is no wonder that sociology arrived rather late. It occupies itself with the most complex phenomena of all.

Comte had set it as his goal to make the science of society the final piece of the positive sciences. However, he realized that sociology, as a brand new science, still had a long way to go to reach the level of sophistication that other positive sciences had already achieved. In his day and age, much of social philosophy was still used in a theological or metaphysical sense, as could be witnessed by the frequent use of concepts such as *'divine rights'*, or *'sovereignty of the people'*. The first concept is typical for theological thinking and the second is metaphysical. More than a hundred years later positive sociologists would fulminate against the use of vague and abstract, if not mythical concepts such as 'the general interest of the public'.[66]

As a reason for the late emergence of sociology Comte mentioned the complexity of social existence, which encompasses all other phenomena. As organic beings, the laws of physics, chemistry and biology govern human beings. Besides, complex and stubborn psychological and social forces limit our ability to discover and manipulate particular social processes. Another complication is that social scientists form a part of the subject matter they study. Critics of positivism have argued that it is precisely this complexity that makes the search for general laws unattainable. They also argue that objective social research is unfeasible because of our involvement in social affairs. Undoubtedly, these are strong arguments. However, it does not seem wise to abandon all efforts to be as objective as possible and to seek for theories that are valid in the widest possible range of social contexts.

Other than leaning on its preceding science in the series, each new type of science also introduces a new method of explanation. It is impossible to obtain a good explanation of a complex phenomenon by reducing it to explanations based on the characteristics of its less complex parts or on the more general phenomena studied by the preceding sciences. Thus, biology has a relative autonomy with regard to physics and chemistry, despite the fact that biological organisms are subject to physical and chemical laws. There also are biological phenomena that are only characteristic for living organisms. Therefore, they can only be explained by biological insights that have no use for physics and chemistry. In a similar fashion sociology is relatively autonomous from biology. Human beings are influenced by former generations: they have learned from them and will pass this knowledge on to the next generation. But people can and will change some of their views on reality and change their way of life. This is not the case with plants and animals. The latter do not have the potential for accumulating knowledge and experience in the course of history. The accumulation of knowledge is one of the motors of social change. So sociology's main contribution to positive science is the necessary introduction of historical comparison. The historical method helps us to detect social laws that determine social development.

Each class of science has contributed to the development of the positive sciences. Mathematics has helped to develop our capacity for logical reasoning. Astronomy has taught us to make good observations and to propose hypotheses. Physics has introduced the experiment as a good method for testing hypotheses, and chemistry has taught us that the introduction of a nomenclature can be very helpful. Biology introduced quite new concepts such as the organism, organic functions, systems and subsystems, statics and dynamics, and necessary conditions for survival. Biology introduced complex classifications of the world of plants and the animal kingdom. Even more important is its introduction of synthesis as a scientific method. Long ago, analysis had already proven its great value within the realm of inorganic chemistry. Synthesis is of the greatest importance for the study of organic matter. Within the realm of biology it is impossible to explain the functioning of a part of an organism if one does not take into consideration the whole organism.

Some comments seem in order. Though the living organism is always a whole, one can do useful research by cutting off small pieces and analyze them carefully. Even very small pieces of a dead organism can render many insights. The whole discipline of pathological anatomy is based on this idea and has proven its great value for medical science. Cutting extremely thin slices of an organism (dead or alive), subsequently treating it with a large range of physical and chemical processes, can bring to light all kinds of characteristics that never could be discovered otherwise. The introduction of synthesis does not mean that there is no use for analysis in biology and sociology. Both methods are needed.

However, Comte was a holist. He was convinced that it is impossible to understand social phenomena, unless one situates them in the context of the social whole. There always is a spontaneous harmony between the whole and the parts of the social system, the elements of which must inevitably be combined in a mode entirely comfortable to their nature. For Comte, it was evident that not only most political institutions and social customs must be mutually connected with prevailing ideas and manners. This consolidate whole must further be connected with the corresponding state of development of humanity, considered in all its aspects, of intellectual, moral, and physical activity. Even during revolutionary periods, when harmony seems at its lowest point, it still exists. A minimal degree of harmonious interconnectedness is needed to prevent the dissolution of the social organism.[67] In similar vein, one cannot fully appreciate the period of the Restoration if one does not understand the Revolution that preceded it. And one cannot comprehend the emergence and the course of the revolution if one does not take in account the monarchist period before the revolution. But if one follows this line of thought, one encounters an obvious difficulty: to understand one moment in the evolution of the French nation, one must refer to the entire history of the human race. The logical consequence of this principle is that the object of sociology is the entire history of the human race. Even if this would be true for the whole field individual scholars and even large research groups have to satisfy themselves with partial knowledge of specific topics. Fortunately, we can learn a lot that way.

1.9 Industrial society

Like all founding fathers of sociology, Comte has studied the emergence and early development of industrial societies. He has noticed the workings of two crucial forces: science and industrialization. He saw the paradox of their promise and their threat: the promise that they can liberate all men from the age-old tyrannies of poverty and power, but also the threat that they may dehumanize them. All this has been analyzed by the great sociologists of the early days: Karl Marx, Ferdinand Tönnies, Emile Durkheim, Georg Simmel, Werner Sombart, Max Weber, and others, each exploring and highlighting different aspects of modernization. They all witnessed a remarkable evolution or even a revolution of social structures and social institutions. They all sought to understand these changes, their causes and the conflicts that emerged in their wake. They sought to understand them in order to be able to remedy the problems that these changes brought about. And all have been concerned with issues and principles of social justice.

Raymond Aron distinguishes the following six characteristics of industrial society:

1 Industry constitutes a scientific organization of labour. Instead of proceeding according to custom, modern production is organized to create the largest output at the lowest costs.

2 As a result of the application of science to the organization of labour, man is engaged in a tremendous growth of total production and wealth.

3 Industrial production implies a huge concentration of workers in factories. It engenders the phenomenon of masses of workers thronging in industrial areas and the thinning out of the countryside.

4 These concentrations of workers bring about an antagonism between employees and employers, between proletariat and capitalists.

5 Whereas wealth, as a result of the scientific character of labour, continues to increase, there is also an increase in crises of overproduction, which can create shocking poverty in the midst of abundance.

6   The economy of industrial societies is characterized by so-called free enter-
    prise: profit seeking on the part of the management. Some theorists conclude
    that the increase of wealth is larger the lesser the state interferes with econom-
    ic affairs.[68]

The first three points are characteristic for Comte's approach. People have always
been capable of producing more than they could consume. After they discovered
the technique for the preservation of food during longer periods they could systematically accumulate more material goods and capital.

> The fact that this surplus exists and can be maintained beyond the
> time requisite for reproduction, makes the formation of material
> commodities possible. ... (They) increase with each generation both
> of the family and the state, especially when the fundamental institu-
> tion of Money allows us to exchange at will the less durable produc-
> tions for such as descend to our posterity.[69]

The collective material wealth grows, if each generation hands over more wealth
than it has received from their predecessors. For Comte, the formation of a material surplus, an absolute precondition for the accumulation of property and
capital, forms the material basis of social development, but equally or even more
important was its social transmission. This is the first essential basis of all real
civilization. This enhances our capacity to live with a greater number of people
in concentrated areas. The production, preservation, and distribution of material goods and capital require and enable some kind of collective concentration
and social organization. Without a good organization of exchange, transport and
distribution surpluses of good will lose their value and rot before they are consumed. Hence, Comte concluded that techniques of transmission have a greater
influence on the progress of any civilization than direct production.[70]
For the socialists, the most striking features of industrialization are mentioned
under point 4 and 5: the antagonism between the proletarians and the capitalistic
entrepreneurs, and the manifold crises that lead to the scandal of poverty in the
midst of extravagant richness. They are a living proof of the anarchy of the capitalist system. Marx has based his major theories on these two points. The liberals
have put their entire hope on point six. For them, the free market is the most important condition for the wealth of nations.
Comte reproached the economists for dissecting the economy from the rest of
society. Furthermore, he was convinced that they attached too much value to the
influence of the free market on the growth of wealth. He was not opposed to the
concentration of the means of production, but saw this as an inherent mechanism of industrialization. He did not agree with the socialists who think that
such a concentration demands nationalization. He did not think the choice between private property and state ownership that important. At the end of the day,
it always is a small number of persons that determine economic and social policy.

Since each society needs economical leadership, he thought it far better if experienced people with special knowledge of financial and economic affairs execute this leadership. Hence, capitalists and captains of industry should put their capital and means of production at the service of society as a whole, and not use it all for their own whims. They should conceive their function as a social function. Opinions like these came very close to the views that dominate the ideology of Social Catholicism.

Comte did not put much weight on economic crises either. In his view, they are not inherent of industrial capitalism, as Marx would have it, but are pathologies that can and will be healed. If industrial relations run off the rails, it is because society is not well organized yet. Contrary to Marx, he did not believe that there is an essential contradiction between the workers and the entrepreneurs. He acknowledged that there have been fierce conflicts between both classes about the redistribution of wealth, but economic growth would be in everybody's interest. Industrial society obeys only one law, the law to create economic growth and material wealth. Whereas the liberals thought that this law was based on the principles of the free market, Comte thought that organizational engineers (*polytechniciens organisateurs*), created wealth by inventing evermore efficient ways of production that saved costs of raw material and labour. He was very optimistic and thought that the scientific organization of society eventually but inevitably would put everyone in the right place and the right profession. This would also create social justice.[71] The interests of workers and businessmen would converge when industrialization developed further. The workers would develop into politically active citizens. The inhumane conditions of labour would drive them to political demands for the betterment of their situation. They would be the first to realize that their plight could not be explained by the will of God, by their limited talents or by their immoral character. Such explanations could find support from employers, because they were focused only on making profits and not on the well being of their employees. Comte contended that eventually the workers would arrive at positive insights, for their minds were not clogged by the petty worries and preoccupations of the bourgeoisie, nor were their minds being spoiled by the stupidities of traditional formal education.[72]

1.10 The organic society

Comte saw a strong affinity between sociology and biology. Both have a strong interest in 'organic bodies'. He was convinced of the practical use of the organic model for sociological theory:

> *If we take the best ascertained points in Biology, we may decompose structure anatomically into elements, tissues, and organs. We have the same things in the Social Organism, and may even use the same names.*[73]

In Comte's view, families are the true elements or cells of the Social Organism, Classes or Castes are its proper tissue, and Cities and Communes are its real organs.[74] In that way he developed a model of society that clearly reflected the morphology of biological organisms. The affinity between biology and sociology led Comte to divide sociology into static sociology, or morphology, and dynamical sociology that studies social growth and development. A full-grown sociology should engage itself with static as well as dynamic phenomena. Structures and processes supplement each other. Social statics investigates the existential preconditions of mankind and society. Social dynamics studies social development.

In the theological and metaphysical phases it was believed that order and change were each other's archenemies. Theologians defended order as a creation of God, and the metaphysical thinkers tended to favour change and progress. Comte contended, on the basis of his observation of growth in biological organisms, that change and progress could be combined with order and stability.

The first doctrine of static sociology is that society is an organic whole, a whole that is more than the sum of its parts. This statement must have intrigued thousands of people. How can anything be more than the sum total of its parts? Let us take some common examples such as a rifle, a car or a washing machine. Soldiers have to learn how to decompose a rifle as quickly as possible, to clean it, and then to put it together again. If all the parts are spread out on a table and you have a bullet lying next to it, the total is completely useless when an enemy suddenly enters the room. Only when all the parts, including the bullets, have been put together again, then you might be able to defend yourself. So what does make the rifle more than the sum of the parts? It is the structure in which all the parts are assembled in the right way. Only then a rifle, a car, or a washing machine can fulfill its function. So it is the coherence between the parts that creates its added value. A coherence that consists of a putting the parts in the right structure or frame, and the cohesive or clicking mechanism that holds the parts together. In similar vein we can observe that society is more than the sum total of all its individual members. More is needed to constitute a society. We not only need a social structure to put or keep all members in the right place, but we also need a culture, a set of norms and values, customs and traditions, that induces people to support this structure, to legitimize each position in the structure. Functioning societies need a structure and culture. Though the one cannot exist without the other, they can be analyzed separately.

Comte stressed the central significance of the division of labour. His analysis of the nature of society, its units, structural elements, its apparatus and their mutual relations within the social system as a 'whole', rested entirely on the phenomenon of the division of functions and the combination of efforts that arise as soon as a community emerges and succeeds to survive. Thus he presented the first structural functional analysis of the nature social order and social change in relation to the social and ecological environment.

For Comte, the binding material is the *consensus universalis*. That universal consensus gives rise to the necessary cohesion and integration of society. It creates organic solidarity, a term that we will encounter again in the chapter on Durkheim. Consensus, as the binding force of a harmonious society also plays an important role in the theories of Talcott Parsons and Jürgen Habermas. The principle of consensus teaches us that we never should study social phenomena in isolation. We should always try to connect these phenomena to other social phenomena.

The second important theme of Comte's theory of social forms is the *spontaneity* of the social order. He agreed with Aristotle that man is a social being. In his view the individual is a theoretical abstraction. Individuals – individual literary means non-dividable - cannot exist in total isolation. They need a social group, a social context, like fish need water. Hence, social coherence and order emerge spontaneously and not on the basis of a social contract or other forms of rational planning.

The third theme of social statics is the family. Comte viewed the family as the most fundamental social unit. Not individuals, but families are the building blocks of society. The family possesses a certain unity and coherence, and a moral climate. As the smallest unit of the social structure it already possesses a subculture of its own. Family life lays the foundation for the formation of social beings. Here, children are socialized. Here they learn basic norms and standards of social behaviour and core forms of social relations. Three types of social relations characterize the nuclear family: the conjugal, the filial or parental, and the fraternal relation. For Comte, the conjugal relationship was most important of all. It constitutes the basis of all social relations. Hence, he strongly opposed divorce and adultery. In his view, divorce is a manifestation of the anarchical spirit of the times that pervades modern society. The filial relation functions as a major playground for acquiring proper respect for authorities, whereas the fraternal relationship offers good opportunities for the development of feelings of solidarity. From the political or moral point of view, Comte emphasized the necessity of maintaining monogamous relationships and the fact that inequality is inherent in familial relations. Parents, in particular fathers, have or should have a natural authority over their children.[75] It does not surprise us that he was heavily criticized for advocating the idea that wives should never be equal to their husbands.

Whereas the family functions on the basis of love and affinity, the bigger social units need other sources for realizing cooperation and a division of labour. Bigger social organizations need specialized sections. According to Comte, society does not produce cooperation, but cooperation is a necessary precondition for any society. But there is a danger that too much cooperation will lead to too much watching of each other's acts while losing sight of the prerequisites of the whole. Therefore, it is the task of the government to guard the interests of the whole. The further specialization proceeds, the more we need the state to supervise and control affairs. With this view Comte situated himself at a great distance of the liberals. In fact, he believed that modernizing societies needed an authoritarian political system, to safeguard the unity of society. A strong state incorporated the reaction of the whole against the divisive and individualistic actions of the parts.

1.11   A new religion and a new moral

In the last phase of his life Comte wrote a second magnum opus. This one deals with the political system and the religion of humanity. For Comte, social science should address itself to matters that could lead the gradual betterment of society. Hence his device is '*Savoir pour prévoir et prévoir pour pouvoir*'. Translated in a freely manner: knowing to enable forecasting and forecasting to enable effective government. In his view, a better society is first and for all an orderly society. After the chaotic periods Comte had experienced during his lifetime, the return of order, peace and quiet was the issue that fascinated him most of all. To safeguard social order we need two independent powers: a moral or spiritual power and a secular power. No longer the secular power should be in the hands of church leaders, princes and noblemen, but should rest on the shoulders of eminent merchants, bankers, and industrialists. The three most important representatives of these categories should become minister of trade, foreign affairs and state finance. They should be endowed with almost dictatorial power.

It is rather striking that Comte showed much contempt for politicians. As a man of science and the creator of a new, secular or positive religion he strongly rejected most of their ideas and actions.[76] Anyhow, he was convinced that each nation gets the government it deserves. As long as the masses do not show other ideas and desires, it is useless to change politicians and politics. At the end of the day, people have to solve their own social problems. Also he did not attach much value to economic change. In his view, it did not take much effort and creativity to organize the economy in an efficient way. It only is a matter of applying some scientifically proofed insights. For him, the main problem was changing the mind of the people. Like Marx he had his vested his hope on the workers. He was convinced that their poor labour conditions would engender a viable movement for economic and political reform.

He wanted to annihilate the remnants of the feudal and traditional religious mentality, and convince his contemporaries of the anachronisms of war. He had set himself the task to put the whole of mankind on the positivistic, scientific track, to make them see that a rational organisation of society is what modern times need. But also, that social order needs a high-principled moral. The aspect of feeling, which would inspire and sustain co-operation and citizenship in industrial society, could be provided, as Comte strongly believed, by a 'Religion of Humanity', which he designed himself. This new and positive religion should be based on a 'demonstrable faith'. The full establishment of the humanitarian religion required a set of solid dogmas, a set of moral rules and a system or cult of worship, and last but not least an organizational structure modeled after the Catholic Church. Now that the inadequate foundations of the dubious doctrines of traditional religions had been exposed – the true core of religious feeling and duty remained. And this was no more and no less than a compassionate concern for mankind; an aspiration towards the achievement of the highest human ideals; and a direction of one's efforts to the improvement of both the conditions of man and his nature. In this context, Comte formulated the following slogan: '*Love is the principle, order is the basis, and progress is the goal.*' The true core of religion is moral commitment, in feeling, thought, and activity, to the service of mankind. In his view, it was the only true and complete 'religion'. It is the replacement of the love of God by the love for mankind. It is man's duty to love humanity. It is on this score that Comte has been most attacked. Fletcher thinks that it is a great pity that his teachings on this subject were obscured by the detailed prescriptions of numerous rituals and ceremonies, copied from the Catholic Church. In this last exercise of zeal, Comte was carried away by the power of his feelings for Clotilde de Vaux. Nonetheless, the core of what he had to say is the ground of morality of the majority of modern people in our day and age.[77]

In Comte's view, it is the task of sociologists and social philosophers to provide and to maintain a social morale. They must contribute to a positive ethic based on altruism, a word also coined by Comte. Three groups, women, workers and philosophers must support this social ethic. In the perspective of Comte and most of his contemporaries, women should stay at home and take care of the upbringing of their children. Thus, they play a crucial role for society. They have to see to it that nobody forgets that matters of the heart prevail over reason. John Stuart Mill, his erstwhile friend, fellow advocate of positive science and comrade in the fight for the improvement of the human condition, strongly disagreed with this conservative view on the role of women. He very much propagated equal political rights for men and women. This was one of the differences of opinion that drove them apart.

The workers have to provide the material products we need, and philosophers must give us wisdom. Sociologists only have a modest role, but their problem solving capacity could speed up our voyage to a perfect world, in which all individuals are free and have ample space for personal development.[78]

1.12 Epilogue

Comte was very disturbed about the dislocation of post-revolutionary society. Hence, it is no wonder that it was his main objective to reorganize society into a peaceful and ordered whole. In our day and age, we have become very skeptic about the possibility to construct or reconstruct society according to a well-designed plan or blueprint. So, we tend to be amazed by the huge ambitions of Comte's project. He still believed in the possibility to improve society. He was no reactionary, nor a revolutionary. He was an incurable reformist, an assertive propagandist of 'Order and Progress'. Hence he found that there was a great need for a positive science of society that would generate theories and discover general laws that could support social evolution.

Comte mainly focussed on the broad coherence of the social world. All his life he would occupy himself passionately with problem of a disorganized society. He did not see the French Revolution as a national, historical incident, but as the turning point in the history of mankind. The *Ancien Régime* had fallen to pieces, shown to be totally inadequate for the new changes in society, science and industrialization. Government was in disarray. There were great cleavages between knowledge and belief. And the feelings of man lacked coherence, confidence, and worthwhile objectives. Morally, man was adrift. In the aftermath of the French Revolution Comte assigned himself with the great task to investigate the nature and causes of the demise of the Christian religion, and to search the various ways that could lead to a reconstruction and revitalization of society.[79] His main problem was to bring about the right synthesis of order and progress. Alas, his theoretical 'solutions' did not convince his fellow countrymen, but they made a great impression on a group of French intellectuals that had sought asylum in Brazil. This explains way the slogan 'Order and Progress' has got a place on the Brazilian flag.[80]

Comte still is a controversial figure. His first works had all the hallmarks of a genius, but his later works were a different matter. However, not all the critique he got and still is getting is justified. Partly, this is due to the fact that his work is not studied very well nor presented in an unbiased way. Whole generations of students have been misinformed about the contents of his oeuvre. In particular the positivist approach to science, which he ardently promoted, has been misinterpreted and distorted. For many decades Comte's positivism was and still is depicted as a caricature, for instance, as a form of research that leads to a random gathering of miscellaneous and uninteresting facts. But then one tends to forget that Comte already warned social scientists for such a trivial way of doing research. He always emphasized that empirical research should be connected with theoretical frameworks.

In some respects Comte was an archconservative, but certainly not in all. He denied the poor a say in politics, but strongly argued for free public education, medical care and houses with seven rooms. He did not like capitalists. In his view, small businessmen were parasites. He wanted to concentrate capital in the hands of a small number of excellent specialists. But this group should not be allowed to use this capital for their own ends. Also his idea to assign moral power to sociologists and social philosophers surely was not conservative in his day and age, but put in very traditional forms in our view at least. As modern 'priests of the religion of humanity' they should guard the new moral. Each society needed a kind of religion and the religion invented by Comte should create a synthesis between matters of the heart and the matters of reason. As a passionate system builder he elaborated his ideas to a very high degree, designing temples, services of worship, prayers and religious holidays, entirely modelled according to the example offered by the Catholic Church.

Fletcher treats the weaknesses, extravagances and intellectual shortcomings of Comte much milder than most of his critics. Of course, it is rather easy to find elements that deserve to be criticized, but it is more satisfactory to study his best ideas and insights.[81] So it seems in order to finish this chapter on a positive note. At least we should thank this linguistically talented man for coining terms like sociology, biology, altruism, and positivism. We should thank him for his great effort to put sociology on the scientific map and to argue that it rightly deserves the status of a valid and autonomous science, a science that cannot be deduced from biology or psychology. He was the first who made clear that social phenomena could and should be studied in an objective way in order to free it from a purely philosophical study of ideas. Admittedly, the great advocate of scientific observation was not very talented in this respect. He did not produce dazzling insights based on personal observations of social reality. But, we should praise him for enriching sociology with interesting focusing points for further theoretical development and even more for his efforts to sketch a clear methodological approach that turned sociology into a 'real' science, although this latter view still constitutes a bone of contention. For that reason his work on methodology deserves reading and rereading because sociology always attracts scores of people who are eager to renounce 'positivism,' without realizing that already Comte shared some of their views about its limits. Maybe, close reading Comte could open their eyes for its positive potential.

2

KARL MARX

CRITICAL INVESTIGATOR AND FIGHTER OF CAPITALISM

In 1989, on a dark November night, after weeks of peaceful demonstrations, the Berlin Wall began to crumble. Tens of thousands of enthusiastic Eastern Germans flooded into West Berlin and were warmly welcomed as long lost friends. At last, the communist specter, once heralded by Karl Marx, was expelled. It had haunted Europe for more than seventy years. Does this mean that we can also destroy the works of Marx, works that have occupied the thoughts of whole generations of social scientists, political activists and intellectuals? I don't think so. Large parts of it are still worth studying because they are of significance to our present society.

Karl Marx was a scholar, a prophet, and a political activist. As a social philosopher, he conducted critical and perceptive analyses of the mechanism of the capitalist system. However, as a prophet, he wrongly predicted the inevitable demise of capitalism. As a political activist, he failed to establish and lead a political movement that could accelerate that fall.[1] But his revolutionary ideas formed the basis for exceptionally brutal regimes, headed by devilish dictators that brought fear, misery, and injustice to half the world during many decades and led to the imprisonment and killing of millions of people. Fortunately, his writings also have awakened the consciousness of many people and urged them to improve social conditions for the poor. They have understood his alarming message about the plight of the underclass, but refrained from advocating a violent revolution. In many countries, social democrats, liberals, progressive Christians, and Muslims have successfully tried to increase the well being of the workers, the poor, the old, the sick, and the disabled.

The focus of this chapter is on the academic work of Marx. After this introduction and the section on his biography, section 2.2 is devoted to some of the ideas of Georg Fredric Hegel that had a great influence on him, such as the idea of dialectical progress. Section 2.3 shows his philosophical trajectory that departed from the pseudo-theological philosophy of Hegel, via Feuerbach's focus on the human being, to his historical materialism in which he focused on the economic and social conditions of people, in particular the deplorable conditions of poor workers and their families. Section 2.4 gives an impression of Marx's view on the formation of two opposing social classes who are heading for a major class struggle. Section 2.5 proceeds with a discussion of his study of industrial capitalism as presented in the Communist Manifesto and in Capital. This analysis brought him to conclude that capitalism had severe inbuilt flaws that would cause its fall. Section 2.6 presents his views on alienation, the negative effect of being forced to carry out boring, repetitive actions under bad working conditions. Section 2.7 deals with some of Marx's contributions to the sociology of knowledge. Then there is a section on the role of the state after the revolution. Section 2.9 tries to answer the question whether Marx changed some of his views in the last phase of his life. The chapter ends with some concluding remarks.

2.1   Biography

In 1818, on the 5th of May, Karl Marx was born in Trier. Political events had a great influence on the life of the Marx family. First, the French Revolution liberated them from the Jewish ghetto. Then, it was made possible for Jews to become civil servants. But in 1813, after the annexation of Trier by Prussia, the old restrictions were restored. Perhaps, in order to circumvent these discriminatory laws, Marx's father decided to convert to Lutheran Christianity. To remain a lawyer would otherwise have been impossible and he would have faced unemployment and perhaps poverty. However, Marx' daughter Leonora once wrote to a biographer that her grandfather gave up the Jewish religion freely and not for purely practical reasons. Hirschel Marx even changed his first name to a typical German name as Heinrich. The whole matter did not emotionally affect him, because he was a fervent supporter of the ideas of the Enlightenment. When asked, he would say that he believed in Voltaire.

2.1.1   Childhood and student years

Karl was raised in this liberal-democratic climate. His mother, Henriëtte Presburg, came from a dynasty of Hungarian rabbis. Her father, Isaac Presburg, had settled in Nijmegen, a Dutch town near the German border and had earned a small fortune as a merchant and moneylender. He gave his daughter a substantial dowry when she married. So, by birth, Karl Marx was half German and half Dutch, but he did not like it at all when his mother called him 'Kareltje', the diminutive of the Dutch Karel.[2]

Karl did not excel at secondary school, but he was a good writer and was full of ideas. His neighbour, baronet von Westphalen, noticed his curiosity and stimulated his passion for classical literature and the Renaissance. He lent important books to Karl and held lengthy discussions with him about learned topics. Jenny, the attractive daughter of the baronet, fell heavily in love with Karl, who was four years younger, even though she could have made a far better catch than Karl, who was to lack a steady job and a income throughout his life.

At the age of seventeen, Karl went to Bonn to study law. He became an enthusiastic participant in the typical leisure activities of students. Soon, it became apparent that he could not manage financial affairs. His father ordered him to exchange the merry lifestyle of Bonn for the much more serious climate of Berlin.[3] This worked well. From now on, study became his highest priority. Even his leisure time was filled with intellectual activities such as studying foreign languages, translating classical texts, and writing poetry, novels, and plays. No wonder that he became overworked and had to take a rest cure.

During Karl's studies, professor Eduard Gans treated Hegel as a progressive thinker whose main object was to change society. However, Friedrich Carl von Savigny, his other philosophy professor, emphasized the conservative aspects of Hegel's thought. Karl learned even more about Hegel when he became a member of the so-called Doctor's Club – a bunch of radical, freethinking, young and marginal academics such as Bruno and Edgar Bauer, and Max Stirner. These young men liked to debate the finer points of Hegelian doctrines for hours on end in Berlin's beer-cellars. The academic schooling in two different aspects of Hegel's thought, added to the critical approach of the Doctor's Club, and ensured that some of Hegel's ideas would always keep a hold on Marx. In the beginning, he was attracted by Hegel's idea that 'what is' is closely connected with 'what should be'. Marx always believed that philosophical and social knowledge should be applied to achieve certain ends. He disputed the division of labour between scientists and politicians, as recommended by positive science. In contrast, he appreciated the fusion of social analysis, social critique, and political action to construct a new world based on the outcomes of objective and critical analyses. However, he did not foresee that the strong commitment to create a better world could lure scientists and politicians into practices that would distort the truth and harm society.

Marx was the youngest member of the Doctor's Club. Though still a student, he had a great influence on the ideas of most other members. These young men behaved as if they already were the equals of the greatest philosophers. The discussions with the Doctor's Club were very important for his intellectual development. A direct consequence of his membership was that he abandoned his study of law and turned to philosophy. It also ruined his academic career, for all members of this radical group became politically suspect. His PhD thesis of 1841 was a philosophical study of Epicurus. In this book, he already presented some important ideas about alienation that he would work out later.[4] Marx saw Epicurus as the destroyer of Greek myths and divinities. He agreed with Epicurus that: *'Not he is heathen, who rejects the Gods of the masses, but he who attributes the images of the masses to the gods.'* In his view, images of gods have no right to exist in the Land of Reason.[5] He praised Epicurus for the attempt to free people of the fear of Gods. Such fears are alien to the essence of man.

2.1.2   *Exile*

Since Marx was already known as a strong critic of society, he did not have the slightest chance of making an academic career in a political climate that was utterly conservative. He got a job as a journalist for a newly founded paper. Within six months, he became the editor-in-chief. Under his radical leadership, the paper quickly headed for a collision with the government. Despite the painstaking activities of a conscientious censor, the government could no longer stomach the anti-Christian and anti-Prussian articles and stopped the presses. Already severely annoyed by the censor, Marx did not mourn long for the loss of this job.

His journalism had opened his eyes to the pains of poverty. From then on, he felt a strong urge to write frankly about the plight of the deprived and the misery of their social conditions. He noticed that there was a sudden rise in the number of lawsuits regarding the theft of wood. The reason was a clash between traditional common law, which allowed people to collect fallen branches for their stoves, and the new legislation that gave foresters the right to stop this. Marx sided with the people who were too poor to buy firewood. Throughout his life, he felt strongly committed to the plight of the paupers. Whenever he raged against the miserable conditions of factory workers and manual labourers, he always did this with a clear image of what he had seen: undernourished children, humiliated and worn-out men and women, living in overcrowded houses lacking all comfort. He was never to forget their misery.[6]

With an academic career that never even got started and a journalistic career that was quickly aborted, there was no future for Marx in Germany. He had to seek refuge in another country. In 1843, he went to Paris, hoping to find steady employment. He did manage to find work, be it as a mere freelance journalist. In Paris, he met all kinds of radical thinkers, artists, and political activists. He held discussions with socialists and communists of every persuasion, such as anarchists, utopians, and Christian socialists. Many of them were immigrants and refugees. With one of them, Heinrich Heine, the poet, he became friends. Their friendship was never tested by quarrels. This was exceptional, for Marx had a confrontational nature and did not agree with Heine, who was not a communist. Somehow, Marx found that great artists had to be treated differently than his fellow social philosophers, with whom he would disagree sooner or later. Besides, according to family legend, Heine once saved the life of little Jenny, by putting her in a bath when she had an attack of cramps. At that awkward moment, Karl and his wife Jenny, who were rather incompetent parents, had had no idea what to do.[7] He also met the Russian anarchist Bakunin. For Marx, all these meetings were important. They sharpened his radical thinking and opened his mind to entirely new perspectives. He became a vigorous communist, which signified a definitive breach with his bourgeois and liberal-democratic origins. This conversion became all too manifest in his articles for a radical German paper printed in Paris. Once more, he aroused the anger of the German leaders. They finally succeeded in pressuring the French government to get him expelled from France.

So, in 1845, he moved to Brussels after promising the Belgian government that he would not take part in political activities.

2.1.3 A lifelong bond with Friedrich Engels

In Paris, Marx met Friedrich Engels. They immediately became close friends. It was a friendship that would last until Marx's death. From 1842 to 1844, Engels had worked in Manchester. This inspired him to write *The Condition of the Working Class in England*. It is a long, full report, based on rather distant observations of the real conditions of workers. In fact, Engels had very few face-to-face encounters with members of the proletariat, but acquired much information from Peter Raskell's book about the manufacturing population of England. In those days, Manchester was both the shock town and exhibition center of the Industrial Revolution. Cutthroat competition and technological innovation created working conditions that were unsuitable for human beings. It produced an exploited class of workers that was driven to oppose the capitalists.

The cooperation with Engels had a great impact on Marx's political and development as a scholar. In Marx, he had found a lifetime loyal comrade and supporter. They had similar ideas and political motives. Moreover, Marx needed Engels' help and stimulation for his opus magnum: *Capital*. Together they prepared many publications. Though they formed a perfect match intellectually and politically, Marx and Engels were strikingly different in character and lifestyle. Engels was a gentleman who enjoyed life, leisure, and good food, whereas Marx was much more frugal, badly dressed, and deeply serious. Unlike Marx, Engels had first-hand experience of the system of production. He was the son of a patriarchal textile-mill owner. He grew up in Wuppertal, during the onset of the Industrial Revolution and became an unusual sort of 'double man': by day, a capitalist, helping to run his father's firm in Manchester, and by night, so to speak, a communist. Engels had declared himself to be a communist before Marx did. In 1844, he wrote *Description of Recently Founded Communist Colonies Still in Existence*. Herein he declared that communism simply meant 'community of goods'. He tried to dispel the objection that this was a utopian aspiration by pointing to its realization in three American communities: the Harmonists, the Shakers, and the Rappists. In these sects money was abandoned and there was free choice of work; yet an abundance of goods was produced. A religious bond characterized all these colonies, but Engels asserted that their success would be even greater if they had freed themselves of 'religious nonsense'. It was obvious to him that we cannot do without our fellow men. Therefore, he wanted to reorganize society on more rational principles by setting up a central planning authority that would organize the production of necessary goods. During the stage of transition from capitalism to communism, governments should introduce basic education for all children, organize a system of financial assistance for the poor, and introduce a progressive tax on capital.

Marx worked like a typical German scholar: conscientious, thorough, and precise. As a consequence, his work progressed slowly. Moreover, political activism often lured him away from his desk. Therefore, Engels often had to finish his texts. During his years in Paris and Brussels, Marx studied economic issues. This helped sharpen his political views and also distanced him from the young Hegelians. This break became clear with the publication of a book sarcastically entitled *The Holy Family,* in which he attacked the ideas of Bruno Bauer and his two brothers. These left-Hegelians squandered their time and energy on pointless philosophizing because they were blind to social reality with its great lack of social justice.[8] Already many critics had previously attacked Hegel, but so far, they had never attacked the essence of Hegel's philosophy. And precisely this was the objective of Marx and Engels.

Many people have observed that Marx was the type of man who is full of energy, willpower and an unshakable conviction. This make-up led to the systematic expulsion of any member of his committees or associations who dared to deviate from the Master's Voice. Some opponents were honored with a lengthy essay or pamphlet. Proudhon was treated in this fashion when he lectured Marx on his vindictiveness and dogmatism after he had denounced his friend Karl Grün. Proudhon wrote:

> *Let us have decent and sincere polemics. Let us give the world an example of learned and farsighted tolerance. But simply because we are at the head of the movement, let us not make ourselves the leaders of new intolerance. … Let us never regard a question as exhausted. … Under these conditions I will gladly enter into your association. Otherwise - no!*[9]

In this letter Proudhon already anticipated that he would receive a caning from Marx. The occasion of this beating arose only a few months later when he produced a two-volume work on *The Philosophy of Poverty.* Like Comte, he preferred gradual and orderly change, rejected revolutions, and even denounced strikes. Marx demolished his utopian socialism in a publication with the hateful title: *The poverty of philosophy.* It was a merciless critique of the highly talented, but autodidactic Proudhon. He mocked his lack of economic understanding, his wrong interpretations of Hegel, and the many contradictions in his work.[10]

In Paris and Brussels, Marx's thinking underwent a significant shift from anthropological philosophy to political economy. This was a result of the association with Engels. Engels had always been in close contact with the ideas and activities of the capitalists. He fed his friend with much valuable information about capitalism. Marx understood that he had to learn the basics if not the essence of economy. While he studied the works of Adam Smith, David Ricardo, and James Mill, he worked on a critical analysis of their ideas, but it took almost a whole century before these writings were put in print to become available to a large audience.[11] Hence, it was not the early Parisian writings that would inspire the communist labour movement, but *The Manifesto of the Communist Party* and *Capital*. These were written in London. They present a concise theoretical framework for the final attack on capitalism.

2.1.4   Isolated in England

After Marx and Engels had to leave Brussels, they went to London. There, the German association for the education of workers asked them to write an easily understandable pamphlet about their views on communism. The Manifesto began with the famous phrase: '*The history of all hitherto existing society is the history of class struggle*'. That first sentence revealed in one stroke the essence of Marx's social analysis. From then on, he would always stick to this analysis. He would only underline and further clarify these central ideas. In 1848, a few weeks after the manifesto was published, revolution broke out in Paris and Germany. Immediately, Marx returned to the continent. First, he visited Paris and then went on to the Rhineland, where he became editor of a radical paper.[12] The revolution failed, but it had frightened the ruling classes of Europe. They responded in a reactionary way. Once again, Marx had to seek asylum in England. He would stay there until his death in 1883.

Marx failed to become accepted by the English labour movement. More and more, he retired in the confinements of his home or to the library of the British Museum. Meanwhile, he remained hopeful of a rekindling of the revolutionary fire in Germany and France. Even the economic recession of 1857 did not set the powder keg off. Without a steady job, Marx was often penniless. From time to time, Engels gave him some money or wine. But even when his family suffered from unbearable poverty, Marx would not lose his bourgeois taste for good wine. Often, Engels wrote Marx's articles for the *New York Daily Tribune*, for which Marx was a correspondent. His reason for doing this was that Engels had more expertise in certain economic or political topics and that he could handle the pen more easily. Meanwhile, Marx was deeply immersed in the writing of *Capital*. This had to become the main intellectual instrument for the emancipation of the working classes.[13]

In England, Marx tried to establish an international communist movement. As the leader, he molded the political program to his own will. As soon as the organization gathered momentum, European governments watched it carefully. However, the organization would always be plagued with internal struggles that mitigated its potential power. Dogmatic conflicts dominated the first four international congresses, but Marx stubbornly held on to his ideas, as published in the Communist Manifesto and the first part of Capital. He vigorously defended his theory that the way to a new society would involve many conflicts. He remained strongly convinced that a well-organized working class would win their war against the capitalists. True socialism could only be reached through a necessary transition period in which the proletariat would seize power. It could not happen in any other way. Hence, he fiercely rejected the ideas of his anarchistic opponents, who advocated the destruction of the state apparatus, which, in their view, would allow a reformation of the economic system, dominated by many small businesses and cooperatives.

For several years, Marx could compliment himself on the fact that he had formulated the right theory of capitalism, and also that he was heading an international organization that would put a stop to the oppression of the working class and the misery produced by the capitalist system.[14] In 1872, during the last congress in The Hague, the first one he attended personally, Marx gained supremacy. He succeeded in expelling the anarchist Bakunin and his followers. Marx fiercely rejected their idea that not only the state, but also all hierarchical organizations, should be demolished, by violent means if necessary. Alas, it was a Pyrrhic victory that heralded the demise of his international movement. Mutual rivalry and embitterment had risen to such an extent that further cooperation became impossible between the South European anarchistic factions, with their penchant for direct action and their dislike of legal political involvement, and the labour unions and labour parties of Northern Europe.[15] In a meeting held in Amsterdam, right after the congress, Marx showed that he had lost some of his belief in revolutions as the panacea for social change in all situations. He told a hostile audience,

> We are aware of the importance that must be accorded to the institutions, customs, and traditions of different countries and we do not deny that there are countries like America, England, (and if I knew your institutions better, maybe I would add Holland) where the workers can achieve their aims by peaceful means. However true that may be, we ought also to recognize that, in most of the countries on the Continent, it is force that must be the lever of our revolutions; ...[16]

From this quotation we can see that Marx had learned some valuable sociological lessons from history, especially from the revolutions that had failed. Nonetheless, he remained a revolutionary until his death.[17]

After the breakdown of his international organization, Marx retreated from the hustle and bustle of the world. Once more, he immersed himself into reading and writing. Various illnesses, boils, and ulcers plagued him during these years. His family suffered from many setbacks. Poverty drove Marx to visit his relatives in Germany and Holland, to beg them for financial help. More than once, he visited his uncle Lion Philips in Zaltbommel, the grandfather of the Philips brothers who started the bulb factory that would develop into one of the biggest multinationals of the 20th century. Sometimes, his wife Jenny was sent on a begging tour to Holland. During one of her absences, Marx impregnated their housekeeper Helene Demuth. In June 1851, he fathered a bastard son: Henry Frederick Demuth. However, Marx denied paternity and the boy was adopted by another family. Although this was a great blow to Jenny, she helped to cover up this blemish on Marx's reputation; Helen remained the competent housekeeper of the family.

Till the end of Freddy Demuths life, in 1929, nobody suspected that he was Karl Marx' son.

Karl and Jenny lost three of their seven children at a very young age. Only Eleanor and Laura outlived their father. Eleanor never married, but lived together with the notoriously unreliable Edward Aveling. When she discovered that he had secretly married a young actress, he proposed a suicide pact to solve the crisis. However, when she had swallowed the lethal dose of prussic acid, Edward did not follow suit, but left the house, to die only four months later. Laura was married to Paul Lafargue. Three of their children died at an early age. Also Charles and Harry Longuet, two other grandchildren of Marx, died when he was still alive. Precisely in the years that most of their financial troubles had been solved, the family was plagued with severe illness and many cases of early death. Karl's health deteriorated after 1873, and in 1878 his dearly beloved wife got cancer. She died on December 2, 1881. A little over a year later, his eldest daughter Jenny died. Only two months later, on 17 March 1883, Karl Marx died. There were only eleven mourners at his funeral at Highgate cemetery. One of them was Friedrich Engels, who predicted that Marx's name and work would last through the ages.[18]

2.2   Hegel and Marx: Thesis and antithesis

When the student Marx arrived in Berlin in 1836, Georg Friedrich Hegel had already been dead for five years, but his influence was still very great. Marx would always remain loyal to some of Hegel's philosophical theories, but denounce others completely or turn them upside down. As Hegel had an important influence on Marx's view on historical evolution, we ought to pay some attention to his ideas. This is absolutely essential for a good understanding of his work. However, rendering a short introduction to some of Hegel's ideas is far from easy, for it is considered to be 'awesomely complex' and 'monstrously ambiguous'.[19] His philosophy is idealistic and completely directed at pure reason. He was convinced that the mental world was the primary reality, from which the material world was deduced.

2.2.1   *World history and the realization of the Absolute Spirit*

In Hegel's belief, self-consciousness, to stand up for your own rights and personal freedom can only be reached through a power that he called The Spirit. This highly abstract phenomenon lives in the consciousness of individuals and is incorporated in an objective form in cultural products, such as the legal system and the 'absolute morality' of the state. Above The Spirit is The Absolute Spirit, which expresses itself in fine art, religion, and philosophy.[20] The Absolute Spirit coincides with The Whole, in all its complexity and infinite character. It is completely autonomous. Only a spiritual reality can be unlimited and completely independent. However, The Spirit, as conceived by Hegel, has not yet unfolded all its potential. This can only happen when it has full insight into itself, has become conscious of its complete self.[21] The history of mankind, of human culture is a learning process in which human freedom will be fully realized, in the form of insight into its own freedom and in the ultimate insight that nature and society are externalizations of the essence of The Spirit.[22] Hence, history has a goal. Once it has reached that objective, we will witness the end of history.

> It is the essence of The Spirit to learn to know itself, to see itself and to realize itself as it is. That will be accomplished in the history of the world. Thus, the ultimate goal of world history is that man grasps what he really is… and that he … makes himself into that what he is.[23]

This quotation shows that Hegel toyed with the concept of 'entelechy', the concept of a telic principle. The essence of The Spirit contains something that has to reveal itself someday, just like seed produces a plant or animal, a blossoming flower or a tree full of fruit. Nowadays it is generally assumed that this kernel can be found in the genetic code, in the DNA-structure. Hegel did not use the biological analogy of the full circle, in which everything remains the same after each cycle. He also seems to have forgotten that one seed can only fully develop itself if it overshadows other seedlings that thus whither away. He ignored the fact that a plant can grow and develop in an optimal way only under favourable physical conditions. He favoured a developmental model of unconditional progress. For him, the advancement of world history is inevitable. It continues its journey to its true and final destination. Every period is determined by its predecessor and determines its successor. The power of thinking pushes history ahead and elevates man and society to a higher level. Marx supported this view but replaced the intellectual motor by a materialistic one. At this point he upturned Hegel's philosophy, though he contended that he put historical theory back in its proper position. Anyway, the end of history does not coincide with the end of mankind, but with the fulfillment of human emancipation. It is an eschatological theory, a doctrine of salvation. For Marx, this process ends in true communism, that is, the political situation in which all people can realize their true selves.

2.2.2   Hegelian dialectics

Hegel's main theme is the opposition between the Absolute Spirit and the world, the opposition between thought and matter. Our world is the materialization of The Spirit. But as The Spirit objectivates or externalizes itself, it becomes alienated from itself. The worldly object is 'alien' to the spiritual subject. Thus a dualism emerges between The Spirit and its material 'negation,' that is, its part that is objectified in the material world. This opposition or tension can be removed when it leads to a kind of 'purified' return to the original situation: the alienated element comes back to the wholeness of The Spirit. But this is not really a repair of what has been. Something has been added: the consciousness of what has happened. Thus, the spiritual unity between subject and object is regained and lifted to a higher plane. That is the triple meaning of the German 'aufheben': firstly, in the sense of removing an obstacle or discontinuing a law; secondly, in the meaning of keeping in reserve and thirdly, as lifting or elevating something to a higher level, where the oppositions can no longer operate as oppositions.[24]

As long as an individual does not do, say, or think anything, he only exists as a biological entity. He exists only for himself. As soon as humans do, say, or think something, they produce something that exists outside them. It can even be strange for a person to realize that he has said or done the very thing he just said or did. But the subject and that what he has externalized will be united as soon as he acknowledges that he really did, said, or thought this thing. Through this process, people become wiser and sadder perhaps. The subject has become more mature and more self-conscious. In that sense, individuals arrive at a higher level, thanks to the objective act, the alienation that it aroused, and the final appropriation of the act as a personal act.[25] This is dialectics in process.

The complicated concept of dialectical movement means far more than an interaction between a thesis and its negation or antithesis. The full movement has to lead to a synthesis that adds something new. The synthesis should bring theory and practice to a higher level. At first, there is an idea, a theory or political movement based on a specific thesis or doctrine. It is assumed that such a thesis will bring forth its antithesis; for the seeds of the antithesis or countermovement are already present in the thesis, since it is imperfect, e.g., since it is one-sided or has other weak spots. The antithesis or countermovement is directed against the thesis, especially against its imperfections and weaknesses. Thus, a real conflict is aroused. The original meaning of dialectic is dispute, a conflict about arguments. It is assumed that this argumentative struggle will result in a kind of compromise in which the oppositional stances fade away, a compromise that eradicates the weaknesses and joins the positive elements of the thesis and the antithesis. Thus, they are elevated to a higher plane. [26]

Figure 2.1

Perhaps the explanation of dialectics presented here is already sufficient. On the other hand, the explanation of this crucial concept cannot be clear enough because many questionable interpretations of this concept are used in books and articles. Hegel, and especially Engels, may be blamed for these faulty applications, because they equated dialectal development with the purposeful advancement or growth (entelechy) that we see in biological organisms; take for instance the absurd idea that the seed is the negation of the flower. Confusing examples like these recur in introductory books and even in well-known novels. Karl Popper argued that we should be careful in using the term dialectic. He even thought it would be best, perhaps, not to use it at all. [27] He acknowledged that the dialectical triad could sometimes be used as a description of processes in philosophy in which a certain thesis, because it has some weak spots, entices opposition. The philosophical debate between the two parties may lead to some sort of solution, which, in a sense, goes beyond both thesis and antithesis by merging the good parts of both.[28] There may also have been a few periods in history that could be described as a progressive dialectical series of thesis, antithesis and some kind of synthesis. But surely the large majority of historical epochs did not show a similar sequence of events. Most historical periods evoked negative reactions, revolutions and counter-revolutions. However, to end this section on a more positive note I will give an optimistic example of a dialectical historical movement.

Nature vs nurture

For nineteenth century America and Europe the ever increased control of nature was a clear sign of progress. Sacrificing nature for food production, chopping wood or coal was considered a reasonable prize to pay. People took pride in their skills domesticating animals and killing beasts of prey, in growing and cultivating plants, in channeling rivers and in controlling the sea by building dykes and thus reclaiming thousands of acres of land. However, in the following century, a growing number of people worried about the destruction of nature and opposed new plans for constructing housing estates, factories, and office buildings. They opposed plans for new motorways, bridges, dams, and tunnels. This was the wake-up call for the antithesis. Public opinion and political parties followed suit. Everyone agreed that man should no longer place himself above nature, but should realize that he is a part it. The preservation of nature, the preservation of rain forests and endangered species, became of vital importance to mankind and engendered the synthesis of a profitable relationship with nature combined with careful stewardship. In this synthesis nature remains a rich source for mankind, which we can use without harming our ecological environment, e.g., by planting a new tree for every tree that is felled for industrial and domestic use.

Box 2.1

2.2.3   What is or what ought to be

As we have seen, for Hegel, history is the process in which The Absolute Spirit unfolds itself and humans become more conscious of their own nature. The role of philosophy is to support this process. Each new phase in history reveals that the previous phase was less rational than it appeared to be during its glory days. Philosophy can only clarify with hindsight why a former phase was not perfect and had to be replaced by a new era and a new worldview. This means that dialectical philosophy is a method for interpreting the past; it is not a useful method for running ahead of historical developments. However, in other instances, Hegel contended that successive philosophical systems are advancing the development of the truth. They have a critical function, as long as history has not reached its final goal, that is, as long as society has not achieved its ultimate condition of reasonability. Until that moment, negative critique has to break through societal complacency and inertia, and must pave the way for new social and cultural possibilities.

An important strand of Hegel's philosophy is anti-utopian. Herein 'To be' prevails over 'Ought'. Thus, the idea could easily be supported that he sanctioned the existing social order. We have to be careful here. His rational philosophy can also be interpreted as a demand to make reality reasonable. But his often-bandied aphorism, 'That what is real is reasonable' can much more easily be explained in a conservative than in a progressive manner. In the final stages of his life, Hegel fully accepted the actual situation of Prussia. For him, this manifested the realization of the Absolute Spirit. He was convinced that individual freedom had come to terms with the general interest. In his view, the end of history had finally arrived, and philosophy had, thanks to his own contributions, fulfilled its most important task. The only thing to be done was to protect western society from a backlash and to spread the reasonable situation among all the peoples of the world.[29] Marx could not reconcile this view with the squalor and the misery he observed everyday. Obviously, the world was still far from perfect. Considering the misery of the masses, there still was a great need for a truly critical social philosophy. For Hegel, the wrongs of the (Prussian) world were only minor hiccups, which had no significant effect on reality. For Marx, they were clear signs that society was heading for a revolution.

2.2.4   The dialectical method

Is there such a thing as a dialectical method? Marx mentioned this several times but he never explicated what he meant by this. However some people seem to be pretty sure what he meant. For example, this is true for a Russian critic, who, in 1872, gave a description of this method that is so clear that Marx quoted him in the preface to the second print of *Capital*, although without mentioning his name. This anonymous analyst stated that Marx not merely wishes to know the laws that control social relations in a specific historic context, but that he, above all, wants to come to grips with the sociological law that explains the process of change of social structures and relations, in other words, the theory that describes the transformation from one situation into the other.

> As soon as he has discovered this scientific law, he will investigate its
> social consequences into the smallest detail. ... It completely suffices
> that he can proof that the historical necessity of the present ordering
> necessitates the future ordering, in which the first is compelled to

transform itself, whether the social agents believe this or not, whether they are conscious of this process or not. Marx sees this historical movement as a natural process, determined by social laws that are independent from the will, the consciousness and the intentions of individuals, but, rather determine the will, consciousness and intentions of the people involved. ... But, one is inclined to respond, the general laws of the economic system remain the same, whether they are applied to the present or the past, do they? Marx denies precisely this. In his view such abstract laws do not exist within social science ... As soon as life has gone through a certain period of development, has passed from one stage to the next, it will be controlled by other laws. [30]

This appears to be a good summary of Marx's views on historical materialism. It is historic, because each epoch has its own social laws. And it is materialistic, because each new technology determines the character of society. A new phase in technology, a new way of manufacturing products leading to a new division of labour renders new living conditions, thus renewing society as a whole. All this generates a new way of viewing life in general and people and their social relations in particular. So there is nothing obscure or oblique in the aims or the methods of the dialectical method. Marx was a real empirical researcher. He was always looking for reliable data. He found them not only in official reports, but also by close observation of factories and the houses of poor labourers.

2.3   From dialectic idealism to historical materialism

In 1841, Feuerbach presented a fierce critique of Hegel's abstract 'theological' ideas and presuppositions. He argued that the basis for any study of mankind should be the 'real' human being, living in a real, material world. Feuerbach stated that the Absolute Spirit or Divine Power emerges from real life and not the other way around. The divine is a human illusion; the gods are simply a projection of typical human characteristics projected on impersonal forces, placed as a deity outside the world and above the self, thus belittling oneself on the one hand and alienating oneself from one's own true self on the other. They endow these self-created gods or Divine Spirits with special features such as sacredness, purity, and perfection, whereas they depict themselves as sinful, powerless, and imperfect.[31] Feuerbach urged philosophers to stop thinking about the Absolute Spirit or Divinities and to think only about humans who are by nature egocentric, is continuously looking for personal happiness. Study the here and now; observe and examine mankind as a natural being. Stop using speculative concepts, but direct your attention solely on that which really exists, for only there the truth can be found. The senses can only register truth and reality. These are identical. Man does not exist from abstract, metaphysical and theological realities, but from concrete, tangible, visible things.

2.3.1 *The dialectic triad constituted by Hegel, Feuerbach, and Marx*

Feuerbach rejected philosophical idealists like Hegel. They detach thinking from being. The real subject matter of philosophy is man as a physically existing and thinking being.[32] Feuerbach built an important bridge that connected idealism with materialism. At first, Engels and Marx were pleased with this move, but after a while, they realized that Feuerbach did not go far enough. In their view, he was still too much involved in a religious way of thinking. A fully materialistic approach is more adequate, for the problems of modern society are based on material causes, such as the structure of capitalism with its unequal distribution of money and power. As we saw, the materialistic approach of Marx and Engels stands diametrically opposed to Hegel's view that the material is only a reflection or an externalisation of what is in our minds.[33] For Marx and Engels, consciousness always equals being conscious of concrete things and persons. Feuerbach opened the door to that view. He passed the barrier from the 'Absolute Idea' to human thought. Thus, he realized the passage from idealistic philosophy to anthropology. Marx and Engels went one step further. They moved from anthropology and humanistic philosophy to social philosophy and sociology, toward the being and the consciousness of real humans in their social-historical context. Furthermore, Marx steered sociology towards a conflict approach. He stressed the eternal war between interest groups, the incessant struggle between dominating and dominated classes, thus ending a purely evaluative philosophy. He opted for a critical analysis of the real world. He wanted to unearth the mechanisms that produced and reproduced inequality, injustice and oppression. He wanted more than theoretical abstractions. Above all, he wanted *praxis*, a valid intellectual reflection that is highly useful for political action. He wanted ideas that could revolutionize social relations. Like most philosophers, Feuerbach did not consider *praxis*, the practical activity directed at social change. This led to the famous eleventh thesis against Feuerbach:

> *The philosophers have only interpreted the world in different ways; the aim is to change it.*[34]

2.3.2 *Basic materialism*

The term 'materialism' is likely to suggest the doctrine that nothing exists except matter. Marx did not hold this view. For example, in his theories, much hinges on his analysis of marketable goods, in other words, objects of exchange or commodities. Commodities are the basic form of wealth in capitalism. But Marx put much emphasis on the fact that commodities also have non-material properties that are vitally important for understanding their nature. They have exchange value, and this value can extinguish all material characteristics. Besides, the market value of a commodity can vary daily or even hourly. Often enough there is no longer a direct relation between material costs and labour costs of commodities.

Nonetheless, materialism is the basis of his philosophy.[35] Matter is the basis of our physical and social existence. For Marx, the material is the sensuous reality, that which is visible, hearable, and tangible. It is something that not only exists in our consciousness, but also out in the world. It is that which we can observe using the methods of positive science. The spiritual exists only in our minds. It is our consciousness. Man exists and thinks; there is being and also a consciousness of being.

The form of materialism strongly associated with Marx is historical materialism. He did not use that expression, but frequently referred to the material basis of his scientific method.[36] The existence of real human beings constitutes human history. The first fact to be established, therefore, is the physical constitution of these individuals and their relation to nature. Whatever else human beings may be, they are first and foremost physical organisms. They have to eat and drink. They need a habitat, clothing, and many other things. Hence, the first historical act is the production of the means to satisfy these needs, the production of material life itself. As long as people have to engage fully in satisfying basic material needs, there is no time and energy left for intellectual and political activities or aesthetic pleasures.

The crucial distinction between humans and animals is not that humans think, but that they produce. According to Marx, people begin to distinguish themselves from animals as soon as they begin to produce their means of subsistence. Marx was foremost interested in a form of labour that is exclusively reserved for humans as opposed to more instinctive forms of production reserved for animals. One could almost say that Marx disliked it when nature's offerings are plentiful and man does not have to work hard and use clever survival tactics. Only then nature keeps man in hand, like children in leading strings.[37] Humans distinguish themselves from animals as soon as they ingeniously invent products and methods of production. By ingeniously producing their means of subsistence, they indirectly produce their whole way of life. How they actually do this depends on the available means of production, which they have to maintain, to reproduce, and to upgrade in order to remain successful producers. [38]

The mode of production is the basis for society. Hence the mode of production must be the starting point for any social analysis. The level of technology has a great impact on the structure of society; it determines the division of labour. It shapes the history of mankind. In premodern societies, there was hardly any division of labour. All men went fishing or hunting using self-made tools, they all chopped wood and built their own simple huts or houses. The women gathered fruit, nuts and plants and cooked meals for their families. They made and mended their own clothes, if any. Real specialization emerged later in the history of mankind. Then men became fishers or farmers, bakers or builders, tailors or tradesmen, soldiers or priests, inventors or copycats. Each new form of production and level of specialization produced its own form of property relations. First, there was the small tribe with its collective tribal property. When tribes merged and formed larger societies, the idea emerged that all major property belonged to the entire community. In feudal times, this was superseded by a system of land-owners who possessed many acres of land with serf labour chained to it. And finally, capitalistic relations put the ownership of land, machines, and buildings in the hands of a few. As the scale of economic activities increased, tools and machines became too expensive for the individual craftsman or skilled worker. Only the owner of large shops, factories, ships, and office buildings could afford and possess these expensive (private) properties often financed by shareholders or state subsidies.

2.3.3   Basis, superstructure and false consciousness

The whole system of forces of production, technology and the organization of producing goods shapes the economic structure. But more than that, it also shapes the political and judicial superstructure. The superstructure is a very broad, general, and loosely defined concept. In the theoretical system of Marx and Engels, it comprises almost the whole of social life, with the exception of the real economic basis. The production of the means of subsistence is conceived of as the *basis* of all social relations. Of course, this is only an analytical construction. In real life, the economy is not separated from the rest of society. We should also keep in mind that the superstructure is not another word for culture, the collective conscience, or the whole set of ideas that exist within society. It is more. Culture is only a part of it. It also embodies the political and judicial institutions, organizations, ideas, and regulations. It also covers social elements that have a real 'material' existence. In fact, the superstructure covers two meanings. There is the political-judicial element, including the whole political and legal machinery, and there is the cultural and ideological superstructure.

Marx and Engels did not invent the term ideology, but they have helped to make it a central Marxist concept. Whenever they used this term, it was in a derogatory sense, almost always in connection with false consciousness.[39] This could give the wrong impression that ideology and false consciousness are synonyms. Though there is a definite affinity between these two concepts, it is not wise to use them as different referents for the same thing. Ideology is a much broader concept than false consciousness. Individuals and social classes can suffer from false consciousness with respect to their actual social position and their objective social condition and this can partly be affected by a prevailing ideology. For individuals, an ideology functions as a shared consciousness of the collective condition and their social interests and objectives. Consequently, this ideology determines their social actions. From this, it follows that an ideology can refer to real as well as to false consciousness. False consciousness occurs when individuals or groups have a wrong view of their actual social position, in particular their position within the economic basis. As long as the ideology of the workers is founded on false consciousness, it will not elicit the right actions for improving their position.[40] On the basis of the abovementioned, it is possible to sketch a four-layered model of society that reflects Marx's ideas about the structure of society.

Scheme 2.2   Basis and superstructure

basis	1 the level of production forces or state of technology;
	2 the economic relations determined by the production forces.
superstructure	3 the legal-political order that emerges from this economic foundation;
	4 the ideology that supports the economic order and the connecting legal-political system.

In the course of time, sliding walls are placed between the political and economic relations obscuring the coherence between both levels. However, it remains a fundamental fact that political relations are somehow an adequate expression of economic interests. Admittedly, as any social institution, the state is inclined to become rather independent. A thorough analysis will show that this dependence still exists.[41] The progressive unfolding of the economy has brought forth groups with conflicting interests. Thus, a strong need has arisen for judicial and political regulation and this is responsible for the birth and growth of the state. The constitutional state has to mend what went wrong socially. In the jargon of Marxists, this is described as a situation in which society has enmeshed itself in an irreconcilable contradiction.[42] Whenever such conflicts have to be solved, the state will side with the ruling class. Once more, this underscores the Marxist view that the legal-political superstructure is closely connected with the economic relations. The state does not solve the contradiction but lets it fester. It suppresses the working class and maintains law and order in the interest of the dominant class.

How does the state run its affairs in these matters? It does not shun the use of violence. But the principal method is the creation of a certain image that legitimates its actions. Firstly, there is the image that the state has so much power that any resistance is useless. Coupled to this image is the Hegelian idea that the state in its present form is necessary and reasonable: There must be order; there simply is no alternative. Thus, the state miraculously succeeds in persuading the oppressed classes that the existing state of affairs is sensible and wholly legitimate. On the basis of his personal experience and thorough study of the hard facts of life, Marx argued that social conditions, in particular economic power relations, determine the form and functions of the state. Instead of criticizing the state, it is better to criticize society. The state is simply an instrument of power for the ruling class. In the nineteenth century, this was accentuated by the fact that workers (and women) had no right to vote. Only people who paid a certain amount of income tax were entitled to vote and to be elected. Therefore, the poor had no representation in any parliament or government. Hence, Marx believed that the state would not play a role in breaking down the relations of production; these revolutionary forces would have to come from society itself.

The economic foundation of society influences the ideological views of the government. This is particularly true for the legitimacy of the methods used for maintaining order, or for the way in which the state attempts to solve conflicts. The state authority also supports other ideological opinions, such as the justification for a highly differentiated system of positions and salaries. In Marx's view, all the prevailing opinions regarding the right organization of society can be deduced from their functionality for the economic base. It has to be admitted, however, that well-established ideological representations can become partially autonomous forces. Their dependence on the base is indirect. Political views are faced with alternative representations. This encourages an autonomous reflection upon the present state of affairs. Besides, society is not static but dynamic. New developments lead to new conflicts over the organization or the need for re-organization of society. This generates new ideas and new solutions. We witness a strong interaction between the economic base and the ideological superstructure during periods of significant social transformations. This should make clear that the basis only partially determines what goes on in the superstructure. Nevertheless, it must also be stressed that Marx and Engels always showed a strong inclination to fall back on the statement that, in the final instance, the economic foundation determines the prevailing set of ideological representations.

2.4   Class struggle as the prime mover of social progress

The work of Marx is closely connected with the mainstream of European philosophy. This is in particular true of his great trust in progress. In the 18th century, Leibniz was one of the first great thinkers to draw attention to the idea that every organic creature goes through a series of stages. It was his assertion that nature does not jump, but develops gradually; that nature is always burdened by its past and is pregnant of its future. The progress of science made Leibniz optimistic. He truly believed that mankind was heading for an ever-increasing measure of happiness.

2.4.1   *The origin of the idea of social progress*

Most Enlightenment philosophers believed that progress would be realized in a gradual and orderly fashion. But some thinkers cherished a completely different idea. They followed Ancient Greek philosophers such as Plato, who argued that progress was based on disputes and conflicts. Another philosopher, Herakleitos, argued: *'Struggle is the father of all things.'* Moreover, he said that everything tends to change into its opposite. Immanuel Kant, the great philosopher of the Enlightenment, also thought that conflict was the driving force behind social progress. Why? Humans must live in groups but they are also egocentric and this produces conflict. Kant was convinced that this conflict would generate progress, simply because people are compelled to solve such problems in order to cope with living in groups. Without this problem-solving capacity, people would forever live like a flock of sheep. Solving social problems and managing conflict lead to perfection. Hence, social progress is not a consequence of the actions of single human beings, but the result of the problem-solving actions of people in groups.

2.4.2   The emergence of social classes

What did Marx see as the seedbed of social conflict? By nature, people are compelled to work for food, clothing, and shelter. They have to struggle with nature for a decent level of subsistence. But man is an insatiable animal. As soon as his primary needs are fulfilled, new needs and desires emerge.[43] The energetic attempts to fulfill new desires force people to co-operate leading to increased specialization. However, as soon as this division of labour crystallizes, groups or classes emerge with opposing interests. Broadly speaking, Marx asserted that individuals who live under similar economic circumstances or situations, whether they are conscious of this or not, objectively constitute a class. Different social conditions create different interests and lifestyles that put classes in a hostile opposition. *'They form a class in so far as they have to carry on a common battle against another class.'*[44] These opposing classes are the star players in the epic history of mankind.[45]

The concept of 'class' is a vital part of Marx's theory of social evolution. In his view, only two groups are essential: the dominant or upper class and the oppressed or lower class. The dominant class has a big stake in reproducing the system whereas the opposing class has a great interest in changing the system to emancipate itself from its marginal position. Between these two major classes are a few in-between classes, for example the petty bourgeoisie or the lower middle classes. But Marx theoretical thought that these in-between classes were unimportant. They will be squeezed between the capitalists and the working class. Parts of these classes will join the upper class because of their possessions and ability to hire labour, whereas other parts will be driven towards the lower class because they no longer own any means of production or are unemployed. It stands to reason that this part of Marx's theory has provided much food for critical thought. His model of a dichotomized society was and always will be too simple. Besides, it completely underestimated the social function, expansion, and flexibility of the middle classes. In Marx's simple sketch of the class structure, the owners of capital goods, such as factories, production machines, and means of transport, constitute a social, legal, and economic class – the bourgeoisie. This class clearly distinguishes itself from the labour class or the proletariat. The workers have no capital or means of production. They only possess their skills and the energy to work. This objective difference is a necessary criterion to distinguish the concept of class from other concepts that describe specific social categories, such as those of married and unmarried people or the young and the old. But Marx also needed a subjective ingredient to define a social class. Only if workers realize that they are being exploited and use this consciousness to get organized, they will be able to form a real class. Before this class-consciousness emerges, they form a latent or potential class, a class in itself (*Klasse an sich*). For instance, he suggested that, in the epoch of feudalism, the serfs did not constitute a manifest class, neither did the peasants. Only when members of a social category are aware of being exploited and use this consciousness as a basis for collective resistance, does the latent class turn into a viable class, a class by itself (*Klasse für sich)*. We see that Marx could not maintain a purely materialist position. He had to acknowledge that class-consciousness plays a crucial role in history, that it is an essential prerequisite for revolutionary action. Nevertheless, he believed that class-consciousness would inevitably be aroused after deterioration of the material conditions of the workers. In the long run, even the capitalists, always in competition, will join forces in order to defend their interests against a mobilized working class.

Many conditions have to be fulfilled to transform a class of itself into a politically conscious class for itself. There has to be a rising number of significant class conflicts about the distribution of incomes and labour conditions. It helps when other conditions frustrate the working class, such as the absence of upward social mobility. This will give them the feeling that individual efforts will be fruitless and that only concerted actions can lead to success. It certainly helps when large numbers of workers are being concentrated in industrialized urban areas. If this is the case, communication and political agitation can be organized more easily. To mobilize the working class in an effective way, the support of a political organization with a persuasive ideology and capable leaders, that is, the communist party is urgently needed. Kautsky and Lenin later redefined the role of the communist parties: making transparent to the working class its 'true' social position, so as to transform its spontaneous but non-revolutionary 'trade union consciousness' into real 'political consciousnesses'. Like the pope, the party could not be wrong. It is on such grounds that Communist Parties have justified their leading role, and oppressed and slaughtered thousands, if not millions, of people to defend them, wherever they came to power. This was, it should be pointed out, not Marx's own position.[16] Nevertheless, it should be added that Marx, during all the years that he was politically active, relentlessly expelled all members and fellow-revolutionaries of the associations and committees that dared to deviate slightly from his views. He was convinced that it was his revolutionary duty to criticize, attack, and expose without mercy any utopian charlatan or pseudo communist who showed the slightest signs of a bourgeois or liberal affinity. As he said more than once *'Our task must be unsparing criticism, directed even more against our self-styled friends than against our declared enemies.'*[47] This device has besieged the communist movement during its entire history.

2.5   The analysis of capitalism

Capital is Marx's most famous book. It was issued in three parts. After his death, Engels edited and finished the last two volumes. In his major work, Marx intended to uncover the social and economic mechanisms of modern society. Understanding and fundamentally changing capitalist society was his main goal. His ultimate objective was the liberation of the oppressed. He was convinced that the laws that determine the development of modern economy are decisive for the functioning and the transformation of society. Therefore, he hardly took other social factors, causes, or forces into account. According to his doctrine, the opposition between capital and labour is decisive for the development of modern society. Everything centers on the inherently antagonistic character of capitalism. He was certain that these antagonisms would bring down capitalism. The strong conviction in his own theory fuelled his need to propagate this view as widely as possible and to urge the workers to speed up this process. Therefore, it is impossible to distinguish Marx the social scientist from Marx the political activist.[48] This is very clear in The Manifesto of the Communist Party, which he and Engels published in 1848. This little book already contains the core of the analysis of capitalism. Stylistically, it does not resemble an academic text at all, but that does not diminish the great value of the insights collected in it. Essays have rarely been written that contain so much ideas in so few pages. This political pamphlet, full of burning rage, offers a concise summary of a complete, scientific doctrine: historical materialism. The fundamental ideas of the Manifesto can be summarized in the following three statements:

1   The level of economic production and the societal structure that it generates in each historical period establishes the basis for the political and cultural history of that particular era.
2   The entire history has been a history of class conflict, a history of class struggles between the oppressed and the oppressor.
3   This class struggle had now reached a level in which the exploited class can no longer emancipate itself from the dominant class, unless it liberates the whole of society from exploitation, oppression and class conflict forever.[49]

This inflammatory publication has had an enormous effect on modern history. The preface opens with the following well-known statement: 'A specter is haunting Europe – the specter of Communism.' Let me quote another paragraph to show that this classical text is far from boring.

> The bourgeoisie, wherever it has got the upper hand, has put an end to all feudal, patriarchal, idyllic relations. It has pitilessly torn asunder the motley feudal ties that bound man to his 'natural superior', and has left remaining no other nexus between man and man than naked self-interest, than callous 'cash payment'. It has drowned the most heavenly ecstasies of religious fervour, of chivalrous enthusiasm, of philistine sentimentalism, in the icy water of egoistic calculation. It has resolved personal worth into exchange value, and in place of the numberless ineradicably chartered freedoms, has set up that single, unscrupulous freedom – Free Trade.[50]

Enough impressive rhetoric, back to the basic idea: class struggle. In order to stay in power, the bourgeoisie must continuously invest in innovations. In doing so, she continuously rearranges and changes the process of production and so the conditions of labour. In the age of capitalism, we can witness an incessant pressure to innovate in order to increase profits, and to stay ahead of the competition. The growing wealth of one small group coincides with the growing misery of the masses. This broadening gap will sooner or later produce a revolutionary confrontation. The expanding proletariat will constitute a real social class that will seize power to reform society once and for all. The difference between this and former historical revolutions is that this will be a revolution of the majority against the minority and not, as before, a revolution of one elite trying to topple another one. The capitalist system incites revolutionary forces. It can only increase profits by means of exploitation. In a market economy, capitalists are compelled to lower their prices as a consequence of growing competition. Thus, they are forced to cut costs. Otherwise they will not survive. The best way to cut costs is to cut labour costs, which boils down to a decrease in the purchasing power of workers. As a consequence, sales will drop, and so will profits. Once more, businessmen will start looking for opportunities to cut costs. This downhill slide cannot be stopped. It drives small entrepreneurs into bankruptcy. The middle classes will dwindle and society will polarize into two opposing classes. Finally, this will incite a class struggle that will revolutionize society.

Above, I have outlined many of Marx's best-known economic theories. Now, I will discuss them more systematically:

a The theory of surplus value

In a modern society the exchange value of certain goods is expressed in money. Thus the value of a kilo of bake meal can be compared to the value of a liter of fuel, a hammer or a domestic service. The common denominator of all these commodities or services lies in the fact that in all these cases labour had or has to be carried out to put them on the market. Quality has to be transformed into quantity to make exchange possible between goods and services and money. Exchange must be conceived in terms of the equation of labour-time. The average labour time is the yardstick for the comparison of the prices of goods and services. The workers and their families need all kinds of goods for their survival. Say, that they have to work 30 hours a week to earn the money they really need to make ends meet, but their employers do not pay them enough per hour. Thus, they are compelled to work longer, say 48 hours a week, to raise enough money. In this way, the employer gets many hours of labour for free. This exploitation renders him so-called surplus value. The factory owner or shopkeeper will use this surplus value for further investments.[51]

b Accumulation theory

This theory refers to the way in which the capitalist utilizes his profits. He could spend it on consumptive goods, but this is unusual. The prestige of an entrepreneur depends on the value of his possessions, the size of his enterprise, and the value of his machines, sales, and profits. To stay in the race and to defeat his competitors, he is compelled to reinvest his profits. He must forever innovate and expand. Only clever investments, ingenious innovations, and shrewd marketing strategies will get him ahead of his competitors. Thus he becomes increasingly rich.

c Theory of concentration

The theory of monopolization states that the winners of the incessant game of competition will gain a growing amount of capital. With their accumulated capital the best businessmen will buy the most modern machines. They will overrun and ruin their weak competitors, because they can produce better products, more cheaply and more quickly, while still making profits. Or in Marx own words: *'One capitalist always kills many.'* In the long run, the few that will have expropriated the many will become monopolists that put the whole market mechanism out of order. By then, centralization of the means of production and socialization of labour reach a point where they have become incompatible with free market capitalism.[52]

d The crisis theory

Classical economists had observed that periods of economic growth and decline follow each other time and time again. Markets get satiated with similar products, and production has to be cut. Factories close down, workers lose their jobs and many businesses go bankrupt. After a while shortages emerge, demand rises, and levels of production rise in response to rising demand. As profits rise, businesses start to expand again. Since businessmen operate on a strictly individualistic basis they tend to invest too much into new machines, technologies, and factories. After a while this generates overproduction. Thus, the cycle of economic growth, overproduction and subsequent decline will occur all over again. According to Marx, these economic crises will reappear after shorter intervals and get more severe.

e The pauperisation theory

Every new round of industrial innovations will make specific forms of craftsmanship obsolete. So, the workers will have to adjust and renew their skills time and time again. Those who cannot adjust to new technologies will loose their jobs. Marx observed a steady process of pauperisation. Sharp competition forced capitalists to lower the wages, lengthen the workweek, or organize the labour process more efficiently. The outcome for the workers is a lower income and increased unemployment. This downward spiral went on until the workers only earned a minimal wage, just at or below the subsistence level. But the growing level of exploitation feeds the motivation of the working-class to revolt. Therefore, Marx and Engels finished *The Communist Manifesto* with the following battle cry:

*Let the ruling classes tremble at the communist revolution. The pro-
letarians have nothing to lose but their chains. They have a world to
win. Workers of all countries, unite!5³*

2.6   Alienation

*All costs to raise capitalist productivity will be laid on the shoulders
of the individual workers. All means to enlarge production will
turn into means for their oppression and exploitation. They mutate
workers into mere appendixes of machines.⁵⁴*

Marx wished to explain more than just poverty. He also wanted to show how specific changes in the mode of production, which have created particular forms of
ownership, have estranged the workers from their own true selves. During this
explanatory process he was constantly looking for negative qualitative turns. He
liked to uncover situations in which the outcomes of human actions take sides
against the very people who have created them. The following quotation gives a
good impression of such a 'negative dialectical' change.

*In our days everything seems pregnant with its contrary. ... At the
same pace that mankind masters nature, man seems to become
enslaved to other men or to his own infamy. ... All our invention
and progress seem to result in endowing material forces with intellectual life, and in stultifying human life into material force. This
antagonism between modern industry and science on the one hand,
modern misery and dissolution on the other hand; this antagonism
between productive powers, and the social relations of our epoch is a
fact, plain, overwhelming, and not to be disputed.⁵⁵*

2.6.1   Alienation before Marx

Marx developed a sharp eye for so-called social contradictions, that is, situations
in which society clearly gets counterproductive and creates social abuses, such
as economic and political oppression and alienation. The concept of alienation
has a long history. Rousseau outlined already that men are good by nature, but
are corrupted by society; that men are born equal but are treated unequally. He
was convinced that people could rid themselves of suffering caused by social
abuses, by constructing a new community and by freely subjecting themselves to
the 'Common Will'. His accusation against society became an important theme
for social philosophy. On the rebound the 'wholeness' and 'naturalness' of small
well-integrated historic communities were idealized. In this climate Schiller contended that man was mentally torn apart by the division of labour. They became
little cogs in the machinery of industrial society. Diminished to a little fraction,

they would never be able to develop to the full. But, not only individuals are constrained in their development; the same is true for society as a whole. State and church have been torn apart and so have law and morality.[56] Hence there is an urgent need for a new integration of man and society.

For Morelly, inequality was caused by the injustice that sprung from private property. Man had lost its innocence by defending and enlarging private property. Thus focusing only on egoistic interests. In his view, the only acceptable form of private property is the property needed for daily use. The rest should be distributed over all members of the community.[57] Marx seconded this view. He too blames private property as the main source of alienation, and contends that the real problem lies in the ownership of the means of production, in the ownership of land, machines, factories and huge sums of money. Money is the source of all evil. It turns man into commodities. As a commodity, man assumes a 'double character': an economic 'value form' and a 'natural' form. As commodity – that is, as incorporated labour – something is worth a certain sum of money. As commodity its natural characteristics are hardly relevant. Similarly, individuals, though physically very much alike, may have very different values for society. Here again, the physical appearance is irrelevant, whereas the commodity value of the person is quite another matter. For instance, a young heart surgeon has much more economic value than an equally young bus driver.[58] On the other hand, personal differences fade away in the light of equal economic values. One civil servant can easily replace another civil servant. The same is true for factory workers or sailors. Realizing that you are as easily replaceable as any pencil or screwdriver can also be a rather alienating and sobering experience.

What is a commodity?
According to Marx a commodity has two sides. It is or has a *use value* – that is, it 'satisfies human needs of whatever kind'; and also an *exchange value* – that is, it exchanges in certain proportions against use-values.[36] The distinguishing feature of a commodity is that it is not merely useful but enters into *exchange*. It is produced for that purpose, rather than merely happening to enter into exchange. Although exchange may occur peripherically and accidentally in many forms of society, it predominates only in capitalistic societies. Where commodities predominate, their circulation must give rise to capital.

Box 2.2

2.6.2   Alienating humans from human nature

Marx did not think that the main source of alienation lies in the great distance between life in industrial society and the simple and often romanticized life in premodern societies, in which humans are supposed to be in very close contact with nature. On the contrary, the productive power of industrialization generates numerous possibilities for the future development of mankind, which could not have been possible under prior levels of technology. However, the social and economic relationship within capitalism fails to realize these historically generated possibilities. The character of alienated labour does not express a tension between 'man in nature' and 'man in society', but between the potential generated by a specific form of society – capitalism – and the frustrated realization of that potential.[60] In principle, work is no problem. Producing something will give people satisfaction and contributes to self-realization. Under the right conditions work is intrinsically motivating.

It is important to take good notice of Marx's view on the evolution of man, for it is a truly sociological perspective. What distinguishes humans from highly developed animals is that human faculties, capacities, and tastes are shaped by society. The isolated individual is a fiction. No man exists who has not been raised in a social group, and thus is shaped by a society. His interactions with the social world contribute to the further modification of that world. Each individual is thus the recipient of the accumulated culture of the generations that have preceded him. 'Individual human life and species-life are not different things'[61] It is man's membership of society, with its technology and culture, which confers his 'humanity' upon him. Many animals have similar sense organs and biological needs as man; but the perception of beauty in nature, art or music is a human faculty, a creation of society. For man sexual activity, or eating and drinking, are no simple satisfactions of biological drives, but have become transformed into actions that provide manifold satisfactions.[62] In principle, alienation is not brought about by an increased separation from nature. A certain measure of separation from our biological origin is normal, for we can only become human through interaction and coexistence with other man, in other words, through living a social life. However, under capitalism the worker no longer works for the satisfaction of his personal needs, but for a market system. The product is taken away from him. No longer does he have a say in the matter. Thus the worker gets alienated from his product and his work. Work has become a duty, a means to satisfy the needs of others.

2.6.3   Objectification

Marx underlined that the forces of production are the result of the outcomes of human forces, which confront their creators as if they are alien forces. This is entirely the consequence of an uncontrolled division of labour, in particular the separation of the producers and the ownership of the means of production. This has created social forces that are independent of the volition of the individual. These economic forces have acquired the appearance of natural forces that follow the mechanical laws of physics.[63] Therein lays the answer to the question why people can become a slave to their products, why work has become so boring and burdensome that the worker can only feel contented during leisure activities. For Marx, this touched upon the essence of man, for he needs work to fulfil himself. When he gets estranged from work, he will be alienated from his true essence. Therefore communists must do everything in their power to dismantle the existing society by putting the means of production in the hands of the community, that is, by expropriating the expropriators. He sincerely believed that, from then on, people would be able to decide for themselves which goods should be produced and how they should be produced.[64]

Marx wanted to detect the causes behind these perverse social forces. So, in the summer of 1844, he started to work on the first draft of his *Economic writings*. These early manuscripts were not published during his lifetime because other political and intellectual assignments distracted him. Many of the positions taken up in 1844 were further elaborated in the *Grundrisse* and in *Capital*. In the first part of these manuscripts Marx describes different ways in which the worker's relationship to his product results in his alienation.[65] But first he had to settle some scores with other political economists. They start with the fact of private property, without an explanation. From their perspective, the only causal forces that keep the economy going are greed and competition - the war of the greedy. They have not tackled the contradictions in their doctrines, for example, how monopolization kills competition.[66] So Marx wanted to spell out the essential connections between private property, selfishness, the division of labour, landed property, capital, exchange and competition, and the degradation of the workers. Under capitalism the worker

> *... does not fulfill himself in his work but denies himself, has a feeling of misery, not of self-being, does not develop freely a physical and mental energy, but is physically exhausted and mentally debased. The worker therefore feels himself at home only during his leisure, whereas at work he feels homeless. His work is not voluntary but imposed, forced labour. It is not the satisfaction of a need, but only a means for satisfying other needs. Its alien character is clearly shown by the fact that as soon as there is no physical or other compulsion it is avoided like the plague. Finally, the alienated character of work for the worker appears in the fact that it is not his work but work for someone else, that in work he does not belong to himself but to another person.* [67]

For Marx it was an indisputable fact the more production increases, the poorer the worker gets. The more commodities he produces, the cheaper he becomes, and the more he resembles a commodity. Labour in a capitalist system not only produces goods; it also produces labour and it molds men into profit making machines. Thus the employer will not hesitate to replace these dehumanized machines for a real machine or robot as soon as it becomes more profitable. This merely proves that the product of work confronts the workers as an alien being, as an independent power. The product of labour has solidified itself into a thing that can be exchanged for money. That is the objectification of labour. Labour has even become an object. Nowadays the worker can only get a job and hold it with the greatest effort. At irregular intervals he will be unemployed or 'between jobs'.

For Marx, it is evident that the more the worker produces for his employer, the more powerful, alien, and hostile the objective world becomes that he helped create, the poorer he becomes in his inner life. Putting your life into the production of marketable objects means that your life no longer belongs to you but to the object. One could say that the worker belongs to the employer, but also the employers have become slaves of the system that sacrifices individual lives for the sake of the Money-God. Men have created a world of objects that exist outside him, independent and alien, which has become a self-sufficient power that confronts them in a hostile way, and has turned them into slavery.

Marx repeated this kind of reasoning time and again. For instance: the more the worker produces the less he has to consume, the more value he creates the more worthless he becomes, the better designed the product, the more deformed the worker, the more civilized the product, the more barbaric the work and the worker.[68] To us, who have grown up in a modern welfare state, these mantras might appear to render a rather negative, one-sided picture of capitalist working conditions of the mid-nineteenth century. But it is undeniable that in those days, and also in the first half of the twentieth century, working conditions in the western factories, mines, textile mills, and sweatshops were horrible.[69] These conditions have exhausted, injured, and killed many adults and children. Presently, this is still going on in many underdeveloped countries. Nonetheless, even during the growing pains of industrialization there must have been conditions in which workers might have enjoyed some pleasure in their work and some pride in their products. Also many workers might have enjoyed incomes that enabled them to buy cheap mass-produced products; otherwise industrialism would have stopped right after it started. The more mass products the workers produce, the more products have to be consumed by the masses. So, we are able to detect weaknesses in Marx's theory, in particular in the many occasions that he indulges himself in presenting long series of completely deterministic dialectical negations as we have just presented here, without any sight of a synthesis that would ameliorate the painful consequences of industrialism.

Nonetheless, a large portion of industrialized work had and still has caused serious side effects, including alienation. Life is a means to sustain life and to procreate new life. Animals only act to live, to survive and to generate offspring. Animals are vital activity, nothing more, nothing less. Man, however, makes his vital activity into an object of his will and consciousness. That places him outside the realm of animals per se. Animals produce only under pressure of immediate physical need, whereas man also can and will produce freely from physical need. Animal only produces itself, but man reconstructs nature. He is free to shape his life to his liking. But alienation reverses this relation. It turns the conscious being into a mere means of existence.[70]

Objectification is inherent to human existence. People have to express their ideas, wishes, wants, and desires in order to get understood by other people. This process of externalization renders ideas, thoughts, wishes, and desires an objective character. This is most obvious when people produce material objects, but it would be incorrect to underestimate the objective character of immaterial products. Also ideas can acquire an objective materialization in the form of laws, contracts, religious rituals, and habits. Objectification does not necessarily lead to alienation. This only happens in systems in which people are more or less forced to work for employers. Then production and the things that are being produced have become powers to which the workers believe they have to submit themselves. When this is the case, liberation amounts to disowning the capitalists, the owners of the means of production.

2.6.4   Money: the source of all evil

Money is the alienating essence of work and human existence; that essence controls him and he worships it.[71]

Alienation occurs because capitalism has evolved into a system in which a small group possesses all the means of production and decides over products and working hours. Instead of producing for themselves in a wholly natural way until their needs are satisfied, workers have to produce for entrepreneurs, and often have to contribute to a work process that gives them not any satisfaction whatsoever and has no meaning for them either. In capitalism the worker simply is a cost item like machines or crude material. The production process becomes an alienating process of objectification instead of a process for self-realization. The worker looses his humanity and is compelled to act as just another instrument for profit making. So, in the end, the items produced by man enslave them.

The main reason for Marx to fight capitalism was his conviction that capitalism is the key cause of alienation and dehumanization. The following quotation reminds us of Schiller's statement mentioned before.

...[The capitalist] producers ... distort the worker into a fragment of a man, they degrade him to the level of an appendage of a machine, they destroy the actual content of his labour by turning it into a torment; they alienate from him the intellectual potentialities of the labour process in the same proportion as science is incorporated in it as independent power; they deform the condition under which he works.[72]

Capitalism is troubled by two characteristics that enhance alienation. To increase production it has to refine the division of labour and the mechanization of production. Both methods change work into a monotonous series of disagreeable activities. Marx believed that communism would offer far better opportunities for individual self-realization and self-expression, because it would rid itself of an unnatural division of labour. Thus labour would become more diversified and more challenging to everyone. Within communism making profit has no high priority, and therefore constructing a system for making labour more efficient at all costs will not have priority. However, hitherto all large-scale experiments with communism have failed terribly. Instead of creating more freedom and less alienation, working conditions worsened and became more alienating than the working conditions in modern welfare states.

The foregoing clarifies what Marx has written in various and distinct ways about alienation. The primary source of alienation is sometimes contributed to the division of labour, the emergence of two opposing classes in which one class owns the forces of production, the competitive market system or the role money plays. Of course, all these phenomena are closely interrelated. Further, Marx has mentioned various forms of alienation. Therefore it might be better to list them separately. We present them once more as a kind of résumé.

- First, man is alienated from the process of labour as soon as he cannot oversee what he is doing and therefore loses control.
- Secondly he is alienated from the object of his labour. It has become an object in which he no longer can realize himself.
- In the third place, man alienates from his fellows, for the other is dehumanized and have become instruments for achieving one's own goals or the bosses' goals. Man increasingly sees each other as competitor or enemy.
- In the fourth place, man alienates from the world that has completely changed its character as a consequence of rationalization and specialization. Thus the world has lost its function as life-world.
- In the fifth place, man is alienated from nature. They have to work long hours in noisy factories, suffocating offices, shops, or mines instead of in the open air. Most of them have to live in slums without greens, gardens or trees.
- Finally, the different domains of life alienate from each other. A capitalistic economy cannot harmonize with ethics, the agrarian sector alienates from the urban world, and the state bureaucracies alienates from the civilians it is supposed to serve.

Alienation equals the frustration of one's own development, one's own realization into one's true self. In a highly materialistic world people are indoctrinated to focus their actions on 'having' and not socialized for 'being'. Marx's ideas about alienation still seem to be valid, although some critical remarks seem in order. Specialization, so despised by Marx, can enhance work satisfaction for many people. Industrialization not only has created inhumane jobs, but also destroyed many inhumane jobs, thus making life more pleasant for scores of workers.

2.7 Sociology of knowledge: ideology and false consciousness

Marx maintained that human thinking is determined by social conditions. The material conditions even determine the way people think, the way they see the world. This idea is briefly described in his famous dictum that 'social existence determines consciousness'.[73] In short: being determines seeing, or being determines thinking. This statement has become a crucial article of faith for the (Marxist) sociology of knowledge. Nonetheless, he granted that there would always be a few individuals capable of developing thoughts that are detached from their own social position and class interests. But this would never happen to groups.[74] Of course, Marx never doubted that he was such an exceptional person, that he had cleansed himself successfully of the prejudiced mindset of his bourgeois background. Therefore, he could see what others overlooked. But he distrusted all others in that respect. For instance, in his Circular Letter to the leaders of the German socialist Party, he warned them that if people from other classes join the proletarian movement, the first condition must be that they should not bring any remnants of bourgeois or petty-bourgeois prejudices with them but should wholeheartedly adopt the proletarian outlook. However, in his experience, most of these gentlemen are chock-full of bourgeois and petty-bourgeois ideas that will adulterate the political aims of the Worker's Party and castrate its revolutionary vitality. So they had to be ousted sooner or latter.[75]

Marx attempted to analyze the functionality of ideas for their inventors and their propagators. He did not go as far as contending that all bourgeois thinkers present similar ideas. He distinguished between ideas that were being promoted during the awakening of capitalism and the ideas that prevail during the heydays of capitalism. In his view, each society already creates the basic elements for its successor. The new society will already announce its arrival explicitly during the fall of the old order. In a dialectical process the existing order will generate its own antithetical successor. This qualification does not mitigate the materialistic determinism of his sociology of knowledge. The quintessence of Marx sociology of knowledge is most succinctly expressed in the following statement:

> *The ruling ideas of each age have ever been the ideas of the ruling class.*[76]

For him the ruling ideas simply are the intellectual expression of existing relations of production. Also religious ideas appear to serve the interests of the ruling class. Likewise material interests generate the state, ethics, and religion. The interests of the have-nots, and the ideas that clarify their interests, are being ignored or labeled as forms of 'false consciousness'. The same is true for the proprietors who do not recognize that form of alienation. In general, both lack the right insight in the nature and course of social evolution.

Marx acknowledged that the representatives of particular interest groups possess a certain variation in their stock of ideas, though they stay within the demarcations imposed by their class. They are driven to the same problems and the same solutions to which their material interest and social position has steered them.[77] It always boils down to the assertion that our ideas, norms, and values are built on the materialistic basis of our society. Later Engels would qualify this strong statement a little by adding that this is so 'in the last instance'. By this he seemed to imply that the most important elements of the superstructure are determined by the basis. Of course, this can lead to circular reasoning. Each time someone shows that something is not determined by the material basis Marxists respond that this particular topic is of no great importance for the superstructure of society.[78] Marx could never admit that the superstructure of society could be relatively autonomous. In fact this would force him to choose another metaphor, because the basis or foundation will always support what is on top of it.

All critical remarks cannot hide that Marx has done a great job to draw our attention to the strong connection between the ruling ideas of any society or social group and the interests of the ruling class. The ideas of the ruling class are the ideas that fit their main interests, and, as a ruling class, they tend to succeed in making their ideas the dominant points of view for the whole of society. This connection between ideas and interests can be generalized to any group of importance, to any pressure group in society. So, tell me your social position and I tell you your ideological perspective. This is particularly true for the representatives of political parties, labour unions and associations of employers, but also for all other interest groups, whether they are consumer organizations, associations of homeowners or one-issue groups like Greenpeace or Amnesty International. Their ideas will always be one-sided and bear witness to tunnel vision. After Marx, every social scientist, historian, or journalist will bear this in mind. Peter Berger presents the telling example of an undertaker who is convinced that an expensive funeral shows the right respect for the deceased.[79]

2.8   The role of the state after the revolution

His economic theories forced Marx to conclude that the periodic return and aggravation of economic crises and the increase of pauperization will end in a violent revolution, a revolution that shall be won by the proletariat. Thus capitalism generates its own demise. This will also be the end for the present role of the state. No longer is the state needed to help the capitalistic system survive, let alone flourish. Via an intermediate period in which the proletariat will be in power, communism will be established for good. This will mean the end of private property, in particular private ownership of the means of production. They will fall under the jurisdiction of the proletariat and will be centralized to enlarge production. Of course, in the beginning this drastic shift of the economy and the polity will cause a slowing down of production. Adjustments to the new system will take time and will go hand in hand with some loss of resources. That's why there is a temporary need to stimulate production by paying higher salaries to the most productive workers: *'each to his abilities, each according to his achievements.'*[80] But this a temporary phenomenon, only condoned during the transition period.

The *Communist Manifesto* presents a clear plan of action that must be executed during the rule of the proletariat: expropriation of land; introduction of progressive taxes; confiscation of the possession of all people that have left the country to seek refuge in a non-communist country; centralization of financial institutes, banks and transportation, a work duty for everyone and the establishment of work armies for agriculture; a merger of agriculture and industry and the eradication of the difference between urban and rural regions; and, finally, free public education for all accompanied with the immediate abolition of child labour in factories. With the exception of the introduction of free public education all these measures are of a negative kind, intended to eliminate all excesses and manifestations of capitalism as soon as possible.

Through all these measures the state will lose its raison d'être, for the only function of state was to defend the interests of capitalists with a host of legal and oppressive measures. In Marx's frame of mind this is quite logical. The capitalists are in power. They constitute the ruling class, and they steer political decisions. Politicians merely are their accomplices and errand boys. In a communist society different, opposing classes no longer exist. Therefore there is no need for a bureaucratic state apparatus to regulate conflicts of interest in the interests of the ruling class.

Here Marx's sociology is most vulnerable. His predictions about a stateless society seem very unlikely, in particular because they are based on weak assumptions.[81] Firstly, Marx suggested that only economic conflicts are conflicts that require a legal-administrative system to solve them. Unless one expects a heaven on earth, we can assume that conflicts will be inherent in any kind of society, capitalist or not. In our day and age we need only point at the many religious and ethnic conflicts that torment our world.

There is another reason to pause for some critical remarks at Marx's prediction of a stateless communist society. In other instances he appears to be a fervent advocate of a planned economy to bring national production in line with the crucial needs of the people. He wants to put an end to the free play of market forces, but, clearly, this requires a large and well-organised governmental planning bureau. How else would it be possible, if possible at all, to make a detailed and effective plan that coordinates the economy, housing, transport, and education simply requires strong state bureaucracies. Whether these could be more effective than the workings of a free market is another question.

2.9   Is there a third Marx?

Of course not all Marx has written is clear. Besides there certainly are instances in which he seems to contradict himself. This is understandable in view of his prolific writing, which also showed a certain evolution. So, Marx's texts do not form a seamless web. In the course of more than forty years of ardent academic work he has amended some of his views. Hence, many scholars make a clear division between his early writings and his later writings. It might even be more useful to distinguish between three periods: early, middle and late writings. The early writings end when he started to co-operate with Friedrich Engels and produced major works such as the *Manifesto, Grundrisse*, and *Capital*. But from the mid-1870s onwards we can discern the beginnings of a counter-discourse. The best example of this is to be found in the drafts of his 1881 letter to Vera Zasulich. This letter deals with the Russian peasant commune, the *mir* or *obshchina*. Then, Marx started to see that particular form of social organization as a possible basis for a distinctive kind of socialism, allowing Russia the chance to bypass the 'fatal vicissitudes of the capitalist regime'.

He argued that the Russian peasant communities of his time still possess primitive characteristics, which it must lose if they are to develop an element of collective production. For Marx, one of the most important advantages which differentiate the *mir* or *obshchina* from more primitive variants of archaic societies, is its having broken from the strong tie of the natural relationship of kinship of its members, and the development, within it, of private property in houses and yards, and the periodic redistribution of communal land so that each farmer tilled the various fields on his own behalf and individually appropriated its fruits. All of these characteristics permit a strong development of individuality and capitalism, which are incompatible with less recent types of 'primitive societies.' According to Marx, its future lies in huge scale mechanized cultivation, ironically made possible by the capitalist production in the West. However, among the debilitating features of the Russian commune, he adds, is its isolation, the lack of connection between the lives of different communes, its nature as a localized microcosm, which provides the basis for despotism.[82]

What is new in 'late' Marx is an explicit repudiation of the inevitability of the dissolution of the primitive commune to make room for forms of industrialization and forms of economic development that he witnessed in Germany and England. What Marx now acknowledges and would not have acknowledged previously is that the primitive Russian communities had incomparably greater vitality than the Semitic, Greek, Roman and a fortiori the modern capitalist societies. Therefore, Sayer supports Shanin's view that 'late Marx' contains the germs, and no more than that, of a very different view of history, which not only acknowledges a plurality of different roads to modernity, but also questions the inevitability and singularity of that destination itself.[83] Marx never reworked his overall vision of history on the basis of these late insights, maybe because his days were numbered. Besides, there is no doubt that he remained a modernist to the end, impatient of those 'prophets facing backward.'

2.10   In conclusion

Marx's forte lay in the synthesis of different theoretical ideas, such as the ideas of the German philosophers, French socialists, and British political economists.

What is original in the result is not any one component element, but the central hypothesis by which each is connected with the others, so that the parts are made to appear to follow from each and to support each other in a single systematic whole.[84]

Marx's theoretical heritage is enthusiastically accepted by many social scientists and elaborated into a Marxist paradigm for sociology, political sciences, ethnology, psychology, economy, and history. His ideas have strongly influenced adherents of the conflict and social critical approach in social science. Their main characteristic is a historical materialistic perspective, which views relations of production as the core element of the social structure. Technological change and changes in the relations of production are the motors of historical development. A second main characteristic is that each society contains groups with opposite interests. The most important ones are the labour class and the bourgeoisie. Marx was the first icon of sociology to address the issue of inequality and the plight of the working class with so much vigor. A third important contribution is his intellectual input in the sociology of knowledge. Rather convincingly he has made clear that ideas do not emerge from nowhere, as highly unexpected and spontaneous manifestations of processes in an individual brain, but cohere with material circumstances and material interest of specific groups. A fourth characteristic is the macro-sociological approach. His study of social phenomena is always placed within the context of the total social system. Moreover, and this is the fifth feature, every aspect is being explained by references to the class conflicts generated by internal contradictions of the capitalist system.

All these perspectives have been of great importance to the further growth of the new social sciences. Some qualifications are in order, though they will not devalue his impressive oeuvre. As we know, history can also take its course without the interference of a violent class struggle. Besides, not all forms of inequality are a consequence of the contradictory interests of social classes. Rather often, ethnic factors play an important role or add too the problem at hand. Nor is it true that all the ruling ideas are the ideas of the ruling class, though this provocative assertion can easily be immunized against any critique by simply to redefine every 'ruling' idea that does not seem to be in the interest of the ruling class, as a 'secondary' idea, and not a prevailing one.

It is not easy to make an objective evaluation of Marx's work. We should not forget to reckon with the social conditions under which he lived, the historical context of his epoch, and the level and type of academic debates in which he was involved. Now we live in an entirely different world. Labour conditions and the level of social security are incomparable with the social conditions of the 19th century. Now, we also are familiar with the horrific excrescences of Marxist-Leninism, Stalinism, and Maoism. Already during his life Marx has encountered some false interpretations of his work and remarked: *'If that is Marxism, then I am no Marxist.'* I am sure that he would have repeated this much more vigorously in the 20th century.

Is Marx responsible for all that is wrong in the communist regimes of the past? At least we can say that some of his political and sociological ideas have helped leaders of communist parties to seize power and to remain in power with the help of very harsh and inhumane dictatorial policies. Undoubtedly some of his ideas have released evil spirits that could manipulatively translate some of his ideas into legitimating the suppression of millions of individuals, all based on the idea that the revolutionary party could never be wrong, as the mediator and stimulator of an unavoidable and predetermined historical evolution that would lead to the communistic heaven on earth, in which all future generations would live happily, free, emancipated, un-alienated but fully developed according to their own unique identity. Biographies and historical studies show that leaders like Stalin, Mao and Pol Pot predominantly were driven by an obsessive will to power and other infamous drives than by the political philosophy of Marx and Engels. They were very ingenious in finding ways to abuse their ideas for their own goals. They could always find some 'dialectical counterargument' that could justify all their deeds or the decrees of their central committees. The main responsibility is theirs and not that of Marx although Bakunin had warned him that after the revolution the new leaders of the communist states would soon forget that they had to serve the interests of the people, but would primarily serve their own interests.[85]

The essence of his scientific doctrine and his political thinking was historical materialism. He propagated this approach as an important alternative for the one-sided idealistic and rather metaphysical philosophy that prevailed in German academe. Yet, it seems opportune to ask oneself whether Marx did not sway too much in the other direction, thus ignoring or belittling the autonomous influence of ideas and their development. One might also criticize his strong undercurrent of economic determinism that leaves hardly any room for other social factors or the free will of individuals. His underlining of the importance of a dialectical explanation deserves to be evaluated positively. Especially in the domains of philosophy, economy, and politics many forceful and strongly appealing ideas and goals tend to arouse equally forceful counter forces. It many cases it can offer a strong antidote to the far too simple linear thinking that still prevails in the social sciences.

Marx's prediction of an unavoidable chain of events leading to successful revolution of the proletariat, by way of accumulation, concentration, polarization, pauperization, and the mobilization of a revolutionary class, did not come true. The first three processes still happen to day, though not always in a linear way. He did not foresee that capitalism was flexible enough to take quite another route in which it incorporated legislation that improved the incomes and working conditions of the masses, without hindering the increase of production and consumption. In fact, in response to the demands of the labour unions and various progressive democratic parties, modernized capitalism succeeded in giving the workers so much to consume and enjoy that they no longer could be mobilized to start a revolution. In modern welfare states they simply have to loose much more than their shackles. Also his vision that capitalist societies were heading to a social structure, in which only two opposing classes would play a major role, appeared to be false. The structure of modern societies has become far more complex instead of less. Many in-between classes have remained and new ones have emerged with the rise of new technologies and new categories of jobs and businesses.

Although Marx ascribed a crucial role to the economic sector, one should not conclude that he was a hundred percent determinist. Such a stance would not agree with his strong adherence to a dialectic view on historical evolution. He full well realized that there is a continuous feedback and mutual exchange between various social domains and sectors. For instance, it is impossible to explain the emergence, rise and fall of religions or political movements by only referring economic factors. Yet he was convinced that these phenomena are influenced by economic variables, if not a predominant way, then at least in the last instance. It is undeniable that in *Capital* Marx comes dangerously close to a complete determinism. Hence, it is no wonder that so many disciples tended to overlook the slight nuances in his texts.

With respect to his political views, we can conclude that he did not take all consequences into consideration. Simply put, he rather naively thought that the creation of a class struggle and the victory of proletarians would provide the right and sufficient conditions for a better, more humane world. He did not indicate what had to be done after the revolution to make this happen. As political activist he remained too much an academic who preferred to analyze the past and the present. Also he believed too strongly that progress was unavoidable. As a strategist he failed in designing a consistent long-term policy. Of all the characteristics that are essential for a politician this was least well developed.

3
ÉMILE DURKHEIM

SOCIOLOGY IN PRAISE OF SOCIETY

Émile Durkheim once said 'If you wish to mature your thinking, devote yourself to the study of a great master.' Nowadays all students of sociology benefit from his work and would even benefit more if they studied his books with real academic commitment. Durkheim has produced fascinating theories on important social phenomena such as the growing specialization in the work force or the division of labour, the dangers of the disintegration of society, the history, content and objectives of education. He showed a particular interest in moral education, the social definition of deviant behaviour and the role it played in maintaining social cohesion and social control. In spite of being raised as a Jew, Émile Durkheim became an agnostic in his teens, but would always view the social practice of religion as positive for the functioning of society. His study of the social origins and functions of religion is widely recognized as a landmark study in the field. In particular his idea to study religion in its most simple form, as practiced by 'primitive clans' in Australia, is seen as a brilliant methodological move. Methodology was one of his strong points. He analyzed the foundations of the methods of sociological research and applied them to his empirical study of the social causes of suicide, which is another milestone in the field of sociology. Great masters like Durkheim had a keen eye for the complexity of modern society and for the important changes that were taking place. They were gifted describers and interpreters of significant aspects of these transformations. With the help of new concepts and theories, they enlarged insights into social structures and processes. Many of these insights are still valid today. It certainly is stimulating to study their writings in depth. This chapter on Durkheim's great contribution to sociology will start with a short biography, highlighting main events in his youth and academic career. Then we will discuss Durkheim's views on the scientific character of sociology as the study of social facts with a real objective and supra-individual character. This will be followed by a discussion of his general theoretical orientation: classical functionalism in which society is seen as a dynamic organism that fulfills all kinds of functions to maintain and reproduce itself. Then more sections will be devoted to specific theories such as his theory on the division of labour, his views on mechanic and organic solidarity. Any chapter on the work of Durkheim has to pay a lot of attention to his work on suicide or better on the sociological explanation of significant and persistent differences in suicide rates. The large amount of data he gathered and analyzed proved that lower suicide rates are related to social integration and regulation in a curvilinear fashion. His outcomes implied that too little but also too much integration can lead to an increase in the of suicide rate. The same is true for the amount of regulation. Before the chapter ends with a final discussion of his work his analysis of socialism will be treated in the penultimate section.

3.1   Biography

David Émile Durkheim was born on April 15, 1858, in Épinal in the Northeast of France. He was the youngest son of a rabbi. He grew up in a happy, stable Jewish family, which provided him with a clear model of a disciplined and closely-knit community of virtuous people. This model has played a major influence on his studies of society.[1] Descending from a long line of rabbis, he studied Hebrew, the Old Testament, and the Talmud after regular school hours. However, as a teenager, he turned away from all religious involvement and became an agnostic.

At secondary school, he was an excellent student. He was recommended to go to Paris, to attend the Lyceum Louis Le Grand in order to prepare himself for the entrance exams to the École Normale Supérieure. The ÉNS was, and still is, an extremely selective educational institute. Of all students who take part in the yearly competition for admission, only few are selected. Success came after his third attempt and in 1879 he could mix with the intellectual elite of the nation. At the ÉNS, France's best professors urged their students to study hard and when the students were not studying, they engaged in heated philosophical and political debates. Durkheim was a skilful debater, much admired by his peers. The ÉNS formed a little world of its own, in which the students relied very much on each other. Friendships that started at the ÉNS often lasted a lifetime. Durkheim befriended Jean Jaurès and Victor Hommay. In 1886, the latter committed suicide. According to Lukes, this tragic event inspired Durkheim to research suicide sociologically.[2]

Émile was not satisfied with the standard of teaching at the ÉNS. He found that the curriculum put too little emphasis on science and too much weight on literature. Nonetheless, he was inspired by some of his professors, in particular by Renouvier and Boutroux. Durkheim valued Renouvier's uncompromising rationalism, his central concern with morality and his emphasis on the dignity and autonomy of the individual, together with his theory on social cohesion based on the individual's sense of unity with and dependence on others. He supported Renouvier's view of the role of the state in establishing social justice in the economic domain; his advocacy of associations, such as co-operatives for producers, independent of the state and his argument for secular education in state schools. And surely, Durkheim was influenced by his intention to reconcile the sacredness of the individual with social solidarity.[3]

Boutroux often stated that each science must explain its subject matter by 'its own principles', as Aristotle also put it. Durkheim confirmed his belief in this method by reading Comte, who asserted that sociology could not be reduced to biology, just as biology is irreducible to chemistry. This kind of argument, aiming to show the relative autonomy of 'higher' versus 'lower' orders of reality, played a major role in Durkheim's thought. But he did not share Boutroux' hypothesis that the role of causal determination diminished and the role of contingency increased as one moved from lower to higher orders in the hierarchy of sciences presented by Comte. For Durkheim, laws were no less to be expected in sociology than in mechanics.[4] He was a positivist who strongly believed in objective methods and law-like social processes.

Durkheim also admired the historians Gabriel Monod and Fustel de Coulanges, who both applied rigorous methods. Fustel, the author of the well-known *The Ancient City*, abhorred dilettantism and indifference. In his view, history is not an art, but a pure science. Hence, historians should not seek facts and explanations by imagination or logic, but by meticulous observation of texts. He emphasized that 'preconceived ideas' were the most common evil of his time. This idea was reflected in Durkheim's statement that sociologists must systematically discard all preconceptions.[5]

3.1.1   Academic career

During the last year of his studies at the ÉNS, Durkheim was ill for a long time. As a consequence, he finished at the bottom of his class. He started his career as a teacher of philosophy at the Lyceum at Troyes. For five years, he taught there with great pleasure. Then, he received a grant to study the system of higher education in Germany and to write a report for the Minister of Education, who thought that France could learn something from the German system. In Germany, the experimental studies of the psychologist Wilhelm Wundt aroused Durkheim's curiosity. He admired Wundt's precise and objective approach and wanted to research society in a similar way. He was also impressed by Wundt's sociological approach to the study of morals. The latter showed a clear affinity with the idea that social phenomena constitute a reality of their own. Hence, social phenomena must be explained by other social facts and not by individual behaviour.

Durkheim wrote two reports about his stay in Germany. The high quality of his reports and essays was noticed. Hence, in 1887, he was asked to teach pedagogy and social sciences at the University of Bordeaux. The victory of the Republicans and the loss of power of the Catholic Church had opened the way for the appointment of an agnostic professor of Jewish descent. This would have been unthinkable in an earlier period. Nine years later, he became the first professor of sociology in France.

In 1887, Durkheim married Louise Julie Dreyfus. The couple had two children: Marie and André. In addition to taking care of the children and many household chores, his wife, who was well educated, often assisted her husband with his academic work. She copied his manuscripts and corrected his proofs. She did administrative jobs, handled parts of his correspondence, and filed it.[6] Without this help, even the industrious Durkheim would not have managed to produce so many essays, book reviews, reports and three books during his fifteen years in Bordeaux. In 1902, he moved to Paris to substitute for the professor of pedagogy. Four years later, he was officially appointed. It took seven more years and much lobbying before he succeeded in having sociology incorporated in his professorate at the Sorbonne. Thus, he became one of the first professional, university-based, sociologists. That became his self-definition and chosen vocation, though he spent much of his time lecturing on pedagogy. He did not limit himself to the confines of a single discipline and he also bridged the gap between the old era of wide-ranging social philosophies and the modern era of narrow, academic specialization.[7]

On 17th July 1914, a French nationalist murdered Durkheim's friend Jean Jaurès, leader of the socialist party, diligent advocate of the peace and opponent of compulsory military service. One day later, Austria-Hungary declared war on Serbia as a result of the murder of crown prince Franz Ferdinand, three weeks earlier, by a Yugoslavian nationalist. This last murder formed the overture to the First World War. The Great War brought tremendous damage to many countries, disrupted many families, and ruined the lives of numerous young men. Durkheim's life also changed drastically. The majority of his students were sent to the battlefield; half of them were never to return. He could no longer concentrate on his academic work, lost his objectivity and turned into a nationalist who wrote political pamphlets against the German enemy. In January 1916, his son André, whom he loved dearly, was reported missing in action. He was overpowered by anxiety and asked his friends not to visit him. A few months later, it was established that André had been killed in Serbia. Durkheim could not cope with his grief. He refused to talk about it and withdrew from social activities. Things got even worse when Durkheim, who was born in Alsace-Lorraine and had a German name, was accused by Senator M. Gaudin de Vilaine (*nomen est omen*) of being a spy for the German Ministry of War. Thanks to the unanimous disapproval of the Senate, the Senator was forced to withdraw his ludicrous accusation. Despite his imperfect health, Durkheim resumed his many activities for innumerable committees and organizations concerned with the war. A few months later he had a heart attack. The doctors advised him to take a lengthy rest, but he never fully recovered. Émile Durkheim died on 15th November 1917, 59 years of age, much too early to finish his treatise on morals.[8] After his death, eight more books were published, but the four books published during his active career have always been the most influential.

3.1.2   *Durkheim and politics*

Durkheim was twelve years old when the Germans defeated the French. This was a severe blow to the national pride. In the same year, 1870, there was also a communist revolt in Paris. These historic events made a great impression on the young boy. They also made clear that France had serious problems concerning national unity, solidarity, and stability. The percentage of industrial workers increased from 23% in 1870 to 39% in 1914. Simultaneously, the rural population dropped to less than half of the total population. Industrialization created a large and poor working class in rapidly expanding cities. Potential class conflicts posed a great threat to the nation. Hence, the plight of the urban working class became an important issue on the political agenda. Durkheim was concerned by the danger of a revolutionary conflict supported by militant socialists and communists. He also feared a reactionary backlash. The reactionaries very much wanted a return of the monarchy and a strong influence of the Catholic Church. In 1885, they attempted to topple the government, but their coup failed. It is no wonder that themes such as social cohesion, integration, order, and stability occupy a prominent place in his sociology.

Nevertheless, we must guard against the inclination to explain all the writings of Durkheim from this turbulent social and historical context. It is also possible to shed a totally different light on this period. Henri Peyre describes the epoch between 1870 and 1914 as a stable period. It was a time of strong economic growth. The center of Paris teemed with joyful people going to theatres, shows, restaurants, bars, and dances. For that reason the nineties were called *la belle époque*. Unfortunately, only the elite could afford these leisure activities and other luxuries. The veneer of conspicuous consumption did not deceive Durkheim. This earnest man from the provinces remained sharply focused on pathological social phenomena.[9]

The Dreyfus affair was such a case of social pathology. Esterhazy, a French high officer from the aristocracy, had been caught in the act of selling military secrets to the Germans. However, he managed to put the blame on Captain Alfred Dreyfus, a lower ranking officer and also a Jew. Due to anti-Semitic sentiments, Dreyfus was convicted. He was degraded and dishonored before the troops. On the parade ground, his commander tore the epaulets from his tunic and the medals from his chest; he also broke his sword. Dreyfus was sent to the labour colony on Devil's Island. But soon doubts arose about his guilt. Emile Zola, then the best-known novelist of France, wrote an open letter to the president of the republic, which started with the well-known *'J'accuse'*. When Zola was taken to court, riots broke out, Ministers were forced to resign, fights broke out in the National Assembly, and students battled in the streets. Some university professors protested publicly.[10] Durkheim was one of them, though he did not take a stance during his lectures, only when he held speeches at other public meetings. He believed that the academic had a right, indeed a duty, to express his views on major political issues, but professors should not use their academic authority to exercise any political influence over their students.[11] The affair divided the nation into two camps. It was almost impossible to stay indifferent in this matter. Durkheim was on Captain Dreyfus' side. Therefore, the reactionaries, who hated all left-wing intellectuals, attacked him. They viewed the Dreyfussardians at the university *'as anarchists of the lecture-platform, in particular those mad and arrogant sociologists who treat our generals as idiots, our social institutions as absurd and our traditions as unhealthy.'*[12]

What were the political views of Durkheim? His socialism was of a peculiarly idealistic and non-political variety. It was not anarchistic, nor revolutionary. He was a reformist and a revisionist, like his friend, Jean Jaurès. He was opposed to agitation, which disturbs without improving, and to social changes that destroy without replacing. He realized that the revolutionary socialists intended to build a new and better society on its ruins. But Durkheim was pessimistic about the outcomes of a total revolution. Instead of hoping for the bright sun of a new era, he feared a return to an age of darkness. Like Comte, he favoured a harmonious liaison between order and progress. In some respects, he was also a liberal, yet in other respects he was clearly a conservative. As a socialist, he pursued social equality. As a liberal, he favoured the expansion of individual freedom. In the economic sphere, he aimed at fair relations between employers and employees. As a conservative, he advocated a strong state and rejected anarchistic tendencies. Above all, he propagated a belief in a moral revitalization of modern society. In his view, the state had to safeguard both individual rights and collective order. However, he also advocated influential independent non-governmental associations that could counterbalance the state whenever it became too repressive.[13]

3.2   The Rules of Sociological Method

Comte argued that social phenomena constitute a set of facts that are not agreeable to the biological or psychological characteristics of human beings. Durkheim agreed that they constitute a *sui generis*.[14] Social facts are generated by other social facts; they have characteristics that are typical of social facts that are produced by other social phenomena. Social facts have a real and objective nature. They endure over time while individuals die and are replaced by others. Not only are they external to man, as a biological entity, but they also are *'endowed with coercive power ... by which they impose themselves upon him, independent of his individual will.'*[15] Thus, social processes create a reality that can no longer be explained in terms of the properties of individual human beings. *'The determining cause of a social fact should be sought among the social facts preceding it and not among the states of the individual consciousness.'*[16]

3.2.1   *Social facts*

In a Durkheimian sense, official laws and regulations and less formal customs and social obligations, are hard social facts. We encounter them, ready made, as soon as we are born. The vast majority of them will still be around after our death. In a sense, they exist outside and beyond individuals. During the first stage of his sociological thinking, Durkheim defined social facts by their exteriority and constraint. In this period, he focused on the operation of the legal system. Later, he was moved to change his views and stressed that social facts, such as moral rules, become effective only to the extent that they become internalized in the consciousness of individuals. He saw constraint no longer as an outside control on individual will, but rather as an inner-felt obligation to obey the rules. In this sense, society is *something beyond us and something in us.*[17]

Durkheim described social facts as ways of acting, thinking, and feeling, external to the individual, endowed with a power of coercion, by reason of which they control him.[18] To us, it might seem odd to see ways of thinking and feeling as exterior to the individual. Living in a highly individualized and psychologized world, we are likely to renounce this idea and maintain that our thoughts and feelings originate inside our own heads. We cherish the idea that these are our personal and unique thoughts and feelings. Currently, many people are seriously engaged in a quest for the Holy Grail of their unique feelings and authentic identity. No doubt, Durkheim would evaluate such a view as naïve and unsociological. He would explicate that we are all born in a ready-made world in which we encounter all kinds of long-existing patterns of action, and ways of thinking. We are born and grow up in a world in which people tend to act the same in similar situations that recur time and time again. We are raised to act in the same manner, to share the same views, and to show the right form of emotions under similar circumstances. In most cases we are not even aware of the social constraints and influences that steer our feelings, thoughts, and actions. We simply take them for granted.

3.2.2 *The coercive nature of social facts*

To Durkheim, it was clear that social facts have coercive power. When we fully consent to the prevailing norms, customs, and traditions, we hardly notice this power. But as soon as we violate a law, we run the risk of being penalized. And when we deviate from the dress code of our class or friends, we attract ridicule. This is one way in which society exerts its influence. This power is imposed on all individuals, irrespective of their will. Therefore, a social fact can be defined as any social phenomenon manifesting itself in a manner of acting of individuals or groups that is capable of exerting external constraints on the individual. Durkheim did not regard this social influence in a negative way. He stressed that social existence is an absolute precondition for human beings. Besides, social facts create opportunities that would not exist if human beings did not live in social groups. This refers not only to mere chances of survival, but also to opportunities for personal development.[19]

Constraint has a precise meaning in everyday language. However, Durkheim used this term in a variety of senses:

1 The authority of legal rules, moral maxims, and customs, as manifested by the

sanctions brought to bear when a person violates them.

2 The need to follow certain rules, procedures, or methods in order to carry out certain social activities successfully, such as speaking the language of the country of residence or using the latest techniques of production to survive in a competitive environment.

3 The causal influence of ecological and infrastructural factors (such as roads, railways, channels, rivers, and networks of communication) on the direction and intensity of patterns of social contact, trade and migration.

4 The psychological compulsion in a crowd when collective movements of enthusiasm, sorrow, pity, indignation, or even hate and aggression carry us away in spite of ourselves.

5 The cultural determination and the influence of socialization as when certain socially given ideas and values are internalized by young people, who thereby acquire certain beliefs, wants, and feelings.[20]

Lukes supported Sorel, who stated that Durkheim stretched the concept of constraint too far. This is particularly true for the last three meanings. They refer to influences on people, but all of these are not experienced as outright forms of constraint or obligation to which one has to fully and immediately consent. Hence, it would have been better if he had called this social influence instead of social constraint. People can become attracted to certain rules, ideals, and values, especially when one is born and bred in a group in which these rules, ideals, and values prevail. One can feel attached to many elements of the culture of that group.[21]

At specific points in time, 'social currents' or forms of mass psychology that emerge within a crowd can determine our behaviour. Durkheim spoke of social currents because, in these cases, there is no crystallized and stable form as is the case with laws and traditions. Therefore, he thought that their influence on society was less deep and less durable. Hypes and sudden changes of fashion are other examples of strong but temporary social influences. They urge people to engage in new activities or to buy new clothes long before the 'old' clothes are threadbare, simply because a new season offers new styles, shapes, and colors, making last year's clothes old-fashioned. Thus, we run the risk of being ridiculed when we hold on to our favourite clothes once they have gone out of fashion. Although we are not used to speaking of coercion in the case of fashion, it is clear that a change in fashion produces constraints and restrictions. If certain styles or colors are out of fashion, it is almost impossible to buy clothes in these particular styles or colors anywhere.

Durkheim was convinced that the presence of many social influences and constraints leave little room for individuality. Yet, he observed that, when people internalize social facts such as customs, rules, norms and values, they can and will make a few minor variations, in accordance with their aptitudes, affinities, and preferences, thus creating individual habits and lifestyles.

This is why every one of us, up to a certain point, forms his own religious faith, his own cult, his own morality, and his own technology. There is no social uniformity, which does not accommodate a whole scale of individual gradations; there is no collective fact, which imposes itself on all individuals uniformly. Nevertheless, the area of variations that are possible and tolerated is always and everywhere more or less restricted.[22]

Durkheim's main concern was to impress the potency of social forces on his students. Hence, he reacted strongly against the individualistic philosophies of his day and age, and rejected the 'methodological individualism of economists, who assumed that all individuals are egoists, solely pursuing their own interests.' In his view, sociology could not be based on a theory that was constructed on the assumption of a pre- or non-social individual. All individuals are socialized human beings. Hence, they are constrained by social forces, which they have internalized and made into a second nature. That is why Durkheim spoke of a *homo duplex*. In addition to being born with a biological nature, which can be egoistic, humans have also developed a social nature based on conceptions of reality and on morals derived from the collective in which they grew up. Unfortunately, Durkheim's desire to stress that sociology had its own subject matter, which could not be explained by purely psychological or biological factors, led him to overstate his case on many occasions, mostly by underrating the importance of the psychological and biological aspects of human existence.

Durkheim was not an anti-individualist. He was convinced that industrial society entailed specialization. Hence, society had to cultivate individual differences and autonomy. In his view, this was clearly leading to the creation of a 'cult of the individual'. This cult did not emerge because men are essentially egoistic, but because modern societies produce it and give it further shape. Besides the functional individualistic demands of an increasing division of labour, there was also a cultural demand for an expansion of individualistic values, brought forward by the philosophers of the French Revolution and the Enlightenment. They were concerned with the dignity and value of human beings. Modern society should enhance the welfare and self-fulfillment of all members of society.[23]

3.2.3 Institutions and collective representations

Durkheim used a tiered model of social facts based on the degree in which social facts were crystallized. This may be thought of as a continuum with numerous gradations. The morphological level is most crystallized and also most visible. The next level is the institutional level. The least crystallized level is that of collective representations.

Scheme 3.1   Three level model of social phenomena[24]

1   Morphology (material domain)
   Volume, density, and dispersion of the population: Material objects incorporated in society: physical geographic characteristics, buildings, roads, railways, canals, and channels of communication.

2   Institutions (normative sphere)
   Formal rules and norms, official laws, moral precepts, religious doctrines, political and economic rules
   Informal rules and norms generally applied within the realms of economy, religion, politics, and business; collective
   habits, beliefs, and opinions.

3   Collective representations (symbolic sphere)
   Social values and ideals; self-images of a society, legends, myths, religious representations, and symbols;
   Free 'social currents', emerging from a sudden collective inspiration or euphoric sentiment, which is not yet solidified in
   a definitive shape; collective, creative formation of ideas and plans

According to Durkheim, social life rests on a substratum of morphological facts that determine the shape and scope of institutional social phenomena. In his view, morphological factors play a major role in the genesis of institutions, but this influence declines in later stages, when other social factors, including other institutions, come to exercise a more immediate or direct influence. From this, Thompson concludes that Durkheim was not averse to giving a materialistic explanation, whenever it was appropriate.[25] Institutions are sets of convictions and practices, opinions and patterns of behaviour. They have acquired an obligatory character and refer to continuously present or recurring social affairs. The well-known examples are laws, moral rules, religious prescriptions, norms of decency and civilized behaviour.

On one of the few occasions that Durkheim ventured to give a definition of sociology, he described it as the science of social institutions, their origin and their functioning. But in *Suicide*, he wrote that, essentially, social existence is based on *collective representations*. These collective representations differ from the mental representations of individuals. Collective representations concern every way in which a group perceives itself in relation to the phenomena that influence her. Collective representations arise from collective affairs and not from individual phenomena, because the social characteristics of the group differ from the nature of individuals. This hierarchical analytical model, which was never made explicit by Durkheim, represents a distinction between matter and structure, on the one hand, and immaterial phenomena, on the other hand. Whether social facts have a material or an immaterial character, they can all be used for the explanation of social phenomena. Moreover, they are interrelated. Material aspects such as extreme poverty, together with great but unrealistic expectations about the social and economic prospects in big cities or foreign countries can cause migration from rural to urban areas. Migrants are convinced that big cities or wealthy nations can offer them jobs, decent houses, good schools, and modern medical care. Furthermore, the flux of migration is aided and guided in specific directions because of geographic, historical, social and political relations between regions and countries. A sociological explanation therefore depends on a great variety of social facts.

3.2.4   Social facts 'as things'

Durkheim's main doctrine was that social phenomena must be explained by social facts. His second doctrine was that sociology should use similar rigorous methods of research as the physical sciences. Hence, social facts should be researched 'as if they were things'. He did not contend that they are similar to physical things such as bricks or bridges, but stressed that they must be studied through observation and inspection and not by means of empathy or intuition. Hence, his dictum was not an ontological, but an epistemological principle. It tells us how we can learn to know social phenomena. Society is more than the mere sum of individuals. Therefore, social facts should not be examined by investigating the motives and intentions of individuals; that is the subject matter of psychology. The social system, formed by the association of groups of individuals, represents a reality that has its own characteristics. Durkheim admitted that nothing collective can be produced without assuming individual consciousnesses; but this primary condition on its own is insufficient. Social life results from a certain combination of individual consciousnesses and is, consequently, explained by it. For this reason we must speak of a collective consciousness that is distinct from individual consciousness. Individual minds, forming groups by mingling and fusing, give birth to a collective being, a being of a new sort. Hence, the group 'thinks', 'feels', and 'acts' quite differently from the ways in which its members would, if they were isolated. Therefore, if we begin our explanation with the individual, we will not be able to understand what takes place in the group. Every time that a social phenomenon is directly explained by a psychological phenomenon, we can be sure that the explanation is false.[26]

Durkheim even contended that, as far as social facts are concerned, many people still have the mentality of primitive men. They still believe that real social miracles are possible, for example, that a legislator can create an institution out of nothing by a mere injunction of his will. Or that a politician can transform one social system into another, just as the believers of so many religions have upheld that the Divine will can arbitrarily transmute one thing into another. But social phenomena, and certainly social systems, are complex and difficult to understand.[27] From this, we may conclude that it is even more difficult to steer society in a carefully planned direction, because we have to take into consideration the inflexibility and the immense complexity of the order of social things. Durkheim maintained that sociologists should not overestimate themselves in thinking that they know a lot about certain social phenomena, just because they are faced with them daily. In general, our ideas about social phenomena, for example, education or politics, are still insufficiently grounded on the outcomes of scientific research. Many are even based exclusively on common sense. In this respect, the social sciences resemble the first phase of the natural sciences. We all know that several centuries have elapsed since Galileo revealed our mistaken illusion that the earth was the centre of the universe. The idea that the sun moved around the earth was based on *notiones vulgares* or *praenotiones*.[28] In a similar vein, social scientists must be aware that social structures and processes cannot be understood by spontaneously applying naïve concepts in everyday life. We must be conscious of the fact that many of our ideas on justice, morality, the family and the state existed long before the advent of social science. Therefore, the only way to discover the truth about social facts is through objective research, through the application of a rigorous logic and through a painstaking analysis of data.

Next to the need for analysis, there is also a great need for synthesis showing that a large variety of theoretical elements can be subsumed under one general concept. This is the justification of general sociology. However, Durkheim did not make much progress in developing general sociology. He truly was one of the first specialists. Analysis was his forte. He always wanted to look beneath the surface of social life; he felt a strong urge to look for internal causes and impersonal hidden forces that moved individuals and collectivities.[29]

3.3   Classic functionalism

For Durkheim, functional analysis was just as crucial as the search for historical causes and origins. Sociological explanations should firmly stand on two legs. We have to explain its emergence causally and make clear how it survives by fulfilling specific functions. Causal analysis alone does not suffice, because society is a whole of interrelated social facts. A change in one of its parts has consequences for other parts. Functional analysis should reveal how a particular social fact affects the working of the whole system or its parts. So, already in his first book Durkheim wanted to discover the function of the division of labour, what social needs it satisfies.

3.3.1   *The necessity of functional explanations in sociology*

Durkheim conceived of society as a kind of organic whole. Societies and other organisms can be discerned from inorganic things because of their growth and development. Expansion often means an increase in complexity and differentiation. And differentiation in structures goes hand in hand with differentiation in functions. Furthermore, each part of the organic social whole is a micro-organism in itself. But we should not stretch the analogy with biological organisms too far. Whereas biological organisms stay alive by a circulation of material elements, societies survive through a circulation of immaterial elements, such as common values, ideals, and collective representations.

The analytical legacy of early functionalists such as Durkheim can be summarized as follows:

1 Functionalists view the social world in systemic terms. Such systems have needs and requisites that have to be met to assure their survival.
2 When viewed as a system, the social world is composed of interrelated parts; the analysis of these parts focuses on how they fulfill requisites of systemic wholes and maintain system normality, homeostasis, and equilibrium.
3 Functionalists tend to view systems as having 'normal' and 'pathological' states.[30]

Durkheim reacted against Spencer, who tended to view society as a set of means created by people to satisfy their needs. He flatly renounced this reductionist explanation. In his view, the social originates from the social, that is, from the co-existence of people in groups, and not from physical and psychological needs of individuals. Individual goals are simply too diversified to shape a force that can engender a social phenomenon without the help of some collective orchestration that already is social by nature.[31] Society is a social system that creates and further develops itself. It creates and fulfills its own needs. Therefore, causal explanations that look for their cause in premeditated acts of social actors cannot suffice. Durkheim's conception of social functions and social needs cannot be set apart from his view on the autonomous nature of social entities.[32] There must be a correspondence between social functions and social needs.[33]

Durkheim defines the function of a social entity as its significant effect on the general condition and development of society. He considered any phenomenon as dysfunctional if it endangered the survival of the social whole. He preferred 'function' to words like 'goal' or 'objective', for only conscious individuals can set goals for themselves. In his perspective, social needs are not related to or derived from individual needs. Personal needs are outcomes of social processes. Hence, social needs must be interpreted as immanent tendencies of the social whole in order to influence its parts.

As society develops, new needs are developed to sustain this development. Time and again, Durkheim has indicated that when structural changes of society occur, certain functions of its parts or subsystems have to change in the same movement. This is a basic assumption of all structural-functionalists. It shows that Durkheim did not ignore social change. On the contrary, he acknowledged that social functions and needs could change. That is why each society must be endowed with an immanent capacity to change its constituting parts in order to warrant its continuation.[34]

3.3.2   *The functionalist explanation*

It is clear that the functionalist method of explanation is different from the causal model of explanation. Perhaps they are two completely different paradigms.[35] Functionalism has been under heavy flak from epistemologists. Added to this was the ideological critique that functionalism is only directed at the explanation of the existing social order and thus, implicitly helps to maintain the status quo. Hence, functionalism would be useless for a critical sociology or praxis that wants to explain social conflicts and transformations in society. However, this critique misses the point that prominent functionalists such as Durkheim, Parsons and Merton have devoted a large part of their academic work to the explanation of social change. The so-called inherent conservative nature of functionalism rests on a biased and partial reading of their work. But the fallacy is rooted much deeper, namely at the level of scientific presuppositions. In that rather dark cellar of science, many sociologists have hastily developed the idea that order and stability cannot co-exist with social change. This misunderstanding frequently goes hand in hand with the false idea that sociologists wanting to understand social order by definition must be conservative and consciously or unconsciously help defending the political and social status quo.[36]

Functional analysts are not interested in the question whether variable a is causally related to variable b, and whether b in its turn causes c. They want to discover whether system S will survive or disintegrate if a specific subsystem or part degenerates. Furthermore, they find it relevant to know what constitutes the connection between parts or subsystems p, q, and r, and their relation to the system S as a whole. They want to understand how, for example, p co-operates with q to keep the whole system going. In other words, what q needs from p to go on functioning and contributing to the continuation of the systematic whole, including all its subsystems. This type of reasoning can be clarified by observing a living organ. It makes sense to say that the heart 'causes' the circulation of the blood, which 'causes' the transportation of food and oxygen to the cells, oxygen that was put in the blood by the lungs. In turn, the heart and the lungs need food for their own cells, which is transported to these cells by the circulated blood pumped around by the heart. But doesn't it make much more sense to speak of functions instead of causes here, for instance the pump function, the transport function, the nutrition function, the filter function, and so on?

In my view, the difference in method stems from a difference in perspective. The functionalist prefers to explain everything from the perspective of the social or organic whole and investigates what function each part performs for the benefit of the whole. Causalists restrict their analysis to sub-processes only, even when studying live organisms. The reason why is purely pragmatic. They believe the whole system is too complex for a complete analysis. Functionalists are not deterred by this challenge. They are driven by a strong wish to understand the coherence of the whole system and the mechanism that sees to its endurance. In contrast, they have no taste to research minor details or partial explanations of a few small causal steps in a long chain of events. This is exactly the prerogative of causalists who believe this the only way to go about it.

3.3.3 The social construction and functions of deviant behaviour

Durkheim's view on deviant behaviour and crime differed strongly from that of most of his contemporaries. For him deviant behaviour and crime are not intrinsic pathological phenomena but entirely normal actions of individuals and groups. In a typical Durkheimian sense, deviant behaviour and crime are 'normal' phenomena, for they exist everywhere. No society has ever succeeded in eliminating them. His main point is that we should not say that an act shocks the public conscience because it is criminal, but that it is criminal because it shocks the public conscience.[37] We cannot specify the intrinsic nature of these collective feelings, for they are too much varied. They are not related to any vital interest of society or to minimal requirements for justice. In general what is classified as deviancy or crime is rather arbitrary. Different cultures have different views on the legality of certain forms of behaviour. For instance, not all countries have the same laws concerning the production, selling, and consumption of alcoholic drinks, soft drugs or hard drugs. The same is true for the possession and use of firearms. So, Durkheim has a point here.

From a societal viewpoint, the only thing that is necessary is the continuance of social cohesion. It seems possible to enhance social cohesion by defining specific acts as illegal and to punish offenders for these acts. It appears to be completely arbitrary which acts are defined as deviant or criminal as long as certain acts are defined as such. Whatever the definition of deviancy or crime may be is unimportant. Their main function is to bond people and to unite their righteous consciences. So, for Durkheim the main function of punishment of deviancy, misdeeds and crimes is to keep the large majority of people on the straight and narrow and to enhance social cohesion between those who abstain from deviancy and crime.

According to Durkheim, crime still has another social function. Deviant behaviour can trigger social change and innovation; without it cultures and structures will fossilize. There are many acts that at one time were deemed illegal, but are now no longer so. Deviant behaviour confronts society with alternatives, which can prepare it for change. Often patterns of behaviour that were defined as deviant in the past turned out to be the heralds of a new moral. Take the example of so-called deviant behaviour as a herald of a new norm. In earlier days people did not speak of euthanasia but of homicide. Nowadays, in the Netherlands at least, there is a policy that strictly regulates in which cases doctors, after consulting a colleague and after following strict procedures, are allowed to make an end to the life of terminal patients who are suffering greatly and have a clear death wish. This example supports Durkheim's view on the innovative force of deviant behaviour. Yet it is difficult to imagine that any type of deviation could herald a change of social practices. Could incest ever be accepted as a legitimate form of sexual activity? Considering what we know about the traumatic consequences for the children involved, this does not seem very likely to say the least.

Surely, deviant behaviour can produce cultural innovation. But the possible change of certain norms and values appears to be a side effect and not a crucial function of deviancy. Social change can also, and most often will, arise from other changes that precede it. Strictly speaking, society does not need deviant behaviour to create new norms and values. They can also emerge spontaneously during some euphoric event or develop unintended within the context of normal behaviour. History has shown numerous cases of making some forms of behaviour illegal that were widely accepted or condoned before. Think for instance of the caning of disobedient pupils that, the first half of the twentieth century was still widely accepted in many western countries. Nowadays, teachers will be severely reprimanded or temporarily suspended for slapping or spanking a pupil. Once more, this shows that much of what is defined as deviant or criminal is closely related to historic and cultural conditions. However, I have already made it clear that I am not sure whether this means that deviancy is completely relative, as Durkheim seems to imply. He certainly shocked a large part of his audience by insisting that defining certain acts as criminal is a rather arbitrary affair, but with respect to some forms of deviant behaviour such as murder, rape and incest this point-of-view is hard to stomach.

3.4   Specialization and social integration

As an agnostic Durkheim did not languish about the ebbing of religious life, but he did worry about the possible disintegrative effects on society. He had also noted many negative side-effects of industrialization when a large number of people had left the countryside to find jobs in factories, which created new rapidly expanding urban areas. In the cities, life was freer and more hectic. Social bonds and social control were far weaker than in the villages where everybody knew each other, was related to each other or had other ties that forged mutual friendship and solidarity. Many observers feared that specialization would destroy social cohesion, because it would mean more individualization and professional segmentation. At the time, it seemed very likely that individualization and specialization could erode feelings of solidarity. These social tendencies inspired Durkheim to investigate the social impact of industrialization, which was a radical economic transformation.

3.4.1   Mechanic and organic solidarity

Durkheim attempted to answer the question of social integration with some concepts that he had developed in *The Division of Labour*, his thesis and first major book. Herein he distinguished and discussed two forms of solidarity: mechanic and organic solidarity.[38] He stated that mechanic solidarity prevails in those cases in which individual differences are minimized, that is, when all members of society look alike, carry out the same tasks, and adhere to the same set of norms and values. It is solidarity of resemblance. Solidarity based on similarity is strongest when the collective conscience encompasses our entire consciousness, when all collective ideas are reflected in the ideas of the individuals. In this case, society is coherent because the individuals are not yet differentiated. Durkheim spoke of mechanic solidarity because he compared the social bonding of human beings with the bonding of atoms in a bar of iron. If the bar is moved, all iron atoms have to move with it. They do not have a will of their own.

The other form of solidarity is based on functional coherence. It is the outcome of the division of labour in society. In this case individuals have specialized in all kinds of jobs. They no longer hold the same set of values. No longer do they share similar opinions or show similar attitudes and lifestyles. The collective conscience is reduced to its bare minimum. The cohesive force lies in the practical and functional interdependence of all members of. Durkheim called this organic solidarity, because it resembled the interdependence of the parts within living organisms. Although organisms have very different parts, they must all cooperate to keep alive.[39]

Durkheim defined the collective conscience (or consciousness) simply as the set of convictions and feelings that are characteristic for the modal members of society.[40] He wrote that we have two consciences: *'... one which we share with our entire group, which, in consequence, is not ourselves, but society living and acting within us; the other which, on the contrary, represents only that which is personal and distinctive to each of us.'*[41] He added and this makes it sociological, that this collective conscience leads a life of its own, and follows its own course of development. Analytically, the collective conscience can be discerned from the individual conscience, but of course, it is also connected with it, for the ways of thinking and the feelings of individuals are the carriers of the collective conscience. Durkheim assumed that at the beginning of mankind the collective conscience represented almost all members of society or the social group. Everyone shared all convictions and beliefs. The unanimous and collectively shared manners in which all convictions and practices are shared render them a specific, almost religious intensity.[42] The collective conscience is less visible in modern societies because it is overshadowed by the variation in individual opinions and beliefs. The average norm is less binding, and the reactions to deviations of the norms tend to arouse less indignation.

In Durkheim's view, these two forms of solidarity coincide with two extreme forms of social organization. In the beginning of social evolution societies were characterized by a high degree of mechanic solidarity. In the Stone Age, all members of the clan were very much alike. So, everyone was easy to replace. Mechanic solidarity is closely related to the segmental structure of the tribal society. It is a homogenous system of segments that are alike. This type of society has a complete hold on the individual. He has no relation with things that fall outside the perimeter of his social segment. Within the boundaries of his own tribe or clan the individual is closely bonded to his social and physical environment, to familiar customs and traditions. Because his social perspective is focused on a very limited part of the world, he has a very clear and concrete conception of his own society. (Note that Durkheim uses a typical morphological or structuralist mode of description and explanation here) In the beginning these segments were based on clans. In a later stage of evolution, the segments no longer consisted of groups of the same parentage, but were organized along territorial lines. Segmental social structures were further characterized by a low degree of interdependence: what occurs in one segment is less likely to affect the others. Each segment is highly self-supporting. [43]

Early in his career, Durkheim asserted that only so-called primitive societies are characterized by strong systems of shared beliefs and convictions. Later, he changed his opinion and emphasized that also systems with a strong degree of organic solidarity need a collective conscience. Only if the large majority of a society is connected to a set of collectively shared views, it can warrant its unity. Otherwise, each social unit, primitive or modern, would fall apart. The difference, however, is that the collective conscience within modern societies is more abstract, and contains norms that leave more space for individuality and variety of lifestyles, norms and values. The consensus is brought to a more abstract level, leaving more room for differentiation. The main thesis from *La Division* is that modern societies will not disintegrate. But the foundation for integration and stability shifts from a strong accent on mechanistic to an emphasis on organic solidarity.[44]

3.4.2   *The explanation of increased specialization*

As collectivistic societies preceded the more individualistic ones, Durkheim opted not to look for individualistic explanations of the division of labour, but to look for causes in the social conditions that preceded it. The utilitarian explanation posited that specialization emerged because people discovered that specialization and cooperation improve productivity. Durkheim was convinced that it was the other way around. So, in his view, the personal individuality of social units was able to form and grow without causing society to disintegrate. Organic solidarity, based on specialization and co-operation, developed from within a pre-existing collectivistic social environment. It remained adapted to it, whilst detaching itself from it.[45] Changing conditions made co-operation not only possible, but also necessary. The expansion of co-operation and interdependence would not be possible if social sentiments had not paved the way. How could prehistoric man, if, by nature, he were an individualist, have resigned himself to an existence that goes so strongly against this fundamental inclination? From autonomous individuals nothing can emerge save what is individual; consequently co-operation itself is a social fact, subject to social rules, which can only arise from social facts. Durkheim cherished this idea all his life. The centre of his sociological approach has always been that the individual is born of society and not the other way around. Therefore we must explain individualization by the state of the collectivity and not the state of the collectivity by individual phenomena.[46]

The utilitarian explanation, unequivocally rejected by Durkheim, implied that people already had become aware of the fact that they varied in character, abilities, and skills, before society had produced the different tasks and jobs that demanded variety of skills and abilities. In Durkheim's view it was the other way around. However, his hypothesis seems rather difficult to test. Undoubtedly, in prehistoric times, social conditions were far less differentiated then what they are now. But there is no reason to assume that the genetic variation between individuals was significantly less diversified than nowadays. Hence, also in ancient times, individual people must have perceived that some of them were better hunters or fishermen, or better suited to maintain order than others. There has always been a genetic basis for individual variations in abilities and the development of all kinds of skills. So it seems wiser to assume that the evolution of society, including the increase in specialization and the shift from mechanic to organic solidarity, has evolved in an interactive and mutually reinforcing process. During this long process individuals must have influenced the course of social events and vice versa.

The only explanation for increased specialization that Durkheim deemed valid was the increased population density. This manifests itself in an increase in material and moral density. Material density is the same as the degree of exhaustion of natural resources. When more people have to survive in the same area and must live of the same land, then social or moral density increases, because more people have to interact, communicate and co operate with one other. This results in an intensified competition that leads to social differentiation.[17] Here, Durkheim used Darwin's hypothesis that the more organisms look alike, the tougher the competition is for scarce resources. Social differentiation is a peaceful solution for the struggle for life. Differentiation enables more people to live closely together. It mitigates competition, because no longer everybody is a direct competitor, but only the competitor of the other members of a subcategory with the same specialization in social activity. Specialization gives people some freedom to contribute in his or her own way to the continuation of the social whole. Aron summarizes this as follows: *'Social differentiation, a phenomenon characteristic of modern societies, is the formative condition of individual liberty. Only in a society where the collective consciousness has lost part of its overpowering rigidity can the individual enjoy some amount of autonomy of judgment and action. In this individualistic society, the major problem is to maintain that minimum of collective consciousness without which organic solidarity would lead to disintegration.'* [48]

Durkheim would acknowledge that even in societies that allow individual freedom, there is more collective consciousness than we are aware of. Organic differentiation would otherwise not endure. It needs a substantial collective fund of norms, values and things held sacred to bind individuals to the social whole.[49]
The increase in the division of labour enlarges the need for contractual arrangements. As always, Durkheim gave priority to a collectivistic explanation over an individualistic one. Individuals agree to make contracts on the presumption

that both parties have similar norms for honouring contracts. Thus, the organic society is not characterized by a replacement of mechanic solidarity or commitment to the community by several contracts agreed upon by individuals. These contracts are emanated by the strong increase in specialization. We should not reverse the historic and logical order of things. Only on the basis of social developments can we understand the emergence of individualistic man and learn why individuals are capable of closing contracts with each other.[50]

3.4.3 Anomie

Marx and Durkheim both noticed the negative effects of industrialization. It mutilated the worker, transformed him into an alienated being, and reduced him to a nut or bolt in the economic machine. But according to Durkheim, this was a consequence of an unfortunate organization of labour. It was something that could and should be repaired. To Marx, it was an unavoidable effect of capitalism that could only be solved by the destruction of the whole system. In Durkheim's view, the soaring inequality between the numerous poor and a small group of extremely rich people constituted a great risk for society: it undermined the feelings of solidarity. In his eyes, industrial society was on the verge of disaster. It created too many far-reaching changes, which led to moral confusion. One of those threatening forces was the migration of hordes of peasants and farm workers to urban areas. Being used to the small scale and well-organized structures of the countryside, they had great trouble adjusting to the hectic life in the cities, where many traditional norms and values had been lost.

Like Marx, Durkheim viewed people as beings with boundless desires. In contrast to animals, they are not satisfied when their biological needs are fulfilled. *'The more one has, the more one wants, since satisfactions received only stimulate instead of fulfilling needs.'*[51] These unlimited desires must be kept within bounds. Thus, well-organized societies have established a set of social norms and controls to restrain individual bents and passions. Without sufficient social control, individuals have to rely on their own strategies. This creates a state of anomie, that is, a social situation that is no longer sufficiently regulated. (The Greek term *nomos* means rule or law, so anomie means without rules and laws. The word was coined by Guyeau and quickly borrowed by Durkheim to describe the possible anarchistic, hence pathological consequences of too much individualization.[52]) Anomie describes a state in which most norms and values have lost their legitimate attractiveness and credibility. Sudden far-reaching social changes can generate a situation of anomie. When an economic recession results in lower incomes for large groups of people, this is experienced as a painful disruption of their lives that has great influence on their self-respect and lifestyle. Demoralization can be so great that people give in to deviant behaviour. Sudden wealth can also lead to a loss of moral standards. All quick changes in social position or in the social structure can cause an anomic situation. Anomie plays a major role in Durkheim's explanation of social differences in suicide rates, which is discussed next.

3.5   The sociological explanation of suicide rates

During his entire career, Durkheim sought for explanations of social order and disorder. Already in 1888, he was convinced that a consistent rise in the number of suicides attested to a serious upheaval in the organic conditions of society.[53] Many statistics showed that the number of suicides had increased three- or four-fold during the nineteenth century. It was a major social problem. Durkheim argued that there are no societies in which suicides do not occur, indicating that suicide is a 'normal' social phenomenon. Statistics show that suicide rates vary significantly between countries and regions. But, these different national and regional rates have stabilized over many years. This shows that suicide rates are related to social factors. Hence, suicide rates are also social phenomena.

3.5.1   Altruistic, egoistic, and anomic suicide

For instance, within a group of sixteen countries with comparable data from about 120 years ago and from the turn of the twentieth century, the average increase was 1.6 per cent. Hungary and Finland show a spectacular increase of 20.9 % and 17.9 % respectively. Belgium, Ireland and Japan show a rise of about 9.5 per cent. On the other hand, Denmark enjoyed a drop of 11 %. [54]

Table 3.1   Suicide rates per 100,000 inhabitants in 15 European countries plus Japan: 1881-1890 and 2001-2005 (In parentheses the ranking order of each country)

	1881-1890	1999-2001	Increase	1999-2001 (males - females)
Austria	16.1 (5)	18.6 (5)	2.5	27.3 - 9.8
Belgium	11.4 (7)	20.6 (4)	9.4	29.4 - 10.7
Denmark	25.5 (1)	14.5 (8)	-11.0	20.9 - 8.1
Germany	20.9 (3)	13.8 (9)	-7.1	20.2 - 7.3
England/ UK	7.7 (10)	7.6 (15)	-0.1	11.8 - 3.3
Finland	3.9 (14)	21.8 (3)	17.9	34.6 - 10.9
France	20.7 (4)	14.8 (7)	-5.9	26.1 - 9.4
Hungary	9.6 (9)	30.5 (1)	20.9	47.1 - 13.0
Ireland	2.3 (16)	11.4 (12)	9.1	18.4 - 4.3
Italy	4.9 (13)	7.2 (16)	2.3	11.1 - 3.4
Japan	15.8 (6)	25.3 (2)	9.5	36.5 - 14.1
The Netherlands	5.5 (12)	9.7 (13)	4.2	13.0 - 6.3
Norway	6.8 (11)	13.2 (11)	6.4	19.5 - 6.8
Spain	2.4 (15)	8.2 (14)	5.8	12.4 - 4.0
Sweden	10.7 (8)	13.8 (10)	3.1	19.7 - 8.0
Switzerland	22.7 (2)	18.3 (6)	-4.4	26.5 - 10.0

As a self-conscious founder of the new science of sociology, Durkheim was eager to show that the interpretation of what at first sight might appear to be a wholly 'individual' phenomenon could be linked to and explained by social facts. Nevertheless, he stuck to his stance that a strict analytical separation must be made between the explanation of the regional differences in suicide rates and the causal explanation of individual cases of suicide.[55] As usual, Durkheim put much energy into crushing some popular non-sociological explanations. He dismissed the suggestion that rates of mental illness are related to the number of suicides. In fact, most people who have actually committed suicide were never diagnosed as insane before. They did not suffer from neurasthenia, hallucinations, or aggressive obsessions. Depressions are related to suicide at an individual level. Durkheim also observed that more women than men suffered from mental illness, but the suicide rate of men was three or four times higher than that of women.[56] A similar opposite relation exists amongst Jews, who are reported to suffer more from mental illness but show a relatively low rate of suicide. Moreover, the rate of suicide increases with age and is particularly high in old age; however, the highest rate of mental illness can be observed between the ages of thirty and forty.

Durkheim defined suicide as *'... any death which is the direct or indirect result of a positive or negative act accomplished by the victim himself which he knows will produce this result.*'[57] It is clear why 'direct or indirect' and also 'positive or negative' are needed. If a man refuses to eat and dies of starvation this is suicide to the same extent as if he eats something lethally poisonous. Durkheim's definition is broader than what we usually see as suicide. According to this definition, the Dutch captain Van Speyk, whose gunboat fell in the hands of the Belgians on February 5th. 1831, committed suicide when he deliberately exploded his ship, taking with him most of the crew. In Dutch history books Van Speyk is not pictured as a tragic victim of suicide but as a hero. Following Durkheim's definition, the widows of India, who, according to old traditions, had to be burned together with their deceased husbands, committed suicide. In Van Speyk's case, he would have called this facultative or optional altruistic suicide and, in the case of the Indian widows, obligatory altruistic suicide. The actions of Japanese samurai, who disembowel themselves after the defeat of their leader, and of the Kamikaze pilots of the Second World War, are other examples of altruistic suicide. These types are based on a strong collective conscience, which regulates individual actions to such a high degree that individuals are even prepared to sacrifice their lives for a collective value. Durkheim mentions many examples of religious fanatics who killed themselves by jumping from a high rock to show the strength of their belief.[58] Modern-day examples of altruistic suicide are for instance the Palestinian suicide bombers who kill themselves by driving cars full of explosives into crowded Israeli streets or market places.

The opposite of altruistic suicide is egoistic suicide. As people become freer and less constrained by society, they become more individualistic, autonomous and lonesome. This makes them more susceptible to suicide. Durkheim speaks of egoistic suicide, meaning individualistic suicide. In general, he stated that religion provides a certain bond within a particular social community. People from integrable religious communities go regularly to church, the synagogue, the mosque or special meetings. They participate in organizations for volunteers, or send their children to denominational schools. This explains why there are fewer cases of suicide amongst religious people than among non-religious people. As there are more non-religious people in the cities than in rural areas it follows that suicide rates are also higher in the cities.

However, not all religions offer the same shield against suicidal tendencies. Statistical data from many countries and regions show that suicide is much less frequent amongst Catholics than amongst Protestants. Protestantism stimulated the development of modern, moral individualism. This denomination attaches great value to individual Bible study and their maxim is 'Investigate all and behold the good'. Not a single Protestant should follow the official doctrines of the church or its ministers without question, because Protestants believe that after death each and everyone will have to justify his own actions before God. Therefore, Protestantism renders more freedom to its believers than does Catholicism, but this individualism has a price: fewer shared convictions and fewer commonly shared rituals.[59] The relatively high level of individual autonomy within Protestantism can exert too much mental strain on some of its members. It depends on the encouragement of free inquiry, in which all believers have to rely on their own instincts with respect to the correct interpretation of the Holy Scripture. Whether they err or not in this respect, they can never be sure that God will save them and lead them to heaven. According to the doctrines of Luther and Calvin, all men are born as sinners and not even a life of good works can save them from an eternity in hell if God has predestined this terrible destiny them for. In contrast, the Catholic Church grants more respite to its members. Confession periodically relieves Catholics from the burden of their sins. They are taught that good works and frequent prayer matter. They are presented with indisputable doctrines, approved by the pope, who is supposed to be infallible. In other words, the Catholic Church offers more social support to and solidarity with its members than does the Protestant Church.

Durkheim related the decline in the number of suicides during wartime to an increased level of nationalism. This political explanation contains hints of the general law that suicide rates vary in inverse ratio to the degree of social integration.[60] However, when war breaks out, other factors figure. Social existence breaks its normal pattern. It loses its power to restrict the conduct of its members. We then witness the prompt emergence of an anomic situation. People suddenly become more susceptible to the inclination to commit (anomic) suicide. Many studies show that a sharp increase in suicide rates occurs at the beginning of a war and near the end of a war. For instance, there was a sharp increase in the number of Jews who committed suicide in May 1940, directly after the Germans invaded the Netherlands. Just before the end of World War II, many Nazi leaders, including Hitler, killed themselves and their relatives. The same is true of the people who collaborated with the oppressors during this war. Similar increases have been reported following the fall of the Berlin wall. With the fall of the Berlin wall, for many Eastern Europeans their whole world also fell apart as their entire lives and careers had been invested in the Communist system. Overnight, their future seemed dark and treacherous.

Above, we saw that the occurrence of altruistic suicide indicates that social cohesion is strong. But, when social cohesion is weak we witness a high level of egoistic suicide. This leads to the conclusion that the suicide rate in a social group or nation is related to the level of social integration in a curvilinear way. The number of suicides is lowest when social cohesion is moderate, allowing enough space for individual freedom, but not too much as not to make one feel isolated or closed in. People must feel connected with the rest of the group and have the feeling that they can count on the attention and solidarity of the group whenever they feel a need for this. Relatively high levels of suicide occur when individualization goes too far or when the collective bonding becomes suffocating or too demanding.

Durkheim has often been accused of adhering to a collectivistic and moralistic philosophy with a strong focus on restricting individual drives and desires, and redirecting this energy to collective tasks to fulfill the needs of society. But his treatment of obligatory or altruistic suicide shows that he was aware that societies or social groups could put an excessive strain on individuals. He firmly believed that a severe disorganization of society could be fatal for many people, but he also realized that too much cohesion and social constraint could be just as disastrous.[61]

3.5.2   Suicide, marriage, and gender

Is suicide a male phenomenon? A great deal more men than women commit suicide, regardless of age. This has been confirmed by a host of studies carried out in many countries. However, there are indications that, when attempted suicides and successful suicides are taken into account there is less difference between men and women.[62] Perhaps part of the sex difference can be explained by the fact that men seem to be more drastic in their attempts and tend to opt for strategies that cannot be reversed once started. But even if this is true, there still exists a significant sex difference in the suicide rate. A regional Dutch study showed that 60 per cent more females than males were medically treated following a suicide attempt.[63] However, the number of registered suicides by women is about half of that of men. This pattern remained roughly the same throughout the twentieth century, despite a general rise in the overall suicide rate in the second half of that century. In this particular Dutch study, analysis showed that most suicides could be categorized in two groups. The younger age group (15-29 years) was single, living alone or with their parents. The middle-aged cluster (30-49 years) was divorced, living alone, and economically inactive. A high percentage of this category reported physical and mental abuse by parents in childhood, as well as physical and mental abuse by a partner later in life.[64] No doubt, Durkheim would label both clusters as egoistic suicides, because they seem not only poorly integrated in society at large, but also in the micro-society of their families.

In his attempt to explain the gender difference, Durkheim echoed some popular prejudices about the disposition of women. First, he observed that women were much less educated than men, which was true in his time. But he also asserted that they were fundamentally conventional by nature without great intellectual needs, He did acknowledge, however, that the level of literacy of women was much higher in England than in France. This seemed to be at a price as the comparative ratio of suicides in England was higher than in other European countries. He also observed that Negro women in the United States were better educated than Negro men. Again, this was reflected in a relatively high proportion of suicides among black American women. All this seemed to indicate that the increase in education boosts suicide rates. However, Durkheim made clear that we should not blame the increase in education per se, but should look at factors that are usually related to a higher level of education. In his view, the increase in suicides is due to deteriorating traditional beliefs resulting in moral individualism. There is no increase in the suicide rate when education does not undermine traditional values and high moral standards.

Durkheim noted that marriage and the start of a family may keep people from committing suicide, which can be viewed as social integration on micro societal level. Marriage decreases the suicide rate, although Durkheim noted that marriage at a young age does not. Especially in cultures where honour plays an important role and shotgun marriages, when the woman is pregnant, are common. In a footnote, Durkheim contended that this type of suicide might be called fatalistic suicide, the opposite of anomic suicide, when it is a consequence of excessive regulation or cultural demands, as may be the case in societies in which marriages are arranged.[65] Nowadays, arranged marriages still occur in traditional Hindu and Muslim immigrant communities. Many Westernized daughters of such families refuse to accept this and some see no other way out except by committing suicide. Durkheim held on to his hypothesis that the protection enjoyed by married people must be attributed to the influence of the domestic environment. This environment consists of two different elements: the spouse and the children. Based on French statistics, Durkheim showed that married men committed one third less suicides than unmarried men. If the marriage did not result in offspring, then the advantage is less obvious. As protection against suicidal inclinations, marriage is somewhat less advantageous for women. If the marriage does not produce offspring, their suicide rate even increases. A century ago, married but childless women in France committed suicide 50% more often as unmarried women of the same age did. This shows that marriage offers some protection against suicidal inclinations, but that the procreation of offspring seems to be more significant. Living with a partner and having children are clear forms of social integration and thus help prevent the incidence of suicide to some extent. In Durkheim's own terms, the higher density of the family explained this positive effect. If the size of the family shrinks, its social vitality also shrinks.[66] In general, in small families, there are fewer interpersonal relationships and interactions, so that domestic life languishes and the home is occasionally deserted.

At the end of his chapter about egoistic suicide, Durkheim attempted to explain why women can endure life in isolation more easily than men. As women traditionally spend more time outside of the community than men do, they are less infused by it; society is less necessary to them because they are less impregnated with sociability. Because her social life has always been simple, simple social forms satisfy all her needs. Men, on the contrary, are beset in this respect. They are raised to become complex social beings; they need to find more points of social support outside themselves. Because their moral balance depends on a larger number of conditions, it is more easily disturbed. If Durkheim was not entirely beside the mark here, a sharp increase in the suicide rate may be expected as soon as women participate more fully in society at large. Data from the second half of the twentieth century show that Durkheim was right. The increase of female participation in education and the labour market concurred with an increase in the suicide rate among women.

The increase in the suicide rate during the twentieth century could easily be explained by the combination of hypotheses put forward by Durkheim over a century ago. Secularization led to a steady decline in participation in religious communities. Fewer and fewer people got married, more people got divorced, and the birth rate declined sharply. These trends show a steady individualization of society resulting in an increased number of egoistic suicides.

In the twentieth century many occurrences of a sudden rise in anomic suicide appeared, for instance, during the financial crisis of 1929 and the Great Depression that followed. Other manifestations of this can be observed during the beginning and the end of the Second World War and also in the period following the demise of the communist empire in many central-European countries.

In modern, western societies altruistic suicide is in decline. The opposite trend can be seen in the non-western world. Buddhist monks who set themselves on fire clearly belong to the category of altruistic suicide. Recent examples from the Muslim world have re-introduced the model of the Kamikaze pilots. For the sake of what is seen as a holy war, they combine altruistic suicide with horrific attacks on their enemies, whether these are Israeli schoolchildren on a bus, holidaymakers on the island of Bali, Iraqi shoppers in a market place, a Russian audience in a theatre or thousands of Americans in the Twin Towers of the World Trade Centre in New York. Unfortunately the topicality of these examples show that Durkheim's theories and concepts still help to explain events today.

3.6   The elementary forms of religious life

From the days when the Jacobins had tried to destroy Catholicism in France and attempted to fill the gap by inventing a Religion of Reason, French thinkers had grappled with the problem of how morality could be maintained without religious endorsement. Like Dostoevsky's Ivan Karamazov they posed the question: *'Once God is dead, does not everything become permissible?'* Durkheim was concerned with a similar problem. In the past, he argued, religion has been the cement of society – the instrument with which individuals could change their everyday concerns into a more general devotion to sacred things. He feared that the end of traditional religion could be the prelude to the dissolution of collective solidarity and morale, heralding a total breakdown of society.[67] As an agnostic, he started a quest for a functional equivalent for traditional religion in a non-religious age, which he thought to find in moral education.

3.6.1   Points of departure

Durkheim's fascination for this topic was aroused by the work of Robertson Smith. This Scott had presented some interesting theories on the cults of Australian clans. He viewed these cults as the most elementary forms of religious life. Furthermore, he conceptualized the social functions of religion, such as its power to unite people and to reaffirm their common bonds. This book inspired Durkheim to develop his own ideas in *The Elementary Forms of Religious Life*. Herein he shows a sharp insight in the importance of rituals and ceremonies for the maintenance of religion, for social cohesion and for holding on to a concomitant system of norms and values.

Durkheim was convinced that the cults of Australian clans represent religion in its simplest form. Technically and culturally, these clans still lived in The Stone Age and could not have borrowed religious ideas or practices from other primitive groups. He was quite certain that the religious ideas and practices of the clans offered a valid model for the origin of religious life in human societies. He found that the study of religion in its most basic form could teach us much about the essential elements of religious thinking, because it already contains the necessary requisites for all religions.[68] According to Aron, the idea that it is possible to get a thorough understanding of the essence of social phenomena by studying them in their most elementary form in one or in very few cases is one of the most brilliant methodological ideas of Durkheim.[69]

3.6.2   The cult of the totem

Because Australian cults did not entail divine personalities or spirits, Durkheim did not think that Gods or other supernatural entities are an essential element for the establishment of a religion. In his view, the crucial thing is the divide between the profane and the sacral. Holy events, places, sacred things, and acts are strictly separated from profane periods, locations, things and activities. Holy matters are treated with great respect and awe. They are placed on an entirely different level. As a consequence, people who engage in religious rituals and ceremonies have to cross some kind of frontier. When they engage in religious ceremonies for the first time, they have to undergo rites of initiation (*rites de passage*).

The bifurcation between the profane and the sacred is not sufficient for the definition of religion. Also specific practices, such as rituals and ceremonies are necessary. Every religion has a 'church' or 'church community', an organized group of religious people. Religion truly is a collective phenomenon. It binds people, in full agreement with the etymological meaning of the word. This is clearly expressed in Durkheim's definition:

> *A religion is an interconnected system of religious beliefs and practices concerning sacred things, that is, things that have acquired a separated role and are tabooed. The religious convictions and practices unite all people who belong to it in a specific moral community that is called a church.*[70]

The basic model for the organization of aboriginal Australian societies is a system of clans. The clan has two important characteristics. The members consider themselves kin, because they all share the same 'family name': the name of the clan. They need not be blood relatives, though, nor do they need to live close together. They may be scattered over different parts of the tribal territory. Secondly, the name of the clan is the name of the totem, which has a special meaning for all members of the group. Each clan has its particular totem. In general, these are normal, worldly things. In most cases, it is not a unique object, but a class of objects, for instance a certain type of animals, which are declared taboo. Members of the clan are forbidden to kill and eat them, maybe with the exception of special occasions such as sacrificial ceremonies.

But the taboo is the prototype of the sacred.[71] Its holy character also covers the image of the totem and all members of the clan. In most 'primitive' religions, all members of the community are considered to be sacred, but a select group that lives an exemplary life can be more sacred than others. They possess specialized knowledge about their religion, its rites and ceremonies. Being accustomed to European religions, all former researchers had overlooked the fact that members of the clan considered themselves to be holy as well, at least to a certain degree. In contrast to Europeans the aboriginals of Australia do not make a sharp distinction between themselves, nature and the entire cosmos. They see themselves as part of nature. The scope of religion encompasses everything; nothing can escape from it. Outside reality there is nothing that can be the source of a 'divine' power. The power of the sacred has to be found within the clan itself. According to Durkheim, 'primitive' tribes relate the feelings produced by the dominating power of society to the image of the totem, to the most characteristic symbol of the group. Thus, the principle of the totem is nothing else than the clan personified and represented by that which functions as totem.

3.6.3 The origin of classifications and fundamental categories of thought

The distinction between totems and totem groups produced a system of classification. Scientific classification stems directly from this first conceptual arrangement.[72] In 'primitive' groups, the system of classification is based completely on the distinctions of the religion. As religions develop further and the number of gods increases, each god represents a specific group of phenomena. Later, in the more secular phases of history, the close connection between the gods and classifications disappear all together. But even then, Durkheim insisted that the system of classification still reflects the original religious and social origin of the group. His point was that societies are the most obvious examples of logical arrangements or orderings, which can also apply to nature. In nature, there is no natural distinction between good and bad, between superior and inferior. Only human groups make this distinction. Hierarchical thinking is also reserved for human groups. In contrast to Kant, Durkheim did not believe in modes of thought that *a priori* exist in the brain. In his view, it is society that endows people with the idea of supernatural powers, with the concept of forces superior to human force.

Durkheim contended that all our knowledge and all our fundamental categories of thought are the products of social existence. In short, he completely sociologized Kant's epistemology.[73] Fundamental categories of thought such as time, space, number, and cause are the result of collective experiences we share with fellow human beings. This does not mean that the perception of physical forces is completely determined by the organization of society. Of course, individuals use their senses. Certain regular patterns are so obvious that it stands to reason that people will use them for their classifications. Day and night, light and dark, light and dark colors can all be put together in the same category. However, the sensorial input, which we experience from the things in the world around us, is vague and variable. The extremely abstract concept of a classification that can be used to group things that have something in common requires sharp demarcations. Often, this relapses into simple, binary oppositions. Thus, the vague and abstract concept of time is sharpened by the regular pattern of ceremonies and the sense of space is reinforced by the demarcation of tribal territories. 'Primitive' man perceived space as a circle, marked out by the horizon. For that reason, their camps sites are circular.

3.6.4 Homo duplex and the origin of religions

In *The Elementary Forms*, Durkheim devoted so much space to the sociology of knowledge that we run the risk of being distracted from the main topic: the origin of religion and its functions. As usual, Durkheim started his study with a critical attack of prevailing theories. For instance, he did not give any credit to the theory that religion had started with and developed from animism. According to this theory, people deduced from their dreams that they had two identities:

a physical and a spiritual identity. All people have felt that they were somewhere else while they were asleep and dreaming. This seems to imply that the soul or the spirit can exist outside the body. The final and definitive separation of body and soul occurs when a person dies and starts his or her eternal sleep. The body dies, but it is assumed that the soul lives on forever. Therefore, it is possible that the spirits of our ancestors, long dead, are still powerful while wandering around. The animists believe that these spirits from the other world can exert influence on the living. They think that prehistoric people must have considered these spirits to be sacred. From there on, it is only a small step to attach a divine quality to the spirits of ancestors and designate the first ancestor as the primal God that has created the tribe, people, or even humanity. Yet, Durkheim did not see why the other, non-physical side of man should reach a holy status. Moreover, not all prehistoric societies show a belief in an immortal soul. He deemed it impossible that humanity would maintain lines of thought that are easily refuted through common experience. Everybody who has ever dreamt that he was involved in some heroic, adventurous, or romantic action has also come to realize that none of this actually had happened, because the other people involved in the dream deny that anything of the sort ever happened.

In his search for the origin of religion, Durkheim looked in a different direction. He supported the idea of a *homo duplex*, a human being that has physical as well as spiritual or mental experiences, but he did not relate this to animistic thinking. In his view, man is composed of two parts, which can be seen as the worldly versus the sacred, the useful versus the moral, and the hedonistic versus the virtuous, the individual and egoistic versus the collective and altruistic part. In a way, the individual human being hosts a 'spark of divinity', as a consequence of the continuous influence of society on the individual.

> *For society, this unique source of all that is sacred, does not limit itself to moving us from without and affecting us for the moment; it establishes itself within us in a durable manner. It arouses within us a whole world of ideas and sentiments which express it, but which, at the same time, form an integral and permanent part of ourselves.*[74]

Here Durkheim made one of his most daring mental leaps. In his view, religion is a social construction. In fact, it is the deification and sanctification of society. In a way that reminds us of Feuerbach, who stated that the gods are projections of the social forces we all experience. If religion is only a transcendental reproduction of social forces, that is, of the forces that maintain social order, then the loss of traditional religion does not implicate the disintegration of society. All we need is to find rational substitutes for the foundation and continuation of essential moral ideas.

In Durkheim's view, the real origin of religious beliefs is the collective effervescence that sometimes overwhelms particular groups when they are ceremoniously assembled during processions, ritual dances, and songs. It is highly probable that he borrowed this idea from studies of mass psychology. Such euphoric states can give birth to religious ideas or reshape them. The theory that this is the origin of religion is confirmed by the fact that, in Australia religious activity is almost entirely confined to when these assemblies are held.[75] The religious life of the aboriginal Australian passes through successive phases of complete lull and super excitation. In these periodic conditions of collective exhilaration, all members of the group undergo these feelings. In particular, the renewal of collective representations concerning the sacred best takes place during collective rites and ceremonies that arouse great excitement and euphoric sentiments.[76] After the religious ceremony, the aboriginal Australian's mind is still full of heroic and sacred representations. He is still overwhelmed with thoughts about the heroic deeds of his ancestors, which were reawakened during the song and dance. As an active and committed participant in the ceremonies, he has, as it were, taken part in the actual actions of his illustrious and sacred ancestors. Hence, the cult inculcates ideals, role models, and specific patterns of behaviour in his brain. These collective representations gain a certain power over the individual. It is society, the tribe or the clan that thus influences him and steers his behaviour in a socially desirable direction. In this way, a moral conscience comes to life in his inner self, a conscience that forms a crucial part of his entire consciousness. But he does not experience the moral part, the voice that speaks to him when he breaches a rule, as a part of his consciousness, but as the manifestation of a higher power or spirit. As a consequence of socialization, modern man experience similar things.

> In this voice which makes itself heard only to give us orders and establish prohibitions, we cannot recognize our own voices; the very tone in which it speaks to us warns us that it expresses something within us that is not of ourselves. This is the objective foundation of the idea of the soul: those representations whose flow constitutes our interior life are of two different species that are irreducible one into another. Some concern themselves with the external and material world, others, with an ideal world to which we attribute a moral superiority over the first.[77]

Therefore, our consciousness is made up of two parts. One part, the social or collective part, has pre-eminence over the other. In most cases, it can repress our inner egoistic and biological drives. Such is the profound meaning of the antithesis that coexists within us. This means that we belong to the species of *homo duplex*.

3.6.5   *The social functions of religion*

According to Durkheim, religion fulfills many social functions. Rituals prepare people for social life by teaching them discipline and a certain degree of prudence. Religious ceremonies are a gathering of people. Hence, they reinforce mutual social bonds and solidarity. Religious supervision retains and revitalizes the cultural heritage of a group and helps it transfer values to the next generation. It also smothers feelings of frustration and the losing sight of life's purpose, for instance, when a person we love dies or suffers from illness or misfortune. Religion can mend feelings of sorrow and support the idea of the essential virtue of the moral society of which we are members.[78] At the most general level, religion gives meaning to the existential problems of people.

Durkheim viewed religion as the cement of traditional society. It produced the means through which people could forget their individual worries and enabled to devote themselves to more revered things and activities. In that way, religion liberates people from the daily routines and inclinations aimed at pleasure and convenience. Religion is the outstanding anti-individualistic force that inspires human beings to engage in collective devotion to ethical goals. Religious traditions fulfill a major role in all religions. Hence, they cannot be considered to be meaningless. Although their apparent function seems to be to intensify the bond with divine powers, their real function is to tighten the bonds between members of the group and to create and reproduce a social morale.[79] There is no religion without a 'negative cult', that is, a series of commandments, interdictions, or taboos. People who violate these interdictions are sanctioned, in the present or in the hereafter. Sacrilegious acts offend public opinion, which evokes a reaction, resulting in a closing of the ranks.

Religion has a euphoric function too. People become entranced during ceremonies. They behave in unusual ways. They get into ecstatic states. They can no longer control themselves. This gives them an idea of external powers that steer their actions and determine their will. By wearing special decorations and painting their bodies, by using special ceremonial dishes and drinks, the participants feel that they form part of a totally different life, a domain of existence that is sacred. During everyday life, when each person leads its own selfish life, involvement in the community is relegated to the background. Thus, periodically, ceremonies and rites must reinforce the loyalty to the group as a whole. Ceremonial actions are intrinsically unimportant. What is important is their invisible influence on collective thought, on the feeling of being a member of a group of equal minded people, or on the feeling of coming into close contact with something sacred. Whatever the form of religious rites, they are all functionally equivalent; they all fulfill the same function of social bonding. In that sense, all religions are alike and equally sincere, for all are directed at the functioning and bonding of society.

3.7   Socialization and moral education

Durkheim started his academic career as pedagogue. He brooded over questions as: 'What is the role and effect of education as an institution for socialization?' 'What has to be done if moral education is alienated from religious education?' At the time, his sociological approach to socialization was very innovative. It

produced interesting new insights: for example, that the goals and methods of socialization and formal education are determined by social factors. They are neither God-given, nor idiosyncratic prerogatives of individual parents. For Durkheim *education*, which he also called *socialization méthodique*, is a social fact. It
is society as a whole that determines the ideals that education should help to realize. The objectives and methods exist outside particular individuals; they have
a 'compulsory character'. Pedagogical behaviour that deviates too much from
the prevailing norms arouses sanctions. Society can only survive when people
achieve a sufficient degree of homogeneity: education perpetuates and reinforces
this homogeneity by fitting a child with essential similarities that collective life
demands. On the other hand, society also needs diversity: education guarantees
this necessary diversity by being diversified and specialized itself. All this led
Durkheim to devise the following definition:

> *Education is the influence exercised by adult generations on those
> that are not yet ready for social life. Its object is to arouse and to
> develop in the child a certain number of physical, intellectual and
> moral states which are demanded of him by both the political society
> as a whole and the special milieu for which he is specially destined.*[80]

Durkheim was convinced that people could not survive in a humane way without the help of a social community. Without the aid of society individuals would
never develop into social beings, that is, into truly human beings. That is the reason why individuals often have to submit their own interests to the interests of
the group as a whole. That is why Durkheim took so much interest in moral education. Moral conduct is in the interest of the community and sets the boundaries
of socially accepted norms and values. Each child must learn to accept social duties. The normative order of society must restrict the insatiable needs of human
beings. Besides, it is for their own good; otherwise they would fall victim to their
own instincts and desires. The essential thing is to be freed from your own instinctive drives and desires. Only if children are kneaded and plied through
processes of socialization or enculturation, will they become truly humane beings. Without socialization no one can develop into a fully developed member
of society. Take away language, ethics, and culture and you end up with a pack of
animals. Enculturation is the key to social evolution for each new generation.
In Durkheim's view, the newborn baby is a *tabula rasa*. He is not interested in
the idea of an innate nature or similar 'vague and indefinite tendencies which
can be attributed to heredity.'[81] He draws our attention to the fact that with each
new generation, society is challenged with the task to compose social beings
out of this 'raw material'. Fortunately, people, in particular young children, are
endowed with an astonishing pliability or plasticity. We need not view this as a
negative characteristic, for it is this exceptional adaptability that separates people
from animals. This characteristic stands us in good stead when we have to survive in difficult physical and social conditions.

In contrast to his broad elaboration on the social character of socialization and its objectives, Durkheim hardly ever discusses the process itself. Yet, he pointed at three important aspects: (1) imitation, (2) co-operation, and (3) identification. These processes reinforce each other. Generally it is true that children imitate the people with whom they live and interact with. These are the people they tend to love - in particular their parents, brothers and sisters. So, it is rather easy to identify with them. Co-operation implies communication, accepting advice from others, following their example and thus imitating them. In this way, socialized adults guide and support the socialization of youngsters. Via this process children acquire the knowledge, skills, and moral standards of the community or profession for which they are destined.

3.7.1   Elements of moral education

In Durkheim's view moral education is the most important element of socialization. Behaviour that reckons with the interests and feelings of other people is the real cement of society. He distinguishes three aspects of moral education:
1 discipline;
2 attachment to social groups;
3 autonomy.

Discipline accounts for the obligatory element of social norms and rules. If large numbers of people would not act according to the rules set by the collective, then social life will turn into chaos. We then no longer know what to expect. So, in any society there must be an authority that sets the norms and rules of behaviour. There also must be continuity and consistency in these rules. In general, yesterday's rules should still apply today. If social rules, customs, and behavioural patterns would change overnight, this would ruin their reliability and regulative character. Then, too much behaviour becomes unpredictable and society dissolves into a chaotic, anomic state, resulting in total disintegration.

The function of moral rules is to maintain social order, and to preserve society. Responsible social action is action in the interest of the collectivity.[82] This requires strong attachment to one's society or social group. Whereas in traditional societies the collective ideals are relatively simple and comprehensive, modern societies promote a large diversity of ideals, values, norms and opinions. Nevertheless, modern societies have to remain integrated. Hence, they have to stimulate a universal respect for more comprehensive and more abstract ideals, such as individualism, justice, and peace. Moral education, should teach different types of values and ideals, the overarching values of society, as well as the specific values that fit specific social functions or subgroups. Durkheim thought that it was quite well possible to acquire a set of general values, skills, and cognitive elements, as well as a specific set, meant for each particular subgroup or professional category, because human beings are exceptionally malleable.[83]

The third element is autonomy. How can the free will be complied with conformity to the rules and demands of society? Durkheim found the solution in basing autonomy and responsibility on valid and reliable knowledge about society, on its needs and functions. The difference between self-determination and autonomy and the complete subjection to the social group lies in the ability to predict the consequences of all alternative actions for oneself and for the other people involved.[84] The more precise these predictions are the better people can determine which line of action would be best. When people make up their minds about what to do or not to do, they will certainly consider the wishes of the group of which they are a part. In Durkheim's view, it is not enough to respect discipline and be committed to a group. Beyond this and out of respect for a rule or devotion to a collective ideal, we must have knowledge of the reasons for our conduct. This consciousness confers on our behaviour the autonomy that the public conscience requires. Morality no longer consists merely in behaving in a socially acceptable way. The rules imposing such behaviour must be freely accepted too.[85] This requires a new attitude in education. Education should pay more attention to the nature of society and its meaning for the individual. At school, morality should not be preached but taught. Explication is the first and most important assignment. Durkheim acknowledged that modern society experienced a period of great social changes and considerable social unrest. His emphasis on explication suggests that he viewed discussion and intellectual reflection of moral principles as a necessary element of modern education.[86] The authority that emanates from morals stems from 'above.' In earlier periods the source was religion or the Church. In modern times, society has adopted this function. Now it has to be made clear that society, as a supra-individual and objective fact, is the source of moral authority. For, it has to be stressed once more, we owe our humane existence to society. Take away our language, laws, art, and culture, and we are left without any civilization. If we can accept this moral authority as a good thing in itself, then we will obey moral rules for their own sake. Therefore, it is necessary that formal education teaches each new generation that we have to respect the moral rules of society.

The rules we experience, as forces from without or from above, have to be transformed into forces that work from within. Thus, we will follow these rules as if it is the most normal thing to do, as if they no longer need any reflection or discussion. In particular, it is this taken-for-granted quality that makes social life run smoothly. The question whether it is desirable that individuals give up many of their personal desires and needs and thus appear to yield to the demands of the group is answered in two steps. First and foremost, the human being can only attain his true self and develop his own talents and character if he is integrated in society. Secondly, the demands of society can only become the desires of the individual, when the rules and customs of society have been internalized in his inner self, and the values of society have become an integral part of his own goals.

As we already have pointed out, Durkheim viewed man as a *homo duplex*. He *has* a physical body, with strictly biological and individual psychological needs and desires, but he also *is* a socialized being. This second side is connected with the social group; it concerns the collectivity. It consists of the whole set of ideas, sentiments, and practices that express in us the group or society of which we are part; these are collective opinions, religious beliefs, moral convictions, and national or professional practices and traditions. Their totality forms the social being. To constitute this collective conscience in each of us is the main goal of socialization.[87]

Both aspects of the *homo duplex* exercise their force on the individual. This can lead to inner conflicts. Only moral conduct can bring men to the point that they will suppress or postpone their strictly individual impulses. This dualism of human nature manifests two aspects of his existence, an existence as a mere individual and an existence as a social being. Frequently, society commands its members to go against their biological and psychological nature. Often we cannot satisfy the two beings within us. Since society has its own nature, its requirements are quite different from our individual natures. The interests of the whole are not necessarily those of the part. *'Therefore, society cannot be formed or maintained without our being required making perpetual and costly sacrifices.'*[88]

3.8   Durkheim's analysis of socialism

As a student at the ÉNS, Durkheim had frequently discussed important social and political issues with his fellow-students. In those days, socialism was the talk of town. Later, Durkheim developed the idea that a mature sociology could fuel socialism in such a way that it could translate scientific insights of sociology into political practice. Before we conclude that there is a striking similarity with Marx' idea of praxis here, we should remember that Durkheim warned us that sociology was still a very young and fragile science that could not fulfill this role yet. So, for the time being, he wanted to maintain a safe distance from politics and did not want that political views interfered with his work as a scientist. Therefore, like Max Weber, he propagated a strict division of labour between politics and academia.

His socialism was rather vague. He strongly supported abstract ideas such as equality, but did not concern himself with the practical question how to achieve this end. He rejected the economic materialism of Marx for its one-sidedness. He found that most of Marx' predictions and hypotheses already had been superseded, although they still served as means of propaganda. His socialism was aimed at the functioning of society as a whole and not at the functioning of the labour classes alone. He was convinced that the misery of modernity rested on far deeper roots than on a wrong organization of the economy. The social malaise entangled both employers and employees. In his view, the redistribution of power would solve nothing. Instead, he aimed at a revitalization of social morality.[89]

Durkheim criticized economic liberalism. He did not think that competition would create social stability. In his view, it is impossible to explain social order by the egoistic actions of individuals. In his view, the chief problem of industrial society is maintaining order and consensus, creating and maintaining such a strong commitment with the community that it prevents social conflicts and suppresses egoistic conduct.

In his study on socialism, Durkheim emphasized that the idea of organic solidarity presents an answer to the problem of finding the right balance between individualism and collectivism. In a society based on organic solidarity individualism can flourish as soon as basic collective needs are fulfilled and major social norms are obeyed. However, maximizing individual rights seems to be the main value of modern western societies. Each individual should develop his or herself as much as he or she can. So, it is no wonder that modern societies have a great problem with achieving the right level of social cohesion and solidarity. In these societies it is still necessary to establish a collective conscience. We have to respect other members of society. This is an absolute prerequisite for a peaceful cohabitation in spite of the variety in jobs, political opinions, norms and values. Precisely in societies that attach great value to individual rights, sociologists must address the social problem of maintaining a basic set of shared beliefs and convictions. Individualism can easily go too far and degenerate into social disorganization. The more individual rights are propagated, the more it is stressed, implicitly at least, that one does not need to take care of one's fellows. Hence, every society must put limits to individual freedom. It must constrain the insatiable desires of human beings. Living in groups creates tensions between the wishes of the individual and the demands of group. At this point Durkheim arrives at the core of his thinking about socialism, or what he understood as socialism to be. He flatly rejected some core ideas of Marxism. He renounced the employment of violence to attain one's political objectives and also rejected the idea that class struggle forms an essential element of industrial society. Further, he discarded the idea that class struggle was an important force of historical development. Like Comte, he contended that the conflict of interests between workers and employers merely are the result of a bad organization of modern society. They certainly are no harbinger of a new era. He repudiated the thought that the only solution could be found in reorganizing the economic and political structure, but stuck to his favourite idea that the real problem was a lack of moral and social cohesion. This view set him up as a strong adversary of Marx, who never would have accepted that the core of a social problem was situated in the super structure of society.

For Durkheim, socialism simply was a more sensible organization of social life. The goal and result of social existence should be to integrate individuals in the framework of communities that are endowed with moral authority and are capable of performing pedagogical and educational needs.[90] Durkheim asserted that the aspiration 'to pull the industrial machine out of the darkness of automatic functioning' did not merely sprout from the wishes of the lower classes, but from the state. National governments dearly wanted to get a grip on the economy, now that its importance has grown so hugely.

Durkheim made a sharp distinction between the doctrines of communism and socialism. Communist doctrines are almost just as old as mankind. They are based on the battle against injustice and inequality. In the communistic perspective, all men are equal. Therefore they should all find themselves in equal positions and circumstances. This view flatly ignores the hard facts of reality, in which we are faced with significant individual differences everywhere. Communism, in its original and unadulterated form does not put economic activity at the center of its philosophy. On the contrary, it tends to favour a decrease in production to prevent a surplus that could lead to unequal distribution of goods. Socialism is a rather new idea that came up after the French Revolution. After this Great Revolution, a growing number of people perceived some kind of anarchy in the functioning of the economy. They also observed an increasing divide between the rich and the poor. Modern industry seemed to create great abundance and wealth on the one hand, and great scarcity and poverty on the other hand, leading to growing tensions between the rich and the proletariat. Hence, the socialists presented many ideas to reorganize the economy in such a way that the growth of production could be used to fulfill the basic needs of all people and erase poverty in all walks of life. Durkheim renounced this solution, because man is an insatiable beast. How successful we might ever become in improving the conditions of labour, shorter working days, raising wages, laying out social support to the widows, the sick, and the invalids, it would never lead to a complete satisfaction of all possible needs and desires. Social reformists direct their energy to something that is of secondary importance. In his view, the essential problem of modernizing individualizing societies is the founding of a public spirit and discipline that directs and restrains the desires of people. Unfortunately, at the time he could not have read the famous dictum of Bertold Brecht: 'Erst kommt das Fressen und dann die Moral' (Eating comes before ethics). Maybe, then he would have seen that the improvement of the social conditions of the poor also could have a significant effect on integration. It could mitigate revolutionary tendencies and form a basis for a positive identification with society at large, including its moral standards.

3.9   In conclusion

Sociology owes much to the works of Émile Durkheim. He invested his whole career in helping it to come of age. He was strongly convinced that a mature sociology could be realized only with the help of the rigorous scientific methods that had made the natural sciences so successful. He believed that social processes obey laws, just as the laws of physics determine natural processes. He stated that sociologists should investigate social facts as if they were material things. Many of their characteristics, such as their relative inflexibility and the influence they can exert on people, seem to legitimate this approach. His positivistic approach appears to be applicable in many cases, especially where social facts are crystallized in objectified 'things' such as constitutions, laws, customs, and age-old traditions, or types of organizations, and transport systems.

He strongly adhered to the idea that social phenomena constitute a realm of their own. They are a *sui generis*. Hence, sociology should occupy itself with sociological explanations only, that is, with explaining social phenomena with other social factors, and not with the help of biological or psychological factors. He assumed that the reduction of social phenomena to psychological or biological factors would lead to invalid theories and explanations. Nowadays, we would view this perspective as being a bit narrow-minded. Human existence and social life are such complex phenomena that an interdisciplinary approach should be favoured over a strictly disciplinary approach. Nevertheless, sociologists should keep his advice in mind and refrain from an approach that offers little more than an aggregation of psychological data.

One way to avoid this is a further refinement of the possibilities of a structural-functionalistic analysis of social facts, alongside a more traditional study of the causes and consequences of social change. However, we should realize that both methods still face many of problems, in particular in the field of sociology, because social phenomena are complex and dynamic, and because it is impossible or unethical to carry out scientifically controlled experiments with human groups and societies. Once again, these huge problems should not lead us to abandon rigorous methods.

The great value of Durkheim's work clearly lies in the objective examination of so-called social facts and the statistical analysis of their relationships. The *Division of Labour in Society, Suicide*, and *The Elementary Forms* are still landmark studies in our field. Many of the theoretical insights he produced are still valid today. His study still inspires many researchers to dig deeper. He was right to reject the explanations that come first to mind when we only use our common sense and our pre-scientific impression of social phenomena. Moreover, he advised us to keep in mind that the large majority of the subjective meaning people attach to their lives and social conditions, are social facts, and can be examined objectively.

In the field of substantive theories, Durkheim left indelible marks. He was the first to draw attention to the importance of a collective conscience. The collectively shared elements in our mind lead to great similarities in conduct and social cohesion. Moreover, without this collective element in our personal make-up, we could not have become the kind of human beings we are now. Without a common language and a set of shared customs, norms, values, morals, and laws, individuals and societies would not have developed. Durkheim showed a deep understanding of and respect for the value of collective life. In his view, people should almost worship societies, because they owe almost everything to social life, to their upbringing, and to socialization in a social group. According to Durkheim, the good society is the real sanctuary. However, he did not think that all societies are perfect and should never be changed. On the contrary, especially societies that manifest clear signs of anomic should be reorganized to give them more structure and regulations. On the other hand, societies that show too much regulation or far too strong cohesion should be loosened up to make individual life more satisfactory.[91]

Durkheim was more than a pure scientist. He was also a moralist who worried about the negative consequences of modernization manifested in industrialization, urbanization, secularization and individualization. He feared that societies could fall apart at the cost of humanity. Should the moral constraints of religion or the social control of small communities fall away, other constraints must fill the gap. In his view, this meant that formal education should become an institute for preparing new generations for society, intellectually, vocationally, and morally.

4

GEORG SIMMEL

THE GREAT IMPRESSIONIST OF SOCIAL LIFE

Georg Simmel covered a broad range of microscopic as well as macroscopic topics, order as well as conflict, economic phenomena as well as art. He favoured a
rather light and essayistic style, but his insights were far from superficial. His eye
was the eye of the impressionist. He also resembled the artist in his talent for generating original ideas and highlighting the typical. He was fascinated by para-
doxical situations. The following words from him are often quoted:

> For us the essence of aesthetic observation and interpretation lies in
> the fact that the typical is to be found in what is unique, the law-like
> in what is fortuitous, the essence and the significance of things in the
> superficial and transitory...[1]

This chapter will cover only some topics of his highly variegated oeuvre and observe the typical way in which he approaches the social. As usual the chapter
starts with a short overview of biographical facts. Section 4.2 deals with his epistemology. All knowledge starts with discovering oneself as a real existing object
that differs from other objects. On this basis we learn more about today's society
and its history. To Simmel, the subject matter of sociology was 'sociation' or the
process of becoming a social being through interaction with other individuals.
Section 4.4 is devoted to his form sociology. He wanted to reach the essence of
society by studying the crystallized and visible basic forms of the more fleeting
encounters between individuals. Though all sociological forms emerge from a
restless flow of life, they do not remain that way, but turn into more stable forms
that appear to assume a life and a will of their own. Life is a form that produces
more than life. Ironically, social life produces forms that gain some power over
life and restrain it or direct it in unforeseen and unplanned directions. In section
4.5 some examples of Simmel's sociology are discussed such as the stranger and
the adventurer, as well as his very interesting thoughts on the relation between
group sizes and individuality. Section 4.6 covers his views on what he calls the

tragedy of modernity. Modernity produces so many new objects, forms and ideas that it has become impossible for individuals to grasp or enjoy it all. This could lead to strong feelings of estrangement, isolation and exclusion. Section 4.7 raises the issue of poverty, how it is constructed and what function it seems to fulfil. Section 4.8 treats Simmel's analysis of feminism. He rejects the idea that women should be duplicates of men. There should be equal rights and society should free itself from masculine domination to make room for inherently feminine elements. Simmel also offered new views on the form and function of social domination and conflict. In his provocative view there is no domination without some acceptance of it by those who are dominated. Near the end of the chapter, in section 4.10, another major element of modernity is discussed, the growing importance of money, its forms and functions, its huge effects on values and valuations. The chapter ends with some concluding remarks.

4.1   A rich life and a poor career

Georg Simmel was born on the 1st of March 1858, right in the centre of Berlin. He was of the same age as Emile Durkheim and six years older than Max Weber. Georg was the youngest child in a large family. He had five sisters and one brother, Eugen. His father, Edward Simmel, born in 1810, was a wealthy merchant from Sephardim-Jewish descent, who turned to Catholicism. In 1838 he married Flora Bodstein, who originated from a Jewish family that had turned Protestant. The children were baptized as members of the German Evangelical Church. The family moved to Berlin, where the father established a business, which later developed into a renowned chocolate factory. His father died in 1874, when Georg was 16. The music publisher Julius Friedländer, a friend of the family, became his guardian and stimulated his love of music. When Friedländer died, he left his entire fortune to his protégé.[2] As a child, Georg was a bit of an outsider. His relation with his dominating mother was rather distant and his brother and sisters did not share his strong interest in intellectual affairs. Later, he complained that there was not much of a cultural climate in his family, although this can hardly be true, for he received his first piano lessons from his sister Marie.

At the University of Berlin, Georg studied history with Mommsen, ethnic psychology with Lazarus and philosophy with Dilthey, Harms and Zeller. At the age of 23, he presented a thesis on 'psychological-ethnological investigations into the birth of music', but this study was rejected. The professors found his topic rather strange and too broad. Instead they asked him to present his study about Kant's views on the essence of matter as a PhD thesis. For this study he already had received a prestigious award. Though this procedure was exceptional, Simmel gladly accepted this way out and got his doctor's degree after all.[3]

Two years later, Simmel presented his *Habilitationsschrift*,[4] on the philosophy of Immanuel Kant, but to his horror the committee rejected it. At the official event of the dissertation lecture, Zeller criticized Simmel for having a blind spot for the human soul. Instead of politely answering this critical remark Simmel turned the event into a scandal by claiming that Zeller held nonsensical ideas about the soul.[5] As a result he had to try again and finally succeeded in 1885.

In the same year, he became a private lecturer at the University of Berlin. This meant that he had to earn his income by asking money from his students. Fortunately, his lectures attracted many students, whom he inspired to think creatively about a rich mixture of topics. He was a virtuoso at the platform. Whenever Simmel wanted to express the core of an idea, he so-to-speak picked it up with his hands, his fingers opening and closing; his whole body turned and vibrated under the raised hand. This gave the students the feeling that they participated in his thought process. Moreover, they found his perspective on modern times fascinating.[6] So, it is no wonder that students enjoyed his lectures. The drawback was that he formed a threat for tenured professors in residence. Some envied his oratory skills and others realized that Simmel could also outshine them academically.

His lectures about logic, ethics, aesthetics, sociology of religion and social psychology became cultural events that were announced and reviewed in the Berlin newspapers. Hence, they also attracted many foreigners and non-academics.[7] Simmel accepted women as guests during his lectures, long before they were officially allowed to study at German universities. It is highly probable that his famous teaching skills and his progressive attitude to women have harmed his academic career. Many colleagues did not like his ideas or his didactical methods. Another reason could be that he ignored the rules of the game. In his books and essays, Simmel often addressed himself to a non-academic audience, in particular to the members of Berlin's counter culture of artists, authors and other intellectuals. Hence, he often used a non-academic style, leaving out all marks of scholarship such as references and footnotes.

In 1890, Georg married Gertrud Kinel, the daughter of a railway engineer. Her father was a Roman Catholic and her mother was a Protestant. The couple had one son, Hans Eugen, who later became professor of Medicine in Jena but had to seek exile in the USA soon after Hitler came to power. Gertrud Simmel was a fascinating woman. She studied philosophy and published four books under the pseudonym Marie Louise Enckendorff. Georg and Gertrud turned their house into a cultural centre. They received many famous guests such as the poets Stefan Georg and Rainer Maria Rilke and philosophers and sociologists as Henri Bergson, Edmund Husserl and Heinrich Rickert. Also Max and Maria Weber and Reinhold and Sabine Lepsius became friends of the family. Clearly, the Simmel's belonged to the inner circle of renowned Berlin scholars, intellectuals and artists.

Georg Simmel has written more than twenty books about a great variety of topics and themes, such as the philosophy of Kant, Schopenhauer and Nietzsche and the work of famous artists like Goethe, Rembrandt and Rodin. He wrote his essays quickly, as if he had composed them in his mind long before. In his philosophy of culture and art he discussed themes like the portrait, the caricature, the landscape and the Alps. He published books on religion, morals and the philosophy, psychology and sociology of money. Besides, he wrote about 200 essays on epistemology, cultural philosophy and metaphysics. Four of his books are considered as landmarks in the field of sociology.

The first was his book on social differentiation (*Über soziale Differenzierung*). It was published in 1890, three years before Durkheim published his book on the same topic. In contrast to Durkheim his central point is not the division of labour, although this is important, but individualization. For Simmel, individual differentiation is an outcome of the growing density and increased civilization of the population. When groups expand, the desire to cross spacial, economic and cultural borders also increases. This creates more room for individual differences. Like Durkheim, he assumed that in pre-historical times, humans were very homogeneous. But he added that this homogeneity is strengthened by a great hostility to other tribes. This brings him to the following interesting hypothesis: *'The closer the synthesis within the own tribe, the more pronounced the antithesis against other tribes.*[8] If we replace tribe by ethnic or religious group this hypothesis still stands most tests in our own day and age.

In 1892, Simmel published his reflections on the demarcation between sociology and history and made many perceptive remarks about the method of explaining social and historical events and processes. Quite a few of these ideas were adopted and further elaborated by Max Weber.[9] In spite of its title, sociologists certainly should study his Philosophy of Money, published in 1900. It elaborates various themes Simmel had already discussed in earlier works. Hence it is indispensable for an understanding of his critical analysis of the cultural climate of his country in his day and age. The last of his four major sociological books is *Soziologie*, his very bulky introduction to the discipline, which he published in 1908.[10]

His impressive oeuvre never seemed to suffice for a professorship at a renowned university, despite the support of his friend Max Weber and the good words of famous professors like Rickert and Windelband. No doubt, the anti-Semitic climate harmed his career greatly. That his parents had converted to Christianity offered no real defence, nor did his complete assimilation in the German bourgeois culture. Even an attempt to appoint him as an extra-ordinary professor failed. Two years later, in 1900, the faculty successfully repeated the request. But this honorary professorship did not improve his academic power, for only full professors had a real say in university politics.

In 1908, two chairs for philosophy became available in Heidelberg. But even then he was not appointed. When a leading historian was asked to evaluate Simmel's qualifications for the chair at Heidelberg, he wrote to the Culture Department of the state of Baden: *'He is ... a dyed-in-the-wool Israelite, in his outward appearance, in his bearing and in his manner of thinking. ... He spices his words with clever sayings. And the audience he recruits is composed accordingly. The ladies constitute a very large portion.'*[11] These comments were lethal, because they suggested that he was a second rate scholar who attracted a second rate audience. Fortunately, he did not become an embittered man. He enjoyed the recognition and respect of eminent professors such as Edmund Husserl, Heinrich Rickert and Max Weber and was admired by renowned journalists and artists. He was also highly esteemed within the field of sociology and was honoured to give the opening speech at the first national congress of the Association of German Sociologists.

In 1914, 56 years of age, he finally was appointed as full professor at the University of Strasbourg. The academic status of this university outpost ranked far below that of the universities of Berlin and Heidelberg. 1914 was also the year that the Great War broke out and Simmel immediately lost his scientific objectivity and impartiality. He got inflicted with strong patriotic feelings and became a fierce nationalist. His young friend, Ernst Bloch, reproachfully said to him: '*Your whole life you have evaded the (political) position and now you have found the utter position in the trenches.*' Simmel immediately asked Bloch to leave the house. Three years later he realized that the policy of Kaiser Wilhelm II was a catastrophe.

When he fell terminally ill, he asked his doctor how much time he had left. The doctor told him that there was little time left. Simmel immediately withdrew from social life to write his last book on metaphysical perspectives.[12] Simmel died of cancer on the 28th of September 1918, sixty years of age. At his own request only his wife and his dear friend Gertrud Kantorowicz were present at the funeral. His son was still on the battlefield. In his obituary Ferdinand Tönnies evaluated Simmel as an outstanding sociologist. He spoke of the '*magical versatility of his highly skilful thought*' and contended that this insightful man would leave profound traces in the field of sociology. He also asserted that Simmel's mind was totally set upon analysis.

> *No matter how many remarkable examples his profound erudition marshals in support of his fine differentiations, he prefers to seize upon completely timeless, general problems, such as subordination, conflict, secret societies, self preservation of the social group and the development of individuality. These are all significant objects and he treats them with a multiplicity of charming observations, brilliant insights and blinding dialectics; but he never fully attains the recognition that the most proper objects of sociological inquiry are the social structures (Gebilde) which arise out of the thoughts of men themselves, out of their subjects.*[13]

This last critical remark is open for debate and will be treated when we discuss Simmel's sociology of forms and his idea that life not only engenders life, but 'more than life'.

4.2 Sociological knowledge

Simmel's sociological writings are based upon explicit epistemological assumptions that determine the scope and limitations of his sociology.[14] Like Kant, he assumes that no reality is directly accessible to human cognition. Sensual impressions may create pleasant or unpleasant sensations and may influence the cognitive process, but they are not identical with knowledge. To achieve a coherent insight into reality rather than diffuse feelings a specific cognitive effort is required. Pure observation does not suffice for apprehending reality. Understanding presupposes a two-fold process of differentiation. To begin with one has to recognize himself as a knowing subject, as a thinking subject that can differentiate and apprehend reality as a series of objects. Knowledge begins with seeing oneself as a subject and an object.[15] The cognition of the 'I' dialectically evolves into the cognition of the other, of things outside oneself. The recognition of oneself as an object constitutes the first *a priori* condition of any cognitive effort. It recognizes the existence of the individual as real. It gains significance because the conscious affirmation, 'I am', becomes the blueprint for the awareness that 'things are'. The same statement also serves an epistemological function. To discover ego as an object is to discover the differentiating power of a category. If it is possible to experience oneself as an object as well as a concept, to set oneself apart from oneself, then any reality outside the subject can be subjected to the same process. The 'absoluteness' and 'steadfastness' of individual existence are the foundations of man's cognitive discoveries.

For Simmel, life itself is the ultimate reality. Life is first and foremost realized in man himself. All further experiences and cognitions can be related back to the 'original' first experience and cognition of the 'I'. Thus, for Simmel, social cognition and social experience ultimately rest with the individual. Any social event, even the most complex one, can be traced back to him. Even objectified social structures and cultural systems do only become real if they are lived and apprehended by individuals.[16]

The second step in cognition also contains an ontological and a categorical aspect. The ontological statement 'something is' remains confined to the knowing subject, for reality can only be felt, experienced and imagined.[17] There is no purely logical access to reality. There are only pragmatic reasons for assuming that reality is 'real'. We are faced with the problem of survival. We must know our natural environment well enough in order to tackle the problems that endanger our species. We have, as Simmel puts it, practical and theoretical interests in the realities of which we are part. The necessity to know and to act compels us to follow these procedures. To act and to theorize means to make decisions, to select among seemingly countless facets of reality. To get a cognitive hold on the apparent chaos we have to construct a framework of values. Values are superimposed upon reality because their selective and discerning power serves our interest. Yet, we add nothing to reality. Reality itself exhibits a wealth of properties and aspects that offer us the opportunity to attach values to them. Hence, the possibility of evaluation is the second *a priori* of human cognition.

The discovery of ego leads to the discovery of alters. However, the others are not purely and objectively perceived as separate, autonomous individuals, but rather as individuals that are viewed from certain perspectives relevant to ego. In other words, the other is evaluated, whether it is a person, animal or thing. In the case of persons we apprehend them in a typified way. We focus on their role, class, status, gender, ethnicity or lifestyle. The cognition of the 'you' is therefore always the cognition of social association. Although experience teaches us that other people are different from the way we classify them, we still relate to them as to a typified object.[18] Thus we always tend to sell them short. They are much more than we tend to think.

Though Simmel started with the individual as the knowing subject, for him to gain knowledge is an eminently social effort. The evaluative categories have their origin outside us. They are reflections of properties of our social environment. We know about other individuals by rediscovering in them the same individualistic existence we experience in ourselves and we recognize them as participants in a common social environment. But this image of the other is not completely determined by the norms and standards of our society. As cognitive subjects we can choose from a variety of available values, norms and standards, but we will do so in accordance with our own abilities, practical necessities and theoretical interests.

Subjective judgments help to establish the content of our knowledge. But knowledge entails more than sets of cognitive contents about objects. It also is an ongoing process of discovery and investigation of relations between things, processes and structures. Through the apprehension of these relationships we construct a unity between otherwise unconnected elements. Such cognitive constructions are 'true' in a relativistic and pragmatic sense. It is only from the pragmatic perspective that elements of reality are perceived as related.[19] They serve as temporary ordering principles that are to be modified or abandoned as soon as their heuristic purpose is served. All this is terribly important. It is here that the social actors and their interests tend to merge. Individuals, forming groups and associations, integrate into larger entities. At the same time, they are the bearers of the interests that govern such larger social units. Our interests no longer remain outside social reality, but enter into it. Hence, it is from here that cognition of societal phenomena must start.

> *The processes of cognition ... proceed under these, not abstractly conscious, but very fundamental conditions that express themselves in the reality of praxis: That the individuality of each one finds a place within the general social structure, indeed, that the structure beforehand, despite the unpredictability of the individual, is directed at this achievement.[20]*

At this point, Simmel postulates a third *a priori*, one about mediation between society and the individual. This leads to a normative statement about society; it forms a very important basis of his theory of modernity. In direct reversal of the philosophy of the Enlightenment he postulates that there is no equality between the elements of a society. We can only grasp the diversified structures of modern society if we consider many facets and diverse qualities of human beings. Neglecting the uniqueness of individuals will turn sociology into a schematic objectification and metaphysical ossification of society.[21]

The goal of sociology is now established: it is the search for the numerous processes that shape and are shaped by the relationships between individuals. These processes and relationships compose social reality. They change and develop further as time goes on. Simmel's whole sociological work is focused on the mutual effects of individuals and historical situations upon each other.

Scheme 4.1   Simmel's 3 epistemological a prioris

1	People can discover and view themselves as a real existing and knowing object.
2	People can and must differentiate between objects and evaluate them.
3	People can discover and investigate relations among things, including social relations.

4.2.1   Historical knowledge

For Simmel, the kind of understanding which is peculiar to social history is embedded in our view of understanding in general. There are fragmentary, prototypical traces of our intellectual activities in the forms and procedures, which the mind develops in order to satisfy the practical demands of life. These fragmental and prototypical images of the past are conditions for the continuation of life itself. Life would be utterly inconceivable without some awareness of the past. The fragmentary consciousness of the past depends upon analysis and synthesis of the material of life.[22]

Insight into historical understanding depends upon insight into understanding people in general. How can one person understand another? Ultimately our understanding of Julius Caesar, Mahatma Gandhi, Nelson Mandela or George Washington is essentially the same as our understanding of a personal friend. All our understanding has the structure of an integral synthesis of two elements. There is a given object, an empirical phenomenon that, as such, has not yet been understood. The second mental element is the interpretative idea of the subject. Subjects may develop their own ideas or interpretative conceptions or these ideas might be taken from another source. There are three forms of this cognitive relationship between an object and an understanding subject. In the first form the observable activities and expressions of an individual are understood as being motivated. We suppose that an animate mind lies 'behind' all the observable actions of the other. We assume that she or he is not a puppet, but a real person who – under certain conditions – can be understood from within. We believe that we understand the behaviour of another man or woman when we can impute certain experiences, feelings, motives and ideas into the other, because we have had similar experiences, feelings, motives and ideas. On this view, the understanding of the properties of a historical person or a person from another culture is understandable if there is an essential identity between us.

We are obliged to infer the mental states of another person from the appearance of external signs. The little child heard himself crying when it was in pain. Solely on these grounds it could infer that another person whom it hears crying must also be in pain. The same inference can be made in similar cases. But this example is too simple. The act of projection is complex. When children grow older they draw conclusions from the actions of other people based on their observations of the whole person. It is not just the observer's anatomical eye that sees or his ear that hears, but the entire person is involved. His entire set of experiences and knowledge is concentrated on the act of understanding the other. This perception of the total existence is far from complete. It is fragmentary and open to correction. It is susceptible to stimulation and suggestion. Nevertheless, it is the fundamental and uniform mode in which one person approaches, perceives and influences another.[23]

Historical understanding is only an alternative form of our understanding of the contempory. The way to the creation of a complete picture is more taxing. The result will be less complete than the picture we can construct of contemporary events. In this case we can question living persons about forms of behaviour that we do not understand. But even then the picture will never be complete and perfect.

4.3   The field of sociology

In his essay 'The Field of Sociology', Simmel tried to explain what sociology is all about.[24] At the time, there was a host of opinions concerning its contents and aims. Even the meaning of society was disputed. Existence was viewed as an exclusive and concrete characteristic of individuals, their qualities and experiences. Society, by contrast, was considered as an abstraction and not seen as a real object. Even today some theoreticians think that society does not exist outside and in addition to the individuals and the processes among them. Others, like Simmel, state that all what people do and certainly all what they do during interactions with each other, is determined by society and forms part of social existence. So, any science of human beings also is a science of society. Hence, in principle, sociology ought to replace the artificially compartmentalized disciplines, such as history, psychology and moral philosophy. But, according to Simmel, nothing is gained with this broad definition. It only sticks a new label on a pot filled with a variety of already well-established disciplines.[25]

4.3.1   *Sociology between methodological individualism and holism*

Like Durkheim, Simmel strongly rejected the arguments of the methodological individualists. If it were true that only individuals are 'real', historical science would reach its goal only if it included the behaviour of each individual. Yet, even if we could satisfy such a fantastic claim, we would not have solved our problem how to interpret, for instance, how 'the Greeks' and 'the Persians' behaved in the battle of Marathon. The notion of 'the Greeks' and 'the Persians' constitutes a totally different phenomenon, which results from a certain intellectual synthesis and not from a direct observation of isolated individuals. Despite their individual variations, they had enough in common to form the more comprehensive units of 'the Greeks' and 'the Persians'.

Simmel did not think it wise to rob our cognition from all such synthetic concepts. It would deprive human knowledge of its most legitimate contents, such as our grasp of the main characteristics of a political movement, a nation or a religion.[26] The method of reduction would not uncover useful insights into the characteristics and actions that are typical of social groups or societies. This inclination to look for a solid ground for our cognition in the basic elements of social units does not lead anywhere. Besides, it is completely arbitrary to stop the process of reduction at the individual, for the individual too is a composite of various qualities, destinies, forces and biographical derivations, which, in comparison to the individual himself, have the same character of elementary realities as do the individuals in comparison to society.[27]

On the other hand Simmel did not shy away from studying the actions of individuals, either as theoretically pure examples of specific types or as unique, famous historical personalities, such as Michelangelo, Rembrandt, Goethe, Nietzsche and Schopenhauer. His aim in the study of these great personalities is always to disclose the inner unity, its essence, formula or destiny of the soul that underlies the diverse contents and expressions of the subject's life.[28] For Simmel, the ego has two layers. The core is hard or impossible to change. It carries the real sense or substance of our life and gives it coherence and unity. The other one is composed of momentary impulses and isolated irritabilities. The more heterogeneous the peripheral contents, the stronger the appearance of the inner unity.[29]

Many sociologists like to stress that the work of great artists and scientists is the result of the activities and energy of a collective. Sociologists are eager to remind us of the famous statement of Isaac Newton, saying that the only reason why he could see further into the unknown regions of nature was because he had climbed on the shoulders of those giants of science that preceded him. Merton and other sociologists of science emphasized that science can only progress if a host of people help to pave the way for their invention or discovery. In their eyes the so-called individual genius only succeeds in synthesizing or rendering a new perspective on material at hand, material produced by other scientists. From a sociological point of view all these remarks are valid. Nonetheless, they appear to play down the role of outstanding scientists, artists, philosophers or political leaders. Simmel is convinced that the work of great philosophers, scientists and artists is more a function of the personality than of the historical setting or the spirit of the times. Their work not only is receptive, but also a creative expression of really individual genius. Therefore, it has historical as well as a-historical elements. The latter elements give them their great value. The historical elements, such as particular techniques, choice of topics and perspectives that are typical for a specific period, are of little or no consequence. From this point of view, the significance of a philosophical treatise or a work of art lies in the dimensions and the profundity by itself. Though Simmel has rejected the individualistic conception of culture in other domains, he considered the history of philosophy or the history of art as the histories of the great thinkers, writers, poets, painters, composers and sculptors. They constitute forms of hero worship.[30] But this worship should not become excessive and expand itself to all personal belongings, characteristics and experiences of these great philosophers or artists. The personality, which is at stake here, is exclusively the person who appears in his work, the author of these ideas or works of art. We understand the philosopher insofar as we understand his philosophy,[31] but sociologists tend to be more interested in the inner unity, essence, form or function of social bodies and processes.

4.3.2 Sociation, the subject matter of sociology

In der Wechselwirkung gerinnt etwas zu Gesellschaft

For Simmel the subject matter of sociology is the world of symbols and forms of interaction. Society is something individuals do, experience, enjoy and suffer. Society is an intricate web of a variety of social relations between regularly interacting individuals; it's not a 'substance'. It's nothing concrete, but an *event*.[32] So, the subject matter of sociology is *sociation*, in other words the specific forms and patterns of human interaction, and their crystallization into characteristics of groups and collective processes. Hence, sociologists should focus on the effects of collectives upon the individual too. Sociology should study everything that leads people to associate themselves with other people, such as the need for social intercourse, love, and respect. Such drives, and the practical need for knowledge or the hunger for power, constitute social reality. These psychological needs form the ground material (stuff) for the process of sociation, the process of constituting the social. Sociation proper, the process of constituting social processes in company of others, in a cooperative or conflictive way, really starts when being next to each other evolves into being together, interacting together, in being with each other, for each other, against each other - in being of some significance for each or other. Sociability, the need for companionship, the drive to interact with other people, to be with other people, to respond to their actions, leads to social forms, functions, patterns or structures that make society a real society, that is, an organization of associated people.[33]

Whatever the strength of the drive to associate with other people, whatever benefit one derives from the interaction with other people, there is also a price to pay. You can't always do as you like in the company of others. You have to hide some aspects of your personality. People have to learn to restrain themselves, to postpone gratifications and to be tactful; otherwise they cannot function well in groups. People avoid badly socialized individuals as much as possible. They will minimize contact by ignoring their presence, by reluctantly responding to or entirely ignoring their requests or remarks.

Simmel envisioned a sociology that predominantly deals with psychic facts, but it does not do so in order to discover the laws of psychic processes. Rather, the aim is to grasp the manifold forms of human interaction. These various forms of interaction, these modes of reciprocal influence and mutual interpenetration are phenomena of a special kind. We must reach the essence of society by studying the crystallized and observable basic forms of the more fleeting encounters between individuals; structures such as tribes, castes, classes, business companies, and voluntary associations. The frequent, repetitive, and rather intensive interactions Simmel has in mind when he talks about 'society' are crystallized as definable, consistent structures such as the state, the family, the church, and other kinds of social organizations based on common interests.[34] But there are numerous less conspicuous forms of relationships and kinds of interaction that also need to be studied. Think of the secret rendezvous, the flirtation, the joyful greeting, the exchange of gossip, the humorous wink of the eye, or the nod of approval. Taken singly, they may appear negligible, but together they produce society. Therefore, we should not confine ourselves to the large social formations, like the first anatomists confined themselves to the major organs such as the heart, the liver, the lungs, and the stomach. Later generations of anatomists learned that the innumerable unknown tissues were just as crucial for a living organism as the more familiar ones.[35]

Sociation continuously emerges, ceases and emerges again. People are incessantly tied together by the whole spectrum of relations that connects them. They may be momentary or permanent, conscious or unconscious, fleeting or long lasting. Even where the eternal flux and pulsation of sociation are not sufficiently strong to form associations, organizations and political movements, they link individuals, in such a way that they influence each other. The interactions of the 'atoms' of society account for all the toughness and elasticity, all the colour and consistency of social life, that is so striking and yet so mysterious.[36]

4.3.3   *On method*

Simmel denounced both the essentially organistic approach as the intangible, immaterialist or idealistic perspective. The supporters of the latter approach were deeply convinced of the unique character of historical events and the individual volition and capriciousness of humans. Hence they found each attempt to study social processes in a positive way a waste of time. Simmel acknowledged that people are social beings with individual volitions. Therefore, he saw a great need for a specific sociological perspective. But this approach had to supersede the traditional explanations in terms of purely individual actions or divine interference. For him, sociology consisted in the abstraction of certain elements from historical reality and in their recombination for the analysis of specific cases.[37] That the social or sociological standpoint is not perfectly clear yet, is no objection; it is a characteristic of the human mind to be capable of erecting solid structures while their foundations are still insecure. When it comes to the most general and the most profound of intellectual problems, it is the rule and not the exception that the 'foundation' is less secure than the superstructure erected upon it. Scientific practice, especially in new areas, cannot do without a certain measure of intuition and purely instinctive advance. As the sciences move on, by trial and error, by conjectures and refutations, they will gradually weed out false assumptions and misguided conclusions.[38] Step by step they will penetrate deeper in reality and reveal new insights. Naturally, scientific work must never be satisfied by vague, instinctual procedures and ideas based on intuitions. Yet, one would condemn science to sterility if one made a completely formulated methodology the condition of taking even the first step. This is all the more true for the study of the infinite complexity of social life.[39]

Simmel stood at the beginning of a long road to a systematic and truly scientific sociology. So, the fragmentary, essayistic and incomplete character of much of his work should not be held against him. On the contrary, he is convinced that even small fragments of culture can reveal many valuable insights into the culture as a whole.[40] Therefore, fragments should not be mixed up with basic elements because even fragments possess many characteristics of the whole of which they are a part. Apparently, Simmel thinks that it is possible to create a theoretically valid image of reality on the basis of a few loose fragments, in the same manner as famous archaeologists succeed to create a lively image from prehistoric societies on the basis of a thorough analysis of a few pieces of broken pottery and some figurative scratches on a rock. Simmel boldly contended that a well-trained eye could detect very much, if not all of the entire aesthetical beauty of a work of art, from a careful observation of each section of a work of art.[41] Of course, not everyone would agree to this last bold statement, but we can agree that we can learn a lot from fragmented evidence.

4.4   The sociology of forms

Several authors have confessed their bewilderment over the seemingly unsystematic and generally vague manner in which Simmel handles his concepts and theories. Consequently, they have called upon a patient scholar, preferably inclined to the rigorous and tenacious tediousness that some aspects of scientific research require, to compile a list of all the instances where Simmel uses the concept of 'form'. It was hoped that this procedure would unearth the general meaning of this term as intended by Simmel. However, so far, it has not produced a consensus among theorists. Wallisch-Prinz takes quite another route. She is convinced that the right meaning of 'content' and 'form' can be deduced from his epistemology.[42] To Simmel, the forms and contents of life are fluid and inextricably interrelated. Human life produces certain states in which it expresses and realizes itself. It started with inventing simple techniques and procedures for gathering food and building shelters. In a long historical process these techniques, customs and rites developed into modern science, technology, works of art, religions, laws and innumerable other forms. These forms encompass the flow of life and provide it with content and form, with freedom and order. Although these forms arise out of the process of life, they acquire a logic and lawfulness of their own. This places them at a distance from the 'spiritual' dynamic which created them and which makes them independent. Herein lays the ultimate reason why culture has a history. Social life ceaselessly creates forms that become self-enclosed and demand permanence. These forms are inseparable from life; without them it cannot be itself.[43] They have their source in 'values and concepts that do not lie within life itself'. Life as such is unintelligible. This is why we need conceptual constructs to understand aspects of life, to understand the various structures or forms of social encounters between individuals.

4.4.1   The epistemological basis

Aspects of reality can only be grasped as possible objects of experience and knowledge if they fit an existing frame of reference, that is, if they fall under a category, taxonomy or other conceptual scheme that performs an epistemological function. For example, science, history, art and religion are forms in the sense that they specify conditions under which it is possible to have a certain kind of experience and acquire a certain kind of knowledge.[44] Social knowledge is only possible if the manifold human actions and experiences are structured in such a way that specific aspects can be distinguished, such as politics, demography, economics, religion, science, technology, war and peace. Likewise, within the historical domain, different periods must be discernable such as the Renaissance, the Reformation, the Enlightenment and the Age of Industrialization. Periods of growth and progress, stagnation and decline are experienced, observed and cognitively digested within each lifetime. Some other examples of forms are superiority, submission, competition, specialization, solidarity and exclusion. These and similar forms may be exhibited by the most diverse groups and the same interest may be realized in very different forms.

The theory of history synthesizes discontinuous, fragmentary and discrete data into continuous wholes. However, the continuity of this synthesis, for example the interconnections between various styles of classical European music, cannot be derived from reality. The observed continuity within 'the romantic period', which connects composers such as Wagner, Chopin, Liszt and Brahms, is an exclusive property of the historical construct itself. Romantic traits can already be found in the music of Beethoven, who treated the rigid and traditional forms of classical music rather freely. The Romantic period has typical hallmarks such as flexible modulations, a broad range of tones, the use of new instruments such as the saxophone and a more frequent use of changes in timbre and tempo. All this was aimed at making music more sensitive and more imaginative to reflect magic, fairy tales, tragedies, great love affairs, dreams and even the mysterious underworld of the human psyche. History fractures *'the real continuity which subsists within any given temporal process.'* Consider distinctions such as Gothic and Renaissance, revolution and reaction. These distinctions destroy the smooth transition of life itself.[45] But the distinctions that make reality intelligible are a consequence of the immanent requirements of history as a form. Perhaps this becomes clear when I define history as a socially constructed perspective on a sequence of interrelated events that theoretically can be discerned from social events in other periods. Without the awareness of sequences of related but discernable periods with their own typical events and characteristics there would be no history at all, but only a dull and infinite stretch of sameness.

History and the social sciences are no mechanical reproductions of the real properties of given data: just the opposite. They invent, construct and further develop this raw conceptual material in conformity with the theoretical purposes of knowledge. 'Sociological or historical truth' is an intellectual activity or function. It transforms objects into something new, because we have confronted the raw data with new questions. Thus we discover new meanings and values. These meanings and values transform the data into a structure that satisfies the criteria that we impose upon it.[46]

4.4.2   Life as a form that produces more 'more than life'

Simmel gave the concept of life centre stage in his approach. However, there is a very important difference with the approach of Wilhelm Dilthey and Henri Bergson. They emphasized the vitalistic principle, that is, the dark sides and hidden powers of organic life, its irrationalities and its continuity. But they tended to ignore that life can also crystallize and produce structures, forms and functions that seem to halt the continuous flow of life. Certainly, life is in a state of perpetual flux. It is constantly creating, increasing and intensifying its own potentialities. The essence of life is to produce 'more life'. That is 'to produce, reproduce and renew life'. But life also has the capacity to transcend itself by creating new forms, new stable structures that are 'more-than-life'. Although these entities are products of life, they develop characteristics that are independent of life and often go against the strain of life. On the other hand, they tend to be rather crucial for social life.[47]

Simmel proffered many illustrations of the manner in which life creates 'more-than-life'. For instance, the biological instinct for reproduction has evolved into various forms of love – passionate love, romantic love, marital love and polygamy. But the same biological instinct also has lead to arranged marriages, marriages of convenience, extra-marital affairs and prostitution. These forms can become partly or even wholly detached from the original hormonal energies of life that produced them. In a similar way the basic need to gather practical, common sense knowledge for our survival has produced science as an autonomous form. This vital origin has evolved in a specific form in which statistics and methodology have become autonomous fields. In a similar vein, particular specializations, for instance astrophysics, have become totally detached from the human capacity to adapt to their earthly environment. The origin of all forms, for example economics and politics, can be traced to the energies and exigencies of life and its disposition to recreate itself. The same is true for the art of painting. In general it is true that we see for the sake of living, but for great painters like Rembrandt, Van Gogh and Picasso it is the other way around. They lived for the sake of seeing. Some forms can only exist when other forms constitute them. Language is a necessary condition for the constitution of literature and poetry. These sublimated forms of language can be viewed as unintended artefacts of primitive forms of verbal communication that originally evolved as another instrument for survival. This too is an example of a form engendering a new form, language producing more-than-language as soon as people discovered the aesthetic power of sound patterns, rhythm, rhyme and the attraction of intriguing stories and wonderful songs. Simmel loved to present such shifts as dramatic events, as qualitative leaps, in which the practical everyday activity turned into a specific form that obeys rather strict rules and imposes these rules and procedures on us.

4.4.3   Different contents, similar forms; similar contents, different forms

The world is structured by a multiplicity of forms, but many different forms may embrace the same content. Blue is an example of a content that may be constituted by a variety of forms. In optics, it is a wavelength; in modern songs blue symbolizes sadness; in religious symbolism blue represents heaven. So, the same concept can represent a physical fact, a mood, aesthetic evaluation or a religious allusion. Form and content are merely conceptual means to structure our knowledge. Analytically they can be separated because the same content can be put in different forms. This is not only true for liquids, gas or clay, but also for numerous cultural phenomena. The plot of a story can be put in a short story or an epic saga. It can be presented in a poem, a play, movie, opera or musical. In reverse, the basic form of a story, the beginning, the main part and the end can be found in a large variety of other cultural products, such as scientific reports, presidential addresses, jokes and sermons.

There are innumerable forms of social interaction, such as attacking an enemy, leading a business firm or organizing a conference or a concert, that seem to be very different from one another. Nonetheless, they all require planning and co-operation. Simmel was convinced that it was feasible to discover similar patterns or forms in conflicts within families, governments and business organizations, because in all these situations imbalances of power play a major role. He aimed to discover generally valid knowledge about the laws that govern these social forms.

> Events which might be widely divergent in their bearing on life as a whole may nonetheless be quite similar to one another; or they may be incommensurate in their intrinsic meanings but so similar in respect to the roles they play in our total existence as to be interchangeable.[48]

Simmel used the terms form, interaction and function indiscriminately. He talked about functional relations between individuals or groups, sociological functions, functions as pure form, unity of interaction and so forth.[49] He was an enthusiast advocate of an approach that focused on a restricted number of existing forms that are constituted by social interactions. He certainly did not deny that specific historic events were unique and irreversible, such as the murder of Julius Caesar, John F. Kennedy, Olof Palme or Anwar Sadat. But he asserted that it was possible to observe, describe and analyse the similarities between certain aspects of various historical events that could be generalized. Hence, he was not interested in King *George* or Queen *Anne*, but in *King* George and *Queen* Anne. He wanted to abstract from the concrete content of actual social situations and events and zoom in on the general form, just like geometry does not study the real and rough circles we encounter in nature, but the mathematically pure models of circles.

Another example is that of the similarities of behavioural patterns within dogmatic religious groups, political ideologies and philosophical schools of thought.[50] Members of these sectarian movements think that they are endowed with special knowledge, convictions and insights that are unknown and incomprehensible to the rest of the world. Therefore, they exclude themselves from the world to devote their life with the greatest intensity to their particular doctrines. Newcomers present another example. Many sociologists have observed a high degree of similarity in the behaviour of military recruits, freshmen and immigrants. They show the same kind of insecurity. They share the same kind of unfamiliarity with their new surroundings. Therefore they anxiously search for signs. Unlike Weber Simmel never used the term 'ideal type', though he did use 'pure type' and 'pure form'. For Weber the adjective 'pure' or 'ideal' referred to a concept that is constructed in the most rational and pure way. For Simmel, it had a similar meaning, but it also meant theoretically pure, in other words, a theoretical form that is severed from its content.[51] If he would have used the term structure instead of form, he would have been far better accepted by later sociologists, for modern sociological terms like status, role, norms and values as elements of the social structure are closely related to the conceptualization used by Simmel.

4.5 Specimen of Simmel's sociology of forms

Simmel has filled a whole gallery with so called social types, as an addition to his array of social forms. These types are described with a host of details and precision. To give an impression, I present some of his types, starting with the stranger.

4.5.1 *The Stranger and the adventurer*

The stranger is not a passing traveller, but someone who has arrived from a foreign region or country and stays in our midst for a long time. He cannot be accepted fully because he has not been a member from birth. There is no collective memory regarding a multitude of events that have occurred during his youth; events that all others members of the group have experienced and can relate to. Moreover, the native members of the group will always keep in mind that the stranger might return to his home country. Often strangers will surprise us with their peculiar and rather detached view on our behaviour, because they come from a different culture. As the strangers in our midst are both near and distant, they can easily act as mediators. Their approach to the conflict at hand will be more objective and neutral because they have not completely identified themselves with one of the parties. Also, they will be bothered less by the prejudices that exist in each of the conflicting groups. Further, it is striking that people will confide things to strangers that would be rather risky if told to acquaintances.[52]

What is an adventure? What sets it apart from continuity and the wholeness of life? Simmel compared the adventure with a work of art and describes what makes the adventure or the work of art stand out from normal experiences or common products of craftsmen, bookkeepers or bakers. 'Wholeness of life' refers to the fact that a consistent process runs through the singular components of life, how crassly distinct they may be. What we perceive as an adventure appears to stand in stark contrast to that interlocking of life-links, to that feeling that all our experiences, after all, weave an unbroken thread. Nonetheless, an adventure is certainly a part of our existence, adjacent to other occurrences which precede and follow it; at the same time, however, in its deeper meaning, it occurs outside the usual run of affairs. Yet, as a foreign element in our existence it also is somehow connected with the centre. [53]

Each segment of personal experience bears a double meaning: it revolves about its own centre, contains as much breadth and depth, joy and suffering, as the immediate experiencing gives it. At the same time, it is a segment of a course of life – it is both a circumscribed entity and an experience that is connected with a series of other experiences. Yet, to the adventurous experience we ascribe a beginning and an end much sharper than those to be discovered in other forms of our experience. Thus, the adventure is given a special meaning in and of itself. It seems to be wholly independent of the before and after.[54] The more adventurous the adventure is, the more dreamlike it becomes in our memory. If non-adventurous people accidentally get involved in an adventure, they will often romanticize it as something experienced by someone else. After a while, they will find their experience hard to believe.

Adventurers are people who like to experience completely new situations. From time to time, they want to escape from the normal routine. But they also want to come back to tell everybody what exceptional phenomena they have encountered during their adventure. While an adventure falls outside the normal context of life, it falls, at the same time, back into that context. In some respects adventurers resemble artists and gamblers. Artists want to cut a piece of the endless chain of experience. They want to detach it from all connections and give it a self-contained form as though their work of art is defined and held together by an inner core. It is an attribute of both the work of art and the adventure that they represent a part of existence, yet in both the whole of life is somehow comprehended and consummated. Moreover, works of art and adventures are perceived to exist entirely beyond normal reality.

Adventurers and gamblers are strongly inclined to flitter around chance. They like to risk all, even their life and their entire fortune. They drive into the mist, as if the road will lead them, no matter what. This is the typical fatalism of adventurers and gamblers. The obscurities of fate are certainly no more transparent to them than to others, but they are sure that their adventure or gamble must succeed, which justifies their actions. Moreover, as fatalists they believe that nobody can escape his fate. So, why should one worry? Yet, they are certain of their success. Adventurers rely to a large extent on their own strength, but above all on their own luck. For gamblers, we can observe the same thing, though in their case it is a strong but unwarranted trust in an unbeatable combination of wit and luck. Hence, it is no wonder that to the moderate person adventurous conduct often seems to border on insanity.

The decisive point about the adventure, its specific nature and charm, is that it is *a form of experiencing*. The *content* of the experience does not make the adventure. That one has entered unknown territories, faced mortal danger, bankruptcy or conquered an attractive man or woman for a short span of happiness– none of these are necessarily adventures. They become adventure only by virtue of a certain experiential tension whereby their substance is realized. Only when the peculiar colour, ardour and rhythm of the life-process become decisive, only when they, as it were, transform substance only then events change from mere experience to adventure.

1.5.2   Group size: dyads and triads

The simplest sociological formation remains that which operates between two elements. Many general forms of sociation are realized with this form. The limitation to two members determines several forms of interaction and the solidified relationships that it constitutes. So, a careful and thorough analysis of the dyad is highly relevant, because some of its major characteristics are the same for various pairs. Some of these features remain constant even if the two members are collectives such as states or business organizations. The fundamental difference between the dyad and larger groups is that the two elements have a quite different relation to each other than they have to all other people. Each of the two feels confronted by the other, not by a collective above them. Larger groups will continue if one of its members dies or leaves the group, for a dyad this means the end. For its life it needs both participants; for its death, it needs only one. This fact is bound to influence the attitude of the individual toward the dyad.

The characteristics of the triad are rather different. The appearance of the third party indicates transition, conciliation and abandonment of absolute contrast. Of course, on occasion, the third participant can also introduce or incite contrast, but he or she can be replaced. In the most significant of all dyads, monogamous marriage, the child as the third element, often has the function of holding the unit together. Even in our present time, in which divorce is widely accepted as a fact of life, a fair number of couples that no longer love each other decide to stay together until the children are considered old enough to cope with their parent's divorce. Not so long ago, only childbirth would make a marriage complete and impenetrable. The birth (or adoption) of a child tends to strengthen the union of the two and to enhance their mutual love. The relation of the spouses to the child produces a new and indirect bond between them, because it will reveal new aspects of their character and worldview. And it leads to the common preoccupation with the child. Even if the marriage ends in divorce, a marriage with children will never really end. The child will always be a reminder of the other parent.

If the third party really is an outsider, he or she can act as a neutral mediator when the other two are engaged in a conflict. The unbiased mediator can show each party the claims and arguments of the other, without the accusative, embittered or aggressive tone of the other. This can be of a great help in solving their conflict because the wrong pitch can easily arouse negative feelings and worsen the problem. Nothing serves the reconciliation of conflicting parties more effectively as does objectivity, that is, the attempt to limit all complaints and requests to their objective contents. The curtailing of the subjective personal tone is the condition under which the reconciliation of the adversaries can be attained. To put it psychologically, antagonism of the will has to be reduced to antagonism of reason. Though, we should not be so naïve that mediators will be capable of solving all conflicts between warring parties, they certainly help in many cases. Recently the help of a mediator has become more popular when the marriage is at risk and also in cases of conflicts between neighbours, especially in urban districts with many people from a variety of ethnic and cultural origins.

4.5.3   Group size: individuality and social structure

Simmel took a great interest in the correlation between the expansion of a group and the level of individuality. His central hypothesis is:

> *Individuality in being and action generally increases to the degree that the social circle that encompasses the individual expands.*

Social differentiation proliferates when groups or associations get bigger. What once were minimal differences in dispositions, preferences, abilities and affinities now are accentuated by the increased necessity of competing for a livelihood with more and more people. In a Darwinist way, competition develops the special abilities of the individual in direct ratio to the number of participants.[55] Thus, new solutions to the problem of survival are bound to appear. As soon as societies grow, a rudimentary form of social classes will emerge. A social divide arises between high and low, as a simple consequence of the natural alliance of the weak against the strong.

After the process of social differentiation had led to separation be-
tween classes or status groups, the mere formal fact of occupying a
particular social position creates among the similarly characterized
members of the most divers groups a sense of solidarity and, fre-
quently, actual relationships.[56]

When addressing the example of the emancipation of the Prussian serfs, Simmel observed that differentiation and individualization loosen the bond between the individual and those close to them in order to create in its place a new bond – real and ideal – with people more distant. On the other hand, if emancipation is unthinkable, as is the case for the members of the various castes in India, this definitely obstructs the creation of bonds between members of different castes, religions or ethnic minorities. The same pattern of integration and segregation repeats itself in many similar situations. For instance, the former German corporate system was set up to strongly unite guild members in order to create an alliance against competition from outside, in particular from members of other guilds. Voluntary associations, on the other hand, impose hardly any uniformity upon their members. These examples hint at a relation that will be found in many places and periods. The homogenisation of individuals in the narrower social circle and their differentiation in the wider one are found, synchronically, among coexistent groups and group elements, just as they appear, diachronically, in the sequence of stages through which a single group develops.

Simmel assumed that in each person there is, as it were and unalterable ratio between individual and social factors that changes only its form; the narrower the circle to which we commit ourselves, the less freedom of individual 'deviations' we possess. However, this narrower circle is itself something 'individual.' It cuts itself off from all other circles precisely because it is relatively small and unique. When the circle in which we are active enlarges, there will be more room for the development of our individuality.[57] But as parts of this larger whole we are more common and have less uniqueness. The larger whole is less special as a social group. In other words, the elements of a distinctive social circle are undifferentiated and the elements of a circle that is not distinctive are differentiated. Examples of the first case we can find in religious sects such as the Quakers, the Amish or the Hara Krishna. As soon as members of a modern society enter the sect of Hara Krishna, they will adjust their clothing, hairstyle, food pattern and whole lifestyle to the prevailing norm in this sect. So, it appears that they have peeled off their individuality. But, as soon as they go out into the streets to chant, beat the tambourine and try to convert other people they draw anyone's attention because they stand out in the crowd. Thus, they are unique or special only in collective matters. Within the sect their life and mentality is strongly regulated.

Similar patterns can be observed at a macro level. Simmel mentioned the local orientation of the citizens of the New England states in North America. From the beginning, the Protestant immigrants or Pilgrim Fathers founded communities in which the individual was restrained by his obligations to the collective.

Although this unit was relatively small, it was also self-sufficient. By contrast, loners populated the Southern states. There, the first immigrants did not come as members of a religious group or community, but as single adventurers. These somewhat anarchistic individualists formed a colourful bunch of people that was not predisposed to local self-government. The Southern states developed large provinces as administrative units.

The difference in political structure between a highly centralized France and a loosely federalized Germany inspired Simmel to quote the following remark of a Frenchman about the mania for clubs in Germany:

> *It is this that accustoms the German, on the one hand, not to count solely on the state; on the other hand, not to count solely on himself. It keeps him from locking himself up in his particular interest and from relying on the state in all matters of general interest.*[58]

To this he added Bismarck's assertion that there was a much more narrow-minded small-town provincialism in a French city of 200,000 than in a German city of 10,000, because Germany was composed of a large number of small states. Apparently the very large state allows the local community to have a certain mental self-sufficiency and insularity. In a smaller state, the local community can view itself more as a part of the whole.

In stark contrast to Durkheim, Simmel never felt the urge to move away from psychology. He assumed that humans have a psychological sensitivity to differences. But it is a dualistic drive. People also want to belong to a social circle, to be part of a whole and, to a large extent, to be similar to other people. Our existence is, as it were, the sum of two: an individual and a collective existence, a unique and a shared one. Simmel assumed that we have a particular amount of the tendency toward individualism that we either have to realize within our own group as personal individuality or as a member of a rather distinct group, that is, as collective our personality to the affiliation with specific groups, we distinguish ourselves from the broader mass.

The family as a social unit offers its members a preliminary differentiation that prepares them for differentiation in the sense of individuality; on the other hand, the family offers members a shelter behind which that absolute individuality can develop until it has enough strength to stand up against the greatest universality. Sociologically, the family has a double role. On the one hand, it is an extension of one's own personality, a unit through which one feels one's own blood circulating. On the other hand, the family also constitutes a unit within which individuals distinguish themselves from all others and develop a selfhood. This double role of bonding and separating, of integration and segregation, unavoidably results in the sociological ambiguity of the family: sometimes it appears as a unit that acts as an individual and at other times it appears as an intermediate circle that intervenes between the individual and the rest of society or the surrounding social circle.[59]

4.6   The tragedy of modern culture[60]

As soon as life progresses beyond the purely biological level to the
level of the mind and mind in its turn progresses to the level of
culture, an inner conflict appears. The entire evolution of culture
consists in the growth, resolution and re-emergence of this conflict.
For clearly we speak of culture when the creative dynamism of life
produces certain artefacts which provide it with forms of expres-
sions and actualisation and which in their turn absorb the constant
flow of life, giving it form and content, scope and order: e.g. civil
laws and constitutions, works of art, religion, science, technology
and innumerable others. But a peculiar quality of these products of
the life process is that from the first moment of their existence they
have fixed forms of their own, set apart from the febrile rhythm of
life itself, its waxing and waning, its constant renewal, its continual
divisions and reunifications. They are vessels both for the creative
life, which however immediately departs from them and for the life,
which subsequently enters them, but which after a while they can
no longer encompass. They have their own logic and laws, their own
significance and resilience arising from a certain degree of detach-
ment and independence vis-à-vis the spiritual dynamism which
gave them life. At the moment of their establishment they are, per-
haps, well-matched to life, but as life continues its evolution, they
tend to become inflexible and remote from life, indeed hostile to it.[61]

The emergence of these new forms, these new cultural artefacts – self-sufficient
and with an inherent claim to permanence – give culture a historical character.
Life, social life, flows on without pause, but the emergence and disappearance of
distinct forms give structure to the history of culture and society. Sooner or later,
the forces of life erode every cultural form that they have produced. The perpetual dynamism of life comes into conflict with the crystallized forms it has produced. This nature of the process of cultural history was first observed with economic developments. Marx spoke of historical materialism when he described
that the economic forces of any age give rise to an appropriate form of production: slavery, the guilds, feudalism and free wage-labour. When they arose, they
were the adequate expression of the capacities and aspirations of that particular
age. But, from time to time new economic energies will surface that cannot find
adequate scope in existing forms. Therefore, they will gradually or abruptly replace old forms by new ones.[62]
For Simmel, it was the essence of form to claim, the moment it is established, a
more than momentary existence not governed by the pulse of life. This can be
seen even more clearly in intellectual spheres. So, from the outset there always is
a latent tension between objective cultural forms and (social) life. Cultural pessimists believe that this could produce a pervasive malaise in which all forms come

to be felt as something imposed on life. This virus of cultural pessimism always tends to find its most eager victims among intellectuals. This belief in a downward spiral only holds true if we overlook the possibility that counter movements could be triggered and spontaneous innovations could emerge that would gave history a more positive twist.

4.6.1   Objective and subjective culture

Simmel always showed a strong interest in objective cultural products, in crystallized externalizations or products of psychological and social interactions. Precisely these cultural products make that people can understand each other, that they can talk about them and start into relations because they share an affinity or a great dislike for them. Thanks to these objectified cultural products, – common ideas, shared feelings, wishes and desires that have resulted in professions, organizations, customs, laws and concrete artefacts – sociologists can observe and analyse behavioural patterns of people and understand why some relations emerge and survive while others fall apart.

Objective culture is the domain of objects that function as instruments for the socialization of people or as conditions under which they can become social or cultural beings. These objective cultural forms are incorporated into the mind of the individual. However, not all elements of objective culture enter into the subjective culture of individuals. This is particularly true for modern societies. The works of great writers have enriched our language. During many centuries, new concepts, shades of meaning and individual modes of expression have been added. Also the mixing with people from other countries, regions, cultures and classes has added new forms of expression.

> Yet if one looks at the speech and writing of individuals, they are, on the whole, becoming increasingly incorrect, undignified and trivial. As for content, during the same period the range of subjects for conversation has objectively increased considerably as a result of advances in theory and practice, yet it seems as if conversation, both social and intimate and letter-writing are much more superficial, boring and frivolous now ... How many workers today, even in smaller-scale industries, understand the machine with which they work, that is to say, the intelligence that is embodied in the machine? ... As regards the purely intellectual sphere, even the most knowledgeable and thoughtful men operate with an ever-increasing number of ideas, concepts and statements with whose precise meaning and content they are only very imperfectly familiar.[63]

It is clear that Simmel deplored the fact that individuals no longer were able to appropriate all the knowledge and meanings that have been produced by mankind, that they cannot understand all the intelligence and meaning that is hidden in modern machines, buildings, organizations, computer systems, procedures, rituals, traditions and customs, nor all the theories and their applications that have been discovered, invented and further elaborated by numerous generations. But this has to be accepted as a fact of life. Our practical existence is and can only be a fragmentary one. There will always be a discrepancy between the objective spirit of a group and the daily actualised culture and lifestyle of a social group. Only very small, undifferentiated and pre-modern societies form an exception to this rule. There the objective cultural potential will not outstrip actual subjective culture. Here we see a strong parallel with Durkheim's theories about such primitive societies as being cemented together on the basis of mechanical solidarity and an almost complete overlap between collective and individual consciousness. Things seem to go awry as soon as the division of labour starts to stride forward into numerous directions. Then, we no longer understand, only in a very simplified and limited way, what and how other areas of industry are producing. Specialization enhances not only alienation of the workers from their products, but it also enhances the division of social categories and the diversification of norms and values, giving rise to all kinds of subcultures, that are objectified in differences in styles of clothing between social classes – a topic that has been picked up, further elaborated and made topical again by Pierre Bourdieu.

Once again, we should stress that Simmel had a special view on culture and the educational formation of individuals (*Bildung*) that was typical for German intellectuals of his day and age. For him, the real tragedy was that the objective culture, as many individuals, including those of former generations, have formed it, bridles the cultural development of men in such a way that they cannot become the men they should have become. Nonetheless, objective culture goes on using the energy of the very individuals that are being frustrated in their intellectual, spiritual, artistic and physical growth, so that they will never reach the height of their true selves.[64]

We have to accept that our subjective culture is limited. The real problem lays in a highly undesirable discrepancy between objective culture and the individual when the objective culture emerges as an autonomous form that seems to control individuals and to hinder their emancipation. Four conditions appear to be essential for the reification of objective cultural forms. Firstly, the existential content of some area of life – science, religion, politics, art or love – is expressed in specific artefacts of a cultural form such as prescribed methods, rules, specific apparatuses, measures, safety procedures, buildings, et cetera. Secondly, this form becomes an independent entity, self-contained and developing according to its own immanent principles. Thirdly, it becomes estranged from the energies and interests that were originally invested in it. Finally, the development of this form outstrips the ability of the individual or even groups of individuals, to master or control it. They cannot even incorporate these artefacts within their own personal culture or mindset. If this is the case, then we can speak of reification.[65]

Simmel, echoing Marx, contended that this might give rise to feelings of oppression and pessimism. For example, more and more, we realize that we cannot master nor escape the reified world of scientific, technological, political and economic change. We have become sceptical about the so-called progress that is promised with every new discovery or invention. Nevertheless, these cultural forms are necessary conditions for the expression and realization of the energies and interests of life. On the other hand, these same forms become increasingly detached from life, which can give rise to a tension or conflict between the process of life and the configuration in which it is confined. Ultimately, such a tension can lead to the destruction of the necessary condition for these social process-

Objective culture: equality and the guillotine

One of the most-propagated ideas of The Enlightenment was equality. This idea has been put into practice in many ways. In general the process of political democratisation can be viewed as a good thing as well as the trend towards more equal opportunities for all, irrespective of gender, ethnic and social origin. Sometimes the drive for equity can run out of hand. During the French Revolution the Jacobins implemented an extremely radical policy to exterminate all people who hitherto had occupied high functions, such as the top of the Catholic church, the Noblemen and the leaders of opposing political parties. Once the killing of large numbers of privileged people started, it could not be stopped. Many frustrated people had to settle some accounts. In the end hundreds of thousands people were executed, including leaders like Robespierre, who had started the revolution. An interesting manifestation of the ideal of equal treatment for all was the invention of the guillotine. In March 1792, Charles Sanson, the chief executioner of the new republic, complained to the minister of justice that there was a shortage of good swords and skilled executioners. Another problem was that most victims were not brave enough to keep their head still on the block. So, severing their head became a messy job. Sanson demanded equal punishment for equal crimes. Formerly, aristocratic murderers were beheaded and ordinary citizens were hanged. The murderers of kings were quartered. A single, simple, mechanical procedure for all condemned murderers would be more humane and democratic. Henri Guillotin, a doctor and member of the National Assembly suggested the method of the falling axe. The German carpenter who built the first guillotine hoped, by patenting it, to sell this concrete product of the Enlightenment to many French cities. From then on, decapitation became a somewhat neater, almost sacred ceremony: the populace was kept at a distance and the victim had a last word with the priest. The victim was tied to a board and placed under the blade. Then the executioner bowed his head and cut the rope that kept the sharp and heavy blade aloft. Within a second the head was severed from the body. It was the quickest way to kill a victim without unnecessary suffering. The new method was consistent with the ideal that the administration of justice should be equal, 'humane', public and impartial.[68]

Box 4.1

es.[66] For instance, laws and regulations that are invented to make social existence more harmonious, just, safe and predictable, laws and regulations that are intended to avoid or solve conflicts often create new and unforeseen problems. In many essays, Simmel has documented this conflict between life and form, for example between the authentic religious experience of the believers and the dogmatic rules of the Church or between the creative, academic aims of scientists and the highly rationalized division of labour at universities and the academic world at large.

In an ever-modernizing world cultural artefacts become more complex, refined, systematic and complete. But, the process of integrating these new cultural forms in the live of the individual does follow suit. Hence, they become only partially incorporated in the subjective culture of individuals. So, on the one hand, objective culture depends upon the activity of individuals who create things that express the energy of their lives. On the other hand, objective culture becomes increasingly self-contained and self-perpetuating. Nonetheless, although forms of objective culture such as governmental rules and regulations have a tendency to evolve into autonomous and self-contained empires, they can never reach the limit of a total separation from subjective culture. There will always be a mutual relation between objective and subjective culture, between the collective spirit of the times and individual minds.[67]

4.7   The social construction of poverty

Most contemporary sociologists will accept that only few people have become impoverished, purely because of individual fate, stupid investments or other unintelligent decisions. Following Marx, they tend to hold on to the idea that whole categories of people are poor and get even poorer as a result of a combination of unfavourable economic, social and political conditions that amount to oppression and exploitation. Simmel focused on completely different aspects of poverty, its causes and consequences. In fact, he mainly analysed the position of the poor in relation to society and the social functions of helping the poor. For Marx, poverty was a deplorable situation that crippled the lives of many innocent people, but it also is a situation that could be used as a lever for a revolution by mobilizing their frustration and anger.

4.7.1   Labelling the poor

For Simmel, the poor emerge when society recognizes poverty as a special status, as people requiring assistance. It is only from the moment that some official organization or some voluntary association starts to help the poor that they become part of a specific category. In his view, a collective labelling process that gets objectified by actual help keeps this category united. Poverty cannot be defined in itself as a quantitative state, but only in terms of the social reaction resulting from a specific situation. In Simmel's view, poverty is a sociological phenomenon that refers to people who occupy a specific economic position within the whole; but this social position is not determined by this fate and condition, but rather by the fact that others attempt to correct this condition.[69] In fact, this goes even further, because such systems tend to make a sharp distinction between the 'deserving' and the 'undeserving' poor. For instance, widows with children tend to be viewed as 'deserving' poor, whereas single teenage mothers often are labelled as 'undeserving' poor, because they behave in an irresponsible way.[70]

I think that Simmel would have reacted positively to V.S. Naipaul's sharp observations of India. In 1962, when Naipaul visited the land of his ancestors for the first time, he could never overlook the fact that India was shockingly poor. He found the squalor revolting. But later, when he returned for the second or third time, he also observed:

> The smiles on the faces of begging children, that domestic group among the pavement sleepers waking in the cool Bombay morning, father, mother and baby in a trinity of love, so self-contained that they are as private as if walls had separated them from you; it is your gaze that violates them, your sense of outrage that outrages them.[71]

In countries where begging is a normal occupation, beggars believe that they have a right to receive alms. This idea might be underlined by religious rules or duties. For instance, Muslims are obliged to give alms to the poor. To them, *zakat* is a sign of piety and a means for receiving God's grace.[72] In a secular world the beggar addresses his demands to the individual on the basis of the solidarity of mankind. Where aid to the poor has its *raison d'être* in the organic link between all members of society or between all humans, the rights of the receivers are more strongly emphasized than when it is based on religion. Then the obligations of the givers are stressed. In the latter case, the motive for alms resides exclusively in the significance of giving for the giver. Then almsgiving represents no more than a form of 'good works' which paves the way to heaven. Simmel hypothesized that the rise of begging in the Middle Ages was a consequence of the senseless distribution of alms. Arbitrary donations to the poor undermined all creative work, so instead of helping the needy, the givers only helped themselves by giving themselves a good feeling and a higher self-esteem.

Simmel was rather cynical about assistance to the poor. In his view, a view shared by many more sociologists, the rich only give aid to the poor to keep them quiet, hoping that this will prevent them from stealing, robbing or killing. The angst that the poor will become active in a destructive way has been a strong impetus for the establishment of welfare systems. Giving aid to the poor is not an end in itself. It is not intended to end poverty per se, but first and foremost, it is aimed at maintaining order and safeguarding the well being of the better off.[73] Even within the family there are many acts of assistance, not for the sake of the recipient, but so that the family need not be ashamed and lose its reputation because of the poverty of a family member. And the aid that English trade unions granted their unemployed members did not purport so much to alleviate their hardship as to prevent them to accept work more cheaply, which could result in lower wages for the entire trade.[74]

The poor stand outside the group, inasmuch as they are mere objects of the actions of the collective; but, in this case, being outside is only a particular form of being inside. This twofold position of the poor can be found in all members of the group, single or married, educated or illiterate, employed or unemployed. No matter how much individuals may contribute to group life and no matter how strongly their personal life may be tied to the group, they also stand apart from social life. This twofold position, which appears difficult to explain, is a basic social fact. This relationship, this fact of finding oneself simultaneously inside and outside, becomes more and more complicated and more and more visible as the group expands. And this is true not only because the whole then acquires an independence that dominates the individual, but because the most marked differentiations among members of the group lead to a whole scale of nuances within this twofold relationship. Collectivism makes individual persons into objects, into different objects. It treats the poor and the rich differently. Assistance, to which the community is committed in its own interest, makes the poor into objects of the activity of the group and places them at a distance from the whole.[75] This can be emphasized by giving the poor assistance, but also be denying them certain civic rights, e.g. denying them the right to take part in general elections as was common in 19th century or, to take a more recent example, denying the right to marry a spouse from a foreign country if you do not earn enough income to guarantee that your partner will not become dependable of social assistance. In a Durkheimian way we could say that the poor are defined as deviant people to help the middle classes to stay on the straight and narrow. They can give them a good feeling by giving them some aid and also by making them realize that they are far better off. The poor as bogeymen can help parents and teachers with the socialization of children by suggesting that if they are lazy, they will also become poor. In similar vein, uneducated parents will tell their children to work hard at school to ensure a financially better life.

4.8   The goals of feminism

In one of his famous essays, Simmel argued that our culture has become distinctly male instead of human. This situation generates special conflicts that define the predicament of women. It determines the relations between men and women and makes it very difficult to rectify this course of events in a gender-neutral direction. His problem with existing forms of feminism was not if women could perform at the same level as men in the economy, politics, arts and sciences. This would only reinforce an already existing masculine culture. For him, the crucial issue was whether feminism could bring about qualitatively new entities, that are not only a reproduction for women of what already exists for men, but also a creation of objective cultural forms in which the authentic female character is expressed. There were three basic perspectives on gender relations: conservative, liberal and socialist. The conservatives expanded the principle that men and women occupy distinct and mutually exclusive social domains to an ideology that legitimatise the dominant position of men. The exclusion of women from economic and political life was based on a whole set of social, economic, psychological, anatomical and theological arguments. It was believed that the emancipation of women would compromise the authority of the husband and father and would thus demolish the structure of the family. Higher education would turn woman into argumentative and discontented wives. If women would enter the job market, husbands, homes and children would be neglected. Conservatives believed that this was not in line with the intentions of God. Rather conveniently they believed that God had created women to be the assistant of men. Moreover, allowing women to have the same sort of jobs and social roles as men would rob them from their femininity and damage their health.[76]

So, the prevailing conservative doctrine reserved all non-domestic economic production for men, and childcare and household affairs for women, though in the case of upper-middle class women servants performed all these chores. This economic division was closely related to the public/private dichotomy. Men went to their jobs and boys went to school. Women stayed at home. The purpose of female education (at home) was to develop domestic skills and good manners rather than vocational training. All this was related to another doctrine about the separation of the spheres of production and consumption. The men were supposed to be engaged in productive activities outside the home. Thus, in the age of industrialization, most women were confined to the sphere of consumption. This separate-spheres model imposed an ethic of charity, chastity, and sacrifice upon women. The dominant view ascribed cool rationality, authority, and decisiveness to men and emotionality and submissiveness to women.

The exclusion of women from public life, based on the separate-spheres model, has lead to political reactions. Already in 1869 John Stuart Mill advocated a liberal model that stated that there should be perfect equality between the sexes.[77] Mill was convinced that the natural creative capacities of men and women are the same. So, there was no valid reason why women should not have the same rights and opportunities as men. Therefore, women deserve what men already have: the same rights and the same access to public life. Though, Mill granted women the right to also opt for a traditional marriage and family life.

The third model is the socialist model. It embraces the basic ideal of liberalism and its advocacy of equal rights and equal opportunities, but it denied women the right to the ownership of private property or private businesses because the early socialists were against all forms of private property and private businesses. Moreover, they opposed liberalism as an ideology that legitimated capitalism, with its inherent exploitation of men and women alike. In their view, men as well as women had to be liberated from capitalist oppression.[78] The socialists believed that the liberal form of emancipation would only lead to a partial solution of the problem. At best it would slightly improve but not eliminate the economic dependence of women. Therefore, the general aim of the emancipation of women should be directed at the transformation of the capitalist order, to eradicate both wage slavery, which greatly affected working women and (marital) sex slavery, which, in their view, is intimately connected with property rights and industrial-capitalism. The draw back for socialist feminists was that they felt obliged to give higher priority to the greater goal of the class struggle, because, as dogma would have it, the unavoidable and successful class struggle would solve everything, including sex discrimination.

Simmel rejected all three models because they all reduce femininity to one aspect. The conservatives subordinate femininity to motherhood, whereas the liberals and socialists take feminist ideals solely from the basic dreams of economic and political equality. For Simmel, being a woman is a specific form of life that is neither equal to masculinity, nor just motherhood. Quite another problem is that the negative effects of male domination obscure authentic femininity. The fundamental relativity in the life of our species lies in the relationship between masculinity and femininity. We assess the achievements and commitments, the intensity and structural forms of the nature of men and women by reference to certain norms. But, as we know, within almost all existing societies these norms are not gender-neutral. On the contrary, they themselves are of a male nature.[79] The male acquires the status of the generally human, governing the phenomena of the individual male and female in the same way. In various media, this fact is grounded in the power position of men.

> ... [W]omen – their accomplishments, convictions and the practical and theoretical contents of their lives – encounter the absolute standard (which is formed by the criteria that are valid for men). At the same time, this absolute standard is juxtaposed or opposed to a relative standard that is no less a consequence of the male prerogative and often imposes demands that are antithetical to it. This is because the man requires from the woman what is pleasing to him in his capacity as a self-interested party and in his polar relationship to her.[80]

For the sake of the argument, Simmel quite grossly equated the relationship between the sexes as that between master and slave. He was convinced that the master does not always need to think about the fact that he is master. The position of the slave, on the other hand, ensures that he can never forget that he is a slave. Likewise, a woman can never forget that she is in an inferior position. The man as master does not take as vital an interest in his relationship to the female as the woman must do in her relationship to the male. As a result, the expressions of the male nature are easily transposed into the sphere of trans-specific, neutral objectivity and validity. Most judgments, institutions, aspirations and interests which men naively regard as simply objective and gender-neutral are thoroughly and characteristically male.[81]

From time immemorial, domination by oppression has made it its business to provide itself with an objective justification: in short, to transform might into right. The history of politics, the priesthood, forms of the economy, the law of the family, all these are full of examples of this process. The fact that the masculine has become the objective and impartial standard of authority has fateful consequences for the valuation of women. Either they are viewed as angels or devils, as loving and caring mothers or as sinful whores and seducers. On the one hand, we see a mystifying overestimation of women. On the other hand, all misunderstandings and underestimations are a consequence of judging women according to criteria that are created for an antithetical being. On this basis, the autonomy of the female principle cannot be acknowledged at all. As long as this is the case, the emancipation of women remains an unfinished business.

4.9   Conflicts, competition and domination

Marx and Simmel developed contrasting and complementary theories of social conflict. Marx was politically motivated to understand and eradicate capitalism. Simmel did not have such a great passion for social change, let alone revolution.[82] Both Marx and Simmel used the concept of 'dialectics'. From a dialectical perspective, any given set of social relations contains its opposite. 'Goodness' only takes on meaning in reference to 'badness'. And 'order' implicitly makes reference to 'disorder'. In Simmel's view, there probably exists no social unit in which the tendencies for order and disorder, for convergence and divergence, are not inseparably interwoven. An absolutely centripetal and harmonious group is unreal – it might as well be dead – whereas conflicts are sure signs of life.

4.9.1   The civilizing function of competition

Some violent acts that are committed simply for the satisfaction of the desire to behave violently seem to exclude all forms of sociation. If, however, there is any consideration for the other party, if there is any restraint to violence, then there already exists a socializing factor. It is almost inevitable that an element of sharing and commonness injects itself into the mutual hatred or animosity once the stage of open violence yields to negotiations about the ending of the conflict. And even if the conflict ends in a clear victory of one group over the other, this will lead to some union of interests. Even slavery produces a sociological condition in which people have to co-operate. Hence, quite frequently, it produces its own mitigation. Thus, divergence and harmony become inextricably interconnected. [83]

Competition in commerce, politics and sports always involves many socially interconnected participants. Many kinds of interests, which eventually hold the group together, seem to come and stay alive by way of competitive struggles. Yet, usually analysts stress the poisonous, divisive and destructive effects of competition. Modern competition is described as the fight of all against all, but Simmel indicated that it often is a fight of all *for* all. It has immense socializing effects. Nobody will overlook the squandering of resources. The overkill of ads in the media is one case in point. But one should also acknowledge that competition creates an immense cohesive force. It is a wrestling for applause, admiration, devotion, support and other kinds of rewards. It is a wrestling of the few for the many, as well as a fight of the many for the few. In short, it is a web of a thousand sociological threads by means of conscious concentration on the will, feeling and thinking of fellow men. It is an intricate process of the adaptation of the producers to the consumers, of the multiplied possibilities of gaining favour and connection.

The socializing power of competition not only shows itself in the coarser, public cases, but also within families and love relationships. We find two parties competing for a third in numerous relationships. We find it in heated debates over ideological convictions and observe it when people engage in social small talk. Whenever it occurs, the antagonism of the competitors is paralleled by some offering, beguiling, coaxing, promising or imposing, which sets each of them in relation to the third party. For the victor in particular, this relation often attains an intensity, which it would not have without the excitement of the competition and continuous comparison of his own achievement with that of the other.[84]

Man's most valuable object is man. The human being is the most condensed, most fruitfully exploitable phenomenon; and the necessity of winning him over grows in the measure in which his mechanical appropriation weakens. To achieve our goal, especially when we fight with someone else for a third party, be it a lover, a friend, a boss or a prospective client, this can be achieved in a thousand ways, through the means of persuasion or conviction, surpassing or underselling, through suggestion or threat, in short, through social-psychological connection. But just as often, this winning over also means the founding of a relationship – from the momentary relation established by a purchase in a shop to the more enduring relationship of a marriage. So, according to Simmel, as the intensity and complexity of social life increases, the struggle for the most condensed of all goods, the human being, must multiply and deepen interactions that bring individuals together.[85]

4.9.2 *The centralizing function of conflict*

Conflicts are also of great significance for the inner structure of each party itself. Experience shows how a quarrel between two individuals changes each of them. It can distort, purify, weaken or strengthen them. The fighters must also 'pull themselves together'. They have to concentrate all their energies in one point so that they can be used at any moment in any direction that might be required. The same forms of behaviour are required for groups that take part in a struggle. This need for centralization, for the pulling together of all elements, without loss of energy and time, is obvious. Such centralization supersedes even the most perfect forms of democratic decision-making. That's why social organizations, nations, political parties and labour unions quickly change their structure of decision making as soon as the fight get serious. Wars need a centralist, hierarchical organization. For this reason, the organization of the army is the most centralized of all, with the exception perhaps of the fire brigade. The army is the organization in which the unconditional rule of the central authority excludes any dependent movement of the parts. Every order from head quarters must be translated into the movement of the whole without any dynamic loss.[86] If this rule is not obeyed the loss can be terrible.

In his epic book *August 1914* Solzhenitsyn writes, in a fascinating way, how two big Russian armies were slaughtered near the Masurian lakes in East Prussia. The first army was lead by an old general, who only wished to die of old age and not as a hero on the battlefield. Therefore, he interpreted the orders in the most passive form. Instead of urging his troops forward at the demanded speed, he let them move on rather slowly or not at all, while he reported to head quarters that his reconnaissance patrols and advance guards were moving quickly ahead. The other army was lead by a young colonel, who was very eager to advance his career. In contrast, he followed the orders in the most active way and even urged his troops to march forward much quicker than was expected. As a result the two armies were split apart, which dramatically weakened their combined strength. As soon as the general commander of the German army noticed this, he started a ferocious flank attack. The separated armies were defeated quite easily and tens of thousands of Russian soldiers got killed.

4.9.3   *The two sides of authority and domination*

Simmel not only rendered interesting new insights into the structure, dynamics and functions of social conflicts but also shed new light on social relations such as authority and domination. Whatever the degree of inequality or domination, there is always some space for a counter influence by the subordinate party. Even in situations of total repression or subjugation, there is room for mutual interactions. That's why even in these cases Simmel speaks of sociation. The powerful need this mutual relationship. The dominated person has to respond to the wishes and demands of his master. Otherwise this relationship will lose its function. Generally, the power is exerted for a reason. The authoritative person wants to continue this relation in order to make more use of it. If the dominated person refuses to play along, then all is lost. On the other hand, dominated persons must have something to gain from it too. When they truly believe that ending this unfortunate relationship will bring them more harm than continuing it they will not end it. If we condone the suppression by a tyrant, than this is because we fear more negative repercussions of a revolt. Even a tyrant is restricted in his freedom by legal rules and procedures. He cannot sentence people to death or confiscate their possessions at random. In theory and in practice, an absolute monarch can change and remake laws as he likes, but in general he does not do this, because it tends to diminish his authority and enhance the image of a lawless regime and that is an image he wants to avoid. Even dictators want respect of other political leaders. As long as this is the case, the relationship continues and both parties go on 'playing' their roles.

As long as the subordinated accept their position, we can observe a real social relation, a real process of sociation. However, as soon as a leader abuses his subordinated people as means for his own ends, treats them as objects, we can no longer speak of a social relation. For Simmel, once again following Kant, the basic principle of ethics is that one should never use another human being purely as a mere object, though, to a certain degree, all parties use each other. For example, we tend to accept the authority of our boss or chief, because not only he or she has more experience, but also because he or she has the power to influence our income and career. It is possible to restore the balance by making yourself very useful. Then the chief will need you just as much as you need the approval and support of the chief. We should never look at inequality from a one-sided perspective. There is more to it than domination and repression. There are many forms and degrees of inequality. Marxists tend to ignore the aspects of interaction, reciprocity and exchange, but sometimes the roles are reversed. Then followers become leaders and vice versa. For instance, leaders of big democratic parties have to listen carefully to their followers; otherwise they run the risk of losing them. Duke Charles-Maurice de Talleyrand, former Bishop and Minister of Foreign Affairs for Napoleon Bonaparte, once said: 'Look there goes my people. I must follow them, for I am their leader.' In other words, good democratic leaders have to follow their followers, share their main priorities. Otherwise, they will not last long as leader. So, as long as the leader thinks it worthwhile to stay in command and to enjoy the privileges that go with the job, he will lend his ear to his followers, for he depends on the support of his followers.

4.9.4   Forms of leadership and group cohesion

Simmel distinguished three forms of domination: a person, a group or a principle. In his analysis, he combined this formal characteristic with other formal aspects, such as the consensus or disagreement that can exist within groups or the degree of hierarchy in the organization. It matters whether the chief or leader is an insider or an outsider. It also matters whether there is more than one leader. Clearly, when there are more leaders the subordinated possess more opportunities to realize more freedom. Think of children who play off their parents against each other because they have learned that they disagree on some aspects of pedagogy. On the other hand, when both parents act as a unit, they will have more authority over their children.

The submission of a group to one person often leads to increased coherence of the group. This is true for the unity of the group against its leader or for the unity between the group and the leader. For example, if the leader of a political party follows the prevailing ideas of the group but tends to shape them more clearly, this will enhance social cohesion. The creation of a clear distance between group members and the leader can also enhance unity. In this case all members want to get near the leader, but simultaneously keep a watchful eye at each other to maintain the same respectful distance. Of course, differences in social distance to the leader will arise. And thus a hierarchy will develop that can produce greater stability.

The degree of resistance against the leader is also of great importance. Opposition tends to unite the revolutionary group. It is generally believed that a common enemy unites individuals. This is even more so when the common enemy is the leader of the group. Human beings are double dealers in cases of submission. Many people like to be lead and to have someone who decides for them. Also many people need somebody or some organization that sets limits, that steers their actions and is prepared to act sternly whenever this is asked for. They need an organization or an authority that protects them against dangers from outside, but also from dangers from within, against their own unrestrained instincts. Other people hate the authorities, almost automatically resist their leaders and protest against any show of social control. But it is precisely because of this counter pressure that the powerful leader gets more power and becomes more meaningful as a social actor. This situation also helps to mark borderlines more clearly. According to Simmel, not shunning away from psychological assumptions, humans are endowed with both drives. They need both motives to discover and fix their own identity as a leader or a subject.

> *Occasionally the consciousness of being under coercion, of being subject to a super-ordinate authority, is revolting or oppressive – whether the authority is an ideal or a social law, an arbitrarily-decreeing personality or the executor of higher norms. But for the majority of men, coercion is probably an irreplaceable support and cohesion of the inner and outer life.*[87]

4.10   The philosophy and sociology of money

Simmel tended to view society from below, that is, from the perspective of a frog. Doing so, he brilliantly captured the spirit of the times in *The Philosophy of Money*. His friend and colleague Karl Joël said that this book was bound to a single place and a single period, but yet, projected the soul of modern Berlin onto a universal level.[88] It certainly is a landmark in the field of cultural sociology. Therefore, the title is misleading. Though it definitely it contains many philosophical analyses, the book could just as well have been titled *Sociology of Money*, for it deals extensively with the social implications of economic behaviour. Simmel showed that the transition from a traditional system of barter towards a moncy economy had many important consequences, which reached much further than mere economic actions. He characterized modernity as one dominated by money that dumbfounds everything into mere nuances of its own impure colour. To a significant degree we are dominated by money. There is no doubt about it. Money tends to determine everything. Therefore, special attention is given to the question of what are the essential characteristics of money, why did it change economic proceedings so dramatically that it also changed social life completely, including the culture of societies and the mindsets of individuals.

4.10.1   *What is money?*

The system of pure barter could only blossom in times of scarcity. The introduction of money changed everything. Money can be divided in small equal units of the same value. This makes it very practical. Also money is impersonal. It is very different from real objects to which we might have become attached because we have worked very hard to construct them or have inherited them from one of our loved ones. Hence, it is a means that can be used very easily for economic transactions. Money enhances calculation. It is the symbol and the incarnation of the spirit of rationalism. In a money economy social relations tend to become more impersonal. Besides, it speeds up all kinds of business transactions, which enhances personal freedom. Imagine that money was not invented yet and you would like to purchase a bed from someone. But he wants a good horse in return and you do not possess a horse. To achieve your goal, you would have to exchange something with somebody else who has a good horse. It is very likely that you need other swapping transactions to acquire the bed. It would involve many social interactions with people with whom you are familiar, whom you trust and who might expect help from you whenever they get involved in a similar complex transaction that involves a similar chain of exchanges to fix the deal. So, it is easy to see why a money economy is more efficient, more abstract, and less personal and creates more freedom.

Money substitutes durable connections of 'natural' social groups by voluntary (temporal) relations. It also has an egalitarian effect. It puts different things and services at the same level of a financial scale. People with very different professions might earn the same salary. Clearly the introduction of money had significant repercussions for social relations. People became less dependent on their families. After the invention of money people could take economic decisions much more easily. When social relations are being mediated by the sale and purchase of goods in exchange for money, then no longer we are personally dependent on other people. All relations become impersonal and social fragmentation grows rampant. Persons become replaceable. No longer are we interested in the typical personal qualities of a dentist or a plumber. Personal qualities become relative. Does the worth of a baker depend on the quality of his bread, on the prices he asks for his products, on his communicative skills and his personal interest for his customers? For Simmel, only transactions for money have that character of a fleeting relationship that leaves no traces. In particular this is the case with prostitution. By giving money the whore-hopper completely distances him from the relationship. They have settled matters more completely than by presenting a gift, which, by its contents, its selection and its use, maintains a wisp of the personality of the giver. Hence, only money is an appropriate equivalent to the momentary satisfaction of the desire served by prostitutes. Money is never an adequate means in a relationship between persons that hinges on duration and integrity – like love, even when it is only for a short time. But money serves the purpose of getting sexual pleasure most matter-of-factly and completely. In prostitution, the relation is reduced to its generic content. It is limited to the natural act. Individual differences are of no importance. Therefore, the perfect economic counterpart of this relation is money, for it, too, is beyond all individual differences. It can represent any object or service. The indifference with which it lends itself to any use, the infidelity with which it leaves everyone, its lack of ties to anyone, and its complete objectification that excludes any attachment and makes it suitable as a pure means – all this suggests a striking resemblance between the nature of money and the nature of prostitution. The debasement of prostitution lies in the fact that the most personal possession of a woman is considered equivalent to the most neutral value of all, one that is most remote from anything that is personal.[89]

4.10.2   Values and valuations

Simmel started his study of money with an analysis about value. The physical world does not know good from bad. Only humans categorize things into good or bad. The lion that kills his prey is no better or worse than the cow that eats grass. The sea is not better than the land. Evaluation is a strictly human thing. For us, something gets value as soon as we want it or desire it. Because all people have many needs and desires, they continuously busy themselves with valuing objects, events and relations. But this valuation is subjective. Not everyone likes the sun and high temperatures; some prefer a cloudy sky and cool weather. At the same time that farmers hope that it will start raining after a long period of drought, others hope that it will stay dry.

Economic transactions create a field of values that is completely disconnected from the subjective personal values. It does not matter at all what the 'real' value is of an object. The only thing that matters is the price that has to be paid for it at the market, that dynamic institution that has emerged out of countless individual transactions of exchange. Any price is the outcome of the law of supply and demand. The decision to buy or to sell is a process of weighing many arguments in which all kinds of subjective and social values play a major role. For Simmel these economic exchanges are no different from any other transaction of exchange. In fact, each interaction with a fellow human being is a form of exchange. It involves the investment of time. It entails skills to interact with other people and to gather and exchange information about the social value of various objects and services. It encompasses much more than the cost of labour or the costs of production. Hence, Simmel clearly disagrees with Marx. For him, in a way, money is the most pure incarnation of all that exists. Things get their meaning from their relation to other things. The value of goods does not depend on the inherent quality of these goods or the cost of its production, but on the relations between things, on the relative position of things. The value of a good or a service on a particular day depends on the mix of priorities, preferences and solvability of all the buyers and sellers in the marketplace.

Maybe money is a very mundane, even vulgar phenomenon. But in Simmel's view it symbolizes the essential structure of our reality. The philosophical meaning of money is that it constitutes the clearest image and the best incorporation of our existence. It signifies how the value of things and services are related to each other. The value is not fixed in the 'essential' quality of an object, but in our evaluation of that quality. If evaluations change so will market prices. The market is the economic-historical realization of the relativity of the value of goods.

4.10.3   *Modernity and money*

To Simmel, the hallmark of modernity was the continuing transience of everything. Nothing remains. Everything changes; blossoms wither away and are substituted by something else: fashions and fads in cars, clothing, couches and popular music, whatever. Art and architecture seem to demand a continuous process of revaluation, innovation and creative destruction. And the most transient of all is money. Its value changes everyday. Inflation rates can oscillate and the same is true for interest rates. Share prizes can be very volatile as economic crises emerge or end. Old economic powers suddenly start to dwindle and get surpassed by emerging economies. Strong companies can get into financial trouble as a consequence of their own doing or because they are entangled with other companies that have made wrong decisions and got into great debt. And when big businesses get into trouble, also many small businesses will feel the pain and might go bankrupt. All this might change for the better after these companies have solved their financial problems, have reorganized their firm in a rational way and have started to grow and make profit again.

Simmel already envisioned money as pure action, pure movement, long before the Internet was invented and cash could flow all over the world in a matter of seconds. Money that lays idle, sits in a piggy bank, lies in a pot under the floor, largely loses its function. It does not even gain interest. One should put the money in a savings account and collect some interest or invest it in attractive financial transactions to make money with money. But virtual profits have to be cashed in on time to turn them into real profits; otherwise they can vanish into thin air.

4.10.4   *A modern view on the modernity of the past*

Reading some of Simmel's insightful descriptions of one century ago gives us the feeling that he is describing modernizing trends of our own day and age. Therefore, his work still is highly relevant. In his renewed essay on the famous French sculptor Rodin he said that searching for psychological explanations is the essence of modernity. Never before, so much emphasis was being put on experiencing and interpreting the world in terms of inner feelings. Never before, we have witnessed such a striking transformation of fixed contents in ephemeral elements of the soul, from which all substance is filtered out and which forms merely are forms of movement.[90] He focused on a whole array of emotions: love, greed, trust and distrust, gratitude, boredom, getting cynic, feeling blasé or alienated. Especially boredom and feeling blasé are consequences of modernity. In particular inhabitants of big cities are feeling blasé. They have seen it all and experienced everything. They have witnessed all kinds of awesome events and spectacular festivities. And each time, it was more awesome and more spectacular than before. Finally the spectacular has become normal. Boredom is also connected to modern labour organizations. Each day large groups of people have to do the same productive activities in a rhythm of its own, a rhythm that is not connected with the course of the day or the change of the seasons. The implication of this description is that modernity gets identified with the weakening of our contact with the external world and the reinforcement of our inner experiences. The modern experience is transformed from a concrete and conscious historical experience to a fluent, ephemeral, individual inner experience.[91] Modernity turns all our earlier experiences of time, location and causality upside down and changes them into temporality, stopovers and contingency. Thus modernity stands into sharp contrast with Antiquity and the Middle Ages. In these periods change came too slowly to get noticed. Methods of government and production hardly altered through many centuries. Yet, there was not much room for boredom, because of the struggle for life, just above or below the subsistence level, demanded everyone's permanent alertness.

4.11   Conclusions

During his entire academic career Simmel moved from one topic to the next, from one line of reasoning to another. Ortega y Gasset compared him to a squirrel, graciously jumping from tree to tree, always on the lookout for fresh and shiny nuts, scarcely bothering to nibble much at any of them. His refusal to restrict himself to only one discipline worried many of the settled professors. His originality, his sparkling intellect and his ability to move with great ease from one topic to another affronted most of his colleagues and superiors. They felt that only sustained application to one or at most a small number of specific problems suited academic work. In their view any worthwhile scholarship required hard and deep digging, instead of a quick scanning of unexplored fields. But in Simmel's case his versatility did not imply a lack of depth or originality. On the contrary, his contribution to philosophy, the methodology of history, to ethics and to the social sciences shows otherwise. His work in sociology consists of a close scrutiny of many facets of social life.[92] His approach can best be understood as a self-conscious rejection of the organicist realism of Comte, Spencer and Schäf-fle and the ideographic method of German humanities. The organicist approach stressed the fundamental continuity between nature and society. Life was conceived as a great chain of being, stretching from the single-celled organisms to the most highly differentiated social organism. From this perspective it was entirely natural to apply the methods of natural science to social science. Of course, idealistic philosophers vigorously opposed this idea. In their view, the humanities differed qualitatively from physics. Therefore natural laws had no place in the study of social phenomena. They argued that sociology had no real, tangible object of study. There is no society outside or in addition to the individuals who compose it. Simmel rejected both schools of thought. For him society is an intricate web of multiple relations established among constantly interacting individuals. The major field of study is association and the supra-individual structures – the state, the family, the city, the political party and the business organization - that are the crystallizations of these patterned interactions.

Though Simmel considered these larger structures a legitimate field of sociological inquiry, he preferred to restrict most of his work to investigations of what he called 'interactions among the atoms of society'. He focused on the relatively durable and, in his view, limited number of forms that such interactions might take.[93] In Simmel's perspective a host of otherwise distinct social phenomena might be properly understood by reference to the same formal concept. For instance you can not only find various sectarian forms within religious movements, but also in revolutionary cells and in small groups of artists that are devoted to one style work only.

In his last book he celebrated the ultimate victory of life over form, of movement over stasis. Now that he was living under the shadow of death he conceived of life as 'an irreversible current in which each moment dissolves into the next.'[94] However, this last attempt to develop a comprehensive vitalistic orientation did not serve to unify his work. Because he was unable to develop a consistent and coherent sociological system, it is not surprising that he did not lay the foundation for a Simmel school of sociologists. Nevertheless, his influence can be found in various places and with many sociologists who have made ample use of his seminal ideas. The modern critique of mass culture and mass society owes a huge though often unacknowledged debt to Simmel. Moreover, he has added noticeable contributions to Marx and Durkheim's discussions on alienation and anomie. As Raymond Aron and others have pointed out, the author of *The Stranger* is among the foremost commentators of the isolation, uprootedness, pliability and flexibility of modern men. His work gave a major impulse to the urban sociologists of *The Chicago School*. He has paved the way to many studies into the personalities and lifestyles of modern city dwellers and the social distance that can emerge between different categories of people. Robert Merton has acknowledged that Simmel's writings were the most fruitful for the development of theory of reference groups.[95]

His formal method, by which he attempted to transcend concrete events with abstract formal categories, led in Germany to a formalistic form of sociology that lacked his sparkle and brilliance. His search for forms did not inspire American sociology, with the exception of some work in sociography. Simmel's mark on macro sociology is more difficult to trace, though it definitely exists. For instance Lewis Coser's *The Functions of Social Conflict* constituted, in large part, an effort to systematize and extend Simmel's insights into the subject.[96] His systematic use of the concept of social role in classical essays on the role of the stranger, the actor or the mediator laid the foundation for its extensive use in sociology, from which it quickly spilled over into daily life and our collective conscience.

David Frisby has reintroduced Simmel in modern sociology by giving him the clothes of a post-modernist *avant le lettre*. The incorporation of Simmel's essay-istic and impressive oeuvre on lifestyles, fashion, taste, city life and art certainly sits well in the eclectic domain of postmodernism. Simmel and contemporary post-modernists seem to share the same interest in these kinds of topics. Howev-er, Simmel's attempt to find formal concepts that could transcend the supposedly ephemeral character of any modern era does not square with the postmodern idea that we definitely have lost all belief in grand narratives and general theories. No matter what can be said about this, it is undeniable that Simmel has enriched sociology with many sharp insights, intriguing concepts and inspiring ideas. The fact that his work has been kept in the shadow for so long should surprise us more than the renewed interest in his work.

5
MAX WEBER

THE LAST HOMO UNIVERSALIS
OF SOCIOLOGY

Karl Emil Maximillian Weber, better known as Max Weber, was the first and the last *homo universalis* of sociology. He brilliantly covered a wide range of topics and added new methods to address the special character of the social sciences. His interpretative method entailed an approach to understanding that explicitly reckons with the specific cultural and historical context of social actions and the meanings individuals attach to their actions. He also introduced the method of constructing so-called ideal types. The objective was to describe social structures and processes in a cleverly summarized way that focuses on the elements, aspects or characteristics that are most crucial for producing fruitful insights.

Following the usual format, we begin with a short biography. Section 5.2 contains a discussion of Weber's teachings in the field of methodology and epistemology. Here we see how he tried to bridge the gap between the methods of the natural sciences and the specific requirements for studying cultural sciences. He did not reject the claims and demands of positive science, but added what needed to be added. Section 5.3 addresses his four ideal types of social action: instrumental-rational, value rational, affective behaviour and traditional actions. This section also highlights his major topic of sociological concern, the process of ever-expanding rationalization that manifests itself in many forms such as bureaucratization, depersonalization and a growing mastering of nature. Section 5.4 discusses his analysis of the spirit of capitalism, which shows a close connection with the growing impact of rational thinking and action. Section 5.5 shows how he applied his methodological views in *The Protestant Ethic and the Spirit of Capitalism*. This seminal study brilliantly explains how the Protestant Ethic, as the common believers practised it, perfectly fitted the ethos of capitalism. This study also showed that this match between modern capitalism and Protestantism as it was acted out in daily life emerged despite the fact that some of the major doctrines of the Christian faith went against materialism and the objective to become rich. This study alerted all sociologists that conscious human actions could have all kinds of unintended consequences. Section 5.6 charts some interesting aspects of his political sociology, focussing on the rationalization of government and on his three ideal types of authority: traditional, charismatic and legal-rational. The next section presents his ideal typical analysis of bureaucracy. Section 5.8 presents his view on social order. Section 5.9 covers his three dimensional approach to social inequality. He argued that inequality not only is an issue of big differences in income, but that it also has important political and cultural dimensions. The chapter ends with some concluding remarks.

5.1   Biography and academic career

Max Weber was born in Erfurt, on 21 April 1864. He was the eldest of eight children. Alfred, one of his younger brothers, also became a famous sociologist. His mother, Helene Fallenstein, was well educated. She had a keen interest in cultural and intellectual affairs, and an open eye for the problems of the poor. She lived a sober and ascetic life, fully in accordance with her strong Calvinistic beliefs. Taking care of her family was her greatest priority. Max Senior was a distinguished lawyer and politician. He was a member of parliament for the National Liberal Party. In many ways he differed from his wife. He was harsh, self-assured, authoritarian, and hedonistic. Frequently, the difference of character gave rise to tensions in the family. These tensions increased sharply after Max's younger sister Helen suddenly died of diphtheria when she was only four years old. Max's mother mourned Helen's loss profoundly and could not understand that her husband was able to take up his old ways, as if nothing had happened.

At grammar school, Max was a precocious student. He learned several foreign languages and took a great interest in Ancient History. Intellectually, he was extremely talented, though physically he was very weak. Reading academic books became his refuge. At secondary school, he studied them like a real student, writing extensive summaries and making critical notes.[1] He understood and knew everything. Fortunately, the friends and relatives of his parents stimulated him intellectually. Among them were several important politicians, professors, and clergymen, whose discussions he followed with great interest. The political discussions gave him a good insight into German politics. Like his father, he learned to appreciate *Realpolitik,* that is, a feel for the practical feasibility of political ideas. He abhorred the unrealistic demands of left- and right-wing extremists, but did not feel at home in the political midfield either.[2]

In 1882, he enrolled as a student of law at Heidelberg University. There he participated in student life and started to drink heavily. Overnight, he lost his timidity and learned to socialize with people from all walks of life. Once, he was challenged to fight a duel and was scarred in the face as a result. In that day and age, such a scar was a highly valued sign of masculinity. He befriended his cousin Otto Baumgarten, who studied theology. In 1883, he had to interrupt his studies for military service. He was posted at Strasbourg, where he often visited his aunt and uncle, Ida and Hermann Baumgarten. Soon, he fell deeply in love with their daughter Emma. His uncle held a chair in history and Max made a point of attending his lectures; his uncle, in turn, became Weber's political and intellectual mentor.[3] After being discharged from service, he continued his studies in Berlin, where his behaviour changed dramatically. He took up an ascetic lifestyle, stayed away from most feasts and parties, and studied like a man possessed. He developed the rigorous working habit that would serve him throughout his academic career. In Heidelberg, his lifestyle resembled that of his father; in Berlin, it was much more in line with that of his mother.

Until 1889, he put all his energy into his thesis on the medieval history of commercial companies. The quality of this study was so high that the famous historian and Nobel Prize winner Theodor Mommsen declared that Weber should become his successor.[4] In the meantime, his academic interests had shifted to other disciplines such as political economy and sociology. In his *Habilitationsschrift*, a study on the history of agricultural institutions, he presented a sociological, economic, and cultural analysis of Ancient society.

In 1894, he accepted a professorship in political economy at the University of Freiburg. This made him financially independent. He married his cousin Marianne Schnitger, the granddaughter of his father's eldest brother. Of course, this meant a definitive and somewhat painful separation from his first love, Emma. Marianne resembled his mother in many ways, but in sexual matters she was even more puritanical. To her, the sexual part of the marital relation was a 'heavy sacrifice'. The lack of sexual fulfilment could explain why Weber later became involved in extra-marital relationships.[5] The marriage remained childless. In 1896, Weber was called to Heidelberg to succeed Karl Knies, a leading figure of the historical school of political economy. There he took on a heavy workload. Each week, he lectured for many hours and also taught seminars. When Marianne once urged him to take things easier, he remarked: 'If I do not work until one o'clock every night, I cannot be a professor.' In Heidelberg, Weber befriended several famous colleagues such as Georg Jellinek, the constitutional lawyer, Ernst Troeltsch, the theologian, and Wilhelm Windelband, the philosopher. Frequently he met and argued with sociologists such as Robert Michels, Werner Sombart, Ferdinand Tönnies, and Georg Lukács. The home of the Weber family became the meeting place for Heidelberg intellectuals.

Weber always took a great interest in political affairs and activities. He was a member of the National Socialist Group and also took part in the Christian-Social movement. In 1897, he declined the offer of a parliamentary candidacy in Saarbrücken, making it clear that his scholarly work took precedence. However, his academic career would soon be damaged by unfortunate personal developments. In the same year, he had a serious argument with his father. The dispute was over his father's bullying behaviour towards his mother. Soon after this unhappy event, his father went on a trip to Riga where he died suddenly on August 10. Understandably, Max felt guilty that they had parted in this fashion. Soon he began to display signs of mental and physical exhaustion. The symptoms were physical weakness, sleeplessness, inner tension, pangs of conscience, bouts of anxiety, and continual restlessness. After a slight improvement, he started working again, but found his teaching activities too strenuous. In 1898, at the end of the spring semester, he suffered a nervous breakdown. A trip to Lake Geneva and a stay at a sanatorium on Lake Constance improved his health, but not enough to prevent a new nervous breakdown at Christmas. It took more than six years before he was able to lecture again, and still many more years before he was completely recovered.[6]

Gradually he resumed reading history books and historical documents, and further occupied himself with art history and philosophy. He also studied Simmel's *Philosophy of Money*. In studying economic history, Weber came across the theme of rationality in economic life. He started to write long essays, but could not manage to teach full terms. Hence, he felt that he did not deserve a full salary. In October 1903, he resigned his teaching post and became honorary professor. Fortunately, an inheritance from his deceased grandfather helped to solve his financial problems. During these years, Weber travelled a great deal, visiting Corsica, Florence, Rome, southern Italy, France, Holland, and Switzerland. In 1904, he went to America to attend a scientific world congress on the occasion of the World Exhibition in St. Louis. He travelled around the United States for several months and received much inspiration for new essays.[7]

Randall Collins and others have presented various possible explanations for Weber's severe mental problems and physical illnesses. Firstly, there is mention of an oedipal complex. Max, who dearly loved his mother, felt he had somehow killed his father. Another explanation states that he never resolved his loyalty conflict towards his two very different parents. This problem may have served as an ideal breeding ground for mental illness. A third possible explanation points to sexual frustration. For many years, he compensated a lack of sexual fulfilment in his marriage with heroic ethics and an ascetic lifestyle, but around 1893, while still in Freiburg, he developed a close relationship with his student, Else von Richthofen, Marianne's closest friend. After Weber's death, she confessed that the friendship had become a sexual relationship, but this probably did not happen until 1917. Before it came to that, Weber had formed an intimate relation with Mina Tobler, who began to play a significant role in his life in 1911. She not only aroused his interest in fine arts and music, but also rekindled his sexual feelings and contributed to the relaxation of his moral rigour.[8]

During the first Great War, Weber served briefly in the army. He was assigned to manage military hospitals. Here, he observed the workings of a bureaucracy run by amateurs. Nonetheless, he worked hard to increase their efficiency. Meanwhile, Weber became highly critical of the policies decreed by Kaiser Wilhelm. Though he had been a monarchist all his life, his insights now forced him in the direction of the republicans. The war turned into a disaster for Germany, and the people became more rebellious and demanded the removal of the emperor. The latter was forced to take refuge in The Netherlands. Weber participated in a political movement that strove for peace through negotiations and was a member of the delegation that went to Versailles to negotiate the conditions for surrender.

After the war, Weber again became very active. He gave impressive lectures on topics such as *Science as Vocation* and *Politics as Vocation* at the Universities of Munich and Vienna. Alas, this period of activity did not last long. In 1920, Weber fell ill with pneumonia and died on the 14th of June.

5.2   Weber's methodology and epistemology

In comparison to other masters of sociology, Weber has published many texts on method. Yet he was always eager to point out that a strong emphasis on methodology could become a curse instead of a blessing. To him, real progress is achieved by the discovery and solution of substantial problems. Nonetheless, the material object of the social sciences strongly differs from that of the natural sciences. This begs serious questions about the intelligibility of cultural phenomena and the adequacy of the use of methods and criteria developed in physics. Starting with the acknowledgement that social reality is very complex and historically contingent, he arrived at two methods to come to grips with that reality: (1) the construction of *Ideal Types* and (2) the introduction of the method of *Interpretative Understanding (Verstehen)*. His position led to many misunderstandings. Whereas some accuse him of a close alliance with positivism, others blame him for being too much engaged in a historicist's orientation to cultural meaning and the uniqueness of social facts and historical events. Actually, he always tried to find a set of methods that would take care of the special problems posed by human consciousness and individual will and also fulfil some of the rigorous demands of the natural sciences. As long as one claims the predicate scientific, one has to accept that proofs have to be delivered with the help of sound reasoning and strict methods. Hence, Weber scorned those 'soft-minded humanists,' who sailed around such intellectual rigour and relied solely on emphatic understanding and intuition. Emphatic understanding and intuition may lead to new and potentially fruitful ideas, but these ideas have to be tested with the help of 'hard' methods, to turn them in valid scientific insights. Randall Collins links the sharp contrast between Max Weber's parents with his theory of knowledge.[9] The mother functions as the model for idealism or historicism, whereas the father functions as the typical model for realism and the methods of the natural sciences.

As we know, German idealistic philosophy started with Immanuel Kant. He introduced epistemological idealism. According to Kant, all that we can know is mediated through our ideas. He does not deny that there is an external, material world, but contends that we can never know '*das Ding an sich*' *(the thing in itself)*, for we can only observe the world through the lenses of our conceptual framework.[10] Weber fully agreed. He, too, was convinced that we would never learn anything that was disconnected from the concepts we applied to reality. Moreover, we could never learn all there was to know about a thing completely and precisely. This was all the more true if that 'thing' was social, for social reality was and is constituted by an infinite, apparently chaotic set of concrete events, dispersed over numerous people, social interactions, geographical locations, and historical time spans. For that reason, scientists should always attempt to select meaningful patterns from the overwhelming multiplicity of phenomena with the help of ideas that they have already gathered and incorporated in their mind. However, there is a slight problem. All social scientists do not share the same

The discovery of the water mole

In 1798, the physical scientist Dobson studied the stuffed skin of a small animal that Australian colonizers called a water mole. The first specimen that was found was the size of a mole. It had tiny eyes, a dark brown furry skin and a beaver tail. It was very flat and web-footed, but the five toes on its forefeet had claws. Therefore, it could swim with its feet and dig a hole as well. It stayed under water for long periods for foraging, but had to surface for air. In that respect it resembled a fish or an amphibian. The female laid eggs, but breastfed their young, although no nipples could be observed. It was billed like a duck. For all these reasons, it was very hard to classify. The tail reminded the scientists of a beaver, the skin, body, and claws reminded them of a mole and the beak resembled that of a duck. Many years later, new specimens became available for study, but it still was hard to understand what type of animal it really was. Though it breastfed its young, breast glands and nipples could not be found. In 1824, however, Johann F. Meckel discovered mammalian glands. In fact, they cover the whole body, but become visible only during the period of breastfeeding. Thus, it was a mammal after all. Yet it did lay it eggs, and the oviduct did not end in a womb but in a cloaca like that of birds. The debate on the correct classification of this animal, a creature

which averaged about 50 centimetres in length, went on for many years and was finally decided by William Hay Caldwell in 1884, who classified these animals as *monotremes oviparous, ovum meroblastic*. This classification made clear that this was a rare species that combined the characteristics of mammals with those of reptiles and birds. This case splendidly illustrates that observations can be put into words only if we are in the possession of the right frame of reference, that is, only if we have the right concepts. Every new observation has to be fitted in an existing system of categories. But if this fit is a bit awkward, it will induce us to change our system of categories to reach a better match between theory and observations. As soon as we have opted for the category mammal, scientists are motivated to look for characteristics that are typical for mammals. Other scientists who wondered about the birdlike or reptile-like characteristics went searching for further proof to bolster their claims. The history of the discovery and classification of the duckbilled platypus clearly shows that at the end of the day observed facts will overrule wrong theories. It also shows, as the philosopher Charles Pierce would have it, that the torch of truth goes from hand to hand. Doing science resembles running a relay race.[12]

Box 5.1

culturally shaped set of basic concepts and values. In Weber's eyes, cultures are not coherent wholes, but arenas in which contrasting values live as warring gods. Hence, it is the individual researcher or the idiosyncratic group of researchers that shapes meaning. Other researchers may criticize this meaning and amend earlier findings. In this way, social science will renew itself time and again, and stay forever young.[11]

5.2.1   The philosophical roots of interpretative sociology

The German philosopher Wilhelm Dilthey (1831-1911) had a great influence on Georg Simmel and Max Weber. He started as a rational positivist but developed into an advocate of the 'irrational interpretation' of social life and history. He became strongly convinced that it is impossible to understand social life with the help of pure reason. For a complete understanding, we need our spiritual capacities as well as our intellect. Dilthey classified the world into two separate spheres: nature and culture. In a similar vein, the sciences were divided into the physical and the cultural sciences. The crucial distinction was that between things or animals 'without a soul' and humans 'with a soul'. In other words, the physical sciences studied subjects without a conscious mind and the social and cultural sciences focussed on conscious subjects. The contrast between culture and nature, between mind and matter, is reflected in a whole range of other differences. Hence, this should lead to radical differences in methods of research and a thorough reflection on core concepts of the philosophy of science. The focal point of Dilthey's view – and his most original contribution – is his conception of understanding and interpretation, through which meaning is recaptured. However, we must avoid the mistaken view of this understanding as a knack for intuitive insight, a popular notion of the Romantic Movement in German philosophy. Dilthey strove for an intermediary position, which would do justice to the specific character of the subject matter of cultural sciences as well as to the rigorous demands of the objective approach of physics. In his view, history, like the physical sciences, is an empirical discipline. Therefore, it shares with the latter many methods of inquiry such as observation, classification and the framing and testing of hypotheses.

The natural sciences use general concepts that go beyond the exceptional and unique qualities of single phenomena. These 'generalizing concepts' deliberately describe the common elements within a group of phenomena. Consequently, these concepts are used to discover and test general laws that explain specific causal relations between different phenomena. In this respect Wilhelm Windelband (1848-1915) speaks of a nomothetical science, referring to the Greek word *nomos* that signifies law, order, and general principle. The historic-idealistic stance contends that the cultural sciences approach their object with 'individualizing' concepts that highlight the uniqueness and particularity of concrete social, historical, and psychological phenomena. In Windelband's view, the main objective of the social sciences is not the production of general laws, but the ideographical description and interpretation of unique events.[13] To the true historicist, the world is an endless series of unique events that can be understood intuitively, like a work of art. Here, we encounter the philosophical perspective known as romantic idealism. In this approach, the work of social scientists does not differ from that of the art historian. True historicists should keep the typical aspects of human actions in tact. Hence, they are bound to use concepts that respect the uniqueness of subjective experience, whereas the natural sciences deliberately ignore the unique.

Hermeneutics is the doctrine of interpretative understanding. This method is rooted in the new self-consciousness that emerged in historical science during the 19th century. The idea for a hermeneutic understanding of historic events and cultural phenomena came from critical readings of the Bible. The idea was that the texts of the Bible, representing the words of God, should speak for themselves, for they contain the truth. The main principle of hermeneutics is that separate phrases, verses, paragraphs, or sections have to be understood in relation to other parts of the text if not in relation to the text as a whole. This painstaking and time-consuming process of looking for valid interpretations of unclear fragments in fragments that are clearer can lead to circular argumentation that does not cease until all the hidden meanings of the complete text have been clarified. On the basis of his individual, fresh, and critical reading of the Bible Martin Luther dared to go against the official interpretations of the Church of Rome. Modern historians began to apply this method to all of the texts studied and interpreted their content and meaning against the background of all of the available evidence of that particular historical epoch.

Hermeneutic scholars renounced the linear idea of progress propagated by the advocates of the Enlightenment. Their bent for a romantic perspective made them focus on the unique nature and the individual value of distinct cultures and historic epochs. They planned to describe history 'as it really had happened', as the famous historian Leopold von Ranke pretended.[14] In a similar fashion, it would be possible to understand different cultures through the interpretation of parts or fragments of these cultures against the context of other elements of these cultures. This method also puts authors and their intentions at the centre of historical interest. One should, as the philosopher Hans-Georg Gadamer stated, not only understand the intentions of authors, but also why they have failed to realize parts of their plans or why they themselves became confused at certain points in their text. Statements like these clearly highlight the romantic, soul-searching view of the interpretative approach.

To Wilhelm Dilthey, social actors are sensitive, wilful, and reflexive. They maintain a multiplicity of emotionally loaded relations to life. They constitute meaning and coherence. Subjectivity is closely connected with emotionality, with norms and values, and with affectively loaded objectives. Whereas the search for physical knowledge rests on abstracting from emotions, values and desires, and therefore, distances itself ever further from 'full life', the cultural sciences deliberately address the problem of making accessible the relations that spring from these origins. Dilthey tried to show that the specific character of the object of cultural science is the consciousness of the subject, a consciousness that is based on the close connection between experience, expression and interpretation. Humans have to maintain a multiplicity of emotional relations with their social environment. They must express their inner feelings. Without externalisation, they cannot engage in and maintain social relations with other people. Through externalisation, that is, through the expression of inner feelings, the internal, subjective aspect of human existence becomes objectified. However, we must assume that people will not express all their inner feelings, thoughts, and desires. Sometimes, they are not able to express them or dare not do so, for fear of negative reactions. And, as Freud has taught us, often we are not aware of our inner motives. Hence, the method of interpreting human motives is far from easy. Solving theoretical problems is like finishing a complicated jigsaw puzzle of which many of the pieces are missing. Using hermeneutic methods, we have to make educated guesses about the parts of the picture that are still missing. Solving the puzzle is, according to Dilthey, a kind of 'finding oneself in the other'. This is not a completely subjective matter, because all of the activities geared to solving academic riddles take place in the context of the 'objective spirit' of shared norms and values. In everyday life, everyone uses this common culture, bases his or her actions on the assumption that all other members of the group share these norms and values, because they have been born and raised in a particular group or society. To a high degree, each individual lives, thinks, and acts in accordance with these shared norms and values. Thus we can understand much of the behaviour of others within the context of that particular culture or subculture.

5.2.2 Ideal types: construction and functions

Though Heinrich Rickert (1863-1936) had been educated in the tradition of historicism, he did not agree that the cultural sciences needed an entirely different methodology. He believed that it was possible to apply some of the methods of the natural sciences, though not all. Otherwise, these sciences would run the risk of overlooking the cultural and the subjective. His stance was based on a compromise. There are social actions that are so common, that they can be observed in all societies. Hence we can study them with the help of general methods. But there are also social events, aspects, and elements, which are truly unique. Hence, they require an individualizing method of research.

Weber went one step further. He sharply attacked the historic idealistic tradition and asserted that it was impossible to explain particular and unique phenomena without the help of generalized concepts and without some 'nomological' knowledge of causal theories.[15] But he acknowledged the distinction between the natural and the cultural sciences. Whereas the physical sciences searched for general laws of nature, the social scientist wanted to explain particular cases with the help of general concepts and law-like statements that describe the relation between the phenomena described by these concepts.[16] He looked for a third way that would do justice to both approaches. As a consequence, however, his work can be read in different ways. Depending on the selection of quotations and fragments, it is possible to present him as an interpretative historicist but also as an explanatory positivist. That Weber intended to ride two horses can be learned from the following quotation.

> *We want to understand the surrounding reality of life in which we are placed in its uniqueness – that is, on the one hand the relationship and cultural significance of its individual appearance in its present configuration, and on the other hand the basis of its being historically so and not having become otherwise.*[17]

The first part of this quotation clearly shows a historicist approach, whereas the latter part illustrates that Weber wanted more than to merely interpret a phenomenon in its actual social-historic context. He always searched for a causal explanation. To Weber, the practical significance of the cultural sciences lied in the cultural 'self-understanding' of a specific epoch. The cultural critic must be able to sift the significant from the insignificant. What is important in one period need not be important in another. Since human values and their ranking change over time, cultural sciences have to produce changing insights. As soon as the cultural climate changes, social scientists have to change many of their concepts. Otherwise they will fail to produce sensible interpretations. Here, Weber manifested a sincere hermeneutic drive to explain each epoch from within. In other instances, however, Weber opted for a positivistic perspective on the relation between theory and practice and contended that social sciences can produce useful knowledge based on causal relations that can solve problems in our everyday reality.[18]

The solution to the problem of coming to grips with social reality lies in the theoretical construction of 'ideal types.' By way of abstracting from the interminable, meaningless multiplicity of empirical data, Weber wanted to generate general, rationally pure concepts. Subsequently these rationally constructed ideational types would lead us to a better understanding of concrete historical events and social processes. In his well-known description of the ideal-type, Weber stated:

> *This construction has a utopian character, that has been gained through an analytical accentuation (gedankliche Steigerung) of certain elements from reality, ... For empirical research the ideal-type serves as a heuristic means for developing the ability to determine causal factors (Zurechnungsurteil schulen): it <u>is</u> not a hypothesis, but it can indicate the direction for the formation of hypotheses.*[19]

Ideal-typical concepts should function as interpretative guides for the unveiling and explanation of specific concrete social actions. Weber searched for useful concepts that could bridge the gap between an infinitely varied social reality that apparently defied any meaningful understanding and a limited number of well-constructed general concepts that could help us to grapple with this complex and apparently chaotic reality. He looked for the missing link between an overzealous and painstaking description of reality and theoretical abstraction. In his view, the best road to a meaningful understanding of social actions was an analytical highway built on ideal-typical constructions. But this construction must be derived from and constantly be examined against reality, by using the 'imagination' as well as the nomological knowledge of the researcher. The construction of ideal types should serve to link nomothetical and ideographical methods, and enable a good match between a causal explanation and an interpretative understanding. It should mediate one method through the other.[20]

The ideal type is a conceptual construct. In view of their specific problems of investigation, researchers should set aside a large number of elements, and save only a restricted number of related characteristics that are particularly significant to their given study. The elements that have been singled out for the ideal type of a specific phenomenon should necessarily be a great help for its location and description. They form beacons that should be easily recognized by other sociologists and laymen. Therefore, pure types must be composed of the most transparent concepts.[21] Weber introduced a number of ideal-typical descriptions that have become widely known in the social sciences. His ideal types of social action, of authority and of bureaucracy will be discussed later on. As soon as we have constructed a good ideal-typical description of a particular phenomenon, say democracy, then we can use this ideal type as a yardstick for comparing real existing democracies. The ideal types are only heuristic means than can help us to become better informed about our world. Yet, they are absolutely necessary for the social sciences. The ideal type, the type in its theoretically purified form, does not exist in reality. Each concrete democracy differs from the constructed ideal type. For example, the democracies of England, France, Germany, India, the Netherlands, and the United States of America deviate from the pure type. They have their own history and national character. Their constitutions vary, as well as their system of elections, the structure of political parties, the press, et cetera.

According to Weber, rational or scientific knowledge of reality can only emerge through the comparison of our observations of reality with theoretically constructed ideal types. Through this confrontation, we gain a clear image of the distance between the ideal-typical construct and reality and this helps us to come to grips with that specific sector of reality. Clearly, the relationship between theory and empirical reality is very close. There can be no insight into reality without the construction of concepts and theories. Conversely, one cannot gauge the value of certain concepts and theories without confronting them with empirical facts.

The construction of (pure) types is inherent to scientific observation, as Kant has taught us. Our minds demand systemization, categorization, and classification. Each concept must be connected to a series of other concepts in a systematic fashion. Our thinking cannot bear isolated elements, nor can it fit all concepts into one coherent totality. Systematisation plays an important role in locating our concepts between the extremes of unity and diversity. We have to construct concepts that will gap the bridge between the unique and the general, between the individual and the universal. These analytical constructions or pure types might not exist in reality, but they will help us to understand aspects of the human condition. There is no other way of providing some transparency to the grey mass of disparate facts.

5.2.3   Interpretive understanding of social actions

In addition to rational understanding, Weber also put a lot of energy into analysing and discussing what he termed interpretative understanding. This topic was crucial in Weber's line of thought, as becomes clear in reading his definition of Sociology.

> *Sociology is a science that aims to understand social action in an interpretive fashion and thereby explain its course and consequences causally.* [22]

Once more, this definition shows that Weber's intentions are both interpretative and causally analytical. To make any scientific statement about social actions every interpretative explanation must be turned into a verifiable causal statement. From a methodological perspective, Weber counts for two.

Weber always took a great interest in the meanings that people attached to their actions. He defined social actions as these forms of behaviour that concern the coexistence with other people. Social actions refer to all actions in which individuals are aware of each other and therefore are considering the thoughts, will, and feelings of the other. Actions are social if the participants attach meaning to their collective situation. Actions that have no meaning for individuals, that do not take the interest or the perspective of the other into account, are not social actions, and fall outside the realm of sociology. Social behaviour comprises each type of behaviour that is significantly focussed on the past, present, or future behaviour of other individuals.[23]

For Weber, the ultimate unit of analysis is the concrete individual, acting socially. That is the atom of society. It is the only enactor of meaningful behaviour. Concepts referring to collective wholes such as the state, the church, feudalism, or capitalism have to be redressed to actions of individuals.[24] This view directly opposes that of Durkheim. In contrast to the latter, Weber did not speak of behaviour determined by society as a whole, but of behaviour motivated and rendered meaning by the individual. Weber strongly opposed holism. He saw societies and cultures as the products of meaning-giving processes. Social wholes do exist, but they do not act. Only individuals can act on behalf of a government, business firm, political party, or a family. This approach is called methodological individualism. To make social phenomena transparent, one has to start with the observation and analysis of the social actions of individuals. Their subjective meanings form the core elements of any sociological analysis. Here, subjective does not mean 'partisan' or 'untrue', but 'from the perspective of the subject', 'from the motivational drives of the individual'. Sociologists should keep in mind that people give meaning to significant elements of their situation and act on the basis of an objective, a plan or a design of the most-desired situation.

Sociologists should trace law-like generalizations in social behaviour, and uncover the meaning that people attach to their social actions using the interpretive method. The explanation not only has to be meaningful (sinnhaft) as well as causally adequate. Purely causal and statistical analyses can only produce incomplete and unsatisfactory images of reality. They have to be supplemented and filled in with the help of interpretations based on what we know of relevant cultural meanings. In this manner, the cultural sciences deliver an extra achievement, an achievement that lies outside of the range of the methods of physical sciences. Of course, the physical sciences do not need this extra tool, as their objects of study have no mind of their own.

Weber rejected Dilthey's 'romantic' view of interpretation, in which understanding is set at a par with something as uncontrollable as empathy, and is based on an intuitive recreation, or re-living. Instead, he emphasized that the interpretative method also presupposed nomological knowledge that referred to observable patterns in people's behaviour. His main interest lay in understanding patterns of behaviour. He was not interested in the deeply hidden elements of human personality. That domain he left for the psychologists. He explicitly argued in favour of an interpretative sociology based on an objective, scientific approach. He distinguished between immediate and explanatory interpretation and spoke of actual or direct understanding if the meaning of an observable form of behaviour could be understood immediately.[25] Raymond Aron gives the example of a cab driver stopping for a red traffic light. Everybody knows that particular rules have been introduced to regulate traffic in order to prevent accidents and that people who do not stop for red lights run the risk of crashing into another car or being fined. In the course of our daily lives, the meaning of most patterns of behaviour is immediately clear to us, because we have experienced these patterns of behaviour hundreds or thousands of times previously. We are familiar with the cultural context in which these forms of behaviour are perpetually reproduced. We have learned to interpret these patterns during a process of socialization. However, as soon as we enter a social situation that is entirely new to us, as soon as we meet people who have been raised in an entirely different culture, we have some difficulty in understanding what is going on, why people are doing what they are doing.

Another example: In general we think we understand why someone is digging up a tree. He might have made a new design for his garden, or he simply wants to create a better view. Maybe, he hates raking leaves every autumn. But what if we see an angry man uprooting a young tree with his bare hands? Why is he doing this? This scene is played out in an Ingmar Bergman film situated in the Middle Ages. For the viewers of the movie it is an act they can easily understand, as they are knowledgeable of the preceding events leading up to this moment. The man is a father who has just been offered the stained dress of his daughter by the very men that must have raped and murdered his daughter. So the spectators understand why the man is enraged and molests the sapling tree. In their own lives, they have experienced that rage can lead people to break or strike out at inanimate objects. However, as they watch the scene unfold, they do not expect another layer of meaning to be revealed. As the film progresses, it turns out that the father is only getting rid of the most vehement of his emotions. As soon as he has calmed down a bit and is capable of clear thinking, he starts to plan the revengeful killing of these murderers. So, in order to interpret this behaviour we need a good deal of extra information; we need to be more familiar with the historical and social context.

Whenever Weber discusses interpretive sociology, he focuses on explanatory understanding. We should never accept the most evident explanation, but test our hypothetical explanation first; that is, we must test its validity with the help of widely accepted scientific procedures. An explanation is adequate as a meaningful interpretation if the phenomenon has been made comprehensible within the framework of a prevailing set of norms. We have to check and double check whether the explanation we have thought up is really the most likely solution. In doing so, we can fall back upon a huge range of well-known patterns of human behaviour.

Surely Weber did not contend that interpretative understanding of meaningful behaviour is entirely different from causal explanation. On the contrary, he stressed that such an interpretation was a necessary precondition for finding a complete causal explanation. Insight into the motives of individuals is indispensable. Here, it might be relevant to quote an aphorism of Friedrich Schlegel's: 'For understanding someone well it is necessary to be smarter than this person, just as smart and also just as stupid.' These motives, aspirations, and calculations are the real (teleological) causal factors that always have to be taken into consideration. Any explanation that restricts itself only to physical phenomena, such as a bankruptcy, a disappointing harvest, or the birth of child, will fall short of being a good explanation of social actions. The restriction to study only observable behaviour boils down to the exclusion of important assets of human existence. It ignores that individuals are socially acting beings that strive to achieve certain goals and render meaning to all their actions and those of others.[26]

In hermeneutics, the method of *Verstehen* is deliberately used and propagated as an alternative to causal explanation. Weber energetically placed himself at a good distance from this 'anti-scientific' position. As we already have seen, he was not interested in meaning for its own sake; he was after meaning for the sake of causally explaining social action. In many respects, he differed quite a bit from Georg Simmel, whom he respected highly. Simmel tended to focus on meaningful *forms* of sociation, whereas Weber was more interested in the *content* of interactions and in 'complexes of meaning.'

In Weber's view, social acts were often not the result of deliberate intentions, but entirely unintended consequences of well-considered plans. It is this focus on unintended consequences of previous motives and patterns of behaviour which makes clear that his primary aim was the search for causal explanations, explanations that do not consist of mere interpretative understanding of the intentions of individual persons, but have to rest on the interactions of groups of persons within broad complexes of meanings. As a historian and social historian he was oriented to understanding patterns of collective activity and their outcomes, whether they were intended or not.[27] Dilthey, who was a theologian by training, wanted to interpret only, whereas Weber wanted to interpret to be able to explain which set of factors might have caused the occurrence of specific social situations. In this respect, it is opportune to stress that Weber was wary of explanations, which were based entirely on one factor. In his mind, social phenomena were far too complex for such simple explanations.

5.2.4   Freedom from value judgment

Despite Weber's stress on the fact that social actions are embedded in history, and despite his explicit attention to subjective processes, he wanted the humanities to strive for an objective approach. In his 1904 article *Objectivity in Social Science and Social Policy*, he manifested himself as the great champion of practicing social science in an objective way. This is very difficult as social scientists are deeply embedded in their culture and are predisposed with the subject under investigation. In principle, social scientists can study the rich or the poor, medical doctors or quacks, great statesmen or political demagogues with the same degree of distance, but in practice things may be different. Nonetheless, in view of the demand of objectivity, it is extremely important that scientists do all they can to prevent cultural biases and personal political views from interfering with their methods of gathering or analysing data or practising their craft in the broadest sense. They have to consider all facts, even if they go against their personal views.

Most theorists tend to stress that Weber started the 'value freedom dispute.'[28] However, we should not forget that he borrowed from the work of Rickert, and that he really meant freedom of value judgment *(Werturteilsfreiheit)*, a concept that is closely connected to value commitment *(Wertbeziehung)*, a term he also borrowed from Rickert. Zijderveld places some of the blame on Weber for preferring the term value freedom to freedom of value judgment, as this has triggered some unnecessary disputes.[29]Strictly speaking, there is no such thing as value free research, since the goals and norms of science such as seeking the truth and the use of objective methods and sound reasoning are important social values that not only are of great importance to science, but also to the field of law. Weber did not oppose this kind of values, on the contrary, but fiercely opposed science based on political ideology or religious dogma. Science cannot answer the question of what we should do. Like Kant, he found that there was an unbridgeable chasm between science and ethics, morals, and religion. Science can only attempt to find some truths about reality. The demand that research be done in a so-called value-free fashion ensures that researchers do not set up their investigations in such a way that an outcome will be generated that nicely fits the political views of the researcher or the interests of the people who have commissioned the study: for example, by choosing a highly selective sample of probable allies or opponents of a specific issue. It is the task of the research community to monitor their peers and to scrutinize their work for missteps in this respect.

Weber held fast to the twin ideas of a 'tough' science and a full commitment to science. In his view such a commitment was just as value-bound as any other value-bound quest for certain goals. Echoing Nietzsche, he stated that the choice for science was just as rational or irrational as the choice for a career in art, religion or politics. In choosing to do scientific work, however, you also had to commit to an objective, neutral, value free method. You can't have one without the other. Rules of logic and method could never be relinquished if truth is to be found. The rational method alone ensures empirical knowledge in the sense of statements (however subject to correction) that are intersubjectively transmissible in a critical manner.[30]

Durkheim attempted to prove the scientific character of sociology by stressing that social facts could be studied as if they were things. His rules of method can be applied to generate testable knowledge of social phenomena. Recurrent patterns in social behaviour and social organizations can be observed, described, analysed, classified, compared and explained.[31] Weber agreed, but added something very important. His method of justifying a special status for the cultural sciences was based on the fact that social processes and institutions are formed by human actions. In sharp contrast to physical things, people can think and chose. Often they act in a goal-oriented way and give meaning to their actions and the goals they have chosen. By acknowledging this subjective element, without ignoring the rigorous demands of engaging in objective science, the methodological oeuvre of Weber offers a good and necessary addition to Durkheim's rules of method.

5.3   Rationalization as *Leitmotiv*

The speedy process of rationalization of the Western world greatly fascinated Weber. At the beginning of the *Protestant Ethic*, he posed the following question:

> *What combination of circumstances has led to the fact that precisely in the Occident, and in the Occident only, cultural phenomena have appeared, which – as we like to think, at least – lie in a line of development that is of universal significance and validity? Only the West offers 'science' that has reached a stage of development that we today consider as 'valid'. ... knowledge and observation of extraordinary refinement have existed elsewhere, above all in India, China, Babylonia, and Egypt. But Babylonian and any other astronomy lacked – which makes the development of the Babylonian astronomy all the more astounding - a mathematical foundation that was first*

formulated by the Hellenes. Indian geometry lacked proof, again a product of Greek minds, the latter also being the first in creating mechanics and physics.[32]

In other parts of the world, people were engaged in scientific activities, but the Western forefathers of science were the first to introduce mathematical formulas, rational proof, controlled experiments, systematic methods, and the requirement of objectivity. At present, the rational approach to science has penetrated all continents.

The analysis of rationalization forms the guiding principle in Weber's oeuvre. He observed this process in various fields using a broad concept of rationality. Before going into the different ways in which he applied this concept, let us first give some attention to his typology of main motives for social action. This is one of his most famous and most widely used typologies. It forms a good starting point for the discussion of the historical trend towards rationalization. Weber distinguished the following pure types of motives for social action:

1   instrumental or goal oriented rationality *(Zweckrationalität)*;
2   value rationality *(Wertrationalität)*;
3   emotions;
4   traditions, customs and habits.[33]

This typology is based on the distinction between rational and non-rational action. Humans act rationally when they are the conscious and calculative initiators of acts. They act in a non-rational way when they are directed by feelings or habits. Thus, instrumental or goal-oriented rationality is rational because it is directed towards the pursuit of a premeditated objective with the help of carefully selected means that very likely will make the act successful. In view of the best information available, all alternative goals and means have been dismissed because the chosen goals and means appear to be more useful, efficient, or effective. Other translations of *Zweckrationalität* are functional, technical and formal rationality. Another translation could be utilitarian rationality. During the process of weighing the pros and cons of alternative goals and means possible consequences will also be taken into account.

Value rationality refers to actions directed at goals and oriented at absolute values that are not rational, such as the goal to preserve one's virtue or honour. They are based on an absolute and conscious belief in the great value of some ethical, aesthetic, religious or other form of behaviour. Value rationality pertains to the pursuit of absolute ends for their own sake only and independent of any prospects of external success.[34] Value rationality springs from the conviction that a certain action has an intrinsic value *(Eigenwert)*, whatever its use, effect, or consequence. The meaning of the action does not lie in the achievement of an ulterior result, but in carrying out the specific type of action for its own sake. Yet these actions can be called rational insofar as the means are rationally selected, for instance, by taking prevailing norms and values into account that might be based on religious, ethical or aesthetic values. For example, the captain of a sinking ship is supposed to be the last person to leave that ship, even if this could mean a certain death. Were the captain to abuse his authority to safe his own life first, this would be considered a disgraceful and dishonourable act.

Emotional actions are motivated by feelings; for instance, people will cry at the death of a loved one, or get angry with a naughty child. However, if emotional actions are 'played' to achieve a certain goal, for instance, more attention from a parent or partner, then it becomes an instrumentally rational act. The crucial element is whether showing one's feelings is an authentic and uncontrolled and authentic reaction to some exceptional stimulus, or that is has been planned consciously in view of the achievement of a desired goal. In the latter case the emotional drama clearly is a goal-oriented social action that deliberately has taken into account how others would react.

Traditional actions are determined by ingrained habituation. The prevailing habits can be so deeply internalised that most individuals do not bother to reflect on the significance of these actions. In this respect, they mirror purely emotionally driven actions. Traditional and habitual actions form the great bulk of all everyday actions. In everyday reality many social actions are based on a combination of ideal typical motives. Nonetheless, Weber's typology helps us to compare social situations. Thus we can learn whether some ideal type is gaining dominance. Most modern sociologists are convinced that rational, goal-oriented actions have gained predominance over all the other ideal typical motives for social action. In other words, we are witnessing a strong trend towards rationalization.

5.3.1   Different meanings of rationalization

Weber was well aware of the complexity and multiplicity of the motives for social action. He acknowledged that most acts take place in a situation of limited consciousness or total unconsciousness. Yet he was convinced that modern societies exhibit a steady increase of instrumental-rational actions. The efficient application of means is foregrounded. Increasingly, behaviour based on values other than economic profit or self-interest is deemed worthless. The interests of the economy and the technical sciences gain ground at the cost of traditions, intuition, and feelings. Furthermore, Weber uncovered a closely connected tendency towards a rational development of political authority. Rulers endowed with power based on tradition gave way to the authority of the cool, calculating heads of state of our day and age. Modern Western leaders govern within the strict lines of legal prescripts and the guidelines for public governance.

Randall Collins discusses the following three chief meanings of rationalization. The first and most widely known of these is instrumental rationality. It forms the basis of modern capitalism. Most transactions that take place on the free market are determined by goal-oriented actions that serve the self-interest of the actors. No longer are these economic transactions hindered by sacred taboos, traditions, or the privileges of specific groups. Economic utility is the sole motive behind all of these acts. In its pure, ideal-typical form – a form that is non-existent – the free market offers the text book example of instrumental rationality in its positive as well as in its negative sense: positive, in the sense of calculability and effectiveness; negatively, in the sense of the total lack of traditional, religious, and moral restrictions. At other points Weber sets the rational against the traditional. Here, he refers to organizations that succeed in manipulating the world according to their own interests, for instance, by reducing nature to a means for generating profit. Whereas the modernist is constantly looking for new ways of controlling nature, the traditionalist will remain passive and refrain from intervening in the usual course of nature.

A third meaning is that of bureaucratization. For Weber, ideal-typically bureaucracy was a more rational way of organizing administrative activities than the more traditional method of carrying out governmental decisions. An important element of rationality is its predictability and the regularity of standardized procedures. Nowhere are these criteria driven forward as much as in the field of bureaucratic administration and governmental control.

Rogers Brubaker presents a slightly different approach. He does not speak of chief meanings but of core elements that frequently return in Weber's writings. They refer to:

1 The use of human intelligence and the increase in knowledge;
2 Increased control of nature, men, and social organizations;
3 The growth of formal relations at the cost of personal relationships.[35]

The main meanings presented by Collins can easily be listed under the three core elements mentioned by Brubaker. Instrumental rational actions can only be achieved with the help of human intelligence; both sociologists mention control and the growth of formal relations and the decrease of personal relations as typical of bureaucratic organizations. The following scheme charts the manifestations of rationalization relations within various fields.

Scheme 5.1   Significance of rationality in different contexts

science/technology	the increase of knowledge
	the harnessing nature
	experimentation
	proof
economy	instrumental rationality
	usefulness
	efficiency - cost effectiveness
government	bureaucratisation
	depersonalisation
	standardization
religion	disenchantment
	de-mystification
	secularisation

5.3.2   *The introduction of rationality in Western music*

Before elaborating on Weber's discussion of rationalization in the three core fields of society (economy, religion, and polity), I will first sketch the process of rationalization in Western music as an illustrative example. We can assume that the first melodic singing emerged within prehistoric tribal societies. Songs were based on a limited number of tones and a simple rhythm. For many ages, mankind did not observe further developments. It was about a thousand years ago that European monks developed musical notation for their religious songs. A few centuries later, they developed the 12-tone scale. The 13th tone is a sound that is in perfect harmony with the first tone and forms the start of the same scale at a higher pitch. Later people discovered that some notes, for instance the first, third and fifth tone of the scale, could be sung simultaneously, producing harmonious chords, that is, combinations of different notes that were pleasing to our ears. Later more complex chords were discovered. On the basis of these consonances, composers create harmonious compositions in which the main melody is simultaneously supported with other melodic lines or interspersed with counter melodies. With the help of musical notation, all of the performers can learn which sounds they have to perform, at which time and with what speed or rhythm, in order to reproduce the music created by the composer. After preparing themselves individually, professional musicians only need some fine-tuning and extra directions by the conductor when rehearsing with the complete orchestra. Clearly, a very high degree of rationalization is required to realize a brilliant performance of a composition by a symphonic orchestra that consists of a hundred or more musicians. It demands standardization and fine-tuning of musical instruments, perfect control of the sound, the rhythm and the volume. Furthermore, it takes years of training by excellent musical pedagogues, as well as near-perfect bureaucratic organization for planning rehearsals and official performances. All of the performing artists are obliged to maintain strict schedules for collective rehearsing in addition to individual training or training in small groups on a daily basis. In this respect, Western music has gone further than any other form of music. Beautiful melodies, fascinating rhythms, and virtuous artists can be found on every continent, in every country, and in every musical style, but the level of organization, cooperation, mutual adjustment and bureaucratic planning of Western classical music has no parallel elsewhere.[36]

5.4   Modern capitalism

Weber saw the development of Western capitalism in the sixteenth and seventeenth century as part of a much broader process of rationalization. Capitalism is not the same as the impulse towards acquisition. The desire to get more goods and money is as old as humanity, but it is not the essence. The search for profit is an important characteristic of capitalism, but the most striking thing is the calculated and rational manner in which profit making is executed.[37] It is rational, calculable action that steers and limits capitalists. Capitalism may even be identical with the restraint, or at least the rational tempering, of this irrational impulse to get rich, or to put it more negatively, towards the unlimited greed for gain. What characterizes capitalism is the constant pursuit of profit by means of continuous, rational, capitalistic enterprise. This entails calculation in terms of financial costs. Within a capitalistic society, any business enterprise not acting in this fashion is doomed to fail. Fierce competition will drive it out of the market. Weber concurs with Marx on the role of competition in disciplining individual capitalists (and workers). Today's capitalist economy is an ever-present cosmos into which the individual is born. It forces the individual to conform to capitalist rules of action. Otherwise, the manufacturer will go bankrupt and the worker will lose his job.[38] The former has to be continuously alert and must always be on the lookout for profitable opportunities. Hence, he needs reliable calculations of the costs and profit margins.[39] A rational mentality is one of the most important prerequisites of a capitalist economy. In particular, it is the capitalistic organization of labour and its calculability that makes Western economies more productive than other systems. This type of economy is not characterized by a strong drive for high profits, but by an orientation towards enduring organizations that continuously aim for profits.

Modern capitalism involves the appropriation of all physical means of production – land, machinery, tools, et cetera, as disposable property of autonomous private industrial enterprises. Full-fledged capitalism also requires 'free labour'. Workers must be free. But economically they must also be compelled to sell their labour on the market without restriction. The development of capitalism is impossible if such a stratum of have-nots is absent. Like Marx, Weber believes that capitalism needs a class of workers who are compelled to sell their labour. Formally, we can speak of free labourers, because they are no slaves; in reality, they are under the pressure of the whip of hunger. If there is a reserve army of free labourers, the employer can select the best among them, the ones that are healthy, strong, and willing to work. Now he is in a position to sack unproductive and ill-disciplined workers, as he has no personal obligations to them, unlike the owners of slaves.

For Weber, modern capitalism could only flourish in a context of modern law. For instance, it could never have reached this level of calculability and predictability in the Arabic system of Kadi justice, in which judges decide on the basis of their innate sense of justice, and, surely, not within a system based on the cryptic words of oracles.[40] Likewise, modern capitalism could not have flourished in a system of patrimonial politics, in which important decisions depend on the mood of the ruler and someone's social relation to that individual. Under such conditions it is very difficult to make rational financial decisions and to plan ahead. Hence, the rationalization of public government is a necessary condition for the growth of modern capitalism.

In addition, the legal control of the owner over the workplace, the tools, machines, the raw material and the end products are of the utmost importance. Weber speaks of 'the complete appropriation of all material means of production'.

Thus, the entrepreneur can oversee everything. He can plan production and production costs exactly. Here, Weber followed Marx' analysis. But he observed this process of expropriation of means of production within other domains as well. It can be seen in scientific research, governmental bureaucracies, and privately organized services. The main reasons for this are the development of technology and the growth of large organizations. Technologically advanced machines are often too big and too expensive to be owned by individual workers. Technological innovation and the need for cost reduction have sidelined many small firms based on skilled handicrafts.[41] But all of these structural and institutional conditions together do not suffice to explain the striking growth of modern capitalism in the West. In Weber's view, a number of crucial factors are still unexplained. He went looking for these missing links within the cultural sphere: within the spirit of capitalism and the ethic of Protestantism, and the elective affinity (*Wahlverwandtschaft*)[42] that exists between these two cultural phenomena.

5.4.1   The spirit of capitalism

Modern capitalism is very distinct from its predecessors. In traditional societies, people did not strive for a maximization of their income. This is easily verifiable in a number of underdeveloped countries. In faraway places, unconnected to the globalized economy, most people still prefer not to work more than is absolutely necessary. They stop working as soon as they can manage to survive for a few days and will only start working if they really need the money.

> A man does not 'by nature' wish to earn more and more money, but simply to live as he is accustomed to live and to earn as much as is necessary for that purpose. Wherever modern capitalism has begun its work of increasing the productivity of human labour by increasing its intensity, it has encountered the immensely stubborn resistance of this leading trait of pre-capitalist labour.[43]

Expanding capitalism needed a completely different set of values. Admittedly, in ancient history, there have been people with a voracious hunger for wealth and money. At the time, however, their behaviour was seen as immoral. In modern capitalism, getting rich is highly valued. The rich have become the ultimate role models for many people. In particular, the people who have risen from rags to riches are widely envied and admired. Nowadays, this attitude to work in order to get rich is no longer restricted to a few isolated individuals. It has become so widespread that sociologists have begun to study its historical origin and social consequences. Thus, the question arises: How could the search for economic profit change from a vulgar drive into a widely respected motive?

Weber focussed a good deal of attention on the cultural phenomenon he described as 'the spirit of capitalism'. Here a noticeable difference with Marx can be observed. The latter seemed to be solely interested in the structure of capitalism and the functioning of the free market with its cutthroat competition that forces employers to exploit their workers. Weber's focus was directed at the norms and values that supported and legitimised the system of capitalism. His point of departure was the book *Advice to a Young Tradesman* by the American moralist Benjamin Franklin. This book from 1748 contained many excellent examples of the spirit of capitalism.[44] Some telling quotations are:

> *Remember, that time is money. He that can earn ten shillings a day by his labour, and goes abroad, or sits idle, one half of that day, though he spends but six pence during his diversion or idleness, ought not reckon that the only expense; he has really spent, rather thrown away, six shilling.*
> *Remember, that credit is money. … This amounts to a considerable sum where a man has good and large credit, and makes good use of it.*
> *Remember, that money is of the prolific, generating nature. Money can beget money, and its offspring can beget more, … till it becomes a hundred pounds. … He that kills a breeding sow, destroys all her offspring to the thousands generation. He that murders a crown destroys all that it might have produced, even scores of pounds.*
> *The most trifling actions that affect a man's credit are to be regarded. The sound of your hammer at five in the morning, or at eight at night, heard by a creditor, makes him easy six months longer; but if he sees you at a billiard table, or hears your voice in a tavern, when You should be at work, he sends for his money the next day; demands it, before he can receive it, in a lump.*

There is no doubt about the spirit of capitalism in the above mentioned quotations. It is a philosophy of thrift and diligence. It is a song of praise for the entrepreneur who does not squander time or money, who punctually delivers what he has promised, for these traits contribute to his reliability. It is more than a way of life; it is an ethic for doing business and earning money. Failure to live up to these ethical rules is considered as a serious neglect of duty. Franklin's lessons do not constitute a form of business administration, but a doctrine of business ethics. And it was this that interested Weber most, for this ethos was lacking in the economies of the past.[45] He then started to look for the roots of this change of ethics and found the answer in the doctrines of the Puritan Protestants.

5.5 The Protestant ethics and the spirit of capitalism

Weber's most famous study is *The Protestant Ethic and the Spirit of Capitalism*. In this work, he showed that the Protestant ethic stimulated the growth of capitalism. This is particularly true of the Calvinistic variants of Protestantism. His main hypothesis was that the flourishing of capitalism in North-Western Europe, as opposed to wealthier Italy where conditions seemed more favourable, was related to the advent of Protestant morality. He did not deny the importance of material factors in explaining salient social evolutions. But they are only part of the story. The explanation needs to be supplemented with cultural factors.

Above, we already sketched the social conditions needed for the development of a capitalistic mode of production. In many regions, the necessary social and political preconditions, such as a reserve army of wage labourers, a market system and sufficiently developed technology, already existed. Yet capitalism did not bloom in all of those other areas because two crucial elements were missing: the rational-legal organization of the state, which regulated economic transactions and disputes in a sensible fashion, and, the spirit of capitalism. According to Weber, this latter cultural element was crucial. But the spirit of capitalism is connected with a specific historical context. Compulsive working with no time for leisure, relentless miserliness, and a rational approach to financial affairs are no anthropological constants. On the contrary, we can observe peoples with a very different attitude towards life. From a historical perspective, most individuals worked for a living, but did not live to work, as most capitalists seem to do. Somehow, the proliferation of the capitalistic mindset had to be triggered by an external factor.

Weber found religious worldviews essential in guiding human behaviour. A strong belief directs social activity in specific ways, though in his day and age, this impact had lost much of its momentum. To get an idea of the formidable hold religion had on people in the 16th and 17th century, we should keep in mind what nowadays happens in some religious sects or in fundamentalist groups. In those days, as in these contemporary cases, any significant breach of a religious rule could lead to an exclusion from certain rituals or sacraments. It could even lead to excommunication.[46]

Weber started his investigation with a good body of statistical data at hand. He found that Protestants were wealthier than Catholics. They also sent a greater number of children to schools, in particular schools that taught practical courses such as mathematics and bookkeeping. Then, he presented a description of the spirit of modern capitalism, as it was manifested by the attitudes and motives of entrepreneurs. The third step in his argument showed that the specific manner in which the Puritan Protestants approached work and did business, closely matched the mindset of capitalist businessmen. In principle, Protestant theology was not favourable towards making profits. But Weber made clear that the doctrine had been adjusted in a practical fashion that perfectly fit the core elements of the spirit of capitalism. The brilliance of his work lies in his willingness to move beyond the official theological doctrines of Calvin and others in formulating his theory, and looks for the extra growth hormones of capitalism in the doctrines as they were interpreted by local ministers and 'translated' for laymen for daily usage.

To prove his point, he also began to study the relation between the economy and other religions such as Ancient Judaism, Confucianism, Taoism, Hinduism, and

Islam. Unfortunately, his early death prevented further studies of these religions in depth. At any rate, he did show that the ethics of other world religions did not enhance the growth of capitalism, though in some cases, the material conditions were favourable.

5.5.1 The Calvinist ethic

The most important doctrines of Calvinism are that the whole universe is God's creation and that all that exists in this universe only has meaning in the light of God's intentions. God does not exist for the pleasure of people, but people exist for the glory of God. Secondly, the human mind is unable to fathom the deep motives of the Almighty. If it pleases God, humans can discover only small sections of the divine truth. The third principle is the doctrine of predestination. This doctrine says that only a small group is predestined to go to heaven and to receive God's eternal grace. Since God is almighty and all knowing, he has already predestined whether an individual will go to heaven or to hell before he or she is born. There is no way in which people can change their destiny. Even the slightest suggestion that people could influence God's acts is unthinkable. Men cannot interfere with God. However, the acceptance of the consequence of God's *decretum horribile*[47] must have left individuals feeling very lonely, isolated and insecure.

The dogmatic elimination of the possibility of reaching heaven by way of good works, or by simply obeying the teachings of the church, is the crucial difference between the Calvinists and the Catholics. This constituted the apotheosis of a process of disenchantment with the world that had been started long ago. According to the doctrines of the Protestants, there are no sacramental charms for receiving the grace of God. They were taught to trust nobody, not even the clergy. They abolished confession, for one could trust only in God. Life was easier for the Catholics. They could confess their sins regularly to an anonymous priest, who would then absolve them after obliging them to say a number of prayers and asking them to promise to improve their behaviour. For Catholics, periodical confessions offered a great relief. The Catholic Church was always mild toward sinners but extremely harsh towards heretics. For Protestants there was no priest to relieve them of the burden of their sins. Therefore, every new sinful thought or act added to the heavy burden they already had to carry day and night. Calvinism offered believers no means of relief from the daily tensions of a life full of temptations, which they could not always resist.[48] They could not amend their moments of weakness, in which they acted against the divine rules and regulations, with 'good works'. According to John Calvin, God does not accept 'a few good works'. He demands a continuous and holy commitment to work. The combination of hard doctrines on the transcendental divinity of the almighty God on the one hand, and the total corruption of anything related to the human body, on the other hand, created among the Puritans a very negative attitude towards the sensual and emotional aspects of human existence and likewise a strong resistance to the rich adornments and rituals of the wealthy Catholic church. In the mind of the Calvinists, all of this had no value whatsoever in saving one's soul. The latter can only stimulate sentimental illusions and pagan superstitions.

During their daily pastoral activities, the Protestant ministers had to face the enormous worries of their parishioners about an afterlife in hell. Something had to restore the balance. Though believers could not do anything to change God's plans, they could start looking for signs that could indicate that they belonged to the small group of chosen people that would go to heaven. At least, that is how the clergymen presented it to them. The local ministers gave them the following two pieces of advice:

1 It is the duty of all believers to see them selves as chosen. Doubting that you belong to the chosen people is a sure sign of insufficient belief.
2 To gain trust in this respect people were advised to work incessantly. This and only this could take away all feelings of doubt and support the reliance on God.

To Calvinists, the chief goal of life on earth is the glorification of God. By fulfilling his commands, through working hard and living ascetically, and by developing one's God-given talents, Christians could contribute to the glory of God. Believers cannot exact salvation, but they can become convinced that they are chosen to the degree that they can manifest God's glory through diligence and wealth. Thus, the Protestant capitalist may enrich himself as much as he can, as long as he really thinks that this is not a goal in itself, but a manner of serving God. As one with a great talent for doing business, he is obliged to do business as best as he can. In this regard, any legal and morally acceptable activity is right in the eyes of God. Actually, every believer is obliged to grab any legal opportunity to make a profit, for it is God that has created this opportunity, no doubt for a purpose.[49]

5.5.2   Inner-worldly ascetics

Weber used the works of Richard Baxter to shed more light on the main principles underlying Puritan Protestantism. Baxter's books not only gave a clear description of the ascetic ethos, but also an unequivocal prescription for a frugal lifestyle.[50] These texts reveal some striking similarities with those of Benjamin Franklin. Whereas Franklin had argued that time is money, Baxter stressed that squandering time is sinful. In view of eternity, our time on earth is very short. It is absolutely necessary to use this short span of time as well as we possibly can for the tasks that can enhance God's glory.

Weber pointed out that the awareness of the fact that man's life on earth passes quickly already played a major role in religious life, long before the advent of modern capitalism. For centuries, the motto of the Church of Rome had been: *ora et labora*, pray and work. To remind people of the quick passing of time, bells were tolled for each hour of the day, in many towns and villages even for each quarter of an hour. All of this was done to remind people of the necessity to use their time well in the service of God. Among the Catholics the ascetic lifestyle had, however, become a matter for monks. They had retired from worldly affairs to sever themselves from all ties to their family, to give up earthly possessions, and to abstain from indulging earthly passions such as the love of art or sex. This forms an example of outer-worldly (*ausserweltliche*) ascesis. The Protestant reformation turned all believers into monks. All believers had to live a sober life and to refrain from worldly passions. Weber called this a form of inner-worldly (*innerweltliche*) ascesis. Wealth was unwelcome, for it could easily lead to a weakening of morals. One should not be tempted to a life of leisure, but one should devote one's whole life to work in the service of God: the devil finds work for idle hands. It is in moments of idleness that people are tempted to engage in what Puritans call 'an unclean life'. Working hard is a safeguard against sin and offers an opportunity to use one's talents to the fullest. There is no objection to wealth, but people should be warned of the danger that great wealth brings in that it can tempt people to sinful forms of leisure activity. Thus, even very rich people are advised to continue working and not to retire early. It is with some hesitance that Baxter allows them to avoid disagreeable chores and to opt for more agreeable tasks. For all, the message is: work, work, and work. Idleness is a great source of evil. It means squandering time and this is a disgrace to God. Even the time for sleep should be no longer than is necessary for your health. The seventh day of the week is a day of rest, and this day should be used to honour God by studying the Bible, going to church, and singing hymns. Again, this is not a day for profane pleasures and relaxation.

5.5.3   *Unintended consequences of the Protestant ethic*

By now, it is clear why the Protestant ethic stimulated the growth of capitalism.

> *... (It) must have been the most powerful lever for the expansion of an attitude which we have described as the spirit of capitalism.*[51]

It is only a small step from calling the squandering of time sinful, to a policy of minimizing the squandering of time for the sake of higher production and greater profits. It is only a small step from the idea that work is good for the glory of God to the idea that work that is planned and carried out well is even better. Thus the value of instrumental rationality becomes more highly valued. In this way, an extra impulse was created for the expansion of modern capitalism.

Weber puts great emphasis on the idea that the well-intended actions of people can produce unintended consequences. They can give rise to new social structures and new attitudes and opinions. They can have enduring repercussions for the future. After having sketched the important role of Puritanism for the growth of capitalism, he observed that modern capitalism had grown so big, that its structure and cultural acceptance had become so strong, that it could now survive and grow even further without the blessing of a religious ethic. It would survive without experiencing any damage from a process of secularisation. We might even add that an ever-growing capitalism will enhance further secularisation, and have a commercialising effect on those religious practices and organizations that remain.

During his visit to the United States, Weber noted that the economic success of Protestant sects validated his theory. As soon as the idea had taken root that members of a particular sect were not only sincerely religious but also highly reliable in economic affairs, because of their willingness to work hard, their sober way of life, and the strong social control, increasing numbers of people started doing business with them.[52] Therefore, when the ethos of Puritanism leads to economic profit, then this will also create the image that members of Puritan sects have a special talent for doing business. This image will lead to even more economic success. This process played a major role in the United States, in particular with respect to the Quakers and the Mennonites. Businessmen who were not members of one those sects, could not profit from this positive image of business talent and reliability, a reliability that was enhanced by the widely known fact that if a member of the sect failed to fulfil his obligations, other members of the sect would guarantee that the client would be compensated for any financial losses. But such cases were rare, as you had to work hard and show that you were trustworthy even to be accepted as a full member of either of these sects.

5.5.4   Testing the thesis

To test his theory, Weber had to make clear why there was no similar connection between economic growth and the ethos of other world religions. Hence, he studied Confucianism of China, the Buddhism and Hinduism of India, and Ancient Jewry. He started with the question of whether there existed an equivalent of the worldly asceticism of Protestantism within the abovementioned religions. During Weber's lifetime, modern capitalism had not emerged outside the Western world. If modern capitalism was a uniquely Western affair and the same was true of the ethic of Protestantism, then this could explain why these two phenomena were so closely related. Of course there are many other structural and cultural differences between the Western world and other continents, so it is impossible to produce watertight proof of Weber's thesis, but his investigations do certainly provide support for this theory.

Confucians view the world in which they live as the normal and only justifiable order of social existence, as created by higher, cosmic powers. Hence, the goals of life and lifestyle have been determined a very long time ago. From that perspective, it is unwise to change your way of life and to strive for new goals. All that is needed is to take care that life forever remains the same. Within this cultural context, traditional behaviour is rational. Confucians would not understand an ethic like the Protestant ethic that urges people to produce and to earn as much as they can. In their eyes, such behaviour is completely irrational.[53]

In India, the belief in reincarnation vigorously precluded the will to improve one's living conditions. Hindus believe that their soul, if they behave well, will return in the body of person that is much more privileged. This doctrine robs the poor Hindu of the motivation to search for a way out of his misery. Moreover, the belief in the caste system also enhances conservatism. No one can escape the caste into which he or she has been born. Hence, no one can escape the kind of profession for which the caste has been destined. Both stabilizing elements hang together. The caste system could not have survived the ages if it had lacked the support of a strong belief in reincarnation.

Weber could not find the time or muster the energy to perform an in-depth study of the relationship between Islam and its economic ethics. In Economy and Society, he devoted only a few pages to the Muslim world. He noted that soon after the death of the prophet, Islam developed into an Arabic warrior religion led by powerful families that aimed at raising this faith to a master religion, to which members of other religions had to pay tribute. The role played by wealth is diametrically opposed to the role played by wealth in the Puritan faith. Muhammad once stated: '*When God blesses a man with prosperity he likes to see the signs thereof visible upon him.*' The prophet rejected every type of monasticism (*rahbaniya*), though not all asceticism, for he forbade eating and drinking by day during the month of fasting. Since eating was allowed after sunset, even this yearly month of fasting by day, did not set people on the track of a frugal lifestyle that could lead to a steady accumulation of money and increased financial investments in entrepreneurial endeavours. Moreover, Weber thought that the prohibition of demanding (high) interest rates and the restriction against gambling had important consequences for their attitudes toward speculative business enterprises. Another important factor was that the strong belief in providence easily turned into downright fatalism. In the period that the Protestant ethic developed in a direction that was instrumental to the development of capitalism, the Islamic world was still organized in a truly feudal fashion that fully accepted slavery, serfdom, and polygamy. Weber even mentioned that the rule that women wear distinctive clothing negatively influenced the economies of countries that converted to Islam.[54] Maybe it is not the prescribed style of clothing per se, but the specific role and position imposed on woman that is more crucial here. In many Muslim countries, traditional interpretations of the Koran bar women from good educational and occupational careers, thus wasting a good deal of the talent of half their population. We note that Weber has given only a few hints on why the majority of the Islamic world, presently more than 1,2 billion people, lives in poverty. Most nations that can be categorized as Islamic are among the poorest countries in the world, with the exception of two or three countries that profit from huge oil reserves and even there the distribution of wealth is appalling, leaving large parts of the population in dire straits. Since the classical masters of sociology did not explain what went wrong here, it is up to contemporary social scientists to find answers to this urgent question.[55]

5.5.5 Critique and counter-critique

An important line of criticism stated that the essence of the Protestant Ethic, its inner-worldly austerity and asceticism, was not unique to Protestantism, but could be observed in other religions, although not in connection with a capitalist industrial economy, but with an agrarian economy. Other critics stated that a fair share of Protestants did not abstain from the pleasures of life. It is well-known fact that many Puritans, after becoming rich thanks to their ascetic lifestyle, began to indulge themselves in worldly pleasures. However, none of these remarks can alter the fact that in recent history Protestants have fared better than Catholics. As a social scientist, Weber did not intend to prove that all Protestants continuously obeyed the rules of a Puritanical lifestyle, but that the Puritan ethos of the Protestants, wherever it prevailed, fit well with the spirit of capitalism, and thus, on average, resulted in greater wealth among Protestants.

Werner Sombart was the main critic of Weber during the latter's life. He launched three points of criticism at The Protestant Ethic. Firstly, Catholicism, in general, tended to further the growth of capitalism, instead of blocking it. In Sombart's view, the recommendations of Benjamin Franklin were a literal repetition of the writings of the Renaissance philosopher Leon Albert. Weber countered that Albert's writings were aimed at the residents of monasteries.[56] Further, Sombart suggested that the doctrines of the Roman Catholic Church, as formulated by Thomas of Aquinas in the 14th century, already preached the gospel of Reason: *'Reason steers the universe, and has to regulate and control human passions and temptations.'* It is here, rather than in Calvinism, that we must localize the transformation from traditional to modern society. It was this doctrine that robbed medieval men of their traditional roots and passions, and replaced their primitive outlook on the world within a more rational view. Humans were advised to make better use of their intelligence. It was Thomistic philosophy that stimulated a methodically developed economy and condemned laziness and avarice. The condemnation of stinginess referred only to the hoarding of money and not to the lending of money in a profitable manner, to make money with money. Yet, this critique does not offer a strong refutation of Weber's thesis; it only points out that the roots of rational and ascetic thinking had already begun before the Protestant Reformation. Sombart did not prove that this mindset was shared by large segments of the Christian population, nor that it had already affected the economy, let alone that it boosted the economy. His main criticism is that Calvin's doctrine rejected capitalism, for capitalism was focused on mundane affairs. In no way does it constitute a preparation for the afterlife. All the time and energy used for profit making is lost before the eyes of God. Weber agreed with Sombart that Protestantism, particularly the Puritanical strand, had anti-capitalistic strains. Certainly it does not take much effort to find anti-capitalistic paragraphs in the writings of the Puritans. But the point is that the strong emphasis on working long hours and not spending your earnings on luxury items and profane pleasures offered a strong impetus for the capitalist spirit. As a sociologist, Weber was not interested in the precise content of Calvin's doctrines, but – and here he shows himself as a true and gifted social scientist – in the way in which the believers interpreted these doctrines and acted upon them in their daily life. In response to such critics as Sombart and Brentano, Weber stressed that he was interested in:

> ... the influence of those psychological sanctions which, originating in religious belief and the practice of religion, gave a direction to practical conduct and held the individual to it ... This is to speak frankly, the point of the whole essay, which I had not expected to find so completely overlooked.[57]

It should be emphasized that Protestantism did not create capitalism; it merely stimulated its development, because the work ethics of the Puritan Calvinists formed a perfect match with the spirit of capitalism. But, as soon as capitalism gained enough momentum, it pushed ever more groups of people towards a typical capitalist mind-set and a strong work ethos. This helped to stimulate production and economic growth to such a degree that the expansion simply went on and on, even after many people turned their backs to religion, in particular to Christian beliefs. Whole societies embarked on a voyage to ever-greater rationalism, to a world in which materialism replaced mysticism and solidarity and science replaced religion and enchantment.

5.6   Weber's political sociology: rationalisation of government

In whatever way a nation is governed, a business is managed or another organization is led, they all need an authority structure. There is a general need for a legitimate order, an order that is acceptable and transparent to all members. Weber defined power, as 'the likelihood that one actor within a social relationship will be in a position to carry out his will, despite resistance',[58] and defined authority or domination (Herrschaft) as 'the probability that a command... will be obeyed by a given group of people.[59] Anton Zijderveld and others feel that the concept of authority also is applicable to authority that can be derived from public opinion and professional expertise.[60] To Weber, the concept should be restricted to a much more narrow terrain. It is a form of power to which people feel themselves obliged to obey. It implies discipline and habituation, especially in the army, but not only there, so that everyone is prepared to follow orders from superiors promptly, without questioning. Power can be very short-lived, but authority assumes a certain degree of continuation. Therefore, it gives rise to a high degree of predictability in organizations. It helps to create more uniform patterns of behaviour. Thus, in comparison to a one-off occurrence of power in the hands of a particular person, it creates added value.[61]

Weber distinguished between the following pure types of authority: traditional, charismatic and rational-legal. In the first case the main source is the continuation of old traditions. Charismatic leaders can expect obedience because they claim to change the lives of their followers in a favourable manner: here, in the case of secular leaders, or in the hereafter, in the case of religious leaders. Legal-rational authorities can claim obedience on the basis of their position in the organization, a position that they have achieved legally, based on education, experience and expertise. Furthermore, it is made clear by the official rules of the organization on which occasions the individual in question can legitimately expect his or her orders to be obeyed.[62] Whereas Marx focused intensively on one-dimensional power relations, Weber, like Simmel, also shed some light on the interactive character of power and authority relations. Often, it is not a matter of simply being subjected to the exigencies of power, but also a matter of acceptance. Thus, the effectiveness of power becomes much greater. It is likely that the same is true of social stability. After all, when order has to be maintained by force or the threat of force, the dominating party must continuously take into considerations that a rebellion might erupt.

5.6.1   Traditional authority

In pre-modern societies, a form of authority prevailed based on 'sacred' traditions and created by honoured ancestors. Authorities within pre-modern tribes inherited their powers of authority from their fathers. It drew its legitimacy from these origins. In the Arabic world, for instance, many Muslim leaders claim authority and respect on the basis of their direct lineage from the prophet Muhammad. The leaders of small tribal societies did not have a staff of specialized personnel. They executed their power directly. In most cases they were experienced, elderly people of whom it was assumed that they knew best how to act in different situations, especially situations connected with old traditions. Within the realm of the extended family, the power tended to lie in the hands of a patriarch. In modern societies, such traditional forms of domination are hard to find. Presently, even the power of monarchs is tightly restricted. In democratic kingdoms, their function is mainly symbolic.

Traditional authority has two characteristic features. Its legitimacy is based on the fact that relations of domination have been regulated in this manner for very long periods of time. In the past, nobody looked for a different type of justification. The second feature was that there had always been a certain hierarchical division of society: the leader and his servants and advisors always stood in opposition to the people with a much lower status. There was no doubt whatsoever who occupied powerful positions. However, the rules that had to be followed by the elite were far less clear; there was ample room for personal interpretations and preferences. Moreover, traditional authorities did not acknowledge a distinction between the public and the private domain. They had power over their subjects, including their subject's private property. Because of this lack of demarcation between public and private, subjects had to be loyal to not only the leader but also to his close relatives. Thus, a legitimised hierarchical order appeared based on inherited power and privileges.[63]

5.6.2 *Charismatic leadership*

Charisma is a creative, driving force that breaks through long-established rules. Charismatic authority rests on the exceptional characteristics of particular leaders. Followers accept all the demands and desires of the charismatic leader and consider them to be authentic and justified. Thus, they go beyond the direct interest of merely following the rules of the existing social order. We can encounter charismatic leaders in a variety of organizations. World history has produced famous charismatic leaders that have changed whole religions and civilizations; in this respect, we can mention Buddha, Jesus and Muhammad. On a smaller scale, we can find exceptional school leaders, founders of business organizations, or national politicians with charismatic qualities. In the case of religious sects, the charismatic leader succeeds in attracting a group of intimate followers who receive some of the charisma of their leader. In this way, the leader and his circle of intimate followers steer the whole organization. Usually, sectarian leaders create a series of obligations and demand that they be fulfilled. Apart from the leader, who stands head and shoulders above the rest, the sect does not have a clear hierarchy. By chance, any follower can suddenly become a highly respected member of the inner circle of the leader. On the other hand, each member that has a close relation with the leader can fall out of grace and lose his privileged position overnight.[64]

Charisma is a specific trait of personality. Apparently, charismatic people are endowed with supernatural or at least extraordinary forces and qualities. It is of no importance whether these exceptional traits really exist. The only thing that matters is that a group of individuals believe that the charismatic leader possesses these very specific qualities, may be, because he has dark penetrating eyes. Other characteristics are far less crucial, but can become important extras, such as brilliant oratory talents, outspoken courage and heroism or a manifestation of great devotion and extremely high ethical standards. The main thing is the possession of some very striking characteristics. Since charismatic authority is based on the personal impression that the leader exerts on his followers, it has an arbitrary and maverick quality. This creates a potential danger for normal organizations and rational forms of authority. Horrific examples of charismatic leadership from recent world history are Stalin and Hitler. They abused their charismatic leadership at the cost of the lives of millions of people. Fortunately, history has also produced very positive charismatic leaders such as Mahatma Gandhi, Martin Luther King and Nelson Mandela.

Charismatic leaders do not like routine behaviour. They are inclined to unstable, eccentric and individualistic conduct. Therefore, they have to be regulated in one way or another; otherwise, the organization or system can become disorganized. Purely charismatic leadership can only play a positive role during periods of social change and innovation. As soon as the period of turbulence has ebbed away and the social system has stabilized, the need arises to be governed in a highly predictable and regularized mode. In the long run, individualistic, eccentric and arbitrary acts of leadership will harm social systems to the degree that they could fall part. Stable systems need a rather high degree of conservatism, predictability and rationalization.

5.6.3   Rational-legal authority

In modern societies authority tends to be based on rational grounds and is embedded in impersonal rules that are legally established or agreed by contract. Thus lord-mayors, secretaries of state, police inspectors, headmasters and managing directors of business organizations possess rational legal authority. They derive their authority from their professional position.

> *In the case of legal authority, obedience is owed to the legally established impersonal order. It extends to the person exercising the authority of office by virtue of the formal legality of their commands and only within the scope of authority of the office. … the person who obeys authority does so, as it is usually stated, only in his capacity as a 'member' of the organization and what he obeys is only 'the law'.* [65]

In general, a subservient has no personal bond with his boss or superior. He follows his directions and commands within the sphere of his job only. This means that the legal authorities are subjected to an impersonal order. Their behaviour and style of management has to fit this order. An ideal-typical description of legal authority excludes the possibility of the authority of chiefs also being based on other sources of authority. Some headmasters, police officers and prime ministers also have charisma. In this way, they can increase their authority and gain a greater influence over people. Likewise they might compensate certain weaknesses in their education and experience with their charisma.

5.7   Bureaucracy as an ideal type

Bureaucracies belong to a new era, an era in which formal organization prevails over informal and personal approaches to doing business. From an ideal-typical perspective, bureaucracies are based on purely rational principles such as the application of standardized rules. The functionaries apply these rules to all cases without any consideration for the social status and prestige of the persons involved in these matters. Each incumbent holds a clearly defined position with clearly defined tasks and responsibilities. The formal, hierarchical structure of the organization makes it transparent to all members of the organization who should give specific orders and who has to obey them. Thus, key concepts in any ideal-typical bureaucracy are subordination, discipline and formal rationality. They become manifest through standardization, formalisation, depersonalisation and specialisation.

Weber described bureaucratic management as the exertion of control on the basis of expertise and cognition. Bureaucratic organizations need technical knowledge for their administrative and managerial tasks. New knowledge about the efficiency of organisational procedures will be accumulated during routine on-the-job experiences. This new knowledge is used to expand the power base of the bureaucracy. Thus, the operational domain of bureaucratic control is ever expanding. Citizens will steadily be subjected to ever-growing bureaucratic organizations. This tendency is an unavoidable consequence of the demands of industrial production, which creates ever-growing units of production in order to produce mass goods efficiently. Weber did not invent the concept of bureaucracy. Hegel and Marx already used and discussed it and such nineteenth century novelists as Nicolai Gogol, Honoré de Balzac and Charles Dickens satirized it. Weber's achievement was to identify bureaucratisation as a major trend in modern society and to define it as a generic type of social organization. Organizational sociologists took his model as point of departure for the empirical study and theoretical analysis of a huge variety of special-purpose organizations such as government agencies, factories, hospitals, custodial institutions and the like.[66] In Wolfgang Mommsen's view, it is not surprising that some of them found that Weber's concept of bureaucracy – in so far as it overemphasizes the role of subordination, discipline and formal rationality – does not altogether fit the empirical reality of many present-day bureaucracies. But Weber deliberately designed an ideal type of bureaucracy to serve as a yardstick for the comparative study of organizations. Comparisons with the character, size and expansion of organizations in the past and present-day bureaucracies could be used to ascertain in exact terms the tremendous cultural significance which the rise of bureaucracies possessed for citizens living in modern societies.[67] The higher the degree of formalization and depersonalisation, the more societies became an iron cage for their members.[68]

From the perspective of accountability, achievement and usability, pure bureaucratic management is the most rational form of exercising authority, assuming that the leaders of the organization act rationally. As long as we keep in mind the ideal-typical bureaucracy, there is not much need for critical remarks. However, experience shows that bureaucratic authority can also produce rather nonrational actions, actions that often persist despite protest, actions that give great cause for irritation. These excrescences have given bureaucracies a bad name. Nowadays, they tend to be depicted as organizations that produce 'red tape' and offer easy jobs to civil servants who unduly profit from the hard-earned money of innocent taxpayers. Some of this criticism seems right. Indeed, bureaucracies tend to produce an overdose of standardized rules that cannot be applied to more specific cases. Another reason for counter-productivity is rooted in the conflicting rules produced by different governmental bureaucracies as solutions to quite different problems. A notorious Dutch example is the rule that demands that kitchen floors of restaurants be as smooth as possible for hygienic reasons; whereas another rule, issued by another ministry, demands that these floors must have a rough surface to prevent cooks from falling on a slippery surface. Yet, Weber argued that the decisive reason why bureaucratic organization has continued to advance has been its technical superiority over any other form of organization used in the past.

Ideal typical characteristics of bureaucracy

The staff and line of public bureaucracies have a position that ideal-typically has the following characteristics.

a   Civil servants are free citizens; they have to obey the rules and execute the duties connected with their official function.

b   They form part of a fixed hierarchy.

c   They have fixed jurisdictional competencies.

d   They assume their position as civil servant on the basis of free choice and agreement;

e   They are appointed, not elected.

f   They are appointed on the basis of competency; preferably, this competency is acquired through formal education and the attainment of certificates.

g   They receive a fixed salary that corresponds with their hierarchical position and status

h   They carry out their office as their only profession.

i   They make a career for themselves within the civil service and are promoted on the basis of seniority and/or achievement.

j   Official work is entirely separated from ownership of the means of administration and without appropriation of this position.

k   During their official activities, they are subjected to strict, uniform discipline and control.[69]

Box 5.2

To Weber, further bureaucratisation was unavoidable. It formed an important part of the general trend towards increasing rationalization. Modernization leads to a growth of knowledge and to an increase in the number of people that become specialists in their respective fields. Bureaucracies have a great need for the expertise and professionalism of specialists. With the help of bureaucracies, governments attempt to gain greater control over society. Standardization of decision rules, transparency of these rules and the reduction of arbitrariness produce an erosion of authority. As a consequence of depersonalisation, people are freed from traditional forms of power and authority. In view of all this, Weber ventured to predict a number of trends. Firstly, he expected a decrease in distance between social classes, because the great need for well-educated specialists would lead to an expansion of education. History has proved him right. He also foresaw that bureaucratic organizations would foster an impersonal, formalistic attitude. He even asserted that the policy measures directed at humanistic goals could fall victim to an increased level of formalism. In the end, the process of bureaucratisation boils down to a levelling of class differences and a levelling of the differences between personalities. The increased domination of predetermined categories threatens to turn individual personalities into an endangered species. These views are very similar to those ideas of Ferdinand Tönnies on the transformation from the traditional, rather romanticized small social communities of the past into more rational societies of to day.

5.8   Social action and social order

Though *The Protestant Ethic* is Weber's most famous work, the posthumously published *Economy and Society* is considered to be his main work. This treatise on general sociology consists of a rather loose set of texts on the sociology of law, economics, politics and religion. He tried to elicit sociological insights through a unique system of concepts, starting with social action.[70] Action is 'social' insofar as its subjective meaning takes account of the behaviour of others and is thereby oriented in its course.[71] Social relationships are dependent on the existence of a probability that such courses of social action will take place. The content of a social relationship can be wide-ranging – it can be conflict as well as loyalty, hostility as well as friendship. Moreover, the relationship itself need not be 'symmetrical'; even if the parties involved assign different meanings to their actions the relationship can still work. In general, social relationships point to a repeated recurrence of behaviour. Nevertheless, the recurrence of a particular social action that fits a specific social relationship always depends on chance. With humans, one can never be sure of a specific action; no matter how many times this action has occurred in the past. At any moment, a person can end or change a relation and start a different or similar relation with someone else. According to Weber, the fact that social relationships consist of past, present and future 'probabilities of action' warns us against the danger of reifying society as wholes that are endowed with that which only individuals have: a sense-giving goal-oriented will.[72] Individuals always determine their personal goals or adjust their goals in view of changing meanings they attach to their lives and the social events that occur in their immediate environment. Awareness of these probabilities should preserve us from looking at society as a monolithic whole, as a coherent unit that determines the acts of all individuals, as if this social whole possesses a will of its own.

As methodologist, Weber does not favour a sociology that reifies society in the form of a concrete acting and goal-oriented entity. Real people form the units that cause everything that happens in society. He does not accept reified abstractions such as 'Society' or 'The World Spirit' that occupied the minds of so many German philosophers of the 19th century.[73] We never see society as such, but only individuals or groups of individuals. These groups differ to such a degree that Weber thought it nonsense that the majority of civil servants, shopkeepers and labourers would share the worldview of the elite. In a similar vein, he found it inappropriate to summarize India by referring to the caste of Brahmins or Germany by referring to the philosophy of Hegel. The only way to understand societies is to start analysing the great diversity of groups and subcultures, as they exist in reality, the forces that bring them about and help them survive and the forces that regulate their mutual relations and determine their place in society.[74]

In spite of Weber's strong emphasis on methodological individualism in interpreting social processes and structures and in spite of his observation that social life is characterized by ubiquitous conflicts, he never viewed social life as and endless stream of solitary acts and events. As a sociologist, he was primarily interested in the orchestrated, communal behaviour of people and their shared opinions, norms and values. He was not interested in the thoughts and drives of singular individuals. His main focus was the emergence and reproduction of patterns of behaviour, that is, structures of social action that are repeated time and again by groups of people because they share the subjective meaning of these patterns of behaviour.[75]

In discussing these various sociological themes, Weber seems to focus solely on collectives. The subjective meanings of individuals seem to disappear beyond the theoretical horizon. This occurs to such a degree that many readers tend to overlook his methodological individualism and his method of interpretive understanding. This has given rise to a debate on a possible gap between Weber's methodology and his substantive sociology.[76] Yet, he always described structured and meaningful goals for social action of individuals. He discussed the motives and actions of the ideal-typical Calvinist, the charismatic leader, or the civil servant. Such pure types denote sets of uniform orientations, such as the ascetic lifestyle, the heroism or capriciousness of the leader and the reliability, loyalty and punctuality of the official. All of his pure types are focused on meaningful social actions. Mapping meaningful actions through ideal types leads Weber away from an analysis of isolated orientations.

5.8.1   The establishment of social order

The explicit connection between social action (*agency*) and social structure is brought about by specific modes of institutionalisation. A social order can arise through a series of uniform social actions, which Weber calls social usage (*Brauch*). Social usages can come and go, like fads and fashions. Whenever usage rests on long standing it constitutes custom (*Sitte*). Certain customs can become so familiar that they become second nature. Then people will enact them without thinking. Uniform action may also constitute a form of social order when 'determined by the exploitation of a situation that is in the self-interest of a powerful actor or a group of actors.' Finally, action can exhibit uniformity in virtue of its being regarded as morally mandatory by the actors. In that case, we speak of a convention that is a form of usage, which is recognized by many actors as binding and is protected from violation by sanctions of disapproval.[77]

What happens if people deviate from historically established customs and conventions? Depending on the type and degree of deviation, the majority of the group will exert some pressure on the deviant person. The community develops a legitimate order or system of social control and negative sanctions. That control can be laid down in conventions or laws. We speak of a convention when law establishes nothing, but there is a collective need that disapproval must be displayed towards certain forms of behaviour. If needed, the rulers of a society can establish laws that forbid certain types of behaviour vigorously rejected by large parts of society. These laws also state which type or degree of punishment will be given to perpetrators. Conventions and formal laws exist only by the grace of the exertion of punishment.[78] A social order becomes a legitimate order when most group members become convinced that this order is useful and acceptable. The larger the number of people imbued with this conviction and acting on it, the larger the legitimacy of that order. A legitimate order can be safeguarded in two ways: from within, that is, voluntarily, or from without, that is, with the help of coercion. In general, individuals can opt for the acceptance and obedience to socially instituted rules on the basis of:

1   emotional grounds;
2   value rationality determined by a belief in the absolute validity of this order as a manifestation of some ultimate ethical value;
3   a religious belief that the salvation of one's soul depends on obedience to that particular order.

The other perspective is based on the fear of negative sanctions. These sanctions can consist of general but informal expressions of disapproval. In case of the transgression of official laws, society will activate a whole system of professionals who have to treat these trespassers severely but justly. If caught and found guilty they will be fined or imprisoned for a specific period of time.[79]

Weber's theory of social action contains a very fluid element. The expectations that persons have of each other are not fixed or necessarily tuned in to each other's wavelength. While one might think that the relationship is built on true friendship, the other could be maintaining it only as long as it is in his personal interest. The main point is that the relationship satisfies both participants. In addition, the reason for starting a relationship may differ from the reasons for maintaining it. A friendly initiative can shift into a purely economic affair or the other way around. In short, to Weber, social relations and institutions are but manifestations of patterns of interaction in which people attach meaning to each other's actions. They originate and are maintained through patterns of communication, cooperation and mutual enjoyment. The social institutions emerging out of these interactions are not eternal. They are no transcendental 'things' that impose their will on people. People cooperating with each other create states. As this cooperation disintegrates, entire political states can fall apart. This became clear after the fall of the Berlin Wall in 1989. It heralded not only the reunification of Germany, but also the demise of the Soviet Union and the emergence of new states and the re-emergence of former nation states. As soon as (political) ideas and convictions change, they also change the institutions that rest on these ideas. (It would be quite a task to state the basics of philosophical idealism more succinctly.)

In general, the redefinition and re-arrangement of geopolitical landscapes will not occur continuously or easily. It suffices to recall that the Soviet Union, the GDR and former Yugoslavia survived for decades despite continuous acts of resistance and criticism. Weber acknowledges the transience of social institutions, but does not overrate them. Strong old and ossified structures, such as traditional norms, laws and conventions do not give way easily. On the one hand, there is the perspective of structuralism that emphasizes the stability of patterns of expectations that have existed for several generations and are being handed down to new generations. On the other hand, Weber gave a lot of attention to the huge potential for change that is inherent in social action, because each social pattern has to be carried out and reproduced by the members of society. So, in principle, each new generation can introduce some major institutional changes by undermining the ideas on which they were founded.

5.9   Inequality, cultural diversity and social cohesion

Weber had a keen eye for the colourful mosaic of social groups, with all their differences in culture, lifestyle, political views and economic interests. Three main categories determine the most striking features of the social structure: the economy, politics and culture. Social classes belong to the sphere of the economy, parties belong to the field of politics and estates are constituted on the basis of cultural criteria. Take for example a worker who sells his energy, time and skills to a factory owner. Both have different as well as shared interests. They both might disagree on the fairness of the salary of the worker but both share an interest in the continuation of the factory. Most probably they will not vote for the same party, but in times of war they could be mobilized to work together in a national effort to defeat the enemy. In private life, they will live according to the traditions, customs and lifestyle associated with their estate: traditions and customs that have remained the same for many generations. Hence, it is clear that behaviour has economic, political, as well as cultural roots. These three domains determine the space in which we are expected to act. To a large extent, they influence our perspectives on man and society, in particular on the members of other classes, parties, estates or societies.

Like Simmel, Weber saw conflict as an important form of social interaction. Conflicting parties are very closely focussed on the motives and actions of the other. During violent conflicts, the two enemies continuously watch each other and calculate how the enemy would act and react to their own actions. Weber is convinced that most conflicts arise from the human desire to impose their will upon others.[80] He extended Marx's one-dimensional model of stratification, a model that was based entirely on the economic dimension. In Weber's view, society is a complex whole of competing forces, in which groups are incessantly engaged in a struggle to improve their social position by enriching themselves materially, in order to raise their status and prestige and maintain or increase their political power, or to liberate themselves from suppression. The history of mankind is a history of change, wars and conflicts, exhibiting cycles of development and decline of empires, world religions, technologies and economies. Yet, despite these major transformations, there will always be groups that survive and continue to succeed in bonding their members with shared opinions and communal feelings: families, tribes, churches, sects and circles of friends. Social groups are the basic building blocks of society. They bind people together on the basis of similar economic positions, political views, or lifestyles. Within these groups, people develop their social identity, their system of values and their worldview. People are born within separate economic classes, estates and political groupings. But even if they are raised within the same economic class, they can grow up within different religious, ethnic and political spheres. Similar class positions can cover different estates and lifestyles, which can be witnessed among men and women that have experienced upward or downward social mobility. As a consequence, the social, political and cultural domain does not affect everyone to the same degree. To Weber, the most potent forces behind the establishment of groups are economic, political and cultural. Nowadays we would probably mention ethnicity as well. People who hold similar social positions and share similar economic interests, in other words people who belong to the same class, will interact with each other more frequently than those who do not share these positions and interests. There is a high probability that they will unite and establish voluntary or political organizations, with the objective of engaging in collective activities and achieving certain goals. The same is true of political positions, cultural origins and affinities.[81] He stated that class position in itself does not necessarily lead to class-determined social or political action. It is necessary to add the status group or estate as a structural category and determining factor. The political and cultural factors play a crucial role, although they are not entirely independent of economic factors. People with a similar position in the economic system can follow different political leaders, adhere to a different faith, have different ethnic origins or vary significantly in status and lifestyle. All of these dissimilarities can amount to diverse social and political interests. It is not unlikely that they have clashed with each other in the past, in conflicts that have left deep and still aching wounds. Feelings of hate and enmity can be passed on from one generation to the next and stand in the way of united action to achieve goals that are in the interests of both categories. Hence, it is clear that the sharing of economic interests can be a necessary prerequisite for the formation of a class in itself, but it certainly does not suffice for the formation of a class for itself.

Weber devoted a significant portion of his analysis to the unequal distribution of personal qualities important to success. Which qualities are important depends on the conditions in which the competition for scarce goods and desirable positions takes place. Social inequality is characteristic of the human condition. It determines differential chances for biological survival, social status and economic fortune. What is at stake is the dispositional power to attain control over opportunities and advantages, which are also desired by others.[82] There is a strong tendency to monopolise this dispositional power and to exclude others. This tendency is turned against outsiders who have been labelled as such, due to a particular characteristic such as skin colour, religion, lifestyle, dialect or mother tongue, social origin or political affinity. People attempting to exclude the other from goods, services and other advantageous opportunities of interest to both parties. Naturally, the outcome of these competitive struggles will reinforce or break down existing barriers, which have thus far marked unequal distribution. Weber acknowledged that the economy and the polity do not suffice to explain social stratification. Also cultural and religious differences create social barriers between people. Furthermore, social status or estate strongly exerts a great deal of influence determining with which groups of people given individuals will associate, or which people wish to be associated with said individuals. Status groups are bound together by notions of the right lifestyle. This is closely related to the avoidance of associating with people belonging to a lower estate and assumed to be inferior. Higher status groups can only exist if their members are endowed with a high degree of prestige. Only then will a social barrier emerge between different estates, between 'us' and 'them'.[83] Cultural hierarchies provide our world with a certain amount of further definition. Cultural stratification reinforces the socio-economic stratification. Recall the elective affinity between the Protestant ethos and the capitalist system, which made Protestants wealthier than Catholics, at least during a certain period. A second observation makes clear that the economic and political elite always strive to become the cultural elite as well. They want a legitimatized support for their higher incomes and other privileges, for they pretend and want others to acknowledge that they have worked harder and are been endowed with exceptional intelligence, creativity and leadership skills. Even aggressive and successful warlords want the respect of legitimate kings, the blessings of high priests, or to be crowned by the pope.

Weber hypothesized that there is strong tendency to make positions within the three structural dimensions more congruent, especially during periods of social stability. It is then that the rich and the mighty do their best to lift themselves to a higher cultural level. Simultaneously, they try to cover their humble social origin. In times of social unrest, revolutionaries and upstarts do their utmost to disturb the traditional hierarchies, but the groups facing an economic fall try to prevent this at all costs. Social climbers invest even more energy in reaching the top. In general, there is a close statistical connection between people's income and social status, but through an ongoing social dynamic in modern societies, which are more open than traditional societies; the connection between these dimensions will never be perfect. Though certain lifestyles and patterns of consumption simply require a high level of income or capital, it can be observed that people who have experienced a painful fall in income and financial reserves, will do all they can to hang on to their former status and thus to keep the respect of their (former) peers. *Noblesse* obliges them to keep up appearances and to hide their relative poverty. The importance of Weber's more complex sketch of the social structure is that it makes us conscious of the fact that people do not always adjust their lifestyle to their new financial situation or their present modest occupational level, but frequently go on acting as if nothing has changed and still belong to the estate they belonged to earlier. Hence, downwardly mobile people will not always act in a rational manner and will spend too much on products and services they no longer can afford. With the help of Weber's more differentiated method of looking at social positions, it is possible to arrive at more sophisticated explanations of human actions than would be possible with the help of Marx's one-dimensional approach or with a focus on instrumental-rational motives. There is more to social life than class or economic position. In fact, whereas Marx simply states that many workers suffer from false class-consciousness, Weber gives us some of the reasons for this. The dynamics of society produce double or triple loyalties. The need for a more pluralistic view on the social structure becomes even more apparent when we also take race and ethnicity into account.

5.10   In conclusion

The extremely high level and broad scope of Max Weber's oeuvre has remained unsurpassed by later sociologists. Therefore, he fully deserves the title of *the last homo universalis of sociology*. Obviously, it is impossible to do justice to his voluminous and varied body of work within the framework of one chapter. It is even more difficult to summarize that work in a short concluding section. In the first part of this chapter, we saw that Weber undertook an ingenious effort to develop a methodology that, on the one hand, suited the special demands of the social sciences as sciences researching the social actions of humans and the cultural patterns which emerge as a result of those actions and, on the other hand, still fulfilled scientific criteria set by the physical sciences. He argued convincingly that explanations of social phenomena must stand on two feet; on the study of objective social facts as well as on the subjective meaning that people attach to their own behaviour. Both play an important role in the explanation of social behaviour. His plea for the creation and testing of ideal types clearly shows that he realized that fruitful theorizing can only be achieved if we construct ideal types that focus on a relatively small set of variables of significant importance to the problem at hand. The only way to come to grips with a highly complex social reality is by foregrounding a few highly relevant aspects of the topic of study and thus neglecting other factors that are far less relevant.

Weber witnessed far-reaching social changes during his lifetime. In his view, the process of rationalization was the most crucial transformation. It forms the main theme of his oeuvre. He noticed clear signs of further rationalization in science, government and the economy. The rationality concept changes its meaning when it is used in different social contexts; all of these meanings centre round the core concepts of intelligent reasoning, increased control over nature, including human behaviour and a growing level of efficiency within the economy and the government. Even within the domain of the Christian faith, one can detect a strong tendency towards demystification and rationalization. He feared that an unlimited intensification of rationalization would manoeuvre us into a steel cage and rob us of all our humanity. In particular, he feared the negative side effects of increased standardization and over-regulation that went hand-in-hand with a growth of bureaucratisation, and a growing domination of goal-rationality over value rationality.

In view of Weber's exceptional fame it is rather strange that his work did not form the basis for a school of Weberians. The main reason for this could well be his versatility. He covered many fields and refrained from one-factor explanations. We sell him short by calling him either a macro-sociologist or a micro-sociologist. His broad interests in a large variety of topics made him explore both specializations. Substantively, he has carried out many investigations of transformations in great civilizations and the social significance of world religions. As a methodologist, he stressed that the socially acting individual is the atom of social science. He does not fit perfectly in the paradigm of conflict sociology or in that of consensual or functional sociology. Could Weber be seen as one of the theorists who negated Marx' theory of capitalism, or was his main contribution that he extended Marx' theory by adding the religious factor as an important cause of the wealth of nations? Was he an agency theorist who ranked the meaningful actions of individuals higher than the impersonal mechanism of social systems? Are his historical descriptions indicative of an evolutionist approach or did he defend the opposing historicist view, which stated that history is contingent and could have taken many different paths? Randall Collins asserts that Weber is all this and more. It appears that Weber has something to offer to all of the main sociological paradigms. Hence, each sociologist reads him differently, according to his or her own theoretical preferences.[84] People tend to gain experience, as they grow older. Thus they add new insights to their body of knowledge. Therefore it is always worthwhile to reread Weber's work more than once. With the help of a broadened frame of reference rereading will mean discovering new valuable ideas.

6
TALCOTT PARSONS

THE INCURABLE THEORIST OF
THE SOCIAL SYSTEM

The work of Talcott Parsons dominated sociology in America in the fifties and sixties. In those days he was considered to be the most important North-American sociologist of the twentieth century. After 1968, the ideological climate changed dramatically at many western universities. Critical theory, with a strong Marxist flavour, gave short shrift to his theories because they were considered to support the status quo. Hence they were deemed to be irrelevant for students who wanted to change the world. But Parsons enjoyed a new interest in his work just before he died. A few important theorists have reassessed his work in a much more positive way. Jürgen Habermas, another icon of sociology and one of the champions of critical theory, asserts that no theoretical book on sociology can be taken seriously if it does not give due attention to his work.[1] Parsons' work is no purely theoretical affair. It was aimed at describing and explaining empirical reality. His political views were strongly influenced by the rise of anti-democratic movements such as fascism and communism in the 1930s. By synthesizing the work of some of the best European social scientists he hoped to produce a better theoretical basis for liberal-democracy.

The chapter sets off with a short biographical overview of Parsons' life and career. Section 6.2 discusses his first major work: The Structure of Social Action, This theoretical synthesis merged the core elements of the work of Emile Durkheim, Max Weber, Alfred Marshall and Vilfredo Pareto. Here he presents the basic analytical elements of any social act: goals, norms, means and conditions. In section 6.3 his so-called pattern variables are being discussed. With these dichotomies we can compare and analyze the degree of modernity of societies. Modern societies would prefer universalism to particularism, achievement over ascription, reason over emotion and specificity over diffuseness. Section 6.4 deals with Parsons' theory of the social system and his structural functionalism. This is followed by a discussion of his famous AGIL-scheme. This basic scheme tells us that all societies or social subsystems have to cope with adaptation to their changing environment, to realize the main goals of the system and its members and organize itself into a well-integrated structure supported by the right culture. Section 6.6 discusses Parsons' theory of socialization. This is an important subject because it renders insight in the way new generations are prepared for their roles in society. To give some counter-fire against the biased idea that Parsons was only interested in analyzing the status quo, sections 6.7 deals with his sociological views on social change. It also deals with his views on the plight of the American Negro. Section 6.8 pays attention to his analysis of the American value system. The chapter ends with a conclusion.

6.1   Youth and family matters

Talcott Parsons was born on 13 December 1902 in Colorado Springs. He died in 1979, while visiting Germany. He was the sixth and youngest child of Edward Smith Parsons and Mary Augusta Ingersol. His father was a minister of the church, who also taught at a few small colleges and universities. Edward Parsons was not an orthodox Protestant. He had dropped the strict teachings of Calvin and devoted much of his time to a social reform movement: The Social Gospel. The main objective of this movement was to rid American capitalism of its rough bolster. He believed that socialism could only work well if it was based on Christian values. Only this basis could guarantee the rights of individuals, whereas any other variation of socialism or communism easily ignored human rights for the sake of collective goals. Parsons was raised in a relatively progressive climate, more so, because also his mother was actively engaged in political actions for women's rights.[2]

Parsons received his undergraduate training at Amherst College, where he started as a student of biology while contemplating a career in medicine. During his studies he shifted to economics. At the time, sociology proper was not taught at Amherst, though he did get acquainted with some sociological theories when he attended a philosophy course on 'The Moral Order'. Aside from the work of major moral philosophers the course paid some attention to the work of Sumner, Cooley, and Durkheim and also to the work of institutional economists as Walton Hamilton. This started his lifelong interest in the social influences on economic activities.[3] The staff of Amherst College reflected on questions such as: the relationship between Christianity, science and modern society. Amherst emphasized the great importance of a practical religion. It wanted to bridge the gap between Christianity and a modern, liberal curriculum.[4] During his studies Parsons felt best at home with theoretical problems, though, for him, propositions, theories, and theoretical systems always had to be related to empirical facts. If they did not have reference to matters of empirical fact, they could have no claim to be called scientific.[5]

Thanks to financial help of a rich uncle he could go to Europe. He spent his first graduate year at the London School of Economics, where he was influenced by the ideas of Bronislaw Malinowski, a pioneer in the development of structural-functional analysis.[6] Two other influential professors in London were Leonard T.

Hobhouse, who was the first sociology professor of Great Britain and an authority on the evolution of morality and Morris Ginsberg, an expert on the economic institutions of preliterate societies.[7] The next year he went to Heidelberg, on a grant from a newly arranged German-American exchange fellowship program. From 1925 to 1927 he studied at the university of Heidelberg, where he received his doctors degree for his thesis on *Capitalism in recent German literature: Sombart and Weber*. For his thesis he also studied the works of Karl Marx. In his first academic articles he not only pointed at the negative aspects of capitalism but also emphasized the great potential for social reform within the capitalist system.[8]

Parsons was impressed by Max Weber's move to put religious values at the frontier of the rise of capitalism. He translated *The Protestant Ethic and the Spirit of Capitalism*. Though Weber's work on economy and society contained a negative view on the further development of modern societies, this did not shake Parsons' typical American belief in the possibility of a bright future after a positive reform of capitalism.

At the age of 25, Talcott Parsons married Helen Walker. The couple had three children: Anne, Charles, and Susan. His wife worked at the Russian Research Institute. Their first child, Anne, committed suicide in 1964. Anne had great trouble merging her intellectual drive and achievements with the role of an attractive, sociable girl or woman. At home there was a strong emphasis on achievement and individual privacy. Anne missed emotional warmth and complained that her mother did not socialize her into the 'feminine mystique'. Although she did well in the field of academics, she was very dissatisfied with her social life and personal achievements. Unfortunately, psychiatric help failed.[9]

During the war, Parsons' interest shifted to political issues, such as the disparity in the support for democratic governments and the origin of fascist dictatorships. Meanwhile, he gained more academic prestige. In 1944, he was appointed as chair of the faculty. His first organizational act was to transform the Department of Sociology into a Department of Social Relations, for which he also recruited social psychologists and anthropologists. Parsons always viewed sociology as part of a broader science of man and society. In 1949, he was elected as president of the American Sociological Association and soon became chief editor of *The American Sociologist*. Three of his best known students were Kingsley Davis (1908-1997), Robert King Merton (1910-2003) and Wilbert E. Moore (1914-1987). He died on the 8th of May 1979, while visiting Munich, Bavaria, where German sociologists had organized an academic conference dedicated to his work.

6.1.1   A purely academic career

In 1927, Parsons became a lecturer in economics at Harvard University. Four years later he shifted to sociology. It took another five years before he became an assistant professor. In 1939, he was appointed as Associate Professor of Sociology, and, finally, in 1944, he got tenure as full professor. To his own taste, Parsons had been a lecturer and assistant professor far too long. For this he blamed Pitirim

Sorokin, the chair of the department of sociology, who disliked his work. In Sorokin's view it was 'full of shameful academic jargon, without clear meaning, precision and elementary elegance.'[10] In 1944, he became the chairman of the department of sociology, which he chaired until 1956.

In the beginning of his career, his main focus was on topics that could be claimed by economists as well as sociologists. He conceived the idea of making a study of the relations – differences and articulations – between economic and sociological theory. For this he studied the work of two very prominent economists of a previous generation, Alfred Marshall and Vilfredo Pareto. The latter was also a sociologist. Parsons also took a great interest in the work of Durkheim, in particular in his *Division of Labour*, again a sociological book on a rather economic topic. This interest was aroused by the highly negative attitude towards the work of Durkheim that he encountered at the London School of Economics. But the more he studied Durkheim in the original language, the more he came to disagree with his London teachers.[11] All these intellectual activities resulted in a synthesis of European sociological thought that – with the exception of an extensive discussion of Simmel – found his way in *The Structure of Social Action*, published in 1937. This book launched Parsons' career on the path of fame. In *The Structure*, he presented his voluntaristic theory of action. As a real liberal, he made ample space for individual freedom, the freedom to make individual choices. As a great admirer of the work of Max Weber, he also emphasized that individual actions tend to be social actions, that is, actions in which individuals take notice of their fellow citizens, their interests, norms, and values. This consideration for the interests of the other would reduce the scope for individual choices. Durkheim's work also strongly pointed in the direction of socially orchestrated actions of individuals. However, every social arrangement also leaves some scope for individual interpretation. For Parsons, the work of Durkheim, Marshall, Pareto, and Weber could be synthesized in a theoretically fruitful way. In his view, only the notion of a social orchestration of individual actions can explain why society functions and why there is a large degree of consensus about societal values.

6.1.2   Three phases in Parsons' theoretical quest

In the forties, his attention had moved from the social action of individuals towards the study of social systems. In 1951, he published *The Social System*. Herein, he integrated a series of ideas he had developed since 1937. Now, he also tried to fit some ideas of Sigmund Freud in his action theory. In 1953, he published, together with Bales and Shils, *Working Papers in the Theory of Action*. Three years later followed *Economy and Society*, which was the result of a close cooperation with Neil Smelser. These two books mark the start of his third theoretical phase. He now shifted his focus on essential functions of social systems. This new phase produced the famous AGIL-scheme, the analytical model of the four prerequisite functions of any social sustainable system. No system can survive without sufficient adaptation to its environment (A), the realization of its goals (G), its internal structural integration (I) and the maintenance of cultural patterns or a state of latency (L). By creating this model, Parsons threw an entirely new light on the coherence of social systems, on the cohesion between structure and culture and on the role that individuals play in this system.

His theoretical work rendered him the label of structural-functionalist. His functionalism was criticized in many ways and for various reasons. A frequently mentioned critique was that his perspective led to an 'over-socialized' conception of man.[12] Parsons reacted that the individual can be conceived as a socialized being whose individualism was 'institutionalized'.[13] A second major critique stated that his work was too abstract and too general to be of relevance for the study of concrete societies. Not only Robert King Merton, but also C. Wright Mills argued that the 'Grand Theory' that Parsons was aiming for would be unable to make concrete social problems understandable, let alone solvable.[14] In the view of Wright Mills, Parsons' abstract theories were little more than a cover up for essentially simple and mundane ideas about society. A third form of critique was of an ideological nature. From a scientific point of view this form of critique was irrelevant, but from a social-political perspective it was devastating. It labeled Parsons as a right-wing conservative. The latter's defense of America's democracy triggered the accusation that he had no eye for social inequality. But this critique was uncalled for. As a consequence of all these forms of critique his work has played a less important role in American education than is widely is assumed.[15]

Unperturbedly, Parsons went on with the further development of his theoretical work. He learned from his critics and from the problems he faced whenever he attempted to apply his models to empirical situations. In his view, theorists should be concerned with the systematization and explanation of aspects of the empirical world. Parsons distinguished between four levels of systematization. At the most primitive level theorists start with (1) *ad hoc* classificatory systems, which could evolve into more systematic (2) categorical schemes or conceptual frameworks. These can form the basis for (3) abstract theoretical systems and (4) empirically testable theoretical systems. Thus, his starting point for the development of a theoretical system is a workable typology of units composing a categorical system or set of interrelated 'general concepts' of empirical reference. Any well-developed categorical system or sound theory must fit the facts. It must fit the subject matter with sufficient complexity and articulation to describe the interdependence of the empirical systems under study.[16] The body of a theory in a given field at a given time constitutes an integrated system of propositions. It follows that any important change in our knowledge must of itself change the statement of at least some of the propositions of the theoretical system, and by consequence, that of other propositions to a greater or lesser degree.[17]

In the last phase of his life, Parsons' work branched out in many directions. He dived into the depth of micro-sociology through a renewed study of socialization processes. In addition, he went on exploring the macro-space of systems theory. And finally, he went far back into the history of mankind to analyze the evolutionary development of social actions.

6.2   Towards a theory of social action

The Structure of Social Action, Parsons' first major work is based on an extensive and clear discussion of the sociological work of Emile Durkheim, Max Weber, Vilfredo Pareto, and the economist Alfred Marshall. He started this theoretical work with the presentation of an important social dilemma. Though, the western world had put a great trust in the integrity and rationality of the individual, precisely these two crucial tenets of its culture had been tested by the outbreak of two Great Wars, and the atrocities of Communist and Fascist regimes. For Parsons, the root of the problem lay in the theoretical weakness of the intellectual traditions of the West.[18] He thought that fascism and communism could seize power because classical social theory failed to offer the right alternative. Liberal ideology had to be revitalized and reformulated in order to safeguard human integrity and reason.[19]

Parsons opened a ferocious attack on the non-sociological, purely individualistic approach of the utilitarians, because they would not acknowledge any role for collective values and ignored individual emotions.[20] However, there are many situations in which humans act in unselfish ways, respecting social norms and values, responding to altruistic motives and showing a sincere concern for fellow citizens. A horde of pure egotists cannot survive. The rational motive can only explain part of all social actions. As Weber has made clear, there also are other motives, such as emotional, traditional, and value-rational motives to describe and explain social actions. Individual actors are continuously interacting with fellow human beings. Within the social system of which they are members, their position, status, and roles are relatively fixed. Though, Parsons was well aware that social conditions restrict individual freedom in significant ways, he energetically maintained that humans have some freedom to make all kinds of choices. For a true liberal democratic like Parsons it was crucial to stress this element of free will. The whole point of his voluntaristic theory of (social) action was that individuals only have a limited freedom of choice, but he found it very important to stress that there are always options left open. In his view, the freedom of choice of the rational choice theorists really is no freedom at all. It appears that individuals must always put their self-interest first, they must go for the shortest route with the least effort, or the lowest price. For Parsons, people have much more options to make their choices than purely economic and egotistic ones. On the other hand, traditions, customs, norms and values can oblige us to make choices that are not rational at all. They restrict our freedom in many ways. But often this restricted freedom is worth fighting for. For an incurable theorist the best way to emphasize and clarify this limited freedom is to describe its mechanism, including the scope, range and limits of the options. He found the concept of voluntaristic action indispensable for any action theory.

Another major flaw in the approach of stimulus-response behaviourists and rational choice theorists is that their purely individualistic approach cannot explain social order. We need an insight in the meaning of social norms. The motives concerning socially accepted rules of behaviour, norms, and values form the necessary building blocks of society. They play a vital role. Every wish, desire, or objective is embedded in a set of normative considerations, social standards and expectations. They canalize the will of individuals. Thus, social behaviour emerges that not only is based on purely individual wishes and desires, but also takes account of the interests of others. To express this in an apt and succinct way, Parsons spoke of 'institutionalized individualism'. Any form of social behaviour entices a certain tension between personal objectives and the restrictions created by social conditions. What has to be explained is how social order is maintained, even under conditions of social change and evolution.

6.2.1   The unit act [21]

The most significant trait of Parsons' synthesis is that he united the positivistic and holistic ideas of Durkheim with the idealistic and individualistic theories of Weber. For Parsons, the nexus between the individual and the collective still needed further explanation. What does it mean that people start considering the norms and values of collectives? What does it mean that they start and remain behaving within the confinements of a social order and thus help maintain this order? According to Durkheim, the collective conscience demands respect for the moral authority of the social whole. Parsons agreed. Every social unit is regulated by a morally guided system of values that manifests itself in social norms, and simultaneously is anchored in the motives and intentions of individuals, because the latter have appropriated these objective social norms and internalized them.

Thus Parsons not only made a strong connection between the ideas of Weber and Durkheim, but he also bridged the theoretical gap between individual and society. He made clear how the institutionalization of social norms and the recurrent reproduction of these norms, by way of regulating behaviour in behavioural patterns, traditions, customs, laws and norms, always coincide with the internalization of these norms, laws, traditions, by the members of that social group. Like Durkheim, Parsons preferred the internalized, subjectively acquired and consciously anchored moral constraint to the external constraint of social control. Obviously, the fear for punishment does play a role, but is of less importance for the maintenance of society than conflict theorists might think. The inner felt obligation is of much more importance. A social order entirely based on the interlocking of personal interests is a social order based on negative sanctions. In theory, such an order could be envisioned but is extremely hard to realize. Besides, as a liberal, he refused to trust in a police state.

Parsons' model of social action departed from a single actor that sets his goals and chooses appropriate means to achieve these goals. Actors not only are intellectually capable of choosing objectives and instruments, but they are guided to make these choices within the confines of social norms and values. So, actors take the opinions, feelings, and interests of fellow humans into account. Without this normative element there can be no social behaviour. Without this we run the risk of ending up in the camp of theorists who interpret behaviour purely as instinctive reactions to incentives.[22] But humans act out of free will, yet not purely egotistic. They act rational within a context that expects a balance between egotistic and social behaviour.

Initially, Parsons did not choose the individual as the unit of analysis, but the *unit act*. The unit act occurs as one unit in the context of a wider action system, which includes a great manifold of acts. Even for the analysis of one discrete act, an extended set of similar acts must be conceived, for example those comprising a particular role. However, this mini-system is complete and complex. It encompasses personal goals, available means, social norms, and conditions that cannot be influenced by an individual actor. Norms and conditions restrict the range of possible actions.[23] In general, only collectivities can change sets of social norms and social conditions. For Parsons, it does not make much sense to speak of social action if one does not take into account the four essential components of the unit act. When one or two components are lacking it is impossible to make a complete and meaningful description of any example of social behaviour.

Scheme 6.1   Core elements of the social act

	individualistic	collectivistic
idealistic	goals	norms
materialistic	means	conditions

In *Toward a General Theory of Action* Parsons began to view actions as a process occurring between two structural parts of a system – actor and situation. The concept 'actor' was extended to define not only individual personalities in social roles but also other types of acting units, such as collectivities. That's why Parsons attempts to avoid – except for purposes of analogy or illustration – psychological references, such as 'need', 'motivation' and 'intention', attributed to human beings. Thus 'actor' can also refer to a business firm, a political party, or a family.[24]

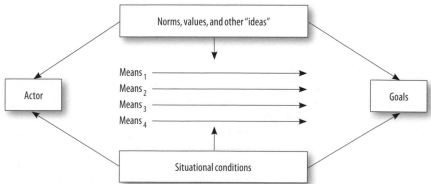

Scheme 6.2   Actions between two structural parts of a system
Social action in context

6.3   Pattern variables and the comparison of cultures

In Parsons' view, it is possible to map the relation between individuals and their social and physical environment in a satisfactory way with the help of a few well-chosen variables, which he called 'pattern variables'.[25] The pattern variables first emerged as a conceptual scheme for classifying types of roles in social systems, starting with the distinction between professional and business roles. In this sense, the concept 'actor' referred to individual human beings as personalities in roles. As we know we all have to play many roles in society. From time to time, policemen have to interrogate men or women suspected of a crime. They are expected to do this in a professional way, that is, by the book. They have learned how to do this during their initial training period, but their methods have been developed further during the early stages of their career, when new recruits were coupled to more experienced cops. During this process they might have learned that it sometimes can be effective to play the good cop/bad cop. Besides the different roles being played during working hours, they also have to play different roles at home as a parent, or as 'a child' when visiting their parents, when they go shopping, participate in a team, team leader, or referee. So, as we all know, each of us has to master many different roles, each of us has to reckon with what is expected from us in different social positions and situations.

Even when we get sick, we have to fulfill a specific role model. Somehow, we have learned to become a model patient. Parsons was the first to describe the role of the patient in an ideal typical way. First, he defined illness as a state of disturbance in the normal functioning of the total human individual, including the biological, psychological and social dimension of his existence. Illness always has a social dimension; it will have an effect on participation in society. People might ask whether 'being sick' constitutes a social role at all – isn't it simply a state of fact, a 'physical condition'?[26] Parsons made clear that there is more to it than simply some dysfunction of the body or the personality. He pointed out that there are four culturally embedded role expectations related to the role of the sick. Despite the huge range of different types of illnesses, it is possible to describe a set of abstract and general aspects of the sick role.

- First, people who are sick are exempted from their normal social responsibilities. If the illness is rather serious we do not expect people to come to work, to participate in sport activities, to go on holidays, or to join parties. On the other hand, we do not expect people to exaggerate their state of illness or simulate an illness when they are healthy.
- Secondly, the sick are not expected to get well by an act of personal will power. Sick persons and the people around them – members of the family, neighbours, friends, and colleagues – must accept that being ill is not someone's fault. They should be regarded as the victim of forces beyond their control. Therefore, they are not expected to 'pull themselves together' and to go on with life as if nothing has happened.

- In the third place, illness is generally defined as an undesirable state. Hence, we expect the sick to do all they can to get well soon.
- Closely related to this third aspect is the fourth, that is, the obligation to seek help from competent and qualified doctors and to follow this doctor's orders. In other words, they are expected to swallow their pills, stop working, stay in bed, change their diet, or, if necessary, to go to hospital for surgery.[27]

Of course all people who are closely related to the sick person are also expected to act according to their roles. The doctor should act in a professional way, take a careful look at the patient's body for the sake of a good diagnosis, and not look at it as a sex object. This example shows that objects do not automatically determine the actor's orientation of action. A chair can be seen as a useful thing to sit on, as a beautiful specimen of antique or modern design, as an object with specific physical properties, or even as a weapon that can be used to defend oneself. So, according to Parsons, actors have to make a few fundamental choices before any situation can have meaning to them.

In the first instance, actors distinguish between a set of orientations and a set of modalities. Orientations concern the actor's relationship to the objects in his situation. These orientations are conceptualized by two attitudinal variables: (1) diffuseness – specificity and (2) affectivity – neutrality. Orientations refer to the psychological need for relating to the object world. Modality concerns the meaning of the object for the actor and is conceptualized by the two 'object-categorization' variables: (3) quality versus performance and (4) universalism versus particularism.[28]

If we relate these four pattern variables to patients and the sick role we can distinguish between patients with a negative, neutral or positive attitude to their particular disease or to diseases in general, to their medical doctor or to the whole field of medicine or alternative methods of healing. Some might start to hate their failing body and lack all trust in the possibility of regaining their health, while others accept their illness as a form of bad luck that could have happened to anybody while trusting that the doctors will help his or her recovery in the shortest possible time. The attitude towards one's illness might remain rather specific, and aimed to quick recovery by strictly following doctor's orders. It can also become more diffuse and lead to a general interest in theories about the causes of this illness and the different methods of healing, or to a membership of a patient's organization or an impulse to become politically active aimed at the goal to implement policies of information about prevention, or intensified research programs to find better medical treatment. On the other hand, if patients have developed a negative attitude to official medicine because of its relation to hard sciences such as pharmaceutical chemistry, painful experiments with animals, the use of industrially fabricated 'spare parts' et cetera, they might turn to alternative non-scientific methods of healing with the help of herbs or rituals.

The example of persons confined to a sick role shows that there is a close connection with the need of humans to relate to the object world in a particularistic or a universalistic way and to evaluate the world on the basis of ascriptions or achieve-ments. They can trust or distrust the achievements of medical science; they can trust or distrust the capabilities of a particular medical doctor or specialist or the entire staff of a hospital; they can trust or distrust a particular medicine or cure, and so on. Furthermore, a comparative study of medical practices in different countries or cultural areas focused on these four pattern variables would reflect striking conflicts between these cultures. Which goals or practices get priority, particularism or universalism, achievement or social origin?

Parson's pattern variables

1 Affectivity versus affective neutrality
This variable refers to the degree of emotional commitment and impulsiv-ity. Within an affective social setting the expectations of ego and alter are guided by the positive or negative feel-ings they have towards each other. In these situations people tend to react immediately. In a neutral social setting people try to suppress their feelings and will react rationally after considering all the options carefully. In general a teacher will behave much less affection-ate towards his pupils than towards his own children.

2 Diffuseness versus specificity
This pattern variable concerns the dilemma of the range of social connec-tions and obligations. An employer will have a broader range of relations with his family than with his employees. The relationship with most of his employees

will be strictly professional, although we can observe many exceptions to this rule.

3 Particularism versus universalism
This variable concerns the evaluation of specific actors or groups of individu-als, for instance your next of kin, or a more general category such as your colleagues or competitors. With this pattern variable the distinction be-tween the in-group and out-group is important. Within a universalistic frame of reference actions are determined by norms that pertain to everybody in an equal way.

4 Ascription versus achievement.
This dimension speaks for itself. Do we find achievements more relevant than someone's ascribed characteristics such as gender, class or race?

Box 6.1

Parsons used his pattern variables when he studied professionals and their func-tioning with clients. In his study of lawyers, doctors or psychiatrists, he found that besides competence, objectivity, and affective neutrality also personal char-acteristics played a significant role. These characteristics can affect the objectivity and neutrality of the professional. We all know that there are too many cases in which the incumbents of these professions have engaged in sexual relationships with their clients. When professionals fail to keep sufficient distance and objec-tivity this will harm their clients or patients.

Of course, reality is more complex than binary models can present. There always are many shades of gray between jet black and snow white. In reality, professionals and their clients can develop a kind of relation that is not completely functional; teachers and pupils cannot help to develop some positive or negative feelings towards each other. This can interfere with the objectivity of the teacher when he or she has to mark a student's work. At some point the shift from universalism to particularism or from affective neutrality to affective partiality can go too far and harm professional relations and effectiveness.

The examples indicate that within cultures there is a tendency to form clusters of categories. Modern societies emphasize objectivity, neutrality, universalism, and specificity, whereas traditional societies lay much more stress on subjectivity, emotionality, particularism and diffuseness. Of course, there are many cultures with a set of values that covers the middle ground.

6.4   The social system

In 1951, Parsons published two books with the word 'system' in its title: *Values, Motives and Systems of Action* and *The Social System*. This shows that his frame of reference no longer was dominated by purely individual social actions, but by actions within a system. From then on, the focus was on one or more actors oriented towards a situation with other social actors. Orientation, this rather vague concept, should draw our attention to the goals of actors within a social system. All social actions take place within a system of actions. They are no direct 'responses' to specific stimuli. George Herbert Mead has put a reflective element of the organism between the stimulus and the response. Parsons related this mediating element to the social system. In his perspective, social actions refer to initiatives and reactions that fit in a system of role expectations. These expectations are not only based on physical and psychological needs, but also on existing action patterns within one's culture, social group or network.

Individuals develop a relatively stable perspective on a variety of social situations. They constitute a whole set of expectations about future developments, options, and opportunities. These expectations and ideas are based on personal needs, knowledge, and the values attached to these objects of desire. In the past, persons might have put a lot of energy in realizing the necessary conditions. These investments are very important. The individual can always choose between doing nothing and waiting how things will develop, or participate more actively, in order to raise the chance of a favourable development.[29] In case someone's life does not render any satisfaction or gratification it will lose its meaning. Then actors will lose all motivation or commitment to act. If too many members get stuck in this kind of emotional situations then the system will fall apart.

Once more, we notice that for Parsons the concerted social actions of individuals keep social systems in process. Therefore, all individuals should get something positive out their interactions with other members of the system; otherwise their motivation to participate will drop below zero. Then, they will no longer put an effort in the maintenance and reproduction of the system. But what someone sees as a positive incentive or a negative sanction largely depends on one's personal affinities and dispositions and on one's cultural background. So, it is important to find the right mixes of egotism and solidarity with the collective.

6.4.1   Structural functionalism

Social systems are very complex. They are not static but continuously 'in flux'. A great variety of processes are going on to keep it alive, to keep all subsystems fulfilling their functions and fighting internal and external tendencies that could destroy the system. Any change in one part of the system entices a reaction in another; all elements are somehow related to each other, directly or indirectly. However, it is impossible to study all these elements, subsystems, functions, and processes at one time. The best strategy to come to grips with complexity is simplification. That is why Parsons always sought to develop relatively simple models. This raises the question how this simple analytical structure has to be linked to the variable elements of complex social systems. Parsons thought that he could answer this question by conceptualizing functions. In his view, system elements are vitally important in so far that they are crucial for the maintenance and reproduction of functional relations between the parts of the social system and between the system and his surroundings.[30]

A logical follow up of the analysis of social systems is the analysis of the functional requisites of those systems. Systems will fall apart if these functional needs are not met. Social systems survive as a consequence of patterned interaction processes between individuals. It is evident that social systems need real members; they need a sufficient number of healthy individuals. Therefore, a viable biological environment is a functional prerequisite. The people that make up the system have to satisfy their biological needs of fresh air, drink, food, and sleep. Furthermore, each social system needs a subsystem to maintain the enduring system of action patterns that the system has developed for its own continuity. Hence, there always must be a sufficient number of people that are sufficiently motivated to work for the system and its continuity.[31] This implies that systems cannot demand too much of their members, otherwise they will stop cooperating. On the other hand, individuals cannot demand too much from the system, because the fulfilling of extreme demands has to be done by other members of the system. So, once more, we see that finding the right balance is crucial for the survival of social systems. Hence, social systems need a subsystem for motivating and controlling members to stay within the system and to remain cooperative. This is another functional requisite. For the analysis of dynamic-functional systems, such as societies, two system-problems are of the utmost importance. In order to survive, any system has to find a solution for the problem of task allocation and for the problem of integration or coordination. In modern societies the core problem is concentrated in the distribution of money and power. Integrative processes have to control the conflicts generated by distribution processes. Social systems need a policy of *divide et impera*, but should not degenerate into dictatorships. It is far better for the system to develop a more subtle mechanism of control than brute exertion of power. So, there is need for the institutionalization of a set of rules that ensures the validity of distribution procedures.

Not all social positions, functions and tasks are endowed with the same prestige. Prestige can vary from very low to very high. Parsons believed that important social positions would acquire a high prestige and thus succeed in attracting sufficient qualified people.[32] This is a typical functionalistic explanation. If a system

---

Solving the problem of task allocation?

In 1945, Kingsley Davis and Wilbert E. Moore published an influential article that has triggered much sociological debate.[33] In *Some principles of stratification* they argued that social inequality is a functional necessity. Therefore, all societies possess a structure of social stratification. *'As a functioning mechanism a society must somehow distribute its members in social positions and induce them to perform the duties of these positions. It must thus concern itself with motivation at two different levels: to instill in the right individuals the desire to fill certain positions, and, once in these positions, the desire to perform the duties attached to these positions. ... If the duties associated with the various positions were all equally pleasant ... all equally important to societal survival, and all equally in need of the same ability or talent, it would make no difference who gets what position. ... But actually it does make a great deal of difference... Inevitably, a society must have, first, some kind of reward that it can use as incentive, and, second, some way of distributing these rewards differentially according to positions. The rewards and their distribution become a part of the social order, and thus give rise to stratification.'* According to Davis and Moore,

inequality is an unconsciously evolved device by which societies insure that the most qualified persons carefully fill the most important positions. If a socially important position is easily filled, it need not be heavily rewarded. On the other hand, if it is important but hard to fill, the reward must be high enough to get the job done. Functional importance is a necessary but not a sufficient reason of high rank being assigned to a position. Scarcity of talents or motivation also plays a role. Davis & Moore gave the example of Medical doctors. In their view, a medical education is so burdensome, takes so much time, and is so expensive that virtually none would undertake it if the position of the M.D. did not carry a reward commensurate with the sacrifice, that is a high salary, high status, and ditto prestige. Besides mentioning the negative side of medical training we could also mention many negative aspects of the actual job, such as frequent contact with people, young and old, with horrible injuries, stinking wounds, or suffering from contagious diseases or even suffering from a mortal disease. In those cases all professional help will be of no avail and you will see them die.

Box 6.2

has a need, and the supply is scarce, then it will see to it that the need is fulfilled by attaching very attractive rewards to these positions that are essential for fulfilling this need, and thus for the continuity of that particular system.

6.5   Parsons' famous AGIL scheme

Social systems are alive. To stay alive, even without growth but simply retaining the status quo, all kinds of processes have to go on all the time to prevent big disturbances and total collapse. Parsons divided social processes into two types: *mechanisms* and *tendencies*. Mechanisms are processes that stabilize social action systems, and tendencies are processes that disturb the state of equilibrium or lead to structural changes in the system. The equilibrium concept is derived from physics. Forces from outside can disturb the equilibrium. The state of equilibrium is the net result of a number of characteristics or variables from the system and influences from outside. Parsons wanted to observe and analyze social systems in the same way as Newton observed and analyzed physical phenomena. He wanted to find out which forces help to maintain the state of equilibrium and which forces could change and disturb it. His great interest in biology inspired him to study homeostasis in social systems. He was convinced that social systems, like biological organisms, could redress disturbances with the help of interdependent organisms of the system, no matter whether these disturbances are caused by forces inside or outside the system.[34] A system is stable or in equilibrium when the relation between its structure and the processes which go on within it, and the interactions with its environment, are such as to maintain those properties and relations that keep the system alive, relatively unchanged, and functioning. To understand this equilibrium act, Parsons was looking for core functions that need to be fulfilled or carried out to keep social systems going. He assumed that all human societies, from the most primitive to the most complex, have so much in common that there must be a small set of fundamental organizing principles shared by all of them.

When Parsons elaborated these ideas further, he arrived at his most important theoretical invention: the discovery and description of four functional problems that are absolutely crucial for the internal integration and the survival of social systems.[35] This invention culminated in a very simple but elegant model, the famous AGIL-scheme. By paying more attention to the other social actors around ego, Parsons developed a keen eye for the social relations between all members of a social system. This shift of attention meant a relocation of the center of his theory from the individualistic aspects towards the collective aspects of behaviour. Existence in social groups generates a system of *status-roles*. Parsons defined status-roles as systems of expectations that are connected with the behaviour of the incumbents of these roles. The evolution of these patterns of expectations leads to the institutionalization of all kinds of customs and enduring relations. This network of social positions and their mutual relations form the skeleton or basic structure of societies.

Parsons did not think it wise to study dynamic social processes before one has acquired a clear idea about the structural frame in which these dynamic processes take place.[36] How did he view this basic structure? From his perspective all social systems are differentiated along two dimensions. The first axis refers to external and internal relations; the second refers to functional problems related to internal stability. By splitting these dimensions in two sides he created a fourfold model that describes four major functional problems: *adaptation, goal attainment, integration* and *latency*. Solving these four problems is crucial for the survival of any system.

Scheme 6.3   Parsons' model of the social action system

	means	goals
external	**Adaptation (behavioural system)**	**Goal attainment (personality system)**
internal	**Latency (cultural system)**	**Integration (social system)**

It is possible to apply this AGIL scheme to any subsystem of the social action system, the behavioural system, the personality system, the cultural system and the social system. To discuss the four functional imperatives it might be better to go back one step from the abstraction ladder and to focus on one of these subsystems, for example a social system, such as a national society. Consequently the same could be done with for instance the polity leading to the following four subsystems each taking care of one functional imperative: A = Administration; G = the Government; I = the Parliament, and L = the Constitutional-Legal System. This could become an endless play of going on to ever-deeper levels of subsystems of subsystems. However, to explain the gist of the model it is best to keep in mind the following model of a normal modern society:

Scheme 6.4   The AGIL model applied to the social system

A	G
The Economy	The Polity
The Culture or Fiduciary System L	The Social Community I

Adaptation – All social systems need resources. Humans need food and drink. Without food and drink, clothes and shelter, they cannot function and are of no use for the system. Nature has to give them the necessary energy so that society can receive energy in the form of meanings and social actions. In modern societies the subsystem of the economy will take care of that.

Goal realization – Goal realization refers to the priorities of system goals and the mobilization of the means to achieve system goals. The social system must have a sufficient number of its members adequately motivated to act in accordance with its requirements; otherwise it will deteriorate or stop to exist.[37] Ultimately, these system goals are the means for individuals to achieve personal objectives. It is the main task of the political system to see that the right balance is found between collective and individual priorities.

Integration – Integration concerns the problem of coordinating and maintaining workable relations between all members of the system, and between all units and subsystems. The stabilization of patterns of interaction must generate workable relations between the units and subsystems of social systems. This process of institutionalization must engender a well-organized network of social positions and social roles. The social community or social system proper has to be well structured and organized in a system of social associations and organizations, social roles, statuses and professions.

Latency – Latency concerns two closely related problems: pattern maintenance and conflict management. Social systems must avoid 'commitment to cultural patterns which either fail to define a minimum order or place impossible demands on people, thereby generating deviance and conflict.'[38] Socialization and education or enticing people to maintain functional patterns of behaviour are the main tasks of the cultural subsystem. Conflict management encompasses the regulation, evasion or mitigation of internal tensions that may arise between members of the system.[39]

Looking at the AGIL-scheme from a second level of abstraction is realizing that social behaviour occurs within four contexts: the physical-biological system, the individual-psychological system, the social-structural context of interactions between individual members and subsystems of the system and their social positions and the cultural context of norms, values, convictions, opinions, knowledge and ideologies. Clearly, a social system has to be well adjusted to all these contexts. Therefore, it has to invest sufficient resources for maintaining good relations with these four conditions. Moreover, it has to solve the problem of coordinating all the necessary functions of the system. Thus, the system has to watch that its priorities are clear. Finally, it has to take care of its internal adaptation function: the socialization and disciplining of the members of the system. The AGIL-scheme not only is a systematic elaboration of ideas that he has published before, but it also is an expression of the shift in his focus of interest from the social act (phase 1), via a focus on the structure of social systems (phase 2) to the functioning of social systems and the interactions between subsystems (phase 3). In the third phase, Parsons focused on the analysis of the functional contribution of social structures and sub systems. What do they do to keep the system going? So, yet another way of looking at the AGIL-scheme is to realize that social systems are based on four subsystems that are interdependent and that all are related to one of the functional imperatives. In modern societies the adaptive subsystem has evolved into the following subsystems: the economy helps individuals to get all society needs for its survival from the wider environment of that social system, including nature, humans, and other societies. The better subsystems such as education, law, science and technology are developed, the better the economy can fulfill its role. Human societies are based on adequately functioning personality systems. To motivate persons to fulfill their roles the system has to satisfy the needs of these individuals. The subsystem that takes care of that is the political system. The organizational structure of the social system consists of defined roles and their institutionalized, that is, personally internalized and collectively shared role-expectations. The cultural system consists of the heritage of shared symbols, knowledge, beliefs, ideas, technologies, mores, customs, habits, laws, standards, norms, and values. The main function of the cultural system is to prepare new generations for their role as social beings, that is, for their role as contributors to the continuation of the system as a whole.[40] Evidently, the four subsystems are closely connected. They have to cooperate to keep each other and the system as a whole alive. At the most general level, the level of the action system, Parsons sketched the following model of interchanging relations between the four subsystems.[41]

Scheme 6.5   The interchange model of the social action system

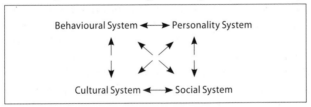

Actually a full description of the model would show several double pointed arrows between all four subsystems to show that energy, material means, information, power, influence, trust, loyalty, motivation and commitment, positive and negative sanctions, money and immaterial rewards have to be exchanged simultaneously between the respective subsystems. This multifarious circle of exchanges has to function sufficiently to create a rather stable dynamic social equilibrium.

6.6   Parsons' theory of socialization[42]

Why is there order? Why are humans not constantly fighting with each other? This is the famous question posed by Thomas Hobbes that Parsons answered by saying that most people adhere to a common set of values to which they attune their goals. This leads us to the next question: how do these common standards come about? To explain this Parsons turned to the process of socialization. His approach offers valuable insights in the mechanism that creates the symbiosis between individuals and society, which is a crucial topic for sociologists. His theory of socialization also shows how he integrated ideas of Sigmund Freud in his own theories. Finally, his approach underlined that he really strove to be a general social scientist and not a purely disciplinary sociologist. Hence he paid just as much attention to the personality system as to the social system.

6.6.1   Freud's legacy

Parsons' brother was a physician. This opened the door for a 'participant observation' of social life in a hospital. Dressed in a doctor's white coat, he made his rounds through the hospital and observed many interactions between patients and doctors. Thus he learned that the praxis of a physician encompasses much more than scientific and rational actions. It also has many non-rational aspects. Hence, his initial interest in conscious instrumental rationality shifted to the role of the unconscious. From studying Freud, he had learned about the early development of young children, and this lead his investigative mind on the path to primary socialization. In particular, he was inspired by Freud's concept of *introjection*, though he preferred the term *internalization*. Individuals appropriate collective norms and values through a process of internalization, in which rules, habits and customs get so deeply ingrained in the human consciousness that they become entirely natural. People get so strongly accustomed to the prevalent norms and values that they no longer ponder on the idea that things just as well could have been arranged differently. This non-reflexive attitude towards the actual state of affairs is enhanced by the fact that young children are strongly inclined to identify with their parents and carers. According to Freud, it is the universal need for love and affection *(cathexis)* that entices children to identify with their objects of love. Through identification and imitation children start to copy their parents. Simultaneously, they internalize their norms and values.

According to Durkheim, social norms are being assimilated in our consciousness. Here, Parsons noticed some similarities with the ideas of Freud. Both put a strong emphasis on moral rules. Freud employed the notion of *super-ego*. On the one hand, this is our moral conscience that speaks to us whenever we are doing something that deviates from the prevailing norms and values. On the other hand, this is a sort of 'Ideal Me', or a highly desirable goal of perfection and maximal personal development. Freud began his theorizing with a strong focus on the individual. Later on, he became aware of the huge importance of the social context. Hence, he started to analyze how the social background was 'introjected' in the personality of individuals. Durkheim departed from the opposite platform: the collectivity. He focused on the institutionalization of collective representations that get ingrained in our conscience. His main interest lay in the way in which external, objective and 'coercive' social phenomena influence the behaviour of individuals. But the longer he studied social facts, the more he realized the importance of individual traits and variations. Both perspectives imply and complement each other. Similar patterns of behaviour are being copied, incorporated, and repeatedly carried out by a host of people. Thus, social behaviour is being reproduced and institutionalized. Moreover, Durkheim pointed out that one should not see social systems as facts that completely exist outside individuals that participate in these systems. Societies can only exist if collective social values are internalized in the majority of their members.[43] Parsons also used valuable insights of Charles Horton Cooley and George Herbert Mead. Following Cooley, he spoke of mutual interpenetration of society and individual. Analytically, society and individuals can be separated, but in reality both are completely imbued with each other. Psychological needs for social interaction, love, respect, and affection, and the social necessity to perform a variety of roles, create the multifaceted interlinking of all individuals with their social environment.

6.6.2   *The personality system*

Since socialization is closely connected to personal development, I will take a short detour to discuss Parsons' view on the personality. He believed that the human personality could be analyzed just as any other system of action. To give a full description of the personality, we have to consider its basic needs and dispositions. Basic needs are essential parts of the biological organism; dispositions are being acquired. They are not genetic, nor of an instinctive nature, but entirely social. As could be expected, Parsons sketched a model of the personality system along the lines of the fourfold AGIL-scheme. Therefore, he had to expand Freud's three-dimensional model to a fourfold one. Freud discerned between *Id, ego* and *super-ego*. The *Id* denotes the purely instinctive element in human behaviour. This element is purely biological and directed at survival and reproduction. To overcome this instinctive level, humans need to develop their *Ego*. The *Ego* directs our behaviour to other goals than the urge to stay alive and to procreate such as a higher self-esteem and psychological well-being. In Freud's view, the *Super Ego* represents the moral pressure from society. It guides *Ego* and bridles *Id*. Parsons situates *id* in the physical or biological domain too. In his view, it functions as the adaptive subsystem that connects the individual with his natural environment. The *ego* mobilizes and coordinates the available means to realize personal goals.

Scheme 6.6   *The Freud-Parsons' model of the personality*

A Id	G Ego
Identity L	Super-ego I

Parsons' concept of the *super-ego* differs somewhat from that of Freud. To fit his AGIL-scheme, the super-ego has to function as the primary subsystem for integration; that is, for the internalization of rules and roles. For the same reason, he had to invent or discover a fourth element to fill the fourth cell. In other words, he had to search for a concept that could symbolize latency or pattern maintenance. This he found in the concept of *Identity*. With the help of the social norms and values individuals give meaning to their behaviour as something that springs from their unique, personal identity, as something that fits their (ideal) self-image. Thus defined, *Identity* forms the stable ground for the personality system.[44] As soon as individuals have become aware of their identity, however constructed or created, they will be predisposed to opt for actions that will be in line with their perceived identity and reject and avoid actions that go against it.

6.6.3 The socialization process schematized

Parsons defined socialization in highly abstract and purely sociological way as follows:

> Socialization is the learning of any orientation of functional significance for the operation of a system of complementary expectations. [45]

In short, socialization is the learning of social roles. For Parsons, socialization is equivalent to the satisfactory adjustment of individual actions to conformity with prevailing norms and values. Through this process of adjustment the social system can remain stable in a homeostatic way. The integrative mechanism of socialization and social control will have the following two effects: 1. The psychological system acquires a structure that becomes compatible with the social structure; 2. Cultural patterns will fit, support, and legitimize social structures.

As mentioned before, for Parsons, it was important to stress that social systems require 'a sufficient proportion of its members that are adequately motivated to act in accordance with the requirements of the role system.' [46] There is no need for everyone to fit the system for 100 per cent. The social system exerts a significant degree of social control, but it does not have absolute power. There is space for individual variation, for individual preferences and individual choice. Secondly, social systems should avoid involvement with cultural patterns that fail to organize a minimum of social order or require actions and sets of goals that are unfeasible for its members. This will engender frustration and conflicts that will be harmful for the continuity of the system.[47]

The acquisition of social roles is a learning process in which the personality system has to be adjusted to the social system. Learning will change the personality system. During this process individuals will face some tensions that will trigger various kinds of psychological defense mechanisms to uphold their identity. However, during socialization or during periods of rapid social change, individuals have to adjust to their environment to a sufficient degree, that is, to a degree in which they will not entice too much acts of social control for reasons of deviancy. With reference to defense mechanisms we could think of cognitive tricks such as accepting that the adjustment is reasonable or is not really that cumbersome. It could mean that we have to postpone some of our beloved actions or give them up completely, but we could make ourselves believe that there still are enough alternatives that will gratify us just as much because satisfaction at a later point in time will give greater joy *(inhibition)*.

On the basis of the foregoing insights that Parsons developed in a number of books it is possible to develop a model that sketches both the individual adaptation – control mechanism and the external mechanism of social control. [48]

Scheme 6.7   A model of the process of socialization based on Parsons' insights

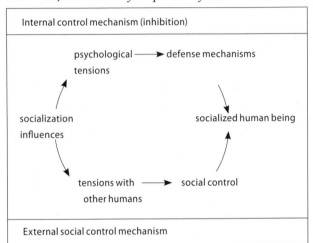

Social control is set in motion as soon as humans start to act in ways that strongly deviate from standard patterns of behaviour. Negative sanctions and positive reinforcements are a necessary part of the process of socialization. It tells individuals what to do and what to avoid in social situations *(reinforcement / extinction)*. It teaches them to distinguish between good and evil, between duty and neglect, between telling the truth and lying, between good achievements and dismal performance. Perhaps the scheme should be expanded with two extra intermediary phases, because the process will always face situations of insufficient adjustment and thus requires some social control, before the tension between ego and the other or the rest of the group has faded away. In that case we see social control as an integral part of the socialization process.

6.6.4   Socialization as learning process

During socialization humans learn to live according to the rules of their social milieu. At the same time they develop their personality. Just like any process of learning socialization follows the law of differentiation and integration.[49] Learning is the effect of the differentiation of an existing and already known structure and the integration of the changes that spring from this differentiation into a new coherent view on a part of reality. During this learning process the personality system grows more complex and acquires more specialized functions. Parsons based his model of learning on a combination of the distinction between differentiation or discrimination and integration or generalization on the one hand, and, the distinction between the cognitive and the affective significance of the object of learning on the other hand. The emotional side of the learning process tends to be overlooked. But a learning object must have '*both* kinds of meaning if it has any meaning at all.'[50] The interweaving of the cognitive and the affective aspects is so strong that it is hard to decide which of the two is most important. Parsons believed that cognitive discrimination always precedes cognitive integration. Individuals are strongly inclined to inertia. Most people are not looking forward to real surprises and challenges that could disturb their peace of mind. Hence, most people need consistent and powerful stimuli to motivate them to learn, because learning leads to new insights and different opinions. In turn, this could lead to new patterns of behaviour. Besides, people have emotional attachments to certain objects, views, and insights. Therefore, new objects for learning have to present themselves in an unequivocal and transparent way, in order to draw ego's attention and to awake him from his inertia.[51] On the other hand, development is a fact of life; therefore, these new stimuli are unavoidable. Social change does give rise to new cognitive objects and the necessity to assimilate them. The same is true for physical growth and psychological maturation. As a consequence both types of growth parents will raise their expectations. If this growth does not manifest itself in new skills, more wisdom and more self-control, parents will be disappointed, something children will soon pick up on, if only because they no longer receive the positive reinforcements they have got used to. To minimize or avoid feelings of frustration or relative deprivation they will try anything to fulfill the new expectations of their parents or educators.

The perceived cause of the relative deprivation, that is the change in behaviour of the parent or caretaker, has to be 'explained.' It must acquire a meaning. Children have to discover or construct the reason for withdrawal of the reinforcement they were used to. They have to discover or imagine a good reason that will restore their positive feelings for their parents. So, children, or individuals in general, need to develop their potential for differentiation but also for generalization in such a way that their need for affection will stay satisfied in the new situation that has emerged. The new learned object has to fit the existing body of knowledge. This can be done by redefining the old object of knowledge as a particular element in a broader category of different, but closely related elements.[52] At the end of this section it has to be mentioned that learning, which is an important part of socialization, not only refers to the cognitive assimilation of objects of culture, but also refers to the appropriation of social structures and systems of interactions.

6.7   Social Change

Parsons is renowned for his preoccupation with social order. However, a quick look at his list of publications also shows a considerable interest in social change and social evolution. This is no surprise, since he felt that there was a great need for a theory that would help us understand the strong tendencies towards social progress.[53] He was well aware of the fact that not all manifestations of social change meant a step forward. History has shown, time and time again, that change can also take a negative turn and herald social ruin and disorganization, ending in the fall of nations and much misery for the people. Social and political change can also result in oppression and exploitation at the cost of liberty and well-being. However, Parsons, as a typical American of his time, still believed that positive outcomes would prevail.

In line with his orderly approach, he started with the assertion that every analysis of change also has to consider the static elements. In studying change and variation there must always be a distinction between what does and what does not change. The intricacies of social change cannot even be identified if there is no stable structure to relate them to. For Parsons, the concept of structure is simply a shorthand statement of this basic point. The structure of a system can be defined as the set of properties of its component parts and their relations or combinations, which, for analytical purposes, can both logically and empirically be treated as constant within a definable time limit.[54] A system is stable or in equilibrium when the relation between its structure and its processes are maintaining those properties and relations. In 'dynamic' systems, this maintenance is dependent on a continuous flow of all sorts of processes, which neutralize either endogenous or exogenous sources of variability, which otherwise would change the structure. A classic example is the continuity of nearly constant body temperature by mammals in the face of variation in environmental temperature. Next to equilibration processes, there are also processes that bring about structural change.

In 1961, Parsons presented his first theory of evolutionary social change and described it as a process of structural differentiations of functions accompanied by concomitant processes of reorganization. The necessary social adjustment includes the upgrading of capacities, new modes of including units in the larger social system, and reinterpretations of norms and values. At an abstract level, social systems change by further differentiation supplemented by processes of integration and re-integration. Most changes produce a further division of labour and create an ever-growing number of different functions, while simultaneously obliterating others. Comte, Spencer, and Durkheim only analyzed one dimension of change in which society is learning to function better. As society grows more efficient, it produces more goods at lesser costs, just like factories produce more at lower costs than the old handicraft industries. Societies can also change in the opposite direction and get less differentiated. Nonetheless, Parsons focused on modernization processes that show growing differentiation, specialization, and individualization.

Increased differentiation engenders significant cultural changes. To adjust for this growing complexity, society has to develop collective values at a higher level of abstraction. The core values of society must acquire a more universal character. That is the only way to make them fit the proliferation of specific opinions, norms, and values that develop in a context of new professions. Gradually, traditional values such as localism and particularism must be replaced by cosmopolitanism and universalism. This generalization implies that growing complexity in the form of increased cultural and ethnic diversity due to immigration should be 'countered' by the development of a set of collective values at a higher level of abstraction.

Like Spencer and Durkheim, Parsons realized that growing differentiation requires extra coordination and new forms of integration. The greater the number of distinctive professions and occupations, the greater is the need for mechanisms of integration. The emergence of an urbanized, industrial society requires a system of public education to fulfill the need for qualified workers, civil servants, and professionals. Again this could be extended to a situation in which ethnic diversity is increasing significantly. In that case all children have to be socialized within the system of core values to ensure that they can live and work together as adults despite significant differences in culture and lifestyle.[55]

Modern societies are changing all the time. Scientific and technological innovations form a strong motor for social change. Presently, nobody can overlook the impressive results of science, in particular technology and medical science. Nor can anybody shut his eyes for the less positive side effects of 'progress.' Scientific discoveries and technological innovations have changed human existence in dramatic ways, in ways that go much further than lightening the burden of physical labour, lengthening life expectancy, and improving modes of transport and exchanging information. In the process, many skills and jobs have become obsolete, but also many new skills, jobs, and professions have emerged. As a consequence, educational systems have expanded and undergone dramatic changes. Moreover, all this has affected family-life and the social roles of men and women. Parsons was mainly interested in the cultural effects of social or structural change. To explain long-term-changes he tended to follow Weber's approach in describing historical change. But unlike Weber, he thought political struggle far less important as a motor for social change. For him, the value system is the most important cohesive for society. Social shifts spring from shifts in value priorities. Like Weber, he was convinced that significant cultural shifts tend to be triggered by great charismatic religious leaders such as Jesus, Muhammad, Luther, and Calvin, or great political leaders such as Martin Luther King and Nelson Mandela.[56] In the long run, the introduction of some new values or the recovery of some old values, as preached by great prophets and leaders, tend to be less important for the change of the cultural system since they can only change those aspects of the traditional culture that were potentially open for change.[57] This begs the question how and why some aspects of traditional culture have opened the potential for change, while others have not. Is this a purely spontaneous and unpredictable process, induced by new ideas from great minds or mundane inventors, or can we predict that inevitably some change will emerge as a consequence of the failure of systems to maintain stability and equilibrium? What would open the potential for cultural change were it not for the impetus of charismatic leaders? In view of the idealistic-collectivistic inclination of Parsons and his tendency to attach great value to entire systems, we can interpret his view as an attempt to stress that cultural changes only get support and stick if the new ideas and values are integrated in a renewed and coherent system of ideas and cultural values.

6.8   The American value system

In view of Parson's strong interest in norms and values it is no surprise that he wanted to study the prevailing value system of his own society. In *A Tentative Outline of American Values*, he made a serious attempt to analyze this topic.[58] This essay remained unpublished during his lifetime. All this is rather odd, since he had lectured about this theme for over thirty years. But he had published three articles about important aspects related to this major sociological topic in which he tackled McCarthyism, social tensions in the US, and the distribution of power.[59] In all three cases, his views differed strikingly from that of his colleagues.

6.8.1   *Criticizing popular sociological analyses*

The prevailing interpretation of McCarthyism, a right-wing political frenzy to silence and penalize all people suspected of communist sympathies, was that it manifested an American form of fascism that could lead to the same horrendous events that fascism had brought about in Europe. His interpretation was less alarming. In his eyes it was a form of populism fed by strong feelings of resentment of the middle classes. These feelings of frustration were an outcome of far reaching changes in the economy and the political position of the US in the world. Many Americans had got the feeling that the enlarged communist block was getting the upper hand. Moreover, the United States also got burdened by filling in the power vacuum that had arisen after decolonization; a process that strongly mitigated the power of many important European nations. Suddenly the US had become a super power facing serious threats by The Soviet Union, another super power in possession of atomic bombs. The fast transformation of the US into a leading empire had cost a huge amount of money and numerous human casualties. The resentment was also a reaction against the modernization of the economy in which tens of thousands of small shop owners were eaten by new and fast growing chains of super markets. It changed the whole character of small towns and inner cities and their typical way of life.
Parsons did not ignore the fact that the hunt for American communists was a serious threat for democracy, but he predicted that this frenzy would be short-lived.

It could not remain, and could certainly not generate the necessary power to destroy the existing political system. History proved him right. Parsons believed that he had revealed the superficial hysteria of a specific brand of journalists and intellectuals. As a champion of grand theories and a way of thinking along long evolutionary lines, he had become allergic to highly politicized intellectual fads. He found it his task to prove the power of less fashionable and far more thorough sociological analysis, by destroying the highly dramatized but ephemeral analyses of sociological ideologists and journalists that were fed by short-lived hypes. He had great doubts about the disturbing messages of extremely popular books such as David Riesman's *The Lonely Crowd*, C. Wright Mills' *The Power Elite*, and *The Sane Society* by Erich Fromm. He feared that these studies reflected old ideological biases that tended to depict the United States as an uprooted society with a mass culture without any authenticity. After rigorous reading they appeared to reveal very few original and tenable ideas.[60] He rejected their treatment of culture and personality, their macro sociological application of psychoanalysis and their overstatement of the influence of power structures.

6.8.2   *The Christian foundation of the American Value system*

From the late forties on, Parsons hired research assistants and PhD-candidates to investigate all kinds of institutional arrangements. The project got extra momentum as soon as he recruited Winston White. Together, they wrote several papers and articles and produced seven draft chapters for a new book with the provisional title: *American Society*. Unfortunately, White left the university and the book was never finished. For this project, Parsons and White reread the work of Max Weber to find valuable clues for a more thorough analysis of the American value system. Most popular interpretations described the US as a society in turmoil, disturbed by rapid social changes that drove generations apart. Obviously, the older generations could not cope with the speed and scope of the changes. Moreover, the character of some of these changes seemed to question their core values and ridicule their life style. Scores of authors predicted the erosion of the highly developed work ethos and individual responsibility. They feared the eroding of democratic social relations and the demise of community spirit. But it is typically American to announce loud and clear that the American nation is at risk.[61] Parsons and White wanted to show that the American society still functioned and would remain functioning on the basis of enduring cultural forces. Yet, they acknowledged that the US was facing some major problems. No doubt, the peaceful integration of religious, social and ethnically different groups posed a huge challenge. The nation had to cope with a pluralism that was showing segregating tendencies. Nonetheless, they believed in fundamental 'system forces' that would guarantee the continuation of American society, including its basic values. Furthermore, they wanted to explicate that a large, complex, modern society like the US could not be dominated by specific groups or practical institutional complexes such as the established elite, the speculators of Wall Street, the 'manipulation mob' of marketing and advertising specialists, or the so-called military-industrial complex.

It is clear that Parsons did not engage in a completely value free project. He employed a typical American middle class perspective, full of trust in social progress and the great value of American institutions. On the other hand, he had a keen eye for certain shortcomings, such as ongoing racism, the dominance of economic values, and the anti-intellectual spirit of the nation. That last mentality manifested itself in the eagerness to solve social and political problems quickly, before a thorough analysis had been made of its cause. Like Weber, Parsons viewed the inner worldly *ascetics* as a core element of Northern America's culture. In his comparative study of European Puritanism and Chinese Confucianism, Weber had interpreted Confucianism as a doctrine of rational adjustment to the world, and Protestant Puritanism as a doctrine of the rational control over the world. In stark contrast to other eminent scholars, Parsons did not think that the American value system was falling apart. In his view, pragmatism or, as he preferred to call it, instrumental activism still prevailed. Signs that seemed to show that the traditional work ethos was loosing ground did not distract him, nor did the often-mentioned decline of achievement motivation and community values. He did not overlook some shifts in value priorities, but distrusted their power to engender a fundamental change in American culture. This belief was supported by the absence of strong causal factors, such as influential charismatic movements. Following Weber, he was convinced that charismatic movements often acted as prime movers of societal change. He was not even impressed by the rise of consumerism, because, as he justly noticed, one could only consume more if one earns more, and to earn more one had to work harder and achieve more. In other words, instrumental activism was a necessary condition for a rising level of consumption.

What was the theoretical foundation upon which Parsons based his trust in the survival power of typical American values? Firstly, he assumed that there is a coherent and dominating value system within any social system. The second assumption was that the value system of a well-established society remains stable during long periods of time. Following Weber and Durkheim, he considered societal values as categories that are deeply anchored in culture. They form the core layer of any cultural system. In contrast to opinions and attitudes, categories that are much closer to the surface of culture, they are hardly susceptible for change.[62] In *A Tentative Outline,* Parsons wanted to prove that, at a general level, the American value system has not changed since colonial history. To support his thesis, he sketched a system of categories that he deemed crucially important. He started with his concept of functional prerequisites. These prerequisites refer to the culture and structure of societies, and the psychological and physical make up of the members of these societies. He stated that there has to be another layer, above the top layer of culture that refers to non-empirical phenomena, a layer for religious or mystical matters. This brought him into the field of metaphysics. According to him, there are normative components, capable of steering human behaviour, which cannot be derived from the norms and values of the lower order of existential conditions. Whatever one may think of the meaning of such ultimate values, for Parsons there was no doubt that we have to face a fundamental choice whether we want to see the primary source of moral authority as coming from within our world, as Durkheim would have it, or from a supernatural force outside our world. In other words, do we assume a secular source or a religious source? The second choice that we have to decide upon concerns the fundamental dilemma between an internal and an external orientation. Do we want our actions to have an effect on internal relations within the social system or on the relations between our social system and its surroundings? The third fundamental choice concerns the primacy accorded to instrumental effects of our actions or to expressive or 'consummatory' effects? Social actors cannot avoid these choices. Actions that immediately lead to the realization of goals can be found within the secular and the religious domain. Think of actions that solve a social problem or actions that lead to a religious conversion. A religious-instrumental orientation aims at the expansion of the number of churches, temples or mosques, whereas a secular-instrumental orientation for example aims at the expansion or improvement of schools, hospitals, roads, and viaducts. All this is done in the hope that this will contribute to the well being of citizens.[63]

Where does this theoretical framework lead us? If we make all the possible combinations of three fundamental choices we end up with eight possible types. Here, I will not start a discussion of these eight types, but follow Parsons in his ideal typical description of the American Value system. For Parsons it was clear that the American culture basically had a *religious orientation*. It has been created out of a mingling of immigrant groups from various predominantly Christian European countries. In the sixties, when he wrote this article, the White Anglo-Saxon Protestants or WASPs, still dominated American culture. They had transferred their Christian values to Afro-Americans, who were forcefully transported to the US as slaves. Despite some secularization still a very high percentage of Americans is religious. According to Parsons, again leaning on Weber, the primary implication of the religious component was *activism*. Protestants had to use all their God-given talents to master and control the world. The main objective is to control, to influence, and to manipulate nature, social situations, and individual behaviour so that men would not sin. This activism is the opposite of letting affairs have their course.

The *instrumental* side of the American value system turns activism into the direction of matters that are of value in this world, and not in an afterlife or another spiritual world. Americans fully denounce fatalism. Activism has to be directed at development and improvement of the present situation. It has to lead to a more desirable social situation than the one we live in now. For Calvinists individual activities must contribute to the realization of the Divine Plan. For pragmatic reasons its realization was turned into the more concrete objective of becoming a 'righteous individual.' To be a righteous man or woman was to be socially responsible and to contribute through high performance in secular 'callings'. In religious terms, then, the American value system clearly belongs to the category of 'worldly asceticism'. It is the farthest antithesis to the type of religious other-worldliness that puts escape from human society and its obligations as the highest religious goal.[64] The value that scores highest is achievement or, to be more precise, individual achievement within one's social role. The universal standard used for evaluating individual achievements is the contribution to the realization of societal values, the contribution to realizing a more desirable society.

6.8.3   Full citizenship for Afro-Americans[65]

In 1965, the scholarly magazine Daedalus organized two conferences to mobilize the resources of the American intellectual community to address the problems of Black Americans. Parsons presented an important paper. He began with a discussion of Thomas H. Marshall's analysis of the concept of citizenship. Citizenship refers to full membership in the societal community.[66] It focuses on solidarity or mutual loyalty. It constitutes the consensual base underlying one's political integration. So, in cases of full citizenship we can speak of Black or Afro-Americans, to show that they first and foremost are Americans. During the period of slavery the Negroes could not be called Negro Americans. In those days, they were called American Negroes to indicate that they lived in America but were not viewed as full citizens. They had hardly any rights and certainly were not fully accepted as members of the societal community. Segregation and subordination were facts of life in most social domains. The modern notion of Afro-American indicates that they are supposed to have more in common with other Americans than with other members of their race in the rest of the world.

The transition from slavery to full citizenship has taken a long time, and even now there are cleavages that can be related to a long history of racism.[67] Parsons agreed that the international fight against colonialism has stimulated the struggle for full citizenship, but he emphasized that the main impetus for this major transition has been internal to the development of American society itself. The conditions in the USA were and still are intimately linked with the process of differentiation. This has produced an increasingly *pluralistic* social structure, in which ethnicity should and does not determine all social participations. More and more, occupation, education, work organization, and political affiliation become independent of ethnic background: more and more careers are based on achievement instead of ascription. In this context it is essential to make a clear distinction between *inclusion* and *assimilation*. In his view, full inclusion and multiple role participation are compatible with the maintenance of a distinctive ethnic or religious identity. It is worth noting that already in 1965 Parsons expressed what later was to become the first article of faith of multiculturalism.

Thomas H. Marshall distinguished between three dimensions of citizenship: (1) the civil or legal, (2) the political and (3) the social dimension of citizenship. According to Marshall, legal citizenship developed first. This gave people certain rights and freedoms, such as individual security, property rights, and freedom of speech, religion, assembly and association. These civil rights provided the legal basis for Negro Americans and other minority groups to organize themselves in associations that strove for equal rights in all sectors of society. The extension of civil rights was followed, rather slowly, with political rights to participate in local and national elections. In general, social rights that protected people against poverty as a consequence of sickness, invalidity and old age came last. But equal rights can remain empty if opportunity is not equalized. Even absence of discrimination is empty if remediable handicaps continue to prevail. For individuals to be able to take advantage of available opportunities they must have the financial and educational resources to do so. Legal decisions are crucial but they only are a first step. Much more is needed to make them effective. The mobilization of political pressure was required to insure that blacks could enjoy both formal political rights and actual participation in the political process and the governmental apparatus. In the beginning, the police force and in some cases even the federal army had to be mobilized to safeguard the implementation of these rights. But legal rights and political participation are no more than necessary conditions. They are far from sufficient. Full inclusion also requires that all the historically created social handicaps must be taken away.

The emergence of the relevant social movements is very crucial. Such movements tend to gather strength as the strain of conflict between the normative requirements for inclusion and the factual limitations are translated into pressures to act. According to Parsons, the ultimate social grounding of the demand for inclusion lays in the commitment to the values that legitimize it, in this case, the constitutional equality of American citizens. However, he hastens to add that this value commitment is not the only factor we have to deal with. There also are long-existing stubborn structural and cultural factors, which can create all kinds of setbacks. Of central concern is the vicious circle of factors related to poverty, bad health, low educational standards, family disorganization, juvenile delinquency, and other anti-social phenomena that are mutually reinforcing. This kind of argument has been severely and routinely criticized as a form of 'blaming the victim'. Though, two decades later, it was largely echoed and supported by new arguments and new empirical facts presented by William Julius Wilson in his book *The Truly Disadvantaged*.[68] Naturally, Wilson stressed the enduring negative consequences of historical and contemporary racism and discrimination in inner-city ghettos. But he also made clear that family disorganization, *in casu*, families headed by teenage mothers, and juvenile delinquency related to severe drug abuse added to the bleak situation of blacks. Another important new factor is the absenteeism of positive role models now that the black middle class has moved out to the richer suburbs. Although this was made possible by the victory of the Civil Rights Movement, it aggravated the plight of the black ghetto underclass. Moreover, modernization obliterated most jobs for people with limited educational credentials. All these factors and processes have been devastating for social life in the ghettos. What makes Wilson's analysis so convincing is his serious treatment of a whole array of causal factors other than racism. He rightfully points at economic, demographic, cultural, and social factors to explain for the tenacity of ethnic segregation and the deprivation of large parts of the black minority. This kind of analysis gives due attention to the complexities of social existence and the manifold factors which are involved in changing or reproducing social conditions.

Two decades earlier Parsons discussed four categories of factors. The first is the commitment to the values that legitimize that the goal of inclusion itself is desirable. Here the Civil Rights movement has played the paramount part. In this respect he draws special attention to the role of the church, manifested by charismatic leaders such as Dr. Martin Luther King and Jesse Jackson, and also by the support of prominent representatives of the Protestants, Catholics, and Jews. All this shows that the support for the Civil Rights of the Black Americans had become very broad, if not nation-wide. This extensive value-commitment had to be articulated in a full acceptance of members of minority groups as equals, as people that are in no way inferior to members of mainstream society. Everybody should acknowledge that the only tolerable solution to the ethnic tensions within the US lies in the constitution of a single societal community with full membership for all. The continuing mobilization of these loyalties and commitments on both sides of the racial line is the second crucial factor in the process of inclusion. Besides these two 'idealistic' factors that are crucial for social inclusion there also are 'real' or 'materialistic' factors at play, that is the political and the economic factor. Essential as government is, it does not stand alone in implementing major political changes. The political problems of integration involve all fields of organizational decision-making. Business firms and public organizations should accept Afro-Americans in employment. Colleges and universities should admit them for study and employment, to give a few examples. However, attempts to enforce compliance with equal rights acts or forms of affirmative action are all-too-often ineffective. Nevertheless, at certain crucial points its mobilization is clearly an essential factor. It includes decisions that make inclusion processes binding as obligations on all members of the collectivity, whether governmental or private.

Note that the use of power has a double effect. It mobilizes sanctions against recalcitrant persons that try to obstruct the implementation of the law. Second, it asserts that the policy of inclusion is taken seriously and that noncompliance will be sanctioned. Parsons thinks that economic interests are the most neutral as far as integration is concerned. Businesses want to make profits. The option to employ or serve people from disadvantaged groups will largely depend on the prospects for the firm. Will they gain or lose customers by hiring people from minority groups or promoting them to higher positions? In Parsons' view, generally businessmen simply will not move, unless the balance of the other factors shifts towards integration.

Although Parsons' analysis lacked the empirical basis, his theoretical skills saved him from a biased and one-dimensional analysis that boils down to an explanation that only blames the whites for everything, thus implicitly disempowering the blacks and rendering their specific cultural and ethnic features of no consequence whatsoever. Parsons' analytical strength lay in his focus on the emancipation of individuals of all categories from diffuse particularistic solidarities. This must be seen as a further differentiation of the role-set in which the individual is involved. By being included in larger community structures, the individual need not cease to be a member of the smaller ones, but the latter must relinquish certain controls over him or her. This reasoning applies to privileged as well as to disadvantaged groups. According to Parsons, we have been witnessing major steps in the extension and consolidation of the societal community of the us, although Wilson's study shows that still much has to be achieved to arrive at the equal society that was proclaimed by the American Constitution established in 1789.

6.9   In conclusion

Parsons has been criticized on empirical, theoretical, ideological and pre-suppositional grounds.[69] There are two main types of critique on Parson's suppositions. One category of critics sees him as someone who has fallen victim to a typical belief of cultural scientists, that is, the belief in a complete freedom of choice and the complete absence of social constraints that strongly limits anyone's options. Some critics only detect this flaw in his early work; others see it reappear in all his writings. Another group of critics see clear manifestations of Parsons' idealistic approach in his recurrent emphasis on social-normative and social-psychological restrictions of complete freedom of action. Note that these critics observe that Parsons is aware of all kinds of immaterial phenomena that direct and restrict human actions. Their main reproach is that Parsons does overlook restrictions of a material kind, such as poverty created by an unjust distribution of scarce goods. In stark contrast to Marx, the materialist, Parsons seems to be obsessed by purely immaterial systems of norms and values. Where Marx tries to explain inequality and social conflict by exploitative relations of production, he draws our attention to social tensions that could be caused by unsuccessful forms of socialization. This line of critique is initiated by David Lockwood, although he acknowledged that conflict theorists like Marx also need idealistic points of departure, and that a materialistic approach to sociological theory can be made compatible with theoretical notions as system and function.[70]

A second type of critique asserts that Parsons did not really present a voluntaristic theory of action, since notions of social constraints and moral restrictions overcrowd his theories. Atkinson clearly misreads Parsons as a functional theorist that pictures man as the plaything of social forces, without any freedom of choice and without the ability to control his own life, because the social systems in which he plays his role simply demands him to play his predetermined role and nothing else. For Atkinson, functional imperatives leave no room for real voluntary actions.[71]

Of course, it cannot be true that Parsons presented theoretical models that completely ignore social constraints and also, according to other critics, that his models are flawed because of his 'over-socialized' conception of man, a conception without any freedom of action. Both biased readings ignore that he believed in the existence of the freedom of choice, albeit it freedom of choice that is restricted by existing social structures, norms and values. This view reeks of a compromise between the idealistic and materialistic approach to sociology, as well as a compromise between an individualistic and a collective approach, but I think we have to admit that this is a very sensitive compromise, or to put it more positively, a highly valuable synthesis of distinctive theoretical perspectives, a synthesis that could only be the result of a combination of theoretical skill and clear observations of empirical reality. Certainly, Parsons was no 100 per cent philosophical idealist or materialists, nor was he 100 per cent individualist or collectivist. Nowhere in his numerous publications will we find an exact percentage to gauge the real balance between those perspectives. We will not even find a statement that says which is more important the individual freedom of choice or the collective restraints that limit the freedom of choice. He only stressed that we need all four approaches to get a valid picture of social actions and social systems.

How can we explain these biased readings of Parsons? Is the only reason that people start reading Parsons with a fixed set of prejudices, pre-notions and a strong preference for their own beloved perspective? Or is it even worse, and will most people refrain from reading Parsons own work and stick to a critical analyst of their own theoretical or ideological persuasion? The explanation for a purely collectivistic reading of Parsons might be found in the fact that he tended to take individual freedom for granted and that he, as a sociologist, was focused on collective phenomena and social constraints, and also because of his great concern with socialization and social order.

His ideological intentions are clear. They remain directed at individual liberty within the framework of a well functioning social system. For him, that is by definition a system that gives individuals enough space for personal development. Further it is undeniable that Parsons' theories are strongly rooted in an empirical basis. Everyday humans take all kinds of decisions although not everybody can do what he wants. Everyone has to reckon with the interest of fellow-humans. Hence, all we do, all our actions, all our choices, have to be made within the ranges of what is socially acceptable. Therefore, Parsons never forgets to take individual interests into consideration when he is theorizing about functional prerequisites. It is a prerequisite that members of societies and social organizations can realize a sufficient number of their goals.

Referring to his first model of four scientific perspectives which all have some validity, and all have to be considered simultaneously, and also referring to his AGIL-scheme, I conclude that he has created ingenious syntheses and that he has elaborated these syntheses further in fruitful ways, despite his inclination to go on applying them to fields and situations that have little value for social scientists.

Parsons' main contribution to sociology is his great attempt to give this science a major theoretical impulse. Active social scientists always call for better theories, though most of them are not doing innovative theoretical work. They tend to carry out straightforward empirical studies, which, in view of the problematic nature of our field, is difficult enough. For most sociologists, already Merton's goal of developing theories of the middle range seems to lie out of their range of imagination, let alone the hard work of sketching and improving so-called *grand theories* that Parsons was after. Therefore, we have reasons enough to show high esteem for his oeuvre and use it as a source of inspiration. Despite all its shortcomings, it is unique, valuable, and applicable in many situations. It deserves to be studied by each new generation of social scientists.

7

NORBERT ELIAS

MASTER OF HISTORICAL SOCIOLOGY

The sociology of Norbert Elias is not as widely recognized as it should be. In view of the great quality of his oeuvre it deserves a much wider audience. Maybe this very chapter will help to widen the circle of his admirers and the number of sociologists that will apply and further elaborate his ideas. A major reason for the relative lack of familiarity with his work was the very slow progress of his career. Born in Germany in a Jewish family was a terrible disadvantage. When the Nazis seized power he found it better to move to Paris. A few years later he sought refuge in England. There he finished his major work The Civilizing Process, but in 1939, there was little interest in a German book about the history and socio-genesis of civilization in Europe. After the war it still took three more decades before it was publisted in English.

This chapter starts with more details about his life and career. After the biographical section his ideas about general sociological theory are presented in section 7.3. His approach to conceptualize social phenomena in terms of figurations was new in many respects. It emphasized that individuals are units in a dense and dynamic web of social relations. Modern societies are very complex and function on the basis of a myriad of interdependent relations between numerous individuals. Section 7.4 discusses his major work, The Civilizing Process, while section 7.5 handles some of the major critiques directed at his central thesis that a long historic process of state formation and centralization, leading to a typical court society in the capital of these new nations, produced new forms of behaviour that could be defined as more civilized. In the view of Elias, civilized behaviour is characterized by more self-restraint, more concern for the feelings and interests of others, and more rationalization than was common in medieval times. Section 7.6 discusses his book *Outsiders and the Established* in which he and his co-author John Scotsman analyzed the problematic relations between two fractions of the working class in a city in Northern England. Historic factors plus cultural differences created segregation, tension and conflict. The next section renders a short exposé of the relationship between individualization and globalization, and the shift in

I-We balance. Section 7.8 offers a discussion of his views on the implementation of social science. Elias points to the necessity to find a balance between involvement and detachment. The final subject that will be treated here is his theory on the social construction of time. The chapter ends with concluding remarks.

7.1   A life and career

Norbert Elias was born on June 22 1897. He was the only child of Hermann and Sophie Elias. Together they formed a small, but happy Jewish family. They lived in Breslau, a city that had been Germanized for centuries. This Polish border town became Wroclaw again after 1945.

7.1.1   *Child, student, soldier, and student again*

As a child Norbert was often too ill to go to school. Hence he was often privately taught. He was an eager pupil, always motivated to expand his knowledge and gather new insights. This quest for scientific truths remained his major occupation if not his major obsession during the rest of his life. Though he claimed that this obsession absorbed so much time and energy that not enough of it was left for a partner, he found enough spare moments to write poems. Anyhow, even long after retirement, he used to start his working day at 11 o'clock and then went on until 10 o'clock in the evening. So, he never really retired from science but went on writing books and essays until the last day of his life. At old age he grew blind but even that did not stop him from producing new texts, although he now needed the help of an assistant to write them down. Thus, he energetically added new books and articles to an already impressive oeuvre.

His father owned a profitable textile business. The family lived in a spacious apartment with ample personnel. His father was a real Prussian. In fact, the entire Jewish community in Breslau considered themselves as good Germans or Prussians. They looked down on people who doubted their German identity.[1] In spite of their German mind-set they occasionally suffered from anti-Semitic incidents. Norbert attended the Johannes gymnasium, an outstanding grammar school with a distinguished staff. There he acquired the foundation of humanistic, classical education. He loved the works of German literary giants, such as Goethe, Schiller and Heine. However, during the First World War and the economic depression that followed he came to realize that their esoteric philosophical orientation was badly connected to the hard realities of life.[2] Elias always identified himself with the cultural tradition of Germany, though he never became a nationalist. He found the Kaiser ridiculous and was strongly opposed to the war, but when he finished secondary school, he became a reluctant soldier in the Signal Corps. It was his task to maintain and repair Telegraph lines between the front and headquarters, a task that easily could have killed him. Later he speculated that the physical part of army training had been good for his health.

Moreover, his war experiences steered him in the direction of sociology, for these hard experiences had taught him that the individual was rather powerless against social forces.[3]

After the war, Elias studied philosophy and medicine in Breslau, but this combination was too much. He quit medicine, though he was fascinated by some of its topics. In particular, the anatomical lessons showed the extremely complex connections between the skeleton, the muscles, the nerves and the organs. These lessons left a long-lasting impression and would be reflected in his sociology. Time and time again, he would emphasize the strong bonds between the biological and social aspect of human existence. His medical-biological knowledge did not always agree with western philosophy. Descartes had been the first to make a clear distinction between the subject, in the form of a grown up individual with an independent 'internal' mind, and a reality outside that consciousness. These autonomous subjects were supposed to be able to study the external reality in an objective way. But Elias had learned that there always was a close connection between the internal mind and the external world. When, for example, someone had a funny thought this would immediately manifest itself in the expression on his or her face. There is a very close relation between mind and body. But also the relations between people have a biological basis. The social aspects of a smile or the sound of laughter cannot be separated from the physiological aspects. This made Elias realize that human beings, by nature, are social. The facial muscles of human beings are much more differentiated then those of primates. Humans are meant to live together with other people. In a long-term evolutionary process, people have developed complicated forms of communications and the physical requirements to make speech possible. Facial expressions, such as smiling or crying, are forms of communication too. These expressions and the inner feelings are both aspects of the same reaction to something that is happening around us. When people are growing up they learn to control their feelings by not showing natural reactions. For instance, shop assistants are trained to remain friendly even when a customer is unreasonable. Their friendliness no longer is authentic but acted.

7.1.2   An academic life outside academia

Let us return to biographical matters. In Breslau the philosopher Richard Hönigswald made a huge impression on Elias. He was a brilliant and original neo-Kantian philosopher, who taught him to trust his intellect, that thinking can be productive and innovative.[4] He also admired Hönigswald's indifference to philosophical fashions. Elias 'inherited' this academic virtue. Alas, this virtue is seldom rewarded, because it does make one an outsider. Elias interrupted his studies at Breslau to study a semester with Heinrich Rickert and Karl Jaspers in Heidelberg and Freiburg. He started to work on a philosophical thesis. In this he showed great skepticism about some central Kantian tenets of Hönigswald, his supervisor. In opposition to Kant, Elias was convinced that basic categories of thought – space, time, causality, and fundamental moral principles – stem from social experience. They are not inherent in the human mind. For Elias all ideas are the products of the intellectual development of scores of generations. Hönigswald was not pleased by the attack on some of his cherished ideas. In view of the power relations between a supervisor and a candidate and the unripeness of some of his ideas it is no wonder that Elias had to rewrite important parts before his thesis was accepted. After this humiliating experience he turned his back on philosophy and moved on to sociology.

Unfortunately, his father had financial trouble as a result of the hyperinflation of the twenties and he could no longer support him. Elias had to look for a job. He became an export manager for an iron foundry, which taught him a lot about the practical side of life. After two years, he started to study sociology in Heidelberg where Alfred Weber had now succeeded his brother Max. At the time, the intellectual field was strongly politicized between the bourgeois and liberal-democratic tradition of Max Weber, Ferdinand Tönnies and others and the socialist tradition that followed the teachings of Karl Marx. Elias did not want to take sides, but he somehow had to choose a supervisor. He approached Alfred Weber with a plan for his *Habilitationsschrift*. Weber accepted his plan but did not offer him a job. He earned some money as a free-lance journalist but this was not enough. Once more he needed the financial support from his father.

Elias took a strong interest in the subjects studied by Alfred Weber: the history and sociology of culture. Alfred Weber argued that the development of the economy and science showed clear signs of progress, but this was not the case for culture. He found it impossible to discern progressive or regressive developments in art, religion, and general culture. Yet, at that time, Elias was already pondering on one of his most beloved theses: cultures do not develop in a haphazard way but in a specific direction, implying some kind of evolution or progress.

In Heidelberg the young and brilliant lecturer Karl Mannheim drew much attention and soon Karl and Norbert became close friends. Mannheim introduced him to the salon of Marianne Weber, who, together with Alfred Weber, did all she could to keep the memory of Max alive. Mannheim was a renowned specialist in the sociology of knowledge. In his view, and to a large degree, all ideas were socially conditioned, and therefore were also restricted, biased or even corrupted. Hence, everyone had to be very skeptical about the validity of his or her ideas. For Mannheim, this was a rather disturbing thought. He looked for a way out. His solution was based on the idea of independent intellectuals, freed from restrictive and corruptive social influences. They should be able to discuss their ideas freely with their equally independent academic friends and colleagues. Thus they could act as *frei-schwebende Intelligenz* (free floating intelligence). If new ideas stood the test of this intellectual forum, then they could be considered valid.[5]

Also Elias held on to the goal of revealing irrefutable truths. But in his opinion, sociology still had a long way to go. Only just real objective methods were being developed. He was convinced that objective social science is possible, but that it still had to face a hard and time-consuming learning process, just what the physical sciences had had to face a few centuries ago. These sciences too had to emancipate themselves from all kinds of pre-scientific thought, such as mythical and theological dogma. Nonetheless, Elias remained an optimistic believer in the possibility to invent and develop images of society that were more congruent with reality, thus helping to demolish all kinds of ideological myths.[6]

In 1929, when Karl Mannheim became professor in Frankfurt, Elias became his first assistant and a candidate for Habilitation. The Department of Sociology at Frankfurt was housed on the ground floor of the famous Institute for Social Research, later known as the *Frankfurt School*. The institute employed many Marxist social scientists such as Theodor Adorno, Karl Deutsch, Max Horkheimer en Erich Fromm. Once again Elias kept politics at a distance. Though his sympathies were on the left, politics was not his cup of tea. He could not ignore the partisan explanations, the half-truths and the impractical promises of politicians.

In 1933, Hitler seized power. Elias sensed that Germany, and the German Jews in particular, would soon be facing a hard time. He had attended a public speech by Hitler and was greatly disturbed by his message and even more so by the fanatic response of the audience. He noticed Hitler's charisma and ability to manipulate a large crowd. Therefore, Elias decided to finish his thesis for Habilitation as quickly as possible. But it was to no avail. After the Nazi's took power Jews had to abandon all hopes of an academic career, or any career for that matter. In 1933, he went to Paris.[7] His life in Paris was very difficult. He did not get a job at a university. After two years, he decided to go to England, though he could not speak English. In London he received some financial help from a charity and spent most of his days in the library of the *British Museum*. For three years he worked hard on *The Civilizing Process*. In those days it was very difficult to find a German publisher for a book written by a German author of Jewish descent. In 1939, his father found a publisher in Switzerland. Alas, not many copies were sold.

7.1.3   Late vintage

It did take a very, very long time, before the great value of Elias' work became widely recognized. Apart from the political situation in Germany and the unfortunate moment of the publication of his masterpiece, there still are other reasons for his late recognition. His approach did not fit in one of the widely accepted traditions of sociology. *The Civilizing Process* is not a purely sociological book, but also has historical and psychological elements. Moreover, it did not offer schemes, definitions or statistical analyses and lacked explicitly formulated hypotheses. And last but not least, it did not contain critical discussions of the work of other theorists.[8]

After a while, Elias received a scholarship as *Senior Research Fellow* at the *London School of Economics*. This seemed to mark a positive turn in his academic career, but he was unlucky again. Even in England the war blocked his career because all Germans in Great Britain were now interned in camps. The compulsory residence in these camps was disagreeable to say the least. People felt that great injustice was done to them. But the war had even worse experiences in store for him.

In 1938, Elias had met his parents for the last time. He could not persuade them to come to England. As assimilated Jews they believed that they had nothing to fear in Germany. Besides, his father said: 'What can they do to me? I have never done wrong to anyone – I've never broken a law in my life.' This turned out to be a terrible misjudgment of the intentions of the Nazi's. Though his father died a natural death in 1940, his beloved mother was murdered in the gas chambers of Auschwitz one year later. Thinking about this horrific death would always be very traumatic for Norbert.[9]

After the war Elias failed to get a job at a British university. He had to survive doing freelance jobs, such as teaching evening classes at schools for adult-education. In those days he met with important psychoanalysts and subjected himself to psychoanalysis. He also started to analyze patients himself. In 1954, at the age of 57, Elias received his first full-time academic position at the University of Leicester. Despite his advanced age, he had to start as a junior lecturer. A few years later he became a senior lecturer. In Leicester, he soon became a highly regarded and influential teacher. Yet, his reputation in the Department of Sociology was also controversial. He did command respect for his intelligence and erudition, but was also considered a bit odd and old-fashioned, a typical pre-war continental scholar, learned and talkative, but not quite abreast of all the latest developments.[10] He retired in 1962, at the age of 65.

The 1950s and the 1960s were an unfavourable time for the type of historical sociology favoured by Elias. Before the war sociologists thought it quite natural to study historical developments in order to get a better understanding of the present. But after World War II the spirit of the times had changed. Social scientists 'retreated' in the present. Almost all attention was directed at the understanding and solution or amelioration of social problems, tensions and conflicts in modern capitalist societies. Most sociologists were engaged in empirical studies, analyzing large amounts of data. Others occupied themselves with the abstract schemes of Talcott Parsons, or were deeply involved in the explicitly normative approach of critical theory as advocated by the members of the *Frankfurt School*. So, even in Leicester he remained a solitary academic. Another important reason was that his work still was not translated into English. This was a major handicap because only very few English colleagues could read German. Part of this was a consequence of his interference. Twice he was not satisfied with the translation *of The Civilizing Process*. The problem was that he wanted to rewrite the whole book and add new material about masturbation.

After his retirement, in 1962, he went to the University of Ghana as Professor of Sociology. During this short interlude, he began to collect African art. What attracted him in African art was a strong and direct appeal to the emotions. The same thing attracted him to the work of Picasso;[11] Elias was already over seventy when his work received wide recognition. In 1969, *The Civilizing Process* was reissued in German and finally published in English. In 1970, his book *What is Sociology?* was also published in both languages. He owed much of this breakthrough to the Dutch sociologist Johan Goudsblom who had already developed a great interest in Elias' work as a student. From 1969 tot 1971 Elias was a visiting lecturer in Amsterdam and the Institute of Social Studies in The Hague. Many young Dutch social scientists fell under the spell of his forceful personality. They applied Elias' approach to a huge variety of topics. By the mid-1970s, Elias had ceased to be a mere academic celebrity in the Netherlands. In Germany, he was also invited to lecture at several universities.

Once, Elias was the victim of tragic-comic event. He had written a book-length typescript on *The balance of power between the sexes* and piled-up all the drafts on the floor in his room in the Department in Leicester. When he was in Germany, the cleaning lady took the opportunity to tidy his room and got rid of the whole pile. The book was lost for posterity.[12] Hence, we do not know much about his stance on the emancipation of women. In his preface of a Dutch study on women who had left violent husbands, he made some remarks on the problematic situation of women. In his view, these could not be separated from the problems of society, *in casu* the welfare state, nor from the problems of men. The problems faced by women are different from the problems faced by men, but they are interconnected. Both categories are involved in a long-term power struggle. For Elias, power relations are an integral aspect of all social figurations. We can never get rid of them. So, the only solution is to find a way to control these imbalances. In other words, we have to create a consensus about some forms of inequality that make marriages work. Should and could there be something like harmonious inequality? Should and could there be something like a figuration in which men and women both have to accept some imbalances that sometimes favour women and sometimes favour men?[13]

In 1978, he went back to Germany, the country that had forced him into exile and had ignored the value of his work for more than three decades. He took residence at the Center for Interdisciplinary Research in Bielefeld. There he greatly enjoyed the swimming pool, the surrounding woods, and the intellectual climate. Germany also made amends for the past by conferring on him numerous honours. The most important one was the title and pension of Professor Emeritus of the University of Frankfurt. In 1977, Elias was the first recipient of the Theodor W. Adorno Prize, conferred by the City of Frankfurt. His ninetieth birthday in June 1987 was marked by two academic conferences in his honor and by a special issue of the journal Theory, Culture and Society. Pierre Bourdieu and other admirers from several countries paid their tribute.

In 1990, on the first of August, when he was working on the introduction for *The Symbol Theory*, he dozed off and died peacefully.

7.2   On sociological theory

In *What is sociology?* Elias presented a new sociological approach in response to the fashionable perspectives that he had vehemently criticized. He strongly opposed a theoretical model of society that was still prevalent with many sociologists and the general public. This model resembles a series of circles within circles. People locate themselves in the center circle as an 'I' or 'Ego.' All the rings around this inner circle resemble sections of society. Closest to ego is the ring of the family, followed by the school or the organization they work for, further rings represent the system of education or the labour market, and the most outer ring represents the state, with its political and administrative system. [14]

The main flaw of this egocentric model is that people see themselves as if they are separated from their social environment. It fails to depict the most essential feature of social life: the enormous interdependency of all people. Individuals form multiple ties in dense social networks or figurations. For instance, before our food arrives on our dinner table most of it has traveled a long distance and undergone all kinds of production and distribution processes, carried out by anonymous workers in far away places. Thanks to our globalized economy, we can eat Gouda cheese or French Camembert, and oranges from California, Israel, Morocco, Spain or South Africa. This is the objective, structural, and horizontal side of figurations. However, there also is a subjective, cultural, and vertical side, forming a kind of supportive superstructure. After all, this economic network cannot function without national and international programs that teach people to communicate, co-operate and reckon with each other. It can only function if enough people have been educated and trained to do all the jobs involved in the production, trade and shipping of these articles. We need an elaborate system of law, norms and values to support this complex system. Most of these activities are being regulated and supported by legal rules and government institutions, to safeguard the quality of products, the financial security of businessmen, and the safety of transporters. In our modern world it is easy to see that a prolific division of labour and social functions entices a high level of interdependency. Everyone has become dependent on the work, knowledge and skills of an innumerable number of people all over the world. This functional interdependency is a key concept of Elias' theories.

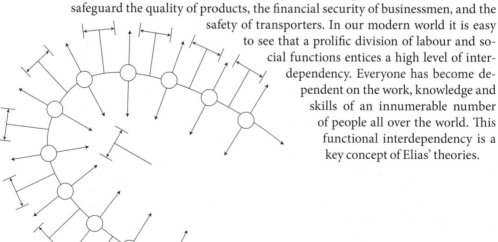

Figure 7.1   Figuration model of Norbert Elias as presented in What is Sociology

In this rather simple sketch of a social network or figuration of individuals the little circles represent individuals that stretch out in many ways to make social connections with other individuals. These social relations with other individuals are characterized by a more or less stable balance of power. Examples of such figurations are a group of friends, a family, a town, a school, a social class, and a nation. Individuals within a social figuration will see themselves as a member of such a figuration and will speak of my friends, my family, my school or my country. From this perspective it is clear that individuals are important parts of social groups or the larger society and do not stand outside these groups, families, circles of friends, and more formal social organizations.

In the model rejected by Elias the individual is viewed as an autonomous unit, as a singular ego, in the center of various objective social frames. This objectification of social structures is understandable, at least to some degree. People feel the presence of social influences. They experience social constraints as forces from outside. So what seems more natural than to ascribe these impositions to concrete things? For Elias the major task of sociological theory is to enlarge the insight in all forms of social constraints. Sociologists should fight the tendency to see social structures and processes as objective, autonomous things that could exist without and outside individuals. Such a view would reinforce processes of reification (*Verdinglichung*). It would dehumanize social structures and processes. But one should never forget that social processes could not exist without the actions of real people.

Before a scientific study of natural and social phenomena was possible, people explained them with the help of models that emerged from their personal experiences and the social forces they exerted upon each other. Thousands of years did pass before this magic-metaphysical thinking was exchanged for a more scientific approach, based on systematic observations, experiments and tests. The new models of physics give a far better idea of the immanent autonomy of natural phenomena. There are no wrathful Gods that make clouds crash to create thunder and lightning to frighten people. But there are high electric powers that have to be released. The tiresome attempts to get better insights in social structures and processes are comparable with those of physics in earlier periods. Social scientists have to make similar spectacular breakthroughs. But first of all, they have to get rid of egocentric thinking.[15] Sociologists must constitute an entirely new science. Already more than one and a half century ago, Saint-Simon and Comte presented this path breaking insight. They were the first who saw that social phenomena function at a higher level of co-ordination and integration than the physiology of biological organs. Hence, the social cannot be deduced from the physical or biological. It is a phenomenon *sui generis*. Elias supported this view wholeheartedly. He saw it as his most important task to search for sociological concepts, theories and models that refer to dynamic social networks of chains of interdependence. However, he expected that it would take many generations to come before people would be familiar with this new scientific approach.[16]

7.2.1   *Figurations or processes?*

Elias introduced the concept of figuration to make an end to the idea that individual and society are two separate entities. In his theoretical framework each individual is the junction of a great variety of social relations with other individuals. The course of social actions sprouts from the mutual dependencies of all the members of these networks. However, the outcomes of their interactions cannot be deduced from the characteristics of the individual actors. Time and time again Elias tells us that these figurations influence the course of events autonomously.[17] For instance, the course of a game of cards is unpredictable, especially when the players are of equal strength. It is contingent on how the cards are distributed and on unpredictable errors of a player. This can change the mood of the players and influence the way they play. It is equally possible that the game gets so exciting that the players temporarily forget everything around them, raise their stakes in irresponsible ways, and go on for hours, though they had not intended to play that long or to take such high risks. The card play becomes a dynamic social event, which gathers momentum on its own and in a way that cannot be explained by the intentions or behaviour of the individual players. All this is even truer for team sports. The two teams and the referee constitute a complex figuration that can change at every moment. A nasty foul of a player can arouse many unpredictable reactions. The same is true for an inconsistent referee or a blundering goalkeeper. Events like this can change the whole atmosphere and turn a defensive team into an aggressive one or vice versa. It can lead to many irritations that can manifest themselves instantly or later in the game. Also a beautiful cross ball or a lucky goal can make a big difference. At such moments even a team performing badly can get wings and start to produce whole series of successful actions, get into a winning mood and make it happen for them. With examples like these Elias wants to clarify that besides the complexity of the game, the mutual dependencies of the team players, autonomous and unpredictable factors play an important role in the course of the game.

Elias' has also introduced the notion of 'double-bind figuration'. They emerge and spontaneously develop in situations in which two competitors strive for the same prize. Like many people, Elias saw the risk of a nuclear war arising not because any group of people seriously wants to start such a war, but because the bipolar struggle between the superpowers of the Cold War had assumed the form of a double-bind figuration. The compelling force of such an unplanned social process cannot be understood simply in terms of the perceptions, plans and intentions of one side. For the perceptions, plans and intentions of each side are in considerable part formed in response to the perceptions, plans and intentions of the other. They are locked together like boxers in a 'frozen clinch', neither able to escape for fear of exposing himself to the blows of the other. Moreover, a double-bind situation tends to be self-escalating for several reasons. In the nuclear arms race each side accumulated more arms in response to the other's growing striking power. Each side invested ever larger sums of money and employed ever more engineers and scientists to invent better bombs. The reciprocal danger enhanced emotive fantasy and unrealistic ideology on both sides. However, Stephen Mennel draws our attention to the hypothesis of Godfried van Benthem van den Bergh, a specialist in international relations, who employed Elias' theory in a more optimistic way. He argues that nuclear weapons had unintended benefits: they forced the great powers to conduct themselves in a much more prudent and restrained manner than in pre-nuclear times, because they were well aware that a nuclear war would produce no winners. There would only be losers on either side plus the rest of the world.[18]

Elias favoured the figuration concept to describe the process of rendering form. He wanted to draw attention to two elements that are inherent to social phenomena. There always is a structure involved, which has the character of a network. At the same time, there is a dynamic process going on, which gives rise to all kinds of developments. This concept has to counterbalance frequently used and rather static terms like 'structure' and 'system', to which Parsons paid so much attention, which annoyed Elias much more than it should have.[19] A serious drawback of concepts such as structure and social system is that they seem to refer to objective things that exist outside and completely separated from individuals and their acts. In contrast, figurations have to be viewed as: *'networks of interdependent people, with shifting, asymmetric power balances.'*[20]

Dimensions and aspects of social figurations

The social figuration is a very rich concept that can be used to diagnose, explain and predict – in a probabilistic way – changes in culture and mentality.

1   It has a physical dimension: its network structure covers short and large distances;

2   It has a social dimension, encompassing many types of social relations, roles, functions, constraints and possibilities, and varying balances of power;

3   It has a mental dimension because everyone perceives these social relations and takes them into consideration.

4   It has a dynamic historical dimension. The roots of figurations lay in the past, and they go on developing dynamically.

It is a phenomenon *sui generis* that can develop autonomously and influence people.

Box 7.1

Later, after many followers had adopted his ideas, his brand of sociology got labeled as figurative sociology. He did not like this at all, because it could give the impression that his ideas had engendered a new school of thought: the figurative school. This he abhorred, because schools of thought tend to become dogmatic and counterproductive for the development of new ideas. That is why he preferred to speak about process-sociology; firstly, because this fitted his intentions far better; secondly, because process is a very common word that could hardly be misused as a label for a new paradigm. On the other hand, Elias did not want to get rid of the concept of social figuration, because it pointed to basic tenets of his whole work. Sociology is about a plurality of people who are bonded to each other in many ways (interdependency), and whose life evolves around the dynamic social network structure they constitute and reproduce together. Continuously social relations are changing. Most changes are of minor importance and hardly noticeable, but some modifications are highly significant and change major features of society. The inherent dynamics of social figurations is largely autonomous. It is hard to grasp, neither by its participants, nor by the sociologist who are observing them.[21] The interweaving of individual actors produces all kinds of patterns and processes; in short, it leads to what sociologists call 'emergent properties'. These principles are so evident, that all sociologists will back them. Yet, they are often forgotten.

An important element of Elias' critique at traditional sociological concepts is his notion of process-reduction. He protested against the widespread inclination to reduce social processes to steady states. An example from our perception of nature is 'the storm is howling around the house', as if the storm is an entity that can blow. In reality the storm is the transportation of a strong stream of air from a high-pressure area to a low-pressure area. The movement of air and the sound that is produced during this process are two aspects of the same phenomenon.[22] Elias believed that European languages are insufficiently equipped to describe complex and dynamic social processes. They have far too many words that emphasize static, material objects, but in reality all social objects are dynamic. Therefore he thinks that there is a great need to coin new process-words for adequate descriptions of social reality. But this is only the beginning. We need to invent words that can describe the complexity, the simultaneous interconnection and character of the processes of social phenomena.

We should also keep in mind that phenomena can change. Therefore, also the meaning of the concepts that describe these phenomena will shift. Take for instance 'bourgeois'. The content of this concept has changed as soon as the social context for the bourgeoisie has changed. Hence, the meaning of bourgeoisie in the Middle Ages is quite different from today's meaning. Nonetheless, both concepts still are connected to each other through a long chain of connecting shifts in meaning. If these historical modifications are taken into consideration, we can still use these concepts. Evidently, sociology cannot manage without rather vaguely defined concepts such as 'organization', 'institution', and 'community'. For the time being, we have and can proceed with the help of these concepts, although we always have to keep in mind that social reality is complex and dynamic, and that it refers to figurations of interdependent human beings.[23]

7.3   The Civilizing Process

We all like to see ourselves as 'civilized.' To be civilized is to be polite, good mannered and considerate towards others. In the thirties, Elias noticed that the concept of civilization expressed the self-consciousness of the West. It summed up everything in which the Western World believed itself superior to earlier societies in Europe or to 'more primitive' ones outside the Western World. With this term it sought to describe what constituted its special character and what it was proud of: the level of its science and technology, the quality of its performance, the development of its worldview.[24]

7.3.1　French civilization and German culture

Clearly, this concept is loaded with evaluative meanings. But Elias did not intend to write a study that would increase the self-satisfaction of westerners. He had noticed that most Europeans tended to consider their medieval ancestors as 'uncivilized.' However, medieval people did not consider their behaviour to be coarse and inconsiderate. Hence, they saw no reason to change their conduct. Yet, since then, feelings of shame and embarrassment have increased, and many norms have changed. That is why Elias called this a civilizing process; however, without adding a normative judgment whether this was good or bad. He asked himself:

> How did this change, this 'civilizing' of the West, actually happen? Of what did it consist? And what were its 'causes' or 'motive forces'?[25]

Elias started his book with an analysis of the sociogenetic process that led to our current conception of terms like civilization and culture. In France the word *civilisation* was used in the connotation of being civilized, of inherently being more civilized than people in the French colonies and, for the aristocracy and the bourgeoisie, of being more civilized than the lower classes. In the 16th century, courtiers used the word *civilité* to describe their own 'courtly' modes of behaviour. Thus they also distinguished themselves from the more rough conduct of their forbears. Later on, the French intellectuals took on many of the ways and attitudes of the elite at the royal court. Trickled down via the intelligentsia and other 'upstarts' the term *civilisation* came to be associated with the progress and identity of the nation as a whole. This happened partly because the French court was relatively open. For the leaders of the French bourgeoisie, which had become a politically active class, the process of civilization was still in progress. It had to be expanded to all classes and to all sectors of social life. For them, civilization ought to include more than refined manners and the pacification of the country by the king. Government should be efficient and democratic. Education should be expanded and improved and justice should be less barbaric. Citizens should be better educated, freer and more humane.

In Germany things were different. There, *Zivilisation* had taken on quite another shade of meaning. In Germany there was no single state or political centre. Instead, there were numerous small courts, all of them French speaking and relatively exclusive. There, it was very hard for outsiders to get accepted. Princes and courtiers regarded the German language as vulgar. The thinly scattered German-speaking intellectuals of bourgeois origin associated the word *Zivilisation* with polished but superficial manners. In their view, it only scratched the surface of human experience. For them, *Kultur* was much more important. For them *Kultur* came to be associated with depth of feeling, sincerity, virtue, intellectual and personal development (*Bildung*), in short, with all that was real and genuine. The word *Kultur* was used by the intelligentsia to distinguish themselves and their achievements from the established courtly circles 'above' them and from the mass of commoners 'below' them. The German intelligentsia had no political power. The social distance between intelligentsia and aristocracy always remained very big. On the other hand, they had a great influence on the mentality of the people. They helped to make the national character more bourgeois.

Elias concluded that the process of civilization reached a kind of provisional endphase near the turn of the 18th and 19th century. At that time nations like France and Germany had become convinced that their civilization and high culture, their scientific, technological and artistic achievements had reached a level of great superiority. And, this idea of superiority seemed to legitimize their dominant position. It gave them the right to bring their way of life to other countries and legitimized acts of colonization.

7.3.2   *State formation, civilization and increased self-constraint*

In the next part of his book Elias makes a study of how this process of civilization took place. He took proof from a great many sources: including literature, paintings and drawings, and other historical documents, but mostly from so-called style books. From the 13th to the 19th century these books had set out the standards of acceptable behaviour for well-bred people. He used many examples from books meant for the education of the children of the elite stating all kinds of rules that are now taken for granted. For instance, he quoted from *Der Deutsche Cato*: 'Do not spit across the table in the manner of hunters.' And from the medieval bestseller *De civilitate morum puerilium (1530)*, by Erasmus he quoted:

> *Turn away when spitting, lest your saliva fall on someone. If anything purulent falls on the ground, it should be trodden upon, lest it nauseate someone.*

If we keep with this example of spitting, we can notice that manners got even more 'refined' in the next century. From Courtin, *Nouveau traité de civilité* (1672):

> *Formerly, for example, it was permitted to spit on the ground before people of rank, and was sufficient to put one's foot on the sputum. Today that is an indecency.*

And another century later we can read in a book about Christian civility (La Salle, 1729, 1774):

> *When you are with well-born people, and when you are in places that are kept clean, it is polite to spit into your handkerchief while turning slightly aside. ... After spitting in your handkerchief, you should fold it at once, without looking at it, and put it into your pocket.* [26]

Nowadays, all western children have to learn to behave in a 'civilized' way. Already at a very young age they are being trained to eat decently, not to speak with a full mouth and to chew with their mouth closed. They learn to refrain from belching, spitting, farting, urinating or defecating in public. In our day and age, all this is so much taken for granted that to read about all these specific instructions is quite hilarious. According to Elias, it is a kind of sociogenetic law that each child has to pass through the same processes that his society had to undergo during its long course of history.[27]

Why can't we simply explain eating without proper plates, forks and knives by the sheer poverty of the Middle Ages, by the fact that common people simply had not enough money to buy these utensils? Why can't we explain public urinating and defecating in the open air, from a lack of proper lavatories, sewer systems and water closets? According to Elias, it is the other way around. We do not need a materialistic explanation, but a cultural one. The emergence of feelings of shame and embarrassment about our natural functions led to a growing demand for sanitary equipment.[28] Technically, it was no problem to produce enough spoons, forks, and knives at low cost. However, the available techniques and resources were used (or abused) to demonstrate the richness and wealth of the secular and religious elite. They had silver spoons, crystal glasses, knives with ivory or ebony handles, golden dishes, porcelain cups, et cetera. Yet none of this led to a change in the common way of eating with hands from an ordinary dish, sharing a platter and so on. To eat in this fashion was taken for granted and suited the people.[29]

But, after certain table manners had been developed at the courts this custom implied that people who did not belong to these circles and did not have these manners, were coarse and uncivilized. After the middle and lower classes developed feelings of inferiority, they started to change their ways and began to imitate the higher estates. From then on, parents started to train their children to behave decently and show 'good manners'. Finally, these new manners and attitudes spread over the entire population.

But this leads to the next question. Why did the well-born people at the courts change their behaviour? To answer this, we have to grasp the social figuration of the noblemen in the Middle Ages. Then, within the borders of their property, knights could do what they liked. They were hardly constrained by governmental rules, tax collectors and scores of other laws and social obligations. There was no need to be considerate with all kinds of people, nor was there a continuous demand for good manners. Knights were lord and master of their manor. Yet, they were not entirely free. They were part of a social figuration, bound in a network with their servants, serfs, farmers, and craftsmen and with other knights and their helpers, soldiers and bondsmen. They were expected to defend their territory against all competitors and to expand it as soon as the opportunity arose. Their whole existence was based on this perpetual competition for the defense or the expansion of their domain. They had to defend their farmers, bondsmen, wives and children against killing, rape, and robbery.

Protection and suppression are closely related social functions; this certainly was the case in those days of knights and castles. In fact, the social pressure was so huge, that knights really had no choice. Knights that could not fight well lost their worldly possessions, their status and prestige. Often they also lost their lives. They simply had no alternative but to fight and to fight well. The social pressure executed by the figuration stemmed from the will of every knight to acquire more land. And the will to gain more land stemmed from the figuration constituted by the knights.[30] This sounds like a circular argument, but it is not. It is based on the interplay between the individual and the collective. Besides, we should keep in mind that different generations are involved here. The will to expand their property is being instilled into each new generation during their youth. They are being socialized to become brave and chivalrous knights with a strong will to defend their land and honour. We can safely assume that knights were not born as aggressive fighters, but were socialized to become courageous defenders and vigorous attackers as soon as the need for it emerged. They had been trained to follow the tracks of their ancestors, to follow their rules and to add to their glory. Thus, that social figuration is reproduced in each new generation.

Somewhere in history this led to a significant concentration of power and the formation of states, although this was never planned. It was the outcome of a process in which knights did not want all the land; they just wanted the land next to their own. This simple and precise formulation expresses well how, from the interweaving of countless individual interests and intentions, something comes into being that was not planned by anyone, yet has emerged from their actions. This is the whole secret of social figurations, their compelling dynamics, regularities, process character and autonomous development.[31] This process led to a centralization of power. The strongest knight became king and ruled over all the land he had won. The 'common' knights had to submit themselves to central rulers that became increasingly powerful. So most of the dominated knights lost their sovereignty and had to adjust themselves to the straightjacket of a life at the royal court. There they had to behave in quite different ways than what they were used to, much more diplomatic and with all the required courteous manners. No longer were they supposed to fight with lethal weapons on the battlefield, but with subtle non-violent measures, such as persuasion, wit, cunning, and intrigue.

7.3.3   Growing interdependency and psychologization

To Elias it was plain that significant changes in social conditions lead to salient changes in the way people have to live with each other. These transformations will affect their patterns of behaviour, their feelings and their consciousness. He drew our attention to a great variety of consequences of social transformations and renounced any attempt to explain major social changes with the help of only one factor. New techniques of farming, craft, transport and warfare, and last but not least, demographic growth and the emergence of cities also had a great impact.[32] The more differentiated social functions become, the closer the social network of interdependencies. Naturally, this demands more self-restraint from everybody. Each one has to take into consideration the feelings, intentions and desires of a greater number of people. Even the high and mighty must show self-restraint. This is so, because their conduct has repercussions for the conduct and daily life of a great many of people. If they behave in uncivilized and unpredictable ways, they will endanger many links in the social figuration of which they form a crucial part.

Elias clarified how sociogenesis gets connected with psychogenesis. Civilization entails psychologization, rationalization, and growing feelings of embarrassment. The ongoing proliferation of social functions means that people have to reckon with a growing number of other human beings. This requires thinking ahead and guessing how people will react. By trying to think how other people think, humans will develop a better idea of the other. The other becomes more specific and unique.[33] In the old world, which was much more dangerous, people had to make quick decisions about strangers: is he good or evil, dangerous or trustworthy? A wrong decision could mean an untimely death. In the old world people lived a simple life. Hence they did not depend on strangers for food, clothing or shelter. They had no need to appease strangers, to acknowledge their feelings and interests. But as soon as interdependency passes a certain level, social life needs more constraint and predictability. Then, individuals have to show more self-restraint. This is manifested in the book of manners written by Erasmus of Rotterdam. It does present much more psychological insights than similar books from earlier periods. For Elias, this was the first sure sign of the 'courtification' of the higher classes. Precisely, the court society demanded a sharp observation of all the noble competitors. Court life was full of intrigues and conspiracies. Everyone had to consider his own deeper motives and strategies as well as those of his peers. In earlier periods, most people were not aware of the inner motives and drives of other human beings. They were more committed to their personal safety, social position and status.

Historians have detected an increase of feelings of shame and embarrassment since the 16th century. Elias defined shame as the fear for social degradation, the fear that significant others would disapprove of your behaviour, or even worse, would stop seeing you. People feel this inner fear and will acknowledge their inferiority whenever their behaviour has put a part of them in conflict with the part that has accepted the general norm. Feelings of shame appear when one perceives that one no longer can control one's feelings. Feelings of embarrassment are very similar. However, embarrassment is engendered by the acts of another person. Embarrassment is the feeling of discomfort that arises when somebody else threatens to breach a rule that you yourself have internalized in your conscience. Shame and embarrassment are being fed by the awareness of social risks. That is why shame represents the dark side of rationalization. The ego and superego of our personality have a double function.[34] They regulate mutual relations and, at the same time, they are involved in attempts to control themselves. Hence, the increased need of previewing potential events and consideration with the other gave rise to the 'foreign politics' of rationalization and the 'home politics' of an extension of feelings of shame.[35]

The process of rationalization started to gather momentum in the 16th century. This trend forms the leading thread running through the oeuvre of Max Weber. Elias has put this social trend in a broader perspective. He drew our attention to its repercussions for a change in the structure of our personality. People have always been capable of rational thinking, of planning ahead and of empathic acts. However, what is of great interest for us is why these rational acts have become so much more dominant in that age, why instinctive impulses and the expression of feelings are being restrained much more than before. At the time, more and more people were willing to postpone short-term gratification for the achievement of highly valued long-term objectives. At the courts people strove for higher status, even if that would ruin them. Within their social and cultural context aiming for higher status seemed more rational than looking after financial affairs. The rationality of the nobility differed hugely from the rationality developed by the bourgeoisie. Since every society, estate, class or group has its own conception of reality, of the most valued goals in life, they also have their own rationality. There always is a calculus of profit and loss of social status or financial wealth.

7.3.4   Summary of the civilizing process

Elias warned us that we should not be content with the conclusion that the interweaving of human actions gives rise to an autonomous dynamic. Though it is a correct observation in itself, it does not dig deep and leaves everything open to all kinds of interpretations. Without the content of concrete historical examples that show how these figurations emerge and influence social actions it simply is an insight without substance. It is significant to notice how changes in the social structure are coherent with changes in behaviour. It also is important to see that socio- and psychogenesis go together. This thesis is founded on the assumption that the human mind is extremely flexible. In principle, each generation can be socialized in new patterns of behaviour. Hence, each historical epoch can produce its specific type of people.

We need a sociological explanation to account for the marked change in behaviour towards more self-control. In the second half of the Middle Ages, political and demographic processes gave rise to a process of the concentration of power.

In many regions stronger knights conquered the weaker ones. Their territories were added to the territory of the conqueror, which in turn led to the emergence of large kingdoms. After loosing their primary function, many noblemen went to the royal courts to become part of the administration or the coterie of the King. There, they had to participate in various ceremonies and to adjust to the strict rules of many protocols. Within the small world of these courts salient hierarchies emerged, reflecting the distance to the Prince or King. Many were competing for a small number of lucrative and honourable positions. Hence, they were continuously scheming to acquire a better position and a higher status. In this social figuration self-control became an important asset. Within this small but overcrowded community of noblemen one had to be much more considerate with the interests and feelings of their fellows, than they had been with their former servants, serfs or enemies. Lack of self-control could lead to emotional outbursts that revealed one's real motives, one's hypocrisy and insincerity. Besides, it would mean the loss of the esteem of many peers and superiors.

There were only a few options to relieve the growing tensions at the royal courts. Some adventurous knights became explorers or colonizers. Another way out was the creation of all kinds of new specialized functions. Specialization could help to mitigate the pressure of fierce competition. Then you only had to compete with people with similar specialized skills. And when the new specializations fulfilled important social needs, other people became dependent on them, thus creating a significant lengthening of the chain of mutual dependence. Elias showed that this process of specialization could indeed be observed at the courts. Survivors had to obey to a Darwinist law of social evolution.

The most central element in the civilizing process is the increase of self-constraint. On the basis of historical books on different manners, Elias showed that the aggravation of self-constraint was a structured process and not an accidental sequence of occurrences. Though it did not answer the characteristics of a rational plan, Elias strongly believed that the process followed a specific path. Undeniably, the trend leads to a further concealment of our animalistic functions that are connected with excretion of bodily odors, sweat, phlegm, mucus, urine, and faeces. This trend has increased our feelings of shame for many of our bodily functions. Emotional sentiments and rational acts of individuals interlock continuously. Increasing interdependency is reinforcing this process. This trend is set spontaneously. Human beings are unable to foresee everything. They cannot even grasp all what is happening today or what has happened in the past. Nevertheless, they must take all kinds of decisions daily. Hence, unexpected reactions and side effects are very common. Even the best intentions can work out rather negatively. The complexity of society and the large restrictions of our knowledge have convinced Elias that long-term-developments cannot be foreseen and planned. Hence, for Elias, the intended actions of individuals are never the starting point for a sociological explanation. The roots of every social development are hidden within the complex social figuration that preceded this development. Even the intentions of individual people are rooted in a specific social figuration with a long history.[36] Or, according to Goudsblom: *the unintended consequences of yesterday are the unintended social conditions for our intentions of today.* [37] And sooner or later the latter will generate new unintended consequences.

7.4   The end of the civilizing process?

Since Elias put forward his theory, we have experienced more permissiveness and 'informalization.' Behaviour that was once unthinkable is now widely accepted. But does this trend refute his theory of civilization? For example, in many western European countries the casualness in the way children address older people has grown. Nowadays it is very common to address parents with their first name. Also many teachers in primary and secondary schools insist on being talked to by their Christian names. Furthermore, in many European countries the use of the informal you has become much more widespread ('tutoyer' or 'duzen'). Social restraints regarding sexual behaviour have shrunk. Today sexual matters are openly discussed. And the dictum to abstain from sexual intercourse before marriage has long since lost its validity. Many modern movies show an overkill of violence and explicit sex. Numerous porn films are produced, sold or hired. Would Elias still maintain that these are forms of behaviour that show an increase of self-constraint?

Whatever might have been feared, the vigorous attacks on conservative and suffocating rules, customs and traditions did not result in an 'anything goes society'. Of course, significant changes have taken place. An analysis of the moral message of a famous Dutch women's magazine showed that it significantly altered its tone and content between 1950 and 1975 where sexual and marital relations were concerned. No longer were women advised to stay loyal to their husbands and to salvage their marriage at all costs. In the seventies, this magazine asserted that teenagers did not always have to obey their parents. Parents were advised to reconsider their views and take account of shifting norms and values. The new message was that individual rights such as the right for self-actualization could outweigh the collective interest of the family. New norms emerged about personal freedom and collective duties. A model of negotiation replaced the old authoritarian relations between husband and wife, between parents and children. These negotiations lead to new rules about fair treatment and a somewhat fairer division of tasks. Emotional arguments became more important. People were advised to make choices that made them feel good. Systematic content analysis of the magazine over a 25-year period shows a shift from moralization towards psychologization.[38] An observation like this nicely fits Elias' theory of the trend towards more psychologization.

All the above-mentioned examples designate a significant relaxation of etiquette, moral standards, and self-control.[39] But do they also indicate an element of decivilization? It must be said that modern history already had shown periods of moral relaxation before, for instance the *fin de siècle* period at the end of the

19th century and the *Roaring Twenties* of the 20th century. Already in 1939 Elias had observed similar trends, though, at the time, he did not develop them into a theory that would fit his general thesis of the civilizing process. He wrote that traditional modes of conduct had become problematic for the young. Where the fathers stop thinking, the sons start asking questions: Why is this allowed and something else that is quite similar, forbidden? In the sixties and seventies, restraints became even weaker and some have disappeared completely. But according to Elias these are rather mild counter movements.[40] Moreover, the more skin is shown by girls or women in public, the more men have to restrain themselves not to show any sexual excitement. Later Elias described the morally relaxed lifestyle of modern times as a manifestation of 'controlled lack of control'. In his view it did proof a higher level of civilization if men could restrain themselves in settings in which women started to wear mini skirts and topless bikinis without risking sexual harassment. He was convinced that this development could only take place in a society in which a high degree of restraint is present. In this respect it is even more important to note that women in 'civilized societies' can mix, work, go out and dance with men without the need of a chaperone.

7.4.1   A return of barbarism?

For many, the first and most obvious critique at *The Civilizing Process* was that some main events of the 20th century are clear manifestations of a return to 'barbarism'. The atrocities of the First and the Second World War, in particular the systematic killing of millions of Jews, plus thousands of homosexuals, Jehovah's witnesses, and gypsies by the Nazi's, but also the less systematic but numerically far greater terror of Stalin and other Communist dictators as well as the many terrible violations of human rights executed by the fascist regimes of Franco, Salazar and the Greek Colonels seem to deny all notions of cultural or moral progress in Europe.

Since control of violence is a central theme in the theory of civilization, the widespread perception that today's world is more violent than ever before seems to undermine that theory. It is generally believed that there is more violence on the streets, more aggression from stressed drivers, and more hooliganism. However, once more studies have shown that perceptions can be deceptive. Among historians, it is common knowledge that each new generation of aging adults complain of the increase in violence. If we take the long-term view, former centuries have been much more violent, not only for travelers, but also for the residents of villages and towns. It is not a coincidence that medieval towns and castles had high walls and would close their gates at nightfall. On the other hand, if we only analyze the available data from the last three or four decades, then we might observe some definite increase in violence. The use of illegal substances has yielded a significant rise in drug-related crime. It is also clear that hooliganism around big football matches has become much more widespread than four decades ago. In those days people went to the stadium in their best Sunday clothes. Now we can witness many half-drunken and half or casually dressed supporters ready to start a fight with any steward or policeman, or any supporter of the other team. Hence, some researchers have concluded that countries like England are experiencing an actual 'decivilizing' upsurge in violence. It certainly is not easy to say whether this represents a minor short-term fluctuation or a more definite reversal of a long-term trend.[41]

As yet we do not fully understand the ups and downs of civilization, or the conditions under which society moves in a certain direction or reverses its trend. Historically speaking there is nothing unusual about the mass murder of defeated enemies or about pogroms against outsider groups. However, there are some negative and positive aspects of modernization worth mentioning. First, the large-scale, methodical, bureaucratic organization of ethnic cleansing carried out by thousands of Nazis and supported by millions of their followers is a typical product of modern technology and modern propaganda. Secondly, the manifestation of widespread disbelief and revulsion when all this became widely known is also a reflection of a modern mentality. The latter reaction is symptomatic of the extent to which most modern people are capable of identification with the sufferings of their fellow human beings. Maybe we must also add another aspect that could be interpreted as a positive sign of further civilization, and that is that many people refused to believe that such atrocities could take place and were actually happening in a country with such a host of famous scientists, brilliant composers, painters, writers and poets. This refusal to see the obvious was even true for German Jews. That is why many Jews, like Elias' parents, did not leave the country in time.

7.4.2   Evolutionism and ethnocentrism

Elias described and explained the cultural development in Western Europe without calling this progress. He only observed that a growing division of labour went together with growing interdependency, giving rise to higher levels of social control and self-control. In his view, this manifested a social and mental development 'in a certain direction'. He explicitly used development in a certain direction to avoid the value-loaded concept of progress. Nonetheless, Anton Blok, a former aficionado of Elias, reproached him for being a unilineair evolutionist. In his excellent monograph on the life and works of Elias, Mennel briefly explains the origins of this accusation.[42] Classical anthropologists always have contended that complex social organizations and societies have developed out of less complex ones. In the 19th century, they shamelessly used terms such as 'primitive societies' or 'savage tribes', and considered modern societies to be much more civilized. New generations of anthropologists rejected this approach. It implied an up-going movement towards social progress that could easily generate dichotomies in which the less complex societies would be described as rude, primitive, lower, uncivilized, or less advanced than modern societies. Evidently, evolutionary classifications can fuel racism. Therefore, modern anthropologists, headed by

Franz Boas, favour cultural relativism. In their view, other cultures could evolve in other ways and directions. And this could and should explain the manifold cultural differences we may observe.

Cultural relativists claim that cultures cannot be compared in a reasonable way. Each culture and each epoch has its own set of prevailing norms and values. Therefore, outsiders are not justified to describe them as primitive, inferior or backward. Although Elias had never written anything negative about preceding cultures or so called 'primitive' societies, the sheer discussion about civilization seemed to imply a wide gap between civilized and non-civilized cultures, and hence, a negative evaluation of those peoples that could be described as less civilized. Blok went even further and accused Elias of ethnocentrism and racism. To me, this last accusation seems to be totally uncalled for. Elias was a victim of the most outspoken racist policy of the 20th century. Racists had brutally killed his mother, forced him into exile, and severely damaged his career. Moreover, Elias had shown that the French and the Germans, both belonging to the European 'race', could develop a whole new set of manners, to a new level of individual self-constraint, within the range of a few centuries. Plainly, levels of self-constraint or civilized behaviour are not related with ethnic origin, but are purely cultural manifestations. So, with his data, theory and terminology, Elias clearly showed that race had nothing to do with it. From hindsight, one can only wonder what spirited people like Blok to their fierce attacks.

Elias supported most of the assumptions of cultural relativism, but he did not think it wise to eliminate all models of development. He did not use the concept of evolution lightheartedly, because the political climate of the thirties had made him well aware of the possibility of a link with a type of reasoning that would divide nations into super humans and sub humans. Initially, Elias favoured the multilinear model. He studied specific societies and their development in *The Civilizing Process*, in *Court Society* and in *The Established* and *the Outsiders*. We can detect a more unilinear approach in his later work, for instance in *The Society of Individuals* and *The Symbol Theory*. In these essays he focused on humanity as a whole. And when one's goal is to study the social development of mankind, one cannot avoid creating a yardstick that is supposed to be universally applicable. In *Court Society* Elias produced a preliminary list of four criteria for such yardsticks:

1   The number of routine contacts between people from different classes, age categories and gender;
2   The number, length, density and strength of chains of interdependence;
3   The central balance of social tensions. According to Elias, the number of power centers increases with the further division of labour. At the same time, inequality will decrease.
4   The degree of control over nature, of people over each other, and of each individual over himself.[43]

Maybe, the list needs further elaboration. For the moment items 1 and 2 offer loads of work that will be enjoyed by those sociologists that love quantitative research. Item 3 will fuel macro sociology and politicology. Item 4 refers to the trio of basic mechanisms of control, of which the last one is highlighted in civilization theory. This list and the following quotation reveal that Elias indeed cherished a spark of optimism about the possibility of social progress with the help of the social sciences.

> *Civilization ... is set in motion blindly, and kept in motion by the autonomous dynamics of a web of relationships, by specific changes in the way people are bound to live together. But it is by no means impossible that we can make out of it something more 'reasonable', something that functions better in terms of our needs and purposes. For it is precisely in conjunction with the civilizing process that the blind dynamics of men intertwining in their deeds and aims gradually leads towards greater scope for planned intervention into both the social and individual structures - intervention based on a growing knowledge of the unplanned dynamics of these structures.* [44]

7.5   Inequality among equals

The study of cultural change occupies a central position in the work of Elias, but he was also interested in the phenomenon of inequality. However, his work on this topic does not fit the main approaches to this major theme of sociology. He did not think that inequality could be fully explained by relations of production, nor did he support the Weberian idea that the Marxist explanation had to be adjusted to variations in estate and political preferences. For him, power was a polymorphous phenomenon, shaped by all the social interdependencies of the social figuration. That is why he searched for concepts that would enable him to understand the dynamics of social inequality. This quest led him to construct a theory on the social relations between the established and outsiders. In this theory, he connects balances of power to differences in cultural habits, manners, and lifestyle, just like he did in *The Civilizing Process*.[45]

In 1965, *The Established and the Outsiders: A Sociological Inquiry into Community Problems* was published. It was a study about the social tensions in Winston Parva, a rather isolated district of Leicester. Winston Parva was divided into three zones. Zone 1 was the lower middle class area. It had the highest prestige. The two other zones were lower class areas. They featured the same type of council houses. Nevertheless, zone 2 had a far better image. It was located in the center. In it were all the important buildings such as churches, shops, pubs, and a cinema. People living in zone 2 considered themselves to be respectable citizens. In contrast, the inhabitants of Rat Alley were viewed as second-rate citizens. The people living there were considered to be noisy, coarse, and dirty. They were viewed as troublemakers who could not raise their children properly. In reality, all these negative labels only fitted a small minority of the people from zone 3.

Social cohesion was much stronger in zone 2. They saw themselves as descendants of 'old established' families. It was a community in itself and not a category of loosely connected individuals as in zone 3. How did all this come about? Naturally, Elias started to dig in the history of the district. He learned that the center part, zone 2, was the oldest part. It was built round 1880. Families, who had moved in when these houses were built, had stayed there, raised their families, and produced grandchildren. For them, there was no need to move. They always had found employment and had liked the neighbourhood. Within the span of three generations they had the feeling that they were living in a kind of village. The bigger and more expensive houses of zone 1 were built in the 1920s. The new inhabitants were welcomed as a group of people that rendered Winston Parva more status and prestige. The houses of zone 3 were built in the thirties. During World War II, a London weapon factory was relocated to Leicester. The Londoners who worked in this factory rented the empty houses in zone 3. However, the newcomers could not fit in, though they were manual labourers like the majority of Winston Parva. But the latter noted too much difference in behaviour and lifestyle and were unwilling to socialize with them. As a consequence, the Londoners did not integrate well. They disliked the cool welcome and arrogance of the 'villagers', who were offended by the jovial and loud ways of the cockneys. As a consequence, a process of segregation started. Soon some pubs became known as pubs for the 'villagers' of Winston Parva, whereas another public house became the favourite pub of the Londoners.

Also, the negative image of the newcomers was greatly advertized. Soon they were being labeled as uncivilized, loudmouthed, dirty, and criminal. Frequent gossiping supported this image building. Some of it might be based on facts, but most of it was highly exaggerated. The deviant behaviour of a small minority of newcomers helped to establish a very negative image for the whole group. Of course, there were also misfits in the established group. But now, these deviant persons were seen as exceptions to the rule. In a rather arbitrary way the image of the newcomers was based on the behaviour of the worst members of their group, whereas the positive image of the established was based on a minority of the best.[46]

Why weren't the newcomers able to improve their image? The answer is simply because their social figuration lacked the right connections. They did not occupy important positions in the labour union, the church, the sports clubs or other voluntary associations. A network of 'establishment' occupied all these positions, and they were not willing to make room for newcomers. Their position was further weakened by their inclination to agree with the general view that Londoners behaved less well. To use a concept coined by Elias: newcomers were far too willing to accept the negative They-image that the people of Winston Parva had created of them. In short, this segregation was the outcome of a combination of exclusion followed and enhanced by self-exclusion.

According to Elias tensions and conflicts are an intrinsic element of all status hierarchies. People with a low status only consent to their low prestige if this is imposed on them. Improvement is difficult. This is the case even when the low status group outnumbers the high status group. Numbers are not decisive. The social cohesion within a network is much more important than the expansion of the network. A small, but tightly knitted network can be superiour to a large, but loosely coupled network. In Winston Parva, the network of 'old stock' families constituted such a forceful source of power that a powerful minority occupied all key positions in the community. [47]

With this study, Elias wanted to reveal the shortcomings of theories that explain relations between insiders and outsiders by an exclusive referral to prejudice and discrimination. He explicitly denounced interpretations based on the motives, intentions and acts of disconnected individuals. He deemed such an explanation too psychological.[48] Instead, he always aimed for multi-causal and multi-dimensional explanations. In his view a good sociological explanation revealed dynamic historic, contextual and internal social causes. Certainly, this rule applies to the explanation of any social figuration established by two interacting groups, in particular when one of these groups consists of migrants. The history of mankind is soaked with tiresome processes in which new groups have to join and fit in into established groups. In general it takes more than one generation to finish this process of acculturation and integration. As soon as the balance of power gets more equal, also the idea of a positive we-group and an inferior they-group will fade away.

Recent history shows many head-on attacks on racism and sexism. How did Elias explain this new movement to get rid of inequality and unfair treatment of various categories? He thinks that this social movement is the outcome of an ongoing process of functional democratization. Increased levels of interdependency must transcend into a functional democracy. You cannot go on discriminating people on which you depend without harming your own interests. In a complex society, you continuously need the help and efforts of all kinds of craftsmen, service people, and specialists. In particular, those categories that carry out specialized jobs that are crucial for the functioning of society can demand more rights, a better pay and a higher status. If they would go on strike, they could bring society to a standstill. Increased complexity and interdependency will surely lead to mutual acceptance and a multidimensional execution of power. Nowadays it is unthinkable that one person or a small oligarchy will possess all the power of the state and the economy. Elias spoke of multi-polar control and polyarchy.[49] The ever-growing chains of interdependence and the proliferation of functional differentiation demand a strong increase in social co-ordination and integration. This can easily lead to new forms of inequality. Unlike Marx, Elias did not think that only economic or material resources are relevant for explaining inequality. He certainly was right to draw our attention to non-material sources and non-economic forms of social distinction and also revealed that there could be serious conflicts and strong tensions within the working class.

7.6   Individualization and globalization

What is more real and concrete: the individual or society? The simplest answer to this false question is that individuals are real and society is not. Everyone can see, hear, feel and smell people. Cannibals can even taste them. Since society is not visible or touchable, it can easily lead to the idea that it merely is a theoretical invention. Margaret Thatcher, the first female prime minister of Great Britain, became the laughing stock of social scientists when she stated: *'There is no such thing as society. There are only individuals.'* But Elias asserts that even renowned sociologists such as Simmel and Weber tended to lapse into methodological individualism.

7.6.1   *The rise of the I-identity and the fall of the We-identity*

Another mistake of some philosophers and sociologists is treating individuals and society as different entities, instead as two different aspects of the same human existence. This aberration of thinking cannot be understood without a consideration of its implicit ideological content. On the one hand, there is a strand that sees society as the highest value, and, on the other, a strand that posits the wholly self-sufficient, free individual, the 'closed personality' or *homo clausus* as the highest value. It is not easy to harmonize these two 'highest values' with one another. In some situations they are plainly irreconcilable. But usually this problem is not squarely faced.[50]

The work of Émile Durkheim forms a strong antidote against methodological individualism. He studied 'social facts' that transcend the existence and consciousness of individuals. For Durkheim, society was an objective and autonomous phenomenon created by collective actions. He tended to lean over to the other extreme. But, according to Elias, the right escape route is to acknowledge that the social bonds between individuals are just as real as the individuals themselves. The social cohesion is just as theoretic as gravitation. Both forces are invisible, but their effects are noticeable.

During social evolution there have been long periods without concepts such as individual or society, certainly not in the meaning we attach to them now. The current meaning of the concept individual seems to suggest that each man or woman is an autonomous being and should also remain so; a being that is unique and different from other human beings, at least in certain aspects. Each society has produced a certain balance between the I- and the We-identity. But Elias believed that this balance has been disturbed. In modern societies too much emphasis is put on the I-identity.[51] Long ago things were very different. Ancient Rome offers a classic example of a society in which the We-identity was much more important than the I-identity. The most important identification was identification with your family or tribe. The antique languages did not even have an equivalent of the modern 'individual'. In Latin it meant impossible to divide and *persona* meant masque. This referred to the fact that people were supposed to play specific roles. Precursors of words like private person had a negative sound. They referred to outsiders and idiots. This very brief excursion into ancient history learns that specific concepts or labels are social products that will change with society. When a society becomes more individualized there will also be words to describe this process and its outcome. We must assume that people have always have had individual characteristics, but as long as these individual differences were of no importance to society at large, they tended to be ignored.[52]

The modern emphasis on our I-identity has to be explained with the structural modernization of society. Industrialization gave rise to social mobility. A growing number of people got jobs that did not exist when they were born. On the other hand, technological progress had obliterated many of the jobs carried out by their fathers. No longer it sufficed to class people as members of the state or the class of their father. Social climbers no longer fitted the traditional categories. They came from a lower class or estate but now belonged to a higher one as a result of their achievements. In fact, they did not really belong to a class or estate. They became more unique, more individual and less a member of a group. In the 17th century, people started to make clear distinctions between one's category of social origin and one's actual profession.[53] Social mobility led to unique professional trajectories. Thus, people got more unique, more individualized. This led to a greater need to discuss, emphasize, and verify this uniqueness.

Elias preferred the historic perspective and he did not flinch from demanding his readers to imagine the social conditions of the 'cave man' and to compare this with their present situation. The cavemen lived in small groups. Most members of the group were related and in most characteristics fairly equal. The most important function of the group was ensuring survival. From a purely biological standpoint nothing much has changed since the days of the cavemen. But if we look at social organization, we see striking differences. In prehistoric times, individuals were much stronger connected to their next of kin. For help one could rely on them only. Others could not be trusted or lived too far away. In contrast, modern welfare states developed formalized support systems for people in need. In modern societies the state has created many organizations that can function as rescue teams for all kinds of emergencies. The modern nation-state fulfills a double function for its citizens. On the one hand it 'dehumanizes' people by registering them as numbers indicating level of income, taxation category, gender, age, marital state, and so forth. It treats all members of the same class or category alike. On the other hand it gives them a lot of freedom. The state does not interfere with the choice of your spouse, your friends, your place of residence, hairstyle and clothing, whereas there was no such freedom in traditional societies.[54]

If we compare ourselves in turn with the cavemen, the ancient Greek or the Mediaeval Europeans, then we can easily see a shift in the We-I-balance that is related to the rising complexity of these societies. The social organization of a Stone Age tribe was extremely simple. Its hierarchy was almost non-existent. The worldview of these tribesmen did hardly go further than the horizon. 'We' could be interpreted in one way only: it referred to all members of the tribe and to no one else. Everyone else belonged to the rest of the world. We were 'we' and they were 'they'. During later stages of mankind, societies grew more complex. There were more layers and more categories. Thus, modernizing societies created more 'We-groups'. Nowadays, people belong to several groups and categories at a time. Besides the family, they also belong to a profession, a religious denomination or not, a town or region in a country. Some people extend this multi-membership to political parties, sports clubs or other organizations. As the We-identity gets more complicated, there also emerges more room for a personal composition of one's I-identity. The growing differentiation within societies offers more options for everyone. It provides more options for the choice of friends or partners, and more options for influencing one's personal development.

For Elias, Descartes' famous dictum: *cogito, ergo sum* (I think, therefore I am) was the first clear manifestation of individualization. With this insight, Descartes not only constructed a foundation for epistemology, but he also gave an important impulse to individualistic thinking. This was reflected in modern literature. More and more the main characters of novels were presented as pure I-identities, pure egos. From then on great novelists not only must be great story-tellers, but above all great psychologists. This individualistic way of philosophizing has become the hallmark of western philosophy and art. Quite wrongly western thinkers and artists believe that they are engaging in a purely individualistic act on without outside influence. And if they admit to be influenced by important thinkers or artists, they will present this as a deliberate, but very personal choice. Especially artists believe that they are engaged in activities that originate from their unique and most inner self.

7.6.2 *Towards a world society of individuals?*

According to Elias, economic and political globalization enhances individualization because it loosens our bonds with the local community and expands our range of options. The establishment of international organizations and agreements such as the United Nations, The World Trade Organization, the IMF, Amnesty International, the Red Cross, and many other NGOs, shows that we are leaving the orbit of nation-states. In particular, the Declaration of Human Rights shows that the individual is getting more attention. Now, humans have rights that cannot be dismissed by national governments. As we know, not all states have ratified the Declaration of Human Rights yet, let alone that they put these international laws into practice. Major political innovations tend to take a long time before they are generally accepted and implemented. But for Elias, it is clear that this development proceeds in the direction of increasing individualization and also an expansion of the We-identity that eventually could encompass the modern world as a whole. Obviously, not all social scientists share this view. For Elias this was no problem. He remained focused on salient long-term trends. Plainly, the traditional We-identity has shifted from the small local community or tribal group to the level of national and international communities. The last change still is in progress. Broad networks that branch out in different directions are replacing strong bonds with the members of the small community of our birth. Modern people can partly choose and create the branches of their global network. The number of bonds has increased. The strong, but small number of bonds with a localized community is exchanged for a large number of weaker bonds with members of a globalized community.

Elias observed manifestations of globalization in the appearance and rapid expansion of one-issue organizations that focus on problems that need a worldwide approach. Problems such as pollution, human rights, international migration, trafficking, and political refugees, child labour, child soldiers and child prostitution have ramifications that do not stop at national borders. NGOs like the Red Cross, Amnesty International, Green Peace, *Terre des Hommes* fill a widespread and growing need to intervene in all kinds of political and environmental disasters. As soon as the radio, tv, and papers report a new disaster, show shocking images of people starving, dying or being maimed for life, we want to act in some way. The world has become a global village and this affects our feelings and identities. The decrease of the mental distance with the rest of the world has enlarged our commitment with others in far away countries. All this enhances our global We-identity.

Identification as a world-citizen is not the same as commitment to a global society in the making. Plainly there is a dwindling influence of the individual on the worldwide whole. Whereas, voters in small democratic still have a tiny possibility to exert some influence on government policies, their influence has shrunken to almost nothing in large states, or unions, such as the European Union, the United States of America, or the United Nations. The integration of people in a global society implies a decline in the influence of individuals on the decisions made by the political leaders. Clearly, a global society needs new forms of political representation and decision-making. For the moment, we can see that the influence exerted by NGOs seems to fill the gap. They help to reconstruct our we-identities as well as our I-identities, because they link us to worldwide networks and commit us to very specific issues.

Even people who oppose the negative effects of globalization cannot avoid global arrangements and organizations. Doubtless, Elias would even interpret the anti-globalization movement as a form of resistance that supports his theory. Clearly the anti-globalization movement is a global reaction against globalization, conveniently based on the advantages of global mobility, communication, economy, banking, politics and human rights. Besides, this protest movement has opened our eyes for negative consequences, in particular for ecological consequences and the precarious position of poor people in underdeveloped countries. So, in so far as the anti-globalization movement will have an impact, it will be an impact on a worldwide scale. Presently, it is hard to ignore that the process of globalization described and analyzed by Elias is a social process that seems to have started and is being directed from the western world, in particular the USA, the economic and military power centre of the world. Therefore, we can easily conclude that globalization is serving the interests of western civilization or the elite within the western world. We can also see that it renders more options to individuals in the rest of the world. It sets standards of political freedom, human rights, and welfare that have an impact on local political aspirations. It opens a window on an individualized culture and opens a door, even if it is a backdoor, to leave your home, perhaps break with your traditional culture, and migrate to a developed country, creating Diasporas that further connects distant parts of the world.

7.7 Elias on science

Doubt is as an essential aspect of science. The core question was whether nature as we observe it really exists? For Descartes this doubt had become an obsession. He was always looking for a solid basis of his philosophy of knowledge, for a basis of hard facts that could not be doubted. Paradoxically he found the solution in his own doubt. After all, one cannot doubt that one doubts. So, it was his very doubt about reality that rendered him a secure fact about reality: *Cogito ergo sum (I think, therefore I am).*

7.7.1 *The social basis of knowledge*

This insight marked the beginning of a new era in epistemology. For Elias it also marked the foundation of a view at science that was too individualistic. In reality, breakthroughs can only occur if the scientific field and the cultural or political climate are ready. For centuries all doubts about reality were forbidden. Doubt equaled heresy and heresy could mean the stake. It implied doubting the existence and power of God, the creator of the universe. So, in the past, all scientists and philosophers had to be very careful. Nonetheless, little by little, they produced cracks in the glazing of theological dogma. Without realizing it, and without any rational plan, they prepared the transition from a religious world view to a secularized one. Hence, Descartes could profit from their insights and from the positive effects on the climate for critical thinking. But even then the climate in France was not mild enough for independent thinkers. Descartes had to take refuge in Amsterdam where the climate was more liberal.

According to Elias, Descartes merely put a clearer focus on some scientific problems. His contribution to the philosophy of knowledge merely was a further elaboration of work in process and carried out by a large figuration of forerunners and contemporaries. But even the breakthrough created by Descartes was not a total rupture with the ideas of the past. It only meant that theological thinking was losing impact and humanistic thinking was gathering momentum. Gradually the center stage was seized by physical science. The discoveries of physics had produced many new insights in natural processes that all caused hair cracks in the steel coating of theology. People had learned to intervene in nature without the help of magic, or the prayers of a priest. Thus they could enter the era of Enlightenment. From then on humans became more self-conscious. And as their image of nature changed, so changed their self-image. They started to believe in the force of reason, in the ability to understand nature and to control it on the basis of observation and reason, without recourse to secular or divine authorities.

> *It evolved as a symptom of and a factor in a specific transformation which, like all such changes, simultaneously affected all the three basic coordinates of human life: the shaping and the position of the individual within the social structure, the social structure itself and the relation of social human beings to events in the non-human world.*[55]

Science is a learning process, not of the individual person, but of mankind as a whole. Whatever the genius of some individuals, they could not have manifested their genius if they had to start from scratch. They all profited from innumerable predecessors. Isaac Newton told us that scientists can see further because they stand on the shoulders of the giants of the past. Though we always should acknowledge this, it does not mean that there is no role for geniuses in science. They can shed a whole new light on things and come up with very innovative ideas, synthesize hitherto separate ideas and thus come up with new concepts. But Elias prefers to underline that all this can only happen because other ideas had paved the way. Hegel and Comte had already clarified this process. Hegel came up with the idea of an ever-growing Absolute Spirit and Comte with his model of the evolution of thought in three phases. Nowadays it is one of the basic tenets of the sociology of science that our whole body of knowledge is based on social processes, on the efforts of a collectivity that encompasses all ages and continents, on the specific efforts of a community of co-operating and competing scientists in the past and the present. However, this insight seems to run against the present high tide of individualization.[56]

7.7.2   The biological character of science

The growth of knowledge is impossible without the unique ability to hand over knowledge to new generations. All pieces of information, whether it is Einstein's formula $E = mc^2$ or the mundane statement that the water is boiling have to be communicated in the same way, that is, with the help of symbols. The transfer of knowledge requires the help of a large number of people, people who can explain, write, print, and use computers. Senders and receivers have to command a common form of communication; otherwise the receivers will never grasp what the senders are or were telling. If we dig up information of senders that died centuries ago, we can only profit from this ancient knowledge, if we solve the riddle of their symbol system first.

The first striking element of Elias' symbol theory is that he devotes a lot of attention to the biological aspects of speech and knowledge. The ability to communicate with the help of an elaborated language is based on a number of biological characteristics that humans do not share with other beings. We can communicate a countless number of different messages with a countless number of sound patterns and use these as symbols. At some stage in evolution, humans, who always lived in groups, have made the transition from a restricted set of sounds to an elaborated set of sound patterns that were taught by their parents, further elaborate and transfer to fellow human beings. Elias called this crucial step in evolution *symbol-emancipation*.[57] It freed people from the cloisters of their instincts. According to Elias, this step in biological evolution was synchronized with a step in social evolution, a significant change in the development of social relations within human groups. Speech, the most cultural skill of all human skills strongly depends on our biological constitution. Our larynx, throat, teeth, tongue and palate play a crucial role in our potential to make a great variety of sounds. But this fantastic instrument would not serve us one bit if we had not learned the meaning of all these sounds during socialization and if we had not learned to develop this system of sound patterns further.[58]

The prevailing philosophy of science seems to neglect the biological and linguistic basis of science. But science is a system of messages that is being produced and reproduced by standardized patterns of sound. These standardized sound patterns serve as means of communication, means of orientation and as instruments for thought. Knowledge or information is encoded in sound patterns that symbolize real experiences or events.[59] With the help of these symbolizations we can execute thought experiments, in which we can test specific solutions with the help of our imagination. We can discuss these experiments and their outcomes with other scientists, just as we can discuss the set-up and outcomes of real experiments and debate the truth of conclusions based on these outcomes.

However, it is good to note that Elias avoided the concept of truth. He opted for reality congruency, because this term elucidates the relation between symbol and that what is symbolized. This relationship is not about similarity. What astronomers know about the sun does not resemble the sun as we see him. What astronomers have done is reducing the content of our fantasies about the sun, its powers, its creation and its life span. They have described its movement and its location in the universe. At the same time they have enlarged the reality congruence. This last concept draws attention to the degree of similarity between the physical or social 'objects' and things we know about them.[60] Or take for example the word 'human being.' The notion refers to people like you and me, or anybody else for that matter. This symbol can be used to make something clear to another person. But, the question is whether this symbol is reality congruent. Is a human being a product of biological evolution or a creation of God? Is our image of men or women corrupted by nasty experiences or naïve fantasies?

Knowledge is the realization of a biological potential by way of a social learning process directed at gathering reality congruent information. This learning process was triggered by our drive to survive, by the need to solve vital problems. In many cases our sense organs warned us for existential problems, for matters of life and death. To develop knowledge and to transfer this knowledge to fellow human beings, people had to translate all significant sense experiences into symbols that could be interpreted by all. In particular this is true for those lethal dangers that could only be prevented or overcome with the help of others. So, for Elias, the evolution of knowledge and science goes hand in hand with the development of collective symbol systems. In other words, languages are essential. Without the advancement of language systems science would never have come off the ground.[61] The discovery of phenomena that were hidden calls for new words to describe them. And these new concepts can engender new ideas about the possible existence of related phenomena. In turn this can give rise to new investigations and new discoveries.

In the framework of evolution the reason for gathering new information and new insights on reality is the survival of the species. Like all evolutionists Elias is optimistic. Our ability to speak and to manipulate a great variety of sound patterns enables us to expand and transform the whole set of symbols to make them more congruent with reality.[62] In prehistoric times, our body of knowledge did hardly grow at all. The diffusion of knowledge went on very, very slowly, because of the limited travel distances of people and the lack of modern means of communication. Elias believed that his symbol theory offered the right means to see that science actually offers a rather coherent set of symbols that evolve during a long-term process. In modern times, science and technology proliferate at a high pace. New scientific ideas and results are spread all over the world in a matter of seconds thanks to the internet. New technological inventions help to improve communication technology to spread information much faster than the speed of sound. In recent history, the rapid development of science was very much enhanced by the invention of print and libraries. But first societies had to develop means of producing enough food to support people who could devote their working time to the further growth of knowledge without having to toil the earth for food. Without all these preliminary steps and preparations the modern evolution of science is unthinkable.[63]

As long as a new theory, a new concept or new insight still wanders in the mind of a single scientist, as long as it is not written down and not presented to an audience it could get lost forever. But publication of this new theory or concept is not enough. It has to be reproduced, further developed and applied to make it fruitful. It has to become a tiny step in the unending evolution of science.

7.8   Involvement and detachment

In 1956, Norbert Elias published 'The problems of involvement and detachment' in the *British Journal of Sociology*. In this essay he attempted to tackle an old dispute in social science: to what degree is it possible to do 'objective' research? In his view, social scientists should always strive for value neutrality, though he did not believe in a sharp distinction between neutrality and commitment. He was convinced that there never could be total commitment or absolute detachment. At most commitment and detachment vary between 10 and 90 percent. He thinks that this is rather fortunate, because extremes will only lead to chaos. Extremism is a sure sign of immaturity. The survival of social order depends on the mutual adjustment and fine-tuning of individual instincts, drives, desires, thoughts and acts. Thus human impulses for commitment or detachment have to be kept in balance.[64] Instead of using terms as irrationality and rationality, objectivity and subjectivity, Elias explicitly used terms like commitment and detachment. Thus he wanted to avoid that these psychological features are being interpreted as separate entities. There is no individual or individual researcher that is purely rational or irrational, purely objective or subjective. The way in which members of social groups experience things and give them a meaning depends on the standard forms of coping with or thinking about these experiences.

Nonetheless, the advancement of knowledge requires a high standard of detachment and thus a high degree of self-constraint. It also demands outflanking movements to make distant or detached observations that are not distorted by too much emotional involvement. To make his point, Elias loved to recount Edgar Allan Poe's story about the fishermen in the maelstrom. In this story three fishermen were caught in a whirlpool. One man falls overboard, is pulled down in the vortex, and drowns. The second fisherman is so frightened that he can hardly think and just holds on tightly to the boat. The third one pulls himself together and starts to observe what is happening. Soon he notices that round objects are not drawn in the vortex in contrast to all oblong and square objects. So he sets himself in an empty fish ton that he has put overboard. The frightened fisherman does not dare to follow his example. Alas, he drowns when the boat is pulled under water. The cool and observant fisherman is lucky, because he stays afloat until the whirlpool had lost its momentum. The lesson is crystal clear. Restrain yourself, even in the face of mortal danger. Those who cannot restrain themselves run a great risk of dying. Only people that stay calm and look for a good strategy to survive stand a good chance of survival.[65] In similar vein, we can hypothesize that only cool and detached observations will result in good theories or successful solutions. It is better to take your time, make some cool observations, analyze them and ponder about the consequences of some of the actions you want to take. This procedure helps us to understand and control nature better. But the very process that has made humans more independent of nature has made them more dependent on each other. And this will endanger sociological research, because it presses sociologists towards more involvement and less detachment. This leads to the conclusion that detachment is hardest when it is needed most.

7.9   The social construction of time

Elias considered his book *Time: an essay* to be one of his most important books. The time dimension plays a major role is his work. All social processes take place within the dimensions of space and time. Therefore, Elias wanted to grasp the phenomenon of time and its measurement, and also the changes in the social meaning of time. He was convinced that a thorough investigation of time could reveal many aspects of man and society. But time is a tough subject. It does not lend itself easily for investigation. One cannot touch time, hear or see it. It does confront us with hard questions such as: 'Do clocks measure time? Or are they merely measuring the end of a working day or the speed of an athlete?'[66] Plainly, humans use clocks to orient themselves within a succession of social, biological, and physical processes. Clocks serve people as a means to adjust their behaviour to the actions of others. Learning to deal with clocks is an important part of the civilizing process. In prehistoric times, tens of thousands years B.C. (Before Clocks), humans had no means for orientation in the dimension of time other than by observing the rhythm of day and night, the change in the shape of the moon, or the change of seasons, or the repetition of the trek of certain birds or animals.

The perception of particular events as a sequence in time, presupposes a unique capacity for synthesizing, a capacity to connect specific symbols with specific events. Humans had to learn to relate events that happened before to events that happened later.[67] This capacity, which heavily leans on our memory, enables us to relate things of the past with things in the future. Or to put all this in common language, it was totally meaningless to know that it is four o'clock if you haven't the slightest idea that it was two o'clock two hours earlier and that it will be six o'clock two hours later. Any useful sense of time and its measurement is closely connected to the notions of the past, the present and the future.[68]

The ability to handle symbols, to synthesize, to think is crucial for the survival of mankind. Humans have to develop these skills during socialization. Then, they not only have to learn essential things from their parents, but also a whole body of essential knowledge that has been accumulated through the history of mankind. Our experience with time merely is a means of orientation that has developed during the course of many millennia. Our awareness of time is still very different from that of people who lived in the Middle Ages or in Ancient Rome. These changes have followed a specific path and will go further in a direction that can be explained and predicted.

As always, like Durkheim, Elias denounces the aprioristic explanation of Immanuel Kant. The great philosopher of Königsbergen argued that people are born with an *a priori* notion of time, space, substance and cause. The only thing children are endowed with at birth is the potential to think, to make syntheses, to connect different things and experiences with each other. However, what they should relate to each other must be learned from society. Others will teach you what is relevant to relate. Kant ignored the huge body of collective knowledge that all modern individuals could use as a rich source for all kinds of insights if only other people would lead them to that source. The present level of abstraction and synthesis was unavailable for the members of prehistoric tribes. Their body of knowledge about time was very limited and probably only related to the shift from day to night and vice versa, or the change of seasons. When social evolution produced agriculture and cattle breeding they still did not think in years, but in seasons for sowing and seasons for harvesting.[69]

7.9.1   *The measurement of time*

Time is yet another concept that was sacrificed by our culturally manipulated disposition to reduce processes to fixed states. For modern people it is very difficult not to think that time, although intangible, is something like a streaming river, a river on which we are floating, whether we like it or not. Meanwhile, people have gotten used to watching the clock, keeping appointments, and consider time as something that really exists. For them time is a reality that passes by at a fixed rate, continuously, without interruption. The clocks and calendars that we have developed are so practical, efficient and reality congruent that for us it has become very difficult to discern between the symbols and the reality they represent. But it is not the time that goes on; it is life that goes on – life passes as things change in our bodies, in nature, and in our society.

There is no experience of time outside social life, although the impression might be otherwise. That wrong impression is a product of the generalization of objectified time measurement. Time, as we have constructed it, steadily and regularly goes on while we are sleeping. It goes on when we are working. Sometimes, when we are totally absorbed by some event or experience that commands all our attention, we seem to lose all sense of time. Afterwards, we will always be amazed that we could have lost all sense of time, for keeping track of time is crucial in modern, strongly rationalized societies. The second reason is that the advanced time measuring instruments that have been invented go on measuring the time flawlessly without our help. They can function autonomously during very long periods. This double layer of relative independence is very misleading. Standardized clocks only have meaning in societies where everybody uses them. They would lose their meaning as soon as everybody would develop his own system for measuring time.

What do we do when we measure time? We ascertain a relationship. In order to measure time, people need at least two continua of changes, of which one is used as a frame of reference for the other. One always needs three continua: humans that maintain relationships in their mind, and two or more continua of change, of which one assumes the function of standard continuum, to which the course of time of the other continuum of change can be measured.[70] Humans started to measure time with simple standards like the shift from day to night and night to day. Prehistoric people tended to think that some days were favourable for the start of specific procedures or rituals. The first agrarians believed that some days were best for sowing, planting or harvesting. Favourable or unfavourable days were related to the full moon or the new appearance of the rising moon. However, when the sky is very cloudy it can be very hard to ascertain whether the new moon has arrived yet. Yet, they thought that picking the right day was crucial for the success of certain actions. So the task to detect the arrival of the new moon was delegated to the high priest. As soon as these priests were certain that they had observed the new moon, they started to announce this as loud as they could. (The Latin stem of the word calendar is derived from the verb *calare*, which means to call.)

One could hypothesize that humans started to measure time by referring to their own life history. But Elias believed that prehistoric people were very collectivistic beings. Before the introduction of counting years like the Jewish or Christian era, humans could not tell when they were born or how old they were. They could give only very rough indications like 'before our great leader was killed' or before the big fire, earthquake or flood. It did take a very long time before people were able to use their own individual life as a frame of reference for timing events, processes, and changes. Besides, in these cases they implicitly use a socially evolved continuum of changes, such as the era reckoning of calendar years.[71]

In its most basic form *timing* means ascertaining whether a change has taken place before, during or after a specific event: for or after harvest time, for or after sleeping. The degree of precision with which people can determine time is closely connected with the development of social existence. As soon as people get busier and have more tasks and obligations, precise appointments become more important, hence fixing and sticking to an exact time for the appointment becomes crucial. In prehistoric times things were arranged in a relaxed way. One went to sleep as soon as one felt tired, ate when one was hungry and had found something to eat. Now things are completely different. We have adjusted our biological rhythm to the schedules of business life. And sometimes, when our workload and our deadlines demand it, we are prepared to postpone our meals, lengthen our working day and even sacrifice some hours of sleep. Again this is an example of the transformation of social constraints into self-constraint, with which we all are familiar. Presently, social regulation dominates natural or biological cycles.[72] This is an important element of the civilizing process and therefore also an important element of our socialization. The strong disposition to work on schedule and finish assignments on the arranged date and time is so deeply imprinted in modern people, that they have developed a strong dislike for wasting time. We even tend to think that people with full diaries, who have to rush from one appointment to another, lead a much more interesting life than those people that do not lead such a hectic life. We have grown accustomed to this kind of life, and seem to take all the negative side effects for granted, such as stress, heart attacks, and accidents at work.

So, the analysis seems to direct us to a kind of paradox. First, Elias concluded that time as such does not exist. There are only changes in nature and society. Then he describes how humans have constructed a very ingenious system for the measurement of time, finally, he tells us that our own social construction of time has become so dominant that we now tend to be governed by the very hands of the clocks we have made. In a Durkheimian sense time has become a social fact that has gained power over our lives. For Elias, time has become a powerful symbol of self-constraint. Time management tends to regulate our periods of leisure. People always ask what we are planning to do in weekends and during vacations. *Dolce far niente* no longer is an option.

7.10   In conclusion

Elias developed his own theoretical approach because he found the accepted perspectives unconvincing, too static and out of focus. We have to thank him for that. His approach offers new views for understanding society. Marx sketched society as a structure with two layers, an economic basis and a mainly cultural superstructure in which only two significant parties – the haves and the have-nots – played a discordant role in the social drama. The groups in the middle would fade away, either by being forced to join the proletariat or by joining the capitalist elite. Bourdieu elaborated this conflict model, by introducing a view on society as a field of numerous fields in which the better off always were fighting the worse-off in order to defend their privileged positions. He also expanded the range of weapons that were used in these conflicts. Besides the financial capital, he also pointed at the value of cultural and social capital. Parsons elaborated and streamlined the organic model of society, by focusing on four subsystems that he found essential for all systems. In Parsons' view these four subsystems had to carry out the following four functions: adaptation, goal realization, system integration and latency. If applied to a social system, for instance a nation-state, we could connect these four functions with the following four subsystems: the economy, the political system, the social system or system of relations between individuals, and the cultural system or value system. The first two functions maintain good relations with the world outside the system (nature and persons) and the latter two have to keep the system intact, structurally and culturally. All these subsystems have to co-operate rather harmoniously, to keep the whole system going.

It is possible to see the Marxist-Bourdieu perspective as a vertical perspective on society and the AGIL-scheme of Parsons as a horizontal blueprint of society. The figurative model of Elias renders another perspective, a perspective of dynamic chains of interdependence or elongated networks of individuals that create an infinite number of links between these layers or fields, parties, and subsystems. For Elias individuals actually function as social knots connecting people to other people, because they carry out and are responsible for many functions. For Elias, functional interdependence is the cement of society. I am sure that he would prefer another metaphor than cement, for example sticky and flexible threads that hold a collective social system together, that is both open and continuously in process of reconstruction.

It appears also that Elias' model is individualistic and not collectivistic like the models of Marx and Parsons. But appearance is deceptive. Elias explicitly renounces an individualistic approach that pictures the human being as a *homo clausus*, as a closed entity that can be separated from society. He also renounces the approach of methodological individualists that try to reduce social processes to rational actions of individuals. For Elias, the individuals are socialized beings that have learned to execute a limited set of specific functions that tie them to many other socialized beings at other positions with a partly different set of skills and positioned in a social and cultural setting. For Elias, a pure individual, or some sort of lone wolf, does not exist. Individuals are socialized beings that can only function in a social setting. On the other hand, society can only function thanks to the unplanned but orchestrated actions of numerous interdependent and socialized individuals.

For me, it is plain that Elias' approach is a valuable addition to the theoretical toolbox with which we can approach social structures and processes. I also think that his conceptions are closer to those of Parsons than he would like to admit. In my view, Elias has been too polemical where the work of Talcott Parsons is concerned, but this was perhaps a consequence of affinities and similarities that Elias was aware of but did not like to acknowledge. They were contemporaries. Both had started their academic studies in related disciplines, biology and medicine. There they had learned about organisms which were reflected in their sociological theories. It had inspired Parsons to study the workings of entire social systems, to study the interconnectedness of various subsystems and how the functioning of one subsystem filled a social need of another subsystem or the whole system. Anatomical lessons inspired Elias to coin the concept of functional interdependency and present a view of individuals interwoven in expanded social networks that resembled intricate nerve systems. As young sociologists, both had sniffed the spirit of Max Weber. Both had been fascinated by the ideas of Sigmund Freud and both rejected main ideas of Marxist sociology. And both wanted to bridge the conceptual gap between individual and society. Though Parsons' model seems to focus on four essential social functions, each connected with a particular subsystem such as the economy, the political system, the social structure, and the culture, he did produce elaborate models that clearly showed that these subsystems were interdependent and could only function when all kinds of exchange processes were carried out between them. He mentions the exchange of money, power, and information. Elias does not give much attention to the kind of things that interdependent people exchange to help each other. He focuses on the structural elements of the long chains of interdependence.

There are many similarities between the work of Parsons and Elias, though they used different concepts and tended to highlight different aspects of social phenomena. They both stressed that society is dynamic and not a static, objectively observable, concrete structure. Nowadays, all modern sociologists share that view. Social organizations emerge, grow and develop, thanks to the functional relations between individuals that make them dependent upon each other. Engaging in functional relations of mutual dependence with other humans does not take place in a vacuum, but in a dynamic setting that already has developed many social figurations or networks of long chains of interdependence. Overlooking the historical dimension will lead to biased descriptions and poor explanations. Although Elias has made some very critical remarks about some of Weber's individualistic explanations, he owes a lot to the work and approach of this great master of sociology. As we have seen both scholars emphasize the closely knit relations between individual and society. Weber directed our attention to social actions, actions of individuals reckoning with the feelings and interests of the people with whom they interact. But Elias went further in his attempt to show the strong link between individual actions and macro-sociological phenomena such as entire civilizations. He did this by accepting Durkheim's idea that there are relatively autonomous collective social facts that are real, because they influence people, by constraining or arousing specific actions. Whereas Durkheim was inclined to see such social facts as completely autonomous forces, Elias hold on to their status of relative autonomy, because he did not think it right to ignore that social figurations can only exist and survive if they are supported by the actions and ideas of individual actors, of biological human beings that think about their actions. He became never weary of clarifying this point. Thus he has succeeded in convincingly connecting the micro- with the macro level of the social domain. He has shown that the individualistic and the collectivistic approaches can be joined to create a more valid perspective on society and social processes.[73]

He also never became weary of pointing out that societies are very complex entities that encompass uncountable figurations and networks of numerous chains of interdependencies. Hence, he concluded that this dynamic complexity would make it impossible to make valid predictions about major future developments. This chapter should have made clear that modern sociologists owe a lot to Elias' insights. Assimilating his insights means getting a far better grip on the typical characteristics, the dynamics, the complexity, and the figurational structures that make up the social world.

MARY DOUGLAS

BRILLIANTLY BRIDGING ANTHROPOLOGY AND SOCIOLOGY

In 2001, Mary Douglas received an honorary degree from Brunel University. By then, she was already eighty years old, yet still very active. At this festive occasion she was described as probably the most distinguished active anthropologist in Europe and as a unique figure in British social anthropology. But calling her an active anthropologist is selling her short. She has developed herself from a specialist in African anthropology into a broad social scientist, covering many disciplines, ranging from social anthropology to cultural sociology and social philosophy. Mary Douglas shows a strong interest in typical Durkheimian topics such as religion, classification, the differences and even more striking the resemblances between traditional and modern societies. When she analyzes 'thought collectives or thought styles' she builds further on ideas presented by Ludwik Fleck, but also on Durkheim's concept of the collective conscience. Of all the modern icons of sociology and anthropology she is the most Durkheimian. When she analyzes a classification system, like Claude Levi-Strauss, she observes that binary systems are often at the heart of any culture; the opposition between nature and culture being the most central one because it distinguishes the human from the animalistic, the civilized from the uncivilized, and the pure from the impure. To discuss this phenomenon she not only makes extensive use of her observations of the Lele, an African tribe, but also builds her arguments on a close reading of the bible book: Leviticus. Mary Douglas does not accept Levi-Strauss' model completely. She finds his fixation on binary models too simplistic to be of use for a broad range of cases. In stead, she has introduced a basic scheme for cultural analysis. This so-called grid-group model has four extreme positions in which the group variable as well as the grid variable can be either weak or strong. The model describes the following four types: individualistic societies, sectarian societies or enclaves, hierarchical societies, and isolates. As a cultural analyst she remains deeply rooted in structuralism as she always wants to reveal how cultural patterns and social actions are linked to a specific social structure.

After the introductory section, the chapter gives a short overview of her life and career. This section will draw attention to her formative years at a traditional Catholic convent school. The convent school would often figure in her work as an important model for a good society: socially cohesive and well-organized. Section 8.3 discusses more deeply how her work is linked to that of Emile Durkheim and presents her views on the pros and cons of structuralism as it was advocated and practiced by Claude Lévi-Strauss. Section 8.4 is devoted to the social function of rituals and the reasons for the decline of rituals. Section 8.5 is a lengthy section that deals with her famous group-grid model, how the model was presented and reworked, how it was linked to theories of Basil Bernstein, the famous sociologist of education. Then the section will discuss the pitfalls of cultural analysis with the help of the group-grid model. Section 8.6 offers an application of the model. It deals with the striking difference in strategy between the British and Swedish peak labour organization. This application paves the way for section 8.7, which treats her great support for Ludvik Fleck's views on the operation of a group mind. It shows how the collective representation of syphilis as a punishment for sinful acts has blocked path-breaking developments in medical science. Section 8.8 offers another interesting example of cultural analysis by Mary Douglas, once more using her group-grid model. It highlights the typical reactions of members of these four types of the group-grid model to the outbreak of AIDS. The chapter ends with concluding remarks.

8.1   Life and career

Margaret Mary Tew was born on 25 March 1921, in Italy, when her parents were en route for home leave from Burma. She was the first child of Phyllis Margaret Twomey and Gilbert Charles Tew. When she began school in 1926, she was left with her grandparents in Totness and felt abandoned by her parents who had to return to Burma where her father served in the Indian Civil Service. She was only twelve years old when her mother died of cancer. Coming from a Catholic family she educated at the Sacred Heart Convent, a boarding school in Roehampton. Within the building, the rooms were imbued with religious significance: each room was referred to by the name of a Catholic saint, and religious representations packed the walls of the schoolrooms and dormitories. The whole space of the school was enclosed by notices, which restricted access to visitors. The girls did not meet even their closest of relatives without the presence of a chaperone. Strict rules governed the routes the uniformed girls followed through the building. Equally strict rules governed the meals, including the seating at the dinner tables. Numerous prayers divided the day in a highly regulated series of activities and fixed time slots. Needless to say, a whole system of small rewards – like the right to talk during lunch – and sanctions enforced obedience to these rules. The purpose of the strict rules was to build a certain type of character. For Mary Douglas, the years at Roehampton made a strong imprint on her life and view on society. She found stability and a sense of belonging in this secure and secluded women's world. The organization of this convent school serves in her later work as an implicit example of her description of hierarchical organizations with a focus on loyalty, commitment, and order.[1]

What did she learn at Roehampton? Mary Douglas recalls that she developed a broad background in the humanities, with an emphasis on Catholic social theory. As part of the curriculum the girls had to study the papal encyclicals that defined the social doctrine of the Church, in particular Rerum Novarum (Of new things) issued in 1891 by Pope Leo XIII and Quadragesimo Anno (In the fortieth year) published by Pope Pius XI in 1931. Rerum Novarum was a late attempt of the Church to respond to industrialization and the dismal living conditions of the workers. It was designed as an alternative for the highly critical analyses of capitalism by socialists and Marxists. In stark contrast to the doctrines of the Marxists the Church taught that certain inequalities are inevitable, that to suffer and endure was the lot of humans; that their final end is not here but hereafter. However, the Church rejected classical laissez-faire economics and argued that the State should not only protect private property but ought also to encourage the wide distribution of property, ensure payment of just wages and implement regulations that should improve working conditions. The encyclical supported the role of voluntary associations, such as trade unions. It also offered a vehement rejection of extreme individualism. Forty years later, Quadragesimo Anno elaborated the line of argument set forth in Rerum Novarum. It sketched an organic model of society in which the producers (owners of capital and workers) and the consumers were to form functional groups based upon cooperation. The functional groups would determine the right policies for each industry and a hierarchical organization of such functional bodies would furnish the charter for a reconstructed social order.[2]

After leaving Roehampton, in 1938, she spent six months in Paris where she attended the Sorbonne and attained a '*Diplôme de civilization Française*'. To pass her Oxford entrance exam she spent some months at a 'crammer' in the Cotswolds. A small bursary and low cost accommodation for students established by The Order of the Sacred Heart allowed her to study at Oxford University, which would have been impossible had she been entirely dependent on her father's modest pension. Her first year at university was a rather unhappy one as she ran into a crisis of faith, which seems a common lot of cradle Catholics, and especially an inquisitive one like herself.[3] In 1943, she graduated with a BA in Modern Arts. As she had quite some trouble with the mathematical side of economics, she achieved only a second class honours degree. From 1943 to 1947, she fulfilled her war service in the Colonial Office. There, she became acquainted with anthropologists and developed a special interest in Africa. After a few years, she returned to Oxford and attained a Masters degree in anthropology, followed by a doctorate in 1951. She studied with the famous anthropologist Edward E. Evans-Pritchard and later wrote a book about his life and work.[4] From 1949 to 1951 she did extended fieldwork in The Belgian Congo. This study rendered the material for her first major book, *The Lele of the Kasai* (1963). It was largely descriptive and ethnographic, but it foreshadowed more exciting things to come.

In 1951, she married James A. T. Douglas, a civil servant, who had just joined the Conservative Party Research Department as an economist. Their daughter Janet was born in that same year. In 1954 and 1956 James and Philip were born. James's background was similar to Mary's in many respects. His Englishness came from his father's side and his Catholicism from his French mother's side. James' father had been serving in the Indian Army before serving in France during the First World War. So, the families belonged to the same Anglo-Indian world. James was born in India and brought up in Paris after his father retired in 1922. James' great knowledge of economics and politics, his bilingualism and wide curiosity outside academia constantly provoked his wife to look beyond the limitations of conventional anthropology.[5]

Purity and Danger (1966), her second book, earned her widespread recognition. It is a classic monograph on an African society, in which she forged a synthesis of Western Philosophical ideas, social scientific theories, and the beliefs of the Lele people. The book shed new light on how people deal with both purity and pollution. During the sixties, she also published many essays on a great variety of topics proving that her intellectual curiosity drove her to other social sciences and social philosophy.[6]

From 1951 to 1977, Mary Douglas taught anthropology at Oxford and London. She recalls being happiest at University College during the two decades when Daryll Forde was head of department. She produced research reports and wrote many articles. In 1977, she joined the Russell Sage Foundation in New York to become Director for Research on Culture. As president of the foundation, Aaron Wildavsky had secured her appointment. He was an enthusiast advocate of Douglas' cultural theories, applying them widely in his own work. Douglas and Wildavsky collaborated to write Risk and Culture. In which they studied perceptions of risk and focused on the concerns of the American ecological movement.[7] In 1981, she went to Northwestern University, just outside Chicago, where she was appointed as Avalon Foundation Professor in the Humanities. This was a joint appointment with the department of Religious Studies. There she renewed her interest in theological themes. She also became a visiting professor at Princeton University. Her move to the United States had become possible after her children had finished their education and her husband James Douglas retired.[8]

Her breakthrough books were the above-mentioned *Purity and Danger*, with its brilliant interpretation of pollution and taboo, and *Natural Symbols: Explorations in Cosmology*, published in 1970. In the same year she was offered a personal chair at University College London. The number of books she has published in the eighties and the nineties bear witness to her continued exploration of new fields, and to her astonishing productivity: *Essays in the Sociology of Perception* (1982), *Risk and Culture* (1982), *How Institutions Think* (1986), *Risk and Blame* (1992), *In the Wilderness* (1993), *Thought Styles* (1996), *Missing Persons* (1998) and *Leviticus as Literature* (1999). Today, her work is a major point of reference for social theorists, for sociologists and economists dealing with risk and consumption, for biblical scholars, for literary theorists, and for everyone who writes about ritual, institutions, systems of classification, or collective memories.

8.2 Douglas, Durkheim and Lévi-Strauss

From all the major modern sociologists discussed in this book, the work of Mary Douglas is the most Durkheimian. Not only does she frequently show a strong interest into typical Durkheimian topics such as religion, classification, and the striking differences between modern and pre-modern societies. But she also builds further on concepts such as collective conscience and has followed the Durkheimian method of drawing on the cultures of small pre-modern societies to illuminate the general nature of social processes such as the development, institutionalization, and disintegration of cultural patterns.

8.2.1 *Durkheim's legacy*

Following this founding father, which she also views as a founding father of anthropology, she favoured theories that try to explain changes in religion or processes of secularization by changes in the social structure. The more open a community, the less its members are coerced by common beliefs. So, from this perspective, secularism and the privatization of religion is a consequence of a social factor, a consequence of a change in the social structure.[9] And last but not least, like Durkheim, she intends to do social science in a positivistic way, based on empirical observations and searching for law-like generalizations in reality.

In her foreword to the English edition of *The Gift* by Marcel Mauss she frequently refers to Durkheim's work. *The Gift* focuses on solidarity and reciprocity. It makes clear that there is no such thing as a free gift. Though charity is meant to be a free and voluntary gift, even a religious virtue, we know that it causes emotional distress. She once worked for a charitable organization and quickly learnt that recipients do not like the givers. You need not be a cynic to see that the volunteers do not work for free. Though they do not want money or other material gifts, they still want something in return: gratitude. Gratitude boosts their self-esteem. It gives them a good feeling about themselves. Douglas believes that Marcel Mauss, a famous student and colleague of Emile Durkheim, did get the idea of a morally sanctioned gift cycle from his knowledge of Hindu religion. According to the Vedic principle, the sacrifice is not a simple gift, but a devotional offering which compels the deity to make a return: *Do et dus* – I give so that you may give. For Mauss, the whole idea of a free gift is based on misunderstanding. A gift that does nothing to enhance solidarity is a contradiction. What is wrong with the so-called free gift is the donor's intention to be exempt from return gifts from the recipient. Instead, in Melanesia and elsewhere, anthropologists like Malinowski had found that gifts were matched with precisely calculated return gifts. In fact, commerce and gift are similar activities. In both cases fair deals keep the exchange process going. During the whole history of civilization the major transfer of goods has been carried out by cycles of obligatory returns of gifts. Gift cycles engage individuals and groups in permanent commitments that articulate the dominant institutions. These systems get their energy from individuals who are due to lose from default. They will be ostracized or otherwise disgraced if they do not fulfill their obligations. They will feel bad, experience lower self-esteem, a strong fear of angry spirits or the punishment of God. The system would not work if it did not include social control, personal emotions, and religion.[10] So, Mauss formulated a 'collectivist' exchange theory. He posed the question: 'What force compels the recipient to make a return?' The answer is society. The social group produces the coercion that forces people to reciprocal acts. 'It is groups, and not individuals, which carry on exchanges, make contracts, and are bound by obligations.'[11]

The most fertile idea of Marcel Mauss was to present the gift cycle as a theoretical counterpart to Adam Smith's invisible hand. Even in modern society gift systems complement the market economy in domains where the latter is absent. Douglas notes that *The Gift* was part of an organized assault on English utilitarian political theory that was carried out by Emile Durkheim and some of his predecessors, such as Jean-Jacques Rousseau and Alex de Tocqueville. They criticized its impoverished, utterly non-social concept of the person. Utilitarian theorists ignored the role of social norms in shaping individual intentions and in making social actions possible.[12] Durkheim, Mauss, and Douglas favour a political system in which a fair amount of individual self-awareness is allowed, a system in which the demands of the individual are in balance with the demands of the collective; in other words, a third way between liberalism and socialism.

Unlike Durkheim, Mary Douglas was much less inclined to separate culture from structure. She concentrated on culture itself, concerning herself with its internal patterns, rather than its ultimate causality or determination by external factors. Like Peter Berger, she approaches culture primarily from the angle of everyday life. For him, the mundane knowledge of everyday life serves as a vehicle for studying more abstract modes of knowledge and legitimization. For her, everyday life itself is the focus of interest. It is the centerpiece of her investigations.[13] Hers is a world of ordinary symbols, rituals, objects, and activities that constitute and fill our daily life. She has a special interest for the observable artifacts of culture, for its material goods, including food, its ritualized practices, its habits, manners, and tastes. Our attitudes towards these manners and material goods reveal implicit meanings or cosmology of the social group we belong to.[14] By implicit cosmology Douglas refers to the beliefs and values that are used to justify our actions. Our implicit cosmology is centered round the ultimate justifying ideas that tend to be called on as if part of the natural order.[15] Our attitudes towards food and other material goods manifest our views of what is clean or dirty, good or bad, nice or ugly, decent or indecent. In other words, they reveal our basic norms and values. However, most of the differences that are vital for social existence did not emerge naturally. For example, what makes some plants into weeds and others into flowers? Categorizations such as these are social constructions. Once they have become institutionalized they tend to be defended vigilantly. They create order and clarity. The only fault of weeds is that they have come, uninvited, to a place, which, in our opinion, ought to be neatly cut into lawns, paths, vegetable plots and flower borders. Weeds spoil the harmony, even if they have a nice fresh colour and smell good. They play havoc with our design and thus we want to uproot or poison them. And what is rubbish, what is dirt? Rubbish and dirt are simply things 'out of place.' We love to see beautiful hair, clean and shiny, but find it disgusting when found on our dinner table. There is a place for everything. This feeling is so strong that chemical companies had to design distinct names and labels for flasks containing identical detergents, after they learnt that people would not dream of using the same detergent for the bathroom and the kitchen. In these as in other cases the obsessive attention devoted to fighting dirt and putting things in their right place is motivated by the need to make our world orderly and hence livable.[16]

8.2.2   Criticizing Lévi-Strauss

In many ways, Mary Douglas went further than Emile Durkheim did. The latter was strongly inclined to explain all social facts with other social facts, preferably, facts referring to characteristics of social structures. As opposed to Immanuel Kant he did not think that people were born with ready-made conceptions about time, causality, space, mass, extent, and hierarchy. From his analysis of studies of religion and social cohesion in pre-modern tribes Durkheim speculated that people gradually acquire a sense of these categories. For instance, from their experience with the eternal cycle of seasons emerged the notion of a generalized experience divided into units of time. This experience was strengthened by the introduction of religious ceremonies connected to the change of season. And from their nomadic travels in search for food came the conception of space. Like Durkheim, Douglas realized that there is a social basis for human thought, and the thrust of her work is the application of that insight to the belief systems of modern society.[17] Her theoretical work is also indebted to the structuralism of Claude Lévi-Strauss, but she borrowed selectively from his approach, remaining very critical of some of its more general assertions. Most French structuralists conceive cultures as systems of classification. Claude Lévi-Strauss wanted to uncover the principles that give shape to the logical relations within these diverse cultures. He assumed that there must be comparable patterns, despite the great diversity of cultures, since all cultures are products of the universal structure of the human mind. Hence, he searched for a basic structure below the observable manifestations. In his view, the purely cognitive meaning of myths, rituals, and kinship relations can be found in the basic paired oppositions they reflect, pairs of oppositions that can be analyzed without reference to the ethnographic context. However, for researchers like Mary Douglas, who have done a lot of empirical fieldwork, the context always remains an important point of reference. She agrees with Lévi-Strauss that the structuring of experience often comes about through a system of paired opposites: dark/light, night/day, good/evil, purity/dirt, life and death. Even the concepts of male and female tend to be viewed as a pair of opposites. These are the kind of distinctions that make us realize that we have encountered a symbolic boundary. In everyday life these patterns are constantly constituted and reconstituted. They are regularly affirmed and reaffirmed in customs, ritual, and speech.

As we have seen, not only deviance, but also dirt is very important to Mary Douglas. They reveal our systems of norms and values. Cultural classifications make our social existence orderly and meaningful and give direction to our actions. They tell us what to do or not to do. That is why they form the very basis of our social demarcations, the basis of the boundaries and lines of division that we continuously construct and reconstruct. However, she does not go as far as Lévi-Strauss that all classifications are based on paired opposites, which are balanced against one another, or that the secret to comprehending these classification systems is to identify parallel patterns of opposites in other domains. Binary classifications can be a useful analytic tool, but reality does not always manifest itself in pairs, let alone opposite pairs. To begin with, there are many situations in which we need more complex classifications. Often we encounter phenomena or organizations of a third or fourth kind. Therefore, Douglas tells us to be suspicious of anyone who declares that there are two kinds of people, or two kinds of reality. For her, it often is problematic whether a symbolic boundary exists at all. The real challenge is to discover how clearly a boundary can be seen, how permeable or impassable it is now or tended to be in the past. For instance, nowadays it is even possible to cross the boundaries between male and female with the help of kilos of pharmaceutical products, a series of ingenious surgical operations, and help of specialized psychologists. She grants that Lévi-Strauss has rendered a monumental analysis of the structure of symbolism, but finds that he did not come up with any interesting hypothesis about cultural variations since his insights are set on what is universal. His analysis of symbolism lacks an essential ingredient. It has no hypothesis. It is utterly irrefutable. Given the materials and the technique for this kind of analysis any researcher can and will succeed and reveal a pair of contrasted symbolic elements, which will finally be resolvable into the contrast between culture and nature.[18]

8.3   The good, the bad, and the holy

Defilement is never an isolated event. It cannot occur except in view of a systematic ordering of ideas. Hence any piecemeal interpretation of the pollution rules of another culture is bound to fail.[19]

Mary Douglas always gets annoyed when the beliefs of 'primitive' peoples are mangled in Western attempts to understand them. The history of the ethnographical study of religions offers many instances of a downright pejorative approach to their religion and rituals. This constructed opposition between 'them' and 'us,' between believers of primitive religions and believers of great religions, is in urgent need of deconstruction, and she is eager to lend a helping hand. For this she has two reasons. Firstly, this construction creates a theoretical divide that has no foundation in empirical reality. Secondly, this approach can only lead to misunderstanding. Hence, she tackles this problem by first stating that so-called primitive religions and rituals have their equivalents in the great world religions, and secondly by arguing that such beliefs and rituals fulfil positive social functions, even in a secularized world. In spite of strong tendencies to get rid of all rituals, even secularized, modern people cherish certain forms of belief, have their taboos, and engage in all kinds of rituals.[20]

8.3.1   The Lele system of classification

In the fifties, Mary Douglas studied the Lele, a tribe living in the southern margin of the tropical forest of the Kasai District of The Congo. The tribesmen grow maize, weave raffia, and drink palm wine, but hunting is their most important activity. So it is not surprising that the richest vein of symbolism is derived from reflections on the animal world, on its relations to the human sphere, and on relations between the different breeds of birds and beasts. For the Lele the forest contrasts with the barrenness of the grassland. The forest is seen as the place of powerful spiritual beings, the source of all they need: maize, raffia, wine, meat, fish, water, and firewood. Not only for the Lele, but also for the large majority of mankind, the basic distinction is the opposition between humans and animals. This basic idea is expressed most usually by relating it to one dominant value, the virtue of *buhonyi*, which is shame, shyness, or modesty. Animals have no *buhonyi*. They urinate publicly, eat filth, and mate incestuously. The strongest form is sexual shame. Therefore, all sexual intercourse should be hidden. *Buhonyi* is a sense of decency and civilization; it is related to the fear of offending accepted rules of behaviour. It is a product of culture and not a natural virtue. Infants do not feel it, but have to acquire it during socialization. They have to learn that parents and elderly people must be treated with respect. A Lele father feels constrained in the presence of his son and the son stands silent and respectful before his father or elder brother. But Lele women interact less formally. They tend to be less sensitive to *buhonyi*. Mothers and daughters can go to the stream together and wash each other's back without the least embarrassment. This kind of behaviour is unthinkable for fathers and sons.

Another basic distinction is that between dirtiness and cleanness. All bodily dirt is *hama*. *Hama* refers to rotten, smelly things such as corpses and excreta. The word is extended to anything that produces a feeling of disgust: Vermin, frogs, toads, snakes, urine, faeces, and used clothing. Most modern people can empathize with this, but perhaps not with the idea that for adult Lele drinking cow's milk is revolting. It also is a matter of shame to have contact with the hair shavings or nail-clippings of people of different status. According to Mary Douglas, one of the basic definitions of dirt is *matter out of place*. Everything that leaves the (human) body passes a boundary. That's why most people consider spit, saliva, blood, mucus, milk, urine, faeces, tears, sperm, sweat, hair, nails, scabs and flakes of skin as unclean. Within many cultures, all natural functions are embarrassing and should be performed in private. Even eating can be embarrassing, so, in some cultures men and women eat apart, either in separate rooms or at different times. In the majority of these cases the men eat first or sit in the best room.

The importance of hama as a dominant theme in Lele culture can hardly be exaggerated. Avoiding contact with dirt is the earliest lesson of childhood and forms the constant preoccupation of women in their work at home, and in cooking. It is natural that it should provide the culture with vivid intelligible symbols. The emotional power of the contrast between human and animal is largely based on the idea of hama, animals, particularly dogs, are unaware of it.[21]

In any culture insults are the most illuminating indications of accepted values. Insults tend to carry the strongest implications of contempt, which the symbolism of the culture is capable of concentrating into one word or a single phrase. In the Lele tribe the most damaging insult is comparing someone with an animal, that is, with a shameless being, or with excrement, which is the dirtiest of all dirt. To call someone a dog and tell him to eat excrement can lead to murder. So the Lele show awareness of two important cultural themes, man's superiority to animals, and the need to avoid dirt. This idea of superiority allows Lele people to eat animals, but certain 'dirty' animals are considered inedible: rats, dogs and cats, snakes and smelly animals such as jackals.[22] There are different rules for children and for men and women too. Women can enhance their respect by fastidiousness, by abstaining from many kinds of food that are loosely associated with *hama,* but that are not strictly forbidden.

Scheme 8.1   Binary classification of the Lele

nature	culture
animals	humans
shameless	shame (Buhonyi)
small children	adults
dirty (unclean)	clean
danger	safety
bad	good
barren	fertile
left	right

Rules of cleanliness largely amount to an attempt to separate food from dirt. People should wash their hands before cooking and eating. Cleanliness requires the Lele to use the left hand for dirty work, the right for noble work and for taking food. The left is therefore associated with *hama*. This very rule is still obeyed in many other parts of the world; especially in groups were food is eaten by hand from a collective dish. Over there it is a grave insult to offer anything with the left hand. Also in western societies children learn to present something with their 'good' hand. In the fifties and sixties of the last century left-handed European children were obliged to learn to write with their right hand. And also the origin of the modern political distinction between left and right is related to a historical distinction between good and bad. In this perspective, the good politicians were the representatives of the nobility and the clerical elite, whereas the revolutionaries, the liberals, egalitarians and socialists were seen as the bad guys.

8.3.2   *The Bible and the classification of tabooed food*

Let us return to the discussion of food. Normally, the Lele only eat vegetarian animals or animals with a furry skin. Carnivorous animals form a special category for two reasons. For one, they prey on the human sphere. They enter the village, steal goats and chickens, and are thought to be sorcerers in disguise. To eat them is to run the risk of indirect cannibalism. Secondly, an animal that fights and kills its fellow creatures symbolizes men as a warrior. Mary Douglas draws our attention to the fact that the fox does not figure in the diet of any European country. Though, most western people do not think about these matters, they follow similar rules. They stick to cows, pigs, horses, hares, rabbits and deer, as far as mammals are concerned, but scorn the meat of wolves, foxes, dogs, cats, mice, rats, and other carnivores. There seems to be something universally repellent about an animal that preys on its fellows, though, in quite a few Asian countries people eat dogs. The division could be based on distinctions between the type of hooves or in case of animals that live in the water, whether they have fins and scales or not. Prescriptions like these can be found in the Torah, the Koran, and other Holy Books.[23]

But why should the camel, the hare and the rock badger be unclean? Why should the frog be clean and why should the mouse and the hippopotamus be unclean? What have chameleons, moles, and crocodiles in common to make them unclean? These rules cannot be based on a sound medical basis. People will not get sick by eating most animals as listed in the biblical books of Deuteronomy or Leviticus. For instance, many people all over the world eat pork without damaging their health. And Moses Maimonides, the great twelfth-century rabbi, physician, theologian, and philosopher,[24] although he managed to find hygienic reasons for all the other dietary restrictions of Biblical law, confessed himself baffled by the prohibition on pork, and was driven back to an aesthetic explanation, based on the revolting diet of the domestic pig.[25] The negative religious laws are assigned pedagogical aims and purposes. The prohibition to eat the flesh of certain animals, birds or insects is expressly associated with the idea of holiness. Its real object is to train the Hindu, Jew, or Muslim in self-control as the indispensable first step for the attainment of holiness.[26] Others have pointed to the fact that the religious lawgiver sternly forbade all animals of land, sea or air whose flesh is the finest and fattest, like that of pigs and eels, knowing that they set a trap for the most slavish of senses, the taste. Some have simply given up all attempts to find a sound explanation. They think that these regulations are not by any means to be rationalized. They believe that their origins are too divers and go back beyond recorded history.[27]

Mary Douglas opts for another solution. For her it is clear that the positive and negative precepts are held to be effective. They are not merely expressive. Observing them brings prosperity, infringing on them draws down danger. Thus, she treats them in the same way as 'primitive' rituals whose breach unleashes danger to the members of the tribe. The religious precepts and ceremonies are focused on the idea of the holiness of God. In this perspective, men prosper by conform-

---

Biblical prescriptions

From the bible: Deuteronomy XIV
You shall not eat any abominable things. These are the animals you may eat: the ox, the sheep, the goat, the hart, the gazelle, the roebuck, the wild goat, the ibex, the antelope and the mountain sheep.

Every animal that parts the hoof and has the hoof cloven in two, and chews the cud you may eat.

Yet of those that chew the cud or have the hoof cloven you shall not eat these: The camel, the hare and the rock badger, because they chew the cud but do not part the hoof, are unclean to you. And the swine, because it parts the hoof but does not chew the cud, is unclean for you. Their flesh you shall not eat, and their carcasses you shall not touch.

Of all that are in the waters you may eat these: whatever has fins and scales you may eat, And whatever does not have fins and scales you shall not eat: it is unclean for you.

You may eat all clean birds.

But these are the ones which you shall not eat: the eagle, the vulture, the osprey, the buzzard, the kite, after their kinds; every raven after their kinds; the ostrich, the night hawk, the sea gull, the hawk, after their kinds; the little owl and the great owl, the water hen and the pelican, the carrion vulture and the cormorant, the stork, the heron, after their kinds, the hoopoe and the bat.

In Leviticus more animals are listed as unclean:
Yet among the winged insects that go on all fours you may eat those, which have legs above their feet, with which to leap upon the earth. Of them you may eat: the locust according to its kind, the bald locust according to its kind, the cricket and the grasshopper according to its kind. But all other winged insects, which have four feet, are an abomination to you. And by these you shall become unclean; …

And these are unclean to you among the swarming things that swarm upon the earth: the great lizard according to its kind, the gecko, the land crocodile, the lizard, the sand lizard and the chameleon. …

Box 8.1

ing to holiness and perish when they deviate from it. Justice and moral goodness may well illustrate holiness and form part of it, but holiness embraces other ideas as well, such as avoidance rules and taboos. Holiness means separateness of all that is unholy, corrupt, and polluted. Holiness is purity, wholeness, and completeness. Much of Leviticus is taken up with stating the physical perfection that is required of things presented in the temple and of persons approaching it. The animals offered in sacrifice must be without blemish, women must be purified after childbirth, men who have come into contact with unclean animals or their carcasses have to wait until nightfall before they have got rid of their pollution. Priests may only come into contact with death when their own close kin die. But the high priest must never have contact with death.[28] The wholeness of the body as a perfect container is also extended to signify completeness in a social context. An important enterprise, once begun, must not be left incomplete. Interruption of new projects was held to be bad in civil as well as in military contexts. Other precepts extend holiness to species and categories. Hybrids and other confusions are detestable.

> You shall not let your cattle breed with a different kind; you shall not sow your field with two kinds of seed; nor shall there come upon you a garment of cloth of two kinds of stuff (Leviticus xix, 19).

Mary Douglas concludes that holiness is exemplified by purity and completeness. Holiness requires that humans shall conform to the class to which they belong. Holiness requires that different classes of things shall not be confused. So, fundamentalists who strictly follow these rules should not eat pork, nor strive for upward mobility or marry a spouse from another race, religion, caster or caste. They also should object to crossbreed or inter-fertilize animals and plants to create new species.[29] Many precepts refine the basic rule. Holiness not only means keeping distinct biological categories apart, but it also involves correct definition, discrimination, and order, because this order is God-given. This also applies to moral rules. Incest, adultery, and homosexuality are against holiness according to the rulings of the Torah, the Bible, and the Koran. It also is unholy to steal, tell lies, give false witness, cheat in weights and measures, and create contradictions between what seems and what is.

For Mary Douglas, a convincing analysis of a cultural phenomenon should also take historical and structural conditions into account. Hence, she thinks that a convincing explanation for the clear division between livestock and wild animals could be found if we keep in mind that the Israelites, like other pastoral people, disapprove of people who live by hunting, because they view their own way of living as herdsmen as a higher form of civilization, as more cultivated. Hunting definitely is seen as a way of life that stands too close to nature. So, to be driven to eat wild meat is a sign of less cultivation. From this perspective, cloven-hoofed, cud-chewing ungulates are the model of the proper kind of food for a people that is dominated by herdsmen and farmers. If the need might arise to find additional food by hunting, some scope for hunting wild animals that also are cloven-hoofed and cud chewing is allowed.

The main key in understanding the religious rules about clean and unclean animals is the degree to which they belong to a specific class that is seen as the 'natural' class of animals. Since birds have two legs and two wings with which they can fly they tend to be viewed as the standard, whereas bats and other flying creatures that have more wings or more legs are seen as unholy. The same holds true for the creatures in the water. Most fish have fins and scales. So, those that lack fins and scales are abominations. In general, this is true for all animals that seem to have a rather unnatural way of locomotion, like snakes, slugs, worms, and other teeming, trailing, creeping, crawling or swarming animals. Also the animals that cannot walk, swim or fly 'properly' are defined as unclean. Therefore, most amphibians and reptiles are listed as unclean, though the list is far from complete and not entirely consistent.[30]

An important social function of observing these rules or the main reason for following these rules to stay pure and clean is to separate you from the rest of the world. Supposedly, all humans that belong to other peoples, tribes, and nations are not holy. By rules of avoidance holiness was given a physical expression at every meal. Observance of the dietary rules is a meaningful part of the great liturgical act of recognition and worship.[31] The cognitive basis for these rules is the idea that things should be as normal and orderly as possible within the context of a specific culture. If strange, ambiguous, and anomalous things appear in any society people are inclined to see this as a big problem that has to be solved as soon as possible, because it can spell all kinds of doom. Mary Douglas lists five options for dealing with events that do not fit in:

1 Reclassification: for example, the Nuer treat strongly deformed babies as baby hippopotamuses, accidentally born to humans. Thus, they believe that the appropriate action is to lay them in the river.
2 Extermination without ingenuous reclassification: to some West-African tribes it is natural that women only give birth to one child at a time. In their view, twins are unnatural, so they have to be killed.
3 Avoiding anomalous things for example by observing dietary rules.
4 Labeling anomalous events as dangerous. Attributing danger is one way of putting a subject above dispute.
5 Ambiguous symbols can be used in rituals for the same ends as they are used in poetry and mythology, to enrich meaning or call attention to other levels of existence.[32]

The opposition of men and animals, of herbivorous and carnivorous animals, of cleanliness and dirt, the symbolism of right and left, and the avoidance of bad food and the presentation of good food, produces a body of rules and categorizations that can be called secular symbolism. Of this, discrimination between various animal foods leads us straight into religious symbolism. Thus, we can observe that the crude symbolism of everyday life provides a basic vocabulary on which religious symbolism draws; though Mary Douglas does not exclude the possibility that it could be the other way around. Anyhow, the secular and the religious are two aspects of the same collective representations that give societies their distinctive structure.

When Mary Douglas studied the Lele it took her quite a while before she got an inkling of the framework of metaphysical ideas that underpins the symbolism involved in various cults. At first, she assumed that the connection between the hunting and fertility cults was only a historical one, highly eclectic and based on the assimilation of elements of the cults of neighboring groups. However, soon she learned that the Lele divide the world in three spheres: humans, animals, and spirits. But there is interaction between these three spheres and the whole is regarded as a single system. A major disorder in the human sphere is presumed to disturb the relations with and within other spheres. In principle, the animal sphere does not impinge on the human sphere. Animals will only molest a man, woman, or child unless made to do so by sorcery. Nor will a hunter succeed in killing an animal unless the spirits are willing. Hence, for a successful hunt, people have to uphold harmonious relations with the spirits. The hunt really is the

The Fertility cult of the Lele

All Lele men who have fathered a child form a specific cult group, the group of the Begetters, that allow them to eat delicious young animals that otherwise would be ranked as hama. In their view, only fathers have attained full manhood. Therefore, it is believed that the Begetters can safely risk eating very young animals and the ribs of animals. The Lele believe that eating ribs is rather dangerous, because it could harm your own ribs.[33] Another privilege of the Begetters is to eat carnivorous animals. The cult of the Begetters is ranked below that of the Pangolin cult, the latter are higher because they have children of both sexes. Rather strangely, this is the only cult group that has an animal as a cult object: the little pangolin. This scaled anteater figures as a symbol for fertility. The highest cult group is that of the Twin cult, which honors men and women who have been blessed with multiple births. Multiple births indicate extraordinary if not divine fertility. The qualification for membership of any of those cults is not something one can achieve by one's own efforts. The Lele believe that the spirits must have mediated between the human and the supernatural. Without such mediation men and women will remain sterile. In the animal world certain creatures are supposed to mediate between animals and humans. Among these the pangolin is pre-eminent. For one reason, it is hard to classify. It has scales like fish, but lives on dry land and in trees. Moreover, it does not run away from humans as other hunted animals do. When they are hunted they simply roll themselves into a ball, with all their hard scales as a bullet-free vest. The hunter simply has to wait a while before the pangolin relaxes and shows his head again.

Box 8.2

activity in which the three spheres coincide. Its significance far surpasses its primary object – the supply of meat. Food, fertility and health are controlled by the spirits and may be thwarted by sorcery. If the hunt fails, the Lele fear that their other enterprises also are in danger. They will believe that their future will be unfortunate. Unsuccessful hunting parties have a bad influence on the daily life of the village. Accusations will be heard; rituals will be discussed or speeded up. People accused of sorcery or contact with sorcerers could be expelled or killed, in particular when new hunting parties also fail to bring in the goods.

8.4   Rituals

In *Natural symbols* Mary Douglas is searching a formula for classifying relations that can be applied equally to the smallest band of hunters and to industrialized nations.[34] This strong statement makes clear that she wants to find law-like statements that are valid for all humans. She does not like to theorize in a purely relativist or postmodernist fashion. She has not abandoned all hope for discovering generally valid theories. Besides, she is not afraid to go against ideas that seem to have a long standing in the social sciences. For her, the idea that prehistoric man must be deeply religious is nonsense. On the basis of her knowledge of a host of anthropological studies she is convinced that all the varieties of skepticism, materialism and spiritual fervor are to be found in the whole range of ancient and present day tribal societies. They vary as much from one another as any chosen segment of a modern metropolis.[35] The illusion created by anthropologists, that all primitives are very credulous and subject to the teachings of priests or magicians has probably impeded our understanding of our own civilization more than we would like to admit. For example, Douglas mentions that Fredrik Barth, a renowned anthropologist, started a series of fruitless research activities when he came across the Basseri, a non-religious tribe of Persian nomads who took no interest whatsoever in the religion as preached by the mullahs, and were indifferent to metaphysical problems. In his Durkheimian perspective every tribal society must have a religion of some kind, to account for all kinds of social forces. So, he redoubled the vigor of his enquiries, and squeezed his data as hard as he could to make it yield an overall superstructure of symbolism that could be counted as an elementary form of religion. But he only found a striking poverty of ritual activities and got so frustrated that he was driven to write a special appendix to clear himself of the possible charges of insensibility to religious behaviour. By the way, this is another telling example of the great influence of institutional thinking, one of Mary Douglas's favourite topics, which will be discussed later.

8.4.1   *The death of ritual life*

A striking poverty of rituals aptly describes modern societies too. It is one of the rather mysterious features of modern times that we explicitly reject rituals as such. When Mary Douglas wrote *Natural Symbols*, ritual had become a bad word signifying empty conformity. Those were the days of revolt against formalism and the powers that be. The protest movement of the sixties reminded her of Luther, the German monk who, in 1530, nearly 500 years ago, protested against the rituals of the Roman Catholics, which they found meaningless. For her, these modern protests were echoes of the Reformation and its complaint against mechanical religion, against mindless recitation of litanies in Latin, a language common people did not understand. These Protestants wanted to return to the austere purity of the Gospel. They wanted it preached straight from the heart without intervening ritual forms. But the pejorative approach to rituals has a much longer history. It started with the way the Hebrews looked at magic. Much later this was mirrored in the way the Protestants viewed Catholicism, to them it all was mumbo-jumbo, meaningless ritual, held to be sufficient in itself to produce results without and interior experience of God.[36] A contrast between interior will and exterior enactment goes deep into the history of Judaism and Christianity, in particular Protestantism. In wave upon wave the Reformation has continued to thunder against the empty enactment of ritual. They will never stop saying that external forms can become empty and mock the truth they stand for. This has created a long and deep-rooted tradition of vigorous anti-ritualism.[37] With the help of modern science, further rationalization and disenchantment anti-ritualism has become a major strand of western thinking. It has created a series of homologous distinctions that have organized debate on the distinctions and similarities between 'great religions' and 'primitive religions.' Thus the relation Protestant/Catholic is analogous to relations such as: Hebrew/pagan, monotheism/polytheism, Muslim/Hindu, religion/magic, interior will /external enactment, belief/ritual, and so forth.[38] Despite its present day negative connotation, rituals can also have a neutral meaning, a meaning that is more useful for the description and explanation of certain acts. It is fair enough that 'ritualized' ritual should fall into contempt. But it is illogical to despise all ritual, to renounce all symbolic action as such. Social scientists need a word like ritual for actions in the symbolic order. They need a neutral word to analyze symbols of genuine conformity as well as one for empty symbols.[39]

How can we explain this revolt against ritualism? One of the usual explanations of anti-ritualism and the recurring revolt against established hierarchical systems (of religion) is that they stem from the deprived and the disinherited. These ideas stem from Sigmund Freud and Max Weber. It assumes that the principal function of religion is to cope with psychological maladjustment. According to some theorists, there is a sudden need for a new interpretation of their social position when particular groups are being marginalized. Insecurity and neglect prompt a need for readjustment that new sects may provide. This line of argument does not convince Mary Douglas at all.[40] To begin with, there is no indication that the first groups of Protestants were poor. As a theory it is too easy. We can add the example of contemporary immigrants who find themselves uprooted and marginalized. What status could be more insecure and anxiety-prone than that of the unskilled worker from rural Ghana, Morocco or Turkey in Western Europe? Yet, they do not create new sects. On the contrary, many of them cling to their religious traditions. But in social science the argument, which seeks to explain behaviour as a logical consequence of maladjustment and deprivation, or as an understandable reaction against oppression, discrimination and deprivation, is always fair game. The deprivation thesis is deeply embedded in sociology. Perhaps Jean-Jacques Rousseau gave the first and most emphatic vision of the individual enchained in society and liable to revolt after a certain pitch of despair has been reached. Nonetheless, social scientists ought to dig deeper. Anyone who uses the idea of strain or stress in a general explanatory model is guilty of leaving his sociological analysis long before it is complete.

Mary Douglas signposts three phases in the move from ritual behaviour:

1   First there is the contempt of external ritual forms. Often the denunciation of irrelevant rituals leads to a rejection of ritualism as such. Again, we must remind ourselves of the start of the Protestant Reformation. Protestants will never stop warning us that external forms can become empty and mock the very truths they stand for. Hence, with every new century we become heirs to a longer and more vigorous tradition of anti-ritualism.[41]

2   Secondly, there is the private internalizing of religious experience. The denigration of standardized expressions goes along with the exaltation of the inner experience. The religious protesters show a strong preference for intuitive and instant forms of knowledge. They reject mediating institutions. In its extreme forms anti-ritualism turns into an attempt to abolish communication by means of complex symbolic systems. We can think of the first generation of Protestants who ruined many churches and cathedrals by demolishing statues of Saints.[42] But soon after the initial protest stage, once the need for organization is recognized, once the need for a coherent system of expression is felt, rituals will reemerge. Nonetheless, there is a loss of historical continuity. Only a narrow range of historical experience is recognized as antecedent to the present state.[43]

3   In the third place, there is the move to humanistic philanthropy. When the third stage is under way, the symbolic life of the spirit is finished. No longer is there any belief neither in spirits nor in the positive function of rituals.

For each of these stages social determinants can be identified. Mary Douglas hopes to disclose these social determinants by considering small-scale, pre-modern cultures. However, little has been done to extend the analysis across modern and pre-modern cultures. There is no common vocabulary yet: sacraments are one thing, magic another; taboos are one thing, sin another. So, according to her, the first thing is to break through the verbal hedges that arbitrarily insulate one set of human experience from another one. To begin with, she defines ritualism as a heightened appreciation of symbolic action. This is manifested in two ways: the belief in the efficacy of instituted signs and sensitivity to condensed symbols. Authentic ritualism is an earnest concern that specific acts are carried out in a traditional and precisely prescribed way and that the right words are pronounced in the right order. Only then these rituals are expected to be efficacious.

Douglas, the staunch Catholic, does not make a distinction between the faith in sacraments and the belief in magic and miracles. Since Robertson Smith drew a parallel between Roman Catholic ritual and primitive magic, she has gratefully taken the hint. In all religions the power of miraculous interventions was believed to exist, but there was a certain way of harnessing it. It was as different and as similar as Islamic *Baraka* or Teutonic *Luck* or Polynesian *Mana*. For her, the Christian doctrines of the incarnation and the resurrection are highly magical. Hence, it is impossible to make a tidy distinction between sacramental and magical practice. So, what we learn about the conditions in which magic thrives in primitive cultures should apply to sacramentalism in other religious groups or sects. The devotion to religious sacraments and magic depends on a frame of mind which values external forms and is ready to credit them with special efficacy. Therefore, the search for new symbols or a revitalization of old ones can be a total waste of effort if the prevailing culture and lifestyle manifest no real interest in external symbols. The perception of symbols in general, as well as their interpretation, is socially determined. The advantage of taking belief in efficacious signs as the focus of the comparison between primitive and complex religions is that other aspects of religious behaviour largely coincide with variations on this score.

8.4.2   Decoding mealtime rituals

There is more to eating than putting food in your mouth. Although eating basically is a purely physical affair, it has become heavily influenced by our culture. Preparing food and the ways in which to eat it at particular times, alone or in the company of others, is highly ritualized. We already discussed how menus differ from culture to culture. Westerners may shrink from the thought of eating insects or singing birds, but we know that grubs and grasshoppers, blackbirds and larks are served as food elsewhere.[44] The social organization of a meal can be analyzed as a ritual ceremony. Moreover, we can observe to what degree these ceremonies are upheld or seem to whither away. Already Douglas's own account of mealtime rituals in Britain in the seventies seems to be partly outdated. She describes how decent middle class and working class families organize their dinners together, seated around a special table in the dining room, nicely covered with a white cloth, plates, forks, and knifes neatly arranged in fixed positions. Father and mother both have their own place at the table, showing the hierarchical pattern within the family. Children also have their own place that emerged as they grew older. The dinner itself is structured; it starts with a starter, a salad or soup, followed by a main dish, and finished with a desert. Each dish, in particular the main dish will consist of predictable combinations of staple food, meat and vegetables. This could be examined in terms of structuralist categories and binary opposites such as cooked and raw, solid and liquid, staple food and non-staple food, but as we already have seen, this does not take her strongest interest.

In a Simmelesque way Mary Douglas draws attention to the huge contrast between dinner and breakfast. At dinner everybody is expected to arrive on time, hands washed, properly dressed or at least tidied up to an acceptable standard, shirt tucked in, hair combed. Breakfast is a far less formal and a much more individualistic affair. Breakfast is taken at a simple kitchen table. There is no fancy tablecloth with napkins, and people eat what they like, if they eat any. There is no fixed time at which all members of the family have to be present. They come individually; some of them still half at sleep. They are allowed to appear in pajamas and to grumble a bit or to hide behind a newspaper. Moreover, they are excused for not taking part in light conversation. All this stands in stark contrast to the rituals that have to be enacted at dinnertime. Here the assembled family resembles a tight community that has come together to reaffirm group sentiments. For that reason there is a general prohibition against discussing topics that might cause argument and would highlight individual views. During dinner the family group should show cohesiveness. Light dinner conversation is a sign of good group membership en enhances the feeling of a tight collective. All this is in striking difference with the breakfast situation, which is a much-atomized meal, in which formal rules are minimized and rituals are individualized. Nevertheless, the behavioural patterns of each member of the family are very consistent and highly predictable. Nowadays, much of dinnertime ritual described by Mary Douglas has vanished, because of huge transformations in society. I will mention only the fact that no longer only fathers have a job outside their home. Furthermore, the number of leisure activities has increased dramatically which means that some members of the family are obliged to eat early or later, depending on the time when they have to take part in sports events, training, fitness classes, evening classes, meetings et cetera. And, last but not least, there is the arrival of tv. So, in many households dinner has become just as highly atomized as breakfast. Like Durkheim, Douglas is a great believer in the function of rituals for the production and maintenance of social relations. Hence modernity should have created alternative forms that keep families together, but did it? It is hard to say whether functional equivalents have been installed for the lost dinnertime rituals. But it is not hard to acknowledge that familial cohesion has deteriorated during the last four or five decades. This period has witnessed a huge increase in the number of broken families. The extinction of sharing daily meals might have further weakened family relations that already were weakening for a whole set of other external and internal reasons.

8.5 The group-grid model

Mary Douglas has constructed a typology that enables social scientists to meet important conceptual and methodological challenges. The group-grid model was designed to be able to take into account the total social setting and the interrelationships of individual members with each other and their context[45]. So far, she has presented and remodeled her model in three major works. In *Natural Symbols* she elaborates on Basil Bernstein's work, on linguistic codes and on social control through pedagogical practices in families and schools.[46] She really admired his work.

8.5.1 Borrowing basic ideas of Basil Bernstein

Before Bernstein's ideas got rooted in socio-linguistics, specialists tended to treat language as an autonomous cultural agent, and failed to relate its formal patterns to the structure of social relations. Certainly, to a large extent, language follows its own rules. Therefore, for a long time, speech was treated as a datum, or simply as medium for communication. But it is an interesting area to investigate whether symbolic forms are purely expressive, merely the means of solving specific problems of communication or whether they interact on the social situations in which they arise, and whether their effect is constraining and conservative.

Basil Bernstein started with the idea that there are two basic styles of speech that differ in a social and a linguistic way. The restricted code arises in small-scale local social situations, in which all speakers have access to the same experiences. All members of a small community, a family, a tribe, village or hamlet, are familiar with the history of the group. They know everyone's roles, business, goals and aspirations. In such groups the collective memory and collective conscience cover a very large part of what everybody has experienced. One needs only a few words or non-verbal signs to communicate with one another, because all share the same fount of information. Here speech exercises a solidarity-maintaining function. The other type, the elaborated code, is employed in situations where the speakers do not know each other very well. In these cases one cannot assume that the other is familiar with all what you know. Hence speakers need to be much more specific in their use of concepts, in their references to specific events, the period, the time of the day, the people involved, and the things that went on. This kind of speech prevails in what Durkheim called organic societies, in societies in which people have very different roles, functions, and positions. To Bernstein and his co-workers the strong tendency of lower class people to practice a restricted code offered an explanation for the less successful school careers of their offspring.[47] In contrast to the restricted code, the elaborated code used by the middle classes fitted nicely with the language used and taught at schools, because teachers tended to use this elaborated code as well. Besides, it also was the language style used in schoolbooks, the style, grammar and vocabulary that were tested in all assignments and exams.

Basil Bernstein has introduced yet another variable for explaining class differences in educational attainments. He distinguished two modes of socialization: a personal and a positional mode. In the personal mode, which is the predominant mode of the middle classes, children are treated as young individuals with unique characteristics. Middle class parents seriously try to understand the feelings of their children and take their level of cognitive development into account. They tend to convince and persuade their children that the things they want them to do are in their own interest. According to Bernstein's theory, which he had based on his personal observations as a young residential family caseworker in East-London, lower class parents are much less considerate with the uniqueness and feelings of their children. They use a so-called positional mode, in which children are treated as immature human beings that are not able to understand reason and cannot oversee the risks of their actions. Hence, they need to be watched and commanded all day. In particular, lower class parents tend to demand strict obedience of their children without giving them reasons for the things they order them to do or to leave.

Scheme 8.2   Basil Bernstein's socialization theories

linguistic code	**restricted code**
	Is used within homogenous, close-knit communities. Few words are needed for effective communication.
	(Mechanical solidarity: collective conscience is maximal)
	elaborated code
	Is used within socially and culturally diversified groups. Most things have to be explained and made explicit to avoid misunderstandings.
	(Organic solidarity: Collective conscience is minimal)
mode of socialization	**positional mode**
	Children have to obey their parents. They must behave as 'civilized' or well-trained boys or girls of their age.
	personal mode
	Children are addressed as unique individuals, with specific traits and feelings. Parents do not want their children to obey them as well-trained dogs but to agree with them because parental demands are 'reasonable'.

Mary Douglas reworked Basil Bernstein's dichotomies of a restricted and an elaborated code and of a positional and a personal mode of socialization into two independent variables: group and grid. At first, she defined group as the variable that denotes the experience of a bounded social unit. Grid refers to the rules that relate one person to others.[48] Splitting both variables in a strong and a weak side, and combining them in a fourfold table renders a typology of four types. The horizontal (group) axis presents the degree to which the boundary insulates members of the group from other groups, separating insiders from outsiders. Castes, classes, and religions are strong group variables. They create clear divisions between people. The vertical (grid) axis represents the degree to which the individual is personally insulated from the other members of his group or society. Douglas has applied this model time and time again, though not always in a consistent way. However, some later shifts in definition have lead to a model that is used by many others in a successful way.

In 1982, when Mary Douglas once more described and elaborated her typology, she decided to start with the issue of allegiance to a group. Some groups can be joined quite easily while others are very exclusive. For any social context we can also recognize appropriate measures of group commitment, whether to ancient lineage, to a learned profession or to a military regiment or a church. So 'group' refers to the strictness of group boundaries or the rules or arrangements for inclusion and exclusion, and also to the degree of social bonding or social cohesion within the social unit. The stronger the social cohesion, the more people interact with each other, the more they can fall back on a collective memory and a restricted code. The weaker the social bonding, the less familiar are people with one another, the more they need an elaborated code. Grid, the other core concept, concerns the extent of regulation of social actions within the group. The extremes run from maximum regulation to maximum freedom. The military regiment with its strictly prescribed rules of behaviour contrasts with the lightly committed and unregulated voluntary association. In strongly regulated social organizations people are addressed as representatives of their position, status, and main role. Again this closely connects with Bernstein's conceptualizations of the positional mode and the restricted code. In weakly regulated social settings people are treated as individuals with unique traits, views, and wishes, which relates to Bernstein's types of personal mode and elaborated code. Combined, these two bipolar dimensions give four typical models of social life as presented in scheme 8.3.[49] The qualitative scholar can use the model to interpret and explain how constructed contextual meanings are generated, taught, and transformed. The quantitative investigator is provided with a matrix to classify contexts and draw specific observations about individuals, their values and belief systems, and all kinds of behavioural variables.

Quadrant A (weak grid, weak group) describes the competitive, individualistic social context that allows a large range of pragmatic options for social mobility and for choosing (temporary) friends and allies. Individual sports, markets and liberal-democratic societies are good examples. Other examples of weak-group/weak-grid settings are a government, a parliament or a flea market. The social system of the flea market is in constant flux, as transient individual vendors enter the community, set up shop, move on to another market or leave their trade.[50] The same holds true for cabinet ministers and members of parliament. Cell B (strong grid, weak group) fits any loosely integrated setting in which individuals do not belong to well-articulated groupings and have few commitments to each other, but are controlled by many rules and regulations. Typical examples are prisons or transfer camps for political refugees. Quadrant C is the environment of large institutions where loyalty is rewarded and hierarchy respected. This is the model in which Mary Douglas was raised: the Catholic Church and the convent school. Another good example might be the army, and more specifically the Marine Corps or the Green Berets. During tough training exercises individual thinking and initiative is played down and group loyalty is strongly reinforced. Group spirit is enhanced by the long and exhausting training exercises and the collective experience of risky operations in which they have to endure much hardship together and learn to appreciate the value of collective actions and become aware of their dependency of the group for their survival. The recruits will also be indoctrinated with the idea that they have been selected to become members of an elite corps and that all this hardship and loyalty is necessary to maintain the high standards of an elite corps. Cell D refers to a social setting in which only the boundaries for membership are clear.

Scheme 8.3   The grid-group model of Mary Douglas[51]

	weak group (weak cohesion)	strong group (strong cohesion)
weak grid (weak regulation)	*A* **Individualistic societies** *(markets; the group of Ministers and Secretaries of State)* individualism	*D* **Sects/enclaves** *(extremist political parties)* factionalism egalitarian collectivism
strong grid (strong regulation)	**Isolates** *(prisons, refugee camps)* atomized subordination mass alienation *B*	**Hierarchies** *(the convent school; the marine corps; government bureaucracies)* ascribed hierarchy communitarianism *C*

As a consequence many other statuses are ambiguous and open to negotiation. Sects can emerge through self-definition by a rejection of the social environment in which they are embedded. After some sorry misunderstandings of the earlier versions of *Natural Symbols* Douglas has come to abjure the word 'sect', because it had become a term of reproach or even contempt. She now prefers the neutral word 'enclave.' By definition this is a bounded group that is encapsulated within a larger society. However, she still retains the word 'sectarian' to describe a cultural bias that favours polarized arguments, dividing the world in two sectors: evil and good, and nothing in between. Sectarianism means adopting an idealized approach to political and social problems; often a simplistic metaphysics, even an anti-intellectual and anti-scientific stance, and an uncompromising ruthlessness towards opponents.[52]

8.5.2   *The dynamic interplay between grid and group*

In *The Active Voice*, also published in 1982, Mary Douglas presents a more dynamic, symbiotic relationship between grid and group. She wants to underscore the dynamic interplay between the individual and the social setting. She uses 'grid' for a dimension of various degrees of individuation and 'group' for a dimension of degrees of social incorporation. Again grid refers to the degree to which individual choices are constrained by formal prescriptions such as role expectations, rules and procedures. For instance, in school organizations teachers' and students' freedom of choice tend to be constrained by national rules that regulate holidays, timetables, curriculum, teaching methods, grading, national exams and standards. The local school board might even add more rules and regulations.

Classic strong-grid settings have inherent structural networks that insulate the individual from others outside his or her particular religion, estate, class, subclass or caste. In strongly regulated settings there is a sharply regulated division between insiders and outsiders. One of the strongest examples of boundaries can be found in the Indian caste system. People from the 'untouchables' can never mix or interact with members of the Brahmin caste. They cannot even stand in their shadow and are forbidden to let their shadow 'touch' the other or his food. Fortunately, for the Brahmins at least, the Indian caste system has many intermediate castes to ensure a functioning society, otherwise they would perish. Even now, Hindus living in a traditional Indian village are not allowed to mix with members of other classes. They have to follow strict rules. This case of very strong group boundaries results in a highly regulated social system in which social strata are segregated and reproduced. There is scrupulous observation of the rules that protects each level of hierarchy from contamination by the levels below it, not to mention the equally scrupulous rules to protect families from the shame that a daughter does marry a boy from a lower caste or a different religion.[53] The Medieval European system of estates does resemble this, but its boundaries were less strong. The nobility would not easily engage into a marriage with a spouse who belonged to the commoners. But they would take less distance and accept commoners as servants in their home or castle, as page, soldier, and so on. The class system that has evolved in industrial societies is one step further down the ladder of strictly regulated boundaries, but still has not reached complete openness.

Food for thought

In *Sir Vidia's Shadow* Paul Theroux writes the fascinating story of his long friendship with Nobel Prizewinner Vidia S. Naipaul. The latter descends from an Indian family that migrated to Trinidad a few generations ago. But even after a long residence in Trinidad and England the Brahmin habitus still is very much alive. Theroux mentions Naipaul's behaviour at some dinner parties in which he refused to take food, although the host had offered special vegetarian dishes. Asked why he refused to eat anything Naipaul told Theroux that the vegetables were tainted because one of the dinner guests had touched the vegetables with a serving implement that had come into contact with the meat dish.

Box 8.3

To estimate autonomy in any setting, one could ask how freely a person disposes his own time, selects his goods, and chooses his collaborators. Strong-grid contexts constrain personal freedoms in these areas. Weak-grid environments promote individual liberty and autonomy. Where roles are ascribed, controls are strong, classificatory distinctions are valued, and there is little or no competition for status. Where roles are achieved, constraints are minimal and individuals can strive for rewards and higher status in open competitive surroundings. Hence, the issues of social control and competition are inversely linked with each other. The group dimension represents the degree to which members value their social unit, its continuation and their life within it. Group denotes the degree to which humans are committed to a social unit, organization or culture. Naturally, both dimensions can reinforce each other or cancel each other out. Group deals with the holistic aspect of social incorporation and the extent to which people's lives are absorbed and sustained by corporate membership. In strong-group environments the survival of the group becomes more important than the survival of its individual members. The primary goal of social interaction is the continuation of the life of the group. The strongest effects are to be found where the group incorporates and unites its members by segregated residence, shared work and leisure time, shared resources and recreation, and by inserting control over marriage.[54] Within multi-ethnic and multi-faith societies we see examples of segregated minorities that choose ethnic segregation as a strategy to maintain their own language and culture and ward off assimilation. Extreme cases of group strength can be seen in monasteries, religious sects, or social communes where private property is renounced upon entering, and the members rely on the social unit for their physical, emotional, and social life support. The kibbutz (a Hebrew word which means 'collection') in Israel represents a good example of a strong-group environment. All property belongs to the kibbutz, and members who work in the kibbutz get kibbutz goods and services for their work rather than cash that could be spent outside the kibbutz.[55]

8.5.3   Pitfalls of cultural analysis

Mary Douglas describes cultures as packages of values. These coherent packages can shape institutions. Stable institutions are upheld by a fixed set of values. If they are viable but in a process of change, we can assume that some values are becoming less important while others gain prominence. Institutions require external favouring conditions to keep them in being as well as holding on to the appropriate set of values. Since there is no guarantee that these favourable conditions will appear spontaneously and regularly enough to account for stability, we must also accept the functionalist premise that a stable organization possesses some capacity to stimulate the enforcing conditions that will enable it to survive.[56] Once again it becomes clear why Mary Douglas does not have a high opinion of explanations that are wholly based on a relationship with a set of values. If we want to explain social change, we also need insights in changing social conditions or changes in the capacity of social organizations to adjust to new circumstances. However, most cultural analysts take things more easily.

> In social theory the word 'culture' becomes an extra resource to be wheeled in after other explanations are defeated. It is the flexible, powerful residual factor where other reason fails. It works because of what it can say implicitly, drawing upon the reserves of understanding created by discourse in the regular culture. However, because it remains implicit it is the weakness at the core of the so-called social sciences.
> You can recognize culture being misused in sociological explanations when you hear behaviour being explained by reference to a cultural value cherished by the actors. Enthusiasm for work (or its absence) is explained by saying that the workers subscribe or do not subscribe the work ethic. Authority being successfully exerted is explained by a deferential culture. A difficulty in establishing consensus is explained by the value placed on individualism or independence. The submission that we make here is that any explanation by appeal to a dominant value is tautological. It just says again the thing that is being wondered at. Furthermore the values have not been analyzed. There is no hint about where values come from or about how to explain them. These questions fall outside common discourse, but they should not fall outside sociological inquiry which needs to link a careful analysis of the values to the institutional forms. [57]

These are strong statements. Maybe they are a bit too strong. Not all purely cultural explanations of cultural facts are completely tautological. It is possible to sketch an explanatory model in which values are seen as the most basic dispositions of individuals or collectivities to prefer certain states of affairs to others. Our values are mutually related and form value systems in which some values have a higher priority than others. Values are inculcated in our minds early in our lives and determine our attitudes, beliefs and opinions, consciously as well as unconsciously. Hence, knowing someone's value priorities can help explain political party preferences or specific views and opinions. Nonetheless, Mary Douglas seems to argue that cultural phenomena should always be analyzed with reference to historical and social conditions too. She has given some excellent examples of her favourite modus operandi.

8.6   Secular sects: the case of the British peak labour organization

Mary Douglas contends that cultural analysts can make sense of a lot of otherwise inscrutable data by using two, three or more kinds of stable types of institutions. It is not always necessary to study all the four types presented in the grid-group model (scheme 3). Often, three types suffice, because the fourth type is not always relevant. This complete or incomplete typology has become an essential instrument in the toolkit of any cultural analyst. For example, in the field of politics the hierarchies with which we are most familiar are the bureaucratic hierarchies of government and civil service. Here strong grid and group combine. The completely opposite case is the bottom left-hand cell. Within the political field here we find the individual ministers who form the government. They constitute a highly competitive market for the politically gifted. The diagonal that links these two cells is where a great deal of power in society is located. It is here that government-to-industry relations take place. It is here that bureaucracies of large firms recruit their top-managers.

Mary Douglas and her followers have applied this grid-group model in a great variety of cases. In her article about 'institutions of the third kind' she discusses salient differences between the political tactics and strategies of the British and the Swedish peak labour organizations.[58] The most remarkable distinction is that the British TUC has always been very much against the employers and the government, whereas the Swedish Labour Organization (LO) always has taken a much more co-operative stance. How can we explain this difference?

Most economic and sociological analysis concentrates on hierarchies and markets, but the third kind, the sect or the enclave, also represents a distinctive and viable form of organization. Though sects have been studied almost exclusively in the context of religious practices, the sectarian pattern is quite common in the secular world as well. The Swedish labour organizations correspond to hierarchies, but the British TUC and also the British Employers' Confederation are not hierarchies by any test. They constitute collectivities of autonomous individual organizations. Moreover, many singular organizations stay outside any overarching collective organization and count as isolates. That the TUC resembles a sect implies that we have found already one reason why it acts different than the Swedish LO. It has quite a different culture or, put in different words, cherishes a different set of values. At least, it strongly differs with respect to one crucial value. This was already so from the beginning of its existence. As an institution survives, it entrenches its values in the minds of its members. Thus it cumulatively transforms itself and its environment. When the British labour movement started at the end of the eighteenth century its enemies likened it to the conspiracies that preceded the French Revolution. The local labour organizations were seen as secret and dangerous societies. From the start they had been placed in the position of requiring freedom from government interference. Successive legal reforms gave them immunity from the charges of conspiracy. Isaiah Berlin has called this negative freedom, freedom from control by others. It is the primary sense of freedom. Positive freedom signifies autonomy, the freedom to be in control of your live, which ultimately leads to taking a share in public responsibilities voluntarily.[59] Rousseau is associated with the idea of negative freedom, with freedom from external constraints, with the freedom to resist intrusion. The social philosophy of Marx is connected with the idea of positive freedom or the idea of unrestrained opportunities for personal self-determination and self-realization. The positive sense of the word liberty derives from the wish of individuals to be their own master, from the wish that their life and decisions depend on their own volition, and not on external forces of whatever kind. Modern individuals want to be somebody. They want to be self-directed and not acted upon by external nature or by other men. Positive freedom gives humans ample room for conceiving and realizing their own goals and policies, for being an independent thinking, willing and active individual.[60]

Scheme 8,4   Isaiah Berlin's types of freedom

negative freedom	freedom:
	• from oppression and social constraints;
	• from the demands of other people or the claims they might have on you.
positive freedom	Autonomy or freedom
	• to develop your own talents, in particular the talents you enjoy developing most.

Mary Douglas uses these two contrasted ideas as pegs on which to hang an account of the differences between the British and the Swedish labour organizations. The British have embraced the concept of negative freedom and the Swedes cherish the idea of positive freedom. Her analysis connects a particular value preference with two distinct institutional structures, because, in practice, when one form of freedom is entrenched in the mindset of an organization, it tends to exclude the other. The inclination to resist interference from outside will stand in the way of the penchant to co-operate with outsiders. Though both labour organizations aimed at a better social security for workers, redistribution of wealth, and political representation they ended up with quite different organizational structures and political strategies.

Around 1900, when the Swedish union movement was grounded, the conspiracy model already had been superseded. Naturally, the Swedish employers originally fought the growth of trade unions, but soon they recognized the unions' right to organize and to negotiate wages and labour conditions. Thus, from the outset the Swedish LO was not placed in an enclave but derived power from its ability to negotiate at a national level. Thus it could take control of part of its environment. According to Douglas these initial orientations lay the trail for the development of a hierarchical institution in the Swedish case and for a sect-like organization in the British case.

Sects tend to build a strong wall between insiders and outsiders. Sects have certain specific problems requiring specific solutions that, in turn, lead to the adoption of particular values. Originated as a group of dissenters, protesters, or revolutionaries it has to settle for voluntary membership and will tend to make a virtue of it. Religious sects and revolutionary cells tend to be highly selective. They certainly will not accept all individuals that want to join the group. The real problem is how to keep members from leaving the sect. The leadership constantly fears that its followers will stop following. To meet such problems, those committed most deeply to the group and its goals build up a strong moral condemnation of the whole outside world. This results in the sectarian trap; it becomes morally and politically impossible for any member to deal with outsiders except in a confrontational form. Insiders who co-operate in one-way or another with the enemy will be scolded. These are all manifestations of a high-group, low-grid situation, in which high bonding and strong commitment still imply a few rigid rules like not to fraternize with outsiders. As the community establishes a stable form, it proceeds to redesign its environment. It flourishes on opposition and directs its opponents in a similar pattern of behaviour and a similar organizational structure. So, it is no wonder that the British employers are, as they always have been confrontational too. Moreover, they use the same forms of war rhetoric.

Mary Douglas does not suggest that the TUC is as sectarian as a religious sect, but merely that the analogy with sectarian religions helps us to understand some of its distinctive characteristics as a peak organization of the British trade union movement. It helps us understand why its tactics and strategies tend to be far more adversarial than those of the Swedish LO or that of other labour organizations on the continent. There, the labour unions as well as the unions of employers are much more centralized and hierarchical, and also much more accustomed to co-operation. Often, this long tradition of co-operation is established in regular meetings of representatives of three parties, the government, the employers and the employees. During these meetings most of the issues that could polarize industrial relations will be de-politicized to prevent strikes and other outburst of protests that could harm the economy and social stability. In many other European countries, such as The Netherlands, we see a similar pattern. There the labour organizations are strongly inclined to strive for consensus, because they know that strikes and unrealistic demands for pay-raises can harm the economy, which indirectly will harm the income position and social security of their members.

Mary Douglas rejects the explanation that the differences between the structure and operation of both organizations can be deduced from class differences, though admitting that the British system was and still is more oppressive than the class systems of Sweden, Germany, Austria or the USA. Class differences exist and existed in all these countries workers, but this does not explain why the Scandinavian and Dutch labour unions use significantly more co-operative tactics than the English. Here, we meet again one of the basic principles of Douglas' logic. For a valid explanation of striking differences between organizations and their success or failure as an organization, between their social structures or their organizational climates, we need at least to consider three important aspects. First we need to look at the historical setting when the institutions emerged and came of age. What were the reasons for its emergence? Which problems had to be solved and what were the available means to solve these problems? All these conditions will have a lasting impact on them.

8.7   How institutions think

Once a structurally complete and closed system of opinions consisting of many details and relations has been formed, it offers enduring resistance to anything that contradicts it (Ludwik Fleck)[61]

As a topic for social theory institutions constitute a big and important theme. In Mary Douglas's view such a theory is long overdue. In fact, she admits, she should have written it twenty years earlier, before she wrote *Purity and Danger*. This particular book and many others could have profited from this attempt to understand institutions better. *How institutions think* begins with a discussion of the hostility that greeted Emile Durkheim when he talked about institutions or social groups as if they were objects that acted with one mind. Among social scientists the very idea of a supra-individual cognitive system stirs a deep sense of outrage. However, the manifestation of this particular collective outrage is in itself evidence that above the level of the individual another cognitive hierarchy is influencing the individual protesters. Unfortunately, the very idea of supra- or extra-personal knowledge domains arouses images of nasty totalitarianism, as if Big Brother no longer was satisfied with watching our deeds, but had developed the ultimate Brain Scan scanning and controlling all individual minds. This would boil down to the perfect totalitarian state in which the last illusion, the illusion that at least our thoughts are free, has been shattered. According to Douglas, the whole idea has made many able thinkers so nervous that they prefer to dismiss this theoretical problem. However, this topic has to be faced despite the many difficulties with which it confronts us. It cannot be dismissed because *Institutions Make Life and Death Decisions.*[62]

But surely only individuals have a mind of their own, don't they? At least that is a widely shared assumption. This assumption holds that individuals calculate what is in their best interest and act accordingly. And yet, in practice, we get the contrary impression. We observe that most individuals do contribute to the public good generously, unhesitant, without obvious self-serving. That is why Durkheim imagined that individuals must have two sides, that the individual is a homo duplex with an individual and a collective mind. The collective conscience reflects the will of society and makes people often forget their immediate personal interests for the sake of the common good. This internalized collective conscience acts as an inner voice that warns us not to deviate from the prevalent norms and values. This internally appropriated collective conscience has filled our minds with all kinds of classifications, ways of thinking and arguing, and, above all, with the sense of the *a priori* rightness or falseness of certain ideas. However, by upgrading the role of society in organizing individual thought, Durkheim downgraded the role of the individual. Since he did not spell out the precise steps of the process in which the collective conscience unconsciously became internalized in individual minds and souls, he seemed to be invoking some mystic entity. As a functionalist he seemed to endow the social group with super-organic, self-sustaining powers, powers that would be immanently conservative. In spite of certain weaknesses, Douglas thinks that his idea still is too good to be dismissed.[63]

Fortunately, the medical doctor and philosopher Ludwik Fleck has elaborated and extended Durkheim's approach.[64] In his book on the identification of syphilis, he went far beyond Durkheim. Both were equally ardent about the social basis of cognition, about the social basis of our most basic categories, such as time, space, and causality. For Durkheim, they represent the most general relations that exist between things. They dominate all the details of our thinking. If humans do not agree upon these essential ideas at any moment, if they do not share similar conceptions of time, space, causality, number, etcetera, all contact between their minds will be impossible, and with that, all social life will come to a halt. Fleck sings a similar song. In his view, cognition is the most socially conditioned activity of man. Knowledge is the paramount social creation. On the one hand, this is very good, because it helps us to gain infinitely more useful knowledge than we could have gathered as single individuals. Though, on the other hand, it also can hinder further developments in science and explorations of new fields. The general opinion tends to be conservative and is strongly inclined to reject new insights that do not square with the prevalent way of thinking. For instance, the discovery of the cause of syphilis was greatly hindered by the fact that it was widely seen as a punishment of God for improper sexual behaviour and not recognized as an illness that could be cured like most other illnesses.

A century ago, Paul Fauconnet and Marcel Mauss already concluded that the basis of social existence is a broad and rather coherent set of collective representations.[65] Ludwik Fleck elaborated this further. In his view a social community or group is a 'thought collective'. Any social, religious, or professional community develops a more or less disciplined, consensually agreed set of principles about the world, about what is fact and what is speculation. This thought style leads human perception, trains it, and adds new ideas to the stock of knowledge that is gathered by the social group. This coherent set of collective representations renders the preconditions of any cognition. It determines what can be counted as a good question and a good answer. It provides the context and sets the limits for any judgment about reality. The individual within the collective is hardly ever conscious of the prevailing thought style, which almost always exerts a compulsive force upon his thinking. For Fleck, the collective thought style is directing the individual thinker. [66]

Fleck realized that thought styles have a strong influence on all members of any social group that cherishes closed systems of opinions. In the case of thought styles that dominate specific scientific disciplines for many decades Thomas Kuhn, who was influenced by Fleck, has proposed the term paradigm. Any established scientific thought style or paradigm has a strong tendency to resist new notions that do not fit the system of concepts, basic assumptions, theories, and widely shared opinions.[67] Kuhn distinguishes the history of science in periods of normal science, in which scientists accumulate a lot of new knowledge based on the basic assumptions of that particular paradigm. However, when ever more data are being gathered and hypotheses are being put forward and tested then there comes a moment at which scientists are faced with outcomes that are totally unexpected within their theoretical framework. The new outcomes that do not fit the prevailing paradigmatic theory are called anomalies. For a while, the group of scientists could try to ignore this outcome and blame it on specific conditions or faulty procedures during data gathering, but if the number of anomalies is growing this will lead to a crisis and an intellectual revolution that might lead to a new paradigm which succeeds in convincing the majority of scientists in this field to accept a changed set of axioms and assumptions. Kuhn's theory of major developments in science has been summarized as follows.

Paradigm A → normal science under the auspices of paradigm A → anomalies → crisis → scientific revolution → paradigm B → normal paradigmatic science under the auspices of paradigm B → ... [68]

Fleck observed an active approach to defend the old system or paradigm. In well-established fields a contradiction to the established theoretical system simply appears unthinkable. For instance, in the fifteenth century, when scientists tried to explain that the earth must be round and not flat, most people argued: '*Could anyone be mad enough to believe that there are antipodes, that there are people standing with their feet opposite our own. Is there really a region on earth where trees grow downward, and where it rains upward?*[69] Today we have rid ourselves from this restricted view on the concepts 'up' and 'down'. 'Down under' the rain falls down from the sky, just like it does on all the other continents. Secondly, there is a very strong tendency to ignore facts and arguments that do not fit the system of collectively shared views. Fleck mentions the ignorance of sexuality in young children. Everyone has been a child, yet it took psychoanalysis to reveal children's sexuality. Thirdly, if a contradictory fact is noticed, it is either kept secret or laborious efforts are made to describe it as an exception and explain it in a way that does not contradict the system. Such effort demonstrates that our first priority is theoretical conformity. Thought collectives try to maintain their well-established logical order and apparently coherent set of classifications at any cost. And even when contradictory views can no longer be overlooked, the members of the thought collective remain focused on circumstances that support the main elements of their thought style.

> *The tenacity of systems of opinion shows us that, to some extent, they must be regarded as units, as independent, style-permeated structures. They are not mere aggregates of partial propositions but as harmonious holistic units ... determine and condition every single function of cognition.*[70]

Nonetheless, also Fleck was quick to point out some distinctions. He distinguished the thought collective from the thought community. The first comprises the true believers. The second, much wider collective, comprises all members who formally belong to a certain social group. We could think of the distinction between fundamentalist, moderate and non-practicing Muslims or between orthodox, moderate, liberal and secular Jews or Christians.

Thomas Kuhn was the first since 1937 to draw attention to Fleck's ideas. He noted that Fleck's position has some fundamental problems that cluster around the notion of a thought collective. A thought collective seems to function as an individual mind writ large because a whole group of people possesses it or is possessed by it. Kuhn is sharing discomfort with many liberals who maintain that only individual persons can think. Can other translations of *Denkkollektiv*, such as 'cognitive community' or 'thought world', take away some of the discomfort? Nowadays, we have become familiar with terms like Art Worlds, coined by Howard S. Becker to state that collective efforts produces a work of art, even though it is attributed to a particular artist.[71] Surely, the celebration of the individual artist is a relatively recent phenomenon in the history of mankind. Great and prolific painters like Rembrandt and Michelangelo delegated part of their painting, such as filling in backgrounds and clothes to assistants, so that they could concentrate on the most essential parts of picture such as the composition or the faces and their facial expressions.[72] But even the very individualistic contemporary painter depends on an anonymous collective of suppliers of paint makers, framers, distributors, art galleries, the public, and last but not least all the artists before him who have invented certain methods and developed certain styles. In this way, every artist is embedded in a social network or figuration, as Norbert Elias made clear.

For me it is also relevant to observe how each path breaking artist still fits in his artistic field, while he also manages to change his field 'single-handedly' by enriching it with a new perspective, style or technique. Only the great masters of art and science create innovations that will be considered as breakthroughs in the evolution of art and science. All the little masters and great servants simply copy them, rework them, but fail as real innovators, just like the millions of biological mutants that emerge every day but are not fit to survive and form a new species. Only the great masters that managed to change the field give meaning to a well known, slightly rephrased, statement of Tacitus: *'Paintings have changed and so have our eyes'[73]* Sir Ernst Gombrich treated the history of art as a continuing tension between the stability of style and the struggle against it, the struggle of an artist 'to win freshness of vision'. He gave many examples of the artist's ambivalence towards tradition, cites the many exercises in copying the masters, and the common fear of becoming a slave of tradition. But Gombrich's main objective was to explain why innovation is so difficult. A current style imposes a closure on the possibilities of perception. It is a contemporary organization of experience. *A style, like a culture or climate of opinion, sets up a horizon of expectation, a mental set which registers deviations and modifications with exaggerated sensitivity.[74]* Each time an artist succeeds to create a brand new style, despite the pressure of the dominant views and preferences of his day and age, he also succeeds to highlight his own approach by highlighting the difference with the prevailing style. Clearly, for most artists it is very hard to create a new style that will convince the connoisseurs and the general public of art lovers that their innovative approach really is of great value and not just a pathetic protest against an existing widely accepted and appreciated style.

Now we have got used to terms such as art worlds, the stage may be set for the Durkheim-Fleck program for the sociology of knowledge, though there are two grave objections made against it. The first objection is the argument against loose functional explanations. For instance, Fleck has his own version of a self-sustaining functional loop.

> *The general structure of a thought collective entails that the communication of thoughts within a collective, irrespective of content or logical justification, should lead, for sociological reasons, to the corroboration of the thought structure.[75]*

Not all readers might be convinced that the 'sociological reasons' hinted at by Fleck offer a valid explanation of the frequently observed commitment of individuals with a larger social whole and its concomitant worldview. Nonetheless, Fleck has been explicit enough in mentioning the widespread psychological need to hold on to traditional views and to share 'sensible reasoning' and 'consistent theories that seem to be very logic'. People need a strong illusion of having come to grips with their apparently orderly and explainable world. They also need a feeling of belonging. By means of developing a thought style institutions confer identity, establish boundaries, similarity and difference, and organize meaning in apparently coherent sets of classifications. In strong, solid, and durable institutions such conceptual systems tend to become naturalized over time. They cease to be mere constructs and turn into essences, into phenomena that can no longer be perceived differently; they turn into social facts that appear just as natural as the burning heat of the sun or the cooling shadow of a tree.[76] Besides, social control mechanism help to maintain adherence to a prevailing thought style. Maybe the more interesting question is why some groups or communities, including communities of scientists sharing a paradigmatic approach, have a much stronger influence on the thinking of their members and even develop distinctive thought styles than other groups and communities, and what factors play a crucial role in opening up thought styles to help them come to turns with 'unthinkable' new insights and new evidence, or entirely new interpretations of well-known facts?

8.8   Aids and the risks of sexual encounters

Let us be careful not to idealize community. It does not always deal kindly with its members.[77]

Rational choice theorists like George Casper Homans assume that individuals always act in their own interest. Hence, they predict that individuals will avoid taking great risks. But the rational choice axiom that people have a strong tendency to make benefit-maximizing decisions based on their priorities is too simple. Mary Douglas proposes the thesis that humans take risks or avoid them according to a predictable pattern of dealings between the person and others in the community. In other words, under certain conditions even people that normally are very prudent can turn into high-risk takers. Self and community emerge in the course of social interactions in relation to perceived risks. For Mary Douglas, the crux is the attitude to knowledge. To make her point, she presents a cultural analysis of group reactions to AIDS, which highlights four main reactions to the question of the acceptability of the medical profession's advice on how to be protected against a deadly virus.[78] As usual she begins her analysis with assimilating the unfamiliar to something she is already familiar with, allowing previous cases to be rehearsed and reworked. This enables her to reason from very broad analogy. For example, when she embarks on an analysis of the risks of modern societies, she looks for a vocabulary that always has been of great help in earlier studies. So, in her treatment of reactions to AIDS she applies her favourite grid-group model to show once more that cultural analysis that takes variables such as the inclusiveness or exclusiveness of groups into account as well as the level of autonomy within these groups or social categories will shed more light on the situation than simply assuming that risky or risk-avoiding behaviour is connected to rational choice.

In 1981, the world was alarmed by the discovery of a new epidemic, caused by the extremely dangerous HIV virus. At first, it appeared that only homosexuals got ill and died shortly afterwards. Later, also other groups got ill. People became scared of direct contact with HIV-positive patients. Many patients got fired because their colleagues no longer wanted to work with them. After a while medical science established a relationship between the illness and sexual behaviour. Later insights became more precise. Science discovered that the AIDS-virus enters the body via the bloodstream. This can happen by sexual penetration or by contact with blood through open cuts, such as infected hypodermic needles. Left outside the body the virus dies quickly; one does not catch the disease by simply touching each other. Hence, people are advised to be less promiscuous and to use condoms. Since many people were kept in the dark about these facts, or could not afford contraceptives, the number of patients rose sharply in continents like Africa and Asia.[79]

This grave threat to the world community generated a debate about the sources of the infection, the priorities of medical science, and the body's vulnerability. Sociological research has revealed different perspectives on the body that are related to specific responses to official medical information. The following scheme shows four models ranging from the idea that the body is rather weak and defenseless to the idea that the body is very strong and endowed with effective natural defense mechanisms.[80] The models 2 and 3 cover the middle ground and could be merged into one model that assumes that the body is half-protected but could be successfully shielded with the help of a prudent society that takes all kinds of precautionary measures to prevent illness and works hard to hasten progress in medical science and practice.

Scheme 8.5   Models of the body

basic idea	main characteristics
1 the weak and porous body	The body is completely open to every dangerous invasion of viruses and bacteria. Therefore, illness is a fact of life and an early death can happen to anyone.
2 the half-protected body	The body is protected by the skin, which is a good protective layer, but not sufficient. We also need a strong 'social skin'. Society must control the level of hygiene and teach everybody to avoid health risks.
3 the body as a repairable machine	The body is a machine that has its own protective shield, but this can be pierced. So, always take medical precautions, and, if necessary, seek trustworthy medical help as soon as possible to repair the damage.
4 the strong body	The body has an effective immune system. It can cope with almost any infection. Actually, too much hygiene can weaken this defense mechanism. Stick to natural healing methods and evade modern medicine.

Using her familiar approach leads Douglas to the following grid-group typology for the different group reactions towards the AIDS epidemic:

- The central community operates as a rather strong group, with a strong grid. It accepts the authority of the established medical profession, which is part of the central community, and it favours the model of the half-protected body or the body as a repairable machine that always needs extra protection by a community that does not take unnecessary risk, but takes all the required hygienic measures. Its responsible members look for professional help from medical doctors as soon as the need arises. Initially they also try to separate themselves from the people who are viewed as a great risk for their own health and safety. This reflex already manifested itself in ancient history by erecting walls around cities, closing the gate doors for people suffering from diseases such as the plague or leprosy.

- Every large community has dissenting minorities. Their ongoing protest against the centre community marks their attitudes. In their perception the dominant group has pushed them into an enclave by rejecting their non-conformism. They not only denounce some of the core values of the dominant group, but also reject its high level of structure and regulation. In the past, all homosexuals would be categorized as deviants or dissenters. Nowadays, in many countries homosexuality is widely accepted and discriminating them is forbidden. Therefore, nowadays many homosexuals belong to the central community, and only part of them could be labeled as dissenting enclaves (strong group, weak grid) who favour the model of the strong body. These dissenting persons are stigmatized for their non-conformist behaviour. Therefore, they feel a strong urge to oppose all the ideas of the central community that are labeling them. Thus they enlarge the divide between themselves and the established. This process might drive them into the field of other dissenting groups like the people who strongly reject official medical science but belief in a natural lifestyle, alternative medication and macrobiotic food.
- The category of individualists among heterosexuals and homosexuals supports the model of porous or half-protected body (Weak group, weak grid). Individualists are iconoclasts as well as pioneers in taste and fashion, in art and science, and in commerce and industry. From time to time they come up with new designs, techniques, inventions and products that are useful for the central community as well as for the dissenters. They like to take risks and lead a hectic life style that might put too much stress on their body. When they fall ill they will eagerly look for any kind of official, innovative or alternative medical treatment that might help them recover as soon as possible.
- Isolates appear as a residual category. Like the individualists, they are not incorporated in any social group. With reference to the topic of analysis here the proverbial examples are drug addicts and prostitutes, in particular drug-addicted prostitutes. They find themselves in a situation without autonomy. They have lost control over their body. Their whole live is regulated by their dependency on illegal drugs and the need to get the financial resources to pay for the drugs or to earn enough money for their pimp (Weak group, strong grid). Because they are so isolated they do not have to legitimize their actions towards their fellows. They do not want to take risks but are not expressly averting risks either. Their choices are very idiosyncratic. Because of their isolation their ideas can also be completely ad odds with the common opinion.

Members of the central community share core values and criticize anyone who clearly deviates from the group norms. Local leaders in the liberal professions, law, medicine, and the civil service all belong to this dominant group. The centre community has much social influence. In Bourdieu's terminology they are well endowed with economic, cultural and social capital. Moreover, since they are closely interconnected, e.g. through marriage, they share the same view on good health, good food, and safe sex. Actually, after the AIDS pandemic emerged, the use of condoms has increased strongly. The central community rejects alternative medicine, folk medicine, and popular 'panaceas'. Since it sees 'deviant' sexual practices as the main cause for the outburst of the epidemic, they focus their attention on the married couple as the norm and enduring monogamous relations as the best practice. In the beginning of the AIDS epidemic they also wanted that the centre community and the groups at risk such as prostitutes, drug addicts and promiscuous homosexuals would organize their own segregated lives. Mary Douglas even feared that the centre community would be very reluctant to invest a lot of money into medical research that apparently would only be of interest for a relatively small and well-defined category of 'deviant' people. By now, we know that responsible governments of modern societies and the pharmaceutical industry have invested a lot financial resources in this line of research, maybe because it soon had become obvious that complete segregation of groups was an illusion and the centre community also had become a group at risk.

Dissenting minorities are always present in the city. Because the center core is seen to be hierarchical and oppressive to the dissenters, the latter espouse equality. In this case, the dissenters are the people whose sexual practices are very risky. The dissenters that constitute modern cultural enclaves reject the knowledge base of the central community. A characteristic enclave style of knowledge emerged in the last century, in particular among artists, architects, and non-academic intellectuals. They introduced healthy fashions in taking exercise, clothing, eating, and emphasizing natural products, unadulterated by chemicals and other artificial materials. They believed in the strong body that should be taken care of in a natural way. They were and still are highly suspicious of the intentions and products of the pharmaceutical industry and the tests, diagnoses and deeds of doctors. In their view surgeons seem far too eager to cut open everybody's body and to remove essential parts or to replace them with artificial substitutes. Not all homosexuals belong to this group. Actually many homosexuals belong to the central community. Many do not show their homosexuality, live a respectful public life like ordinary people, and keep their sex-life to their private sphere, whereas others feel no restraint to hide their homosexuality, are completely open about this and often are inclined to show their sexual nature to everyone. And there are typical cases that thought that the connection revealed between aids, promiscuity and homosexuality was just another myth produced by the established heterosexual community to stigmatize the homo scene.[81]

In general, homosexuals support the idea of the two skins. Besides the natural skin one needs an extra skin based on precautionary measures, such as using condoms, but also by avoiding contact with the saliva or blood of HIV infected patients. Many homosexual citizens, after being labeled as groups at risk, developed solidarity in shared adversity. Pressed to give up promiscuous sex, they asked the establishment to grant them the same rights as heterosexual couples, such as the right to be married and to adopt children. However, very few governments did grant them marriage rights. So, for Mary Douglas, it is no wonder that the general mood is one of hostility to the central community. Rejection triggers rejection. In the beginning of the epidemic, when no cure was at hand, they appeared to belong to a doomed community in which friends and buddies were dying or expected to die soon, whereas those who were not ill jet feared to be HIV-positive because they had been in intimate contact with HIV-positive friends in the past. In some cases, this atmosphere led to heroic fatalism. Many homosexuals started to glorify risk and to deride the cult of safety. Who would rightly want to live a safe life if that means no love, no passion, and no ecstasy?

A new group at risk are the MSM's (men that have sex with men, which could be heterosexuals, for example men in prisons) who, because of condom fatigue or other reasons practice bare backing – a general term for having sex without condoms. This practice, although only executed within a minority of a minority, emerged in the mid-nineties, probably because new forms of medical treatment of AIDS prolonged the life-chances of patients considerably. From then on some MSM's estimated that the risk of engaging in unprotected promiscuous behaviour had become very low. It seemed to have lost its lethal character. Others engaged in this risky behaviour just for the sake of getting more media attention, or because they romanticized making love without protection, or because they were stimulated by widely available pornography that showed this kind of sex. Some healthy people take part in group sex with HIV-positive patients, or so-called conversion parties, for reasons of solidarity; an act that almost certainly will lead to their conversion to the status of HIV-positive. Prostitutes who offer unprotected sex do this for reasons of attracting more clients. All these developments took place after Mary Douglas did write the essay 'The Self as Risk-taker'. This category could be labeled as dissenters of dissenters, because in a way everything is relative.

As all individualists, homosexual individualists do no belong to any exclusive group. You can find them in every educational and income level, though they tend to prefer types of occupations that offer much autonomy, such as the professions, the arts, show business, and brokerage. They are iconoclasts and innovators, pioneers and trendsetters. They are incurable risk-takers: their lifestyle involves them in a heightened risk of heart failure. But whenever they fall dangerously ill, they tend to remain hopeful and will look for entrepreneurial therapists who will try the latest medical techniques and medication. They will avoid quacks but search for doctors with a high reputation. Their attitude does remind us of the mind of the adventurer, described by Georg Simmel. On the one hand they are fatalists, but on the other hand they have a strong feeling that they are special and that fate will treat them favourably. Mary Douglas quotes the answer of one homosexual with a risky lifestyle: *I have always had the feeling, since I was a child that I would live to be old.*

In general, individualists accept that the body is porous. Hence anybody can fall ill; that is a fact of life. But as to therapy, they are always hopeful. As experienced entrepreneur, innovator or trendsetter, they prefer entrepreneurial therapists, who are prepared to try the latest in surgical techniques and pharmaceutical help.[82]

We see that each type shows a different attitude to the knowledge of professionals. This variety is related to differences in level of education and income. In the central community the authority of the medical profession is accepted. They acknowledge its ideas about hygiene and diet. In fact, the norms and prescriptions of the medical professions are generally considered as core elements of the prevailing system of norms and prescriptions. In contrast, the real dissenters reject the knowledge base of the central community along with its authority. For them, the learned professions are suspect. The dissenters have segregated themselves from the centre in many respects. They tend to be unimpressed by the prestige of the medical establishment, and stay completely open to alternative medical advice. However, enclaves of aids patients, like all enclaves, tends to gather around charismatic spokesmen, who favour alternative therapies or methods of prevention such as 'healthy eating', in particular macrobiotic food. Modern 'enclave medicine' is based on a long tradition of people, in particular artists and intellectuals of the Arts and Crafts movement that introduced healthy fashions in taking physical exercise, clothing, eating. It emphasized natural products, raw foods, and consistently placed itself against 'artificial' food and clothing. It protested against surgeons, which they compared with butchers, plumbers, or constructors, and the pharmaceutical industry that they did not trust at all but saw as greedy profit makers who mistreated animals in all kinds of horrible tests and did not care about the negative side-effects of their pills and potions. The enclave developed a coherent thought style that counseled against adulterated foods, against stimulants and sedatives, against artificial additives and protested against the mass production of fast foods. They prefer homespun, folkloristic remedies.

8.9   In conclusion

This chapter should have made clear why the work of Mary Douglas is not only widely used in anthropology but also in sociology. Mary Douglas has always advocated a broader scope for anthropological research. In her view, the day that anthropologists give up their attempts to ground meanings in politics and economics will be a sad day. The loss will not so much be for themselves as for the social sciences and social life in general. Anthropology should be relevant for pre-modern as well as for modern societies. Like all modern anthropologists she does not think that the natives of developing countries are fundamentally 'other' than us. There is no basic natural difference between people that our predecessors called primitives and us; the difference is cultural and socially constructed. Human beings, in all their variety, are busying themselves about two things: trying to make sense of the world and trying to coordinate their lives with the people around them. Therefore, things we can learn and discover by studying humans on far away isles in the Pacific Ocean, deep in the heartland of Africa, or in the damp rain forests of South America, can be very relevant for modern post-industrial societies. This is one of her most cherished mantras. She is convinced that we cannot understand modern societies if we do not understand traditional societies and civilizations. She will often remark that anthropological insights in non-western cultures can be very useful for solving scientific questions about our western society. Hence, anthropologists should engage in all the major social and political issues of the modern world. They should engage in social theory in its broadest sense.[83] I doubt whether the majority of anthropologists have followed her call, but she surely has turned her own advice into good practice.

Richard Fardon has thoroughly studied the work of Mary Douglas. This resulted in a whole monograph, simply titled: Mary Douglas. Herein he discusses her life and her work extensively. He concludes, rightfully, that she has covered a broad range of topics, refusing to be deterred by disciplinary boundaries, and always manifesting a startling amount of cultural imagination.[84] He admires the way in which she combines the mundane and the esoteric, the common and the scientific, the funny and the serious in her treatment of the classification of the good and the bad, the clean and the unclean, the safe and the dangerous. She has presented valuable new insights in religion and secularization, ritualism and anti-ritualism. She went on investigating topics that most of her colleagues shied away from, because they were deemed to be fruitless or just conservative topics. In the age of individualization she dared to return to Durkheimian topics such as the collective conscience or the thought styles of groups or societies. Precisely, the amount of critique this aroused was a clear manifestation of the existence of a dominant thought style within modern anthropology, sociology and affiliated disciplines. I assume that her work will be of longer lasting value than the more effervescent products of most self-declared modernists and postmodernists. Of course, this is just a hypothesis, which may be refuted within a few decades. For the moment, I think it is a good thing that some eminent scholars stick to the further analysis and investigation of what it is that binds groups, what does keep them functioning, and what functional equivalents emerge after important institutions appear to loose their grip on society. These issues will always remain relevant, no matter one's political affiliation.

9

PETER L. BERGER

AN ALTERNATIVE INTERPRETATION OF MODERNITY

Peter Berger introduced sociology to me. After two years of studying mathematics I read his *Invitation to Sociology*.[1] I was immediately fascinated by this original and lucid introduction. Three weeks later, I decided to become a sociologist. I am sure that this book has invited thousands of students to sociology, for Berger is an inspiring author. During his childhood he lived in Austria but after Hitler invaded his country he first moved to Israel and in 1946 migrated to the USA where he was granted citizenship. He studied in the USA and spent his whole academic career there. Peter Berger is the second American sociologist whose work will be discussed here. Though American, the work of this icon of sociology always remained strongly rooted in a European scholarly tradition made up by people like Karl Marx, Emile Durkheim, Max Weber and Alfred Schütz. However, Berger was also influenced by Herbert Mead.

This chapter will cover a wide range of examples of Berger's sociology, but in section 9.1 we will first present a short overview of his life and career. Section 9.2 attempts to characterize his work, which is not easy because it shows many influences. He, himself would rather call it humanistic, because it features a great concern with problems of the human condition. The aim of sociology should be to generate knowledge that helps to ease human suffering, but the limits of our knowledge should save us from big revolutions based on grandiose utopian plans. Hence, progress has to be achieved in a step-by-step approach. In section 9.3 his most famous book is discussed: *The Construction of Social Reality*. This is a sociological masterpiece that he produced in close cooperation with Thomas Luckmann. The construction of social reality is an on-going process of externalization, objectivation and internalization where society gets deeply ingrained in the individual and individuals become the carriers, producers, and reproducers of society. A special subsection is devoted to the way we experience our daily reality. This part of his work is inspired by the existential phenomenology of Alfred Schütz. Socialization plays a very important role in this process. This is dealt with in section 9.5. It features topics such as primary socialization and the issue of identity formation, which is a delicate issue in modern times. Section 9.6 presents more of Berger's views on modernity. He has not joined the big male choir of cultural pessimists who love to indulge in strong overstatements on the doom and gloom of modernity. This section treats Berger's insightful addition to the common sociological explanations of secularization. His defence of the social functions of traditional marriage is presented in the next section. In section 9.9, his views on capitalism are presented. His book *The Capitalist Revolution* presents a huge amount of data showing that in many respects capitalism is to be preferred over a centrally planned economy. Capitalism creates more wealth, more social equality and more democratic freedom. The chapter begins with Berger's invitation to sociology, so it is with some regret that the chapter has to end with a discussion of his article titled 'Disinvitation to Sociology'. Near the end of his career he had become extremely critical of mainstream sociology. He then uttered harsh critiques about the triviality of much empirical research, and cosmopolitan sociologists that remained quite parochial in the choice of their topics, perspectives and conclusions. He identified this and other tendencies as major reasons for the stagnation of sociology.

9.1   Life and career

Peter Ludwig Berger was born on 17 March 1929 in Trieste, Italy's most Austrian city, but was raised in Vienna. In his youth Hitler invaded his country. Although the Berger family was Lutheran, the Nazis classified them as Jews. Aware of the danger, they left Austria to seek refuge in Israel, but they did not settle there. In 1946 they migrated to the United States and Peter Berger started to study theology. After one year he changed to philosophy and social science. In 1949, he graduated from Wagner College with a Bachelor of Arts degree and he continued his studies at the *New School for Social Research* in New York City. This academic institution acted as a safe haven for illustrious foreign philosophers and social scientists that had fled Europe after Hitler seized power. One of his famous teachers was the phenomenologist Alfred Schütz.[2]

Peter Berger received his M.A. in 1950 and his doctorate degree in 1954. He then he went back to Germany to work at the *Evangelische Akademie* in Bad Boll. From 1956 to 1958 he was assistant professor at the *University of North Carolina*. In 1958 he became associate professor at Hartford Theological Seminary. In 1963, he returned to the *New School for Social Research*. A few years later he was offered a full professorship at Rutgers University in New Brunswick. Since 1981 Berger has been Professor of Sociology and Theology at Boston University. In 1985 he became the director of the Institute for the Study of Economic Culture. A few years ago this research organisation was transferred into the Institute of Culture, Religion and World Affairs.

Peter Berger is married to Brigitte Berger, who is also a renowned sociologist. Like him, she has written several important books and is also a full professor.

Together they published an introduction to sociology and other books.[3] A photo on the back of the cover of *Redeeming laughter* shows Berger in his role of proud grandfather.

Berger has a great interest in the sociology of religion, which provided the topics for his first two books, *The Noise of Solemn Assemblies* and *The Precarious Vision*.[4] He passionately contended that the mainstream churches had failed to keep pace with social developments. They had done little more than legitimizing the existing political and social situation. Moreover, they lacked the religious sincerity and moral commitment required to confront the great social problems of modern society. At the time, these books had a great impact on the religious community of the US.[5] He would often return to this subject, careful not to treat it as some kind of religious marketing research, a type of research he abhorred. He labelled his own approach as methodological atheism. It featured a rational disposition and ascetic value-neutrality, as stipulated by Max Weber.

In the sixties, Peter Berger became very famous with the subsequent publication of three books. The first was the abovementioned *Invitation to Sociology* from 1963. Three years later he published *The Social Construction of Reality*, together with Thomas Luckmann. This bestseller was studied by a whole generation of students and is still in print today. The third one, *The Sacred Canopy* from 1967, also became very famous.[6] His fame rose considerably during the seventies, but started to dwindle in the eighties. Yet, I am convinced that Berger's work will hold his ground in theoretical sociology for many years to come.

The Vietnam War raised his political awareness. This led in 1970 to the publication of *Movement and Revolution*. He wrote the first part: *Between System and Horde: Personal Suggestions to a Reluctant Activist*. Richard John Niehaus, his good friend and theological sparring partner, wrote the second part of this political pamphlet.[7] Together with his wife and Hansfried Kellner he aired his displeasure about modernity in *The Homeless Mind: Modernization and Consciousness*.[8] However, he was not completely satisfied with this book, because the political perspective was pushed into the background. Within a year he produced a new monograph *Pyramids of Sacrifice*.[9] Here, he clearly distanced himself from both the capitalist system and the communist system. At the time, he did not believe either system was proficient for solving the huge problems of developing countries.

In the eighties, Berger started to re-evaluate capitalism based on the study of a wide range of literature on the theory and practice of communism and capitalism and a thorough analysis of empirical data from various economic studies. Since then Berger no longer viewed capitalism and communism to be on a par. His findings drove him towards the conclusion that capitalism was much better equipped to solve important social problems than communism was. His former reservations were based on his observations of the negative effects of capitalism in Latin America. Now he had become greatly impressed by the positive developments of emerging capitalist countries in East Asia. In 1987, two years before the demise of communism in Europe, he presented his new insights in *The Capitalist*

Revolution. The book contained a list of fifty propositions on affluence, equity, and freedom. It is a bold attempt to write a non-Marxist theory of capitalism. Politically, he had moved towards the right and evolved into a neo-liberal, although he preferred to be labelled a 'progressive conservative'.

In 1981, Peter Berger and Hansfried Kellner published *Sociology Reinterpreted: An Essay on Method and Vocation*. This sequel to *Invitation to Sociology* arose from their intention to redefine sociology in a concise and clear manner. They had noticed a significant change of climate in the field. Confusion was growing about presuppositions and procedures. Sociologists started to show a widespread and deepening dissatisfaction with their profession. The belief in the possibility of steering social developments and planning the world was quickly losing ground. Two World Wars, the holocaust, atomic bombs, economic crises, and ecological disasters had shattered Enlightenment optimism, while the tenacity of social problems such as poverty, racism, and crime did not help either. At the time, Berger and Kellner still believed in the potential strength of sociology and its power to render valuable insights in social structures and processes. With this essay they intended to revitalize sociology by revitalizing Max Weber's interpretative approach and a return to the big questions put forward by the founding fathers of sociology: How is the modern world different? What are its essential structures? Where is it going? How did it get that way? These questions were crucial to Comte, Marx, Weber, Durkheim, Parsons, and many others. According to Berger and Kellner, sociology cannot ignore these questions without losing a core element of its intellectual substance.[10] In the nineties, however, Berger became even gloomier. Instead of a new sequel to his earlier invitation he now wrote a 'disinvitation'. He repeated many of his former critical remarks about the state of the art of sociology, especially about its provincialism and triviality.[11]

At present, his oeuvre counts more than twenty books and numerous scientific articles. Already during his active career a complete volume was published with critical discussions of his work. Because Berger was given the opportunity to respond to his critics, we are now in a good position to find out what he really thinks. The title of this anthology (*Making sense of modern times*) perfectly fits Berger's oeuvre.[12] Just like all canonical sociologists he has made great efforts to interpret modern society. No wonder that one of his books is called *Facing up to Modernity*.[13]

9.2   Characterizing Peter Berger

If you want to characterize Berger's approach you have to begin with his strong affinity with the 'soft', non-quantitative side of sociology. In general, he does not have much faith in 'hard' variables such as birth rates or patterns of migration, but is far more interested in the significance attached to having a family or the subjective reasons for migration. But he does not stop here. Berger has always taken a great interest in the connections between social actions and the objective structures of society.

9.2.1   *The input of existential phenomenology*

The necessity of this double focus is made crystal clear in *The Social Construction of Reality*. Theoretically, Berger owes much to Marx, Durkheim, and Weber. He is indebted to Marx for his contributions to the sociology of knowledge. From Durkheim Berger borrows the methodological rule that society should be studied as if it were an object. He agrees with Weber that subjective meanings attached to social actions are the subject matter of sociology. He does not see these as two conflicting perspectives, but as complementary positions, because social reality has a subjective as well as an objective side. As these two sides constantly influence each other, a 'dialectical' approach is needed. He also owes a lot to Alfred Schütz who was his teacher at the New School for Social Research. Both Berger and Schütz were strongly influenced by the work of Herbert Mead, the founder of symbolic interactionism, a theoretical approach closely linked to phenomenology.

The primary focus of the existential branch of phenomenology is individual freedom or the free will. The major tenet of this perspective is the intentionality of human actions. Consciousness is always directed at specific objects.[14] With this concept of intentionality, phenomenology tries to bridge the gap between empiricism and intellectualism, between objectivism and subjectivism. Empiricists are convinced that human existence can only be understood by assuming that all things are separate, external to each other and causally related in such a way that each phenomenon is influenced by other objective phenomena. In this vision, there is no explanatory role for consciousness. On the other hand, philosophical idealists think that physical entities only become 'real' in our consciousness. They deny that the material world exists independently from our minds. Phenomenology attempts to connect these contrasting views. It argues that our consciousness is a consciousness of external objects. Obviously, the term external object has to be taken very broadly. We should not restrict ourselves to houses, rocks, and rivers, to people, plants, and animals. Also our own consciousness can be the object of our thinking.

Edmund Husserl, the founder of phenomenology, succinctly described the ubiquitous existence of the connection between consciousness and the reality of external objects. Perception is awareness of something. Desire, love, and hate always are directed at something or somebody. There is no such thing as a completely autonomous thought, a thought that is not related to something real. You are always thinking about something, remembering, fearing or fantasizing something. In short, you can only perceive, hear, feel, smell, or taste if there is something to perceive, hear, feel, smell, or taste. You can only think of something if there is something real to think about. So, phenomenology is the doctrine of the intentionality of all subjects directed at really existing objects. This theory also assumes that consciousness will be corrected or sharpened in the interchange between subjects and objects.[15] The world of objects corrects our mind. You cannot run away from reality. Perceptions of the world will always enter your mind. They are imposed on us and often thrust deeply into our awareness. This is certainly true for the social world. However, this is not to say that we will perceive everything in all its detail, completely, and in a pure form. Far from it, but the objective world has a corrective potential that adjusts most misconceptions.

It is quite easy to accept the major tenets of phenomenology as long it is concerned with the perception of the physical world. This is different once we address the social world. Then the question arises what we perceive when we perceive aspects of the social domain. In that case, according to Schütz, we perceive a universe of social relations between individuals. That world of interpersonal relationships constitutes an objectively perceivable reality, a reality that already existed before we were born, long before we started to think about these relationships. In fact, one of these interpersonal relationships brought our biological parents together to create our person.

Berger subscribes to the close connection between subjectivity and the world of real objects, which he thinks is applicable to the perception of one's own body and mind as well as to social institutions. He emphasizes that a human being not only *is* a biological body, but that it also *has* a biological body. In reflection, individuals can situate themselves outside themselves and look at themselves in a critical and observant way. They can ask themselves difficult questions: Who am I? What motivates me? What turns me on? What frightens me and why? People perceive their own selves as not identical to their biological existence. Their experience of themselves oscillates always between their whole being and their biological existence. A similar relationship exists for social facts or, if you prefer, social artefacts. They can only exist as a result of the social actions of individuals. As soon as they come alive, they start a life of their own that can be observed and analyzed by the individuals that have created them.

9.2.2   Humanistic sociology

The subtitle of *Invitation to Sociology* is *A Humanistic Perspective*. Berger has always shown a great compassion for the human condition, for the capabilities and limitations of human beings, with all their socially determined convictions and lifestyles. He is deeply aware of the fact that our knowledge is limited, and that our insights are biased by our social environment. It is important to realize this, because it prevents us from developing arrogant visions of the world as it should be. For this reason, he is very sceptical about revolutionary policies and utopian plans. All these plans are based on insufficient knowledge about today's world and an even greater ignorance about the future. Hence, we need to be very careful with any designs for the transformation for society, as the cure might be worse than the disease.

Modesty and prudence is advocated for other reasons too. Sociologists tend to analyze social phenomena from very different and even opposing perspectives and value systems.[16] The ideal social scientist should be interested in a broad spectrum of problems, issues, cultures and historical periods. Berger distrusts extreme specialization and the same is true for a fixation on methodological and technical aspects of research. In his view, data and statistical analysis can only turn into sociology if the outcomes are explained by a sociological theory. The tables in a research report become sociologically interesting only when they teach us something about social meanings, values, and institutions. Too much concentration on techniques is lethal for sociological imagination. This is not to say that Berger denies the usefulness of rigorous methods or correctly applied statistical analysis. On the contrary, they are essential for doing science. He only wants to emphasize that method and statistics merely provide the means for furthering social science. They are no end in themselves.

If we were to label Berger as a philosopher of science, we would call him a champion relativist. The realization that our knowledge is limited and also tainted by our culture turns him into a modest scientist and reluctant activist. Paradigmatically he feels at home in the realms of phenomenology and interpretative sociology, although he seriously attempts to bridge the gap between these approaches and a more objectivist and structuralist approach. His humanist disposition is manifested by a theoretical focus that has the human condition as its centre and circles around the idea that human beings incessantly are forced to construct and reproduce a social environment that continuously is influencing them. Undeniably, his political commitment is humanistic too. It is directed at a step-by-step approach to reduce human suffering. Because of the great risks for creating chaos, sorrow, and despair, he rigorously rejects revolutionary ideologies.

9.3   The social construction of reality

In all his studies Peter Berger emphasizes the constants of the human condition.[17] People can survive in almost any climate or geographical area. Once more this proves that humans are very flexible and malleable. At birth, the human organism is 'unfinished'. In comparison to other mammals, their biological instincts are underdeveloped. Hence, humans have to develop alternatives for their limited instinctual make up during early childhood. Moreover, humans can control their biological instincts, at least to a certain degree. Therefore, they are freer and less bound to their biological programme than animals. As a consequence, and in contrast to animals, people face an 'open world'. This terminology is typical for the phenomenology of Schütz, who asserted that the social world has the potential to expand continuously. By necessity, it is an open world. Hence, it makes sense to contend that man constructs his own nature or, more simply, that man produces himself.[18]

9.3.1   The foundations of Knowledge in Everyday Life

Man produces himself, but not on his own. He cannot survive as a solitary individual. Our body is equipped for a rather stable social environment that protects us against extinction or an existence at a subhuman or animalistic level. Social processes must create what our biological nature does not provide. Humanity is acquired by the activity of making sense of reality; this is a never-ending process.[19] We are condemned to make sense of everything, to make choices, and to take decisions. In that sense there is no absolute freedom. In the view of existentialists such as Sartre, our freedom to make choices and to take responsibility of the consequences of our decisions is the quintessence of our existence. Berger agrees. Even when someone threatens to kill us if we do not obey him, we still have the liberty to decide how we will respond. We can always reject the demands of our oppressors, as the stoic Epictetus taught us two millennia ago, though it might mean that we will be killed. Fortunately, most of the time social coercion is less extreme. Nevertheless, according to Sartre and Berger, it is a form of 'bad faith' if we forego our own choice or completely give in to social pressure. Precisely, by ascribing our yielding fully to these pressures, we help to reproduce these impositions. This view reveals a consistent ethic: there always is a margin of freedom, but we must never presume that man has complete freedom.

At the very day of his birth, each individual is confronted with a socially constructed social reality, imposed on him from day one. On the other hand, each individual has its own genetic idiosyncrasies and potential structure of character, which can in turn be imposed on his social environment. This reciprocal interchange between society and the individual, with its continuous tension between individual freedom and social coercion, was already on the agenda in *Invitation to Sociology*. Chapter four is titled 'Man in Society', followed by a chapter called 'Society in Man'. A few years later this theme is developed in *The Social Construction of Reality*.[20] In subsequent publications, Berger tries to maintain a theoretical balance between society's power over its members and the capability of people to reconstruct society. Continuously, he emphasizes the essential man-made character of the social world. The social order and its maintenance are always dependent on the manifold social actions of people compelled to execute specific actions because of their biological 'deprivation', in the terms of Gehlen.[21]

In a way, *The Social Construction of Reality* is an academic treatise on the sociology of knowledge. The concept of knowledge has to be apprehended much more broadly than scientific knowledge, philosophical ideas or religious beliefs. According to Berger and Luckmann, it should encompass everything that passes as knowledge in society at large. It should also concern the practical, common sense knowledge of ordinary people, the familiar knowledge that they need to live their lives.[22] Society and social beings could not survive a single day without the commonplace insights that guide conduct in everyday life. Hence, the knowledge of ordinary people is a central topic for sociology.

Traditionally the philosophy of knowledge occupied itself with the ideas of philosophers, politicians, and high priests, categories that make a profession of creating ideas or transferring ideas to others. Often their ideas evolve into complete worldviews.[23] However, according to Berger and Luckmann, worldviews and scientific theories are not that important. Although each society has such systems of thought, they only form a small part of the whole set of collective ideas. Only a few people are professionally involved in this kind of knowledge. But all people, including scientists, base most of their actions on knowledge that is not supported by scientific tests. This common knowledge forms the foundation of meanings on which the whole construction of society rests. That is why the sociology of knowledge should focus on social reality, as ordinary people perceive it. Traditional sociology of knowledge is chiefly occupied with the notion that human thinking is determined by the social-historical context, with the exception of mathematics and physics. The Ancient Greek scholars already made sensible guesses about the social determinacy of worldviews and dominant values, and Blaise Pascal too had already asserted that what is truth on one side of the Pyreneans could be untrue on the other side. It was Karl Marx who stated the basic tenet of the sociology of knowledge most succinctly: *'das Dasein bestimmt dass Bewustsein'.*[24] This could be translated as 'Existence determines consciousness.' or 'Being determines seeing'.

9.3.2 The holy trinity of social construction: externalization – objectivation – internalization

Society has an objective and a subjective reality. Every sociological explanation should include both aspects. Both will get due attention if society is seen as a kind of dialectical process that encompasses three sub-processes: externalization, objectivation or objectification, and internalization.[25] Only when we understand the interconnectedness of these three movements, can we acquire an adequate, empirically based view on society.[26] These three processes do not constitute a progressive dialectical process as described by Georg Friedrich Hegel. Objectivation is not a negation or an antithesis of externalization, and internalization is not the synthesis that brings the whole process to a higher level. The difference is that Hegel recognized a dialectical process in the historically logical sequence of social evolution, with the Absolute Spirit externalizing itself in the objectively observable behaviour of individuals, groups or even whole nations, bringing about a sort of learning process for the Absolute Spirit. Berger and Luckmann use this notion of objectivation to describe the production or constant reproduction of society as an interchange between actions of individuals and the collective norms and values that emerge when they engage in social action. The third step involves the return from the collective or social objectivity, to the consciousness and subconsciousness of individuals.

Externalization refers to the need of humans to confront the world with their words and deeds. Social agents have a need to show their feelings and intentions to other people. They have 'to tell their story' to friends and relatives, to colleagues and partners, and, when no one else is around, even to perfect strangers. These manifestations give rise to patterns of behaviour and social structures that acquire an objective character. The products of externalized behaviour, material as well as immaterial, acquire a type of transcendent reality that will be experienced as an objective fact external to the producers. As a consequence, these objectified structures start to have an impact on individuals.

Internalization is the process of subjectively re-appropriating the structures of the objective world. People transpose these objectivations to their own subjective values and meanings. It is a process of incorporation that involves learning to accept these objectivations and introjecting them as the most normal and sensible reality one can think of. No need is felt to question this reality, and in general, people do not even feel the urge to criticize a socially constructed reality, because they do not realize that it is socially constructed and it might just as well be different. This 'self-evidence' is the result of a socialization process that has been very successful in blinding people to the possibility of alternative social constructions and in making them believe that their life-world is the only sensible life-world.

Society is a human product, a consequence of the externalizations of all individuals. Through objectivation it becomes a *sui generis* and through internalization individuals become social beings.[27] The social construction of reality is, as suggested by Hegel and Marx, a consequence of the constant need of human beings to externalize. Man is an expressive being. But there is one more human constant, the disposition to socialize, or the need for what Simmel has called 'sociality'. A truly solitary existence from birth, assuming that this would somehow be possible, would imply an animalistic existence.

From the three components – externalization, objectivation, and internalization – the process of objectivation still is rather vague. How does objectivation arise from the social actions of individuals, how does a recognizable, observable, tangible, objectified social structure come about? In other words, how can individual actions give rise to a regulated collective behaviour, to social structures that acquire an object-like existence with some coercive power? The easiest answer is that each individual is born in an already structured world in which the majority presents or regards certain social phenomena as social facts, as objects or things that should be taken into consideration, taken care of, followed and kept alive such as traditions, norms, values, rules and regulations. Hence, social reality seems to the actor to be independent of the actor's apprehension of it; it appears already objectified, pre-given.[28] Therefore, it imposes itself on the actor to such a degree that he no longer sees it as imposition. It is taken for granted. From day one the infant learns to adjust to this apparently well-ordered social world. The young child has to adjust; it does not see any alternative. So, it learns to make sense of all these structures and learns to imitate the apt patterns of behaviour. This ensures that social order will be recreated continuously.[29] This habitualization has the important psychological advantage that not every action involves reflection. There are however more sides to the process of objectivation, as will become clear from a consideration of the phenomenon of institutionalization.

9.3.3   *Institutionalization and the social construction of reality*

As soon as individuals establish certain habits, institutionalization follows. From then on regular patterns, rules, and programs or ways of organizing are imposed on individuals by society.[30] At the macro-level subsystems such as education, the

economy, and the law are big and complex institutions that catch the eye immediately. But there are many smaller and less complex institutions of social organization. Wherever habitualization takes place, institutions arise as soon as the
group expects its members to conform to these newly created rules. This mutual-
ity is important. It is crucial that the majority of the group obeys the established
group rules and follows its customs. Institutions are crystallized customs that
have become law-like rules, prescribing specific types of behaviour for specific
occasions. They 'determine' what has to be done in particular situations. For example, judges should sentence the guilty according to certain preset boundaries
for a particular crime. Within this range they can take the circumstances of the
felony and, if relevant, the social background and the psychological state of the
accused into account. We expect the lawyer to do his utmost for the defence of his
client so that he may be acquitted or may be sentenced with only a minimal sentence. On the other hand, we expect the prosecutor to present his case as strongly
as possible, to present the court with all the necessary evidence and to plead for a
maximum sentence.

Institutions have causes and effects. They have a history and imply social control.
In general, they emerge gradually and not overnight, and once they are crystallized they start to control and canalize social behaviour. This element of control
is most evident in social institutions with a legal basis, that establish, in turn, a
complete subsystem of social control. When institutions lack such a formal legal
basis, their power is derived from the 'force of habit', a force strong enough to
influence people and to regulate their behaviour. Significant deviations from the
standard patterns evoke critical reactions and might lead to severe sanctions.

Institutionalization processes carry out the social construction, maintenance,
and reconstruction of social phenomena. But individuals have to sustain and legitimize this on a daily basis. That is why the human being, according to Berger,
is not only a *homo socius*, but also, as conceptualized by Marx, a *homo faber* – a
creator of the world and a cultivator of its culture. Society is a work in progress,
a never-ending story, involving a continuous activity of world-constructing. All
the time people are reproducing, renovating, repairing and re-establishing its
features. As a result society acquires a thing-like quality. Here Berger pays tribute
to Durkheim's view. The culture and structure of society remain real only in so
far as they are confirmed and reconstituted in and by the social actions and relations of individuals.

All institutions lean on the regulative pattern of language. Each institution depends on a language for the verbal presentation of all its inherent classifications,
concepts, and prescriptions. It is the first institution encountered by a young
child, who cannot invent his own language, at least not one that is understood by
others. Only when he starts to use signs, sounds or words that can be recognized
by adults, a meaningful communication will emerge.

Language is the most fundamental of all institutions because it structures the
perceived environment. Moreover, it helps to objectivate that reality. The continuous stream of experiences is crystallized, partitioned, and labelled into separate

objects that all appear to have group names such as cats, trees and houses. With the help of language, relationships can be established. For instance, the young child might soon learn that the red cat lives in the white house next to the tall tree. Language makes the social world more real. It describes its relations and by doing so it gives social elements an extra dimension, underlining their status as real existing phenomena; it objectivates the rules that control social reality. The does and don'ts of social behaviour are consistently specified by language. With the help of these linguistically fixed patterns we can easily learn the social rules and roles, including our own. Moreover, roles are institutions that also represent social institutions. The parent that punishes his or her child represents society – a society that judges his behaviour as deviant and undesirable. So, the role of the punishing parent represents the moral system of society.[31]

9.3.4   Main characteristics of institutions and the danger of reification

Institutions are recognizable by a few essential characteristics: externality, objectivity, social force, moral authority and historicity. An institution is something that exists outside the individual. It represents a 'hard' reality that can be distinguished from immaterial thoughts and feelings. For instance, one can have a rough encounter with the judicial system, with cultural traditions, or with group mores.

Institutions are real. They have an objective reputation. They are visible and their effects can be either directly or indirectly discerned. Legislation has been debated in parliament or congress, it has been written down in legal books, and it has been interpreted in real court cases and it has resulted in concrete penalties. In time, all this will result in a clear interpretation of the law and a just punishment for the offender. In similar vein, the majority of speakers of a national language agree about its proper usage. Grammar and spelling are described in instructive books and dictionaries. Already existing inconsistencies in grammar or spelling may become an accepted fact, which makes protest against the new rules useless. As a direct consequence of these characteristics, institutions have power. Individuals cannot ignore the external and objective reality of institutions, or wish them away. Those who neglect to fulfil their duties towards their friends or employers, run the risk of becoming lonely or losing their job. Incomplete integration in the dominant institutions of a society can mean a severe handicap. For example, migrant children with a limited proficiency in the language of instruction are severely disadvantaged and are likely to achieve less than their native peers that are fully socialized in the national language of education.

The acknowledgement of the objective and powerful character of institutions does not imply that they will never change. On the contrary, most institutions change continuously, albeit incrementally, because they are the product of meaningful actions of numerous individuals. Take language. New words or meanings flourish while other words become obsolete, depending on changes in the means of production, in value systems, in society or in the world.[32] In the legal domain, too, we see that new rules and regulations are introduced and other laws are changed or abolished. Nevertheless, most institutions are rather stable. Changes take place at a slow pace. Often, alterations are resisted or held up. The introduction or abolition of laws requires lengthy political procedures before they are accepted and put into practice. The same is true for major innovations in the content and structure of education.

This excursion brings us to the two last characteristics: moral authority and historicity. Institutions assert their legitimacy. Those who do not obey the rules, run the risk of being sanctioned. The over-ambitious intellectual, with his misplaced jargon, will sooner or later learn that he does not quite fit in. The same is true for the migrant worker who, after many years of residence, still mixes up his second language. The non-middle class policeman, who tries to speak impeccable English, may make peculiar mistakes because of hypercorrection of grammatical rules. The cross he bears is imposed on him by a category of people who always use the legitimized, standard language; a point also highlighted by Pierre Bourdieu.

Institutions are historical facts. Some emerge at present, and certainly more will arise in the future, but most institutions that exist today have a history that dates from before we were born. Hence, individuals always are confronted with habits, rules, and customs that already existed before they were born. Numerous ancestors have imprinted specific meanings onto these institutions. Although these ancestors passed away long ago or even centuries ago, the institutions they have established are still very much alive.

To what extent is an institutional order objectivated as a non-human entity? This is a question of great theoretical interest. Reification (*Verdinglichung*) is the apprehension of socially created phenomena as if they were non-human things – such as facts of nature or manifestations of divine will. Reification implies that people tend to forget their own authorship of the social world. It implies that the interaction between the human producer and his product is lost to consciousness. This happens easily with institutions that already existed long before we were born. These are experienced as strange entities, alien products and beyond control of ordinary people, for example 'the government', 'capitalism' or 'the law'. But as citizens, we should never forget that even ancient laws, customs or traditions can also change or fade away. So, as soon as an objective world is established, we must be aware of the fallacy of reification, of the effect that the social world, its rules and organizations, are experienced as something outside ourselves. Sociologists should never cross the thin line between objectification and reification and always alert people to this fallacy.[33]

Reification is the ultimate step in the process of objectivation, when the objectivated world has lost its comprehensibility as a human enterprise which is subject to change because it is affected, produced and reproduced by humans. The available ethnological and psychological evidence indicates that reification is widespread, especially with children and in pre-modern societies. Not long ago, marriage was reified as an imitation of the divine act of procreation, as a holy fulfilment of God's law to fill the world with new generations, as the necessary consequence of biological or psychological forces, or, if you wish, as a functional imperative of the social system. What all these reifications have in common is their obfuscation of marriage as an ongoing human institution. Nowadays, marriage has lost its aura of holy matrimony. Presently, it is simply seen as a personal choice of two people. A formal marriage is no longer required to legally establish a family or regulate the sexual drive. Roles too, for example, may be reified and apprehended as an inevitable fate. Individuals in specific roles often say: 'I have no choice. As a mother, father, chairman, or headmaster I have to act this way.' In fact, they dehumanize both themselves and their role, forgetting that the set of role expectations is socially constructed and subject to change.[34]

Berger does not believe that society fully determines human behaviour, or that individuals are moulded according to a pre-designed blueprint. I refer to the sections on his theory of socialization, although the intriguing question of where social influence stops and individual self-determination starts is not answered here. Like all other social theorists Berger cannot give even a rough indication of the proportion of human behaviour that can be accounted for by social determinants. For him, it suffices to emphasize that the individual is not completely moulded or controlled by social forces. There is room for each individual to act according to his own will and intentions; what is more, this is how he really interacts with his social environment. Society does not unilaterally impose its will on the individual. Evidently, the assumption that there is some playing field for individuals to express their autonomy is necessary to the idea of mutual interactions and a mutual influence between the objective and the subjective side of social reality. Without this elbowroom for individual manoeuvring, there is no 'dialectic interaction' between society and the individual. Without such reciprocity, individuals would just be puppets on the strings of social forces, and society would always stay the same and never alter. It is obvious that this is not the case. So, we can argue by *reductio ad absurdem* that, to a certain extent at least, man has a free will.

9.3.5   *The experience of everyday reality*

Once it is established that the social world is the product of human actions, we can tackle the question what everyday reality looks like. Berger insists that at first the world appears to us as an unintelligible chaos. We are compelled to filter and cluster information in order to come to grips with that complexity. Specific symbols are attached, for example, to certain facts while simultaneously a host of others are ignored. We only use a dozen different words to distinguish all the colours of nature, for example, although eye specialists have found that it is theoretically possible for us to differentiate between more than six million colours or shades of colours.

A second basic tenet of Berger's ideas is that everyday reality is overwhelming and tends to dominate everything. Building on the phenomenological work of Schütz he asserts that we construct a world that we share with others, a world that can be called everyday reality. Phenomenological sociologists investigate the many ways of digesting social reality, by dividing it into specific sectors and separate categories.

In everyday reality, a great importance is attached to the here and now. We perceive our immediate surroundings as very real. The same is true for whatever is happening now. We experience time as a phenomenon that irrevocably proceeds from the past to the future. Bygones are bygones; there is no 'back to the future,' no 'replay function' for the past. Whenever we turn to memories or speculate about the future, we are enclosed in the confinements of our minds, in our world of dreams and fantasies.

Thirdly, everyday reality is perceived in pragmatic terms. It is the world of labour, of production, a world where people are evaluated and classified on the basis of their useful contributions to society. This is seen as the real world. This world can claim our full attention, our full commitment. Here we have to accomplish our most important goals.

The fourth characteristic of everyday reality is the constant need for full alertness. We always have to be alert not to miss splendid opportunities that might come our way or for potential danger that may destroy our (social) life. This constant need to be awake at all time is essential for the daily reproduction of everyday reality.

The fifth characteristic is our disposition to ignore any doubts about everyday reality. Here we see a clear difference between our everyday reality and reality as perceived by scientists. It is a basic disposition of every scientist to cast doubt on every aspect of life and to research whether his doubt can be grounded on observational data or test results. Ordinary people would be very much annoyed if everything and everybody was doubted. A general lack of trust in people will reduce social participation, collective action and the economy.[35]

Finally, Berger believed that everyday reality is partitioned into small pieces. Every partition demands a partial commitment of all our skills and knowledge. The skills we use when driving a car are different from those we use when cooking. We constantly try to reduce the complexity of our world so that we can concentrate on the task at hand. This increases our effectiveness considerably. As a consequence, we live in an efficient world, an orderly world where most events take place in a routine fashion. It is a relatively safe world, a world we can trust. Only in very exceptional cases will the physical world take us off guard with unsuspected disasters, such as floods, earthquakes or avalanches. Only in exceptional cases will the social world confront us with deviating lifestyles, shocking opinions, riots, acts of terrorism, revolutions or even wars. In general, we know what to expect in our part of society. Its orderly and predictable character makes social life rather simple and easygoing for most of us. Because we all operate on the basis of a common set of meanings, we quite easily socialize with other people from the same society.[36]

Assumptions about everyday reality held
by Alfred Schütz and Peter Berger

1 We perceive everyday reality as an orderly and conveniently arranged whole, because we filter out chaos and reduce complexity

2 We experience everyday reality as the all overpowering reality that we share with others

3 We see the practical, concrete reality of work and production as the most essential reality

4 We have to be alert all the time, because everyday reality is full of opportunities as well as risks

5 We are inclined to ignore all doubts about everyday reality.

6 We divide everyday reality into sectors. This helps us to concentrate on specific tasks. It makes reality more practical and behaviour more efficient.

Box 9.1

9.4   Comic relief: a necessary interlude

One of Schütz's major contributions to our understanding of everyday reality and human existence was his specific delineation of what people experience as reality and what as extraordinary. He was particularly interested in the relation between the reality of the ordinary, everyday life, which he called the paramount reality – Berger prefers to term them 'sub-universes' – and those islands within the latter, which he called 'finite provinces of meaning'. The paramount reality is the reality which is most real to us. Sub-universes are experienced as the individual temporarily leaves the paramount reality of ordinary life. Examples of taking leave of ordinary life are dreaming, day-dreaming, experiencing sublime works of art, getting high from taking drugs, being overwhelmed by beautiful music, enjoying orgiastic sex, undergoing an intense religious experience, or seeing or hearing something so comic that one bursts into uncontrollable laughter. Though these examples all still are part of the wider reality of human existence, they can bring people into a trance, or generate a state of ecstasy, which is derived from the Greek *ek-stasis*, meaning standing outside. Moreover, they are set apart by a specific 'cognitive style' and one has to pass a psychological barrier or undergo a kind of shock to get back to ordinary reality.[37] Instead of the positive examples given here there are also bad experiences of the extra ordinary, such as finding yourself in a very bad dream, a terrible nightmare, or in a real terrifying situation such as a car crash, a bombardment, or being shot at by a sniper. All these are also forms of sub-universes that have their own logic, such as giving the highest priority to your own safety, ignoring the fact that your partner or child needs to be saved too. This has happened to people trying to free themselves from a crashed and burning plane. Adults may have lost control over their sphincter muscles and dirtied themselves like a baby as a consequence of an extreme angst for dying. Berger has written an interesting book about laughter and the comic experience, one of the positive sub-universes of reality. His point is that laughter brings relief, relief from the tedious, serious and tragic sides of human existence. It acts like a counterforce against subordination. The stronger the sense of powerlessness, the greater the need to make jokes about the powers that be. The capacity to laugh and make jokes is a unique and a universal human talent. We may observe animals at play, but animals behaving comically or making fun of each other do not exist. Maybe because animals aren't aware of the fact that they are mortal, they have less need for comic relief. They do not understand the whole concept of the comic, that is, the emergence or creation of situations that stand so far apart from the everyday events in life that people feel a strong impulse to laugh about it. Often this occurs when the high and mighty is unexpectedly put in a weak and vulnerable position or when traditional roles are reversed.

Berger ends his book Redeeming Laughter with a theology of the comic. Here he observes that all the monotheistic religions, the world religions stemming from Abraham, hardly ever mention laughter or the comic side of life.

9.5   Symbolic interactionism and socialization

When Berger introduced his theory, socialization was mainly described and explained from the perspective of social control. Primarily, socialization was seen as the imposition of social control, supported by a system of reward and punishment. At the time, sociologists were accused of an 'over-socialized' conception of man.[38] Berger does not deny that each individual is confronted with numerous attempts to control his behaviour. *Every individual is born into an objective social structure within which he encounters the significant others who are in charge of his socialization. These others are imposed upon them. Their definitions of his situation are posited for him as objective reality.* [39] From the moment of their birth, babies interact with their physical and social environment. Their social background will determine whether they will be nurtured with the bottle or breast-fed by their mother or a wet nurse. Certainly, it will determine the type and quality of their clothing and the frequency and sort of attention they will get from their parents.[40] In this way, newborn babies are in close contact with the macro-world of society as a whole. The prevailing views on child rearing will have an impact on their biological functioning. If mothers or other caregivers adhere to a rigid scheme of feeding times, the body will adjust and the infant will be hungry at the right time. With this impressive example, Peter and Brigitte Berger illustrated the impact of macro social forces on the micro world of families and newborn babies.[41]

9.5.1   *Socialization and social determinism*

A child is born and raised in a country with a vast array of customs, laws, rules, and regulations that it is expected to obey. The state has established an entire organization of professional controllers and supervisors: policemen and women, prosecutors, judges, and prisons wardens, to mention a few. And, last but not least, each household develops its own rules for maintaining a peaceful co-existence. Deprivation of love and affection is a very effective way to correct undesirable behaviour within this social micro-world. Yet, Berger is convinced that everybody has the means to escape from intolerable social pressure. In the first place, social control can never be total. Even in a police state it is impossible to control everybody at all time, day and night. Moreover, the rules can be changed, circumvented and manipulated. If people no longer want to remain loyal to the system, they can protest or move to other places. Hirschman summarized these options as exit, voice, and loyalty.[42] Merton mentioned the following options besides conformity: innovation, ritualism (or fake-conformity), retreat, and rebellion.[43]

People can try to discuss the legitimacy of the imposed rules and demand change or abolishment. Berger notes that processes of ideological critique have preceded every revolution. He considers the non-acknowledgement and the alternative definition of social norms as a potentially revolutionary action.[44] He has a keen eye for the possibility of a redefinition of norms and values. This, once more, shows that he does not see socialization as a one-purpose instrument for social control and society-maintenance. In his view it is also an instrument for individual development.

According to Berger, the fundamental processes of socialization are interaction, identification and internalization. This triad of processes is very similar to the one put forward by Durkheim, who used similar terms, though he mentioned co-operation instead of interaction. Individuals learn to recognize, accept, and appropriate the attitudes, norms and values from the socializing agents with whom they interact frequently. Through empathy they learn to identify with someone else's role. Finally, through internalization, it becomes a part of their personality. Thus, socialization creates the basis for an understanding of the meaning of social events, for the apprehension of the world as a meaningful reality.[45] To a great extent, this involves learning to understand fellow-human beings. Socialization is the process of a child's learning to become an active member of society. To a great extent, socialization is the imposition of social patterns on individual behaviour. It can be a very powerful process. This is all the more so, because young children have no idea of the possible alternative patterns of behaviour in other regions, countries, and classes. They will experience the culturally determined patterns of their upbringing as the normal and valid form of pedagogy. They simply take them for granted. Only much later, they learn that alternatives do exist; that other social groups have different customs and values. The stability and uniformity of the child rearing practices and other social patterns offer young children a solid basis for getting a grip on their social environment.[46]

Growing up also implies becoming a person with a well-established objective and subjective identity. These can be further developed, although society tries to keep people in their prescribed role and place. One can view socialization as a top-down process within which the child is stuffed with all kinds of rules and customs from society, supported by a process of social control that functions thanks to a rigid system of sanctions. One can also approach this from a more positive angle and see socialization as a prolonged process of initiation into the social world of adults.[47] Socialization enables children to prepare themselves for a world that is already out there and waiting for them, though it is not waiting for children but for civilized and well-trained grown-ups. Without socialization there simply is no social life. Socialization makes the world less strange, less chaotic and more meaningful. Gradually, the world becomes recognizable, reasonably safe, and self-evident. Thus we learn to participate in and contribute to this social world. Simultaneously, we also acquire a clear view on our social position and develop our social identity.

It should be emphasized that socialization is not a one-sided, top-down process. There is no such thing as a passive victim of socialization. Even the very young show a will and express disgust or their preferences. They may cry or smile. With these emotional expressions they can exert an influence on their parents, a potential that gets stronger as they grow older. They learn to predict how their parents will react to specific actions. When they start to talk, they can explicate their wishes and desires and they learn to reject, argue, and talk back effectively. Socialization, therefore, is not a case of a mechanistic determinism, but involves a long process of communicative interactions in which the ego has an active role too.

9.5.2   The legacy of Herbert Mead

Herbert Mead strongly influenced Berger's theory of socialization. Mead's work forms the basis for symbolic interactionism and deserves some closer attention here. In this approach a central role is attributed to the verbal and non-verbal interchange of symbols that represent specific intentions and meanings. Mead was a contemporary of Durkheim and Weber. He was a modest man, who lived a quiet and unobtrusive life from 1863 to 1931. But, according to the great American pedagogue John Dewey, he had 'the most original mind in philosophy in America of the former generation.'[48] Mead was strongly influenced by the pragmatist William James, by his colleague Charles Horton Cooley and by his friend, John Dewey.

For contemporary scientists, who are continuously pressed to publish papers, articles, reports, and books, it is quite remarkable to learn that Mead hardly published anything during his lifetime. He had written a great deal, but never saw it fit for publication. His main ideas were published posthumously by some of his best students who had taken many notes from his lectures, titled *Mind, Self and Society*, as well as *George Herbert Mead on Social Psychology*.[49] As that title shows, psychology was to Mead more important than sociology. Yet symbolic interactionism is a very important current of sociological thought, even though some consider it too unsystematic and *'an intentionally constructed vagueness'*.[50] Zijderveld's evaluation is much more positive, although he asserts that you will not find any systematic theory in Mead's work.

The basic tenets of symbolic interactionism	
1 People act in reaction to things and events on the basis of the meanings that these things and events have for them; 2 These meanings are the product of	social interactions; 3 These meanings are adapted and remodelled by each individual when he or she receives and interprets the signals of fellow human beings.[51]

Box 9.2

The theoretical starting point for Mead is that man is a thinker, someone able to reflect upon himself and others. He is conscious of himself as himself. In a manner of speaking human beings can observe their actions and evaluate them as if they were objectively evaluating a stranger. Other animals do not have this capacity for critical self-reflection. According to Mead, this is the crucial difference between men and animals. This difference is enlarged by our capacity to handle symbols. A symbol is a sign with an agreed meaning for everyone involved in regular interaction processes. As a psychologist Mead was very much interested in thought and consciousness, and his sociological disposition made him realize that the emergence and further development of thought is closely connected to the interaction processes between people. He agreed with William James that human thought is developed by the search for the solution of all kinds of practical problems that arise from the co-existence of people. Thinking is like a discussion between two partners, an internal discussion with the 'generalized other' in our consciousness. Before we take a decision, we reflect on the most likely or entirely predictable reactions of significant others. We frequently experience such internal discussions, about for example a job application, changing places, ending friendships, including trivial decisions about what present to give to a friend.

The precondition for the development of self-awareness is that we, in our daily contacts, learn what others think and how others tend to evaluate a situation. Mead has called this process role taking. Children as well as adults continuously try to understand everyone who is close, a process that presumably involves trying out various interpretations. Mostly, the other reacts according to our initial interpretation or expectations. If this is not the case, we evaluate the situation quickly and try other interpretations that make more sense, that is to say, that fit a more general frame of reference for the interpretation of human behaviour. As soon as children learn to talk- and maybe even before that - they can correct invalid interpretations of the actions of their parents, siblings, and others. They also learn to distinguish between gestures that support or contradict the verbal communication and learn to distil the 'real' message.

When discussing the process of socialization, Berger follows Mead's theoretical concepts closely.[52] First, children learn about social roles from their mother or father. They start to imitate these roles as they grow up, playing 'mother', for example when playing with other children. Soon they also learn to understand and imitate the roles of other people. These are what Mead called the *significant others*. This then is generalized when the circle broadens and the child becomes familiar with the *generalized other*. At this stage, the new roles are no longer linked to concrete persons, but are like representations of larger groups or social categories, such as the typical, expected roles for men and women, specific age groups or professions. By mentally adopting the role of others, individuals also learn more about their own roles and social position. The interaction with other people helps us then to establish a well-organized and stable self-identity.

Analytically Mead divides this self-understanding in 'I' and 'Me'. 'Me' encompasses the residue of everything that is internalized of the 'Generalized Other'. It is the social component of the 'Self', the social component of identity. 'I' refers to the 'essential' individual component, to the authentic, expressive element that is not socially determined. The foundation of 'I' refers to the unique characteristics each individual is endowed with by birth. In Mead's view both the 'I' and the 'Me' constitute human behaviour. Social action is the result of the internal communication between both components of the self. It is the result of a discourse about what the individual really would like to do and what his socially constructed inner voice, representing the 'generalized other', tells him to do or not to do. For Peter Berger, the attractiveness of this approach lies in this tension between both components. This proposition of an internal discussion with society counters the one-dimensional image of a completely socially determined perspective on socialization and social integration.

9.5.3   *Primary socialization*

Sigmund Freud, Erik Erikson, and Talcott Parsons sketched socialization as a many phased process. Each subsequent phase can only be reached through a painful emotional crisis.[53] Berger disagrees totally. In his view the process of role learning derives its strength from its 'unconscious' and easy-going character. Children are very flexible and adaptable. Moreover, like most people they simply want to belong and to be liked. They will share experiences with other people and develop reference groups that supply the models to which they can compare themselves and develop their social identity, an identity that suits the social roles they have to accomplish. At the same time, those reference groups present a particular philosophy about the meaning of life and the character of our society.

Berger stresses the importance of a strong emotional bonding with significant others for the realization of identification processes. Young children internalize society through identification with people who already have incorporated the dominant norms and values of society, and already behave in socially acceptable ways. Moreover, they identify with the people they love, like, or admire and so 'understand' the deeds of other people. They see that it makes sense, at least in the sense of 'that is the way it ought to be' or 'it has always been that way'. The voices of significant others become inner voices and constitute a conscience. The net result is that socialized agents tend to stick to the rules of society. Consciously as well as subconsciously they will behave as people are supposed to behave. Thus, they tend to reproduce society with all its rules, customs and traditions.

Primary socialization ends when children break away from the small circle of the family, when they go to school, or become a member of sports clubs or other organization. Outside the parental home, they will encounter new significant others and a lot more less significant others. By then, primary socialization has laid a strong basis for further socialization, strong enough to take the shock of meeting people with strange and hitherto unfamiliar roles, views, and lifestyles. The primary life-world, the life-world that was internalized during primary socialization, was accepted uncritically and has provided the touchstone for assessing significant others. That is why primary socialization takes up a privileged position in the life-long process of socialization. Strong impulses are needed to effect a fundamental change in that basis of accepted role models, norms, and values. Thus, re-socialization into a quite different cultural setting, for example, will require more effort and might cause some tension. For this reason it is often assumed that children of migrants experience difficulties, as they have to juggle two different cultural environments. However, few studies show that these problems exist on a large scale. For instance, research demonstrates that migrant children attend primary school with as much if not more pleasure as indigenous children. Their self-image is not less positive than that of their indigenous classmates or peers.[54] This seems to support the view that young children are capable of a rather 'effortless' socialization, even under relatively complex circumstances, with even some striking differences between the home culture and the cultural climate at school. Apparently, they understand quickly that not all rules apply to all situations. Different situations are connected to different demands, rules and roles. As soon as they enter a familiar situation, they know what actions are expected or not. As highly flexible and intelligent beings they can immediately, within a split second, modulate their 'improper' actions as soon as a parent, teacher, or policeman unexpectedly arrives on the scene. Besides, the culture-clash paradigm seems to overlook the fact that many pedagogical values are the same for all cultures and ethnic groups. All parents want their children to be friendly, cooperative, 'civilized', good humoured, honest and so on. Thus, the cultural differences refer to only a small subset of norms, such as whether an adult should be looked at directly or whether it is more proper to avert one's gaze when addressed. Both acts are in fact concerned with a shared underlying value: respect must be shown to one's elders.

9.5.4   The development of our identity

At some points Berger seems to forget his main assertion that a process of dialectical interaction goes on between individuals and their social environment. He then writes that one's social role is ascribed by society and that society determines, supports and alters someone's social identity.[55] The 'objective' social identity that is imposed on us is acquired through processes of interaction with our socializing agents. These will influence our character and identity, though not in a completely arbitrary way. They react on our position, attitude and on how we present ourselves. We need other people to tell us who we are. Only when enough significant others have confirmed our own sense of identity, can we assume that these descriptions closely fit our perception of what we think is our real identity. In other cases we will reflect on the reasons why there is such a disturbing discrepancy between our own image of ourselves and what other people perceive. In some cases this could lead to an adjustment of our identity or self-image.

Identity is not something 'given' at birth or imposed on us by society, but bestowed in acts of social recognition. Cooley argued that someone's self or identity grows from one's interaction with others. Your self-awareness is a reflection of how others perceive you, aptly expressed in Cooley's well-known metaphor of the self as a looking glass self. This notion is composed of three elements: the imagination of your appearance to the other person, the imagination of his or her judgment of that appearance, and some sort of self-feeling or self-evaluation resulting from those imaginings.[56]

Peter and Brigitte Berger agree with Cooley and Mead that one's personal identity is a product of the interplay between external identification with and by others, and self-identification.[57] Someone who is co-operative and altruistic will acquire this aspect of his identity when colleagues or friends call him as such and when he evaluates his own behavioural patterns from this perspective. These dialectical processes between external identity and self-identity apply also to typical social identities such as male and female. The main characteristics of gender roles are not neatly distributed by biological sex. Both men and women can perform masculine and feminine roles. But in practice there is little room to manoeuvre between socially constructed roles. So-called masculine women or feminine men will receive critical comments. The tomboy might have enjoyed her rough play and outfit during childhood, but will receive increasing pressure to behave like a 'real girl' as soon as she becomes a teenager.

In Berger's view socialization is successful when symmetry emerges between the socially constructed objective reality and a subjective reality. What is 'real' for society should also be 'real' for the individual. However, there will always be some difference between what people think of themselves and what other people think of them. Most people are inclined to evaluate themselves favourably. Moreover, other people can only observe you partly, at given moments. They will rarely get to know all aspects of your character. And, for that matter, will we ever completely understand ourselves?

Depending on the culture or spirit of the age, some of our innate talents and inclinations will be stimulated while others are suppressed. Our genetic make up supplies the framework, society can only help to develop or curtail the talents with which we are endowed. In addition, something spontaneous and uncontrollable that may unexpectedly manifest itself lurks in each individual. When this happens, social institutions will impose their power.[58] The result of socialization is the integration of children into a specific social group or society, but also entails the process of getting acquainted with oneself and simultaneously with society.

9.6   The overstated miseries of modernity

One of the most persistent themes among intellectuals since the end of the 19th century is the belief that modern society is in a state of crisis or on the brink of collapse. Such thoughts gave a strong push to the development of sociology. Marx mentioned alienation; Durkheim feared anomie and Weber envisioned human beings constructing their own iron cage. The Spanish philosopher Ortega y Gasset set the tone with *The Revolt of the Masses.* In his view the emergence of modern masses would lead to great harm for mankind. Nations and civilizations might be destroyed. There had been mobs and masses before, but their subordinate position in society was uncontested. For Ortega y Gasset, the underlying crisis of modern society was caused by the fact that the masses had become assertive and self-conscious. They demanded a legal and political equality and a fair share of the wealth of nations. The peaceful herds of the past now threatened to turn into a stampede, thereby trampling the fragile fabric of civilization.[59]

9.6.1   The cultural pessimism of social critics

The social critics of the *Frankfurter Schule* – who will be discussed more fully in the chapter on Habermas – agreed that modern industrial society was ill. Erich Fromm, for example, maintained that modern society endangered our mental health, for capitalism created 'false needs' such as the materialistic drive to possess more and more. Like Fromm, many believed that modern society was repressive and would lead to further alienation. Arnold Gehlen took a more conservative stance and argued that modern society made people insecure because traditions had broken down and people were forced to choose from too many options. By erasing the traditional certainties of collective social existence, modern society enforces an individual, secluded and mental existence. With the shrinking of the collective conscience the individual mind is challenged ever more.

In the fifties and sixties the economy boomed in Western Europe and North America. Governments became less frugal and expanded the arrangements for social security and social assistance. The nation was protected against the economic and physical hazards of unemployment, illness, disability, old age and poverty. Nonetheless, a new wave of societal critique emerged. Berger believes that the intellectual elite are much more troubled by many aspects of modernization than the rest of the population. The intellectual elite observed the emergence of a mass culture that might even assimilate and corrupt the 'high' culture of the elite. In their view the Pied Pipers of advertising and entertainment vulgarize culture into a dull and tasteless mixture.

The fast expansion of secondary and tertiary education – another token of modernization – was not welcomed as a big step ahead, but interpreted as a lowering of educational standards. According to many pessimistic intellectuals it only increased the bureaucratization of fast growing schools and universities. Methods of teaching had become standardized and routine, while students were no longer challenged to develop a critical attitude and to become independent thinkers. The situation was not much better in primary education. With his smooth rhetoric and attractive style of writing, John Holt became one of the champion opponents of the existing didactic methods in primary schools, designed to train pupils to give meaningless answers to meaningless questions.[60] Reimer even declared that school was dead, whereas Ivan Illich advocated abolishing all schools and replacing them with networks of small groups of individuals interested in the same sorts of knowledge and skills, to be provided by specialists.[61]

At the same time, urbanization went on at full speed. In the USA numerous studies were published about the social problems in the big metropolitan areas. European studies revealed similar situations. Community life seemed to collapse under the pressure of poverty, labour migration and homelessness. This gave rise to many social problems. In inner cities the number of broken families soared, just as the number of homeless people and drug addicts. The rate of criminal offences reached disturbing levels. Once this bleak picture of derelict inner cities had become common knowledge, new studies showed that suburban life was far from idyllic. In these affluent districts no real community life had emerged. Social cohesion was weak and commitment with community affairs was very low. Divorce rates soared, producing more losers than winners. It is no wonder that psychological help became a booming business.

Many of these critical studies offered a description of a new type of individual, such as the mass man of José Ortega y Gasset, the one-dimensional man of Herbert Marcuse, the organization man of William Foot Whyte. Even if the labels are not very precise, the characteristics are clearly sketched. They contain a great deal of negative connotations: modern man is alienated, isolated, depersonalized and even de-humanized. Moreover, he is powerless, confined to the prison house of society, to the state or to the company he works for. His life is boring, empty and utterly meaningless. His only resort is the hedonistic world of make-believe provided by the entertainment industry, withholding real satisfaction or contentment. Most culture critics shared this negative view on modern society. The seedy sides of modernity were accepted by a small number as part of the deal to achieve progress in other domains, such as higher average incomes, higher levels of education, better medical care, better means of transportation, and, in many countries, more equality and liberty.[62]

During his entire academic career, Berger analyzed modernization, but his analyses differ substantially from the usual critiques. It is also striking that he picked up a number of so-called conservative issues, such as religion, marriage and the market economy, as we shall see in the following sections.

9.6.2   *Religion and social order*

Berger sees culture as the all-embracing, socially constructed world of subjectively and inter-subjectively experienced meanings. The social world acquires a certain amount of coherence and intelligence through the inter-subjective sharing of these meanings. This is how the world makes sense. This coherent reality replaces the plasticity of the social domain by seemingly stable and reliable structures. Society is a *nomos*-constructing enterprise.[63] Life would be unbearable without such a socially constructed *nomos*. For each individual this socially constructed order represents the clear and trustworthy side of life, where he can live and orient himself. The socially established *nomos* may thus be understood, perhaps in its most important aspect, as a shield against disintegration, chaos, and terror.[64] But every socially created *nomos* has to be defended and re-established, over and over again, against the threat of its destruction by anomic powers that are endemic to the human condition. Social order has to be maintained despite the frequent experience of suffering, evil and death. These anomic phenomena must not only be endured; they must also be explained in terms of the *nomos* of the society in question.[65] Such an explanation is called a theodicy or sociodicy - terms introduced to sociology by Max Weber. Such an explanation may be both complex and sophisticated', simple and straightforward. The illiterate farmer who attributes the death of his child to the will of God makes use of a theodicy, just as the theologian who writes a treatise to demonstrate that the suffering of innocent children does not negate the conception of an all-good and all-powerful God.

Berger emphasizes that each individual is inclined to contribute to the organizing or order-creating power of society. This disposition places the life of each individual in an all-encompassing network of meanings. It renders meaning to life, including its painful aspects. The individual who internalizes these meanings in the right way acquires a kind of supernatural status. He can interpret his birth, life and finally his death in a way that transcends the unique position of these phenomena in his life. This becomes dramatically clear during certain *rites de passage*. The ritual changes the singular event into a typical event, just as the personal biography merges into an episode in the history of mankind. Individual existence will then be perceived as the fact of being born, of living a life, of suffering and finally of dying. It takes its course just like all our ancestors and just like all our descendents. If people can cope with this, then they transcend their own individuality and unique experiences and learn to situate themselves 'correctly' in reality, that is, correctly as defined by their society. The sheltering canopy of the socially constructed order can make the pain of living more bearable. It can make your *angst* of death less overwhelming.[66] With the help of faith people are more able to undergo the pains of life and death and to render these events with meaning. If faith is that powerful, it should be strong enough to counter the frequent attacks on religion, but Berger noticed of course the demise of religion in the modern world, in particular in Western Europe and pondered on the reasons.

9.6.3   The seed of secularization

Berger usually takes an original turn when searching for explanations and this is not different in the case of his attempt to understand the process of modern secu-

larization. He defines secularization as the process of the successful escape, or
withdrawal, of certain sections of society from the overpowering grip of religion.
There is an objective as well as a subjective dimension to this process. In the western world, an objective divide has emerged between the church and the state. The
church also has lost its power over education, philosophy, art and science. Until
the Middle Ages, religion played a dominant role in all these domains. In our
time, art and science are autonomous secularized fields that defy all influence of
religion. Secularization also has a subjective side, in that most people in western
countries nowadays lack a set of (traditional) religious interpretations.[67] Secularization is by no means universal. In Western Europe secularization has taken
place on a large scale, but many Christian people in the US still attend church
every Sunday or on Saturday night if that is more convenient. There also are successful movements of evangelization in the US and Latin America. Nonetheless,
Christian mainstream communities have declined in many western countries
whereas alternative religious sects and movements seem to enjoy a remarkable
growth albeit on a much smaller scale.

Most explanations for the decline of western religions refer to the growth of capitalist economy, urbanization, the rapid spread of mass media and mass tourism,
causing large numbers of people to experience other cultures and other religions.
Moreover, atheistic social movements, in particular Marxism, have contributed
to the exodus from the Catholic and Protestant Church. Berger does not deny the
validity of these factors, but he wishes to look beyond these familiar accounts.
It is axiomatic, to Berger that we need many explanatory factors to account for
the huge impact of secularization. He is interested in the possibility that religion has produced its own seeds of secularization. Before him, Hegel and other
western philosophers had proposed a causal relation between secularization
and the emergence of the Protestant movement. In comparison to the 'richness'
of the Roman Catholic universe, Protestantism is a very austere and dismantled
religion. The iconoclastic fury of the 16th century robbed many churches and
cathedrals from their pomp and circumstance. The Protestant revolt implied a
return to the pure essentials of religion at the cost of all the richness of religious
forms and rituals of Catholicism. The Calvinists reduced the number of holy sacraments. A much simpler service was exchanged for the Holy Mass, the prayer
for the souls of the dead was abrogated and saints were no longer worshipped.
Protestantism stripped religion from the three most traditional and mightiest
resources of holiness: mysteries, miracles and magic. Protestants do not believe
in a world full of holy objects and holy forces. They will not kiss a cross, touch
a statue in reverence, or kneel down to kiss the earth after arriving in the Holy
Land. Their reality is polarized between a holy, supernatural God and a world
full of sinful human beings.

Roman-Catholics have adhered to the role of mediators between themselves and
the Holy, as with the holy sacraments of the church, the intercession of saints, the
recurrent appearances of the supernatural through miracles. With Protestantism, however, people are thrown back on themselves and have to rely on their

own strengths and weaknesses. In order to elevate the awesome Greatness of God, the world was stripped of godliness. The only connection between God and the people was the word of God, as it was laid down in the Bible. But this precisely made religion vulnerable. Modern science and rational thought had eroded the plausibility of God's word, leading Nietzsche to his famous conclusion that: 'God is dead'. Berger contented that *'a heaven without angels lays open for the scrutinous investigation of astronomers and astronauts.'* He concludes that Protestantism, with its radical sell-out of religious sacraments, ornaments, and rituals, unintentionally provided a great impetus for modern secularization.[68]

9.6.4   *The modern attack on the nuclear family and marriage*

Durkheim's study *Suicide* from 1893 showed that marriage can offer protection against suicide. In his view, a marriage bond constitutes a basic form of social integration that can help people to endure hard times, a hypothesis that is supported by recent studies showing that married people score higher on several indicators of wellbeing.[69] Nevertheless, traditional marriage has lost a great deal of its popularity. In many modern societies more than a third of all marriages end in divorce. No wonder that a lot of people are not even bothered with the official procedures of marriage and opt for less formalized forms of relationship, or even choose to remain single. Many explanations have been put forward to account for the decline of matrimony. Norms and values have changed, in particular values connected with sacred traditions, premarital sex and adultery, as part of a more liberal view on individual freedom in sexual affairs. Berger and other neo-conservatives also refer to the mixed blessings of the Welfare State, with Social assistance levelling the formidable financial barrier against the option of divorce. Nowadays, divorced mothers can rely on a minimal income thanks to social assistance for single parent families.

The decline of the traditional family inspired the couple Brigitte and Peter Berger to write a book with a provocative title: *The War over the family*. The book contains many references to the cultural war against the nuclear family. There are historical roots to this war. The Enlightenment problematized more than two centuries ago, the traditional family, consisting of a father, a mother and one or more children. The central goal of this philosophical and political movement was to free human beings from the shackles of tradition; the family being one of these. However, the bourgeois family ethos survived the 19th century without many problems and positively flowered with the increased education of bourgeois values. It became the kernel for moral standards, especially in sexual matters. It also valued the welfare of children highly; supported the inculcation of values and attitudes conducive to economic success as well as civic peace; valued religious faith or at least the appearance of religious faith; and expressed an interest in the devotion to the 'finer things' of life, especially the arts.[70] Bourgeois women became the shock troops of the movement that sought to evangelize the lower classes with middle-class values. In America and England, Protestant ministers were an important ally in this missionary enterprise. According to the Berger's, the origins of modern social work are to be found in this vast missionary enterprise of ladies and clerics to redeem the lower classes. Early socialists, particularly the Fabians in England, supported this operation. Despite their antagonism to bourgeois class dominance and their reservations about religion, the Fabians wanted the working class to profit from a sound education and enjoy the benefits of cultural refinement. Their project was not to abolish bourgeois family ethos, but to redistribute it.

So, until the 1950s, the middle-class family was perceived as a success story. The family became increasingly child-centred. Women were expected to find their life-goal at home, in the role of mother and the emotionally sensitive companion to their husbands. Yet, a growing number of husbands and wives failed to adjust to these roles. Many women in the new suburbs experienced a kind of social vacuum as soon as their husband left for work in the early morning and the children had been dispatched off to school. Besides, modern technology had alleviated many a household chore, education had taken over much of their pedagogical tasks, and urbanization had taken them away from their friends and relatives. Many wives, in particular better-educated wives, were frustrated by the lack of opportunities for further personal growth and self-realization.

This new radicalism of the sixties and seventies strongly affected the perspective on the family. Not deviations, but the norm itself was perceived as the real problem. Individuals were not maladjusted, society was 'sick'. The well-known feminist Betty Friedan pejoratively spoke of 'the cult of domesticity' and of 'repressiveness'. Most of the social and cultural movements of the sixties fed this anti-family mood. The radical social scientist Barrington Moore even suggested that we should give the family a decent burial. Others were prepared to bury this established institution without any decency, because they viewed the family as a nest of oppression and social pathology. It should be noted that, even when added up, all these radical movements were constituted in relatively small sectors of the upper-middle class. Their influence, though, was much amplified by the media. And, according to Berger and Berger, some of the radical ideas were put to political use by people who were not particularly radical in their own thinking, leading for example to a strong proliferation of Welfare State arrangements and an equally strong proliferation of the 'helping professions'. From hindsight one can see the radical movements of the 1960s as a cultural revolution that prepared the ground for an institutional social transformation through legislation and public policy in the following decades.[71]

Brigitte and Peter Berger address many topics in their book, such as the historical development of the bourgeois family. They also contribute to the debate on the value and future of traditional families. However, they pay little attention to important factors that might help to explain the steep rise in divorce rates or the postponement of marriage and parenthood, such as the effects of the introduction of better methods of birth control. Nor do they give due attention to the effects of the expansion of education. The strong increase in the enrolment of women in higher levels of secondary education and in higher education had an enormous effect on the postponement of marriage and motherhood. It prepared the ground for a greater autonomy of women and brought them to the same or a higher educational level as that of their prospective partners. Obviously, this had a great impact on the power balance between men and women. It led to a steep increase in the participation of (married) women in the labour market, and after a while, even women with young children. The Bergers did not address the multiplier effect of the growth of the divorce rate either. All traditional normative restrictions seemed to have lost their currency and with more single people around, also at the workplace, short or long-term sexual relations without the intention of getting married almost set the norm.

Instead of addressing these factors, Berger and Berger try to construct a reasonable defence for the traditional marriage and family. Since they formed a married couple themselves, it is clear that their discussion cannot be value-free. Their theoretical assumptions might be biased towards marriage and the family. The same could be true about the empirical data they selected and the way they interpreted them. They explicitly warn their readers for this danger, but promise to be as scientifically neutral as possible. On the other hand, they also warn the readers that most members from the anti-family camp tend to be biased in their opinions and arguments. Even those who have discovered the staying power of the family stress its discontinuities and loss of functions and to prognosticate a variety of impending disasters.[72] Most analysts do not take into consideration that many divorced people remarry soon or neglect to acknowledge the negative effects of divorce for many divorcees and their children. The opponents of the traditional family persist in ignoring that a substantial majority of Western societies continue their attachment to the bourgeois, nuclear family, both in practice and as an ideal.

What are the basic assumptions of Berger and Berger on this issue? To begin with, they have no nostalgia for a reactionary and romanticized past. They do not advance a rosy picture from an idealized past to solve the rather problematic reality of the present. But neither do they find much hope in the various 'alternatives' suggested by so-called progressive thinkers. They assume that there was no perfect family in the past and that there will be no perfect type of family in the future. They do not share the Enlightenment faith in general progress, although they think that some progress has been made, for instance, with the abolition of slavery, the recognition of equal rights for women, or the huge reduction in infant mortality. But they warn us that these singular forms of progress can be lost again. Therefore, they must be continuously defended and institutionalized. They believe that the bourgeois family manifested a progress on human values over its predecessors and they further believe that these values continue to be valid even today. Besides, modern alternatives to marriage and the bourgeois family have been tried and tested, and do not really constitute a viable alternative.

9.6.5   Marriage and the construction of social reality

Berger and Kellner had already paid some attention to this topic in *Marriage and the Construction of Reality*.[73] That article started with the above-mentioned reference to the work of Durkheim: marriage as a defence against anomie. This Durkheimian idea sparked off their interest in the nomos-constituting power of marriage. In short, a marriage is the domain of building, maintaining, repairing and modifying a consistent reality that will be perceived as very meaningful. Marriage does not exist in a social vacuum. Through a long and extended socialization process, usually within the framework of a nuclear family, most people have learned to understand and accept their social environment and the social meaning of all that takes place in it. This meaningful social order has to be reproduced everyday. Everyday we also want to get a convincing confirmation of our social identity, status, and position. This is crucial for all of us. The only way to receive this unequivocal confirmation is through the interaction with other individuals, in particular with sympathetic significant others. So, we all need regular contact with significant others who support us, especially when our self-image has been damaged by the actions of other people or by some of our less dignified or less successful actions.

The plausibility and stability of the world, as a socially defined world depends on the strength and durability of relations with significant others, with whom all the ins and outs of this world can be discussed over and over again.[74] According to Berger and Kellner, a good marriage offers an excellent opportunity for such a stable relation. The close and continuous presence of a spouse reinforces the importance of this relation for the confirmation of social reality. Of course, if an unmarried couple has a similar intimate and trustworthy relation it will have the same integrative and stabilizing effect.

In their ideal-typical description of marriage, Berger and Kellner assert that marriage is a play in which two 'strangers' have decided to live together. In most cases the actors have prepared themselves for this play and have redefined their social position and social identity. Both partners have considered their new roles in advance, and have anticipated certain changes. Society has made the rules long ago and sets the stage, supported by a pervasive ideology concerning such salient themes as romantic love, the fulfilment of sexual needs, faithfulness and personal growth through frequent and close interactions with a partner and children.

Married couples, cohabiting couples and nuclear families are specific examples of a more general institution in modern societies: a private sphere that is separate from the public realms of politics or the economy. In modern society, individuals are unable to develop their real self in the public domain. There are too many restrictive norms, rules and laws. Besides, many individuals suffer from the idea that they are anonymous nobodies in the huge mass of people that surround them in work and leisure. The private domain offers a haven where their personal identity is reaffirmed and their self-worth and self-esteem regained, should this be necessary. In the small circle of the nuclear family everybody is somebody. Within the boundaries of this small, familiar and intimate sphere each individual has a real influence on the course of events, on social reality at micro level, which they have constructed together.

Not so long ago, married couples or nuclear families were deeply embedded in extended families or small local communities. Now, the family has turned into a privatized island. Simultaneously, marriage has lost some of its traditional functions while new functions have taken their place. Basically, the married couple does not constitute such a strong foundation for a durable relation. First, the relation is based on the bond between two people who have been raised in different families and communities. They have not shared the first part of their lives, the part of their primary socialization. Secondly, they have to rely on the frequency and intensity of their interactions to confirm, reconstitute, and objectivate their loving relation. But modern society sets very high standards for a successful marriage or cohabitation. Hence, new partners tend to expect too much from each other. The new and much beloved partner has to become the most significant other of all significant others. From now on, the new couple expects to do most things together. This intensive sharing and co-operation can become stressful for one or for both partners. They have to learn to be much more considerate with each other. Society aids and abets by putting even more stress on both partners and expecting them to get the most out of their careers.

The strong commitment to the new partner may also lead to fewer contacts with other significant others, and less time for former hobbies and cherished passtimes. All this entails a redefinition of social roles and identities. Therefore, starting an intimate and close relationship with a new partner involves a break with former life. This rupture has to be repaired as soon as possible. The new *nomos*, based on the new partnership, which also has to withstand possible irritating influences of new ties with in-laws or friends, has to replace the old *nomos*. New partners are inclined to consider these problems as external, temporal and atypical, but by discussing the characters, habits and lifestyle of each other's friends, they will redefine them and quite often this will lead to an estrangement or a final break with some of them.

A new enduring and intimate relationship means a new phase in the life-long process of socialization. This process is quite different from socialization in early childhood. Now both subjects are each other's socializing agents. Both try to re-socialize the other into a good partner. Doing so, they have to discuss many aspects of each other's actions, preferences, and tastes. During these interactions the new relationship is objectivated and crystallized. Moreover, both partners discover new aspects of their personal identities. Both will redefine their personal biography to make their past fit better with their current situation, and remodel it as a convincing preparation for this particular relationship. Many new lovers want to create the myth that they were born for each other. The main function of this social construction and reconstruction of reality is to establish a new stable identity.

9.7   Modern identities

Berger enjoyed tackling the problems of modern society and the identity of modern man. As we will see, he succeeds in posing new questions and suggesting new answers. In doing so, he always started from the sociology of knowledge he had developed earlier with Thomas Luckmann. In this approach, modern identity is constituted in dialogue with the development of modern society. Within this 'dialectical relation' individuals negotiate their objective identity with their significant others. These negotiations are not completely free, but take place within the boundaries set by society. Hence, individual identities also are social constructions.

Traditional societies seldom change. In the past, social mobility was almost non-existent. Sons followed the tracks of their fathers; daughters became mothers like their mothers before them. From early youth a clear connection existed between the objective identity imposed by society and one's subjective identity. Modern times, in contrast, are much more dynamic. New jobs were created because of technological advances, whereas old skills became obsolete. So, there is a lot of social mobility, both horizontal and vertical. More than anybody else, Berger thinks about the social-psychological consequences of modernization and mobility. What will happen if the connection between objective and subjective identity becomes weaker? One of the problems of technological change and increasing rationalization is the strong proliferation of specialization. Specialists can discuss the intricacies of their work only with other specialists. A professional identity is thus constructed. Another reason for the weakening of social identities is the erosion of class differences. What is your class when you are a social climber? Will your lifestyle fit in with the lifestyle of the class you recently have entered or will it still remain most characteristics of the class of your parents? What happens to your subjective identity, your class identity, and your lifestyle, if because of the hazards of life you can no longer keep up with the Joneses?

According to Berger, the crises of identity are among the major manifestations of the perceived meaninglessness of modernity. True enough, not all categories are equally sensitive to such crises. Adolescents are more vulnerable than their elders, who are settled in society and tend to have a steady partner, a job and a home. Berger postulates that members of the higher social classes, in particular intellectuals, are much more vulnerable than members of the working classes, because the former have more latitude without the knowledge what to do with it. Precisely because they are used to analyze everything and to ponder all the pros and cons, the causes and possible consequences of every motive, plan or objective, they run the risk of becoming more insecure and depressed.

Does a clear divide between a public and a private sphere offer a solution for the problem of social identity? According to Berger, this will not help much since the private life too has become more diversified and fragmented. Moreover, radio and TV have introduced the whole world into our private lives. Many radio and tv-programs question our way of life and present a host of alternative worldviews, beliefs, opinions, traditions, and lifestyles. Berger agrees with Gehlen that also our private existence is getting de-institutionalized. Traditions of family life are undermined by the strong and variegated influences from outside. Although the modern, rationalized world has become more institutionalized, the private domain has become more de-institutionalized. As a result, individuals withdraw to their own world of dreams, hopes and fears. It is a flight forward towards a growing subjectivation of human existence, in search for a much-needed foothold to keep us going.

This process can be aptly illustrated with reference to the historical transformation of two ethical principles: sincerity and honour. In traditional Western societies, the quality of man was manifested in 'sincerity' – the openness and integrity with which one performed public roles. Nowadays, sincerity has been substituted for 'authenticity' – the expression of the true self. The contrast is very significant. Sincerity presupposes a symmetrical relation between self and society while authenticity implies a fundamental opposition between them. Whereas sincerity can be found within social roles, authenticity is a characteristic of the individual playing these roles. In a similar way 'honour' is a direct manifestation of status, and a source for equality and solidarity among peers. Honour also implies a certain standard for the interactions with superiors, peers, and others. But the concept has vanished and is displaced by dignity. Dignity presupposes a certain meaning behind or beyond imposed social roles and norms. In short, honour implies that identity in essence, or at least to a significant degree, is connected with social roles. In contrast, dignity refers to the fact that someone's identity is independent from his or her social role and status. The emergence of values such as dignity and authenticity illustrates that the self-evident ties between individual and social identity have been severed.[75]

Berger does not stop here. In his view, subjectivation implies the obligation to think about everything we do and about who we are. This imposed self-reflection is a lonesome activity, shared with just a few others who similarly live a unique, individualized life. An ever-increasing number of people do not have a clue about where their life is heading. In a world without traditions and frequent changes it is difficult to plan ahead anyway. The *self* is vulnerable and dependent on the expectations of a multitude of reference groups. Our ideas about who we really are, are only real as long as they are confirmed by significant others. Because of the dynamics of a hectic modern society, many people undergo a mental crisis about their own social role and identity. So, for Berger, it is no wonder that the demand for professional help of psychologists and psychiatrists has soared.

9.8   The relationship between method and engagement[76]

Berger has devoted much energy to the ethical implications of sociological research. His view on this issue stems from his strong awareness of the limits of sociology. So far, this relatively young science has produced only a rather limited body of knowledge about a complex subject matter. Moreover, this knowledge about society is deeply embedded in the social context of its production. There are therefore no absolute truths in social science. The outcomes of research should be applied with great care when geared to far-reaching plans for changing society. Such planned changes will have great consequences for many, but social science cannot really provide the warranty that the proposed 'improvements' will materialize. Unforeseen, unintended, or negative consequences are to be expected. Should we then leave everything unchanged to avoid any risk? Berger did not think so and tried to find a safe alternative. His solution requires two types of action. The first is the improvement of the methodological basis of our knowledge and the second demands social scientists to be very prudent and modest whenever they endeavour in policy research. In general, immodest sociology is irresponsible sociology. This is particularly true for policy analysis.

9.8.1   *Modesty as motto*

A valid sociology requires a continuous alertness to the great diversity of meanings people attach to different events, and the consequences of these meanings for their actions. Whenever a sociologist wants to gain more insight in reality, he will have to listen attentively to the opinions, convictions and beliefs of his subjects. He must carefully consider all variations in relations and in patterns of behaviour. Therefore, he has to *listen* attentively and show a *cognitive respect* for all the peculiarities of individuals, human groups and their cultures. Such an awareness and attentiveness will discourage people from making ambitious plans to 'educate and lift a people' or to 'make them conscious of their true needs'.

The common denominator of social reformers – from left to right – is their strong belief in their cause. They are deeply convinced that their truth gives them the right to convert other people to their own views and ways. They have little respect for the feelings, convictions, and traditions of 'the other'. This reflects the typical arrogance of many political movements. In the most extreme cases, new intellectual ideas have been packaged into a revolutionary rhetoric and violent political practices that has cost the lives of millions. Hence, Berger rejected violent revolutions and fanatical drives for reform and conversion. He detested researchers who showed no respect for what other people believe and think, and instead imposed their own meanings upon others. Berger's commitment is based on compassion:

> *The only political commitments worth making are those that seek to reduce the amount of human suffering in the world. Much of politics, of course, is too ordinary to evoke commitments of any depths. Most of the rest is crime, illusion or the self-indulgence of intellectuals.*[77]

9.8.2   The practical value of value-neutrality

In spite of the professional ideal of objectivity, the main impulse of positivists is the creation of instruments for improving society. Often they see themselves as members of an intellectual vanguard with such a clear vision that they believe that they can make valid judgments about the real interests of society. Berger assures his colleagues to be more modest and to aim at the purest possible observations of that reality. From this perspective the sincere sociologist attempts to be a good spy or scout, who accurately reports what he has seen. But others will have to decide what moves ought to be made in that terrain.[78]

Berger supports Weber in his view that social scientists should do their utmost to observe, describe, and explain reality disconnected from their own personal interests and preferences. This does not mean that one should not have personal interests, preferences, and priorities and should abstain from all efforts to work in these interests. But Berger wants social scientists to make a clear divide between their scientific work and their social or political activities in other domains of their existence. One should not mix one's political interests with the interests and necessary rigor of scientific activities. Value-neutrality also implies that social scientists seriously reflect on the results of their professional work.

Following the trail of Weber and Schütz, Berger asserts that social scientists should base their concepts on the observations of everyday life. Concepts should be 'meaning adequate'. That is, they should reflect everyday reality and be comprehensible for laymen too. The quest for causal social relations should be founded on the world of social meanings used by common people. Human beings live and act in this meaningful reality. According to Berger, a strongly developed *cognitive respect* for all people can ensure that sociological concepts and explanations remain vivid and meaningful, and prevent them from acquiring the arid characteristics of positivism and their deductive schemes. This suits his rejection of positivistic *social engineering.*[79]

The quest for a social science based on the Weberian criterion that theoretical concepts should be rooted in the meanings used by ordinary people leads to the awareness of the inevitable, exciting, and sometimes frustrating pluralism of social existence. Berger sees the plurality of the modern life-worlds as the most salient rupture with homogenous traditional societies. Modern man is a restless player in a great variety of roles. Social masks are changed with the same ease as we change clothes. A great diversity of social roles, cultural and historical circumstances and personal biographies generate quite different perspectives on the world. As long as cultures, social conditions, and worldviews differ, so will the claims for truth – another reason for social scientists to be prudent and modest.

The modest pretences of Weber's interpretative approach seasoned all Berger's scientific projects. This prudence could be interpreted as a form of conservatism fearful of any change and innovation. But it simply springs from a lack of belief in the maturity and decisiveness of sociology. This scepticism is fuelled by the insight that unintended consequences of social and political actions have given human history many ironic turns. Instead of taking a beeline towards a better world, history has often coursed to disaster. That is why the ideology of social progress is based on a false doctrine. Berger's distrust in great social innovations is doubled as soon as attempts are made to impose these plans with great force. He is a conservative humanist, who accepts people as they are. He acknowledges the value of order, continuation, and triviality for social existence. He can only endorse political plans that show respect for human reality. Therefore, he strongly opposes utopians that will accommodate state policies to their subjective ideas about an ideal world, to their plans for progress and reform. Though Berger is not in favour of perpetuating the status quo, he certainly is an ardent opponent of ideologies that propagate any kind of revolution.[80]

The philosophy of science has stressed continuously that we can never be sure of any claim to truth. Thus, we are condemned to an eternal scepticism and are destined to scrutinize critically each proposed theory and all outcomes of scientific research. We must develop 'the art of distrust' as Nietzsche called it. We do not have to be disengaged fully from all political commitments, but should remain detached from all forms of political commitment based on ignoring our ignorance, on our lack of information about the many consequences of our plans. So, Berger does not advise us to remain completely passive, but urges us to prudently collect all the relevant information and to be wary of unintended consequences and the perverse effects of political actions. His humanitarian compassion dictates a sober ethic of responsibility and keeps him far from the addictive intoxication of an ethic of ultimate goals.

Interpretative sociology certainly does not exclude the utility of political praxis. On the contrary, it encourages us to acknowledge the vulnerability of all established social regulations, institutions and customs. The relentless attempts to interrogate received wisdoms, to modify extreme convictions, this continuous scepticism, are a form of revolution too, designed to safeguard the boundaries of a process of change that is both responsible and compassionate.

9.9   The capitalist revolution

In *Pyramids of Sacrifice* (1974), Berger did not choose between communism and capitalism. However, thirteen years later he wrote *The Capitalist Revolution*, where communism is definitely rejected.[81] Marx had taught that capitalism is a conservative force, interested in blocking the evolution of history. Berger tries to show that capitalism is no conservative force at all, but a catalyst of modernization. He argues that every society that has become capitalistic has changed in many ways. There is more wealth and there tends to be more democratic freedom and cultural diversity.

With this book, Berger intended to develop a coherent social theory of capitalism, based on empirical facts. Such a theory did not exist yet. Even Marx, seen by Berger as one of the most important social scientists, did not meet the standards of social science. *Das Kapital* is a mixture of scientific facts and unscientific prophecies. According to Berger, the non-Marxist attempts to create such a theory had stranded. He refers to the attempts of Weber, Schumpeter, and Hayek, who were, like anybody else, limited by our little knowledge of society and social processes. Therefore, also Berger does not pretend that his book will be the final answer. However, he put his reputation at stake by presenting fifty refutable hypotheses about the growth of the economy and the development of social equality and political liberty in capitalist countries.

Industrial capitalism has succeeded in creating the biggest economic production ever. No other system has been able to equal this. The tandem of capitalism and technological development provide the best condition for economic growth. Berger acknowledges that the transition from a pre-capitalistic economy to a capitalistic economy may create a temporary setback in economic production and a temporary increase in inequality. But he contends that once the dust has settled, inequality will level out and economic growth will emerge. After a while, there will be a stable level of inequality, owing to technological changes and demographic factors. Berger is convinced that governments can help to redistribute incomes, but only to a certain level. Too much equality in incomes will negatively affect economic growth, and so affect the standard of living of the entire population.

In capitalist countries all traditional forms of social stratification will fade away. The ongoing process of industrialization is the main cause of the significant amount of social mobility we can witness in all advanced industrial societies. This economic system always has a great interest in getting the right person in the right place. Hence, educational credentials and experience are more important than social background. Therefore, capitalist societies are more open than other types of society.

Berger contends that capitalism is a necessary but not sufficient condition for democracy. In the case of the state increasingly exerting more influence on the economic system, a point can be reached where democracy cannot function any longer. In contrast, as soon as a state with a communist system gives more leeway to the market-economy, it can shift towards a more democratic system. When capitalism succeeds in generating economic growth, and when large parts of the population can profit from this growth, then this will most certainly lead to pressure for more democracy.

In his discussion of the relationship between capitalism and an individualized culture Berger is a true heir of Max Weber. He starts with the statement that the origins of western individualism date back to a period long before the rise of capitalism. This proto-individualism has smoothed the way for the individualism of capitalistic entrepreneurs. The bourgeois culture of western societies, in particular Protestant societies, has engendered a human type strongly characterized by individual autonomy. In turn, capitalism forms a necessary condition for the survival of individual autonomy. Certain aspects of western bourgeois-culture, in particular its activism, its urge for rational innovations and self-control, constitute necessary requirements for a successful capitalist development. Besides, capitalism requires specific institutions such as the nuclear family and religion to counter balance the negative aspects of individual autonomy.

Since his former writings about the social problems of the Third World, his negative view on the applicability of the capitalist experiment in those countries had shifted 180 degrees. Now, he concludes that the integration of Third World countries in the capitalistic world system will have positive effects on the economy, as many economic studies show. Surprisingly, the inequality in incomes decreased in those countries that opted for the capitalist route. Third World countries that follow the socialist model show less economic growth.

Berger was particularly influenced by his observations of the economic development in five Pacific countries in Asia. In those countries several capitalistic hypotheses were corroborated and anti-capitalistic hypotheses were refuted. In these countries too, there was a strong increase in productivity, as well as a quick rise in the standard of living. Moreover, these countries became more open. In contrast to the history of Europe, the introduction of capitalism did not lead to a temporary increase in income inequality. Inequality diminished immediately, but stabilized at a lower level after a few years. The experience of these five countries demonstrated that underdeveloped countries could profit from a transition to capitalism. Their dependency on the capitalist world system did not hamper their economic growth.

However, the Asiatic experiment offers a refutation for the hypothesis that a market economy cannot succeed when there is a high level of state intervention in economic affairs. The culture of these countries was characterized by a set of core values that strongly resembled those of western bourgeois culture: activism, a disposition for rational innovations, and self-discipline. Obviously, there are cultural differences too. Typical Asiatic values help boost economic growth, despite a much weaker emphasis on individualism than in Western Europe or North America. Berger points at more than one factor that accounts for the rise of capitalism, but he focuses in particular on cultural factors such as individualism, innovativeness, and self-restraint, the very values that were endorsed and stimulated by Protestantism. He locates the main consequences of capitalism in the following domains: economic (higher productivity, higher standard of living), social (less inequality), political (democratization), and a cultural domain (increase of individual autonomy).

Berger presents more arguments against the presumed favourable developments (economic, political, and social) of state socialism, but we need not recapitulate all these arguments. The weaknesses, drawbacks, and shortcomings of the communist experiment in Europe have become obvious to everyone. The conspicuous collapse of communism was a necessary eye-opener that exposed a very strong myth that had bewildered millions of people all over the world. The myth of a splendid future for the working class and the proletariat had made itself immune to scientific critique. All forms of critique were dismissed as bourgeois, reactionary, revisionist, or fascist. Capitalism, on the other hand, lacks such a comforting myth. From experience, everybody knows that capitalism produces both winners and losers. In a capitalist system, no promise is made for a heaven on earth, but its surplus value can be proved in empirical comparisons with communist countries.[82]

Three cheers for capitalism? Berger rejects such a triumphant attitude. He contends that *The Capitalist Revolution* is not a pro-capitalistic book. Not even the comparatively favourable empirical data should be interpreted in that way. Each evaluation of a political or economic system depends on the criteria we choose for this evaluation. If one does not attach much value to economic growth, individualism, or democracy, then one will not be in the least impressed by the empirical facts and the hypotheses mentioned in Berger's book. Nevertheless, Berger thinks he has done all that could be expected of a good social scientist, that is, collecting a set of hypotheses that can, for the moment at least, boast the best available scientific support. He is convinced that his hypotheses have a low chance of being refuted by new research or new practical applications. Therefore, all politicians that want to address an urgent social problem, for example, poverty in Third World countries or poverty in inner-city ghetto's, have no other alternative than to base their actions on the best available research, although even this will always be insufficient and not completely reliable. Alas, the urgency of many problems is so strong, that politicians cannot wait until all the necessary research is done, properly discussed and neatly translated into adequate policy measures. It seems to be in the nature of politics that most decisions are made on the basis of non-scientific arguments.

9.10   Berger's disinvitation to sociology

It will be clear that Berger antagonized many progressive sociologists and thus placed himself effectively outside mainstream sociology, that was, in the in the seventies and eighties, dominated by the liberal and the leftwing. More and more colleagues disregarded his work, which had the regrettable effect that he decided to distance himself from the field. In 1992, he published a farewell essay with the resentful title *Disinvitation to Sociology*[83] He tells us here that he has lost most of his affinity with the discipline and its practitioners. What had gone wrong? Does he really mean to warn potential students against studying sociology? In principle, he still backs the sociology he described and promoted in *Invitation to Sociology*. The main reason for his frustration is that many contemporary sociologists seem to practice another type of sociology from the science that he loved in the sixties.

After realizing that it is impossible to practice an absolutely value neutral social science, many sociologists decided that a partisan perspective might as well be made explicit. Another tendency that he observed and regretted was the increasing divide between theoretical studies and empirical research. He is sorry to see that many leading theorists proudly state that they limit themselves strictly to the analysis of pure, abstract concepts, rather than dirtying their hands with the gathering and analysis of empirical data. He points out several cases where modern sociologists clearly failed. One such case is the explanation of secularization. For a long time, contemporary sociologists assumed that religion was an irrational affair that would not survive the progress of modern science and technology. They had no doubt that modernization would lead to a total secularization of the world. And so, American and European sociologists wrongfully ignored post-war evangelical movements or too hastily dismissed these movements as superficial and second rate. The rise of the new evangelical movement, the vote for Jimmy Carter as president of the USA , a very devote Christian, and the noisy appearance of a 'moral majority' disproved the thesis of secularization. And also the rise of fundamentalism in many Moslem countries disproved the tenets of modernists. Berger emphasizes that social scientists, most of whom are secularized intellectuals, missed the all too obvious signs of their times. The enlightened framework of modern sociology made them ill prepared to recognize the vitality of religious needs and creeds.

Why do sociologists overlook so many important tendencies in society? Berger has thought of some explanations. Firstly, secularized intellectuals are blindfolded as far as religion is concerned. Believing that religion is a thing of the past, they tend to close their minds for counter-information or try to make it fit their beloved perspective. Thus, they do not feel the need to adapt their political philosophy and worldview. Another reason is the parochialism of intellectuals. They think that they are real cosmopolitans, but they only interact with the kindred in spirit at meetings, conferences and seminars. They read international magazines, keep up with international politics and international trends in art, are members of international professional associations and visit international conferences but, at a second glance, all this takes places within a rather narrow intellectual framework. The world of western progressive artists and intellectuals is their congregation. They don't see the rest of the world, let alone analyze it seriously. And if they see it, they only see it through the badly focused lenses of their peers.

Berger includes what he calls leftwing social scientists and journalists in his accusations. Clearly, they supported the Soviet-regime far too long, long after they could have noticed that the drawbacks of real existing socialism were much greater than its positive sides. And when this stance no longer was tenable, they went on a search for 'true' socialism, because, in their eyes, anything was better than the capitalistic system they were part of. Berger touches a raw nerve when he states that this was not simply an issue of *bearing your heart at the left side*. Instead, he diagnoses that their intellect was biased to the left, premised on an uncritically following of the Marxist doctrine that the course of history would irreversibly lead to the downfall of capitalism. It is quite telling that many social scientists spoke of late-capitalism, whereas nobody ever spoke of late-communism before 1989. After the sudden demise of the communist system in Middle and Eastern Europe, which came as a great surprise to almost anybody, including western Kremlin watchers and soviet-specialists, left-wing intellectuals were in a state of cognitive anomie. The demise of communism caused a severe blow to left-wing ideology. Berger is not sure, however, whether social scientists will be permanently cured from ideological inclinations. In his view, new candidates already have arrived at the scene such as feminism, anti-racism, and multiculturalism.[84]

Clearly Berger's goal here is to get even with his opponents. But this does not mean that he is not right in many respects. What does he see as the great mistakes of sociology in the last quarter of the century? He points at four symptoms that already have been mentioned before, parochialism or provincialism, triviality, rationalism, and ideology. How can this awkward situation be overcome? Berger believes that sociologists should hold fast to a really cosmopolitan attitude. We should keep ourselves posted about the main aspects of modernization in our world. Modernization is a complex process that has many faces. To keep track of this we certainly need a comparative approach and study the course of events in many countries, regions and cultures. Berger contends that if we want to understand the western world, we should study eastern countries like China, India, Iran or Japan. Events in the Northern and the Southern Hemisphere should be compared, just as majority and minority groups. Thus our perspective will be sharpened.

Trivial research can be avoided by abandoning the wish to quantify everything. Of course, many research questions can be answered with the help of quantitative methods. But, Berger hastens to add; there also are many interesting research questions that demand a qualitative approach. If the quantitative method would be prescribed for all research issues, a host of trivial outcomes can be expected. This would easily lead to sharp restrictions in the type of questions to be investigated. However, qualitative studies can easily deteriorate into trivial enterprises too, when not delving any deeper than the level of amateur forms of village journalism, with the verbatim presentation of numerous quotations from interviews in lieu of a thorough sociological analysis. Of course, we should keep in mind that both methods could lead to interesting new discoveries as well as to trivial outcomes.

Berger also opposes those sociologists who base their work on the assumption of rationally acting individuals. Pareto had pointed out that most human actions are not logical. And in the sixties, C. Wright Mills offered a similar critique and spoke about the uninspiring deed of mainstream functional sociology.[85] The result was that whole generations of young sociologists went looking for an alternative and plunged head-on into an ideological delirium with strong Marxist overtones. They occupied themselves with the fashionable great issues of sociology, such as the shortcomings of capitalism, the suppression of the labour class, or the exploitation of the Third World. With a cosmopolitan perspective they thought in terms of the economic-political world system. Unfortunately, they did not find the right answers to their questions.[86]

So, the question remains whether the social sciences can be salvaged. In line with the insights derived from his particular sociology of science, Berger remains very sceptical. The only thing that sociology has to offer is the sociological perspective. This perspective focuses on the total interdependence of man and society, on the dependence of contemporary social processes on the recent and not so recent past. It considers that many social factors and processes are intertwined in complex ways. This perspective is grafted on the assumption that social reality is based on a daily readjustment because of the interactions of all members of society. Such a complex perspective is thwarted by parochialism and by ideologically biased worldviews accepting far too eagerly any singular, one-dimensional explanation for social events, but also suffers from the avalanche of trivial studies that only register simple facts without further analysis. At the end of the day, Berger, the arch-sceptic, has only one serious plan: the establishment of a school for the academic elite that takes care of the best students and the best research. Let us hope that sociology can be salvaged by a less elitist plan or even without a plan. There is no reason to doubt that new charismatic and creative innovators will emerge that will put sociology back on track again. As was mentioned at the beginning of this chapter, Berger invited many young people to study sociology. It is a great pity that his great enthusiasm for this field has cooled down, but this cannot obscure the fact that he has produced an impressive oeuvre of exiting sociological studies, studies that can still inspire us enormously.

PIERRE BOURDIEU

FIELD MARSHAL OF MODERN SOCIOLOGY

On the first of August 1930 Pierre Bourdieu was born in Denguin, a small rural village in the South of France, where his father was a postman. He grew up in a strong anti-intellectualist atmosphere. It is extremely rare that someone from such humble origins reaches the top of the academic world. According to Bourdieu's theories this was a big exception to the rule of omnipresent social reproduction. Thanks to his intellectual qualities, he was selected for the highly prestigious *École Normale Supérieure* in Paris. Gaining an entry into that renowned *Grand School* guarantees a great future. Bourdieu's career was crowned with his appointment as professor at the College de France. He has written and co-authored about thirty books. Obviously this chapter can only draw attention to a small part of his oeuvre.

After sketching his life and academic career in section 10.1, the chapter continues with a discussion about his vehement attacks on some strands of sociology he strongly rejected such as rational action theory. This sets the stage for a presentation of his theories. Section 10.3 starts with a discussion of habitus, one of his core concepts, followed by a treatment of the concepts of strategy, sense of practice or feel for the game. In section 10.4 we discuss his legacy to Marx. He has broadened the latter's concept of economic capital to cultural, social and symbolic capital. He thus enriched the field with new analytical tools to get a better understanding of how social inequality is reproduced. The next section sheds new light on the role education and symbolic capital play in the reproduction of social inequality. Section 10.6 offers an exposé of *Distinction*, his most famous sociological study. This fascinating book reveals that whenever the social gap between two classes or class fractions starts to shrink significantly, new forms of cultural distinction are produced to keep the lower strata at bay. The use of language and its pronunciation are also weapons in the war between social classes and status groups. Bourdieu's sociology of language is the subject of section 10.7. Section 10.8 is devoted to his view on the necessity to practise sociology in a reflexive way, meaning that we should always analyze the possible reasons behind all our choices. Why do we pick a particular topic, select a specific method and draw certain conclusions? Do we have a special interest that influences the choices we make? The final section evaluates Bourdieu's work, offering a mixed bag of admiration and critique.

10.1   Academic career

The ENS creates a kind of state nobility with almost the same hereditary power as the traditional nobility.[1] The very demanding, broad and classical curriculum selects students on their cognitive precocity; the school demands a huge amount of knowledge. Moreover, each student is expected to present this large fount of knowledge in an eloquent and persuasive style. Such a highly selective institute has its advantages: it offers bright lower class students a unique opportunity for upward mobility. At the time, however, the atmosphere at the ENS was very Stalinist and authoritarian. Together with other students Bourdieu attempted to break down this dogmatic ideological climate, but failed.[2] He majored in philosophy, but chose not to write a philosophical dissertation but to leave the ENS to become a teacher of philosophy at a provincial grammar school instead. It was the prelude to an excellent career that reached its zenith with his appointment as professor at the famous *Collège de France*. No doubt, this is the most prestigious post in the academic world of France. To win this position he had to compete with renowned colleagues such as Raymond Boudon and Alain Touraine. When occupying this highly desirable chair one has complete freedom to teach whatever subject one likes. Besides, the incumbent of this highly enviable position is not burdened with the usual duties of university professors. The *Collège de France* has no regular students and does not present systematic courses. The lectures are open to anyone who takes an interest. The professors can form research groups and start a research centre of their own. In other words, the college is an academic heaven on earth for the greatest scholars of France.

In 1979, Bourdieu published *La Distinction*. His main theme here is social stratification and the role of culture in reproducing it. He is strongly motivated to reveal the mechanisms that uphold the tenacious structures of inequality. As soon as this book was translated into English, he became one of world's most famous social scientists. His work covers a diversity of interests such as kinship relations, economic change, social inequality, sociology of education, epistemology, methodology, literature, and the worlds of art and science. And what is more, he won his spurs in all these specialist fields, treating old issues and themes in an original and creative way. His influence is not restricted to sociology, but stretches much further afield into disciplines such as philosophy, ethnology, cultural studies and the study of art and literature. His selection of research topics and methods are followed all over the world, and naturally his work, like that of all great scholars, is criticized, scrutinized, widely discussed and analyzed. Bourdieu is a great master of both social theory and empirical research, which is a rare combination. He displays a broad knowledge of social theories, methodology and philosophy,

handles advanced statistical techniques, but does not shy away from presenting simple frequency tables when they fit the occasion. In each domain he seeks
his own theoretical approach and develops his own methods or combination of
methods. He does not abstain from mundane empirical work, nor does he fear
highly abstract theoretical endeavours. He wants to put his theories, concepts
and methods into the service of social practice. Moreover, he critically reflects
his own *modus operandus* and ponders the consequences of his approach for the
outcomes of his research.[3]

If the French saying *'le style est l'homme'* is true, then Bourdieu must have a complex character. He expresses his ideas in a highly complicated style. To avoid any
misunderstandings he produces long sentences full of informative comment
clauses, to describe and explain the very complexity of social phenomena; a complexity that is produced by the fact that many processes occur simultaneously
and influence each other. Later, he expressed his doubts about the success of writing with so many sidelines, nuances, and qualifications, but by then it was too late
to change his style.[4] Fortunately, there are a number of good introductions to his
work and his thoughts are also lucidly expressed in numerous interviews. These
interviews, which were always carefully edited by Bourdieu before publication,
are less complicated and tend to be clearer when he answers specific questions.[5]

10.1.1 Academic productivity and career

In 1956, Bourdieu was enlisted in the French army. He was sent to Algeria, where
the French were involved in one of their last colonial wars. For two years, he observed this conflict at rather close range. These experiences have put their mark
on his scientific approach. To start with, they drove him towards the social sciences. After military service, he remained in Algeria to teach at the University of
Algiers. He began to research the social problems of the Algerians and the French
colonists who lived in a similar dramatic situation.[6] This ethnographic fieldwork
formed the raw material for his first book, *Sociologie de l'Algérie*, issued in 1958. In
retrospect, he qualified his first book as a simple descriptive report of an empirical study carried out by a beginner. But he added that he certainly had learned a
lot from this project.

In 1960, he became a research assistant with Raymond Aron and attended the
workshops of the famous anthropologist Claude Lévi-Strauss. A year later, he
became a lecturer at the University of Lille. In 1964, he got a job as director of
research at the *École Pratique des Hautes Études*. Quite soon, he had gathered a
group of researchers that assisted him in carrying out his countless ideas for research projects. Bourdieu became a *patron*, always the driving force behind the
numerous books and articles he produced together with many co-authors. In the
mean time a new book was issued about Algeria, *Travail et travailleurs en Algérie*,
which was quickly followed by yet another one, *Le Déracinement*, co-authored
with A. Sayad. The book contained an analysis of the uprooting of the rural population during the transition from a pre-capitalistic era to the capitalistic era. In

subsequent articles he wrote about the Algerian proletariat and marital patterns in Kabylia, but also about sexual relations and celibacy among French peasants. Soon new topics emerged such as the perception of art and the social function of education. The reproductive role of education would forever be among his favourite topics. This theme alone led to many famous books, all of them available in English and many other languages. Every sociologist of education is familiar with at least some of these titles, such as *La Réproduction*, co-authored with Jean Claude Passeron, who also collaborated with two studies on French students.[7] The same is true, by the way, for his work on the sociology of art, its producers and consumers, such as *Un art moyen, essai sur les usages sociaux de la photographie* (1965) and *L'Amour de l'art, les musées d'art et leur public* (1966). All these books have been translated into English. In *Distinction* (1979) he stressed the importance of the cultural factor for the reproduction of social inequality.

Another of his major topics is methodology and epistemology. In *Le métier de sociologue* (1968) Bourdieu had struggled with the problem of how to investigate and understand social practices, without distorting social reality during the process of observation and interpretation. In 1972, *Esquisse d'une théorie de la pratique* was published, later translated and revised as *Outline of a Theory of Practice*. This formed a stepping-stone towards *Le Sens Pratique* (1980).

He also critically analyzed the field of academics in his book *Homo Academicus (1984)*. Bourdieu expected or hoped that this book about the intellectual elite of Paris, written by a simple provincial, would shock this very elite. It certainly was heavily criticized, but not burned. It was followed by another book on the academic world, La *Noblesse d'Etat (The State Nobility)*, which focused on the preparation of the elite of the nation in special academic institutes and schools of secondary education.[8] He continued writing academic books and published, in 1992, *Réponses*, together with Loïc Wacquant, a former student who takes great effort in disseminating Bourdieu's work by translating it into English and by also interpreting, applying and defending it. *Réponses* intends to elucidate the internal logic and coherence of his work. Bourdieu thinks that his whole oeuvre centres on his preferred *modus operandi*, on his manner of carrying out all academic projects.[9] Admittedly, his favoured method is important, but that is even truer for his theoretical ideas and some of the concepts he introduced into the social sciences.

In the nineties, Pierre Bourdieu turned into an active political radical. This fitted his character, which had always had a strong inclination to go against the grain. During the nineties there was a rather emphatic shift towards the right; not just political parties, but the entire population also. The mainstream social democratic political parties of England, France, Germany and The Netherlands moved from left to the centre, embracing a so-called third way. In all these countries, governments attempted to stop and even reduce the steady increase in expenditure for social security, pensions, health and education. Bourdieu was a strong opponent of such 'neo-liberal' policies and supported small political parties and political movements 'left from the left.' He delivered speeches to workers on strike or other politicized audiences and published books and pamphlets where this trend was radically attacked.

In the second half of 2001 Bourdieu fell ill. He was diagnosed with an aggressive form of cancer and died on the 21st of January 2002. Pierre Bourdieu is survived by his wife, Marie-Claire Brizard, to whom he was married for almost forty years.[10]

10.2 Scientific friends and foes

Bourdieu admired the work of Marx, Durkheim and Weber. He borrowed some of their important ideas and reconstructed others. With Marx he shared a strong interest in inequality, power and domination. But, like Weber, he invested a lot of his energy in the analysis of cultural factors, in particular class-related lifestyles. He was also influenced by the work of Durkheim and Mauss on classification.[11] He shared a strong interest in socialization with Durkheim and also with Berger and Luckmann, because this process forms the foundation for what he called the habitus, i.e. the lifestyle and tastes that everyone develops. Moreover, the work of Berger and Luckmann on the social construction of reality provided him with the necessary material for his attempt to bridge the theoretical gap between the individual subject and the social object. He calls attention to the process of objectification, where individuals, consciously and unconsciously, are influenced by objective social conditions and constraints, to construct and reproduce social facts. In his view, the concept of habitus, i.e. the mental make up that one acquires during socialization, offers a very promising conceptual solution. The habitus-concept will be discussed more extensively in a later section.

10.2.1 *The attempt to end the objectivism-subjectivism debate*

As a beginning ethnographer Bourdieu was deeply impressed by the structuralism of Lévi-Strauss. But soon he distanced himself from this approach, because structuralists tend to analyze the social world purely as a system of objective relationships. They degrade human beings to pure bearers of the social structure.[12] Structuralists try to grasp objective relations, which, as Marx said, are independent of the human mind and will.[13] Bourdieu reintroduced the social agent as a socialized individual. He knew that individual actions are determined by society, but rejected the idea that this was fully the case. There is some space, in other words, for individual choices.

Like Elias, Bourdieu is eager to bridge the great distance between objectivism and subjectivism and has invested a lot of energy in transcending these two irreconcilable perspectives. Objectivism treats social facts as things, or as objects, as Durkheim would have it, and bars anything that is connected to individual consciousness. Subjectivism takes the opposite view and reduces everything to mental representations. Marx and Durkheim expressed the objectivist position most consistently. Bourdieu quoted Durkheim's remark that '... *social life must be explained not by the conception of those who participate in it, but by the deep causes which lie outside consciousness.*' In this approach, scientific knowledge can be obtained by breaking away from the primary representations or 'pre-notions', as Durkheim termed them. This leads to a search for impersonal causes. But Bourdieu likes to draw attention to the fact that even hard-core objectivists cannot fully ignore individual consciousness. Marx, for example, used concepts such as ideology or class-consciousness and Durkheim characterized men as a homo duplex, that is, as beings with both a subjective and a collective conscience.

One of the most prominent defenders of the other camp is Schütz. In his view, social reality has a specific meaning for each human being. Living, acting and thinking implies that the world has to be interpreted with the help of common sense. Thus, all human beings interpret their world as the true reality of daily life.[14] Consequently, their premature and unscientific interpretations influence their social actions. Therefore, social scientists should base their analysis of social actions on these mental constructions, acknowledging meanwhile that these interpretations are tentative and premature. Social scientists must then build their theoretical constructions on a foundation of mental representations of 'ordinary' people.

As we can see, the opposition is complete. According to Durkheim and Marx, we can only gain sociological insights by cutting ourselves loose from the prevailing preconceptions and false ideologies of common people. On the other hand, subjectivists think that only common sense based knowledge of ordinary people will provide a valid and solid ground for useful sociological knowledge.[15] Bourdieu makes an audacious attempt to summarize this epistemological battle in a few sentences.

> *On the one hand, the objective structures which the sociologist constructs in the objectivist moment, by setting aside the subjective representations of the agents, are the basis of subjective representations. They constitute the structural constraints, which influence interactions. But, on the other hand, these representations also have to be remembered if one wants to account above all for the daily individual and collective struggles, which aim at transforming or preserving these structures. This means that the two moments, objectivist and subjectivist, stand in a dialectical relation.*[16]

Bourdieu stated that the representations of individuals are closely connected with their social position. Once again we hear echoes of Marx, who insisted that the content of our minds was determined by class conditions. In the objectivistic approach, sociology is a sort of social topology, an analysis of everybody's location in the social sphere and the relative position towards one another. This constitutes a necessary but limited part of any sociological analysis, but it has to be complemented with the analysis of social interactions. These interactions can be observed in many different ways by means of audio-visual recordings or standardized descriptive methods. However, social interactions cannot be understood without a clear picture of the positions of agents in social space, their positions in relation to one another. A mere analysis of interaction patterns can easily overlook the substratum of the subjects' relations with the social structure. Only if we know someone's position, can we understand why he or she is acting in a subservient, arrogant or superior way. Then we know how to interpret certain actions and remarks. The observation that someone 'is rather flexible' becomes more specific, for example, when we are aware that this person is a drill-sergeant. So, from a sociological standpoint, it is not satisfactory to reduce social structures to interaction processes, nor is it admissible to deduce interactions completely from the structural positions that people occupy in social space. We need instead to reinforce the positive aspects of both approaches. Firstly, the construction of social reality does not take place in a social vacuum, but is subject to social conditions. Secondly, we need to be aware of the fact that all our ideas have social origins. And thirdly, we should always bear in mind that the social construction of reality is no individual affair but a collective enterprise.

Rejecting the assumption of the fully deterministic character of social behaviour does not necessarily imply that one has fallen for the charms of the idea of the free will of the voluntarists. Conscious and well-considered goals do not offer a sufficient explanation for social behaviour. We must find a middle course between total determination and complete freedom. Structuralism reduces individuals to puppets on a string, as if they are completely subjected to social forces. An individual will or conscience does not appear to matter and consequently people cannot be held responsible for their actions. Rejecting this approach, Bourdieu sought for a solution that would not put him in the same camp as the subjectivists. He found it in a dialectical synthesis, in concepts such as habitus, *sens pratique*, strategy and feel for the game.

10.2.2 *A ferocious attack at rational choice theory*

Rational choice theory was Bourdieu's archenemy. Whereas structuralists underestimate the role of individuals, rational choice theorists tend to overestimate it. Yet they fail to acknowledge the full complexity of the individual, who in this approach becomes a one-dimensional being who always operates in a rational way. His main objections against rational action theory or RAT, as he preferred to call it, were that:

- It locates the whole dynamics of social life in purely rational decision-making. Individual and collective histories which unconsciously generate the ongoing reality of that social life are ignored;
- It substitutes the culturally defined and historically changing rationalities and interests of real life with an arbitrary rationality, namely the rationality of the market, of positive science and self-interest.
- It prevents a theoretical apprehension of the relationships between individuals

and between individuals and their environment, which are the proper objects of social science.

According to Bourdieu, it is easy to understand why RAT may appear to be empirically sound. The idea of individual finalism, which conceives of action as determined by conscious goal setting, is a plausible illusion. Most people like to think that they are independent, that they are rational agents capable of making decisions autonomously. Richard Jenkins states that Bourdieu's attack is not entirely justified.[17] Does not Bourdieu himself set goals and objectives, which he then pursuits? Why cannot this be true for his research subjects too? If one starts to debate the question whether or not people always behave in a rational way and pursue their own self-interest, then we create two opposing camps that never will be reconciled. The question is, really, what can be explained with the help of the model of a purely rational man and what by other motives for social action? It does not take much observation to see that most people will behave in a rational way most of the time. They will not hesitate to take the shortest and safest way back home. They will try to buy the best consumer goods for the lowest price. If they encounter some problems, they will search for solutions that will require minimal costs and physical energy. But it is also true that people often do things that seem to go against their own interest, such as helping a stranger in need. It is clear that we cannot satisfy our sociological curiosity with only one paradigm. Rational choice theory can only answer a certain type of questions. But this is true for any paradigm. Bourdieu, the polemist, was right with his critique of the polarized versions of structuralism and rational choice theory. But this critique should not lead to a complete abandonment of these approaches. On the contrary, from a dialectical stance, such a critical attitude should lead to a kind of synthesis where social structure and individual behaviour both get due attention. In the following sections we will see whether Bourdieu has been successful in creating such a synthesis.

10.3   Core concepts

In 1971, Pierre Bourdieu and Jean-Claude Passeron published the theory of the *habitus,* a term they borrowed from Thomas of Aquino.[18] They had been looking for a concept that could aptly describe the connections between socio-economic conditions and lifestyle, in different social classes. This theory has much in common with more familiar socialization theories that state that we continuously learn from and are influenced by our social and cultural environment. Thus, we appropriate a large number of skills and perspectives, learn to know our position in the social system and acquire our social identity. During our youth, we absorb all the assumptions of the dominant culture and internalize the norms and values of our social group. The social conditions we experience during our childhood years will be deeply ingrained in our minds. This process will create a mental structure of views and opinions that is taken for granted and that will make us uncritical about social life around us. Objective structures and internalized subjective structures converge, rendering an illusion of immediate understanding of our life-world, a comfortable illusion we dare not give up. This mental structure is called the habitus. It is a rather consistent set of perspectives that encompasses observations, evaluations, and predispositions to act in certain ways. The basics for these mental schemes are acquired within the family. Later on, the school also takes up the socialization process; that is, the teachers, classmates and peers followed by our friends and colleagues. Because all this might sound a bit too much like a one-sided process, we should remind ourselves that we partly choose our own socializing agents, in particular our friends and also to a certain degree our colleagues. With some we only interact when strictly necessary, with others we develop more intensive and friendly relations. This kind of voluntarism falls within the range of our own discretion. In most cases this will not arouse negative reactions or other actions of social control. Anyhow, this internalized habitus generates meaningful social actions and perceptions, fitting the social context from which they emerged.

In *Distinction* Bourdieu presents the emergence and the proceedings of the habitus in a rather simple model, after explaining first, far less simply, that the habitus is not only a system that produces social actions, but also a system of classification for evaluating these social practices. With the help of these capabilities the habitus helps us constituting and reproducing the social world.[19] In his typical style, characterized by his habit of using several variations of the same word, Bourdieu states that the habitus not only is a structuring structure, but also a structured structure. At an abstract level this is rather evident. Every structure is structured and only structured processes can change the structure of something else. What Bourdieu wants to make clear is that the principles of producing and classifying practices and evaluations, embedded in any habitus, in turn are themselves the product of internalizing the objective, class based social structure. Because of the fact that the habitus is developed within a world full of concrete class differences, it is adapted to it. We have learnt to recognize and acknowledge these class differences in our society or our 'social space,' a term preferred by Bourdieu to emphasize that all positions are relational. We have learned to classify and judge everything according to the standards of our own social group or class. Thus we create and reproduce the same practices, products, lifestyles, and tastes that belong to our own social origins. Doing so, we underline, support, and reproduce the existing social order with all its social differences and cultural distinctions.

Figure 10.1   Social conditions, habitus, and lifestyle

Social origin	Habitus	Lifestyle/taste
Social, and cultural conditions	The production system of social practices and preferences (taste)	Social practices and products

Despite its new terminology there is a strong similarity with the process of internalization described by other classical sociologists and psychologists. However, theorists such as Durkheim, Parsons and Berger put a very strong emphasis on the formation of moral behaviour. In their view, the conscience acts as a guardsman of social behaviour, to the effect that all individuals stay in line with the expectations of the social group, at least to a sufficient degree. Bourdieu does not belittle this control function in any way, but he likes to focus on the inculcation of dispositions for certain behavioural patterns. The habitus ensures that people can make the right choices without any effort, whenever they are interacting with other people. This can also boil down to self-control and self-censorship. In particular, Bourdieu wants to make clear that our personal lifestyle will not deviate much from the lifestyle we have observed and experienced during childhood, a lifestyle that seems to be apt for people like us. Where the classical theory of internalization deals with the question why people abstain from certain actions, Bourdieu draws attention to the question why people are dispositioned to choose, or seem to prefer, particular actions. Where other classical theorists pay much attention to norms and values, Bourdieu focuses on lifestyle and taste.

Bourdieu recognizes the social determination of our behaviour. Yet, he leaves room for the concept of voluntary behaviour and rejects the notion of the hypersocialized and fully determined social agent. With his concept of a habitus he wants to escape the vision of a totally regulated social existence. The habitus directs our behaviour, efficiently and efficaciously, to certain objectives, even though we are unaware of this. What people say or do not say, do or leave undone, seldom is determined by conscious calculation. The extreme urgency of large parts of our social behaviour excludes a careful consideration of all the pros and cons. Mostly, the circumstances urge us to react in a split second. Because of the necessity to react immediately – for also a hesitation can be interpreted to carry meaning – people have to possess a kind of second nature for apt reactions. In our contacts with other people we are often confronted with unexpected actions or reactions. What will we do when someone attacks us? Will we venture a counter-attack, cry for help or run away as fast as we can? But also in less dangerous situations we have to react quickly and convincingly. How to respond to a difficult and rather awkward, but relevant question during a job interview? Even our hesitation to answer immediately will be interpreted in a certain way. Will we speak the whole truth, even though it might reduce our chances of getting this job? Or will we conceal our lack of experience with specific tasks and exaggerate our skills? Can we bluff ourselves out of this predicament? In situations like this our behaviour strongly depends on our habitus.

But the habitus cannot structure everything. It is impossible to foresee everything and be prepared at all times. People have to improvise. Improvisations and solutions for new and unexpected problems, however, still have to fall within the range of what is accepted in a society. These conditions are predetermined in a long historical process. Arbitrary though they may seem they constitute hard social facts that cannot easily be altered by single individuals. Social and cultural conditions, however, are mostly taken for granted. There is little desire for change, because these conditions are ingrained in the habitus in great detail. So, when we plan our reaction to an unexpected situation, we unconsciously take all these restrictive conditions into consideration. Hence, our mind will not even allow solutions that are only theoretically possible.

We do not act at random, but rather predictably. We act as we do, because we have been socialized to do so. On the other hand, the habitus does not mean we operate as a robot. Within certain limits, there is room for individual manoeuvring. The habitus implies that we have the capacity to react in a flexible but fitting way to all kinds of situations. With this notion, Bourdieu wants to transcend irritating theoretical oppositions such as deterministic - voluntaristic, causal explanation – teleological explanation, unconscious actions – conscious actions. Perceived as social life incorporated, the habitus concept should be able to transcend the quite absurd opposition between individual and society, or, politically, between total individual freedom and totalitarianism.[20] These are two complementary and inseparable parts of one system. By developing his habitus the individual becomes an accessory to the continuation of social life. This complicity assumes conscious as well as an unconscious participation in social affairs. It manifests itself in what Bourdieu calls 'feel for the game' or practical sense.[21]

All humans have their own individual biography, so they all have acquired a habitus that is a variant of the modal habitus of their social group, class or category. Since members of a social group share a great many of social conditions, they also share a large part of their habitus. Thus it is possible to live, work and play together without an ever-present overseer. All the players in this social collective know what is expected from them, when to start, how to play, and when to stop. Besides, the habitus turns necessities into virtue.[22] Humans adjust their subjective expectations, their personal motives, and needs to the objective conditions and probabilities. Thus, the social order is firmly established in the habitus, and it needs no further supervision, in general, no public display of power. Social order is produced and reproduced in our mindsets. That is one of the main functions of the habitus.

It may appear that the notion of 'order' implies a strict application of rules. This view is too simple, for Bourdieu. The social world is far too complex to survive just by prolonging and reaffirming a rigid set of rules. Social order is dynamic and organic. Hence, this order cannot be explained by a concept of behaviour that is completely directed by fixed rules. To survive in a complex social system, people need to develop a sense of practice and a feel for strategic actions.

10.3.1 Strategy, sense of the game, sense of practice

Bourdieu has introduced many new sociological concepts. One of the most innovative is *le sens pratique* (practical sense or feel for the game). The meaning he gives to 'feel for the game' has little in common with mathematical forms of game theory, or with Goffman's metaphor of society as a theatre or play. Undoubtedly, people play games with each other. Often they behave like movie stars and use a whole array of different strategies to manipulate each other. These observations urged Bourdieu to shift his perspective from the vocabulary of social rules to that of social strategies or practical sense. This perspective renders a different outlook on the social actions of individuals. For Bourdieu, it also meant the definitive rupture with structuralism. In his first ethnographic studies he described how culturally given dispositions, interests, and means of production interact with individual skills and idiosyncrasies, with economic, social, and cultural constraints, and with the social effects of historical events. In Algeria, he realized that conjugal transactions should not be perceived as the simple continuation of an already existing genealogical line and specific matrimonial rules, but rather as the result of a complex strategy, that nevertheless results in the repeated manifestation of certain traditional patterns.

Bourdieu developed a growing distaste of the term rule, because it always remains very unclear what structuralists mean when they use this word. Is it a juridical or quasi-juridical principle, more or less consciously produced and dominated by social agents, or is it a set of objectively observable regularities imposed on all those who join a game?[23] Theorists should make a clear distinction between a law-like rule and an empirical regularity. Social life is regulated. It is a place where certain actions take place regularly, where most actions follow well-known patterns. For instance, in many multi-ethnic and multi-faith countries, there are hardly any marriages between partners from different ethnic or religious groups. Also, in many countries, rich people tend to marry the rich and poor the poor. It is the outcome of specific historical and social processes that steer potential candidates for marriage towards a specific process of selection.

Yet, there is a third meaning to the word rule, in the model or principle constructed by scientists to explain social phenomena. If one blurs these distinctions one risks to confuse 'the things of logic with the logic of things' as Marx once phrased it while he was criticizing Hegel. To avoid this, one has to include the real principle behind strategies in the theory of social behaviour, i.e. the practical sense or feel for the game, as sports players prefer to call it. The real principle behind it is the practical mastery of the logic of a game. This mastery of the immanent necessities of the game is acquired by experience and training.[24]

Bourdieu saw a fruitful analogy in sports games, to make clear that a group of people participate in a socially regulated activity, that is, an activity that is not the result of mere obedience to rules.. Each social game that has been developed over a long historical process has acquired an inbuilt necessity. Because of this immanent logic of the game you cannot do whatever you like, without the risk of punishment. The better the feel for the game, the better the game is played by following these immanent rules. Excellent players seem to subject themselves to the inherent logic of the play. The mastery of the game is acquired and further developed during practice, without even noticing it, just like one is unconscious of the way one walks or moves. Besides, not everyone is endowed with the same amount of practical sense. This capacity is not equally distributed and evidently, there are differences in such a feel for the game, differences in ability, aptitude or indigenous talents, Bourdieu is very successful in avoiding such terms, especially when he analyzes the role of schools.

Strategies are not the result of a mechanical structuralism, or of conscious, rational calculation. They are the products of practical sense or feel for the game – an ability that has been developed during children's play and other social activities. The star player is, so to speak, the game incarnate. Every second he performs exactly what the game requires. This presupposes a permanent capacity for invention, which is indispensable for anyone who has to adapt to infinitely varied and never completely identical situations.

> *Nothing is simultaneously freer and more constrained than the action of the good player. He quite naturally materializes at just the place the ball is about to fall, as if the ball were in command of him – but by that very fact he is in command of the ball.* [25]

The activities in team sports may give the impression of automatic actions, as if the players were robots. In reality good sportsmen always act on what they survey of the actual situation. In a split second, they take account of the positions of their teammates and their opponents, including the course they may take, and last but not least, the speed and direction of the ball. When players sell a dummy, it is in anticipation of the anticipations of the opponent. In a conversation, we can observe similar processes. The content and tone of a conversation is guided by the practical sense and feel for the interaction process, which includes empathy with the other. People eager to win a game, catch the ball, or score a point, need to have a feel for the game, just like when they want to marry, recruit a new colleague, acquire a new business partner or a political ally they must have a good feel for the relevant games of society. They must be able to profit from every opportunity that comes their way. They must be creative and able to improvise.[26]

Concepts like habitus, feel for the game and strategy do not square with concepts such as a mechanical obedience to explicit, codified rules. Bourdieu developed these notions to break away from objectivism, from the idea of action without an agent that structuralism presupposes. His description of the double strategies employed in playing according to the rules, while intermittently neglecting these rules when they do not fit personal interests, offers a good example of his theoretical intentions. The most able players will give the impression that they live according to the rules, but are prepared to break a rule whenever achieving one's goal demands it. Take soccer, for example, the game that vividly illustrates this. Rinus Michels, the former coach of Ajax, Barcelona, and the Dutch national team, used to tell his players that soccer is war. So, smart defenders will not hesitate to place a well-aimed kick against the shinbone or ankle of an opponent who threatens to score a goal. But they will make it look like an unintentional accident, an offence that could not be helped but happened in the heat of the moment. However, we can safely assume that these professional artists, these athletes who have trained their body to the limit, really acted in a very deliberate way. The way they react to the referee after this act of foul play is telling enough. They show no concern for the pain of their opponent, only fear for being sent off. When safely retired from sports, years later, some may admit that the foul was deliberate and committed in view of the fact that the stakes were so high and that losing was no option. Another form of legitimization that is often mentioned is revenge: hurting an opponent physically is a quid pro quo for something that happened earlier in the match, or even in another match, perhaps a year ago. These unwritten rules state that fouls are a necessary last resort, to force the game. Even the risk of temporary suspension or a fine is taken into the bargain. This example clarifies that sociologists must always make an effort to look beyond the official rules of the game. Structuralists, as the argument goes, tend to neglect this.

10.3.2   Matrimonial strategies

From 1957 to 1964, Bourdieu was engaged in ethnographic research in Kabylia, a region in Algeria. His topic was the systems and rites of marriage in a pre-capitalist society. This period coincided with the Algerian revolt against the French colonizers, and it was impossible to perform research in a quiet and systematic way. Bourdieu opted for basing his study on a great variety of sources, such as official statistics, historical documents and interviews with local people. Kabylia was chosen because of the intense clash between tradition and modernity at that time. One of the topics that fascinated Bourdieu was the possible consequence of this clash for matrimonial systems.[27] Matchmaking can be subjected to strict rules. The most powerful restrictions emerge from customs related to succession, such as the necessity to maintain a farm or a business that is large enough to be viable. But the rules are not always obeyed. Traditions are often ignored; the rules are bent to achieve personal goals. Social scientists must observe therefore the *practice* of matchmaking, because the laws of tradition everyone speaks about are not reliable. Bourdieu learned that his concepts such as a feel for the game or practical sense can be applied quite well to traditional matrimonial strategies in Northern Africa as well as to the practices of peasants in the Béarn, the region in the South of France where he grew up. He contended that it was indeed necessary to use these concepts, lest we end up with fruitless theories. Practical sense guides people to 'choose' the best partner, in the given circumstances and under certain conditions. For instance, the eldest son in a well-to-do family has better prospects than his younger brothers.[28] The explicit rules of the game define the value of sons and daughters. In that sense, the prevailing norms and values, customs and traditions, determine the outline of the playing field. But within this field, everyone may choose the best strategy for success.

In Kabylia, matrimonial arrangements often are the outcome of power relationships within the family. These relationships can be fully understood by appealing to the history of this group, in particular the social history of previous marriages. If the mother, for example, comes from outside, she will endeavour to reinforce her position by trying to find a match in her own lineage, which will be less problematic the more prestigious her lineage is. But the husband may find it in his interest to find a match in his own lineage. The outcome of this conflict of interests between husband and wife is unpredictable, because it does not follow simple rules. Besides, there are many other strategies that play a role in the matter, for instance strategies of fertility, educative strategies, or economic strategies. Clearly, there is much more to marriage than biological reproduction. Above all, most families want to maintain or better their position and rank.

The interesting question is whether these matrimonial traditions are applicable to modern, open and individualized societies. Bourdieu, who observed the transformation from a planned matrimonial market to a much freer market, noted that the importance of habitus is as great as ever. How else could we explain that birds of a feather always flock together? Moreover, there are all kinds of strategic customs to ensure that the supply of potential partners be restricted to the right kind. There are public dances, exclusive balls and other community gatherings to create some kind of protectionism for the matrimonial market. Within socially and culturally homogenous groups, such as student fraternities or sororities, or mixed sports clubs, a large number of love affairs and matrimonial matches are made. The creation of homogenous social categories largely excludes relationships with outsiders. But the best guarantee for a marriage between equals (homogamy), and maintaining status, is the spontaneous affinity that joins humans with a similar habitus.

The great families of the French aristocracy use matrimonial strategies that are altogether similar to those Bourdieu had observed among peasants from Béarn. In the most famous families of the French aristocracy, marriages are founded on strategic manoeuvres, intended to retain or improve social status. Even important economic decisions, such as business mergers, often are connected to certain relations between families that have been welded by 'arranged' marriages.[29] It is certain that these elite families do all that is in their power to keep their youngsters segregated from commoners, by sending them to prestigious private schools or to exclusive holiday camps. These strategies are, at the core, similar to the strategies of rural people in the South of France or in Kabylia.

Conjugal strategies cannot be dissected from other strategies, such as family planning, financial investments, or investments in the education of children. They all form a coherent set of strategies aimed at the preservation of social positions and high status. This is the theory at its most abstract level. It is a general theory with a high degree of validity. Whatever the social and historical conditions, privileged groups will do all that is in their power to keep their privileged position intact. The drive to improve status and the anxiety to lose it, the desire to improve one's social position and capital, are the main motives behind all these strategies. That is why elite groups choose elite schools for their children. That's why white parents send their children to white schools as soon as the number of pupils from minority groups rises above a certain tipping point. But this is not the whole story behind the social reproduction of inequality.

10.4   Marx revisited and revised

Most modern sociologists have tried to come to terms with the views of Karl Marx in one way or the other. Pierre Bourdieu was no exception. He did not reject Marx' views on social inequality but refined and strengthened them by stating that not only there is an inherent class conflict between the upper and the lower classes, but that these battles occur at every level between all classes and even between fractions of the same class. Moreover, the fight is not only fought over material issues but over cultural issues as well. For that reason the system of inequality is embedded in society far deeper than Marx had foreseen. In this way differences in education, culture and lifestyle help to reinforce the tenacious patters of socio-economic inequality that can be witnessed everywhere.

10.4.1   *Cultural capital and social battlefield*[30]

According to Bourdieu, we have to take notice of capital in all its manifestations to get a good understanding of our social world. Capital is not just monetary, or what can easily be transferred to the monetary. Sociologists have to look further. Economic practices do not exhaust all social practices, and often serve other social practices. Therefore, Bourdieu coined the term cultural capital. There are three forms:
- The corporeal form, that is the form of enduring dispositions, skills, and capacities;
- Objective forms such as paintings, books, software, et cetera;
- Institutionalized forms such as educational diplomas, certificates, and titles of nobility.

Corporeal cultural capital is a form of ownership developed as a part of the habitus: having is exchanged for being. This strictly personal form of capital cannot change hands from one moment to another, as is the case with money. Yet in certain ways and forms it can be transferred. Specific forms of knowledge and particular skills can be taught and so handed down, to children, students, and protégés. To some degree this happens subconsciously, but in other cases this demands a lot of time and energy, for which one often has to forgo beloved leisure time activities.

In his attempt to find a valid explanation for the big class differences in success at school, Bourdieu did not accept explanations in terms of intellectual ability or motivation. He found that achievements at school strongly depend on the cultural capital 'inherited' from parents. Children from the higher classes have developed a habitus that eases their educational career, thanks to the fact that they are raised in an environment of cultural capital and specific investments made by their parents. These parental investments are manifested in a great interest in the cognitive development of children, in particular the correct use of language.

Next to cultural capital there is also social capital. This is the whole set of present and potential resources that arise from one's social network. In this extended concept of capital one finds the strong influence of Marx. Bourdieu was a real conflict theorist. He saw conflicts wherever he looked, not just conflicts restricted to that one big and significant class war or the preliminary fights that herald the final revolution, but the struggles for power, prestige, and money. His concept of a (battle-) field occupies a central place in his theories. The structure of a social field (*champ*) is a state of power relations among the agents or institutions engaged in the struggle. It is also a state of distribution of the specific capital accumulated in the course of previous struggles and it orients subsequent strategies.

> *The most different social fields, court society, the field of business firms or the academic field can function only if there are agents who invest in them, in the different senses of this term, who commit their resources to them and pursue their objectives, thus helping, even when hostile, to maintain the structure of the field or, in certain conditions, to transform it.* [31]

Despite the big differences that exist between fields, differences in the stakes and interests, there are general laws of fields. The functioning of fields as different as politics, philosophy or religion follows invariant laws. That is why the project of a general theory is not completely unreasonable and why, even now, we can use what we learn about the functioning of each particular field to question and interpret other fields.[32] In each field we can observe conflicts between newcomers and the establishment, between upstarts and old stock. Whether sportsmen, artisans, scientists or politicians, as newcomers they all have to prove themselves in the form of a specific talent, knowledge or skill. To gain access to the top regions of their field they must pass certain tests and earn the merit of being a worthy opponent or teammate. This does not stop the elite of a particular field, to defend their privileged position with all the means that can be mustered.

Each field is determined by specific stakes and interests, which are irreducible to the stakes and interests specific to other fields. Talents, knowledge and skills that are important in one field can be worthless in another field. The structure of a field is the state of the power relations between agents and institutions that are caught up in the struggle. One can also say that it is the distribution of relevant capital or capitals. That structure directs the strategies for future battles in the struggle for better positions. The powerful opt for conservative strategies that will not affect the structure of the field. For them, innovations and changes are risky. The newcomers and other less privileged categories tend to put their hopes on change, on new plans and methods, which might offer an opportunity for improving their position. In general they have more to gain then to lose.

Concepts such as field, habitus, strategy and feel for the game are closely related. Each social field is connected with a specific habitus and a specific feel for the game, because it has its own stakes, rules and logic. Think of the fields of professional sports, policing, medicine, science, banking, and building. How the game can be played largely depends on one's position in the field and vice versa. Bourdieu gave the example of the editor or a critic of a progressive paper writing polemic articles with, unaware perhaps, the expected reaction of a conservative paper in the back of her mind. Similar processes occur in political debates. The inner logic of a field can engender unintended actions and unintended consequences. A paper might lose some of its loyal readers and a political party might lose its grassroots support. An avant-garde painter may encounter hostile reactions to the unexpected and unfamiliar works he created in order to distance himself from the former generation of artists. In that case, it is quite unlikely that he will sell many of his paintings. Nevertheless, it is possible that he has set a process in motion that eventually will change the taste for works of art. According to Bourdieu, new consumer goods are introduced all the time, not because producers want to change their products, or consumers demand new and different products, but simply because of the inner logic of a market economy. Within the logic and automatisms of capitalism, businesses are always on the look out for new products that can give them a decisive advantage on their competitors.[33]

10.4.2   Class revisited

Bourdieu's theory of fields signifies a kind of rupture with the classical class theory of Marx. But, since the reproduction of social inequality was his main concern, he couldn't ignore the work of Marx. On the contrary, he reconstructed, refined, and expanded some of the latter's ideas. This was urgent because the socio-economic situation in the western world had changed dramatically. The social structure now is much more diversified than a century ago. In the nineteenth century, the proletariat of unskilled labourers was much more homogenous. All were poorly educated, had long working weeks, earned very little and lived in poverty. There was hardly any time for leisure and certainly no money to spend on luxury goods. As a consequence there was little variation in lifestyle. In the twentieth century this all changed, with new types of jobs and a matching educational system, an expanding economy, pay rises and an improved social security system against the hazards of working life. Clearly, the simple divide between capitalists and proletariat is outdated. Another important reason to expand and refine the class theory of Karl Marx is the need to take other structural factors into account. Economic factors no longer suffice. Gender, ethnicity and geographical stratification are important too. Bourdieu maintained, furthermore, that cultural factors were of great significance.

In contrast to Marx' simple model, Bourdieu painted a more complex picture of a society consisting of many layers and fields. Most are restricted to particular professions and locations, which is why each social class must be subdivided into class fractions. Moreover, Bourdieu paid a lot of attention to the people who find themselves in ambiguous positions, as a result of upward or downward mobility. Another cause of increased complexity is the choice of a spouse from a lower or higher class. A working class man can move up the social ladder by marrying the daughter of a businessman. Eventually, he might even take over the business and become a businessman himself. But these are sporadic incidents. The larger impact comes from structural transformations of society. Think of the huge increase in women with paid work, whereas most of their mothers and most certainly their grandmothers, stayed at home as housewives all their lives. This has boosted the income of many working class families. Thus, the whole concept of a proletariat is fading. Instead, these families can afford a more luxurious lifestyle, buy a car, go on holiday every year and eat in restaurants. In the second half of the twentieth century, this transformation created a triple win situation. The workers became more affluent, the capitalists earned more money, because of the rise in production as well as consumption, and, because of this significant boost for the economy, governments expanded the public sector, offering better welfare arrangements, public education, health care and so on. All this smoothed industrial relations. There were fewer strikes and other forms of class conflict, politics became less polarized and class-consciousness dwindled.

Bourdieu broadened our view on class and class relations. In his view, what constitutes a class is not only determined by the occupation, income, and educational level of its members, but also by secondary characteristics such as the sex-ratio, geographical distribution and a whole range of other characteristics that may function as latent prerequisites for class membership. One is not accepted without the required secondary characteristics. And if, miraculously, people 'of the wrong type' are admitted, they will often have special tasks. For instance, lawyers with an ethnic background will often get the cases that involve ethnic minorities, immigrants and political refugees.

Another important difference from Marx is the focus on the dynamics within each class and class fraction. A class fraction as a whole can rise on the social ladder or climb down a few steps. Technological innovations can lead to an upgrading of occupational categories. The increase of the number of males can do the same for certain jobs that were formerly seen as typical women's jobs. Experience tells us that the status of jobs tends to decline when the proportion of women rises. In the past, an excess in the number of unmarried men was a sign of a class's degeneration. This has been observed in the category of farmers. Bourdieu observed that farmer's sons who were unable to buy or lease a flourishing farm, would postpone marriage, remain single for the rest of their life or choose a different occupation.[34]

The homogeneity of dispositions within an occupational category is partly a consequence of the rules that those occupations impose on their occupants. But it is also produced by the mechanism of selection that makes that those people who are attracted to these occupations already have been adjusted to the social requirements of these kinds of jobs. They have the feeling that they are born for this particular profession. In reality, they are prepared for their job within the modal educational trajectory of their social origin. If some individuals still do not fit in at the beginning of their career, then they will learn to make adjustments in the following years. In general, humans adjust their aspirations to their objective chances. They learn to live with their objective conditions. They become what they are and learn to live with what they have.

According to Bourdieu, Marxists attach too much value to theoretical categories and purely theoretical analyses of classes. They confuse the things of theory with the logic or theory of things.[35] He did not think it right to define a class as a theoretical category, fully based on objective economic conditions. But he also rejected a definition purely based on subjective elements such as class-consciousness. He wanted to embrace both aspects simultaneously. Hence he defined classes as sets of agents who occupy similar positions and who, being placed in similar conditions and submitted to similar types of conditioning, have every chance of having similar dispositions and interests, and thus producing similar practices and adopting similar views.[36] Whether classes get involved in a revolutionary class struggle is not a question of historical determination, as Marx believed, but a question of historical probability or contingency. For instance, a sudden emergence of nationalism can shake up class affiliations. The real status of a potential working class remains dependent on a whole series of social and political conditions, or even the appearance of the right political leader at the right moment. In Bourdieu's view, classes only exist when they are organized as a political party that has fully mandated its leaders to negotiate on behalf of the party and to demand certain actions from the party. The party and the class should be one and the same organizational unit.

It should be clear by now that Bourdieu wished to retain some basic ideas of Marx about social classes. Instead of dismissing them completely as outdated concepts, he refurbished them to make them relevant for the more complex societies of our modern age. His criticism of Marx' theories did not lead to a definitive rupture. On the contrary, Bourdieu said that he was inclined to refer more often to the work of Marx after Marxism lost popularity among social scientists.

10.5   Education and symbolic violence

Bourdieu's contribution to the sociology of education was the first aspect of his work that received wide recognition. Together with Jean Claude Passeron he published a series of books on this topic, but all these books bear the mark of Bourdieu's insights, concepts, and modus operandi.[37] In *Les Héritiers* from 1964, Bourdieu shows that working class children lack the cultural capital that is required for a smooth educational career. At the time, he still thought that state schools were neutral institutions that offer opportunities to members of all classes to meet and to further get to know one another. During the preparations for *La Reproduction (1970)* he realized that schools are no such thing, but rather institutions of 'symbolic violence'. Modern education offers an ingenious solution to the problem of the intergenerational transfer of power and privileges.[38]

10.5.1 Symbolic violence

The concept of symbolic violence represents Bourdieu's elaboration of Weber's theories about authority and legitimization. He shows that the social justification of all kinds of mechanisms of power has no legitimate basis, but is merely based on the cover up of injustice and arbitrariness. Symbolic violence is the imposition of someone's own system of meanings upon the members of other groups in such a way that this is perceived as 'natural' and legitimate. Most of the time the victims do not even realize what is hitting them. Every authority succeeding in imposing certain cultural elements upon the rest of the population, without revealing the real underlying power relations, increase their own power. Precisely the cover up constitutes an insidious and powerful form of suppression, because the people who suffer from this type of violence are unaware of it. It is even worse. They think that everything is okay and fair. Precisely the people who fail in education do not see that it is quite the reverse, that education has failed them. They are convinced that they have only themselves to blame. They were lazy and stupid, weren't they? These self-accusations show that formal education is well equipped to give the impression that everyone gets a fair chance. Qualified teachers teach everyone. Everyone has to study from the same kind of books and everybody receives the same treatment. Everyone will get a pass mark for a good answer and a fail for a wrong one. Everyone is subjected to exactly the same tests. So, lower class children and children from ethnic minorities do not see that middle class children from the dominant group get a head start. They do not see that the content of education is not tailored for their needs. But in fact, only the children socialized with middle class norms and values, from homes where the standard language is spoken, encounter at school the language, pronunciation, choice of words, and grammar they are accustomed to.[39]

The fact that the educational systems succeeds in helping a small group of people with upward mobility, does not contradict the power of the reproductive mechanisms in society. On the contrary, these exceptions reinforce the myth of equal opportunities. They do not alter the overall pattern of social reproduction, but form a kind of legitimization for social inequality. Thus, in Bourdieu's view, education insidiously contributes to the stability in a society that pretends to be a real meritocracy.[40]

The dominant class determines what knowledge should be taught. Thus, according to Bourdieu, the cultural elite takes care that their words and deeds are consolidated as the national standard, that the education system imposes the same standards in language, codes of conduct and other norms and values on all pupils and students, irrespective of their social, ethnic or sub cultural origin. Pedagogical actions include the suppression of ideas and opinions that do not tally with the hegemonic culture, as well as the indoctrination of pupils with the core elements of the prevailing culture. Teachers will do this with great conviction. They think that their actions are legitimate. But no pedagogical action is culturally neutral. Fortunately for them, the consumers of primary and secondary education are inclined to accept this.[41] Schools succeed in passing on the idea that the lifestyle and taste of the upper class is the only valid lifestyle and taste. This is problematic, because schools fail to bridge the gap between the culture of the dominant class and the subculture of socially disadvantaged pupils.

10.5.2   Self-exclusion by a negative reaction to limited opportunities

Thousands of studies from all over the world have shown already that socially deprived children have very few opportunities of becoming upwardly mobile. Over and over again sociologists of education have proven that lower class children lag in cognitive development and educational achievements. They have a significantly higher tendency to dropout before getting a diploma, and, if they finish education with a diploma, their level of achievement will be below average. Not only educational scientists are aware of this fact, but also the population at large. That is one of the reasons why many children at risk give up on the idea of social mobility through school. Many studies show that lower class children and children of minority groups have a negative attitude towards education. For Bourdieu this is yet another manifestation of subjective adaptation to objective opportunities. There is a well-known study by Willis, often cited by Bourdieu, where the behaviour of a group of recalcitrant lower class pupils (*the lads*) is observed. These lads refused to conform to the school system. They tried to create havoc in class by harassing both teachers and well-behaving classmates, called ear holes, because they still listened to the teachers.[42] The lads attempted to imitate the sturdy, macho behaviour of their fathers, who worked in a factory or at a shipyard. Their fathers had never studied, hardly ever read nor did other intellectual things. Instead, they horsed around with their mates and tried to thwart the orders of their bosses. Anyhow, the obstructive behaviour of the lads resulted in the self-exclusion from education, and, at the end of the day, they were included in the ranks of the working class, just like their fathers.

Similar processes of self-exclusion have been reported about ethnic minorities. Fordham describes the extreme pressure executed by peers with an anti-school attitude on classmates who are doing well at high school. Most black high school pupils in the ghettos of an American metropolis strongly believe that higher education is not a black thing but a white thing.[43] Besides, they are convinced that a diploma will get them nowhere, because of widespread racism among employers. Black boys in particular think that it is useless to put much effort in education. Most of their energy is channelled into proving their black male identity by dating girls. And the few who, stimulated by their parents and teachers, persist in studying hard are called 'brainiacs' or are accused of being homosexual. At that age these forms of harassment are not easy to resist. As a consequence, many will give in and join their peers, maybe forever forgoing the chance of a good education and a good career.

Fuller describes a group of black London girls, who try to solve this dilemma by performing an anti-school attitude during lessons, while simultaneously paying as much attention as they can. At home they work hard at their homework, although they flatly deny this should anyone ask. Their school career is not harmed while they remain friends with their less motivated peers.[44] This double strategy offers an excellent example of practical sense, as feel for the educational game. With another group of black youngsters in Amsterdam, this feel was lacking. Sansone observed a group of young Surinamese boys during a period of over ten years. The group counted many dropouts, who subsequently tried to survive with shady deals and other petty crimes.[45] This strategy turned out to be rather hopeless. Some were put in prison for several months or years. They forfeited their chances on a diploma and a good job. After a while, they had to be content with third-rate jobs in the secondary labour market or just went on with their life at the fringe. What we see is a contingency of unfavourable conditions. Education is not carefully attuned to their needs. The lack of school success leads to frustration, lower aspirations and, finally, dropping out without a diploma. They shift the focus of their daily life to the alternative of the subculture of their peers. This is a hedonistic subculture with immediate gratifications in the fields of music, dance, drugs and sex, in most cases financed by petty crime.

10.5.3 Bourdieu's theory of reproduction

Reproduction theorists like Bourdieu and Passeron are right in many respects. But their view on the reproduction of inequality by education is biased. Even a quick scan of the outcomes of educational research shows that the school system not only reproduces intergenerational inequality, but also helps supporting meritocratic tendencies. Nowadays numerous pupils from lower class origin succeed in entering universities and colleges. After graduation, most of them succeed in acquiring a job that suits their level of education. Therefore, it is not right to belittle the emancipatory effects of compulsory education. Besides, in most western countries girls have caught up with the educational level of boys or even have surpassed them. In secondary schools they tend to achieve better. Their marks are higher, fewer have to repeat a class, and they are just as successful with their exams. The only thing that lingers from past traditions for both girls and boys is that the choice for higher education appears to be gendered. On the other hand, however, there still is a big gap in achievement between majority groups and most ethnic minorities. However, outcomes of research show significant differences between various groups. In the United States some minority groups show the same level, or even a higher level, of achievement as the white majority. In particular this is true for pupils who originate from East-Asian countries such as China, Japan and Korea. These groups are also able to secure high status and well paid jobs. A favourable mix of family values and strong achievement motivation seems to explain this.[46]

Despite these meritocratic tendencies, there are also strong reproductive forces at work in education. And precisely these forces have called the attention of Bourdieu. In his view, the reproductive element of education is situated in its middle class culture. Its whole curriculum is catered for children from the middle classes of the national majority. The language of the school is the standard language of the nation. Hence, children from lower class families, or children from linguistic minorities, are disadvantaged from day one. They have far greater trouble to understand the teachers and they lack the right frame of reference for many elements in the curriculum. Many words and concepts are quite alien, whereas children from more privileged groups can easily feel at home at school, because they recognize the language, sayings, norms and values, from home.

But we should realize that middle class parents are prepared to invest more in the education of their children. They put in a lot, to prevent that their children will fail at school. Their children must follow in their footsteps, so as to become members of the same privileged class and acquire similar well paid high status jobs. They will pay for extra tutoring when necessary, or even send their children to expensive private schools if they think that this is necessary for their educational career. They want to prevent a loss of status at all costs. Lower class parents often lack the insight that stimulating cognitive development of their children and supporting their school career is very important for school success, and hence, for upward social mobility. In other words, they lack the right amount or type of cultural capital.

This last perspective has been labelled as a deficit model. Adherents of the difference model assume that all cultures are equally valuable. Therefore, state schools should not give any group a head start by attuning the content and methods of education to the language and culture of one specific group. Some critics have accused Bourdieu of actually endorsing the deficit model, by assuming it, but this critique is completely misdirected. In fact, he is the champion criticizer of this arbitrary and unjust practice to support and legitimize the culture of the dominant class or ethnic group. He always tries to reveal the complicity of education in reproducing inequality with the help of symbolic violence. Whenever he speaks of a lack of cultural capital, it is only in a 'relational' logic. For sure, he does not think that victims should blame themselves. On the contrary, over and over again, he explains that these deficiencies are the result of social constructions, where elite groups have been successful in making their own language, subculture, taste and lifestyle the only valid standard for national education.

Bourdieu started his studies in the field of education by revealing the mechanisms that are accountable for the reproduction of class differences in school careers. However, these studies have shattered his initial belief in the emancipatory function of education. Reasons for the failure of education in this respect can be found in his famous study *Distinction: A social critique of the judgment of taste*. This highly influential study will be discussed in the following section.

10.6   Cultural distinction and social distance

La distinction is the jewel in the crown of a project that has taken more than twenty years. It started with Bourdieu's scientific quest in Algeria. He was fascinated by the manifold cultural variations he encountered. Initially he was content with the explanation that diversity was created to ease the distinction between different tribes and that the differences functioned as markers for ethnic identities. Later, his interest shifted to the social function of differences in lifestyle during the transformation from traditional to modern society.[47] He observed that the adaptation to capitalism imposed by colonizers differed greatly from the process of becoming capitalistic on one's own account. There was no puritan ethos that, according to Weber, had been of such great importance for the flourishing of a capitalistic economy. To Algerians, this transformation only meant imitating the lifestyle of the colonizers, for example by purchasing modern French furniture and luxury goods. Even tribesmen who still lived in tents or very simple houses bought modern furniture and luxury goods to increase their status. It had no other function. In Kabylia, Bourdieu realized for the first time that the struggle for recognition is an essential part of social existence. To get this recognition people make extensive use of their status, lifestyle, and taste.[48]

10.6.1   *The road to a modern classic*

In *Photography, a Middlebrow Art*, originally published in French in 1965, Bourdieu explicitly shifts from the language of differences to the language of distinction.[49] He perceived that photography is not seen as a legitimate art, but as a sort of semi-art. Photography is squeezed between 'real' forms of art such as painting, classical music, and literature and creative expressions that are not related to art, but to taste, such as home decoration, interior design, and dress style. In the socially constructed hierarchy, professional photography is a second rate art at most, just like jazz and filmmaking. Amateur snapshots do not represent art at all, but a social practice. It is easy. Everyone can do it.

For this empirical study, Bourdieu observed village people from Béarn, the region of his birth, workers from a car factory and members of a photography club in Lille. Unfortunately, he did not study the category of professional photographers, whose work is published in important magazines. Nonetheless, even this study highlights class differences. Within each class or social category there is a socially constructed consensus about what could or should be photographed and what not. Photography is particularly associated with family life and its integration. In general, the social function of taking pictures is to solemnize and record those special occasions of social life where the group reaffirms its unity: weddings, christenings, family holidays, but not funerals. There also was consensus about how people and events had to be pictured.

It struck Bourdieu that there are few social practices that are as predictable as taking photos. Certainly, this is true for taking snapshots. Everybody uses the camera (or video camera) to record the main events of family life. It is a way of registering and formalizing the highlights of family existence. These pictorial records support and reinforce the solidarity of the family by reinstating the image that people have of themselves as members of a close social unit. The following quotation nicely shows how Bourdieu, in his typical style, frames ordinary practices that nobody else seems worthy for a sociological analysis.

> *Because taking pictures of the family is a ritual of the domestic cult where the family is subject as well as object, and because it forms an expression of – and therefore a reinforcement – of the festive feeling that a family renders itself, the need for pictures and taking pictures (the internalization of its social function) grows stronger the better the family is integrated and experiences a moment of maximal integration.[50]*

Taking pictures of important family events also has a social function at macro level. It registers the social distinction between different social categories and between the rural-traditional and urban-modern poles. Within the traditional context in particular, photos of weddings and baptisms contribute to the registration and consolidation of the objectified social organization. Thus, the social structure is recorded visually. The captured style of clothing, hairstyle, and jewellery will clearly show forever to which social class this particular family belonged.

Whereas manual labourers and farmers have a simple and direct relationship to taking pictures – they know precisely when and how something should be photographed, taped or filmed – this is much more complex for the *petite bourgeoisie*. They know of 'art photos' by famous photographers who photograph from unexpected angles. These artistic professionals have captured events in an artistic way, creatively employing the special effects of natural and artificial light and the shadows they cast. Their pictures also manifest an experienced eye for composition and alertness for interesting social dynamics or awesome situations. The petty bourgeois really like to be able to take such photos themselves, but they know they lack the skills of these professionals. Hence, they use their camera with far less self-assurance.[51]

If Bourdieu had also studied the practices in the upper class, he would have seen that they too take pictures and make video recordings of weddings and parties. There is one important difference, however, the elite will always hire a professional. Furthermore, the upper class will also take pains to record other main events in the family history: graduations and meetings with vip's. American politicians, managers and professionals indulge in creating an 'I-love-me-wall' showing all their diplomas of higher education and their meetings with vip's. The central piece would be the photograph where one is shaking hands with the president of America. All these photographs objectify someone's social status.

10.6.2   What is legitimate art?

In retrospective, *L'Amour de l'art* from 1966 appears to be a pilot study for *La distinction* too. Bourdieu argues here for the first time that art has a very arbitrary character. He knocks 'high' culture from its high pedestal and presents it as a rather arbitrary hobby of the leisure class. The cultural and social elites have managed to legitimize their taste for art as the right taste.

The middle class eagerly, but often unsuccessfully, tries to imitate the lifestyle and cultural tastes of the higher classes. In a sense, the lower classes seem to be wiser. They do not even try. Experience has taught them that high culture is not meant for them but for a different kind of people. They shall never visit a museum or a concert hall if they can avoid it. They would not enjoy what is displayed or performed and would not like the people who frequent these sacred places of fine art. To legitimize their dislike, they will assert that any toddler could have painted those abstract pictures, or that the disfigured figurative paintings of Picasso show that he should never have left kindergarten.

The demarcation lines between fine art and phoney art, creative artists and ingenious impostures are not only questioned by the lower classes. The frontline between legitimate art and the latest form of avant-garde has always been hotly debated. Nowadays the whole art world accepts that Picasso was a great painter and that abstract paintings can be considered as art. Though some doubts are voiced over the signal heap of bricks deposited in a museum, or Christo's covering of a Parisian bridge and the old parliament of Berlin in parachute nylon. Is it also art, then, if workmen put a scaffolding around these architectural constructions for reasons of restoration? Does Christo produce new works of art by simply wrapping aluminium foil around the Venus of Milo or the sculptures by Henry Moore? Perhaps even the staunchest postmodernist would deny that this is the case. But take another case. A few famous connoisseurs of art assert that two of the three famous sunflower paintings by Vincent van Gogh are forgeries. If true, this could mean that one of most expensive paintings in the world is not a Van Gogh, but a copy by Schuffenecke. It will be clear that the borderline between art and non-art is arbitrary. The question is whether it follows that the classification of art is a purely arbitrary matter decided by the cultural elite and social elite.

10.6.3   The natural gaze: unmasking a modern myth

There are individuals who pretend to have a natural gift for appreciating and evaluating art. According to Bourdieu, this is a myth. Relentlessly he has tried to come up with a scientifically valid theory as an alternative to Kant's aesthetics. According to Kant, the aesthetic gaze springs from a lofty perspective that is free of personal interests. Bourdieu does not agree. In his view, there is no such thing as the interest free and pure gaze, but a disposition that is the fruit of abundance and wealth. Without the worry about naked survival, the elite created time for leisure activities, for instance the creation and appreciation of art. Within the confines of a comfortable and luxurious life, they could afford to distance themselves from the daily worries for survival. In situations like these, one can indulge oneself in 'useless matters', such as art and music.[52]

To arrive at this point art itself had to emancipate; a struggle that took centuries. Firstly it had to free itself from the yoke of church and king. During the historical trajectory towards the movement of l'art *pour l'art*, art for art's sake, artists gradually had stopped considering the wishes and decrees of church leaders and governments. It is no surprise that this particular movement coincided with the scientific emancipation of religious doctrines. At the dawn of a new era artists no longer accepted any obligation that conflicted with the intrinsic demands of artistic creation. Art became an autonomous field. The struggle for power, status and prestige was fought with the customary rules and methods within this field, but this also widened the gap and kept common people outside the field of legitimate art. Only a highly selective group of pretentious connoisseurs believed to have a natural gift for intuitively appreciating the true aesthetic quality of paintings and sculptures.

In *L'Amour de l'art* Bourdieu denounced the hypothesis that one is born with the ability to appreciate art, that it is something that you must have an eye for. More and more he became convinced that this ability is nurtured by upbringing and thus appears to be a natural gift. Direct understanding of a work of art is possible only in those cases where the code of the viewer coincides with the codes of the artist. Therefore, most people do not understand most works of art. People, who seem to intuitively interpret works of art, rely on a so-called gift that is nothing less than a habitus developed in childhood. They grew up in a milieu where art was readily available. Their parents listened to classical music, musical instruments were played and at home art was often talked about. That is why their ability to interpret art is no more than a show off of cultural capital acquired during socialization.

10.6.4   Contested tastes

Tastes differ. Whatever the extent of a difference in taste, they always cause touchiness. This is a common experience of mankind, hence the famous dictum that we should not debate matters of taste: *De gustibus non est disputandum*. A useless admonition, for people are always arguing about good and bad taste. No innocent matter either, as differences of taste may cause couples to separate and the most devastating remark one can make is that he or she has no taste. La Rochefoucauld once observed that our pride will be hurt more by the assertion that we lack good taste than with the statement that our views are wrong.[53] Another reason for the ongoing battle about good or bad taste is that tastes separate social classes. One can immediately recognize cultivated people. They are tastefully dressed, and show good manners and good taste also in other ways. That is why the English say that *'Manners maketh men'*, at least those Englishmen who think of themselves as being well mannered and so have earned the right to judge other people. With his sociological analysis of taste, Bourdieu has touched a nerve.

No doubt, he deserves merit for that. Besides, he has helped to reclaim the study of culture from the realm of conservatism and made it an acceptable terrain of study for all social scientists.

Of all tastes the taste for music is likely to be the most sensitive. The display of musical capital is quite different from flaunting one's knowledge of other forms of art, for music is the most spiritual art of all, and so the love for music offers the best proof of a 'spiritual' personality. Music touches our body and soul. Listening to music can arouse people; it may cause their emotions to be elevated to a state of euphoria, or a state of sacred devotion. It can move people deeply, or cause them to laugh, sing and dance. It can remove tensions and bring people in a very quiet mood. For all this, music is not only the most spiritual form of art, but also the most physical.[54] This does not only apply to classical music, but also to all kinds of popular music. Though Bourdieu tends to emphasize the individual experience of and preference for particular styles of music, he is far more interested in the relationship between musical preferences and the social conditions that have made the development of these preferences possible. This always boils down to a process of class-based socialization. During this process, young people learn to distinguish objects and customs that are associated with good or bad taste. Within this context they develop a personal taste that is only a minor variation on the modal taste of their social group. Nonetheless, this little deviation of the modal form is enough to give them the feeling of a unique personal identity. Each time when they discover something that perfectly fits their own taste; they discover and affirm their personality a little bit more.[55]

In *Distinction*, subtitled '*a social critique of the judgment of taste*', Bourdieu shows that the taste for art is socially conditioned. The statistic relation between educational capital and social origin is matched by a similar relation between tastes for specific forms of art and social class. Different classes develop quite distinctive tastes for art and music, and quite distinctive attitudes towards museums and concert halls. *Distinction* is about the different reactions to works of art, paintings, sculptures, music, literature and poetry. First, if we take paintings, then we can distinguish people who have a naïve and phenomenological attitude. Especially people with a low level of education have a strong affinity with paintings that represent concrete, realistic situations, such as landscapes, portraits, flowers and animals. What is appreciated most are well-painted girls, animals, flowers or fruit that appear to be so real that you feel the urge to touch and caress them or, in the case of food, to eat it. The quality of art is for these people closely connected to the degree to which reality is copied.[56] In their eyes abstract paintings are not art at all, because everyone can make it, even one's little sister. People with cultural capital have learned to appreciate abstract paintings or modern music. With figurative paintings, they tend to ignore the primary image–the realistic representation–and pay much more attention to characteristics of style, technique, and composition and to allusions to other works, myths or certain metaphors.[57] And in the case of abstract paintings there is a lot to be said about style, composition, and deeper meanings. They know even what emotions this particular work of art is supposed to arouse. All this has nothing to do with an intuitive gift for appreciating art correctly, but with a capacity that has been developed during socialization.

It is even more striking that the taste for superior art is concomitant to the taste for clothes and even food. Members of the working class had to work hard under very difficult conditions. Therefore they needed durable clothing. The work of the elite did not require any strong physical effort, so they could afford to wear clothes of fragile and delicate material. Whereas the workers lost a lot of calories during their hard day's work and therefore needed a lot of food, the members of the elite did not use so much physical energy and could indulge in all kinds of refined little dishes that would please their palate. Peasants and miners, dockworkers, carpenters, blacksmiths, and bricklayers, however, all needed large quantities of staple foods to fill their empty stomachs and refuel their muscles. Under these conditions the rich could develop a luxury taste, whereas the poor developed a taste of necessity.[58] This relation between labour conditions and the taste for food and clothing was handed down to the next generation, even when work had become less demanding, because machines took over some of the heavy work.

Styles of home decoration and tastes for food require the same method of analysis as the class-determined preferences for art. The elite have a strong preference for a brilliant presentation of their dishes. They prefer to have a large and varied range of small titbits of food. They dislike large helpings of food, whereas the lower classes like to have their plates full of food in order to fill the stomach. This preference is closely connected with the history of the lower classes; they had to experience periods of poverty when food was scarce or when they needed high-calorie foods in order to get through their working day. So when food is concerned the lower classes still prefer quantity to quality and content to variety and attractive display.

10.6.5   *Distinction through distance, distance through distinction*

Cultural capital, life-style and taste play a significant role in the reproduction of inequality. With this perspective Bourdieu introduced a new explanatory dimension to the familiar array of attempts at interpreting social inequality. Not only did he find that class fractions differ in lifestyle and taste, but he also showed how these distinctions help to maintain class differences. This is the central topic of *Distinction*. Bourdieu argued that it is in the interest of the bourgeoisie to conceal the fact that taste is acquired through socialization. Thus, their familiarity with legitimate cultural products is made into an instrument for maintaining social distinction, based on the crude divide between people with and without taste. The lack of 'good taste' becomes the pretext to exclude members of the lower classes from their own elitist circles and from the market of desirable jobs. So, cultural distinction and social distance are closely connected and remain closely connected, as cultural distinction effectuates social distance and vice versa. The dominant class is rather successful in creating the image that they provide the touchstone of good taste and a lifestyle of quality. Their taste and lifestyle acquire legitimacy, whereas the taste and lifestyle of the lower classes is generally seen as second rate. Life for the members of the elite is relatively easy; they only have to be who they are. For the rest of the world, life is harder. It does not suffice, when you aspire to climb the social ladder, to have the right (educational) qualifications; you need to be able to change your habitus, taste and lifestyle as well, and you must start with a careful imitation of the manners of the higher classes or you hardly stand a chance of being accepted. But even serious attempts to adjust taste and lifestyle will not guarantee a successful route to the higher echelons of society, for, on many occasions, a modest background betrays the 'social climber' or 'upstart'. No matter what volume of cultural and educational capital has been amassed, the social trajectory always plays a significant or even a crucial role. The cultural capital that is consciously acquired by education is static, and a confrontation with new forms of high culture (the *avant garde*) may cause bewilderment. So in the case of social and cultural mobility, there is a tendency to adhere to those forms of high culture that are well established and beyond dispute, just to be safe.[59]

There is yet another reason why it simply is not enough to adjust. In an egalitarian society with equal opportunities, where class differences seem to have faded, it often turns out that, other things being equal, social and cultural capital are decisive factors in acquiring a good job. The right social connections and the right habitus and lifestyle are of tremendous help in anyone's career perspectives. This helps in reproducing, maintaining, objectifying and even legitimizing the connection between parental social class and occupational position of their offspring. This gives people the idea that only members of a certain class have the right social capabilities and cultural level to suit the higher professions. This process entrenches the social distance between social classes.

From this perspective it is quite logical that the majority of people intend to copy the taste and lifestyle of the elite. This is of course intensely disliked by the elite, who prefer to keep the distance at least as large as it is. When the lower classes appear to bridge the gap, the elite will start to think of strategies that can restore it. To keep upstarts and parvenus at a distance they will develop new preferences in leisure activities, food, art and music. For instance, when the average citizen starts to enjoy famous pieces of music, that were formerly only appreciated by the elite, they will instantly play down the quality of that music and start looking for other composers, singers, musicians and conductors. Whenever a piece of art becomes popular, this is a clear sign for the elite to drop it from their 'repertoire' and to move on. This can be a move forward, into avant-garde art, or a move backward into ancient music, played with antique instruments in a style that is supposed to be really authentic. The popularized canon of classical music is now only acceptable if performed under special conditions; say a special location, with an extremely famous conductor, a recently discovered exceptionally talented performer, or an innovative interpretation. In general, social climbers will adhere to that part of legitimate culture that has been taught at school. Since they have been brought up in a milieu that lacked cultural capital they will always fear to do or say something wrong, to reveal a lack of familiarity with high culture and make a showcase of their downright vulgarity and shallowness, and alleged insensitivity for the most sublime in art. Only by staying within the safe limits of acquired taste, can they avoid a complete embarrassment before the born and bred elite. Repetitively, therefore, it was stressed by Bourdieu that there is a difference between primary and secondary socialization, that is, between what has been acquired during your upbringing at an early age and what you have learned in a later period of life, regarding art and other forms of high culture. In the first case, knowledge becomes an integral and natural part of one's habitus. The music lover who is brought up with classical music shall move around with much more ease and shall be prepared to accept new developments more easily, whereas someone who only later in life has learned to appreciate classical music will not be so flexible. This is one more way to identify differences between the old elite and the nouveau riche.

10.6.6   *Theoretical framework of La Distinction*

In *La Distinction* Bourdieu continues the theoretical drift of his earlier studies. Explicitly or implicitly all his core concepts come to the fore: social strategies, habitus, subjective expectations that are adjusted to objective probabilities, and, last but no least, social reproduction. Once again it is a theory about how social practices of groups of people are determined by their social history and the status of their parents and ancestors. All individuals are confronted by the social conditions of class. And, once again, it is about the inbred social conditions, learned opinions and perspectives, classifications and judgments, manners and customs contribute to the reproduction of the existing structure of society.

First, Bourdieu contends that the definition of art is arbitrary and is imposed by the cultural elite, who pretend that they have a natural gift for understanding the fine arts. Thus they seem to imply that they belong to a higher class of people. However, their so-called gift for understanding and interpreting the fine arts is nothing special. It is an acquired capacity, developed during childhood, which correlates with other dispositions, such as a preference for certain types of food, a specific style of clothing, that all are the result of early socialization. The elite have succeeded in promoting their lifestyle, taste and manners as the hallmark of real style or 'class'. Even the people who do not belong to the social and cultural elite are inclined to share this view. This universal legitimating underlines the great success of this form of symbolic power. It supports the social reproduction of social distance and social distinction between classes and class fractions. Step by step Bourdieu's reproduction theory runs as follows:

- Variations in objective social conditions lead to the formation of different social classes and class fractions that divide people according to their positions;
- Similar social conditions and social positions produce a class determined habitus;

- That habitus is a system of mental schemes that generates a system of perception and preferences and classifiable practices;
- These preferences and practices result in a lifestyle that materializes as system of distinctive signs, that reproduces practices of classifications;
- The elite – a fraction of the ruling fraction – succeeds in imposing its lifestyle, taste and practice as the only legitimate one.
- Moreover, the elite succeed in safeguarding its privileged position by a strategic use of differences in cultural capital, taste and lifestyle.[60]

In summarized form it is even more plain that Bourdieu's theory is very deterministic, like all reproduction theories. He observes that changes are taking place, but also notices that the overall structure and the core process of society do not change at all. It may seem that the distance between two particular classes or class fractions have decreased or even disappeared. It may also be that some social categories exchange positions on the social ladder. And it may be that quite a number of individuals succeed in achieving some upward mobility – and in some cases the range of mobility can even be quite spectacular – but all this does not change the structure and overall level of inequality in society.

10.7   The power of words

Nothing is more social than language. Hence it is no wonder that sociologists have given a lot of attention to the phenomenon of language. Elias drew attention to the intricate interweaving of our physical, social and linguistic evolution. And Habermas thoroughly investigated how language or speech could contribute to changes in society and emancipate the oppressed. Bourdieu also links language and social structure.

10.7.1   *The necessity of a sociological analysis of language*

Since language does not only function as a medium for exchanging messages, Bourdieu focused on sociolinguistic aspects, such as the legitimacy and power of linguistic expressions.[61] He preferred to examine language situated right in the middle of the practices that have produced it, that is, a social world with all its imbalances of power, its cultural distinction and mechanisms of social reproduction. By focusing on the social structure, we see how the course of a conversation depends on the acceptability and authority of the speaker. In other words, the attention of an audience depends on the power and authority of the speaker, on his or hers social status, position, experience, expertise and his or her rhetoric skills. With this type of analyses social science is brought in and as a result linguistics loses its purely linguistic character.
Bourdieu has introduced concepts such as the national and international language market with as its necessary corollary, a symbolic capital, but also concepts

such as a linguistic habitus and the legitimacy and power of language users. As we know, the nation-state was and still is a great destroyer of minority languages and local dialects. Most nation states acknowledge only one legitimate national language. That standard language is imposed on everyone by means of a system of compulsory education. The standardization of the national language is perfected by the introduction of an official spelling and grammar, which is disseminated in institutions of primary, secondary and higher education. There is a form of linguistic coercion carried out by publishing houses, language professors and the writers of dictionaries, who provide the standards for evaluating anyone's use of language. When taking an exam or at a job interview, a person runs the risk of being rejected for his limited skills in speaking and writing the standard language appropriately. In many cases, imperfections in the use of the standard language will provide a (silent) reason for refusing someone a high status job.

Within most nation-states, historical contingencies have arbitrarily elevated one local dialect to the status of the national standard. This promotion meant that all other dialects were relegated to a lower league. Besides, the group that speaks the standard language has succeeded in fostering the idea that their speech is more refined and civilized, whereas the other dialects are coarse, vulgar, cheap and shoddy, in other words, uncivilized. This social mechanism has given them a surplus symbolic capital. Their language use has more value than that of people who hadn't learned to speak the standard language at home. The differences in language and dialect both underscore and reproduce the difference between social categories, in particular between social classes. This analysis is a logical extension of the ideas that were presented in *Distinction*.

As soon as people notice that their own dialect is treated as an inferior language, they will shift to the dominant language and use it wherever it seems to offer better opportunities. However, no matter how much they try, most of them will never be able to make this shift completely. Some elements in their choice of words, grammar or pronunciation will reveal their 'inferior' background.

Alongside the national linguistic market there is also an international language market, where similar conflicts of power between rising and falling languages can be observed. Thousands of languages run the risk of becoming extinct whereas only a few will survive the third millennium. At the moment, English is in a winning mood. It is the global lingua franca within the spheres of science, internet, film and popular music. It regulates international air traffic and dominates the hard world of software. In contrast, we can witness the shrinking international status of French, which, for many ages, was dominant with the western elite, the field of diplomacy and that of *haute couture*. To make things worse, French language purists have already noticed a shift towards *Franglais*.

10.7.2   *Linguistic habitus and competence*

Not only have many languages found themselves in dire straits. The same is true for individual speakers, whose social position is connected to their language habitus and competence. Language competence covers the impressive capacity to produce linguistically correct sentences, but also the ability to use language in a socially correct way. It is a matter of appropriate speech at the right place. What is said, or written, to whom, where and when? Such questions have defined the field of linguistic sociology. Bourdieu has broadened the scope for this field in his characteristic way, using his cherished concepts such as habitus, field, and strategy. Our habitus colours the way we master and use languages. It tells us what we are expected to say, or not to say, in a gamut of social situations. Only in completely new and different social situations do we experience a feeling of being at a loss in a communicative sense. We don't know how to take part in communication, partly, because social classes differ in linguistic habitus. The same is true for professions, ethnic groups, and regional areas. The choice of words, or one's accent and intonation, reveal the social, regional and ethnic origin of a speaker. Some social categories speak more loudly and quickly than others. All such characteristics offer further information for classifying the speaker, and immediately affect the reaction of the speakers who are being addressed. So, verbal communication always involves an exchange of more messages than the purely linguistic one.[62]

The language usage of a speaker can't be separated from his position. If a general practitioner addresses his patients as if he were a dockworker, then the patient would immediately doubt his expertise and skill as a doctor. Also the other way around, if a dockworker would talk to his colleagues as if he were an academic, using a posh and elevated language, he would run the risk of being harassed into quitting his job. So, what is conveyed by speech is not just pure language, but the complete social person. For sociolinguists it is no radical innovation to speak of a communication habitus. It will remind them of well-known theories of socialization. But Bourdieu's approach is different. For him linguistic competence is a form of practical sense. Competent speakers will anticipate the reception of their words. It depends on the habitus and competence of speakers whether they foresee the consequences of their interaction. They have to assess the differences in power between both parties involved in the conversation. Speakers proceed on the basis of their subjective expectations of objective probabilities. Their strategies are based on the average chances of success, given his or her past experiences. Within the acquired linguistic habitus most people will have developed a disposition to mind their use of language and will select the right linguistic expressions on the basis of an interiorized standard. The general standard guarantees a mechanism of self-correction and speakers silently acknowledge the legitimate status of the standard language and the demands of a correct and proper use of that language. At home or among friends they will be less strict in their use of grammar and vocabulary, compared to when they find themselves in formal settings or amongst members of the dominant group.[63]

Verbal competence also refers to the ability to force people into listening to what you have to say. One does not only speak to be understood, but also to be heard, obeyed, believed, and respected. Often communicative strategies are directed at the chance of being heard, believed and obeyed as well. Linguists seem to forget that the conditions for successful communication have to be created and recreated time and time again. It cannot be taken for granted that people will be prepared to listen to your conversation or to have a discussion with you. This willingness depends on the position of the speaker and the listener. The soldier has to listen to and obey his sergeant or captain; a pupil his teacher. In hierarchical relations, communication is guaranteed. When this is not the case, the speaker has to find compensation in the power of persuasion. His or her competence in to draw attention and it is crucial to keep the listeners interested. Without authoritative power or special communicative skills, there is little effect in speech.

In the domain of communication, efficacy is more important than efficiency. To achieve a particular goal, one may withhold specific information, or transform it. In general, people will then not hesitate to exaggerate or to play matters down. In order to safeguard certain powerful positions or to impose their will upon others, people even tell lies. Telling lies is a very common thing. Politicians and leaders of important organizations will lie to conceal weaknesses in their policy or in their organizational strategy.[64] Again, this supports Bourdieu's view that humans use double strategies, in particular when they feel attacked or think that their position is under threat. In those cases, communicating reliable information is not the main thing. Then, language is just another medium of gaining or maintaining power.

10.7.3   *The social conditions of the power of words*

Differences in power presuppose differences in social position, which, in turn, presupposes a hierarchical classification, verbalized by distinguishing categories that differentiate between social categories.[65] In this way classification functions as a means to discover or emphasize differences between social positions and groups.

Classifications can be imposed, appropriated even, or rejected. The dynamics of social existence show for example that, under favourable conditions, it is also possible to renounce formerly imposed classifications. Nowadays, the Koori of Australia renounce the label aboriginal, which was assigned by the early colonizers. Likewise, Eskimos demand to be called Inuit now. Another interesting example is related to the word 'black.' The *Black Power*-movement of the fifties and sixties urged what are now called African Americans to call themselves blacks and to be proud of being black. After centuries of slavery and discrimination, the 'negro' had become a stigma in the collective consciousness of Americans. The Black Power movement launched the slogan that *Black is Beautiful*. Linguistically the shift from Negro to Black was not significant, because Negro was the word for black in many Roman languages. Socially, the difference was highly significant, because the term Negro had a very negative connotation because of the frequent and always pejorative use of derivates such as *nigger*.[66] It was urgent for African Americans to regain a positive self-image, because they themselves had taken up the idea that it was better to be light skinned than to be darker skinned. A hierarchy of colours had emerged, with the message that it was better to be honey-coloured than chocolate or other darker shades of brown.[67] A similar approach to different hues of skin can be found in India. Vikram Seth's book *A suitable boy* pays much attention to the efforts of parents to find a suitable boy to marry their daughter. These efforts not only involve finding a groom from the same caste and the same or somewhat higher social status, but also with a light skin colour.[68]

The times keep changing. Afro-American, thought to be more politically correct, as it fitted the general tendency to use hyphenated terms to describe the various ethnic groups in the USA, soon replaced the term Black. Again, from a purely linguistic perspective, this appears to be much ado about nothing, but from a social and political perspective these matters are highly significant. A striking point is that these examples also show that minorities can exert linguistic power over the majority whenever politically correctness, equality, justice and a positive attitude towards cultural diversity have become major values of societies. However, all these changes in terminology have not led to a real social equality for the blacks in North America or in other countries dominated by White or Caucasian groups.

10.8   Reflexive sociology

Scientific rationality does not solely depend on the purely knowing subject. Logical control and epistemological vigilance are both embedded in society. They are founded upon the institutionalization of certain traditions of thought. These customary patterns of thinking are nothing more than a particular academic habitus that helps scientists to control their work.

10.8.1   Critical theorizing as a habitus

Just like other social practices, social research is predominantly steered by internalized dispositions, instead of codified propositions. Research is not directed by the rules in methodological handbooks, but by a sociological sense of practice. The habitus determines which research problem we choose, which type of explanations we offer, and what type of research instruments we use. It is even more important to observe that the habitus determines how scientific questions are expressed, the problems stated, and explanations construed. During many phases of a research project, the academic habitus turns researchers into some kind of 'automatic pilot'. Many important decisions are made unconsciously, but they steer our research into a particular direction. That steering process has been programmed in our brain during our training as a researcher.

Since carrying out research is founded upon a specific habitus and a well-developed feel for the game of doing science, Bourdieu urges us to be much more aware of our scientific acts. Therefore, he urges social scientists to reflect on their own practices. Theoretical work must become a special habitus, where the researcher is prepared to apply and test his or her own theoretical concepts on his personal functioning as a scholar. This reflexive attitude should always have priority. We should aim for a reflexive mode that continuously draws our attention to the risks of the many unconscious and semi-automatic elements of our practices. Every 'spontaneous' scientific discovery has to be complemented, controlled, and corrected by other techniques and mechanisms. This process of control starts with keeping a logbook during the whole research project that contains all methodological and theoretical decisions. Research then becomes more accessible for inspection and control. This is necessary because the habitus tends to evade inspection and control easily.

Of course this is not new, but Bourdieu demands to scrutinize many more aspects of doing research than what is common practice. New is also his emphasis on self-critique and self-control, where other philosophers of science seem to put much more faith in the purifying and cleansing effect of the critical forum of fellow-researchers. He is conscious of the restrictions that hamper every scientific study, and attempts to discover a form of truth that is closer to reality as it is, and not reality as it is theorized. Thus, he also tries to free himself from the restrictions that were created by his own socialization, a process that has conditioned him to see specific things and to overlook other aspects.

Reflexive sociologists realize that scholars invest much time and effort in their studies, and so have a large interest in the results of their work. This personal interest can conflict with the exigencies of a value free and neutral approach to science. The researcher has to discover something that is worth reporting, preferably something that will enhance his reputation, fame, and career. The history of science has revealed that many researchers have been tinkering with their data to 'prove' their own cherished theories. Reflexive social science differs from the sociology of sociology. Reflexive sociology is a critical analysis of one's assumption, methods and interests, whereas the sociology of sociology examines other sociologists, their approaches and biases, their networks, productivity, and power. For that matter, Bourdieu engages in sociology of sociology too, when he points out that this discipline, just like all other sciences, is an arena full of competitors in an ongoing contest for positions, grants, fame and academic power. In this battle for fame and recognition, few will refrain from bending the rules of the game.

10.8.2   *Social change as ultimate goal*

Bourdieu did not only criticize the lack of reflexivity of the modus operandi of most social scientists, but also thought that they were committed to the wrong scientific objectives. Instead of endlessly discussing theoretical concepts they should turn to social reality.[69] Bourdieu thought it more important to offer instruments for a practical strategy aimed at changing our perspective on society. Following Marx, he did not stop at describing and explaining social reality, but he wanted to change it, if possible, in a radical way. Bourdieu wanted a critical science that brings society in an awkward position by revealing situations and processes that social authorities prefer to hide forever. For instance, a society that pretends to offer equal opportunities for all citizens is not at ease with sociologists showing that equal opportunities are a myth, because class differences still are reflected in educational and social careers. Bourdieu argued that sociologists must always carry out studies that bring to light what society wants to keep in the dark. As Bachelard so neatly put it 'There is no science but that of the hidden.'[70]

This leads us to a fundamental issue. If sociology is driven by a pragmatic motive instead of a purely theoretical logic, then it is rather useless to study sociological texts in a purely theoretical way. The only valid way then is the one that leads to a specific practice, or to a transformation of a social practice. We have to appropriate the work of other social scientists in such a way that it can be applied to these practical goals. This is even necessary, because we do not understand reality until we know what a theory can do in practice. One has to reactivate the concepts, theories, and methods of others in a new productive action that is just as inventive and original as the initial scientific action.[71] It is the practice of a productive processing of theoretical concepts that turns social theory into a cumulative affair. Hence, we have to attain a practical mastery of sociological tools. We must incorporate them in our habitus. An active use of intellectual or theoretical tools of the best scholars demands some continuity as well as ruptures. Otherwise, no new knowledge can be generated. Otherwise, there is only imitation and epigonism. Bourdieu urges to think as Marx, Durkheim, and Weber to use their way of thought in order to criticize them. This is how social science is furthered.[72] It stands to reason that one may apply the ideas of one scholar to criticize or to develop those of another. There is hardly any other way to make progress in social theory. We should not satisfy ourselves with attempts to understand the work of great sociologists, but we have to get such a high degree of familiarity with their ideas that we can think along with them to think against them, in order to arrive at new insights. Bourdieu exhorts us to make similarly use of his work for a critical evaluation of his oeuvre or for the furtherance of social science.

10.9   Critique and admiration

Many critics of Bourdieu lament the complexity of his texts. Bourdieu realized that his style of writing was Byzantine, for his long sentences are often interrupted with expressions such as 'In other words', 'in short', 'more precisely'. But he never changed his style. On the contrary, he defended his writing by arguing that a complex reality demands a complex description, for in society many things happen simultaneously and influence each other. Take for instance the process of labelling. The labeller labels himself as someone who has a legitimate right to label people from other social classes or ethnic groups. But in this same action he underscores and reproduces the hierarchical structure of society and the value system and ideology that supports it. That is why Bourdieu writes in a single sentence that social agents who classify other individuals or groups also classify themselves, thus producing and reproducing the existing system of classification and the social system of positions and statuses that is being classified by the system of classification. After a while, the reader gets used to sentences like these.

In science, one of the rules of the game is to show audacity and genius in taking up arms with the greatest scholars in your field. Certainly, Bourdieu did not lack audacity or genius. Therefore, he was soon recognized as a prominent player in the major league of social science. Jenkins observed that Bourdieu dealt in four different ways with the grandmasters of sociology, anthropology or philosophy:

- He completely rejected their work;
- He partly agreed with the content of their work, and held part of their work against them. This was his approach to Marx, Durkheim and Weber, the holy trinity of sociology. It is the approach he advocated for all serious scientists: think along with your masters or opponents and use their very ideas to criticize them;
- He acknowledged the merits of someone's work, but denied that it had any influence on his own ideas whatsoever;
- He belittled their work and suggested that he was so familiar with it that he could summarize and evaluate it (negatively) with his eyes shut.[73]

All these methods require a combination of acknowledgement and distance, and each of these strategies implies a legitimate claim to scientific authority. Without any doubts about his own status, Bourdieu self-assuredly tore down every theoretical approach he did not like. On closer inspection, we see that he started with constructing a rather one-dimensional version that brought to light the greatest weaknesses in the work of his esteemed victim. This is his approach when he criticizes structuralism and rational choice theory. This strategy is rather popular among scholars engaged in paradigm wars. In any case, it did not harm Bourdieu's prestige as a scholar of formidable stature or as best-seller academic. Moreover, we should acknowledge that Bourdieu's academic habitus was formed in the most competitive section of the already very intellectualistic and competitive field of French academia.

10.10   In conclusion

Bourdieu did not want to construct *Grand Theories* in Parsons' style, or restrict himself to purely empiricist and statistical fireworks. Academically he sought to establish a balance between the theoretical acrobatics of modern French Philosophy and the theoretical poverty of quantified empirical studies that prevailed in the USA. Nonetheless, his work offers both these forms of doing science along with a variety of intermediate forms, alternatives and rare combinations. His academic productivity reflects the habitus of a theoretician who is strongly rooted in down to earth empirical research as well as in philosophical analysis and abstraction. He offers a level of skill in these very diverse domains one seldom meets in the broad field of social science.

We can acknowledge that a number of typical Bourdieu-concepts, including those that were introduced by eminent precursors, have become widely accepted in social science and beyond. Nowadays, not only social scientists talk about cultural capital, social capital, and habitus but also a wider audience of intellectuals, semi-intellectuals and journalists use the terminology. We can find proof of this in weekly magazines and the cultural sections of national papers. Of all the theoretical notions coined or re-introduced by Bourdieu, I think that the concept of feel for the game or practical sense and strategy are very important. They offer a valuable addition to notions such as society as drama or a stage, or mathematical game models. With these concepts, in combination with the concept of habitus, Bourdieu has shed a new light on the connection between social determination and individual self-determination. It clarifies the relation between collectively created social conditions and the range of personal options. The social setting seems to determine how far one can go, but the individual develops a feeling for how far he or she can go 'too far'. Thus we are offered with a new insight in the daily production, reproduction and maintenance of the whole social construction. The great merit of concepts such as cultural capital and symbolic violence (concealed repression) is in drawing attention to the more or less hidden mechanisms that reproduce social reality, including injustices and inequalities. With his explicit attention for the close relationship between cultural capital, lifestyle and taste on the one hand, and structural inequality on the other, he has removed the stigma of conservatism from studying cultural phenomena.

The reproduction of inequality was his main topic. Bourdieu has renovated this old theme by adding the role of cultural factors in keeping social rankings alive. He showed how cultural capital, lifestyle and taste are used as sources of power in the struggle to defend age-old or recently gained privileges. The need for acknowledgment, respect, and status is so strong that the relatively better off passionately wish to hold on to their level of status, their privileged position or their amount of power. The other groups are prepared to struggle for improving their lot too. Therefore, conflict is ubiquitous, and variants of class conflicts can be witnessed in every social domain. In modern societies the big clash between the working class and capitalists is now replaced by a multitude of small-scale class conflicts that manifest themselves within families and between families, between and within business firms and factories, between labour unions and organizations of employers, and within these unions and organizations, between and within ethnic groups, between and within urban and rural areas, between and within centres and peripheries – the list can be expanded endlessly. Despite all the different outcomes the overall result will be a reproduction of social inequality.

When social space is depicted as a site full of arenas, one may wonder why societies are not falling apart all the time, why all these micro-struggles and local wars do not evolve in total destruction. One answer given by Bourdieu is that most people learn to adjust their subjective expectations to objective social conditions. This process reduces the pressure in the hottest conflicts. The people with the biggest reason to revolt have learned to accept their situation, including a future that leaves little hope of improvement. Most losers even lose the will to fight for a change. Somewhere along the line, they have fixed their mindset to the idea that everything is based on bad luck and that good fortunes will always befall the already privileged. Often they destroy their last option for improving their situation. As a consequence of all the hidden forms of repression (symbolic violence), underprivileged individuals and groups are inclined to give up the fight for a fair treatment. The net result is that new generations seem to genetically inherit their low status and to become accomplices in the reproduction of inequality.

In my view, Bourdieu has certainly shed a new light on the process of social reproduction, though he tended to underrate the positive forces, unleashed by the Enlightenment, democratization, the expansion of education, literacy, and the media of communication, that result in a general uplifting of societies and opening them to more meritocratic forms of reproduction. However, whatever our critical views on the work of Bourdieu, this chapter must have made clear that this icon of modern sociology has enriched sociology in many ways. He deserves to be studied critically, so that we can take up his advice, and use his work to use it against him, to use it for further theoretical developments. Following Bourdieu's maxim we should not indulge ourselves in a purely theoretical analysis of his theories, or even worse, theoretically analyze the theoretical analyses if Bourdieu-specialists. No, we should rework his concepts, methods, and theories and that of other major sociologists to make it applicable to our own attempts at practicing social science, in order to make social science more practicable and advance its status in the very world it studies.

11
JÜRGEN HABERMAS

CRITICAL SOCIOLOGY AS LEVERAGE FOR EMANCIPATION

The awesome productivity of Jürgen Habermas has drawn the attention of many social scientists, philosophers and intellectuals. At the beginning of his career he was seen as the principal inheritor of the Frankfurt School, a renowned group of philosophers, psychologists and sociologists with a strong affinity with the works of Karl Marx and Sigmund Freud. The Frankfurt School was highly critical of modern society. Later, Habermas would question many of its theories. But, as he said, one can only remain in such a tradition by criticizing and transforming it. Besides, he added, the only traditions that survive are those that change in order to accommodate new situations.[1] So, although he has changed some of his views and themes, he has never abandoned the basic objectives of critical theory, such as its strong concern with equality and emancipation. Because of the broad scope and great depth of his work the lineage of Habermas' ideas is difficult to trace. Each new instalment of his ever-growing oeuvre incorporates insights from a continuously expanding range of scholars. He even feels comfortable with certain theological perspectives, and has drawn widely from empirical studies about economic, political, and cultural conditions. The scope of his knowledge is encyclopaedic. His work not only exhibits an astonishing eclectic attitude, but it also shows his great skill in synthesizing such a huge variety of ideas into new theoretical frameworks, on the scale of the likes of Auguste Comte and Talcott Parsons.[2] After the introductory section, section 11.1 maps his biography and brilliant academic career, a flawless career that was not hindered by his highly critical analyses of society. Section 11.2 discusses the intellectual sources that inspired him; 11.3 sketches his position within the field of critical social theory. It also tackles his debate with the great defenders of positive science. Section 11.4 discusses his views on the tight connection between types of knowledge and their specific interests. Section 11.5 deals with his perspectives on the risks of modernity, in particular the social and political risks created by science and technology, risks that tended to overshadow their more positive potential. His fears about an ever stronger focus on one-dimensional, economic rationality triggered his interest in public debate. Is it possible to create a really democratic public debate in which power and authority have no decisive voice, but it is only the best argument that decides? More than once, he revisited this problem and presented his thoroughly reworked ideas in his opus magnum *The theory of communicative action*. Some of the major topics he raised in this important book are treated in section 11.6. Section 11.7 tackles his views on the struggle for recognition for minorities and for women. Section 11.8 presents his highly critical views on postmodernism. In spite of all the negative turns made by history, Habermas keeps fighting for his project of modernity, for the emancipation of the oppressed and the underprivileged. The chapter ends with some concluding remarks.

11.1   Biography and academic career

Jürgen Habermas was born in Düsseldorf, on 18 June 1929. He grew up in Gummersbach, a little village not far from Düsseldorf. Four years later, Hitler seized power, but life almost went on as usual in this quiet, little town. His parents did not actively support the political ideas of the Nazi's. However, as president of the local chamber of commerce, his father did become a fellow traveller of sorts; otherwise he wouldn't have kept his job. Jürgen became a member of the Hitler Youth, as was expected of every German teenager at that dark time. It was only after the war, when the war criminals were brought to justice, that he became fully aware of the great atrocities of the Second World War.[3] On the other hand, the post-war processes of democratization and exceptional economic growth restored his trust in mankind. These two experiences – a strongly negative and a strongly positive one – would always be reflected in his perspective on human nature and society. He remains convinced that societies create violence as well as peaceful consensus.[4] In his view, the explanation of both the terror of the Nazi-regime and the miraculous economic and political recovery is to be found in the characteristics of German history and culture. Apparently Habermas has a great affinity with a type of explanation that leans on the same internal, causal factors for different kinds of social developments. This is manifested in his unshattered belief in the great ideals of the Enlightenment:

> *Only Reason is capable of healing its self-inflicted wounds; only through a radicalization of its own ideals will the Enlightenment be capable of facing its own dangers.* [5]

Habermas studied philosophy in Göttingen, Bonn, and Zurich. In 1954, he finished his Ph.D. thesis on the work of Friedrich Wilhelm Joseph Schelling. After that, he became a journalist and developed a strong interest in social issues and sociology. In 1955, he married Ute Wesselhoeft. They had three children: Tilmann (1956), Rebekka (1959) and Judith (1967). In 1956, Theodor W. Adorno, who had just returned from exile in the USA, invited Habermas to work at the reopened

Institut für Sozialforschung, far better known as *Die Frankfurter Schule*. In the twenties, this institute was established by a group of scholars who were strongly influenced by the ideas of Karl Marx and Sigmund Freud. They all had serious misgivings about modern society and the positivistic approach to social science. They wanted to construct a form of critical social theory that aimed at producing enlightenment and emancipation. Criticism of capitalism lay at the very heart of critical theory. In their view, capitalism repressed people and prevented them from awareness of their true situation and their real interests. In order to be liberated, the individual should rid himself of ideological illusions and false consciousness.[6] Obviously, there was no room for such a critical institute when the Nazis had seized power. All its illustrious members quickly went abroad to escape imprisonment or worse. This was all the more necessary since most of them came from assimilated Jewish families. Ironically, the majority took refuge in the United States, the very center of capitalism.

After the war, back in Frankfurt, Max Horkheimer started a metamorphosis of the institute. In the wake of the cold war, he kept a low profile and many of the pre-war publications were stashed away in cellars or re-issued in adapted versions. To put possible opponents on a wrong footing, the institute also accepted research grants from employer organizations. This did not lead to the complete erosion of critical theory, but it cut off new members from the intellectual past of the institute. Habermas, more than a generation younger than its founders, was the institute's first non-Jewish member and also the first famous member who had actually grown up in Germany during the Nazi period. For all these reasons it was not possible for him to fully identify with the first wave of Critical Theory.[7] The main result of his co-operation with Theodor Adorno was his study *The Structural Transformation of the Public Sphere*,[8] an analysis of the large difference between the real situation and the ideal-typical, classic liberal model of public discourse. His famous concept of a *Herrschaftsfreie Dialog* was launched here. It presented a vision of a free speech community, where everyone can participate in the public debate without any danger of coercion. All forms of domination and coercion should be excluded from the public sphere, except *'the coercionless coercion of the better argument'*. Horkheimer refused to accept this *Habilitationsschrift*, because of its very critical content. Habermas resigned. Fortunately, Wolfgang Abendroth, professor of political sciences at Marburg, accepted this study. Habermas taught philosophy at Heidelberg from 1961 till 1964. After that, he was appointed as professor of sociology and philosophy at Frankfurt and became the successor of Max Horkheimer, the very man who had rejected his *Habilitation* thesis. There is another irony here, because after a conflict with the left-wing student movement he resigned again and left Frankfurt for the second time, to become the managing director of the Max Planck Institute. This institute was specialized in carrying out research on the human condition in the modern technological world. In 1983, he returned to the Johann Wolfgang Goethe University in Frankfurt to become professor of philosophy, with a focus on Social and Historical Philosophy. He kept this position until his retirement in 1994. During his career he was awarded many prizes and honorary doctorates. The praise for his work has not stopped after his retirement. In 2001 he was awarded the Peace prize of the German Publishing Houses, and in 2004 he was awarded with the Kyoto-Prize for Art and Philosophy.

11.2   Sources of inspiration

Habermas' Ph.D. thesis discussed the work of Schelling, who had tried to connect elements from the Gnostic tradition with standard approaches to philosophy. Gnosticism is characterized by its black and white image of social life, in which evil dominated, hate obscured love, and darkness reigned over light. Jürgen Habermas is fully convinced that evil prevails in modern society: we live in the 'wrong' world. In the history of mankind something has terribly gone wrong. That is why we are now in a world dominated by the negative principle.[9]

European theologians and philosophers have continuously tried to excommunicate the Gnostic orientation from their field. That should not surprise us, for its colourful set of esoteric treatises, ritual prescriptions, myths, and gospels did not only originate in the Judaic tradition, but also stemmed from ancient Egyptian and Persian cults. It had emerged and blossomed on the fault line between Oriental and Western culture, and was diametrically opposed to the main ideas of Classical Greek philosophy. The Greek saw the universe as perfectly ordered, as a divine creature endowed with a psyche and reason. They adored the stars, their purity and immortality, and the regularity and harmony of their movements. They were convinced that human beings were capable of understanding the cosmic order and could use this knowledge to guide their moral life. Thus they bridged the gap between *theoria* and *ethos*, taking the regularity and harmony of the stellar order as the supreme model for the social order. In stark contrast, the Gnostics envisioned the cosmos as a monstrosity of demonic powers. In their view, it was a tyrannical order, a harsh prison from which no escape was possible, and a devilish labyrinth where all people would get lost.

Yet, the Gnostics believed that people had a divine origin and were endowed with a divine particle that was imprisoned in a body beset by low instincts and desires that lured people away from the knowledge of their divine origin and ultimate destiny. Gnostics believed that men had been thrown into the darkness of the world and were separated from the Primal Light.[10] Heidegger too sees human beings as 'thrown' into the world. As a consequence they have arrived in a state of intoxication and oblivion from which they can only be awakened by a 'call from outside'; a calling from the Primal Light, that sometimes breaks through the thick veil of darkness. There are many parallels with Gnostic ideas in *Sein und Zeit*. According to him, human beings continuously flee their authentic inner essence, driven by fear. As these feelings get stronger, they will no longer see the world as normal, natural, and trustworthy. Strong fears teach them that they are worthless, empty, futile, and mortal creatures, incessantly in need of help from other beings. Our greatest fear is the angst for death, a death that is inevitable, because our time on earth is restricted. In Heidegger's view, the voice of conscience acts as the divine. Although it is an internal voice, it appears to call us from outside. Moreover, individuals cannot control this voice that opposes their will. But, if they listen to their conscience, then people can withstand the seductions of life and discover their authentic essence.[11]

In his Ph.D. thesis Habermas discusses Heidegger's conceptual distinction between the *verfügende* (commanding) and the *vernehmende* (serving) disposition. In the course of history the commanding disposition has become stronger and stronger, until it started to govern the pastoral disposition towards nature. Nowadays, many people want to control nature with scientific and technical means. They have forgotten to honour nature and don't take care of it, as a good steward is supposed to do. This technical rationality has raged to such an extent that new forms of pauperism have emerged. Habermas sees it as his main task to expose and denounce this fateful chain of events and hopes to contribute to the revival of a world, where mankind can live in freedom and harmony, and develop its capacities without any constraints.

11.2.1 *The influence of Marx and the Frankfurt School*

Positivist science, technology, and modern capitalism, have always been critically regarded by Habermas, a reason why he has been branded as a Marxist. Undoubtedly, his work shows many signs of Marxist influences, but a series of historical events have gradually affected his views on Marxism.[12] Firstly, as the state now plays a major role in the economy, it is meaningless to consider the economy as the sole determinant of all governmental actions. State intervention has many forms, such as the taxation on the import or the export of certain goods, or the exemption from taxation with other goods. Besides, the state subsidizes business companies or factories in many different ways. Moreover, the government has set up a complex legal system in order to regulate labour conditions, production, transport, trade, and the consumption of goods, so as to protect workers, consumers, and the general public. That is why sociologists should investigate all state actions, as this important area of research cannot be left to the specialists of public administration. The issue of the legitimacy of laws and regulations has become a major theme in Habermas' work. Secondly, the sharply increased standard of living has transformed the forms of economic repression. This requires a thorough reconsideration of the social and cultural conditions of the working classes. Presently, according to Habermas, the oppression of the working classes is manifested in psychological and moral control, rather than in terms of economic exploitation. Hence, there is a need to identify an alternative mechanism that will fulfil a quasi-revolutionary change. Thirdly, he had witnessed the disastrous application of Marxism-Leninism in the Soviet Union, China, and Cuba. The reality of applied socialism had shattered his confidence in communist solutions. These states had established a hugely bureaucratic apparatus so as to orchestrate the economy and bring about a fundamental change in the structure of society, but this did not generate the ideal of a classless society where emancipated people could develop all their capacities in freedom. Instead, these extremely powerful bureaucracies formed a new and effective system of oppression. Still, this deception did not turn him into a supporter of capitalism.[13]

The original program of the *Frankfurt School* was based on an attempt to expand on the theories of Marx, and later also on those of Freud, while remaining loyal to the basic goals of the Enlightenment. The philosophers of the Enlightenment were united by an ambitious agenda concerning secularism, humanism, cosmopolitanism, and liberalism. It claimed freedom in many forms – freedom from arbitrary power, freedom of speech, freedom of trade, freedom to realize one's talents: in a word, freedom to make your own way in the world.[14] The underlying thought was to become emancipated on the basis of rational thought. Immanuel Kant proposed the claim of man to be recognized as a mature, responsible being, reason providing the means for growth and emancipation. Man would emerge from a self-imposed tutelage. He offered the motto of *Sapere aude* (*Dare to know*): to take the risk of discovery, to exercise the right of unfettered criticism, and – this seemed to be part of the deal – to accept the loneliness of autonomy.[15] The scholars of the Frankfurt School agreed with this Enlightenment ideal, but asserted that capitalism obstructed this emancipation process. Thus, they set themselves the task of revealing the inherent faults of capitalism. Critical theorists must unearth and highlight the shortcomings of contemporary society and confront it with a utopian idea of a perfect society, where everyone can realize his or her capacities to the full. Habermas fully agreed to this. It is his political ambition to bring about real emancipation by way of a critical social philosophy, always along the road of non-violence, for he is convinced that the use of violence is the final defeat of Reason.[16]

In the perception of the *Frankfurt School*, these ideals cannot be achieved with the help of applied research on certain policies, as this runs the danger of serving political manipulation. Typical research questions such as how to increase the standard of living for certain categories, how to improve inner cities, how to improve education and health care are to be avoided. Although these studies can be useful in some way, they cannot replace the broad and fundamental perspective of critical theory. First and foremost, critical theory is geared towards exposing why certain research questions have gained priority over others, why certain issues are ignored or not taken into consideration. Such an analysis should lead to a debate that succeeds in making choices about research priorities on a more rational and democratic basis.

11.3   Critical theory

Martin Jay has written an excellent book on the history of the Frankfurt School.[17] The true origins of Critical Theory go back to the mid 19th century, when Hegels immediate successors applied his philosophical insights to the social and political situation of Germany, then a rapidly modernizing society. Like these Left Hegelians, The Frankfurt School adhered to an approach that integrated philosophy with social analysis, and were concerned with the dialectical method devised by Hegel and amended into a materialist orientation by Marx. However, almost one century later the field of philosophy had changed enormously. Not only Karl Marx, but also Arthur Schopenhauer, Friedrich Nietzsche, and Edmund Husserl had criticized Kant and Hegel. Of course, the ideas of these outstanding philosophers had also influenced the fellows of the Frankfurt School. Still more important were the vital changes in social, economic, and political conditions. Capitalism had entered a new phase dominated by growing monopolies and increasing governmental intervention in the economy. Already in the thirties of the 20th century it had become clear that the Soviet Union was not as successful as most Marxists had hoped for. Another hot item was the gradual integration of the proletariat, which dampened the revolutionary spirit of the working class. Most workers had turned into consumers and now had much more to lose than their chains. This was especially true for the United States, as the members of the Institute could easily observe after their move from Nazi-Germany.

In the 1920s, the signs were still unclear. The political system of the Soviet Union wasn't yet transformed into a Stalinist dictatorship. At the time, Max Horkheimer was still convinced that large sections of the proletariat would serve as a revolutionary class, although Lukàcs was of the opinion that the true interests of the workers was represented by the (reformist) socialist party. In the thirties, when the Institute resettled at Columbia University, it changed its tone. In the American context its authors avoided words like 'Marxism' and 'communism'. They were substituted by terms such as 'dialectical materialism'. Not only because they did not want to offend their hosts, but also because this subtle change expressed a growing loss of confidence in some Marxist dogmas. Although Marxism was not completely abandoned, other philosophical notions had been incorporated to develop a new theoretical perspective, fit to make the new situation intelligible.[18] Horkheimer, who set the tone for all research at the Frankfort Institute, was deeply influenced by some views and attitudes of his mentor Hans Cornelius, having absorbed his critical stance and cultural concerns. He tended to agree with Cornelius' cultural pessimism:

> *Men have unlearned the ability to recognize the Godly in themselves and in things: ... Therefore their lives flow meaninglessly by, and their shared culture is inwardly empty and will collapse because it is worthy of collapse.*[19]

11.3.1   *The positivism debate: Objectivity and value-neutrality?*

At the German sociological convention of 1961 Karl Popper and Theodor Adorno were critically feuding on the issue of positivism. This was the start of the so-called *Positivism War*.[20] Since the seminal work of Auguste Comte, positivistic science has been identified with objectivity and value neutrality. It is directed at the study of observable phenomena and the search for general laws that can explain these 'positive' facts. Anti-positivists contend that this empirical-analytical method is not applicable within the social sciences, or only to a limited degree. As people are – in a relative sense in any case – free, creative thinkers and agents, their behaviour can hardly ever be predicted. Hence, social and historical processes can never have the high level of predictability that is characteristic for the 'actions' of matter, plants, or animals. As far as we are able to detect relatively fixed patterns of social behaviour, these are only valid within the limits and constraints of specific historical periods and social conditions. Thus, there can be no universal laws in the realm of social science.

An important bone of contention is the issue of value neutrality. Popper approaches this issue by making an analytical divide between two domains: science and the rest of the world. Within science, values such as truth, objectivity, and scientific relevance are judged to be important. Popper acknowledged that science will always be committed to these typical scientific values. In that sense it is not value-free. This does not mean, however, that there is a license for a science to be partisan and value-ridden. There is always the duty, for the scientific community, to labour industriously in order to achieve these objectives as best as possible. Popper realized that absolute objectivity is unattainable, just as it is impossible to become absolutely certain about the general validity of any theoretical statement about reality. But in his view scientists should never sacrifice these scientific values for the sake of non-scientific values, such as the interests of any social category or political ideal, because that would pave the way for all kinds of biases. Like Adorno, Habermas rejects Popper's analytical division between scientific and non-scientific values. In practice, value-free science means that one should try to remain unaffected by cultural traditions, political affinities, or loyalty towards one's friends, colleagues, and relatives. Certainly, Weber has meant it that way. But Habermas does not accept such a socially constructed demarcation.

Popper agreed that his preference for upholding scientific values such as logical reasoning, objectivity, and inter-subjective testability is based on *'an irrational belief in Reason'*. Precisely this is the point made by Habermas. He thinks that Popper has been too quick in concluding that it is possible, in science, to separate reason from ethics, just as science and politics, or facts and (non-scientific) values cannot really be kept apart. Popper had agreed that good science needs good ethics, as researchers should always strive for objectivity. Only severely tested theories can be accepted as valid theories until they are refuted or surpassed by a better one. So, the progress of science depends on a rigorous control executed by the forum of scientists. What is considered as a scientific truth depends on the prevailing opinion or even on power relations within a particular field or paradigm. This can prevent the breakthrough of new and better explanations. Popper had always ardently believed in the evolution of science by the process of trial and error elimination. He felt supported by the history of science that reveals a host of instances of long cherished and fiercely defended dogmas that sooner or later had to be replaced by better theories.

Habermas thinks that the exclusion of social values leads to an unacceptable restriction of the field of scientific research. In his view, segregation from the political and moral domain could lead to disasters such as the holocaust. For example, marketing research and opinion polls give the impression that all individuals have a say in the matter of production or in political issues. But such studies are merely used to facilitate the manipulation of consumers or voters. So the real questions for critical research are why these investigations are carried out, how they are financed, and with what objectives. These types of questions are not tackled within the traditional, positivist and non-critical research programs.[21] The adherents of critical theory are the self-appointed observers and commentators of mainstream social science. Of course, there is nothing wrong with an indepth investigation into the potential negative effects of positivistic research. But Adorno's attack, supported by Habermas, wasn't a successful attack on all marketing research, let alone on all positivistic social research. Not all of these studies are useless. Some outcomes of marketing research can prevent unwise investments, or lead to products that better match the needs of consumers. Positivistic research may lead to improvements of labour conditions, fewer traffic accidents or better preventions against severe illnesses.

11.3.2   *Manipulation or emancipation?*

It appears that Habermas has two perspectives on positivism. On the one hand, he states that empirical quantitative research can produce useful knowledge. It reveals for instance how many people live below the poverty line or which categories of workers become ill from bad working conditions. Such data can inform a critical analysis of society, or support political struggles for more equality, health, or well-being. On the other hand, Habermas strongly opposes this type of research because it might lead to manipulation. Managers can use these outcomes to improve working conditions for higher productivity and profits, rather than for improving the well-being of workers. Nonetheless, both parties may profit from this type of research. In similar vein, powerful politicians can use the results of poverty research to diminish poverty, not from Samaritan motives to help the poor, but simply for reasons of maintaining social order.

The results of empirical positivistic research may be used in diametrically opposed ways. When a positivist has established some scientific law and explained how it operates, he will assert, for example, that certain causes produce certain effects if specific conditions are fulfilled. Such a law tells us what to do in order to arrive at a desired situation, but the means to obstruct this process have also become available, so that opponents now can block the appearance of vital conditions, preventing the effects from happening. Knowledge is power, surely, but on the condition that it is not available to all parties.

The attack at positivism has created a remarkable paradox. On the one hand it asserts that positivistic research cannot lead to useful knowledge, because social processes are far too complex to apply methods from the 'hard' sciences in a meaningful way. On the other hand it asserts that the outcomes of such research can be put to use for all sorts of ends. Habermas, rather subtly, acknowledges that positivistic methods can be profitable in some cases, although the danger of abusing outcomes of research is never out of sight. He is right on both counts. But, because he is convinced that we live in a 'wrong' world, a world where negative tendencies prevail, he fears abusive use of research will prevail. In his view, immanent laws (*sic*) of industrially advanced societies lead to an escalation of technical control over nature, men, and their social relations. In this complex social system the negative tendencies of positivistic science, technology, industry, and public government are interlocked and reinforce each other.[22]

11.3.3   Should we study aspects of society or its totality?

Adorno asserted that survey research only produces aggregates of subjective opinions. It isolates the particular from the general and never arrives at a study of the 'real' object of sociology: society as a totality. Critical theorists cannot be content with studying only small segments of society, and wish to probe society in its 'totality'. Ideally, their research is concerned with a central question: '*Why are citizens alienated from contemporary society? Why don't they perceive society as their society, a society that is also functioning for them? Why do they perceive society as a rather alien organic whole that reproduces itself according to inherent mechanisms, to a dynamic of its own, without any reference to human goals?*'[23] In the ordinary practice of so-called critical research this is conveniently scaled down to questions about the occurrence of alienation, ethnocentrism, and authoritarianism among specific categories of people. Most followers of the Frankfurt School only used a limited number of positivistic instruments such as the F-scale that was developed in a well-known study of *The Authoritarian Personality*.[24]

Ostentatiously there is an enormous contrast between the scorned study of social 'bits and pieces' and the study of totalities, but in practice no one can study the whole totality of societies. In view of our limited knowledge, scarce financial resources, and lack of time we all have to make do with the investigation of parts of social structures or processes. The claim of approaching social existence as a totality can only mean that one pretends to study broader questions, questions concerning more crucial social issues and covering more aspects than is customary in social research. In practice, critical sociology has committed itself to studies that have the potential to reveal the contradictions of capitalist societies or studies that could foster the emancipation of the oppressed and underprivileged. Habermas takes the angle that we can only intuitively grasp the whole of social life. A dialectical approach conceives the context of social life as a totality that not only influences the objects of research, but also the researcher, including the way research project is set up and executed. Hence, we have to interpret every social phenomenon from the perspective of this totality. But this leads to a circular logic, from which it is difficult to escape. As Salman Rushdie says in *The Ground beneath her Feet,* you can only see the whole picture if you step out of the frame. Social scientists can never step out of the frame of society, like theological exegetes cannot step out the frame of their holy books. This is known as the hermeneutic circle or dilemma. The entirety of a work is to be understood from the individual words and their connections, and yet the full understanding of the individual words already presupposes the full understanding of the whole. Of course, understanding everything will never happen, so we have to pursue the process of interpreting the social world by taking one step at a time. Especially at the start we will make many mistakes. As we go on, some of these failures become visible because they do not match with other observations and interpretations, creating the need to go back, reconsider, and venture new interpretations.[25]

Clearly, we should be more modest in our objectives. It certainly is plausible that we can only come to grips with social reality, if we have acquired sufficient fore-knowledge about this reality, so that the right schemes, classifications, and concepts can be selected. Otherwise, we will soon learn that our approach does not fit reality, will be rather fruitless or bring us only a tiny step along. Though there will always be lacunae in our pre-understanding, there is no other way. In the end, then, there is not much of a difference from Popper's model of the growth of scientific knowledge through trial and error-elimination.[26]

The founders of the Frankfurt School knew very well that it is impossible to step out of the frame of society. They fully realized that sociology, including critical sociology, is always embedded in the very society it wants to analyze. Therefore, critical sociologists are or should be constantly aware of the strong ties with their own social context. Otherwise they run the risk of unreflectively using the dominant social perspective. And, according to Marx, that is the perspective of the ruling class.

11.4   Knowledge and interests

In his inaugural speech Habermas launched another head-on attack at the supposed objectivity and value neutrality *(Werturteilsfreiheit)* of positivistic science. His main argument is that personal, social or political interests have an influence on all scientific statements. Always, specific social interests fuel the search for new knowledge. The viewpoints we have when approaching reality have their roots in our own evolution, history, and culture.[27] They are connected to three anthropological media: work, language, and power. These media are the most important means of collective socialization.[28] Therefore, Habermas distinguishes between three paradigms of science, each with a specific view on methodology and the validity of scientific knowledge: the positivistic or empirical-analytical approach, the historical hermeneutic approach, and the critical approach. The first type is related to the sphere of work and has a technical interest, directed at gathering insights that could lead to practical knowledge. It wants to improve production, transport, medicine, services, and so on. This cognitive orientation propels the development of the physical sciences. It has a deeply rooted interest in explaining, predicting, and controlling. Positivists are convinced that they are discovering objective knowledge that is not related to any other interest than the growth of knowledge. They do not question the social framework of their practices and overlook that they deliver the means for carefully planned interventions in our way of life and its natural context. In other words, the knowledge interest of positivistic science is a strong concern with control.

Scheme 11.1   *The connection between science and knowledge interest*

Type of science	Knowledge interest	Medium/Goal*
Positivistic	**Technical** (Domination/Manipulation)	Work / Survival
Hermeneutic	Ethical (agreement / consensus)	Language / Coexistence
Critical social theory	Emancipatory	Power / Equality and self- realization

The second type is connected with an ethical interest. People have a universal need for mutual understanding and respect. However, during the long march of evolution, societies have evolved in ways that produce and reproduce much inequality, misunderstanding, mistrust and conflict. Without communal interpretation, individuals are not able to live together harmoniously. Therefore, a good interpretation of each other's background, culture and way of thinking is crucial. The third type of science has an interest in social critique and emancipation. Its main objective is to enhance critical reflection on society, and self-reflection. This should liberate individuals from repressive social conditions that severely restrict their full development.[29]

Positivistic or empirical-analytical scientists only acknowledge theories based on a system of statements that allow the deduction of testable hypotheses. They make predictions about relations between observable facts. When these predictions are confirmed, they see this as a corroboration of their theory and feel safe to base certain actions on these theories. Their 'objectivistic illusion' is founded on observations expressed in basic propositions that are supposed to be immediately evident. Habermas, however, renounces the idea of an objective reality separate from observers. In his view, even basic empirical facts are socially constituted. Our entire experience is formed within the functional sphere of instrumental reason, where the divide between subjects and objects is taken for granted. A critical social science will always investigate whether theoretical statements refer to real laws of social action or whether they merely formulate ideologically fixed relations.[30]

The hermeneutic tradition approaches reality by recognizing, interpreting, and positioning meanings and objectives of individuals *(Sinnverstehen)* or texts. Interpretative sociologists place themselves within the frame of reference of those individuals they are studying, or within the cultural context of a certain text. But here too the facts are only constituted in relation to the criteria for perceiving them. Just like positivists forget to make the relation between method and purposeful actions explicit, hermeneutics ignore inherent meanings and opinions that are part of their own situation as researcher. This 'foreknowledge' shapes the production of hermeneutic knowledge. The world of historically transmitted meanings becomes intelligible to interpreters only to the extent that it clarifies their own world. Interpretation creates a form of communication between both worlds; one discovers the meaning of transmitted information, by applying the tradition to oneself and one's own situation. Hermeneutic research generates insights that are motivated by an interest in the continuation of consensus and mutual understanding. Habermas calls this the practical knowledge interest. Rather surprisingly Habermas, the great champion of consensus building, also criticizes the hermeneutic perspective.

The phenomenologist and hermeneutic Edmund Husserl were convinced that positivistic science had cut the connection between pure theory and social practice, between *theoria* and *praxis*. Positivists viewed the world as an objectively existing universe of real facts, with inherent and interrelated laws of cause and effect waiting to be discovered. But, according to Husserl, the knowledge about the world is based on a pre-scientific sphere, on the unquestioned evidences of our life-word. Hence, objectivity is an illusion. Nonetheless, he believed that his brand of phenomenology had hacked itself loose of all social interests because of its strictly reflective disposition. He put self-reflection on a par with pure theory in the classical sense, that is, a theory purified from all those variable, mutating, and insecure factors that characterize social praxis. But Habermas thinks that Husserl became a victim of a kind of objectivistic reasoning that has always been present in the traditional view on theory.[31]

The critique of ideologies assumes that revealing information about all kinds of power relations can initiate a mental process that may change the stage of unreflective consciousness that is part and parcel of social regularities. Critical theory can destroy these law-like relationships. Unscrupulous self-reflection can emancipate social agents from the dependency of social powers. Therefore, critical theory is determined by an emancipatory interest. The interests that guide the acquisition of knowledge are closely connected to the existential functions of human beings who are conditioned to accept their social situation, and have developed a personal identity in the midst of the primordial and ubiquitous conflict between individual motives and social constraints. Thanks to our capacity for critical self-reflection we are able to see the connection between particular types of knowledge and specific interests. That capacity cannot eradicate this knowledge-interest, but, in a way, it can surpass it. In other words, critical self-reflection unites the search for knowledge for the sake of emancipatory knowledge interests.

Habermas could have gone one step further, an important synthetic step, if he had subsumed the technical and practical knowledge interests under the all-covering interest of emancipatory knowledge. But then he would have had to acknowledge more fully that the methods of logical positivism and hermeneutical interpretations can produce useful and even necessary knowledge that may help to emancipate people, especially when emancipatory interests are involved in selecting the topics for research. His view was unnecessarily biased as he overlooked the positive sides and potentials of other paradigms. It is hard to see how people ever could have become aware of real forms of oppression, exploitation, and alienation, without making this apparent with the help of facts, discovered by positivistic methods. It is also hard to see how people suffering from cultural, religious or political indoctrination can be raised to awareness without the help of interpretative explanations of processes that have created, reproduced and legitimated inequality and oppression in a long social-historical process.

Scheme 11.2   Empowering Emancipatory Social Theory

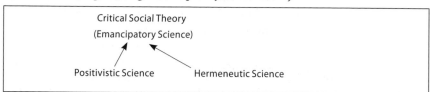

For Michel Foucault it was not enough to gather historical, empirical and theoretical knowledge that could be offered as mental food for the underprivileged in the hope that it would mobilize them into action and emancipate them. He wanted social scientists to apply their newfound knowledge in political actions that would actually help to destroy the power of the powerful and mitigate social oppression and human suffering. In *Making Social Science Matter* Bent Flyvbjerg explains some of the differences between the work and the goals of Foucault and Habermas, and argues strongly in favour of a what he calls phronetic social science, that is a science that actually engages in political actions that bring about change, while using their scientifically acquired knowledge, based on highly reliable data, thoroughly scrutinized and analyzed, and valid theoretical arguments. The phronetic approach shows a strong political commitment by tackling questions the following crucial questions: (1) where are we going; (2) is this desirable; and (3) what should be done? But because of this clear lack of value neutrality and the urge to make a difference that matters, they must be able to base their actions on the outcomes of solid positive science. Otherwise, their arguments would make no impression whatsoever with those who are in power. Without a solid scientific basis they would have no authority at all and their actions would become futile.[32]

11.5   Risks and opportunities of the technical revolution

In his first works about industrial society Habermas directed our attention to new forms of pauperism. He asserted that the gain of less tiresome physical work was cancelled out by an increased psychological strain. The work speed had been raised and for many workers their job had become even more monotonous. He welcomed the increase of income and leisure time because workers need much leisure time to recuperate from the strains of their work, but more pay is only a meagre compensation for the lack of work satisfaction. These rewards were only surrogate solutions, as the real problems were long working hours and mind-numbing jobs. At the time, Habermas hoped for a conscious reduction of consumption in order to decrease production. Hence, he advocated the restriction of advertising, for it only created artificial needs. He also hoped that talented industrial designers would 'package' all new technical products in such beautiful forms, that consumers would become emotionally attached to them and use them carefully, so that they would last longer. Later on, he directed his hopes towards the ecological movement that also argued for a more frugal way of life. Political objectives like these are closely linked to his rejection of an instrumental exploitation of nature and his advocacy of good stewardship.

11.5.1   Degeneration of praxis[33]

Unfortunately, most people with boring jobs are rather uncreative and inactive as soon as they go home. So, the real solution was to make work more challenging, more diversified and interesting. This demands a form of 'social rationalization' that stands diametrically opposed to purely technological or economical rationalizations. Social rationalization is a serious attempt to create an optimal situation for both workers and employers. It wants to prompt a successful combination of the economical demand for higher productivity with the social demand for healthy and satisfying working conditions. At first, this *Human-Relations*-movement introduced popular easy listening for workers at the assembly line. Another method was organizing all kinds of leisure activities for employees. Yet, empirical studies showed that a pleasant work climate was not sufficient. Workers should have a greater say in matters such as their work conditions, their workload, the division of tasks, and the distribution of responsibilities. Only diversification of tasks and greater autonomy and responsibility would diminish the dullness of repetitious work. Besides, studies had shown that a one-sided emphasis on technical and economic rationality might lead to a decrease in productivity. It could make workers sick, disabled or stressed as a consequence of the ever-increasing demands for more efficiency and higher productivity. Social rationalization often demands a lower work pace and a less efficient structure of organization, because people need some latitude for restoring their energy, for socializing, and for a more humane organization of work. Anyhow, Habermas soon realized that instrumental rationality would not correct itself. The economic rationality already had gone too far. It had become too dominant and infected all aspects of social existence.
In industrial society the laws of reproduction demand an ever-growing technical control over nature and an increasingly refined steering of human actions.

In such a system, positive science, technology, industrial business and public administration are closely interlocked. Within this context theory can only prove itself by means of a rational application of techniques that are required for empirical research.[34] Rationality is restricted to a 'neutral' application of the method of science, and, at a policy level, to the predictive and technological application of the knowledge that it produces. Its only function is the reinforcement and refinement of methods that will realize those policy goals. But these objectives can never be justified by a scientific theory. That is why positivistic scientists leave the solution of political and moral problems to non-scientists. Thus, many problems remain unanalyzed and many political decisions remain highly subjective. Effective social theory no longer is directed at arousing the consciousness of the people but at deceitful manipulation. Although even a fully rationalized society cannot dispense with social or moral issues, no effort is made, alas, to solve such issues by bringing about a rational consensus to improve the human condition.[35]

This is why Habermas criticized positivism once again. He believes that positivism conceals its strong commitment to technical rationality behind a veil of value-neutrality. Everywhere positivistic scientists are searching for empirically testable proofs, dismissing all alternative methods as unscientific and meaningless. But there are many situations where we have various options that are equally valid. At such moments we need a second order rationalization to make a valid choice. This can be done with the help of a decision theory, which outlines what rules can be used to select certain specific procedures and set priorities. Decision theory does not shed light on the content of alternatives, but clarifies how the pros and cons of each alternative can be weighed. It will not consider the value-loaded basis of various choices. So, there will always be a kernel of 'irrationality' in the orientation on values, objectives, and needs. If we cannot solve this problem, then there is a big chance that hard criteria of efficiency and profitability will get the upper hand. So, there is no other option than to try to arrive at some sort of compromise or an expression of the will of the majority.

Habermas denounced Niklas Luhman's systems theory as just another variant of second order rationality. Here too a central value is advanced, namely the continuation and reproduction of the system. Systems analysis concerns itself with improving the functioning of systems and facilitating its continuation, by enhancing stability and adaptability. Thus, it serves as an apology for the present state of society. It merely is a theory for technocratic use that eliminates the distinction between Technology and Praxis.[36] For Habermas, the idea of a cybernetic self-regulating organization of social life is the worst form of technocratic thought. In this 'negative utopia of technical control over history' man no longer appears as a *homo faber,* who realizes himself through his products and achievements. He is a *homo fabricatus*, a fabricated being, completely integrated in the technical system. The classical perspective on society, as a system of interactions between people that organize their life in a conscious way, is discarded for the sake of an *'instinctual self-stabilization of social systems'*. In this approach, the emancipation of individual citizens will not have a high priority.[37]

In spite of everything, Habermas still believes in the creation of a better world, a world where people really can be free and equal. Those who support technocratic models of science remain aloof from public discourse. In the decision model, citizens can only legitimize governmental decisions by way of periodic local or national elections. The process of decision-making is kept out of the domain of a rational public debate. Systems theory rationalizes decision-making at the cost of democratization, as power is delegated to professionals and experts. This leaves the public domain emasculated: all its functions are taken away, except that of legitimating the government. A complete victory of the technocratic model implies the definitive defeat of liberal democracy. But we have not arrived at the end of history yet. In view of the problems of contemporary welfare states, there is an urgent need for research programs that will turn the tables and return power to the people.

11.5.2 Democratization and emancipation through constraint-free dialogue

New technologies create new possibilities. These, in turn, may raise new needs, norms, and values, furthering technological development without governmental planning. This largely unplanned process should be made explicit in order to perceive that social interests are subjected to technological and economical interests. But how can the relation between technological progress and social conditions be analyzed and brought under the control of a rational discussion?[38] Rational discourse should not only be directed at the improvement of technical products and gadgets, but should also take into account the social and moral implications of technological progress.

There is a great need for the kind of critical reflection that relates potential technological developments to political goals. But it is precisely this type of reasoning that is overlooked by a technical rationality, because it dismisses any non-technical discourse about social priorities as unscientific. Thus, it fulfils the ideological function of obscuring the social interests that actually determine technological developments. Without critical reflection new technologies unexpectedly penetrate into existing cultural patterns and social activities, exacerbating the mismatch between unbridled technical control and unreflected objectives, fossilized systems of values, and outdated ideologies.[39] A well-considered mediation between technical progress and social action can only be realized when the process of political decision is grounded in a public, constraint-free discussion. Such a debate has to scrutinize issues that have not been discussed earlier. The traditional preconception (*Vorverständnis*) of historically determined practical interests and needs should come to the surface, and earlier social interests that had not been analyzed before will have to be made explicit. The same is true for norms and values, since economic, political, and social interests also determine them. By uncovering the ideologically legitimized repression of collective interests, Critical Theory contributes to the re-interpretation and re-valuation of certain needs and corresponding goals, norms, and values. In this sense, becoming aware of technological potential is an essential aspect of political emancipation. From a democratic perspective, all the proposed technical solutions should be evaluated with reference to the future context where its practical consequences will be felt. Only then, can sensible decisions about the expansion of our technical potentialities be made.[40] Habermas sees democracy as the institutionally guaranteed form of public communication concerning questions of how people can and want to live. At the centre is the idea of a permanent communication between the sciences and public opinion. Public opinion should be formed on a basis of unrestricted acquisition of information and a completely free discussion of matters of general interest. Then it acquires a control function concerning the application of technological knowledge in an emancipatory social practice. In a real democracy everybody has the opportunity to participate in public debate. It is the opposite of manipulation of the masses by a great leader. The big difference between Habermas and all his predecessors at the *Frankfurt School* is that he tenaciously maintains a union between liberalism and democracy. Although he is extremely critical about the current state of affairs, he will never forsake this ideal-typical form of democracy.

The idea of a constraint-free dialogue (*herrschaftsfreie Dialog*) was inspired by the free and democratic climate of English coffeehouses, French salons, and German Table Societies. In these places there was a free exchange of thoughts about literature, art, and politics. There was an atmosphere of parity, as all forms of domination had been switched off, except *'the non coercive domination of the better argument'.*[41] Public opinion took shape in these gatherings and gnawed at the dead wood buttressing the absolute power of states, kings or princes. But in the course of the nineteenth century the stark division between state and society gradually became smaller. Policy making organizations and interest groups began to cooperate more and more. All sorts of things were arranged underhanded, bypassing official political channels and procedures. Thus a social midfield was created between the state and private life-worlds. As a consequence the private life-world (*Lebenswelt*) shrank to the intimate sphere of family life at home. Thus, the consensus that should be established in the field of politics was replaced by political compromise.

Habermas underwrites the analysis of Carl Schmitt, who stated that the public discussion in parliament had squandered its potentials. More and more, important decisions were precooked in back rooms and corridors, reducing the parliamentary debate to a pantomime where politicians glibly tried to sell their party's position to the general public. The critical function of parliament had lost its purpose, and the public was offered some political pillow fighting, just for show. This sketch of political proceedings is over seventy years old, but still valid.[42] In reaction to the decline of liberalism and democratic processes, Schmitt had concluded that the days of democracy were over. He argued for a return of a strong state, towering over the scramble of fighting political parties. His ideas offered theoretical support for the undemocratic ideas of German National Socialists. Although

Habermas supported Schmitt's analysis of the decline of parliamentary democracy, he flatly rejected his recommendations for a new, far less democratic system. Instead, the weakened democratic procedures should be revitalized. Backroom politics should come out in the open to become public again. Then all political interactions and negotiations can be made controllable and widely discussed. In view of the strong conflicts of interest that surround any given topic, however, it will not be easy to reach the desired rational consensus. Therefore, Habermas revisits the theoretical problem of reaching a rational consensus in his magnum opus *Theory of communicative action*.

11.6   The theory of communicative action

In the mid-seventies Habermas shifted his interest from the question of what divides society to what keeps it together. In his view, the formation and maintenance of consensus through communicative action cements society. Already, this perspective had been explored before, but now it was given the full treat of his scholastic skills. The result was a book of well over 1100 pages, titled: *Theorie des Kommunikativen Handelns.* This is the most central work of his entire oeuvre. For a start, it is a systematic reconstruction of classical social theory. Habermas thoroughly discusses many important ideas of Marx, Weber, Durkheim, Mead and Parsons, at least to the extent that they bear on his own theoretical project.[43] But the book has much more to offer. It aims, among others, to solve the problem of rationality. For Habermas the essence of rationality is argumentation, that is, the ability of supplying good reasons for arriving at a common opinion on the basis of sound argumentation. The most crucial element of his vision is that rational argumentation should not be restricted to a discussion of facts only, but should also be concerned with social norms and personal feelings. Thus, our current one-dimensional rationality could be re-established as a broad communicative rationality, that is, rationality aimed at establishing a soundly based consensus *(Verständigung)* built on free discourse. A fair and ordered society is possible only on the basis of communal definitions of social reality, produced by communicative action. The more we deviate from this ideal typical situation, the more social constraints will emerge.

Habermas wants to connect the micro-sociological analysis of speech acts with the macro-sociological analysis of social systems. The problem is that adherents of both camps denunciate each other. At best, they confiscate some theoretical element of the other paradigm to use it in their own approach, albeit in a subservient role. Even a full-blooded synthesizer as Talcott Parsons allowed the systems approach to get the upper hand. Habermas tries to avoid this pitfall by strictly applying both theoretical approaches to the domains for which they are suited. He analyzes the symbolic production and reproduction of the informal life-world with the conceptual tools of agency theories, and the material production with the help of the systems approach. He is able to shed more light on the economic and political intrusions on our life-world.[44] Obvious examples are the demands of employers that want employees to work overtime so that they have to forsake family duties or civil servants that are asked to control whether individuals on social assistance are not sharing their house and bed with someone who could provide for a regular income.

Because Habermas held on to his belief in social progress, a collision with post-modernism was on the cards. Postmodernists no longer believe in the 'Grand Narratives' of progress after the horrific events of the holocaust, the atrocities of the regimes of Stalin and Mao Zedong, or the killing fields of Cambodia. Of course, Habermas had also become sceptical about the great ideologies that offer a wonderful future for mankind. He rejected the Marxian theory that capitalism will irrevocably lead to a great revolution followed by a heavenly communistic world order. The form and content of social evolution is unpredictable and will be contingent with chance occurrences, for the logic and dynamic of development do not strongly hang together. The dynamic mainly depends on unpredictable events. The basis of social evolution is, according to evolutionists such as Kant and Elias, our ability to be critical of our situation, and to generate new knowledge whenever we want to solve concrete practical problems. This process is propelled by the accumulation of knowledge that we can pass on to new generations and by the expansion and refinement of networks of communication. Eventually this will lead to a critical consideration of what is taken for granted in our life-world. Thus, our life-world will be freed from obsolete traditions, foolish superstitions, narrow-minded prejudices and false dogmas. However, this will engender a differentiation in worldviews, ideologies, and opinions that entice a great need for consensus about the validity of specific standpoints.

The concept of developmental logic has been borrowed from Piaget, the famous specialist of the cognitive and moral development of young children. Habermas transposes this concept to social groups, and even to the cognitive, moral, and esthetical development of mankind. Development occurs whenever completely new concepts replace central concepts from an earlier period. Following Piaget, Habermas speaks of decentring. In this process old categories lose their value and are replaced. An entirely new level of development is reached when the capacity to distinguish between physical, moral and esthetical phenomena is further developed.[45] This collective learning process does not depend on the logic of development, but on the dynamic of social development. The dynamic of history is influenced by external circumstances such as technological, economic, and political conditions. This important distinction signifies that history, as it has unfolded itself, could have taken quite another route. In stark contrast to Marx' theoretical predictions, our history has not followed a predetermined path.[46] Nonetheless, on the basis of historic events that lay behind us, many social scientists, social philosophers, and cultural commentators have sketched very bleak images of our future. They all expect that the negative trends will continue and even grow stronger, and they ignore all tendencies that could be interpreted in a more positive way. Habermas vehemently rejects the thought that all of it was unavoidable. Moreover, he keeps reminding us that there have also been positive developments. He is convinced that a greater good can come out of our social evolution, if we broaden rationalization. Moreover, with the help of medical and biological sciences we can overcome hunger and many lethal diseases. With the expansion and deepening of our knowledge of social systems and social processes we might get rid of oppression and inequality.

It sounds rather optimistic, and it does raise the question of why the process of rationalization had gone off course. Habermas tries to answer this question by presenting a rather convincing diagnosis of the problems of modern times. Once more he points at the dominance of instrumental rationality and the separation of social system and life-world as the main source of all problems of modern, western societies. In principle there was nothing wrong with the development of instrumental rationality. It led to the growth of science, more efficient production, and a longer life expectancy. Compared to the Middle Ages, there has also been a striking abatement in social inequality. A negative tendency however was the colonization of the private life-world by capitalism, state socialism, and government bureaucracies. These subsystems had gained so much power that they repressed communicative action with the forceful arguments of money and political power. Habermas put his hope on new social movements such as feminism, environmentalism and the peace movement, the new forces in waging the war against inequality. The new movements demand an open debate about other priorities such as equity, liveability, protection of nature, and people's well-being and safety.

11.6.1   *Pathologies of modern times*

In Habermas' view there is an increase of social pathologies. They are so obvious that he does not think it necessary to give further indications.[47] Besides, a whole array of renowned sociologists had already discussed major negative developments such as alienation, loss of meaning, commodification, reification, and an overdose of instrumental rationality culminating in wasteful production and relentless competition. This was ascribed to factors such as structural differentiation, specialization, and increased complexity. Social units had expanded and the traditional bonds of the tribes and lost their social function as cohesive forces. The trustworthy leadership of tribal chiefs and heads of extended families had shifted into the hands of 'alien' public authorities and their anonymous governors. The modern economic system had obliterated the autarkic, small-scale economies of extended families and tribes. The development of a global market resulted from the inherent logic of an economic rationality that is only focused on increasing profits and cutting costs. A similar inherent development arose from the logic of power, the logic focused on increasing the power of the powerful.

The natural sciences have secularized our worldview and shattered many traditional and sacral myths. Weber had revealed the co-dependency of the evolution of scientific thought and changing values on the one hand, and the development of capitalism and the modern state on the other. Habermas appreciates Weber's broader conception of rationality because it encompasses not only instrumental rationality, but also value rationality. He had also acknowledged that social actions could be based on personal affections and social traditions. Nevertheless, he criticizes Weber for only using these concepts to explain individual actions. As soon as the latter refers to processes of rationalization in society at large, he restricts his analysis to the growing dominance of instrumental reason. This kind of analysis leads to sombre conclusions and predictions. For example, that people will lose any perspective on the meaning of life as a consequence of secularization. They will be thrown back on their own autonomy. Increasingly they will have to rely on their own insights and views. Although this implies emancipation from old dogmas, it also raises the risk of too much individualization, even to the extent that society could disintegrate. In contrast to this tendency, however, bureaucratization and growing social complexity will increasingly restrain individual freedom.[48] Later, Horkheimer and Adorno would share this gloomy outlook. Habermas, however, believed that these pessimistic views originated from an idealized image of the past. He supported their bleak sketch of historical developments in the first half of the twentieth century, but kept hoping for a counter movement and a better future, although his own sketch of our present-day world was in fact rather bleak too. Actually, he noticed that the strong differentiation and rationalization of society extended far beyond the mere formation of subsystems such as politics and economy. His central thesis was that even our private life-world has been subjected to a process of rationalization. In other words, they were too colonized.

However, in line with his adage that both negative and positive factors spring from the same source, he still cherished the hope that our life-world fosters a cure. In archaic societies all interpretative frames of reference were sanctified. Then, there was no distinction between different validity claims. Only in modern societies can we detect a fundamental cleft between the assertions of positive science, positive law and aesthetics. Historically, there has been a growing amount of valid definitions of situations. The belief in evil spirits and witches has died. Emotions have become more authentic; norms are more often consciously justified. In a better world, we do not have to pretend to be different from what we are. We can sincerely show our emotions, mention our strongest wishes and cherish our deepest desires. This evolution is inherent to communicative action. Potentially, what is here today has been there from the very beginning. People can observe and learn and are capable of detecting lies and insincerity, so they have the means to criticize others and correct deviant or insincere behaviour.

11.6.2   *Colonization of the life-world*

As a consequence of the critique on traditional dogmas, people can no longer rely on fixed norms and definitions of reality. Now that the sacrosanct authority of tradition and religion has been undermined, communicative action has become more important than ever. But, with the growing complexity of the social system, political decisions are delegated to professional politicians and bureaucrats. This creates an independent political system that distances itself further and further from the life-world. Even within the life-world there is an ever-growing expansion of instrumental rationality and differentiation, partly because the subsystems of politics and economy penetrate ever more deeply into the private sphere of the social community. Strategic rationality determines the further development of the economy and the polity. Here power and money impose a sort of consensus instead of communicative action. Economic and political claims will be 'accepted' on the basis of positive and negative sanctions and not on a foundation of rational arguments. Economic and political power will drive out any consensus based on a fair and free dialogue. As authentic arguments lose their validity, power and money will become the only valid arguments. That is why Habermas speaks of an empirical instead of a rational co-ordination of social actions.

The life-world yields the sources for establishing mutual understanding. It is a reservoir of existing frames of reference and non-problematized basic convictions. Within the everyday life-world people present existing interpretations as valid statements about reality and assume that their partners are responsible beings. In turn, these interpretations are retained and reproduced through the confirmation of their validity and because the agent behaves in a social and responsible way. Habermas rejects purely culturalistic interpretations of the life-world. In his view, the life-world consists of people who are socialized as responsible social agents. It has institutions that regulate the solidarity within social groups. The life-world is therefore a subsystem of the entire social system. Apart from this symbolic reproduction, he also discerns a material reproduction of the life-world. Primarily, material reproduction is dependent on instrumental actions, whereas communicative actions take care of symbolic reproduction. They safeguard cultural reproduction, social integration, and socialization. Thus, the three building blocks of the life-world – culture, institutions, and personalities – always remain available.

The life-world is a reservoir from which the economic and political system can draw labour and loyalty. Power and money are anchored in the life-world by a socially created sense of justice and a socially determined belief in the legitimacy of political relations. Colonization of the life-world occurs as soon as the economic and political systems are replacing the co-ordination of communicative action.[49] From their one-dimensional rationality, the economic and political subsystems are inclined to trespass into other domains and to colonize the informal life-world. This leads to all kinds of conflicts and pathological developments. Cultural traditions lose their function and coherence as soon as money and power bypass rational communicative arguments. Then, solidarity erodes, and processes of socialization run astray. This process of colonization engenders all the ills that characterize capitalistic societies. Nevertheless, Habermas holds on to an optimistic view on the possibilities of re-establishing a stable and well-balanced society. He has not lost his faith in the capacities of human beings. Precisely the astonishing development of instrumental reason fuels his optimism that other dimensions of rationality can be developed too. Because not all human potential has been used so far, there is a great need for a theory that can explain and erase the single-purposed unfolding of rationality, and bring about a more balanced form of social evolution.

11.6.3   The input of the philosophy of language

In his search for the cement of a just society Habermas turned to the philosophy of language. He maintains that social cohesion is established through linguistic interactions of people who want to come to an agreement. Consensus unites and disagreement divides.[50] This is called *Verständigung* and means agreement as well as shared understanding. But he wants a concept beyond this, *Telos*. This Greek word indicates that consensus is the inherent objective of language, that agreement is the primary goal of communication. Habermas strives for a social consensus, an elimination of cultural and social distinctions, because social distinctions are the main sources of social conflict. Therefore, he plunges wholeheartedly in a thorough analysis of communicative action. What happens when we communicate with each other? To say something is to do something. Often there are clear connections between words and deeds. Examples of the perlocutionary dimension are: 'I will help you, I promise to visit you tomorrow'. So, most speech acts have a propositional and a performative dimension, expressing an expectation, a wish, a promise, an order or a demand. A perlocutionary effect refers to an effect on the hearer that is not grammatically coded by the speech act itself but that will be revealed to the interlocutor. The performative element is used to make clear how the propositional content has to be interpreted: for instance as a request, an order, a threat, or an insult.

We can say something about three worlds or domains and stand in a relation to these domains in different ways.[51] What we say may concern the *objective, physical world (1), the social world (2)* or the *subjective, psychological world (3)*. For each domain, different validity claims are used. Statements about the physical world claim truth. Statements about social relations claim justness, and statements about personal feelings are based on a claim for authenticity.

Scheme 11.3   Dimensions of reality and the criteria for validity

Dimension	Criteria for validity
Physical world (positive sciences)	Truth
Social domain (ethics: law and morality)	Moral justness
Psychological domain (subjectivity, aesthetics)	Sincerity, authenticity

Take the following example. A daughter asks her old, lonely mother to move from the inner-city district where she has always lived, because it has deteriorated. Many houses have become derelict and the streets are unsafe, because of an increase in juvenile delinquency and other forms of crime. Already many people have moved to suburbs with better and bigger houses. Mainly the poor have stayed behind and immigrant families have moved in. Other groups have also taken over the empty houses, such as prostitutes and drug-abusers. The traditional form of social control has disappeared and occasionally there are reported cases of mugging, burglary and even shooting incidents. The daughter uses these objective and undeniable facts to convince her mother that it is no longer safe to stay there. The mother does not agree. She is very much attached to her house where she has raised her family and lived in for over forty years, and she asserts that it is still safe enough to keep on living in their old home. In response the daughter comes up with moral arguments. Now, she emphasizes that the neighbourhood has lost its good reputation, and this will affect the reputation of everybody who lives there, no matter whether they are decent people or not. To this her mother might respond that she still has good relations with some of the elderly neighbours and that she feels responsible for their well-being. She would hate to abandon these old friends who might desperately need their help and cannot do without their regular neighbourhood. So when moral arguments still cannot convince her mother, the daughter launches a new series of arguments, labouring on her mother's feelings, by claiming that she is very worried about her safety. She even asserts that she is lying awake at night every time she reads about another case of mugging, or about shooting incidents. For Habermas it is of the utmost importance that the discussion will lead to a consensus, to an agreement and mutual understanding on the basis of a free, honest, and open exchange of arguments between equals, without the manipulation of facts, amoral arguments or insincere behaviour. [52]

11.6.4   Elements for discourse analysis

A critical discussion about arguments leads to a discourse about the claims for truth, moral justness and sincerity.[53] The difficulty is in finding arguments that are valid for everybody who has a stake in the matter. Discourse rules should have a universal character. If some statement or argument is countered, the foundations of these arguments will be put forward, and people will start to explain or justify their viewpoints. This raises the problem of sincerity, as there is no extrinsic reason to tell the truth, although telling lies only makes sense if the other assumes that you speak the truth. Habermas contends that a discourse about the validity of claims is only possible in an ideal speech situation, when everyone has an equal right to speak and has an equal right to put forward his arguments, when every participant is absolutely impartial and all participants have equal power. Only then consensus can be achieved.

Participants in a constraint-free debate have to cut themselves loose from all bonds with special interest groups or political parties. They even have to break away from their own culture. Such are the conditions for addressing objectively their own sincerity, prejudices, and biases. It is clear that this situation will never occur. It is an ideal-typical situation. Nobody can cut himself completely loose from his social and cultural background. Moreover, there shall never be enough time for discussing the validity of all the arguments that have been put forward. Lack of time also prevents us of getting cornered in an endless regression of arguments in defence of other arguments. For practical reasons, we will have to establish a common ground for those aspects of the discussion that are agreed on anyway, or can temporarily be put aside without further ado. Habermas thinks to find this common ground in the life-world.

Characteristic for communicative action is the opportunity for criticizing all definitions of the situation. As long as all participants are oriented towards the goal of mutual understanding, a rational consensus is attainable, in principle at least. But in many cases, psychological and cultural barriers block a free exchange of all types of arguments. In everyday reality we can only hope for conditions that approximate a situation of communicative symmetry.

11.6.5   Critique and counter-critique

Not every reader will be persuaded by Habermas' model for communicative action and embrace the possibility of a peaceful and rational consensus, if only because we still live in a world full of inequality, social conflicts, and cultural differences. We are far removed from the necessary conditions for an ideal speech situation. Habermas is of course aware of this, but it will not stop him from looking for the ingredients that might produce the necessary conditions. Although the life-world is colonized by politics and the economy, it would still contain parts that are intact and have the potential to revitalize communicative action on a large scale. Habermas tends to fall into the same kind of trap as the romantic philosophers of the nineteenth century, who idealized the naturalness and harmony of the past. He idealizes the informal life-world and overlooks the possibility that it also contains forms of inequality, violence, and differences of opinions or contradictory interests that have not been imported by external processes. In reality, we often lack the necessary preconditions for a free and democratic discourse even in our informal life-worlds. In addition, Habermas does not account for the false assumptions, distorted information, or invalid arguments that may inform consensus. Moreover, he seems to ignore that deep and extensive discussions may lead to an aggravation of conflicts, and reveal cultural or ideological differences that otherwise might have been glanced over.

Another line of critique is that Habermas puts too much emphasis on language as the main bond of society. Of course, language is very important in paving the way towards harmony and consensus, but traditions and customs, affiliations and affections, material possessions and interests can also divide or unite people. At the core of this critique is the questioning of the supposition that language has an inherent aim, an autonomous power to push us all towards consensus with all fellow human beings.[54] But, as has been mentioned before, linguistic interaction may also enlarge our conflicts and misunderstandings. We need more than the ability to speak with each other; we also need the will to come to an agreement. Some conflicts are so big that we need a strong motivation and much perseverance to solve them.

According to some critics, Habermas is inclined to view psychological problems solely as problems that have arisen from blocked communication and restricted rationality. By neglecting the inner drives of people, he arrives at a far too optimistic perspective on the possibilities of socialization and re-socialization that reconcile individuals to society. His view on mankind tends to be oversocialized and underpsychologized. Stephan Mestrovic, for example, argues that Habermas gives too much weight to the cognitive side of people at the cost of a better understanding of the emotional dimension.[55] This critique is partly beside the point, because it is Habermas who has drawn our attention to the validity of social and emotional arguments. But it is true to say that Habermas disregards emotions as the manifestation of our physical instincts or drives, such as lust and desire, and does not appear to recognize that there is no room for careful communicative action in urgent matters of life and death.

Another point of serious critique is the stark divide between the social system and the life-world, between the formal structures of society and the informal organization of our daily lives outside the domains of paid jobs and business relations. Thomas McCarthy, who has studied, commented, and translated much of Habermas' work, makes a point of this. He criticizes the antagonistic sketch of both domains, as if the economy and the polity function purely on the basis of strategic reasoning and the private life-world on communicative action solely. A few observations suffice to see that within the domains of the economy and politics there is room for other forms of rationality than mere instrumental rationality, even though the latter is very dominant. The opposite is true for the informal domains of the life-worlds. Moreover, both domains influence each other and are, in a sense, interdependent. Even the life-worlds of individuals interact with the economy and politics. From time to time they distract instrumental reasoning from its purest forms so that other interests are taken into consideration. Obvious examples are the democratization movements in industry and other business organizations.

Against these critical observations Habermas has responded that he never meant to create an absolute demarcation between social systems and the life-world, although he admits that he might have given this impression in some of his texts. In principle all social phenomena can be analyzed from the perspectives of both life-world and social systems. Nevertheless, he believes that it is still meaningful to retain a conceptual distinction between social systems and life-world in order to describe and explain how society is changing and life-worlds are colonized and ecological interests are sacrificed by economic and political systems. In his view, some phenomena can be better explained with a macro systems approach whereas and other social events ask for a micro life-world perspective.

A last critical remark of McCarthy is directed at Habermas' use of systems theory. He thinks that the application of systems theory is lethal for a critical theory that is worth its salt. The systems approach is inherently focused on order, stability, and continuity, whereas social critique aims for change and revolution. Habermas counters that with the help of systems theory, he has clearly analyzed how modern society is turning means into political ends, with the consequence that meaningful goals have lost priority. Besides, he is convinced that his analysis exposes that the strategic actions of the political and economic system as detrimental for the reproduction of the symbolic structure of the life-world. Cultural traditions, social integration, and the socialization of young people can only be carried out by actions directed at mutual understanding, and not just with the help of power or money. *'Meaning can't be bought, nor extorted.'*[56]

11.7   The struggle for recognition

We can only grasp what is involved in equal rights for women or ethnic minorities, when we listen to the specific demands and requests of these groups, so as to know what rights or which forms of unequal treatment are relevant.[57] Without such a discussion cultural differences and their consequences are easily trivialized or overcharged, distorted or ignored. This could lead to lawlessness or deprivation. Open democratic discussions create the opportunity for making clear which traditions minorities desire to prolong or abolish, how they wish to cope with their past, with each other and with nature.

Habermas endorses Amy Gutman's view that the recognition of minorities includes respect for the unique identity of each individual as well as respect for his or her culture. Constitutional rights protect the integrity of individual citizens, but it is doubtful whether an individually oriented judicial system can handle the conflicts that arise from the clashes between majority and minority cultures, for these conflicts are about the expression and maintenance of *collective* identities.[58] Charles Taylor maintains that warranting collective identities is incompatible with individual freedom and the right to equal treatment. He takes the position of Quebec as an example. Separatist political parties in Canada's francophone region have sought, in their demands for secession, to forbid the French part of the population to send their children to schools where English is the language of instruction, or have campaigned for proscribing that French should be the medium for communication in all enterprises with more than fifty employees. Taylor accepts that it can be necessary to put aside individual rights in order to warrant a collective right. Habermas disagrees however, because he has more affinity with individual liberal-democratic rights. He accuses Taylor of needlessly constructing an opposition.[59] Of course, he perfectly understands that individuals are social beings and that personal identity is interwoven with collective identity. But he argues that overstating the importance of collectivities will erode the basis for individualistic liberalism. Giving priority to collective identities will mitigate anyone's freedom to act as he or she pleases.

However, according to Taylor it is acceptable to execute active policies so as to *create* members of a community within an endangered culture. In Quebec, these kind of political interventions boil down to the imposition to choose for a specific school and a specific curriculum and French as language of instruction. Habermas rejects this kind of coercive policies. He thinks they are unnecessary, for a correctly perceived theory of individual rights does take cultural background into consideration. On the other hand, he is rather critical towards individualistic liberalism for it ignores half of the concept of autonomy. The only way to acquire autonomy (in the sense of Kant) is by being able to see oneself as the constructor of the laws to which one is subjected. Conventional individualistic liberalism denies the common origin of personal and public autonomy. This is no trivial matter, but a conceptually necessary relation. In a true democracy people have made their own laws. They have been constructed on the basis of a free and open discussion. Citizens will only perceive laws as legitimate, if they are produced in this democratic way. Then they will realize that these laws have been established on their own request and in their own interest.[60] A constitutional democratic state has to take account of social inequality as well as cultural diversity. This is possible, if we grant individuals an inter-subjective identity. All human beings are socialized in their own culture, which in turn belongs to their personal integrity. That is why a constitutional state has to acknowledge the right to be different. If this is the case, then, according to Habermas, there is no need for a second form, a collective form of liberalism.

11.7.1   The feminist struggle for equal rights and equity

To acquire a better view on this issue, Habermas ponders the case of the women's liberation movement, which shows that the fight for equal rights is far from transparent, because it also involves a fight for the right to be different. Time and time again we can observe that the advance of women's rights is a tough dialectical process. After a while each victory turns out to be only a partial victory as formerly obscured inequalities come to the surface. Every step forward produces new inequalities, entices new antagonisms, and tends to trigger a backlash to boot. Think, for example, about the traditional situation of the core family in industrial societies. Because of the large differences between the roles of men and women, inequality had become manifest. The typical male had his job outside the home and was the sole provider.. The typical housewife was expected or even compelled to stay at home and look after the children and do the daily chores of housekeeping. The earnings of the husband were seen as family-income and spent on what was necessary for the whole family. So, from a purely financial perspective, it could be said that husband and wife were equally poor or equally rich. Nowadays, women have a paid job, whether they are married or not, whether they have young children or not. This has made them independent from the income of men. But women tend to have lower paid jobs than men. Even if they have the same type of jobs, they still receive lower salaries and are less often promoted. So today inequality in incomes has become much more manifest. New forms of welfare and social assistance have given another push in this direction. So, now women are more independent. As a consequence there also are more single-headed families. Also and closely connected to this is the concentration of poverty in groups of women, especially single mothers. Once more, the fight has to be rekindled to get the process going. Equal rights, when realized, do not automatically lead to real equality and each new step ahead bring about new bones of contention.

There are two possible solutions to tackle the socially constructed, but very tenacious forms of inequality. Affirmative action can give women a head start on the labour market. The other way around is to compel men to take on more responsibilities in the domain of housekeeping and the care of children. For example, the Norwegian government has issued a law that obliges men to take their share of parental leave in case new babies are born in the family. This last approach is criticized by Habermas. He speaks of *normalizing* interventions that amount to a restriction of freedoms.[61] In this case the freedom of choice is limited for those women who prefer to claim the whole period of parental leave.

Habermas is sceptical about the idea of solving all social problems by legislation. As we have seen, the construction of laws that formally arrange for the equality of men and women did not produce equality in all respects. In reaction, many new laws and regulations have been issued to repair this, and many legal regulations in the field of work have been adapted to the new perspective on the social role of women. But even so, many forms of inequality remain. We tend to expect too much from legislation, but we should be careful with issuing new laws because they can generate unintended consequences and even become counterproductive. Again, Habermas emphasizes that laws have to be supported by the majority of the people or the majority of the relevant categories of people. Only an open and sincere discourse can pave the way for a fair distribution of professional work, housework and childcare. Such a discourse about housekeeping and childcare will have a strong impact on the socialization of children. It will influence the opinions, norms and values of the next generation. This could constitute a positive contribution to the solution of gender inequality.

The struggle for equal rights and recognition is a fight against repression, marginalization, and humiliation just like it is for ethnic groups. The feminist struggle is about the lack of consideration, both legally and informally, for gender specific differences. There is insufficient recognition for the self-image of women, their specific needs and their contribution to a common culture. The political struggle for recognition starts as a struggle about the right interpretation of gender-specific interests. Once this is achieved, the collective identity of women will have changed, and so will be the relations between men and women. It will certainly modify, if not damage, the self-image of men and lead to a critical discourse about the whole set of social values.[62]

11.7.2 The recognition of cultural rights of minority groups

An individual's integrity can only be warranted if his cultural context is preserved. Every identity is intertwined with collective identities. It can only be stabilized when the cultural frame is stable, for example when it is embedded in or strongly related to a religion or a particular language. Therefore, liberal-democratic systems should offer ample opportunities for discussions about anyone's identity. Each individual has cultural rights, that is, has the right to be and remain a member of a cultural group, because his identity is connected with a particular collective identity. As a consequence, certain group rights, such as a right to establish and maintain particular schools, churches, et cetera, should be respected. In particular, endangered minority cultures, such as that of the Inuit in Canada or the Maoris in New Zealand, can refer to special moral arguments when claiming support for their culture. In these cases, Habermas thinks that affirmative action might be necessary, although it is uncertain whether this will really help the survival of this particular minority culture. Its success will depend on the economical vitality of such a community and on the degree of attractiveness of the modern, majority culture.

Cultural traditions are transferred to new generations. During the process of socialization, personal identity is impregnated with the culture of the group. Usually, new generations will continue the culture of their parents and ancestors, in most cases without much critical reflection. However, multicultural societies urge people to evaluate and re-evaluate their culture whenever they are confronted with cultural alternatives. This is inevitable, unless minorities opt for almost complete segregation. The state can only create the right conditions for the reproduction and preservation of minority cultures, but it should not force citizens to reproduce their ancient traditions and lifestyle. That would deprive members of minority groups of the choice to either accept or reject their cultural heritage. In multi-ethnic and culturally pluralistic societies the notion of equal rights of co-existence implies that all citizens are assured that they can come of age in a social and cultural world that reflects the world in which they were born and raised. According to Habermas, everyone should have the right to continue in their own culture in a conventional way, or to opt for a way of life in another social group with a different culture. When the members of a group start to reflect upon their norms and values, customs and traditions, then only those cultural patterns will be preserved to which a close connection is felt. Nonetheless, Habermas thinks that minority cultures will change. Somehow they will adapt to the majority culture and will create a new lifestyle, a mix of old ethnic traditions shot through with the new ways of the majority. Research has shown that most immigrant groups will assimilate completely in the course of two or three generations.[63]

Habermas poses the question whether Welfare States have a right to choose a restrictive policy regarding immigration. He favours a lenient policy for the admission and naturalization of political refugees and economic migrants. He flatly rejects a policy of 'Fortress Europe' that keeps its doors closed to almost all sorts of immigrants. Yet he makes the observation that the preservation of the culture of the indigenous majority could be at risk if too many people from entirely different cultural backgrounds would immigrate in a short period of time. It would fuel the fear of the majority that they would become a minority in their own district, town or land. First Habermas tackles the issue of naturalization. Under which conditions does a state have the right to deny citizenship to immigrants? What may be demanded from immigrants with respect to adaptation and assimilation, in view of the integrity of the culture and lifestyle of the indigenous population? First and all, it is not improper to ask that immigrants consent with the Constitution. Militant fundamentalists who want to restrict certain constitutionally guaranteed rights could be denied entry to the country. Legal immigrants who have no objections against the constitutional principles of the country can be granted citizenship. They cannot be forced to give up all their cultural traditions, not even for the sake of naturalization, but might have to give up those traditions or views that go against the constitution of the host country. In theory, a naturalized immigrant group that has grown in number very strongly might in future claim constitutional amendments to bring the constitution in line with their heritage culture and religion. But this is a rather hypothetical case, because the change of constitutional laws often requires a two third majority in parliament. Moreover, generally we can observe that children and grandchildren of immigrant groups shift to the language, core values and lifestyle of the country of settlement.[64] We should also note that Habermas not only acknowledges the right of minorities to opt for the preservation of their own culture and traditions, but also the right to abandon old traditions and opt for the culture and lifestyle of the majority or any other group. Furthermore, he explicitly extends the right to retain one's culture to the majority. This is quite remarkable, because this right tends to be discussed in relation to minority groups only, perhaps because most people think that the preservation of the majority culture is no problem, because the percentage of immigrants is and probably will stay relatively low.

There is another aspect in the debate between Taylor and Habermas that deserves some comment. Both seem to think that the preservation of cultural traditions depends on processes where members of minority groups consciously reflect and discuss all their options, collectively and individually, but seem to overlook that most cultural changes and cultural shifts occur in spontaneous and unplanned ways. Historical studies of processes of migration and settlement have shown that the children of immigrants quite easily adjust to many of the customs, norms, and values of the majority group. Like most specialists in the field of minority issues, both Taylor and Habermas tend to focus on normative aspects. Habermas' approach is purely discursive and legalistic. The right to maintain one's culture is one thing; however achieving this goal is quite another matter. It involves real commitment and active engagement, every day of the week, because the social and cultural environment is not very helpful in this respect. On the contrary, the culture and lifestyle of the indigenous majority might be very attractive to many immigrants, in particular to their children. Culture requires a continuous process of cultural reproduction, restoration and reconstruction. Establishing minority rights merely is a necessary but insufficient condition for the maintenance of language and culture.

Habermas is fully aware of this; hence he advocates a lively discourse about the pros and cons of maintaining traditions, in order to enhance the cultural consciousness of all people. Such a discourse can lead to a greater awareness of the consequences of cultural reproduction, adaptation, and renewal. The outcome of such a discourse will be difficult to predict. Most certainly, it will not lead to the goals one has set, unless one opts for adaptation to the majority culture, for that is the easiest trajectory. If one seriously opts for culture, then this will take the shape of a dialectical process, where the debate must go on perpetually, for the dynamics of social development demands reflection over and over again.

11.8   Modernizing modernity

The peak of the hype of postmodernism was in the eighties. In that decade the word postmodernism popped up in many a magazine and cultural section of the papers. The term has become very broad and vague. Yet, there are a number of ideas that generally are associated with postmodernism. First and foremost, the concept seems to imply that we have left the age of modernism and its concomitant optimism about human progress. Modernization refers to the rise and flowering of positive science and a strong emphasis on individualism and a decline of traditions. Modernity also refers to the development of technology and industry, capitalism and expanding state-bureaucracies. This coincided with a strong growth of the population and with migration and urbanization. In the field of art old conventions were replaced by new approaches. The chronological story line made way for flashbacks and flash-forwards. No longer were narratives focused on one main character; they became plural and open-ended. In modern literature as in psychology, the individual is no longer seen as an integrated personality, but as an extremely complex being with humane and inhumane characteristics. However, this seems to be characteristic of modernism and postmodernism. Postmodernism settles the score with other sacred forms. It denounces the demarcation between high culture and low culture, between official or legitimized art that is exposed in museums or classical music played in concert-halls, and art-like expressions that we can observe in our daily life such as posters, ads, and cartoons. It does not accept a demarcation between high culture, middlebrow art such as photography and jazz, and forms of so-called low culture such as folk dance, naïve paintings, ads, comics, cartoons, or graffiti. Postmodernists reject the existence of a fundamental divide between great and classic and popular novels. To emphasize this eclectic attitude, post-modern art is characterized by an acceptance of a mix of different styles, matching romantic and figurative elements with the abstract and the surreal. The same is true for interior design and architecture. It is typical for postmodernists to make ample use of irony, parody, pastiche, and superficiality. They also seem to have abandoned the concepts of genius, depth, and originality.[65]

Within philosophy and the humanities, postmodernism became quite fashionable. It has left an imprint on the social sciences, in particular in the field of cultural studies. Favourite themes are relativism, instability, change, and the ephemeral. Postmodernists do not think that someone's character or identity is stable. On the contrary, they expect changes all the time, as a consequence of changing social structures, values, friendships and other social relationships. *Panta rei*, all is in flux and often at a very high speed. Think for instance of globalization. Increasingly the world economy tends to ignore national frontiers. The Internet, satellite tv, videos and cds help to foster a globalized culture mixed with local cultures. For the time being, American TV-series, American movies, popular music and paperbacks, and the latest technological products from Japan and other East Asian countries dominate globalized culture and lifestyle. However, in the struggle for supremacy in the domain of food, Italian pizzas and pastas, Mexican tortillas and Spanish tapas, and Chinese, Indonesian, Vietnamese, Japanese and Thai food seem to mount an ever-growing competition for American burgers and donuts. Whatever the outcome of this world-wide competition, globalization has created internationally mixed meals all over the world that seems to have pushed restaurants serving local food into the background.

Globalization does not hamper individualization. Far from it: it helps to free people from their local environment with all its old traditions. It offers them more options for a career and a personal lifestyle. Individualization is also stimulated by other forms of modernization such the processes of liberalization and democratization that emerged in the sixties and the seventies, which in turn were pushed ahead by a process of secularization and de-institutionalization. The loss of the traditional authority of church leaders and the assent of a new liberal and hedonistic ideology made room for thought and reflection, and thus for personal choices, choices to leave your own family, your own social network, your community, religion, culture or nation. But this freedom soon turned into an obligation to be continuously aware of all one's options. Instead of imposing opinions on somebody else, one was asked to answer the question: 'What do you think of this?' The great difference with earlier epochs is that one is no longer obliged to opt for a total package based on a specific religion. Now one can – and thus *has* to choose from a fixed but variegated supply produced by various subcultures and life styles. This leads to the emergence of all kinds of new and unexpected combinations, so that everybody can confirm or reconfirm his own identity.

Postmodernist research nicely fits into this situation. It usually is descriptive, imaginative and qualitative and seems to prove over and over again that there is an abundance of different cultures, subcultures and lifestyles that co-exist in the same geographical and social space. Important elements of postmodern thinking are plurality, individual authenticity and uniqueness, cultural and philosophical relativism and historicism. All this leads to the conclusion that postmodernists have developed a sharp eye for what makes people, groups and subcultures different. They do not show much interest in what people share nor in the question of the universals of mankind.

11.8.1   Habermas contra Lyotard

Habermas strongly opposes the postmodern critique of the Enlightenment as Jean-François Lyotard most vehemently expressed it. Like many other postmodernists, Lyotard started as a Marxist, but already in the forties doubts began to haunt him. Together with other sceptical Marxists he started the political movement Socialism or Barbarism. After a while, he realized that Marxism had committed the same fallacies, over and over again, by claiming universal validity for its totalitarian dogmas, despite its emancipatory intentions. Everywhere, where Marxists seize power, ideology degenerates into a violent institution that has no consideration whatsoever with any deviant opinion. It generates injustice and covers up all conflicts between the political leaders and the workers, between the bureaucrats and their subjects. He concluded that all these failures could not be accounted for by unfortunate contingencies of history, but resulted from some serious fallacies inherent in Marxist theory.[66] As a left-wing intellectual he had no trust in capitalism and also had lost all confidence in Western civilization. The horrific concentration camps of the Nazis and the Gulag Archipelago had made him suspicions of any theory that claimed to offer a valid recipe for a just society. Hence he denounced any attempt to search for a historical, philosophical or ethical foundation for justice. All these attempts would lead to universal pretences and turn into the enforced imposition of ideas upon anyone with alternative views. Hence, Lyotard urges us to abandon all narratives that sketch a grand history or an immanent and unstoppable development of history that promises a splendid future for mankind. He believes that the project of modernity is lost, not because history recently has generated a few horrific political disasters, but because such disasters are part and parcel of each grandiose political theory of society that claims universal validity. Habermas believes that the project of modernity, although it has gone astray, can still be put back on track and redirected towards a satisfying end. He envisions a solution in a further modernization of the project of Enlightenment and favours the broadening of rationality into a communicative rationality. Although science and technology have produced many disadvantages, he does not abandon modernization yet.

In accordance with new developments in epistemology, postmodernism opposes the idea that there is one unequivocal and positive truth in social science. It stresses that our insights are culturally conditioned, in particular in the case of social phenomena. It only accepts temporal and local truths. It dethrones scientific knowledge to make room for other sources of insight. Instead of assuming the possibility of one universal truth it stresses theoretical pluralism, based on ontological plurality. Scholars like Marx, Durkheim, and Weber still were convinced that it was possible to find one objective truth, but in post-modern epistemology such a model of a neutral and objective observation is questioned. Language and theory are no pure descriptions of reality but interventions in reality. Language, science, and art are completely permeated by and interconnected with social historical events. Once more, Habermas takes a position in the middle. He largely agrees with the relativistic view of social science, but persists in aiming for the truth and for the right praxis that can lead to the emancipation of the repressed.

There is another important difference of opinion between Habermas and the postmodernists. Postmodernists criticize him for his strong emphasis on rationality. Though he has included ethical and aesthetical rationality, he still seems to ignore that people not only have a mind, but also have strong emotions and physical needs too.[67] In contrast, postmodern thinking is full of Nietzschean and psychoanalytic motives, such as erotic desires, a craving for recognition and the awareness and fear of mortality.[68] Habermas rejects the main tenets of postmodernists, whose only hope appears to be based on irrational outbursts of emotional and physical energy. Although he does not underestimate the liberating potential of modern subcultures and life styles, he thinks that these are better means for overcoming instrumental rationality. He insists on a continued fight against the dominance of economic rationality with the help of communicative action and stresses the need for an expansion of human rights and an improvement of democracy. In his view, these values are just as important as the values of individual self-realization.

Lyotard has involved himself with language and discourse, just like Habermas, but here the similarity between the two stops, for Lyotard does not believe in consensus at all. He focuses on dispute and does not expect that it will be possible to solve most disputes and achieve consensus between opponents or different minds. Conflicts, he maintains, are not discussed within a universal set of rules shared by both parties. Rather, opponents often have views and arguments that cannot be expressed in a mutually shared idiom or frame of reference.[69] Conflicts tend to be accompanied by injustice and an unequal distribution of power. Injustice cannot be lifted, because the discourse of the victim does not fit in or is not acknowledged by the discourse of the other party. The dominant party does not accept other styles of arguing. For Lyotard there is no such thing as non-coercive dialogue, because of the differences of empowerment that will exist. However, Lyotard seemed to overlook those important moments in history in which power has been taken away from the oppressors and been put in the hands of less undemocratic governments. In these instances the views and arguments of the oppressed have gained dominance despite the forces that wanted to keep them down.

There are more important differences. Whereas the notion of an autonomous, rational subject is upheld by Habermas and safeguarded against the dominance of instrumental reason with the help of communicative actions, Lyotard denounces subjectivity, autonomy and rational action. He considers these notions as dangerously 'humanistic' constructions that should be banned from academic discourse as soon as possible. The human being and its image that has been developed in the course of thousands of years, no longer takes up a centre stage position with Lyotard. In his 'linguistic turn' he denied the existence of the autonomous, goal-oriented subject who acts on the basis of feelings and intelligence. As a post-structural die-hard, he only acknowledges observable speech acts. In his view, these speech acts or phrases are determined by linguistic structures that surpass the level of individual intentions and individual acts. These sentences and other externalizations of human beings (in his perspective: senders and receivers) are the only valid analytical units, the only observable facts. The essence of the subject will always remain a secret. Everyone who thinks that he has found a universally valid theory threatens to start another universalistic, violent war that aims to destroy all other views. That great danger incited Lyotard to oust the subject from social theory and philosophy. That is why his analysis of reality is restricted to an analysis of speech acts.

Through a detour, however, the subject reappears, now as a passive victim, who can suffer pain or be damaged by forms of injustice, for which there is no compensation, because there is no tribunal that acknowledges these particular forms of injustice. These cases are not treated in official law or legal handbooks. According to Lyotard, one (a subject I presume) can also become a victim of the legal discourse for compensating the damage that has been done, if the victim fails to participate in the right legal procedures, because it is blocked off by other discourses. Habermas, however, will never forget the individual subject. He is convinced that humans want and must communicate, because they are social beings. They have to express themselves. They have to interact with other people. They have goals, and want to achieve these goals through agreements with fellow human beings. For Habermas, individuals, in principle at least, are capable of understanding other individuals. This, however, is precisely what postmodernists question. They depart from the opposite platform, namely that, deep down, human beings will never understand the other. Everyone's mind will always remain a black box to the other.

The radical critique of reason worried Habermas so much that he devoted twelve lectures to The Philosophical Discourse of Modernity. His strategy was to return to the crossroads where Hegel and the Young Hegelians, Nietzsche and Heidegger made the fateful decisions that had led to this ferocious attack on the Enlightenment, rationality, modernity and the ideas of progress. Though Habermas has severely criticized the dominance of instrumental reason, he never intended to replace rationality with irrationality. On the contrary, he wanted to broaden and elevate subject-centred reason to the thoroughly intersubjectivist paradigm of communicative action. Habermas agrees that instrumental reason was abused for the organization of the holocaust and strategic actions of politics and economics have colonized the life-world, but he still thinks that the better half of reason can be regained to create a better world. He will not accept the deadly critique of subject-centred reason, because it serves as a morbid prologue for the fatal demise of western culture. For Habermas, there are many valid reasons to criticize modernity, however, he is not inclined to write off Modernity as postmodernists are so eager to do, but sees it as an unfinished project that needs to be put revitalized. Nor does he want to exchange western culture for a hotchpotch of miscellaneous cultures and lifestyles. Where postmodernists and multiculturalists seem prepared to give up their own culture – lock, stock and barrel – and fervently dip into the salad bowl of cultural diversity, he still is concerned with the core values of western culture and modernity, which contains a healthy, if not a universal basis for a great variety of salads.

With these lectures, Habermas intended to resume and renew the counter-discourse that has accompanied modernity from the start of the Enlightenment. His main focus is on the two paths that lead out of the philosophy of Nietzsche. The first path runs through Heidegger and then to Jacques Derrida, the other from Georg Bataille to Michel Foucault. [70] Habermas argues that Heidegger misses the dialectical interdependence between a historically shaped understanding of the world and the experience and practice within its horizon. He does not ignore that our interpretations of the world are heavily influenced by our culture, by a long process of socialization that has shaped our frame of reference, but holds fast to an autonomous kernel that enables each individual to criticize the culturally precooked interpretations on the basis of reason and personal experiences and maintains that individuals can learn other things than what is taken for granted in their society, subculture or life-world. Social practice submits the background knowledge of the life-world to an 'ongoing test' across the entire spectrum of validity claims. These learning processes may well cast doubt on the adequacy of dominant worldviews and trigger forms of critique that may change unjust social practices. Social scientists can be of help here. They can decipher the pathologies of modern life, transform them into sociological terms and test them through empirical investigations.

11.9   In conclusion

Habermas still is a highly esteemed heir to critical theory. He has attempted to make this legacy fruitful for contemporary problems of society. In order to be successful, he decided to bypass important parts of Marxist elements of critical theory. He remained loyal to its normative goals, such as equality and the liberation of alienating social forces and social structures. Nowadays, he is convinced that the only alternative for the political left is social democracy. His political dedication is so strong and so clearly focused on the transformation of society, that many aspects of his work can be interpreted from this perspective. He is convinced that a thorough study of the causes of social pathologies, mainly caused by the dominance of instrumental reason, deserves the highest priority. He honours Weber's sharp insight in the process of rationalization as the most crucial element of modernization and his warnings about the negative consequences of too much rationalization and disenchantment. In the first phase of his career Habermas indulged himself in exposing the manipulative and dehumanizing character of technology and positivistic science. In particular he blamed the one-dimensional interest in finding means for the control of man and nature. His career can be pictured as an endless quest for the exit from this misery. He never falls back on a romanticized myth of the pre-industrial age 'when existence supposedly was good and people easily satisfied'. Neither does he dream of a great socialistic revolution that will produce a new, emancipated and non-alienated human being. Nor can he accept the resignation, stoicism, and cynicism of postmodernist, who appear to be satisfied with an attempt to make the best of life and to enjoy it as long as they can. Habermas keeps making plans for the future and looking for solutions for the problems of contemporary society. He searches for the solution of social conflicts and political disagreement in a further liberalization and democratization of modernity. He thinks he has found the answer to these problems in a broadening of the concept of rationality. In his view, the rapprochement of an ideal speech situation, that is, a situation in which communicative rationality can be realized, would automatically lead to a further democratization, to a greater legitimacy of the legal system, and towards the proper acknowledgement and respect for other cultures and identities. However, he seems to overlook the fact that a completely free exchange of ideas on the basis of the ideal typical conditions of a power-free dialogue may also produce a sharpening of differences of opinion, instead of producing consensus. Of course, this insight does not mean that we should abandon the goal of a real free dialogue. A dialogue without taboos and self-censorship can be an important step on the road to a better functioning of democracy, a greater validity of the legal process and a more peaceful coexistence of ethnic and religious minorities and dominant groups.

Notes

Chapter 1

1 Fletcher, o. c., p 165.

2 J.H. Abraham (1973). *Origins and Growth of Sociology* (p.21). Hammondsworth: Penguin books.

3 Idem, pp. 22-25.

4 Aristotle: *The Politics*: Quoted by J. H. Abraham. o. c., p. 37.

5 Idem: pp. 38-39.

6 I. Khaldun: *Al-Muqaddimah*. Quoted by J. H. Abraham. o. c., pp. 40-41.

7 J. Heilbron (1991). *Het ontstaan van de sociologie*. Amsterdam: Prometheus.

8 R. Fletcher (1971/1972). *The Making of Sociology 1. Beginnings and foundations* (pp. 118-119). London: Nelson University Paperbacks.

9 E. Cassirer (1987/1932*). Le problème Jean-Jacques Rousseau*. Paris: Hachette.

10 J. Heilbron (1991). *Het ontstaan van de sociologie*. Amsterdam: Prometheus.

11 R. Fletcher: o. c., p. 122.

12 Raymond Aron views Auguste Comte as a founding father of sociology and Lewis Coser starts his *Masters of Sociological Thought* with him.

13 R. Fletcher (1974). *The Crisis of Industrial Civilization: The Early Essays of Auguste Comte* (p.4). London: Heinemann Educational Books.

14 Idem

15 R. Fletcher (1971/1972). *The Making of Sociology 1. Beginnings and foundations*. London: Nelson University Paperbacks.

16 R. Fletcher (1974). *The Crisis of Industrial civilization. The Early Essays of Auguste Comte* (p.4). London: Heinemann Educational Books.

17 Auguste Comte died on the 5th of September 1857 in Paris, surrounded by the few loyal admirers that were left.

18 M. Bock (1999). Auguste Comte (1798-1857). In D. Kaesler (Hrsg), *Klassiker der Soziologie. Von Auguste Comte bis Norbert Elias*. München: Beck.

19 G. Simpson, '*What we still owe to Auguste Comte*'. Slightly revised text of a speech delivered before the Dutch Sociological Association on April 23, 1966.

20 M. Pickering (1993). *Auguste Comte. An Intellectual Biography* (Vol.I), Cambridge: Cambridge University Press.

21 Proof that Comte preferred slow and thorough scientific thinking over immediate actions can be found in his second letter to John Stuart Mill in which he praised the latter for not taking a seat in parliament: 'Excellent reasoning alone can have convinced you how infinitely more useful your philosophical career would be if you removed yourself from the all too mundane parliamentary debates, … your decision … runs so much counter to prevailing custom, where everything impels to immediate action. I hope that the evolution of mankind … will derive substantial benefit from it.' *The correspondence of John Stuart Mill and Auguste Comte* (p.39). Translated from French and edited by Oscar A. Haack (1995). New Brunswick: Transaction Publishers.

22 J. Heilbron, o. c., pp. 232-233; J.M.M. de Valk (1979). *Inleiding bij Auguste Comte. Het positieve denken.* Meppel/Amsterdam: Boom, p. 10.

23 Fletcher, o. c., p. 189.

24 S. Andreski (1974). *The Essential Comte. Selected from* Cours de Philosophie Positive *by Auguste Comte.* London: Croom Helm, p. 8.

25 A. Comte, *Système de politique positive ou Traité de sociologie instituant la religion de l'humanité.* This was written in the period from 1851 to 1854.

26 H.P.M. Goddijn, P. Thoenes, J.M.M. de Valk & J.P. Verhoogt (1971, 1974). *Geschiedenis van de sociologie.* Meppel: Boom, pp. 67-69.

27 *The correspondence of John Stuart Mill and Auguste Comte.* Translated from French and edited by Oscar A. Haack (1995). New Brunswick: Transaction Publishers, p. 37.

28 Coser, o. c., p. 39.

29 Introduction by Ronald Fletcher in *Auguste Comte: The Foundation of Sociology* by Kenneth Thompson.

30 Bruce Mazlish (1989). *A New Science: The Breakdown of Connections and the Birth of Sociology.* New York: Oxford University Press, pp. 12-13.

31 B.C. van Houten (1974). Saint-Simon en Comte. In L. Rademaker & E. Petersma (Red.), *Hoofdfiguren uit de sociologie.* Utrecht: Het Spectrum/Intermediair, p. 23.

32 H. de Saint-Simon (1980). Who contributes to Society? In L.A. Coser (Ed.), *The Pleasures of Sociology.* New York: A Mentor Book.

33 R. Aron: o. c., p. 80. (English translation Penguin, p. 63 and further)

34 R. Fletcher (1974). *The Crisis of Industrial civilization: The Early Essays of Auguste Comte.* London: Heinemann Educational Books, pp. 13-14.

35 Comte, quoted by Aron, (English translation.) p. 82.

36 Aron, o. c., p. 83.

37 Coser: o. c.

38 G. Lenzer (1975). *Auguste Comte and Positivism: The Essential Writings.* New York: Harper Torch books, p. 210.

39 Fletcher: o. c., pp. 168-169; Michael Bock, o. c., p. 47.

40 Fletcher: o. c., pp. 125-126.

41 Fletcher: o. c., p. 169.

42 A. Comte (1896). *The Positive Philosophy* (Freely translated and condensed by Harriet Martineau) (vol.II, bk IV, ch. VI.). London: George Bell & sons, pp. 522-540.

43 Idem

44 J.G. Frazer (1981). *The Golden Bough.* New York: Gramercy Books, p. 59.

45 Fletcher: o. c., p. 169.

46 Fletcher, o. c., pp. 168-170.

47 Unfortunately, no sooner had he made the distinction between positivists and negativists, who continued to uphold old pre-scientific dogmas, than Comte began to twist it, and apply it to everything he happened to assert or approve of, because he pretended that all his beliefs and preferences were backed by 'positive' science. Andrewski: o. c., p.9.

48 Idem

49 John Stuart Mill (1866). *Auguste Comte and Positivism.* London: Trübner & Co., p. 6.

50 Comte: o. c., pp. 62-64

51 Comte: o. c., p. 219.

52 Coser: o. c. pp. 5-6. (Coser quotes from the old Martineau translation)

53 Coser: o. c. p. 6.

54 Fletcher: o. c.

55 August Comte in *Course de la Philosophie Positive*.

56 Fletcher: o. c., pp. 172-174.

57 Idem

58 Fletcher, o. c., p. 174.

59 Fletcher: o. c., pp. 171-172.

60 *'Tristes calculateurs, algébristes en arithméticiens'.*

61 Idem

62 Idem, p. 18.

63 *Savoir pour prévoir, prévoir pour pouvoir.*

64 Idem, p. 20.

65 A. Comte (1974). Plan of the Scientific Operations Necessary for Reorganizing Society. In R. Fletcher, *The Crisis of Industrial Civilization. The Early Essays of Auguste Comte*. London: Heinemann Educational Books, p. 176.

66 Karl Dieter Opp (1976). *Methodologie der Sozialwissenschaften*. Rowohlt: Reinbek bei Hamburg.

67 A. Comte (1896). The Positive Philosophy (Freely translated and condensed by Harriet Martineau) (vol.II, bk VI, ch. iii. London: George Bell & Sons, pp. 218-32.

68 Aron, o. c., p. 88 (Engl. translation), pp. 72-73.

69 A. Comte quoted by Ronald Fletcher in *The Crisis of Industrial Civilization*, o. c., p. 246.

70 Fletcher: o. c., p. 247.

71 Aron, o. c., p. 95.

72 Fletcher, o. c., p. 181.

73 A. Comte (1875). *System of Positive Polity or Treatise on Sociology* (pp.239-240). London: Burt Franklin. Quoted by Jonathan H. Turner (1978) in *The Structure of Sociological Theory* (Homewood, Ill., The Dorsey Press), p. 21.

74 Idem, pp. 239-240.

75 R.A. Nisbet (1966). *The Sociological Tradition* (p.60). London: Heinemann Educational Books Ltd.

76 Aron, o. c., p. 116.

77 Fletcher, o. c., pp. 182-183.

78 Aron, o. c., p. 117.

79 Fletcher, o. c., p 165.

80 On Comte's burial memorial there is a plaque of Brazilian positivists.

81 Fletcher, o. c.

Chapter 2

1   G. F. Gottheil has counted 153 predictions in Marx' oeuvre, and checked that most of them failed to come true. See B. Tromp (1983). *Karl Marx*. Meppel/Amsterdam: Boom.

2   J. Gielkens (1997). *'Was ik maar weer in Bommel'. Karl Marx en zijn Nederlandse verwanten.*

Een familiegeschiedenis in documenten. Amsterdam: Stichting beheer IISG.

3   L. Kolakowski (1980). *Geschiedenis van het marxisme* (p. 121). Utrecht/Antwerpen: Het Spectrum..

4   Idem.

5   Kolakowski, o.c., p. 122.

6   Fletcher, o.c., p. 340.

7   Francis Wheen: (2001). *Karl Marx.* London: Fourth Estate, pp. 64-65.

8   Banning, o.c., p. 32.

9   Francis Wheen: o. c., p. 107.

10 Kolakowski, o.c., pp. 240-241.

11 Tromp, o.c., p. 36.

12 *Die Neue Rheinische Zeitung (The New Rhineland Paper).*

13 Coser, o.c., p. 65.

14 Coser, o.c., p. 66.

15 B. Tromp (1983). *Karl Marx.* Meppel/Amsterdam: Boom, p. 140.

16 D. McLellan (1977). *Karl Marx: Selected Writings* (Marx-Engels Werke, 18, 160). Oxford: Oxford University Press.

17 In 1879 Marx and Engels wrote a long letter to the leaders of the German Social Democratic Party warning them not to become too quietist and not to forget to go on preparing a successful class-struggle. They reminded Karl Liebknecht and others that they had stressed the class struggle as the immediate driving power of history … as the great lever of the modern social revolution. Idem, Vol. 34, pp. 405 ff.

18 In November 1911, Laura Marx and her husband Paul Lafarge decided to commit suicide together when they had reached the conclusion that there was nothing left to live for. The main speaker at their joint funeral was Vladimir Ilyich Lenin, who prophesied that the ideas of Laura's father would be triumphantly realized sooner than anyone guessed. See F. Wheen (1999). *Karl Marx.* London: Fourth Estate Ltd.; J. Gielkens (1997). *'Was ik maar weer in Bommel'. Karl Marx en zijn Nederlandse verwanten. Een familiegeschiedenis in documenten.* Amsterdam: Stichting beheer IISG; W. Blumenberg (1962). *Karl Marx in Selbstzeugnissen und Bilddokumenten.* Reinbek.

19 Kolakowski, o.c., p. 73.

20 Banning, o.c., p. 60.

21 L. Layendecker (1981). *Orde, verandering en ongelijkheid.* Meppel: Boom, p. 164.

22 H. Kunneman (1986). *De waarheidstrechter.* Meppel: Boom, p. 130.

23 G.W.F. Hegel (1955/1968). *Vorlesungen über die Philosophie der Weltgeschichte, Bd 1: Die Vernunft in der Geschichte.* Hamburg: F. Meiner, pp. 74-75.

24 Störig, o.c., p. 83; Tromp, o.c., p. 26.

25 Laeyendecker, o.c., p. 165; K.R. Popper (1972). *Conjectures and Refutations.* London: Routledge & Kegan Paul.

26 W. Kaufmann (1991). *Goethe, Kant and Hegel. The Discovery of the Mind* (Vol I). New Brunswick: Transaction Publishers, p. 266.

27 'He thought … that this bud negated the winter, the flower the bud, and the fruit the flower. He laughed foolishly, almost childishly happy, at the image aroused by this elementary dialectics, for the fragile, not yet tangible bud, that green sap deep in the snow-covered belly of

the earth, would not only be the negation but also the fulfilment of the winter. Old Hegel was right. The blinding snow would find her realization in the fresh and blinding green.' George Semprun (1992). *Zo'n mooie zondag* (p.9). Agathon. Popper reminds us of the following utterly nonsensical mathematical example, once produced by Engels. The latter presented a plus – a as-thesis and antithesis, and a-square as their synthesis. Everyone knows that a times –a equals $-a^2$, which is the opposite of a^2, p. 323.

28 Popper prefers to replace this terminology with the terminology he favours, that is, the terminology of trial and error elimination. The search for valid criticisms (or contradictions or negations) of a flawed theory (thesis) is the best way of producing a growth of scientific knowledge. K.R. Popper (1972). *Conjectures and Refutations*. London: Routledge & Kegan Paul.

29 Van Peperstraten, o.c., p. 98 e.v.

30 From *Das Kapital* (Translation into Dutch by I. Lipschits). Weesp: De Haan. p. xxi-xxii.

31 A. Giddens (1971). *Capitalism and modern social theory. An analysis of the writings of Marx, Durkheim and Weber* (p.3). Cambridge: Cambridge University Press; Ritzer, o.c., p. 19.

32 Jakubowski, o.c., p. 21.

33 Jakubowski, o.c., p. 24.

34 Theses on Feuerbach (1854) MEGA I/5, pp. 533-535.

35 K. Graham (1992). *Karl Marx. Our contemporary. Social Theory for a Post-Leninist World.* Hertfordshire: Harvester Wheatsheaf, pp. 9-10.

36 Idem, p. 10.

37 Karl Marx (1867a/1976). *Capital* (Vol. 1, pp. 283-284, 649). Hammondsworth: Penguin.

38 The crucial difference is not that men produce and animals don't, but that men can produce entirely new things, invent new methods of producing, and really can plan their work rationally and not go ahead in a purely instinctive way like bees or ants producing their homes, feeding their larva's, or defending themselves against intruders. See Keith Graham, o.c., p. 11.

39 M. Conforth (1980). *Communism and philosophy.* London: Lawrence and Wisehart, pp. 173-174. Conforth mentions that Napoleon, for example, called certain people of whom he disapproved 'ideologists'.

40 Idem: p. 21 and pp. 173-174.

41 Jakubowski, o.c., pp. 41-42.

42 Jakubowski, o.c., p. 43.

43 T.B. Bottomore and Maxmilien Rubel (1963): *Selected Writings* in Sociology and Social Philosophy. London: McGraw Hill, p. 60.

44 K. Marx & F. Engels (1976). *The German Ideology* (pp. 348-349). Moscow, pp. 348-349.

45 Marx was not the first that recognized the principle of class struggles. In 1780, Gaetano Filangieri already pointed out that a careful reading of all the great books about societies showed that all nations are divided in two irreconcilable parties: the owners and the non-owners or hirelings. The owners will always try to get the work of the labourers at the lowest possible price, whereas the worker will always try to sell his labour at the highest price. Gaetano Filangieri (1826, 2nd ed.). *La Scienze delle Legislazione* (Vol I). Livorno. (Quoted by R. Michels, First Lectures in Political Sociology, 1965), pp. 208-209.

46 D. Sayer (1991). *Capitalism & Modernity. An excursus on Marx and Weber.* London/New York: Routledge, p. 106.

47 F. Wheen, o. c., p. 169.

48 Aron: o. c., p. 148.

49 W. Banning: o.c.

50 K. Marx & F. Engels (1983). *Manifesto of the Communist Party*. New York: International Publishers, p.16.

51 Cuff et al. o. c., p. 86.

52 For Marx, this 'negation of a negation' will not re-establish private property for the producers, but will lead to the expropriation of the few monopolists by the mass of revolutionary workers. Karl Marx (1867a/1976). *Capital* (Vol. 1) Hammondsworth: Penguin, pp. 801-804.

53 Manifesto of the Communist Party.

54 K. Marx (1867a/1976). *Capital* (Vol. 1). Hammondsworth: Penguin.

55 K. Marx. Speech on the Anniversary of the People's Paper, 19 April 1856. In D. McLellan (Ed.)(1977). *Karl Marx. Selected Writings*. Oxford: Oxford University Press.

56 Schiller, quoted by Coser, o. c.

57 Layendecker, o.c., pp. 214-215.

58 This can be checked by looking at the huge difference in the amount of money insurance companies have to pay to the widow when either the surgeon or the driver is killed in a traffic accident. This enormous difference in the economic value of both persons, – let us assume that they both victim were healthy, law-abiding men, responsible husbands, and father of two children – is related to the difference in the income they could have made if they stayed alive.

59 K. Marx (1867a/1976). *Capital* (Vol. 1). Hammondsworth: Penguin. Quoted by Keith Graham

60 Giddens, o. c., pp. 15-16.

61 T. B. Bottomore: 1974: K. Marx. *Early Writings*, p. 158.

62 Giddens, pp. 13-14.

63 Jakubowski, o.c., pp. 34-35.

64 Marx/Engels. *De Duitse ideologie*, o.c., p. 49.

65 D. McLellan. *Karl Marx. Selected Writings*. o. c., p. 75.

66 D. McLellan. *Karl Marx. Selected Writings*. o. c., p. 77.

67 K. Marx (1976). *Selected Writings in sociology and Social Psychology*, pp. 177-178. Hammondsworth: Penguin. (From the Economic and Philosophical manuscripts, 1844.)

68 D. McLellan. *Karl Marx. Selected Writings*, o. c., pp. 78-79.

69 George Orwell (1937). The Road to Wigan Pier. London: Victor Gollancz.

70 K. Marx. *Selected Writings*, o.c. p. 82.

71 K. Marx. *Selected Writings*.

72 K. Marx (1867a/1976). *Capital* (Vol. 1). Hammondsworth: Penguin. Quoted by Conway.

73 Jakubowski, o.c., p. 31. Jakubowski quotes from the preface of Marx'. *Zur Kritik der politischen Ökonomie*.

74 K. Marx: *Selected Writings*, p. 202.

75 K. Marx: *Selected Writings*, p. 574.

76 K. Marx: *Selected Works*, p. 52.

77 K. Marx: The 18th Brumaire (1852). Quoted in Selected Writings, o.c., p. 96.

78 Laeyendecker, o.c., p 235.

79 P. Berger, *Invitation to sociology*, New York: Doubleday. 1963.

80 Karl Marx (1938). *Critique of the Gotha Programme*. (Quoted by W. Banning, o.c.)

81 Aron, o.c.

82 D. Sayer, o. c., pp. 21-22.

83 T. Shanin (1984). *Late Marx and the Russian road.* London: Routledge.

84 I. Berlin (1948). *Karl Marx, His Life and Environment.* New York. (Quoted by L.A. Coser, o. c.), p.13.

85 K. Marx & F. Engels (1957). *Werke* (Vol.8). Berlin: Dietz Verlag, p. 634.

Chapter 3

1   S. Fenton (1984): *Durkheim and modern sociology.* Cambridge: Cambridge University Press.

2   Steven Lukes (1973): Emile Durkheim: His Life and Work. London: Allan Lane, p. 49.

3   S. Lukes: o. c., pp. 54-55.

4   Durkheim, quoted by Lukes, o. c., pp. 57-58.

5   S. Lukes: o. c., pp. 59-60.

6   Chr. Charle (1984): Le beau mariage d'Emile Durkheim. *Actes de la Recherche en Sciences Sociales, 55,* pp. 45-49.

7   K. Thompson (1982): *Emile Durkheim.* London: Tavistock Publications, p. 50.

8   W.S.F. Pickering (1979): Introduction by W.S.F. Pickering. In *Durkheim: Essay on morals and education.* London, Routledge Kegan Paul.

9   Fenton: o.c.

10 R. Collins & M. Makowsky (1972): *The Discovery of Society.* New York: Random House, pp. 80-81.

11 S. Lukes: o.c., pp. 331-332.

12 Idem.

13 S. Lukes: o.c., pp. 321-325.

14 L.A. Coser: o. c., p. 129.

15 E. Durkheim (1950): *The Rules of Sociological Method.* New York: The Free Press, p. 2.

16 Idem, p. 110.

17 E. Durkheim (1953): *Sociology and Philosophy.* New York: The Free Press, p.55.

18 Idem, p. 3.

19 Giddens stresses that social structures have restrictive as well as facilitating characteristics. A. Giddens (1984): *The constitution of society.* Cambridge: Polity Press, p.169.

20 S. Lukes: o. c., p. 12.

21 Idem, pp. 13-14.

22 E. Durkheim (1960): Sociology and its scientific field. In Kurt H. Wolff (Ed), *Emile Durkheim et al., Essays on Sociology and Philosophy.* New York: The Ohio State University Press, pp. 367-368.

23 K. Thompson (1982): *Emile Durkheim.* London: Tavistock Publications, pp.51-52.

24 K. Thompson adapted this model first presented by Jean Claude Filloux in *Les Science Sociale et l'Áction,* Paris, PUF, 19790. See Thompson, o. c., p. 60.

25 K. Thompson: o.c., p. 61.

26 E. Durkheim (1966): *The Rules of Sociological Method.* New York: The Free Press, pp. 103-104.

27 E. Durkheim (1971): *Elementary Forms of Religious Life.* London, Allan & Unwin, p.27.

28 In *The Rules,* Durkheim refers to Francis Bacon, who introduced these terms to warn his fellow scientists not to be satisfied with common sense impressions, which all too easily take the place of facts.

29 E. Durkheim (1964): Sociology. In Kurt H. Wolff (ed.) *Emile Durkheim et al. Essays on Sociology and Philosophy.* New York, Harper Torchbook, pp. 376-385.

30 J.H. Turner (1978, rev. edition): *The Structure of Sociological Theory*. Homewood, The Dorsey Press, p. 37.

31 A. Pierce (1960): Durkheim and functionalism. In: Kurt H. Wolff (Ed.). *Emile Durkheim, A collection of Essays*. Pierce gives six quotations from *Les Rules* and from *Suicide* that put a sharp light on Durkheim's view, pp. 154-169.

32 E. Durkheim (1983): *Le suicide*. Paris: Quadrige, PUF, p. 366.

33 Durkheim never spoke of functions of society as a whole. He only used this term when he discussed a part or an aspect of a social system, for instance, the function of the division of labour or the social function of religion. In turn, he exclusively used the concept of need to express a characteristic of society or an autonomous social system. In his approach aspects or parts of society have no needs but fulfill functions for society as a whole.

34 Pierce: o. c.

35 T. Kuhn (1970): *The Structure of Scientific Revolutions*. Chicago: University of Chicago Press.

36 J.C. Alexander (1982): *Theoretical Logic in Sociology, Volume Two. The antinomies of classical thought, Marx and Durkheim*. London: Routledge & Kegan Paul, pp. 76-80.

37 E. Durkheim (1991): *De la division du travail social*, Paris: Quadrige, PUF. (E. Durkheim (1984): *The Division of Labour in Society*. Houndmills and London: MacMillan.)

38 Idem.

39 R. Aron (1987): *Main Currents in Sociological Thought. Part 2*. Hammondsworth: Penguin Books, p.21.

40 The French 'conscience' means conscience as well as consciousness.

41 *La Division*, p. 99.

42 *La Division*, p. 143.

43 *La Division*, pp. 152-153.

44 A. Giddens (1971/1991): *Capitalism and modern social theory, an analysis of the writings of Marx, Durkheim and Max Weber*. Cambridge: Cambridge University Press, p. 72.

45 E. Durkheim (1984): *The Division* of Labour. Houndmills and London: MacMillan, p. 221.

46 R. Aron (1987): o. c., p. 321.

47 *The Division of Labour*, McMillan, 1984, p. 201.

48 R. Aron: o. c.

49 R. Aron: Main Currants in Sociological Theory (part 2). p. 33.

50 R. Aron, o.c., p. 326-327.

51 E. Durkheim (1951): *Suicide*. New York, The Free Press, p. 248.

52 *Dictionnaire de la sociologie*. Paris. Larousse, 1993.

53 E. Durkheim (1888): Suicide et natalité, étude de statistique morale. *Revue* Philosophique, 46, p. 447.

54 W. Ultee, W. Arts & H. Flap (1992): *Sociologie: vragen, uitspraken, bevindingen*. Groningen, Wolters-Noordhoff.

55 A. Giddens (1971): *Capitalism and modern social theory, an analysis of the writings of Marx, Durkheim, and Max Weber*. Cambridge: Cambridge University Press, p. 82.

56 Some researchers point to the fact that more women attempt to commit suicide than men, but that men take more drastic steps and thus are more 'successful' in this respect, whereas women use methods that are less lethal.

57 E. Durkheim (1852, 1987): *Suicide*. London. Routledge Kegan Paul.

58 Idem: pp. 222-223.

59 Idem, p. 209.

60 E. Durkheim (1852, 1987): *Suicide*. London. Routledge Kegan Paul, p. 209.

61 L. A. Coser: o. c.

62 C. F. Schmid & M. D. van Arsol (1955): Completed and attempted suicides: A comparative analysis. *American Sociological Review, 20*, pp. 273-283.

63 E. Arensman (1997): *Attempted Suicide: Epidemiology and Classification*. Leiden, Universiteit van Leiden.

64 A third cluster was difficult to label.

65 Suicide, o. c., p. 276.

66 According to Durkheim, other individuals such as grandparents or other people who live permanently in the same household could compensate for the low number of children.

67 L. A. Coser: o. c., p. 136-137.

68 E. Durkheim (1971): *The Elementary Forms of the Religious Life*. London: George Allan & Unwin, p. 13.

69 R. Aron: *Main currents of sociological thought*, o.c., p. 51.

70 E. Durkheim: *The Elementary Forms of Religious Life*, o.c., p. 47.

71 Idem, p. 140.

72 E. Durkheim quoted by A. Giddens from: *Primitive Classification*, London, 1963, p. 81.

73 A. Giddens: (1978) o. c., p.84.

74 *Les formes*, p. 376; *Elementary forms*: p. 262.

75 *Les formes*, p. 313; *Elementary forms*: p. 218.

76 *Les formes*, p. 494; *Elementary forms*: p. 346.

77 *Les formes*, p. 376-377: *Elementary forms*: p. 263.

78 L. A. Coser: o. c.: p. 139.

79 *Les formes*, p. 323; *Elementary forms*: p. 226.

80 E. Durkheim (1956): (translated by Sherwood D. Fox). *Education and Sociology*. New York: The Free Press. p. 71.

81 Idem, p. 72.

82 E. Durkheim: Moral Education, p. 59.

83 *Education et sociologie*: o. c.: p. 118.

84 *Education morale*, 1963, p. 34.

85 Quoted by Steve Fenton from E. Durkheim: *Moral Education*, p. 120

86 S. Fenton: o. c.: p. 148.

87 Idem

88 E. Durkheim (1960a): The Dualism of Human Nature and its Social Conditions. In K. H. Wolff (Ed.), *Émile Durkheim et al. Essays on Sociology and Philosophy*. New York: Harper and Row, pp. 337-338.

89 S. Lukes: o. c., pp. 330-332.

90 R. Aron: o. c., pp. 376-377.

91 T. Parsons (1973). *Durkheim on Religion Revisited: Another Look at The Elementary Forms of Religious Life*. In Charles Y. Glock and Phillip E. Hammond (1973): Beyond the Classics: Essays on the Scientific Study of Religion. New York: Harper and Row, pp. 156-180.

Chapter 4

1 G. Simmel (1978): *The Conflict in Modern Culture and Other Essays*. New York: Teachers College Press, pp.71-72.

2 Simmel dedicated his Ph.D. thesis 'with gratitude and love to 'his fatherly friend Julius Friedländer'. See Michael Landmann. Bausteine zur Biographie. In: *Buch des Dankens an Georg Simmel* Briefe, Erinnerungen, Bibliographie. Ed. by Kurt Gassen & Michael Landmann. Berlin: Duncker & Humblot, 1958, pp. 11-34.

3 The dissertation was published as *Das Wesen der Materie nach Kants physischer Monadologie* (*The Nature of Matter According to Kant's physical Monadology*).

4 This is a kind of second Ph.D. thesis that serves as entry exam for full professorships.

5 K. Gassen & M. Landmann (Eds.) (1958): *Buch des Denkens an Georg Simmel*. Berlin: Duncker & Humblot, p. 21.

6 According to Simmel's student Siegfried Kracauer, quoted by David Frisby, o. c., p. 133.

7 P.E. Schnabel (1976). Georg Simmel. In *D. Kaesler: Klassiker des soziologischen Denkens*. *Volume I*. Münich: Beck, p. 272.

8 G. Simmel (1890). *Über soziale Differenzierung. Soziologische und psychologische Untersuchung.* Leipzig: Duncker & Humblot, p. 48.

9 M. Weber: *Roscher und Knies. Logische Problemen der historische Ökonomie*

10 Georg Simmel: *Soziologie: Untersuchungen über die formen der Vergesellschaftung.* Leipzig: Duncker und Humblot, 1908.

11 L.A. Coser (1971): *Master of Sociological Thought*. New York: Harcourt Brace Yanovich, p. 209.

12 G. Simmel (1918): *Lebensanschauung. Vier Metaphysische Kapitel* (Perspective on life: Four metaphysical chapters). Berlin: Duncker und Humblot.

13 Idem

14 In his epistemology of the social sciences Simmel follows the following three staged scheme:
    1 The differentiation of subject and object in the individual mind;
    2 The differentiation of cognitive objects by means of a categorical evaluation;
    3 The heuristic unification of cognitive objects within a pragmatic relativism. See: Wallisch-Prinz: A Sociology of Freedom. Georg Simmel's Theory of Modern Society. Dissertation. University of Bremen, 1977, pp. 84-85.

15 B. Wallisch-Prinz quotes Simmel from the German edition of *The Philosophy of Money*.

16 B. Wallisch-Prinz (1977): *A Sociology of Freedom. Georg Simmel's Theory of Modern Society.* Bremen: Universität Bremen, pp. 86-87.

17 Philosophy of Money, pp. 6-7.

18 B. Wallisch-Prinz (1977): o. c., pp. 89-90.

19 *Philosophy of Money*, pp. 6-7.

20 *Soziologie*, p. 45.

21 *Soziologie*, p. 41-42.

22 G. Simmel (1980): On the Nature of Historical Understanding. In Guy Oakes: *Essays on Interpretation on Social Science*, p. 97.

23 Idem, pp. 101-102.

24 G. Simmel (1964): The Field of Sociology. In *Kurt H. Wolff, The Sociology of Georg Simmel. Translated and with an introduction by Kurt H. Wolff.* London: The Free Press, pp. 3-25.

25 L.A. Coser: o. c., p. 211.

26 *The Sociology of Georg Simmel*, o. c., pp. 5-7.

27 Naturally, these arguments and beliefs do not invalidate the fact that the natural sciences and other sciences too, have shown that a thorough investigation of small elements can lead to valuable insights.

28 D.N. Levine (1965): Some key problems in Simmel's work. In: *Makers of modern social science*. Englewood Cliffs, New Jersey: Prentice Hall, pp. 97-98.

29 Moreover: 'The ego can become more clearly conscious of this unity the more he is confronted with the task of reconciling within himself a diversity of group interests.'

30 G. Simmel: o. c., pp. 198- 204.

31 Idem, p. 203.

32 Idem, p 11.

33 G. Simmel (1970) (original 1917): *Grundfragen der Soziologie (Individuum und Gesellschaft)*. Berlin, Walter de Gruyter & Co.

34 L. von Wiese (1965): Simmel's formal method. In George Simmel & Lewis A. Coser (Eds.): *Makers of modern social science*. Englewood Cliffs, New Jersey: Prentice Hall, pp. 53-55.

35 Simmel uses this organic analogy to emphasize that without the interspersed effects of countless minor social syntheses, society would break down into a multitude of discontinuous systems.

36 Idem, p. 10.

37 (Expand: Note).

38 K. Popper (1963): *Conjectures and Refutations: The Growth of Scientific Knowledge*. London: Routledge & Kegan Paul; Karl R. Popper (1972): *Objective Knowledge; an Evolutionary Approach*. Oxford: Oxford University Press.

39 Simmel quoted by Kurt Wolff in *The Sociology of Georg Simmel* (1950). New York: The Free Press.

40 G. Simmel (1978): *The Philosophy of Money*. London: Routledge, p. 55. (See Frisby)

41 G. Simmel (1896): *Soziologische Ästhetik*, p. 206. (Quoted by D. Frisby.)

42 B. Wallisch-Prinz: o. c., pp 89-90.

43 G. Simmel (1968: *The Conflict in Modern Culture and Other Essays*. New York: Teachers College Press. (*Der Konflikt der modernen Kultur*. Leipzig: Duncker & Humblot, 1918.)

44 G. Simmel (1980): *Essays on Interpretation in Social Science*. (Translated and edited with an introduction by Guy Oakes). Manchester: Manchester University Press, pp. 9-10.

45 G. Simmel (1967): *Fragmente und Aufsätze*. Munich: Drei Marken Verlag, p. 204.

46 G. Simmel (1980): On the history of Philosophy. In: *Georg Simmel Essays on Interpretation in Social Science*, p. 202.

47 A.M. Bevers (1982): *Geometrie van de samenleving. Filosofie en sociologie in het werk van Georg Simmel*. Deventer: Van Loghum Slaterus, p. 199.

48 G. Simmel (1971): In: D. Levine: *Georg Simmel on Individuality and Social Forms*. Chicago: Chicago University Press, p. 187.

49 A.M. Bevers mentions four locations in: *Soziologie*. p. 87.

50 A.M. Bevers: o.c., p. 91.

51 Idem, pp. 154-155.

52 G. Simmel (1971): The stranger. In Donald N. Levine (Ed.): *Georg Simmel on Individuality and Social Forms*. Chicago: The University of Chicago Press, pp. 143-149.

53 G. Simmel (1971): The Adventurer. In Donald N. Levine (Ed.): *Georg Simmel on Individuality and Social Forms*. Chicago: The University of Chicago Press, pp. 187-198. (Das Abenteuer. In: Philosophische Kultur: Gesammelte Essays. Leipzig: W. Klinkhardt, 1911)

54 Idem

55 G. Simmel (1964): In: Donald N. Levine: *On Individuality and Social Forms*, pp. 251-252.

56 Idem, p. 253.

57 N. Elias later developed this idea by pointing to a growing shift in what he calls the We-I-balance into the direction of greater individualism in globalizing networks.

58 Idem, p. 259.

59 Idem, pp 263-265.

60 G. Oakes, pp. 38-42.

61 G. Simmel (1976): The conflict of Modern Culture. In P.A. Lawrence, *George Simmel: sociologist and European*. Sunbury-on-Thames, Middlesex: Nelson, p.223.

62 Idem, p. 224.

63 G. Simmel (1904). *Philosophie des Geldes*. Leipzig: Duncker & Humblot.

64 G. Simmel (1911). Der Begriff und die Tragödie der Kultur. In: *Philosophische Kultur*, pp. 245-277.

65 G. Oakes, o. c., pp. 12-13.

66 G. Oakes, p. 4.

67 G. Simmel: *Brücke und Tür*. Stuttgart. K. F. Koehler: 1957, p. 94 (Quoted by Oakes).

68 A.J. Dunning (1992): *Extremes: Reflections on Human Behaviour*. New York: Harcourt Brace Jovanovich, pp. 69-84.

69 G. Simmel (1971): The Poor. In: Donald N. Levine (Ed.), *Georg Simmel on Individuality and Social Forms*. Chicago: The University of Chicago Press, pp. 150-178.

70 M.B. Katz (1989): *The Undeserving Poor: From the War on Poverty to the War on Welfare*. New York: Pantheon books.

71 V.S. Naipaul (1964): *An Area of Darkness*. Hammondsworth: Penguin Books.

72 H.A.R. Gibb (1975): *Islam: a historical survey*. Oxford: Oxford University Press.

73 This aspect if further elabourated in Abram de Swaan (1988). *In Care of the State: Health care, education and welfare in Europe and the USA in the Modern Era*. Cambridge: Polity Press/ Oxford University Press.

74 G. Simmel (1971): The Poor. In: Donald N. Levine (Ed.), *George Simmel: On Individuality and social Forms*. Chicago: The University of Chicago, p. 155.

75 Idem

76 J.N. Burstyn (1980): *Victorian Education and the Ideal of Womanhood*. Ottowa: Barnes and Noble Books.

77 J.S. Mill (1869): *On the Subjection of Women*. In: Collected Works of John Stuart Mills (1983), Volume 21. Toronto: University of Toronto Press.

78 A. Bebel (1971, orig.1883): *Woman under Socialism*. New York: Schocken.

79 G. Simmel (1984): The problem of the sexes. In Georg Simmel: *On Women, Sexuality and Love*. New Haven: Yale University Press, p. 102.

80 Idem, p. 105.

81 Idem, pp. 103-104.

82 J.H. Turner (1978): *The Structure of Sociological Theory*. Homewood, Ill.: The Dorsey Press, pp. 122-123.

83 G. Simmel (1955): *Conflict*. (Translated by Kurt H. Wolff.). Glencoe: The Free Press.

84 Idem.

85 Idem.

86 Idem.

87 *The Sociology of Georg Simmel*, op. cit., 299 f. Translated by Kurt H. Wolff, 1950.

88 K. Joël quoted by David Frisby, o. c., p. 132.

89 G. Simmel (1971): Prostitution. In Donald N. Levine (Ed.): *Georg Simmel on Individuality and Social Forms*. Chicago: The University of Chicago Press.

90 G. Simmel (1923). *Philosophische Kultur*, p. 196.

91 This definition of modernity closely resembles the definition of post-modernity that emerged almost one century later. Images and appearances seem to become more important reality. Emotions recover from the blows of super rationality and the objective world of science is replaced, at least partly, by hyper nervous subjective world.

92 L. A. Coser (1956): *The Functions of Social Conflict*. New York: The Free Press of Glencoe, p. 4.

93 Idem, p. 5-6.

94 G. Simmel (1923): *Fragmente und Aufsätze*. Munich: Drei Marken Verlag, p. 185. (Quoted by Lewis Coser, o. c.: p. 22)

95 R. King Merton (1957): *Social Theory and Social Structure*. New York: The Free Press, p. 310.

96 L. A. Coser (1956): *The Functions of Social Conflict*. New York: The Free Press of Glencoe.

Chapter 5

1   H.H. Gerth & C. Wright Mills (1848/1982): A Biographical View. In *From Max Weber: Essays in sociology*. Routledge Kegan Paul, London.

2   R. Collins & M. Makowsky (1972): *The Discovery of Society*. Random House, New York.

3   D. Käsler (1988): *Max Weber: An Introduction to his Life and Work*. Cambridge: Polity Press, p. 4.

4   Christian Matthias Theodor Mommsen is generally regarded as the greatest classicist of the 19th century. He received many prizes, including the Nobel Prize for Literature for his main work on Roman History.

5   Marianne Weber (1926/1950): *Max Weber: Ein Lebensbild*. Heidelberg: Verlag Lambert Schneider. (*Max Weber: A Biography*)

6   Idem, p. 10.

7   Idem, p. 14.

8   Idem, p. 16; R. Collins (1986): *Max Weber*. Sage Publications: London, p.14.

9   Collins: 1986, op. cit.

10 Collins: op. cit., p 33-35.

11 J.G Merquior (1980): *Rousseau and Weber: Two Studies in the Theory of Legitimacy*. London: Routledge & Kegan Paul, pp. 146-151.

12 U. Eco (2001): *Kant en het vogelbekdier*. Amsterdam: Bert Bakker.

13 'Idio' is the classical Greek word for 'oneself'.

14 Often Ranke is quoted as having used the words 'wie es wirklich gewesen ist'. However, the correct quotation is 'wie es eigentlich gewesen (ist)'. Maybe, for stylistic reasons Ranke did not use the last word.

15 'So ist eine gültige Zurechnung irgend eines individuellen Erfolges ohne die Verwendung 'nomologischer' Kenntnis der Regelmäßigkeiten der kausalen Zusammenhänge, überhaupt nicht möglich.' M. Weber, *Gesammelte Aufsätze zur Wissenschaftslehre*. 1922. Weber frequently places the term nomological between inverted commas, to indicate that he does not mean invariant objective law-like relations, but so-called 'general rules of experience'.

16 M. Weber (1922); In: *Gesammelte Aufsätze zur Wissenschaftslehre*. Tübingen: J.C.B Mohr/Paul Siebbeck, pp. 175-179.

17 L. Scaff (1989): *Fleeing the Iron Cage: Culture, Politics, and Modernity in the Thought of Max Weber*. Berkeley: University of California Press.

18 H. Kunneman: o.c., pp. 172-175.

19 M. Weber (1922): *Die Objektivität sozialwissenschaftlicher und sozial-politischer Erkenntnis*. In GAW, op. cit., p. 190.

20 Käsler, op. cit., pp. 182-184.

21 M. Weber (1992). Methodologie der Sozialwissenschaften (quoted by W.L. Wallace) In: G. Ritzer (Ed.): *Metatheorizing. Conceptual Standardization and the Future of Sociology*. New York: Sage.

22 M. Weber (1922): *Soziologische Kategorienlehre*, § 1. GAW. Tübingen: J.C.B Mohr/Paul Siebbeck.

23 M. Weber (1968): *Economy & Society*. New York: Bedminster Press, p. 22 . (Orig. *Wirtschaft und Gesellschaft*)

24 L.A. Coser: *Masters of Sociological Thought*. o.c.

25 J.P. Verhoogt (1980): *De wetenschapsopvatting en methodologie van Max Weber*. In M. Goddijn (Red.), *Max Weber. Zijn leven, werk en betekenis*. Baarn: Ambo, pp. 69-73.

26 R. Fletcher: op. cit., pp. 419-421.

27 Merquior: op. cit., p. 160.

28 H. Albert & E. Topisch (1971): Werturteilsstreit: Wege der Forschung. Darmstadt, Wissenschaftliche Buchgesellschaft.

29 A. C. Zijderveld: op. cit., p. 62 e.v.

30 Merquior: op. cit., p. 152.

31 R. Fletcher: op. cit., pp. 459-464.

32 M. Weber (1920-1921): *Gesammelte Aufsätze zur Religionssoziologie I*. Tübingen: J.C.B. Mohr/ Paul Siebeck, p.1.

33 M. Weber (1968): *Economy and Society*. New York: Bedminster Press, pp. 24-25.

34 J.H. Abraham (1973): *Origins and Growth of Sociology*. Hammondsworth: Penguin Books, pp. 268-269.

35 D. Brubaker: op. cit., p. 9.

36 R. Collins: op. cit., pp. 65-69.

37 GAR: p. 4.

38 M. Weber (1974): *The Protestant Ethic and the Spirit of Capitalism*. London: Allan and Unwin, pp. 54-55.

39 The device of striking a balance, the symbol as much as the method of calculation, was invented by the Dutchman Simon Stevin in 1698.

40 *Economy and Society*, pp. 976-8.

41 M. Weber: General Economic History: o. c., p. 277.

42 The word is taken from Goethe. Weber used the tern when he wanted to refer to a form of causality based on an affinity between and a natural matching of social phenomena or cultural features.

43 M. Weber (1985): *The Protestant Ethic and the Spirit of Capitalism*. London: Counterpoint, 1985, p. 60.

44 GAR, pp. 31-32.

45 GAR, pp. 33-34.

46 GAR, o. c.

47 Horrible decision

48 GAR, pp. 114-115.

49 See the parable of the talents in the Bible that states that each individual should make the most of his God given talents.

50 GAR, op. cit., p. 163 e.v.

51 GAR, op. cit., p. 192.

52 M. Weber (1920-1921): *Die protestantische Sekten und der Geist der Kapitalismus*, GAR, pp. 207-237.

53 R. Aron: *Main Currents in Sociological Thought*. o. c.

54 M. Weber: *Economy and Society*, pp. 623-627.

55 Bernard Lewis (2002). *What went wrong?* New York: Oxford University Press

56 Ray refers to the English edition of the *Protestant Ethic* issued by Talcott Parsons.

57 M. Weber (1974): *The Protestant Ethic and the spirit of Capitalism*. London: Unwin University Books.

58 M. Weber (1968): *Economy and Society*, I, Chapter 1, section 16. New York: Bedminster Press

59 Idem, p 215.

60 A.C. Zijderveld (1985). *De dynamiek van macht en gezag.* 's-Gravenhage: VUGA, p. 25.

61 Merquior, op. cit., p. 97.

62 F. Parkin (1982): *Max Weber*. Chichester: Ellis Horwood Ltd.

63 R. Fletcher: op. cit., p. 448.

64 M. Weber: *Economy and Society*, pp. 242-245.

65 Idem: pp. 215-217.

66 D.H. Wrong (1981): Max Weber and Contemporary Sociology. In Buford Rhea (Ed.), *The Future of the Sociological Classics*. London: George Allen & Unwin.

67 W.J. Mommsen (1974). *The Age of Bureaucracy: Perspectives on the Political Sociology of Max Weber*. New York: Harper & Row, p. 19.

68 In sociology the term 'Iron cage' has become the most widely used translation of Weber's 'Stahlhartes Gehäuse', though steel case, steel jacket or steel box might have been more proper. (See for example note 17).

69 M. Weber: *Economy and Society*: p. 220.

70 R. Aron: o. c., p. 550.

71 M. Weber: *Economy & Society*: op. cit., p 4.

72 J.G. Melchior (1980): *Rousseau and Weber. Two Studies in the Theory of Legitimacy*. London: Routledge & Kegan Paul: London, p. 90.

73 Hence, he did not create the book title *Economy and Society*. Marianne Weber proposed this title after his death.

74 Collins & Makowsky: o.c.

75 Stephen Kalberg: Max Weber's Comparative Historical Sociology (1994): Chicago: University of Chicago Press, p. 30.

76 Idem, p. 31.

77 *Economy & Society*, pp. 29-30.

78 Raymond Aron rightly reminded us that Weber used a Durkheimian approach to defining deviancy here. Aron: o. c., pp. 551-552.

79 M. Weber: *Economy & Society*, pp. 33-34.

80 R. Aron: op. cit., p. 552.

81 Economy and Society: op. cit., p. 302.

82 *Economy and Society*: p. 38; WuG, p. 20.

83 L. A. Coser: o. c., p. 229.

84 R. Collins (1986): *Max Weber*. London: Sage Publications, p. 10.

Chapter 6

1   J. Habermas (1981): Talcott Parsons: Problems of Theory Construction. *Sociological Inquiry, 51* (3-4), pp. 173-196.

2   B.C. Wearne (1989): *The Theory and Scholarship of Talcott Parsons to 1951*. Cambridge University Press: Cambridge, pp. 11-18.

3   E.C. Devereux Jr. (1961): Parsons' Sociological Theory. In Max Black (Ed.), *The Social Theories of Talcott Parsons*. Englewood Cliffs N.J.: Prentice Hall, p. 4.

4   Wearne: o. c., pp. 19-20.

5   T. Parsons (1949): *The Structure of Social Action* (Ch. 1). Glencoe; Illinois, The Free Press, p 7

6   T. Parsons (1970): On Building Social System Theory: A Personal History. *Daedalus, 99*, pp. 826-881.

7   E. C. Devereux: o. c., p. 4-5.

8   J.C. Alexander (1983). *The Modern Reconstruction of Classical Thought. Talcott Parsons.*. London: Routledge & Kegan Paul.

9   W. Breines (1986): Alone in the 1950th: Anne Parsons and the feminine mystique. *Theory and Society*: Vol. 15. No. 6 (November 1986), pp. 805-843.

10 P. Sorokin (1966): Quoted by Robertson & Turner in R. Robertson & B.S. Turner (Eds.) (1991), *Talcott Parsons, Theorist of Modernity*. London: Sage Publications.

11 T. Parsons (1981): Revisiting the Classics throughout a Long Career. In Buford Rhea (Ed.): *The Future of the Sociological Classics*. London: George Allen & Unwin.

12 D. Wrong (1961): *The Oversocialized Conception of Man*. American Sociological Review, 26(2), pp. 183-192.

13 T. Parsons (1962): Comment on 'The Oversocialized Conception of Man' by Dennis Wrong. *Psychoanalysis and Psychoanalytic Review, 10*, pp. 322-34.

14 C. Wright Mills introduced the term 'Grand Theory'. He always used it in a pejorative way.

15 R. Robertson & B. S. Turner (1991): *An introduction to Talcott Parsons: Theory, politics and humanity*. In R. Robertson & B.S. Turner (Eds.), *Talcott Parsons, Theorist of Modernity*. London: Sage Publications, p.10.

16 T. Parsons & E.A. Shils (1951): *Toward a General Theory of Action*. Cambridge: Harvard University Press, p.50.

17 T. Parsons (1949): *The Structure of Social Action* (Ch. 1). Glencoe, Ill.: The Free Press, pp. 7-8.

18 T. Parsons (1966): *Societies: Evolutionary and Comparative Perspectives.* Englewood Cliffs, New Jersey, p. 113.

19 J.C. Alexander (1987): *Twenty Lectures: Sociological Theory since World War II.* New York: Columbia University Press.

20 Idem, o. c., p. 22.

21 See Habermas' discussion of *The Structure of Social Action* in his *Theory of Communicative Action.*

22 T. Parsons (1937): *The Structure of Social Action.* Glencoe: The Free Press.

23 Idem, p. 731.

24 T. Parsons (1960): Pattern Variables Revisited: A Response to Robert Dubin. *American Sociological Review,* 25(4).

25 R. Münch (1988): *Theory of Action. Towards a New Synthesis Going beyond Parsons.* London: Routledge & Kegan Paul, p. 41.

26 T. Parsons (1951): *The Social System.* London: Routledge Kegan Paul, pp. 436-437.

27 See also: T. Parsons (1978). The Sick Role and the Role of the Physician Reconsidered. In T. Parsons: *Action Theory and the Human Condition.* New York: The Free Press, p. 21.

28 In response to Dubin's critique Parsons concedes that the fifth pattern variable (self versus collectivity) falls outside these two sets and seems to belong to another level of analysis. See: Talcott Parsons (1960). Pattern Variables Revisited: A Response to Robert Dubin. *American Sociological Review,* 25(4) See also: R. Dubin (1960): Parsons' Actor: Continuities in Social Theory. *American Sociological Review,* 25(4).

29 T. Parsons (1951): o. c., pp. 10-11.

30 T. Parsons (1945): *The Present Position and Prospects of Systematic Theory in Sociology,* in: G. Gurvitch, W. E. Moore, eds. Twentieth Century Sociology. New York: Philosophical Library.

31 T. Parsons (1951): *The Social System,* o. c., pp. 27-28.

32 J. Alexander (1987): o. c.

33 K. Davis & W.E. Moore (1945): Some Principles of Stratification. *American Sociological Review,* X, 242-249. See also: M. Tumin (1953): Some Principles of Stratification. *American Sociological Review, 18,* pp. 387-394.

34 T. Parsons & E. Shils (1951): *Toward a General Theory of Action.* Cambridge: MA, Harvard University Press, p. 108.

35 B.S. Turner (1991): Neofunctionalism and the New Theoretical Movement. In R. Robertson & B.S. Turner (Eds.), *Talcott Parsons, Theorists of Modernity,* London: Sage Publications.

36 T. Parsons (1965): *General Theory in Sociology.* In: *Sociology Today, Problems and Prospects.* New York: Harper & Row.

37 T. Parsons (1951): *The Social System.* New York: The Free Press, p. 27.

38 Idem, pp. 27-28.

39 J.H. Turner (1978): *The Structure of Sociological Theory* (Rev.ed.). Homewood: The Dorsey Press, p. 51.

40 C. Morse (1961): The Functional Imperatives. In M. Black (Ed.): *The Social Theories of Talcott Parsons.* New York: Prentice Hall.

41 Hans Adriaansens (1976): *Talcott Parsons en het conceptuele dilemma.* Deventer: Van Loghum Slaterus.

42 In writing this section the chapter on Parsons' socialization theories by Cees Klaassen
    was of great help. C.A.C. Klaassen (1981): *Sociologie van de persoonlijkheidsontwikkeling:*
    Verkenningen in de socialisatietheorie. Deventer: Van Loghum Slaterus.

43 T. Parsons, (1964): o. c., pp. 56-57.

44 Idem

45 T. Parsons, (1951): *The Social System*: pp. 207-208.

46 Idem, p. 27.

47 Idem, pp. 27-28.

48 The idea for this model was based on his theoretical observations made in the following books:
    Family, Socialization, and Interaction Process. New York: The Free press. (1955, in cooperation
    with Robert Bales and others) *The Social System* (o.c.), and *Social Structure and Personality.*
    New York: The Free Press (1964).

49 Parsons owes this idea to G.W. Allport.

50 Parsons & Bales, o. c., p. 198.

51 Idem, p. 194.

52 Parsons en Bales, o. c. (Piaget has made clear that learning not only requires the integration of
    new elements in old, existing cognitive schemes, but that learning also will involve the creation
    of whole new schemes of thinking).

53 T. Parsons (1964): Evolutionary Universals in Society. *The American sociological Review*;
    T. Parsons (1966): *Societies*: Evolutionary and comparative perspectives. Englewood Cliffs
    (N.J.): Prentice Hall.

54 T. Parsons (1961): Some Considerations on the Theory of social change. *Rural sociology*, 26,
    pp. 219-239.

55 M.J. de Jong (1986): Educational policy in the Netherlands: a plea for integration. *Equity and*
    Choice, II(3), pp. 86-96.

56 History also has produced negative charismatic forces such as Hitler, Stalin, and Mao.
    Fortunately their power and influence appears to be relatively short lived.

57 Collins & Makowsky, o. c., pp. 178-180.

58 T. Parsons (1991): A tentative outline of American Values. In R. Robertson & B.S. Turner (Eds.),
    Talcott Parsons, Theorist of Modernity. London: Sage Publications.

59 See Part III, Structure and Process in Political Systems, in T. Parsons (1960), *Structure and*
    Process in Modern Societies. New York: The Free Press, pp. 17-250.

60 V. Lidz (1991): *The American Value System: A commentary on Talcott Parsons' Perspective*
    and understanding. In:R. Robertson & Bryan S. Turner (Eds.) *Talcott Parsons, Theorist of*
    Modernity. o. c.

61 A telling example is the report A Nation at Risk, published in 1983. The first page opened with
    the statement that no foreign power could have been so successful in destroying the core of
    American society than recent educational policies had succeeded in doing.

62 G. Hofstede (1980). *Cultures consequences, International Differences in Work-Related Values.*
    London: Sage Publications.

63 T. Parsons (1991): *A Tentative Outline*, o. c., pp. 43-44.

64 Idem, p. 49.

65 T. Parsons (1965): Full Citizenship for the Negro American? A Sociological problem. *Daedalus.*
    Vol. 94 (Fall) pp. 1023-1034.

66 This term refers to that aspect of the total society as a system, which forms a *Gemeinschaft*, a term used by Tönnies.

67 W.J. Wilson (1987): *The Truly Disadvantaged*. Chicago: Chicago University Press.

68 Idem

69 J.C. Alexander (1984): *Theoretical Logic in Sociology, Volume Four. The Modern Reconstruction of Classical Thought: Talcott Parsons* (pp. 289-310). London: Routledge Kegan Paul.

70 J. C. Alexander, (1984): o.c., p. 302. Alexander refers to David Lockwood's *Some Remarks on The Social System*, published in 1953. Mills, Dahrendorf, Rex and Gouldner have followed Lockwood's line of argument.

71 Idem, p. 303.

Chapter 7

1   A.J. Heerma van Voss & A. van Stolk (1987): *De geschiedenis van Norbert Elias*. Meulenhof, Amsterdam, p. 16.

2   S. Mennell (1989, 1992): *Norbert Elias. An Introduction*. Oxford: Blackwell, p. 6.

3   S. Mennell, o.c., pp. 6-8.

4   Elias quoted by Mennell, o. c., p. 12.

5   L.A. Coser (1971): *Masters of Sociological Thought*. New York: Harcourt Brace Jovanovich, pp. 429-437.

6   S. Mennell: o. c., p. 15.

7   After 36 years, in 1969, his thesis *Die Höfische Gesellschaft (Court Society)* got published.

8   J. Goudsblom (1974): *Norbert Elias*. In: *Hoofdfiguren van de sociologie-II*. Utrecht/Antwerpen: Aula, Spectrum.

9   S. Mennell: o.c., p. 19.

10 J. Goudsblom, J. & S. Mennell (Eds.) (1998): *The Norbert Elias Reader*, p. 84. Oxford: Blackwell

11 S. Mennell, o. c., pp. 22-23.

12 S. Mennell, o. c., pp. 24-25. The only thing that remained of all this work was the article 'The changing balance of power between the sexes in the history of civilization'. *Theory, Culture and Society*: (4) 1987, pp. 287-316.

13 Norbert Elias: Voorwoord. In B. van Stolk & C. Wouters: *Vrouwen in tweestrijd*. (1983). Deventer. Van Logum Slaterus.

14 N. Elias (1978). *What is sociology?* London: Hutchinson.

15 Idem, p. 17.

16 Idem, pp. 16-18 & pp. 36-52.

17 Idem, pp. 144-145.

18 S. Mennell: o. c., p. 220.

19 M.-J. de Jong (2001): Elias and Bourdieu: The Cultural Sociology of two structuralists in denial. *International Journal of Contemporary Sociology, 38*(1), pp. 64-86.

20 G. van Benthem van den Berg (1971): *The Structure of Development: An Invitation to the Sociology of Norbert Elias*. The Hague: ISS, occasional paper no. 13.

21 S. Mennell: o. c., p 252.

22 Already Benjamin Lee Whorf had drawn our attention to the negative consequences of our incorrect use of language. As a scholar and insurance agent he had detected that many

shortcomings of our language lay at the basis of terrible accidents. Think for instance of an 'empty' oil tank. The tank appears to be empty because all the liquid is pumped out of it, but it still contains a huge amount of explosive gasses. B. L. Whorf, *Language, thought and reality*, Cambridge, Mass. 1986, quoted by Elias in *What is Sociology*?

23 In this respect, Elias denounced Weber's idea of the construction of ideal types, because he feared that these scientifically constructed ideal types could easily lead to new forms of process reduction.

24 Norbert Elias: *The Civilizing Process*. Oxford, Blackwell, 1994/2000

25 Idem, p. xi-x.

26 Idem, pp. 130-131.

27 Idem, pp. 12-14.

28 Mennell: o. c., p. 45.

29 Idem

30 J. Goudsblom (1974): o. c., p. 103.

31 S. Mennell, o. c., p. 72.

32 J. Goudsblom: o. c.

33 N. Elias: *The Civilizing Process*, o. c.

34 Mennell observes that Elias is very much aware of the danger that these Freudian concepts could be reified and degenerate into static entities, but he uses these concepts always very carefully.

35 *The Civilizing Process*. o. c.

36 The widely known Thomas-theorem of William I. Thomas (1863-1947) runs as follows: *If men define situations as real, they are real in their consequences.*

37 J. Goudsblom quoted by S. Mennell: o. c., p. 259.

38 C. Brinkgreve & M. Korzec (1978): *Margriet weet raad*. Utrecht: Het Spectrum.

39 C. Wouters (1977) (with the help of Norbert Elias): Informalization and the civilizing process. In: Human Figurations: Essays for Norbert Elias, *Amsterdams Sociologisch Tijdschrift*.

40 S. Mennell: o. c., pp. 241-242.

41 E.G. Dunning, P. Murphy & J. Williams (1988): *The Roots of Football Hooliganism: A Historical and sociological Study* London: Routledge Kegan Paul, pp. 242-245.

42 S. Mennell: o. c., pp. 234-235.

43 Idem: p. 236.

44 *The Civilizing Process*, 1994, p. 445.

45 S. Mennell: o. c., pp. 115-116.

46 Idem, p. 81.

47 N. Elias & J. Scotson: o. c., p. 41.

48 N. Elias (1991): *The society of individuals*. Oxford: Basil Blackwell, Oxford

49 S. Mennell: o. c., p. 124.

50 *The Civilizing Process*, p. 201.

51 N. Elias (1991): *The Society of Individuals*. Oxford: Basil Blackwell, pp. 155-156.

52 Idem, p. 158.

53 Idem, pp. 159-162.

54 Idem, pp. 180-183.

55 N. Elias (1991). *The Society of Individuals*. Oxford: Basil Blackwell, Oxford, pp. 91-97.

56 *Symbol Theory*, p. 113.

57 N. Elias (1991): *The Symbol Theory*, o. c., London: Sage, p. 53.

58 Idem, p. 6.

59 Idem, p. 111.

60 Idem, p. 112.

61 Idem, pp. 114-115.

62 Idem, pp. 115-116.

63 Idem:,pp. 116-117.

64 1956: p. 227.

65 1983d: p. 46.

66 N. Elias (1993). *Time: An Essay*. Oxford: Blackwell Publishers, p.1.

67 S. Mennell: o.c., p. 211.

68 N. Elias, 1993, o. c., p. 75.

69 Idem, pp. 39-40.

70 Idem, pp. 46-47.

71 Idem, p. 48.

72 Idem, p. 49.

73 Mennell: o.c

Chapter 8

1   Here I borrow much information from Richard Fardon, who extensively quotes Antonia White to catch the atmosphere of the convent school. Richard Fardon (1999). *Mary Douglas*. London: Routledge; Antonia White (1978, 1933): *Frost in May*. London: Virago.

2   R. Fardon (1999): *Mary Douglas*. London: Routledge, pp. 20-21.

3   R. Fardon (1999): *Mary Douglas*. London: Routledge, p. 22.

4   M. Douglas (1980): *Evans-Pritchard*. Brighton: Harvester Press.

5   R. Fardon (1999): *Mary Douglas*. London: Routledge, p. 50.

6   R. Wuthnow et al. (1984): *Cultural Analysis. The Work of Peter L. Berger, Mary Douglas, Michel Foucault and Jürgen Habermas*. London: Routledge & Kegan Paul, pp. 11-12.

7   R. Fardon (1999). Mary Douglas. London: Routledge, pp. 144-145.

8   J. Douglas had been Director of the Conservative Research Department from 1970 to 1975, but was demoted to Associate Director when Margaret Thatcher became leader of the Conservative Party in 1975 and Chris Patton was appointed as the new director. The autonomy of the research department was curbed and its functions were taken over by a number of right-wing think tanks. John Ramsden (1980): *The making of Conservative Party Policy*. London/New York: Longman.

9   M. Douglas (1996). *Introduction to the 1996 edition of Natural Symbols: explorations in cosmology*. London: Routledge.

10 M. Douglas: No Free Gifts: Introduction to Mauss's essay on 'The Gift'.

11 M. Mauss (1954): *The Gift*. New York: Free Press, p.3 .

12 Here Mary Douglas quotes Larry Siedentrop: 'Two Liberal Traditions'. In: Alan Ryan (1979) (Ed.). *The Idea of Freedom*. Oxford: Clarendon, pp. 153-174.

13 R. Wuthnow et al. (1984): *Cultural Analysis. The Work of Peter L. Berger, Mary Douglas, Michel*

Foucault and Jürgen Habermas. London: Routledge & Kegan Paul, p. 77.

14 M. Douglas (1978). *Implicit Meanings, Essays in Anthropology.* London. Routledge & Kegan Paul.

15 M. Douglas (1982c): *Essays in the Sociology of Perception.* London: Routledge, Kegan Paul.

16 Z. Bauman 1990: *Thinking Sociologically.* Oxford: Blackwell, p.57.

17 M. Douglas (1978) O. c. p. xi.

18 M. Douglas (1996). *Natural symbols*, pp. 70-71. o. c.

19 M. Douglas (1966, 1979): *Purity and Danger: An analysis of the concepts of pollution and taboo.* London: Routledge & Kegan Paul, p. 41.

20 R. Fardon (1999): *Mary Douglas.* London: Routledge, p. 85.

21 M. Douglas (1975): *Implicit Meanings: Essays in anthropology).* London: Routledge & Kegan Paul, p. 12.

22 Not all African tribes obey to the same rules. Some tribes are known as rat-eaters or snake-eaters.

23 Believing that Jews (and Christians) had been transformed into apes and pigs and other unclean animals, as divine punishment for rejecting the teachings of the Prophet is widespread in the Islamic world. It is mentioned in the Koran, verse 5:60 and referred to in other verses (2:65 and 7:166) as well as in the Hadith. It is widely discussed among Muslim theologians, and still mentioned by renowned imams in their sermons today. Special Report, Nr. 11. MEMRI, the Middle East Media Research Institute. Retrieved on 3 august 2006.

24 Moses Maimonides is also known by his Hebrew name Moshe ben Maimon. He is posthumously acknowledged as one of the foremost rabbinical arbiters and viewed as a cornerstone of orthodox Jewish thought.

25 M. Douglas (1966, 1979): *Purity and Danger: An analysis of the concepts of pollution and taboo.* London: Routledge & Kegan Paul, p.31.

26 Christians have lifted the ban on biblical food restrictions.

27 M. Douglas (1966, 1979): *Purity and Danger: An analysis of the concepts of pollution and taboo.* London: Routledge & Kegan Paul, p.45.

28 Idem, pp. 50-51.

29 Hence, if the Bible should be updated we should expect to find a law that would forbid genetic engineering for the same reason.

30 Yet, another way to classify food, which also is found in Asian countries, especially China and Japan, is based on the belief that some kinds of food are very good for sexual prowess and fertility.

31 M. Douglas (1966, 1979): o. c., p 57.

32 Idem, pp. 40-41

33 Idem, pp. 18-19

34 M. Douglas (1970): *Natural Symbols: Explorations in Cosmology.* New York: Pantheon Books, pp. vii-viii.

35 Idem, pp. xi-x.

36 M. Douglas (1966, 1979): *Purity and Danger. o. c.,* p. 18.

37 Idem, pp. 61-62

38 R. Fardon (1999). *Mary Douglas,* p. 87.

39 R. Fardon (1999). *Mary Douglas.* London: Routledge, p. 3.

40 R. Fardon (1999). *Mary Douglas*. London: Routledge, p. 5.

41 M. Douglas (1966, 1979): *Purity and Danger: o. c.*, pp. 61-62.

42 Nowadays, we remember the TV-images of the Taliban who demolished age-old Buddhist statues in Afghanistan in the year 2001.

43 M. Douglas (1966, 1979): *Purity and Danger*, p. 18.

44 M. Douglas (1978): *Implicit Meaning: Essays in anthropology*. London: Routledge & Kegan Paul, p. 55.

45 M. Douglas (1982c): *Essays in the Sociology of Perception*. London: Routledge & Kegan Paul.

46 Bernstein sought to apply Sapir's insight about the controlling influence of language on culture. Sapir asserted that the real world to a large extent unconsciously is built up on the language habits of the group. We see and hear very largely as we do because the language habits of our community predispose certain choices of interpretation. For instance women that have sex with many male friends will be labeled very negatively as easy lays, sluts, whores et cetera, whereas men who show a similar pattern of behaviour tend not to be labeled that negatively. The lack of equivalent negative terms for their promiscuous behaviour reflects that society uses a double standard regarding the sexual behaviour of men and women and helps to reproduce and legitimize that double standard.

47 B. Bernstein (1971): *Class, Codes and Control. (Vol. 2)* London: Routledge & Kegan Paul. Jenny Cook-Gumperz (1973). *Social Control and Socialization: A study of Class Differences in the Language of Maternal Control*. London: Routledge & Kegan Paul.

48 M. Douglas (1970): *Natural Symbols: Explorations of Cosmology* (p. viii). New York: Pantheon Books.

49 M. Douglas (1982): *Introduction*. In: Mary Douglas (Ed.), *Essays in the Sociology of Perception*. London: Routledge & Kegan Paul.

50 J. Gross & S. Rayner (1985): *Measuring culture: A paradigm for the analysis of social organization*. New York: Columbia University Press.

51 R. Fardon has given another enlightening overview of the development of the group-grid model during the course of Douglas's work and has presented a series of synonyms she has used to describe the different 'ideal types'. Richard Fardon: o. c., p. 224.

52 M. Douglas: Introduction to the 1996 edition, o. c., pp. xix - xx.

53 V. Seth: A Suitable Boy (1993) New York: Harper & Collins.

54 M. Douglas (1982). *In the Active Voice*, p.202. London/Boston: Routledge and Kegan Paul.

55 The kibbutz was a very popular social unit during the first decades of the establishment of the state Israel. Then youngsters from various countries came to Israel to help its economic development. Nowadays Israel is individualized just like all other modern western societies.

56 M. Douglas (1989): Institutions of the Third Kind. British and Swedish labour markets compared. *The Journal of General Management*, 14(4), pp. 34-52.

57 M. Douglas: Risk and Blame: Essays in Cultural Theory (1994). London/New York: Routledge, p. 167.

58 M. Douglas (1989): Institutions of the Third Kind. British and Swedish labour markets compared. *The Journal of General Management*, 14(4), pp. 34-52.

59 I. Berlin (1958): Two Concepts of Liberty. In: *Four Essays on Liberty*. Oxford: Oxford University Press.

60 Idem, pp.130-131.

61 L. Fleck (1979): *The Genesis and Development of a Scientific Fact*. Chicago: The University of Chicago Press, p. 27.

62 This is the title of the last chapter of 'How Institutions Think'.

63 M. Douglas (1986). *How Institutions Think*. Syracuse NY: Syracuse University Press, pp. 9-10.

64 L. Fleck (1935/1999): *The Genesis and Development of a Scientific Fact*. Chicago: The University of Chicago press.

65 P. Fauconnet & M. Mauss (1968): La sociologie: objet et méthode (1904). In: M. Mauss, *Essais de sociologie*. Paris: Editions de Minuit.

66 . Idem, p.41.

67 T. Kuhn (1962): *The Structure of Scientific Revolutions*. Chicago: University of Chicago Press.

68 G. Ritzer (1981): *Toward an integrated Sociological Paradigm*. Boston: Allyn and Bacon, Inc.

69 There are indications that this fact that the earth was round already had been discovered before, e.g. in Alexandria, which had become the scientific center of the world after Alexander The Great had established this Egyptian town.

70 L. Fleck (1935/1979). o. c., p.38.

71 H. S. Becker (1982). *Art Worlds*. Berkeley: University of California Press.

72 M. Douglas (1986). *How Institutions Think*. Syracuse NY: Syracuse University Press, pp. 14-15.

73 The original aphorism was: 'Songs have changed and so have our ears.'

74 E. H. Gombrich (1960): *Art and Illusio: A Study in the Psychology of Pictorial Representation*. Princeton: Princeton University Press, p. 60.

75 Fleck, quoted by Mary Douglas, op. cit., p. 18.

76 S. Fuchs (2001). *Against Essentialism*. Cambridge, Mass.: Harvard University Press, p. 287.

77 M. Douglas (1990). Risk and Blame. *The Sociological Review,* 38(3), pp. 445-464.

78 M. Douglas (1990). Risk and Blame. *The Sociological Review,* 38(3), pp. 102-103.

79 In 2005 it is estimated that almost 40 million people are infected all over the world. In that same year at least 2.4 million died of AIDS.

80 M. L. Calvez: Composer avec un Danger, approche des réponses sociales a l'infection au VIH au SIDA, Rennes, IRTS de Bretagne.

81 The renowned philosopher and sociologist Michel Foucault really believed this to be true. Though he came from a dynasty of medical doctors, he ignored the advice to be more careful and did not change his lifestyle. He became an early victim of an AIDS-related disease and died in 1984, 57 years of age.

82 Idem, pp. 106-108.

83 M. Douglas (1990): Risk and Blame. *The Sociological Review,* 38(3).

84 R. Fardon (1999). *Mary Douglas*. London: Routledge.

Chapter 9

1 P.L. Berger (1963). *Invitation to Sociology: A Humanistic Perspective*. Doubleday.

2 Schütz earned his living as a financial specialist at the Wall Street Stock Exchange, gave evening classes and at night wrote lucid essays.

3 P. Berger & B. Berger (1972): *Sociology*. New York: Basic Books.

4 P.L. Berger (1961): *The Noise of Solemn Assemblies*. Garden City New York, Doubleday. P.L. Berger (1961): *The Precarious Vision*. Garden City New York, Doubleday.

5   Davison Hunter, James & Ainly, Stephen C. (Eds.): *Making Sense of M odern Times: Peter L. Berger and the Vision of Interpretative Sociologie*. London: Routledge Kegan Paul.

6   P. Berger (1967): *The Sacred Canopy*. Garden City (N.Y.), Doubleday.

7   P. Berger & R.J. Niehaus (1970): *Movement and Revolution*. Garden City (N.Y.), Doubleday.

8   P. Berger, B. Berger & H. Kellner (1973). *The Homeless Mind: Modernity and Consciousness*. Random House, New York.

9   P. Berger (1973): *Pyramids of Sacrifice*. Garden City (N.Y.), Doubleday.

10   P. Berger & H. Kellner (1982): *Sociology Reinterpreted: An Essay on Method and Vocation*. Hammondsworth: Penguin Books, pp. 7-15.

11   P. Berger (1992): Sociology: Disinvitation? *Society: 30*(1).

12   Davison Hunter, James & Ainly, Stephen C. (Eds.): *Making Sense of M odern Times: Peter L. Berger and the Vision of Interpretative Sociologie*. London: Routledge Kegan Paul.13   Peter Berger (1977): *Facing up to Modernity*. New York: Basic Books.

14   *The Social Construction of Reality*, o. c., p. 20.

15   S.C. Ainlay: *The encounter with phenomenology*. In: *Peter L. Berger and the Vision of Interpretative Sociology*, o. c., p. 37.

16   *Invitation to Sociology*, 1963; o. c., p. 55.

17   His anthropological presuppositions are strongly influenced by Marx, Plessner, and Gehlen. See P.L. Berger & T. Luckmann (1966): *The Social Construction of Reality: A Treatise in the Sociology of Knowledge*. New York: Doubleday & Comp., p.17.

18   S.C. Ainlay: o. c.

19   P. Berger cited by Peter Ainlay, o. c., p. 35.

20   In 1986, twenty years after publication, Berger still fully endorses the content of this book. Of all the books he has written together with a co-author, this is the one he least feels inclined to change parts of, and Berger knows that Luckmann feels the same way. Peter L. Berger (1986). Epilogue. In J.D. Hunter & S.C. Ainlay (Ed.): *Making Sense of Modern Times*. RKP: London and New York, p. 222.

21   Ainlay, o. c., pp. 35-36.

22   P.L. Berger & T. Luckmann (1966): *The Social Construction of Reality: A Treatise in the Sociology of Knowledge*. New York: Doubleday & Comp., pp.14-15.

23   M. Scheler introduced the term Wissenssoziologie.

24   Berger and Luckmann note that the sociology of knowledge derives two key concepts from Marx. The one is *ideology* or a system of thought that serves as a weapon in the struggle for economic and political power. The other is *false consciousness,* which refers to ways of thinking that are alienated from the real social being.

25   P.L. Berger & T.Luckmann (1966): *The Social Construction of Reality: A Treatise in the Sociology of Knowledge*. New York: Doubleday & Comp., p. 129.

26   P. Berger (1967): *The Sacred Canopy. o. c.,* p. 4.

27   Berger borrows the terms externalization and objectivation from the work of Hegel (*Entausserung* and *Versachlichung*). They should be conceived as Marx has applied them to collective phenomena. The concept of internalization is derived from the work of G. H. Mead. See *The Sacred Canopy*, footnote 3, p 188.

28   G. Ritzer (1981): *Toward an Integrated Sociological paradigm*. Boston: Allyn & Bacon, p. 199.

29   Berger & Luckmann: o.c. Part II, Chapter 1.

30 Berger en Berger, o. c., p. 66.

31 Berger en Berger, o. c., pp. 68-69.

32 For instance, feminists demand that chairperson and spokesperson replace terms such as chairman and spokesman.

33 Berger, (1965): p. 200.

34 Berger & Luckmann: o. c., pp 89-91.

35 R. Putnam (1992): *Making democracy work: civic traditions in modern Italy.* New York: Princeton University Press.

36 R. Wuthnow: *Religion as Sacred Canopy.* In: *Making sense of the Modern World,* o. c.

37 P. Berger (1997): Redeeming Laughter: The Comic Dimension of Human Experience. New York: Walter de Gruyter, pp. 7-8.

38 D. Wrong (1976): The oversocialized conception of man in modern sociology. In L. Coser and B. Rosenberg (eds): Sociological Theory (4th edn). New York: Mac Millan, pp. 104-112.

39 P. Berger: *Invitation to Sociology,* o. c., p. 131.

40 Berger & Berger: o. c., pp. 46-47; Berger & Berger also refer to the comparative study of Beatrice Whiting (Ed.) (1963): *Six cultures - studies in child rearing practices.* New York.

41 Idem

42 Hirschman: (1970): *Exit, Voice, and Loyalty. Responses to Decline in Firms, Organizations and States.* Cambridge M.A.: Harvard University Press.

43 R.K. Merton (1957, 1965): *Social Structure and Anomie. In: Social Theory and social structure* (revised and enlarged edition). New York: The Free Press.

44 Berger: Invitation to sociology. o. c., p. 139.

45 *The Social Construction of Reality,* p. 130.

46 For instance, children of mothers who are addicted to hard drugs, and who, therefore, cannot structure their own life, are severely retarded in their mental and social development.

47 Berger, 1963, o. c., p 104; 1972, o. c., p.53.

48 Lewis A. Coser (1971). *Masters of Sociological Thought.* New York: Harcourt, Brace & Jovanovich, p. 333.

49 G.H. Mead (1934/1959): *Mind, Self and Society.* Chicago: University of Chicago Press. Other books of Mead that are reconstructed after his death: *The Philosophy of the Present* (1932); *Movements of Thought in the Nineteenth Century* (1936) and *The Philosophy of the Act* (1938).

50 The quotation is from Paul Rock. Quoted by Ian Craib in his *Modern Social Theory: From Parsons to Habermas,* p. 71. For a more positive evaluation see: A. C. Zijderveld (1974): *George Herbert Mead,* in: *Hoofdfiguren van de sociologie, deel 1.* Utrecht: Spectrum.

51 I.Craib, o. c., p. 73.

52 P. Berger: *Invitation to Sociology,* p. 104.

53 T. Parsons (1948): Social Structure and the development of Society: Freud's contribution to the integration of Psychology and Sociology. *Psychiatry, 21,* pp. 321-340. E.H. Erikson (1963): *Childhood and Society.* New York: W.W. Norton.

54 M.J. de Jong (1987). *Herkomst, Kennis en Kansen.* Lisse: Swets & Zeitlinger.

55 *Invitation to Sociology: o. c.*

56 C.H. Cooley (1964): *Human Nature and the Social Order.* New York: Schocken. Quoted by Lewis A. Coser: Masters of Sociological Thought, o. c., p. 306.

57 Berger & Berger: 1972, p 62.

58 1972, o. c., p 61-62.

59 J. Ortega y Gasset: The Revolt of the Masses (1932). New York: Norton.

60 J. Holt (1967, 1983): *How children learn*. Hammondsworth: Middlesex. Penguin.

61 I. Illich (1971): *Deschooling Society*. New York: Harper & Row; Christopher Lash (1978): *The Culture of Narcissism*. New York: Norton; E. Reimer (1971): *School is Dead*. Hammondsworth. Middlesex: Penguin.

62 Zie noot 5 p. 488.

63 Berger 'indirectly' derives his notion of a nomos from Durkheim, by choosing the opposite of his notion of anomy. See footnote 23 on page 189 of *The Sacred Canopy*.

64 *The Sacred Canopy*, o. c., p. 23.

65 Idem, p. 53.

66 Idem, pp. 53-54.

67 Idem, pp. 107-108.

68 *The Sacred Canopy*, p. 109-112. Berger delves deeper into Ancient History, by asserting that the elements of this Protestant Puritanism were already present in the old books of the bible, where monotheism was a central issue. God or the gods and the people did not form part of a collective universe, but Yahweh existed outside of this cosmos. He had created the whole cosmos, including mankind. This implies a great distance between Yahweh and the people.

69 Robert H. Coombs (1991): Marital status and Personal Well-Being: A Literature Review. *British Journal of Medical Psychology, 40*, pp. 97-102.

70 B. Berger & P.L. Berger (1983). *The War over the Family*. New York: Anchor Press/Doubleday, pp. 6-7.

71 Berger & Berger, pp. 16-17.

72 Idem, p 140.

73 First chapter in: *Facing up to Modernity*: *Excursions in Society, Politics and Religion* (1977). New York: Basic Books.

74 Berger & Kellner: o. c., p. 7.

75 zie noot 5 p. 488.

76 O'Leary (1986): The Place of Politics. In: *Making sense of modernity*. London: Routledge, Kegan Paul, pp. 179-196.

77 P. Berger, 1970a, p. 13.

78 P. Berger, 1963, p. 6.

79 J.P. O'Leary, o. c., p. 181.

80 P. Berger, 1970a, p. 23.

81 P.L. Berger (1987). *The Capitalist Revolution; Fifty Propositions about prosperity, Equality, and Liberty*. Aldershot: Wildwood House.

82 The increasing damage to our natural environment is often mentioned as another drawback of economic growth. This is indeed a great problem that Berger does not address. However, he could have riposted the modern antagonists of capitalism that industrial production in communist countries has caused much more damage to the ecological system than in the west. Moreover, the ecological movement is flourishing in the democratic countries and has already won many important victories against polluting industries.

83 P. Berger (1992). Sociology: A Disinvitation? *Society, 30*(1), pp. 12-18.

84 In my view also postmodernism offered a resort for many disoriented Marxists.

85 C. Wright Mills (1959): *The Sociological Imagination*. New York: Oxford University Press.

86 I suppose that one of the main reasons was that their theoretical model was too simple. Basically there were always only two parties involved: a powerful oppressor and a completely powerless victim.

Chapter 10

1   That the two sons of Bourdieu also have gained access to the ENS seem to prove this point.

2   R. Jenkins (1992): *Pierre Bourdieu*. London/New York: Routledge , p. 14. (Derrida was a member of Bourdieu's committee for the defense of freedom. Le Roy Ladurie was an opponent.)

3   P. Bourdieu (1993): Concluding Remarks: For a Sociogenetic Understanding of Intellectual Works. In: C. Calhoun, E. LiPuma & M. Postone (Eds.): *Bourdieu: Critical Perspectives*. Cambridge: Polity Press.

4   Dick Pels (1989): *Inleiding. Naar een reflexieve sociale wetenschap*. In: *Pierre Bourdieu. Opstellen over smaak, habitus en het veldbegrip*. Amsterdam: Van Gennep, p.21.

5   Pierre Bourdieu (1993): *Sociology in Question*. London: Sage; P. Bourdieu (1990): *In Other Words*. Cambridge: Polity Press.

6   A. Honneth, H. Kocyba & B. Schwibs (1986): The Struggle for Symbolic Order: An Interview with Pierre Bourdieu, *Theory, Culture and Society*, 3.

7   Pierre Bourdieu & J. C. Passeron (1977): *Reproduction in Education, Society and Culture*. London: Sage.

8   Pierre Bourdieu (1996): State Nobility: Elite Schools in the Field of Power. Oxford: Polity Press.

9   Loïc J. D. Wacquant (1992): Présentation. In: Pierre Bourdieu avec Loïc Wacquant: *Réponses, Pour une anthropologie réflexive*. Paris: Seuil.

10 Pierre and Marie Claire Bourdieu had three sons: Jérome, Emmanuel and Laurent. Further it is interesting to note that Pierre Bourdieu published a scientific article together with his wife: Pierre Bourdieu & Marie-Claire Bourdieu (1965): Le paysan et la photographie.*Revue française de sociologie*. Paris. Éditions du CNRS, pp. 165-174.

11 R. Jenkins: o. c., p.19.

12 Pierre Bourdieu (1993): *Concluding Remarks*, o. c.

13 Pierre Bourdieu (1990): *In Other Words: Essays Towards a Reflexive Sociology*. Cambridge/Oxford: Polity Press, p. 34.

14 A. Schütz (1962): *Collected Papers, vol. I.: The Problem of Social Reality*. The Hague. Nijhoff, p. 59.

15 Pierre Bourdieu (1990): *In Other Words*, o. c., pp. 124-125.

16 Idem, pp. 125-126.

17 R. Jenkins: o. c., p. 73.

18 Norbert Elias also used the term habitus.

19 P. Bourdieu: *Distinction*. o. c., pp. 170-171.

20 P. Bourdieu: *In other words*. o. c., p. 31.

21 P. Bourdieu (1989): *The Logic of Practice*. Cambridge: Polity Press (*Le sens pratique*, Paris, 1980.)

22 P. Bourdieu (1989). *Vive la crise!* In: Pierre Bourdieu, Opstellen over smaak, habitus en het veldbegrip. o. c., pp. 64-66.

23 Pierre Bourdieu: *In other Words*: o. c., pp. 60-61.

24 Idem

25 Pierre Bourdieu: *In Other Words*: o. c., p. 63.

26 Idem, p. 63. Though Jenkins notes that Bourdieu does not pay much attention to the overwhelming amount of people who are not very competent.

27 P. Bourdieu (1958): *Sociologie de l'Algérie*. Paris: PUF, p. 5.

28 From rules to strategies: interview with P. Lamaison, *Terrains*, 4 (March, 1985).

29 Here, Bourdieu refers to a study he carried out with Monique de Saint Martin.

30 P. Bourdieu (1986): *The forms of Capital*. In: John G. Richardson (Ed.), *Handbook of Theory and Research for the Sociology of Education*. New York: Greenwood Press.

31 P. Bourdieu (1990): A lecture on the lecture. In: *In Other Words*, o. c., p. 192.

32 P. Bourdieu (1993): Some properties of fields. In: *Sociology in Question*. London, Sage, pp. 72-73.

33 *Sociology in Question*, o. c., p. 111.

34 In most western European countries the agrarian sector is facing hard times, despite financial help from the EC. The prospects for the future are very bleak. Each year many farmers quit farming without finding a successor. As a consequence, many young farmers find it very hard to find a spouse.

35 P. Bourdieu (1985): The social space and the genesis of groups. *Social Science Information, 24*(2), pp. 195-220. Also in Pierre Bourdieu: *Language & Symbolic Power* (p. 231). Oxford: Polity Press.

36 Idem, p. 198.

37 R. Jenkins: o. c., pp. 103-104.

38 P. Bourdieu & J. C. Passeron (1977): *Reproduction, In Education, Society and Culture*. London: Sage. Orig. La Réproduction, Minuit, Paris, 1970.

39 Idem

40 Idem

41 R. Jenkins: o. c., p. 105.

42 P. Willis (1977): *How working class kids get working class jobs*. Farnborough: Saxon House.

43 S. Fordham (1988): Racelessness as a Factor in Black Students' School Success: Pragmatic Strategy or Pyrrhic Victory? *Harvard Educational Review, 48*(1), pp. 54-84.

44 M. Fuller (1981): Black girls in a London Comprehensive. In: A. James & R. Jeffcoate (Eds.), *The School in a multicultural society*. London: Harper & Row.

45 L. Sansone (1992): *Schitteren in de schaduw*. Amsterdam: Het Spinhuis.

46 Th. Sowell: Ethnic America, 1980.

47 D. Robbins: o. c., p. 117.

48 R. Jenkins: o. c., p. 129.

49 P. Bourdieu, et al. (1990): *Photography: A Middle-brow Art*. Cambridge: Polity. (*Un art moyen: Essai sur les usages de la photographie* (1965).

50 P. Bourdieu et al. (1965): *Un art moyen: Essai sur les usages sociaux de la photographie*. Paris: Editions de Minuit, pp. 38-54.

51 R. Jenkins: o. c., pp. 130-131.

52 Distinction: o. c., p. 5.

53 P. Bourdieu (1993) Music lovers: origin and evolution of the species. In *Sociology in Question*, p. 104.

54 *Sociology in Question*, o. c., p. 105.

55 P. Bourdieu (1993): The metamorphosis of tastes: In *Sociology in Question*, o.c., p. 109.

56 P. Bourdieu: *Distinction*, pp. 34-37 & 527-528.

57 Idem: pp. 9-18 & pp. 18-82.

58 Idem: p. 372.

59 Idem: p. 65, pp. 333-343.

60 Idem: p. 171. R. Jenkins: o. c., p. 142.

61 P. Bourdieu (1977): L'économie des échanges linguistiques, *Langue française, 34*; L. Wacquant (1989): Towards a reflexive sociology: a workshop with Pierre Bourdieu. *Sociological Review, 7*, p. 47.

62 P. Bourdieu (1991): *Language and Symbolic Power*. Cambridge: Polity, p. 66.

63 Idem, p. 108.

64 A boss of a Dutch broadcasting organization once said about a colleague that he also lied when it was not necessary.

65 P. Bourdieu (1991). *Language and Symbolic Power*. Oxford: Polity Press, p. 130.

66 Once again we see a revival of an old and formerly rejected term. Afro-American and Afro-Caribbean Rappers use the word nigger or niggah frequently in their texts. Still, I think presently it would not be wise for White people to follow this usage.

67 This is also expressed in the following song.
If you're white, you're all right.
If you're brown, stick around,
If your black, stay back

68 In Africa, many black women buy skin creams to make their skin lighter. Some of these creams turn out to be very dangerous, creating scar tissues that ruin their skin forever.

69 P. Bourdieu (1979). Les trois états du capital culturel. *Actes de la recherche en sciences sociales, 30*, pp. 3-6.

70 P. Bourdieu (1993): A science that makes trouble. In: *Sociology in Question*. London: Sage Publications, p. 10.

71 P. Bourdieu, 1985a, pp. 15-16.

72 P. Bourdieu, 1987a, pp. 63-64.

73 R. Jenkins: o. c., p. 166.

Chapter 11

1 J. Habermas (P. Dews, ed.) (1992): *Autonomy and Solidarity, Interviews with Jürgen Habermas*. London: Verso, p. 96.

2 Robert Wuthnow et al. (1984): *Cultural Analysis: The Work of Peter L Berger, Mary Douglas, Michel Foucault and Jürgen Habermas*. London & New York: Routledge & Kegan Paul, pp. 179-180.

3 J. Keulartz (1992): *De verkeerde wereld van Jürgen Habermas*. Meppel/Amsterdam: Boom, pp. 13-14.

4 J. Habermas (1992): *Autonomy and Solidarity*. London: Verso, p. 126.

5 J. Keulartz (1992), p. 15.

6 R. Geuss (1981): *The Idea of a Critical Theory: Habermas & the Frankfurt School*. Cambridge: Cambridge University Press, pp. 2-3.

7   J. Habermas (1992): *Autonomy and Solidarity*. London: Verso.

8   J. Habermas (1962): *Strukturwandel der Offentlichkeit*. Darmstadt und Neuwied: Hermann Luchterhand Verlag. J. Habermas (1989/1992): *The Structural Transformation of the Public Sphere*. Cambridge: Polity Press, p. 96.

9   J. Keulartz, pp. 12-13.

10 Idem, pp. 36-40.

11 Idem, pp. 23-24.

12 J. Habermas (1976): *Theory and Practice*. London: Heinemann, p. 198.

13 R. Wuthnow: *Cultural Analysis. o. c.*, pp. 180-181.

14 M. Jay (1973): *The Dialectical Imagination*. London: Heinemann Educational Books Ltd.

15 Kant cited by Martin Jay, p. 3.

16 H. Kunneman & J. Keulartz (1985): *Rondom Habermas: Analyses en kritieken*. Meppel: Boom.

17 M. Jay (1973): The Dialectical Imagination: A History of the Frankfurt School. o. c.

18 Idem, pp. 43-44.

19 Idem, p. 45.

20 R.C. Holub (1991): *Jürgen Habermas: Critic in the public sphere*. London/New York: Routledge.

21 Idem, p. 27.

22 J. Habermas (1976): *Theory and Practice, o. c.*, p. 254.

23 H. Hoefnagels (1977): Kritische sociologie. In L. Rademaker & H. Bergman (Eds.) *Sociologische stromingen*. Utrecht: Aula/Het spectrum.

24 T. W. Adorno et al. (1950): *The Authoritarian Personality*. New York: Harper.

25 Pierce cited by Jürgen Habermas. In: *Knowledge and Human Interest*. London: Heinemann, p. 170.

26 Karl R. Popper (1972): *Objective Knowledge*. Oxford: Oxford University Press.

27 Th. McCarthy (1981): *The Critical Theory of Jürgen Habermas*. Cambridge, Mass.: The MIT Press, Cambridge, Mass, p. 55.

28 J. Habermas (1965/1973): *Kennis und Interesse*. In *Een keuze uit het werk van Jürgen Habermas*. Deventer: Van Loghum Slaterus, pp. 81-96.

29 McCarthy: o. c., p. 56.

30 Idem, pp. 89-90.

31 Idem, pp. 86-87.

32 B. Flyvbjerg (2001): *Making Social Science Matter*. Cambridge: Cambridge University Press.

33 Thomas McCarthy's book was a great help for writing this section. Thomas McCarthy: *The Critical Theory of Jürgen Habermas*. MIT-Press: Cambridge Mass. 1981/82.

34 J. Habermas (1963). *Theorie und Praxis. o. c.*, p. 254.

35 Idem, pp. 254-255.

36 J. Habermas & N. Luhmann (1971): *Theorie der Gesellshaft oder Sozialtechnologie* (p.170). Frankfurt: Suhrkamp, pp. 81-96.

37 J. Habermas: *Technology and Society as Ideology*, Ibid.

38 J. Habermas (1971): *Toward a Rational Society*. Boston: Beacon Press; London: Heinemann, p. 55.

39 Technische vooruitgang en sociale leefwereld. In: *Een keuze uit het werk van Jürgen Habermas*. Deventer: Van Loghum Slaterus. O. c.

40 O.c., p. 15.

41 J. Keulartz: o.c., pp. 178-179.

42 J. Habermas (1990): *Strukturwandel der Öffentlichkeit*, pp. 305-307. See also the summary of Schmitt's analysis by Keulartz: Keulartz o. c., pp. 171-1/2.

43 H. Kunneman (1983): *Habermas' theorie van het communicatieve handelen. Een samenvatting.* Meppel/Amsterdam: Boom, p. 7.

44 Idem

45 A. Brand (1990): *The Force of Reason: An Introduction to Habermas' Theory of Communicative Action.* Sydney: Allan & Unwin, pp. 51-53.

46 Idem, p. 53.

47 TKH II, p. 447.

48 TKH II, p. 447.

49 TKH II, p 580.

50 See the balance theory of Fritz Heider or the theory of cognitive dissonance of Leon Festinger.

51 Besides, you could also say something about the linguistic world, but it is better this medium to see as part of the three other worlds.

52 This example was constructed by Arie Brand, 1990.

53 There are other alternatives, such as the use of violence or the evasion of an opponent.

54 A. Brand (1990). *The Force of Reason; an Introduction to Habermas' Theory of Communicative Action.* Sydney: Allan Unwin, pp. 51-53.

55 S. Mestrovic, o. c.

56 J. Habermas, 1986: 386-387, quoted by Brand, p. 133.

57 A. Gutman (1995) (Ed.). *Multiculturalisme*, pp. 7-8.

58 J. Habermas (1995). Strijd om erkenning in de democratische rechtsstaat. In A. Gutman (Ed.) *Multiculturalisme*. Meppel/Amsterdam: Boom, p. 129.

59 Idem, pp. 131-132.

60 Idem, p. 134.

61 J. Habermas 1995, o. c., p. 135.

62 J. Habermas 1995, o. c., pp. 138-139.

63 J. Fishman (1972): *Advances in the Sociology of language.* The Hague: Mouton. J. Habermas (1995), o. c., pp. 152-153.

64 P. Brassé & W. van Schelven (1980). *Assimilatie van vooroorlogse migranten.* Den Haag: Sdu.

65 M. Featherstone (1988): *Postmodernism.* London: Sage, pp. 202-203.

66 H. Kunneman (1996): *Van Theemutscultuur tot walkman-ego. Contouren van een postmoderne individualiteit.* Meppel/Amsterdam: Boom, pp. 106-107.

67 In fact, Mestrovic asserts, the same is true for postmodernists. S. Mestrovic (1991). *The coming fin de siècle,* London/New York: Routledge.

68 H. Kunneman: 1996. o. c.

69 J.-F. Lyotard (1986): *Le Différend.* Paris: Minuit, p.24.

70 Th. McCarthy (1987): *Introduction in Jürgen Habermas: The Philosophical Discourse of Modernity.* Oxford: Basil Blackwell.

Index

The author

Mart-Jan de Jong is professor of social sciences at the Roosevelt Academy in Middelburg. The Roosevelt Academy is an international Liberal Arts and Sciences University College. It is one of the international honours colleges of the University of Utrecht.

From 1973 to 1979 the author studied sociology at the University of Utrecht. During that time he combined his studies with teaching mathematics and social studies at a school for secondary education. After receiving his master's degree he joined the department of Sociology of Education and Educational Policies at the Erasmus University Rotterdam.

In 1987, he successfully defended his PhD thesis on educational problems of immigrant children. For this study he observed and analyzed the educational career of over a thousand Rotterdam pupils during their transition from the second last grade in primary school to the end of the second year in secondary school. He published many reports and articles on issues related to these educational issues and on policies related to minority groups. Later his focus of interest widened and shifted to issues of the Welfare State, topics of cultural change and reproduction and social theory.

In 2004, he transferred to the Roosevelt Academy where he is now head of the Social Science Department. He is also coordinator of the research network Sociology of Education of the European Sociological Association.